W9-CQP-475

The Century Studies in Education

EDITED BY WILLIS L. UHL

PRINCIPLES AND TECHNIQUES
OF CURRICULUM MAKING

PRINCIPLES AND TECHNIQUES
OF CURRICULUM MAKING

BY

EDGAR MARION DRAPER, Ph.D.

ASSOCIATE PROFESSOR OF EDUCATION IN
THE UNIVERSITY OF WASHINGTON

D. APPLETON-CENTURY COMPANY

INCORPORATED

NEW YORK   LONDON

COPYRIGHT—1936—BY

D. APPLETON-CENTURY CO., INC.

*All rights reserved. This book, or parts
thereof, must not be reproduced in any
form without permission of the publisher.*

366

PRINTED IN THE UNITED STATES OF AMERICA

EDITOR'S FOREWORD

CURRICULUM construction requires (1) definite information, (2) a point of view, (3) effective planning, (4) ability to conduct an extensive program of research and organization, and (5) ability to administer a course of study. This volume provides for the first three of these items, and it supplies numerous examples that illustrate successful programs of research, organization, and administration. The materials on each item are evaluated with reference to the needs of both progressive and conservative curriculum workers.

Years of work with administrators, teachers, and other students have enabled Dr. Draper to winnow these materials from a much more extensive array. He has included only such materials as are needed by any one who seeks, in a single book, the essentials for curriculum construction. Additional information, historical and contemporary, is cited for workers who wish to carry on a first-hand survey of this important and engrossing field.

Elementary, secondary, and collegiate levels of learning are considered here for the rather obvious reason that a course of study is a vertical as well as a horizontal affair. For the same reason, curriculum construction, if it is to become effective, is an administrative issue. Most important of all, the advancing pupil's development is also vertical and horizontal and as complicated, structurally, as the flourishing banyan tree with its primary and secondary roots, trunks, and branches.

WILLIS L. UHL

PREFACE

TEACHERS and administrators at every level of American education are concerning themselves with problems of curricula and course of study construction. These professional challenges involve the determination of objectives, teaching fields, and teaching materials and also incorporate many stimulating studies of the best methods of directing children in their learning experiences and activities. These dynamic problems invite the teacher and administrator to consider (1) the principles of education, (2) the general objectives of the various curricula in the school, and (3) the specific objectives of definite subject-matter fields. By way of contrast it should be pointed out that as late as 1918, the organization of general aims or principles of learning was regarded as sufficient for the guidance of teachers in the development of learning experiences and activities for the pupils in the classroom. In the last few years, educators have generally agreed that it is essential for teachers and administrators to extend their activities in this field to the development of the specific objectives of the course of study in which they are interested.

The work undertaken in organizing specific objectives in all subjects has opened new fields for investigation. The allocation of objectives of a specific character in any subject-matter field has caused teachers to think of the education of the child in terms of twelve or fourteen years rather than in terms of a particular unit of the school system. It has also convinced those interested in the improvement of education that teaching materials, learning experiences, and educating activities can be organized definitely in terms of the specific objectives. As soon as this point was achieved in the thinking of educators, the necessity of validating the objectives was appreciated by the advanced thinkers in curricula. The waste of time, energy, and finances in developing learning activities for the realization of invalid objectives was unthinkable.

Methods of instruction have received the attention of educators for centuries. At times the emphasis upon methods has tended to eliminate the consideration of teaching materials. The problems suggested in the preceding paragraph were largely overlooked because of the unjustifiable conclusion that the ultimate solution of the problems of education rested upon the determination of a particular method of instruction that could be adapted to all teachers, students, and learning materials. Although this position has lost many ardent advocates in the last decade, the true importance of method of instruction in the reorganization of teaching materials has by no means diminished. Administrators and supervisors appreciate, however, the need for differentiation in the method of instruction in terms of the abilities of teachers, needs of students, and character of the subject-matter to be presented. These considerations necessitate the development of extensive supplementary materials, bibliographies for students, bibliographies for teachers, and the organization of individual- and group-guidance programs in order that almost complete differentiation of learning and teaching may be facilitated.

Every teacher in the elementary school, junior high school, senior high school, junior college, and university should know the techniques of constructing a course of study in his particular field. This involves developing general objectives, selecting and validating specific objectives, determining and organizing the content of the course, selecting a method suitable to his personality and scholarship, the needs of the students, and the teaching materials; planning and developing a testing program that will enable him to evaluate the results of his teaching. The additional items of supplementary materials and bibliographies will merit his attention.

The present volume has been developed to assist the teachers at all levels in the organization of their teaching materials. Since the basic principles are the same, the techniques are presented and analyzed without specific reference to elementary, secondary, or collegiate units. It is the opinion of the author that the book will be particularly valuable for the teacher who is interested in the reorganization of his teaching field, but who does not have the direction of a research expert or advisers in curriculum or academic fields. Inasmuch as the book presents a practical approach to these problems, it can be used as a college text in courses on curriculum and courses of study construction.

Any writer in the field of the curriculum who attempts to present a practical approach to the problem rather than a theoretical treatise naturally owes much to others. The reader will note that the author has used current experimental literature and courses of study freely and has been influenced by the men and women whose names appear in the references of the book. Individual recognition cannot be given to the hundreds of professional people who have made a definite contribution in the development of the manuscript. These include university professors, school administrators, directors of curriculum research, members of curriculum committees, and teachers of boys and girls. The author is greatly indebted to Dean Willis Lemon Uhl, of the University of Washington, and to Dr. Richard E. Rutledge, Director of Research and Curriculum in the Oakland Public Schools, who read the manuscript. Inasmuch as Dr. Rutledge has had extensive experience in curriculum research and course of study construction in one of the outstanding curriculum centers in the country and has taught university classes in curriculum construction, he brought a rich professional training to this work, and his suggestions were greatly appreciated.

E. M. D.

CONTENTS

PART I

INTRODUCTION

PART II

PRINCIPLES AND OBJECTIVES OF EDUCATION

PART III

THE UNIT OF WORK

PART IV

ADMINISTRATION AND ORGANIZATION OF CURRICULUM DEVELOPMENT

PART I
INTRODUCTION

PRINCIPLES AND TECHNIQUES OF CURRICULUM MAKING

CHAPTER I

DEFINITIONS

I. IMPORTANCE OF DEFINITIONS

The construction and revision of curricula is of paramount importance in American education. Teachers, supervisors, and administrators in elementary and secondary schools, as well as professors and administrative officers in institutions of higher education are considering these problems and experimenting with methods of procedure at the present time. In this book it is proposed to present, discuss, and analyze the status of these investigations at various levels of learning and develop a technique of investigation and organization that will enable teachers to improve their work. Many teachers who desire to improve their teaching have little to guide themselves in organizing investigations, establishing valid objectives in their fields, determining teaching materials and learning experiences, selecting methods, or developing reliable and valid tests. It is proposed, in view of this condition, to sacrifice a theoretical and philosophical approach, which might be both scholarly and profound, and consider instead the practical aspects of the problem in a simple, concrete, and definite presentation.

It is assumed that many teachers who are interested in this work will not have the direction of an expert in curriculum or research to guide them in their work or interpret for them the practical applications that may be made of an illusive, philosophical exposition. In order that the reader may work through this interesting problem with the writer, it is essential that the terms to be used extensively in the treatment of the subject-matter be carefully and clearly defined. Much of the confusion in the minds of teachers to-day exists because there is little agreement among writers in the use of terms in this field. At least a part of the emphasized disagreement among the writers on curricula is no more fundamental than a misunderstanding and a misinterpretation of the terminology that has developed with recent curriculum construction. These new terms have been used in many recent books and articles, and in almost every instance, no basic definitions have been presented. It is imperative that these fundamental terms in curriculum construction and course of study organization be defined and discussed in this introductory chapter.

II. DEFINITIONS OF TERMS USED

A. The program of studies. All the teaching materials and learning experiences which are organized in the elementary school, especially the departmentalized type, junior high school, senior high school, or junior college, and the department, school, or college of the university may be spoken of as the program of studies. In so far as the extracurricular activities are organized as educational experiences and are supervised by teachers who are trained to direct them toward specific and definite objectives, which have been determined by the school, they should be classified as a part of the program of studies. The application of this criterion to every subject-matter field in the school would do a great service in clarifying the thinking of teachers regarding the reorganization which could profitably be undertaken in teaching materials.

An illustration of a program of studies (see pages 5 and 6) from a high school of two hundred and fifty students will clarify the meaning of the term. It will be noted that this program of studies is composed of eight definitely organized curricular fields. Four classes constitute a normal high-school course. Thirty-two credits are required for graduation.

A program of studies arranged for a large four-year high school is presented in tabular form in the following excerpt on pages 8 and 9.

It will be noted here that the program of studies in the large high school is not always divided into curricula as in the pre-

1. Language	2. Scientific	3. General	4. Home Economics
English I and II Algebra I and II Language I and II Elective	English I and II Algebra I and II General Science I and II Elective	English I and II Algebra I and II Social Civics I and II Elective	English I and II Social Civics I and II Foods I and Clothing II Biology I and II (Elective)
English III and IV Geometry I and II Language III and IV Elective	English III and IV Geometry I and II Biology I and II Elective	English III and IV Geometry I and II Elective Elective	English III and IV Foods II and Clothing II Biology I and II Elective
English V and VI Physics I and II or Chemistry I and II Language I and II Elective	English V and VI Chemistry I and II Language I and II Elective	English V and VI Physics I and II or Chemistry I and II Elective Elective	English V and VI Home Economics V and VI Physics I and II or Chemistry I and II Elective
U. S. History ($\frac{1}{2}$) Government ($\frac{1}{2}$) Language III and IV Elective Elective	U. S. History ($\frac{1}{2}$) Government ($\frac{1}{2}$) Language III and IV Physics I and II Elective	English VII and VIII U. S. History ($\frac{1}{2}$) Government ($\frac{1}{2}$) Elective Elective	English VII and VIII Home Econ. VII and VIII U. S. History ($\frac{1}{2}$) Government ($\frac{1}{2}$) Elective

5. Stenographic	6. General Business	7. Manual Arts	8. Agriculture
English I and II Business Arithmetic I and II Social Civics I and II Elective	English I and II Business Arithmetic I and II Social Civics I and II Elective	English I and II Algebra I and II Manual Arts Elective	English I and II Social Civics I and II Agriculture I and II Elective
English III and IV Bookkeeping I and II Industrial Geography Business Law (½) Elective	English III and IV Bookkeeping I and II Industrial Geography Business Law (½) Elective	English III and IV Geometry I and II Manual Arts Elective	English III and IV Agriculture III and IV Elective Elective
Eng. V and Business Eng. Typewriting I and II Shorthand I and II U. S. History and Government Elective (½)	Eng. V and Business Eng. Bookkeeping III and IV Elective Elective	English V and VI Physics I and II or Chemistry I and II Manual Arts Elective	English V and VI Physics or Chemistry (Unless Biology was taken) Agriculture Elective
English VI and VII or VIII Typewriting III and IV U. S. History and Government Office Training (½) Shorthand III and IV	English VI and VII or VIII Economics (½) U. S. History and Government Bookkeeping V Elective	English VII and VIII U. S. History and Government Manual Arts Elective	English VII and VIII U. S. History and Government Elective Elective

vious illustration. The possibilities of developing curricula are here, however, and almost endless variations are presented in terms of the individual student.

In this case, Group I*a* is composed of the core curriculum materials or constants. These subjects are required of every student for graduation. Group I*b* presents the variable subjects offered in the program of studies, and through these the individual curricula, emphasizing college preparation, scientific preparation, commercial training, etc., are developed. Group II presents those subjects which are freely elective in the various years of the high school.

This program of studies is not typical of the organization of teaching materials except in larger schools. It will be helpful for the student to keep this fact in mind in thinking through the definitions which follow.

In the university, the organization of work is similar. In the Department of Education at the University of Washington the program of studies includes the following fields : secondary education, tests and measurements, educational sociology, philosophy of education, history of education, educational psychology, modern methods of teaching, administration, supervision, curricula, and practice teaching. These are organized as exploratory fields for undergraduates and as definite curricula for graduate students.

The junior college has been developed to a great extent as an additional two years of secondary-school work and exists in most cases as a part of the secondary school. If it does not occupy the same building with the high school, it usually has a separate building on the same campus. This close relationship has developed the junior college program of studies as a super-high school, and there is little, except the level of work, to distinguish one from the other.

B. Curricula. In the elementary school the program of studies and the curriculum are the same, since the school is concerned with skills, habits, and knowledges that are fundamental in the education of every child. The organization of teaching materials at this level may, therefore, be correctly

9B	9A	10B	10A
Group I (a)			
English (1) 5 Mathematics (1) 5 History (1) World 5	English (2) 5 Mathematics (2) 5 History (2) World 5	English (3) 5	English (4) 5
Group I (b)			
		Mathematics (3) 5	Mathematics (4) 5
		History (3) Med. 5	History (4) Mod. 5
Latin (1) 5	Latin (2) 5	Latin (3) 5 Greek (1) 5 French (3) 5	Latin (4) 5 Greek (2) 5 French (4) 5
French (1) 5	French (2) 5		
German (1) 5	German (2) 5	German (3) 5	German (4) 5
	Geography (1) 5	Geography (2) 5 Biology (1) 5	Biology (2) 5
Bookkeeping (1) 5 Arithmetic (1) 5	Bookkeeping (2) 5 Arithmetic (2) 5	Bookkeeping (3) 5 Shorthand (1) 5	Bookkeeping (4) 5 Shorthand (2) 5
GROUP II			
Voice Culture (1) 5 Chorus (1) 1 Glee Club (1) 2 Orchestra (1) 5 Band (1) 5	Voice Culture (2) 5 Chorus (2) 1 Glee Club (2) 2 Orchestra (2) 5 Band (2) 5	Chorus (3) 1 Glee Club (3) 2 Orchestra (3) 5 Band (3) 5	Chorus (4) 1 Glee Club (4) 2 Orchestra (4) 5 Band (4) 5
Vocat. Info. (1) 5 F. H. Draw. (1) 2½	F. H. Draw. (2) 2½	Typewriting (1) 2½ F. H. Draw. (3) 2½	Gen'l Business (1) 5 Typewriting (2) 2½ F. H. Draw. (4) 2½
Mech. Draw. (1) 2½ Home Science (1) 5 Domestic Art (1) 3	Mech. Draw. (2) 2½ Home Science (2) 5 Domestic Art (2) 3	Mech. Draw. (3) 2½ Home Science (3) 5 Domestic Art (3) 3	Mech. Draw. (4) 2½ Home Science (4) 5 Domestic Art (4) 3
Wood Shop (1) 2½	Wood Shop (2) 2½	Turning (1) 3½	Mach. Shop (1 & 2) 5
Phys. Train. (1) 2½ Swimming (1) 2½	Phys. Train. (2) 2½ Swimming (2) 2½	Phys. Train. (3) 2½ Swimming (3) 2½	Phys. Train. (4) 2½ Swimming (4) 2½

1. The number in parentheses, following the name of each study, indicates the number of the course.

2. The number opposite the name of each study, at the right side of the column, indicates the amount of credit for the successful completion of the course.

3. The number of credits required for graduation is 160. Approximately one-half of these must be taken from the studies in the Eleventh- and Twelfth-Grade columns.

4. The subjects in Group I (a) are required for graduation.

5. In addition the following are required: (a) one year of laboratory science, which may be biology, chemistry, physics, or physiography; (b) one year of physical training; (c) one course in swimming.

Entering January, 1925

11B	11A	12B	12A

Group I (a)

11B	11A	12B	12A
English (5) 5	English (6) 5	English (7) 5	English (8) 5
		History (7) Amer. 5	History (8) Amer. 5

Group I (b)

11B	11A	12B	12A
		Public Speak. (1) 5	Pub. Speaking (2) 5
		Mathematics (7) 5	Debating 5
Mathematics (5) 5	Mathematics (6) 5	Mathematics (8) 5	Mathematics (9) 5
			Pol. Science (1) 5
History (5) Eng. 5	History (6) Eng. 5		
		Economics (1) 5	
Latin (5) 5	Latin (6) 5	Latin (7) 5	Latin (8) 5
Greek (3) 5	Greek (4) 5		
French (5) 5	French (6) 5	French (7) 5	French (8) 5
French (1a) 5	French (2a) 5	French (3a) 5	French (4a) 5
German (5) 5	German (6) 5	German (7) 5	German (8) 5
German (1a) 5	German (2a) 5	German (3a) 5	German (4a) 5
Chemistry (1) 5	Chemistry (2) 5	Physics (1) 5	Physics (2) 5
Physiography (1) 5	Physiography (2) 5	Geology (1) 5	
Biology (3) 5	Biology (4) 5		
Com'l Geog. (1) 5	Com'l Law (1) 5		
Shorthand (3) 5	Shorthand (4) 5	Shorthand (5) 5	Shorthand (6) 5

GROUP II

11B	11A	12B	12A
Piano (5) 5	Piano (6) 5	Piano (7) 5	Piano (8) 5
Chorus (5) 5	Chorus (6) 1	Chorus (7) 1	Chorus (8) 1
Glee Club (5) 5	Glee Club (6) 2	Glee Club (7) 2	Glee Club (8) 2
Orchestra (5) 5	Orchestra (6) 5	Orchestra (7) 5	Orchestra (8) 5
Band (5) 5	Band (6) 5	Band (7) 5	Band (8) 5
History of Music (1) 5	Hist. of Music (2) 5		
Harmony (1) 5	Harmony (2) 5	Harmony (3) 5	Harmony (4) 5
Typewriting (3) 2½	Typewriting (4) 2½	Typewriting (5) 2½	Typewriting (6) 2½
F. H. Draw. (5) 2½	F. H. Draw. (6) 2½	F. H. Draw. (7) 2½	F. H. Draw. (8) 2½
Com'l Art (1) 2½	Com'l Art (2) 2½	Stagecraft (1) 2½	
Art Apprec'n (1) 1	Mech. Draw. (6) 2½	Domestic Art (7) 3	Domestic Art (8) 3
Mech. Draw. (5) 2½	Mech. Draw. (6) 3	Mech. Draw. (7) 2½	Mech. Draw. (8) 2½
Domestic Art (5) 3	Domestic Art (6) 3	Domestic Art (7) 3	Domestic Art (8) 3
		Millinery. 3	
Mach. Shop (3 & 4) 5			
Auto Mech. (1) 5			
Phys. Train. (5) 2½	Phys. Train. (6) 2½	Phys. Train. (7) 2½	Phys. Train. (8) 2½
Swimming (5) 2½	Swimming (6) 2½	Swimming (7) 2½	Swimming (8) 2½

6. Of the 160 credits required for graduation, at least 120 must be from Group I, not over 15 in physical training, and not over 30 in manual training or household arts.

7. Pupils electing a study running through a year must complete the year's work in that study before any credit is given, except in cases granted by the principal. Before receiving credit in any foreign language, a pupil must have completed satisfactorily at least four semesters or courses, except in cases granted by the principal.

8. The arrangement of studies by grades is not restrictive, but indicates the natural order to be followed in any line of study.

9. Before graduation, a pupil must have acquired at least 40 hours of credit in one subject, at least 30 in a second, and at least 20 in a third.

spoken of as a program of studies or a curriculum. This was true, also, of the first high school in the United States (Boston, May, 1821), as every boy was required to complete the following program of studies or curriculum:

First Year: Composition, reading, rhetoric, declamation, geography, arithmetic
Second Year: Continue subjects of the first year adding algebra, ancient and modern history, logic, geometry, trigonometry, navigation, surveying, mensuration, forensics
Third Year: Continue all subjects of the second year and add natural philosophy, moral and political philosophy

The beginnings of the present curricular organization of the secondary school are found in the academy which was established at Philadelphia in 1751. The institution was organized into three schools—the Latin, the English, and the mathematical—and in a general way these correspond to the classical, English or general, and scientific curricula of the modern high school. It was not until about the time of the Civil War that curricula were established in a few high schools. However, by 1890 the effects of the industrial revolution, immigration, and democracy had begun the popularization of the high school, and every secondary school of sufficient enrolment had been compelled to meet the problem of the adjustment of children through the organization of new curricula which were differentiated, in part at least, from the college preparatory materials. The early years of the twentieth century saw the extension of this program until as many as twenty-five or thirty curricula were presented in some secondary schools. The emphasis has changed somewhat in the last decade through the development of the concept of constant or required subjects for all high-school pupils and variables and electives to take care of their individual needs. As administrators and teachers have been working with this new organization of subject-matter, they have developed two distinctly different connotations of the word "curriculum."

1. Administrative curriculum. The program of studies, as
we have noted, consists of an indefinite number of curricula.
These are regulated by the size of the school and the vocational
and trade opportunities which exist in the community. Each curriculum is an administrative device since the child may be assigned to a certain combination of subject-matter fields which
have been developed to enable the children in this organization
to realize definite educational goals. The point may be illustrated
by the freshman boy and his parents who come to the school and
talk over with the principal the educational program of the boy
during his high-school days. It is decided that he shall prepare
his program so that he can enter the university and possibly the
college of engineering. He has indicated an interest in mathematics and science, and it may be that his work in these fields in
the high school will cause him to register in a college of science.
However, the principal has at hand an administrative curriculum, known as the scientific curriculum in his school, and the
student who completes the specific requirements of this curriculum is prepared to enter the college of engineering or the college
of science in the university. There is enough latitude in this
curriculum so that the boy may investigate other interests and
secure a cultural education. The boy is registered in the scientific
curriculum; his immediate problems are solved and his immediate needs filled.

A freshman girl and her mother seek the principal and discuss the work of the girl in the school. It is generally understood
that the girl will not enter the university unless new interests
are awakened during her high-school days and opportunities
present themselves which are not envisaged at the time. The
girl shows interest in secretarial work and hopes for a position
at the conclusion of her high-school work. Administratively, the
principal's problem is simplified by having at hand an organization of subject-matter fields which will provide for the young
lady the objectives which she has mentioned, and at the same
time present opportunities for the exploration of other interests
and the development of cultural backgrounds. She is assigned to
the commercial curriculum. Later, her work may be further

differentiated by the selection of such specialized fields as secretarial training, office practice, bookkeeping, accounting, etc.

The junior college presents little that is new in the discussion of this field, as it has copied again the organization of the high school or has simply extended the program of the secondary school with which it is organized and articulated. However, there are many new terminal curricula designed to meet the needs of those students who will complete their education in the junior college.

If we allow for the organization of colleges within the universities, we find that the organization of subject-matter fields within each college is similar to the secondary-school program. For example, a college of business administration admits students to the following curricula: economics, accounting, business finance, commercial teaching and secretarial training, foreign trade and consular service, management, insurance, marketing, merchandizing, advertising, transportation, labor, public utilities, statistics, and general business. While there are fundamental required subjects in all curricula, extensive differentiation is developed in terms of the objectives of curricula as indicated in the titles given.

2. *Individual curriculum.* In a general way, educators are accustomed to speak of the individual's curriculum as the administrative curriculum in which he is registered. Thus the student's curriculum may be thought of as the scientific or commercial curriculum, but, in reality, his curriculum may vary considerably from that of any other pupil in this curriculum. This variation is accounted for through the elective opportunities which are presented. An exact statement of the pupil's curriculum requires greater refinement than the terms "scientific" or "commercial" imply. An analysis of the curricula of two pupils in the scientific curriculum will illustrate the point.

In the freshman year, these two pupils have four common subjects, three common subjects in the sophomore year, two such subjects in the junior year, and only one in the last year of work. These curricula are similar, but they are easily distinguished from each other through the selection of electives

An Analysis of Two Curricula

Pupil A	Pupil B
Freshman	
Mathematics I	Mathematics I
Latin I	Latin I
History I	French I
English I	English I
Physical Education	Physical Education
Sophomore	
Biology	Penmanship and Spelling
Mathematics II	Mathematics II
English II	English II
Latin II	Latin II
	French II
Junior	
Chemistry	Chemistry
Mathematics III	English III
English III	Latin III
History II	French III
Commercial Law	Public Speaking
Senior	
Physics	Physics
Mathematics IV	Mathematics III
Typewriting	Latin IV
American History and Civics	French IV
	American History and Civics

and the development of different majors and minors. In order to have a clear understanding of the pupil's attainments, it is necessary to analyze his own curriculum. Each administrative curriculum is made up of a large number of individual curricula. The exact number is governed exclusively by the enrolment in the administrative curriculum and the total number of courses offered in the program of studies.

In considering the curricula of individual students, we are

concerned not only with the teaching fields to which they have been exposed, but also with the new attitudes, skills, knowledges, etc., they have realized from the contacts with materials and teachers. Fundamentally, it is not a question of registration in courses or grades secured in subject-matter fields; a student's curriculum may be expressed only in terms of his skills, habits, knowledges, attitudes, and ideals. The grade in the course often measures only inaccurately the student's attainments in the fields of skill, habits, and knowledges and has little, if any, relationship to his development of new and better attitudes and ideals. At present little is known of the real achievement of the pupil. It is manifestly impossible for the parents or the teachers to indicate the curriculum of any student, since the student can demonstrate only through his living his realizations from the subject-matter fields to which he has been exposed. When teachers use the term individual curriculum in this sense they are dealing with one of the intangibles of American education.

Bobbitt says:[1]

The chief conditioners, guides, and supervisors of the good life by the children and youths are the families. The family is then the basic, and the chief, educational institution.

Owing to the complexity of the good life and of much of the conditioning necessary, the family unaided is usually not competent to induct the children and youths into the more complex and difficult activities. For this reason, schools are established as specialized auxiliary agencies designed to give expert assistance to the families in getting those kinds of high-grade activities properly under way. As the school does, so the responsible and socially efficient family will do everything possible to make and keep the activities thus started by the school properly and continuously operative in the out-of-school lives of the young people, and thus relieve the school as early and rapidly as possible of the temporary responsibility delegated to it.

The teacher is primarily a specialist in high-grade human living. It is his function to coöperate with the families in discovering the kind of life-continuity that appears to be appropriate for each individual child or youth. The teacher should see the part that the family itself can and should do directly for itself, and the more

[1] Franklin Bobbitt, "A Summary Theory of the Curriculum," Society for Curriculum Study, *News Bulletin* (January 12, 1934), pp. 2-4.

complex and difficult part that must be taken over temporarily by the school. As the teacher thus discovers as exactly as the conditions permit the course that each individual life should run, he will provide the necessary opportunities, conditioning, and guidance at the school, and counsel and coöperate with the families in their guidance of the much larger volume of home and general community activities.

Each life runs its individual course. Each curriculum then must be an individual thing, different from every other. The appropriate channels can be discovered with exactness only by those in intimate contact with the affairs of the child or youth, namely his parents, his teachers, and himself.

While there are general guiding principles that enable parents and teachers to foresee in advance the long general course that is normally to be run, yet they cannot foresee or foreknow the specific and concrete details of the course that is to be actualized. The current living in the concrete, which is the only form in which it can exist, if it is to be adjusted to the conditions with the greatest practicable exactness, must be planned from day to day according to the conditions that arise. The details of the curriculum then are to be planned currently under the guidance of the general principles that properly govern the several fields of human behavior.

The manual or other printed material that is placed in the hands of the teacher is to assist him in his adherence to, and application of, the numerous guiding principles. The primary purpose of the manual will be to make the general principles clear. A secondary purpose will be to economize the teacher's time and labor by showing the wide range of possible activities in each field as alternative suggestions from among which to select in planning for the concrete situations actually met with.

Even more important than the teacher's educational manual is the one that is to be supplied to parents for their guidance in conditioning and supervising the current living of their children.

Most important of all should be the manual, changed from year to year, that is placed in the hands of the maturing child and youth, as reference help for his own self-guidance. Only as he learns rightly to live his own life, as guided by the inner light of his own intelligence, does he become properly educated. His manual should help him to this intelligence.

C. Course of study. This term, which should not require definition or illustration, has been so naïvely confused by writers and speakers in the educational field with program of studies and curriculum that it is necessary to discuss it in some detail.

PLAN I. A TYPICAL CURRICULAR ORGANIZATION OF WORK IN THE
PROGRAM OF STUDIES FOR THE FOUR-YEAR HIGH SCHOOL

Post-High-School Education	Higher Education	Life in Community	Vocational Efficiency
High-School Grades	Curriculum No. 1	Curriculum No. 2	Curriculum No. 3
FOURTH YEAR	1. Course of study in English for particular curriculum 2. Other courses 3. in 4. curriculum		
THIRD YEAR	1. Course of study in English for particular curriculum 2. Other subjects 3. in 4. curriculum		
SECOND YEAR	1. Course of study in English for particular curriculum 2. Other subjects 3. in 4. curriculum		
FIRST YEAR	1. Course of study in English for particular curriculum 2. Other subjects 3. in 4. curriculum		
Pre-High-School Education	Elementary Preparation	Elementary Preparation	Elementary Preparation

The terms "State course of study" and "high-school course of study" are frequently used in place of "program of studies." Curriculum construction has been used extensively rather than course-of-study construction. Course of study construction is a vital part of developing a particular curriculum and this, in turn, is a fundamental phase of the program of studies, but the terms are not synonymous in either case. The teacher who is beginning work in this field should distinguish clearly between the connotations of these words.

The curriculum is organized to realize the objectives of a particular group of students who are registered in the program of studies of an educational institution.

The course of study is organized to achieve the objectives of a curriculum, and it articulates with previous and later training in that subject-matter field.

The course of study will be analyzed and intensively studied in several of the following chapters, but it is necessary at this time to point out certain general characteristics. The effectiveness of the course of study is measured by the improvement of teaching in the classroom. In order that the teacher and supervisor may utilize the course of study in the most effective way, this instrument must meet certain standards in its organization. It should present the general objectives of the curriculum and of education. The general objectives of the course will then be analyzed into a large number of specific objectives which point out the details of the particular units, jobs, activities, and experiences that have been developed to realize the general objectives. If real and specific objectives have been attained and validated, they will suggest accurately the subject-matter and student activities that are essential. The particular methods that have been found effective in promoting student interest and enthusiasm in realizing the objectives should then be included. This predicates that methods of measuring student achievement through standardized and non-standardized examinations should be included in each unit of the course. Annotated references to the best books and materials in the field should be indicated. If the pupils are to be taken outside the school to observe or engage in activities, these activities should be outlined in considerable detail.

In using the term *course of study,* the reader should not think of a body of subject-matter for a school year or a semester

and studied or recited in class periods of a certain length for
a certain number of days per week during that time. A course
in English may be twelve years in length and the objectives
stated in terms of desirable adaptations and mastery. These
objectives will govern the organization of units within the
course. The objectives and the content of the units will determine their grade placement in the educational program, and for
this reason educators have made the mistake of speaking of
the course of study for a particular grade or semester. In
reality, most courses of study merge into the complete curricular
experience of the child and become a vital part of his educational
development for more than a year. Exceptions can be pointed
out, but these tend to be merged in the basic integrated fields
in the school. The old "courses" of economics, history, civics,
geography, and other social-science subjects are losing their
individuality and are becoming part of the integrated social-
studies course of study, which is a fundamental part of the
complete curricular experience of the pupil.

D. Principles and objectives. These terms are suggested
for general use, rather than goals, aims, and outcomes, as means
of eliminating the confusion that exists in the writing and
thinking of educational leaders. Objectives can be classified
further as general and specific. If educators propose to state
the desirable realizations in a course as general and specific,
it is permissible to use the terms *goals and aims* as synonymous
with general objectives. It is essential that when goals and aims
are used in this way the term *principles* should be reserved to
indicate the fundamental assumptions of our educational philosophy. It is usually easier for the reader to begin with principles and work back to specific objectives, if he is to understand
and appreciate their true relationship to each other. He should
develop the principles of education which represent the fundamental concepts of our philosophy of education. The general
objectives, goals, or aims of each curriculum should then be
stated. This necessitates the organization of objectives in each
subject-matter field that contributes to the objectives of the
curriculum. In order that vital experiences and activities may be

organized for the pupils, these objectives of the course must be subdivided into their general and specific aspects.

E. Outcomes. It is important, in view of the advance which has been made in the field of measurement, that the teacher have a clear understanding of this term. The proponents of the activity school are suggesting that the term be used exclusively in place of objectives to indicate the realized objectives of the activities which have been worked out by the children. It is impossible, according to the activists, to formulate objectives in the activity program, since no person can foresee the results of the activities in which children are engaged. Furthermore, it is their contention that it would be presumptuous to attempt to establish a preview of the societal needs of the children who are at present in our schools. It is possible, however, to recognize and enumerate the results of the program which has been worked out in the educational institution for a semester or year. These results are the outcomes. In case the same program is set up for a succeeding group of students, as is often done, the outcomes of the previous program become the objectives of the teacher and students of the new group. This situation is merely mentioned to show the reason for the misunderstanding in many quarters of the terms *objectives* and *outcomes*. Many people who do not appreciate the significance of the two terms advocate the amusing procedure of defining the outcomes of the educational program before the children have been assembled or the teaching materials and procedures of instruction have been organized. This taboo of the term *objectives* by the older activity group led to loose thinking on the part of others interested in curriculum building with the result that, in many quarters, the terms are regarded as synonymous. The prestige of the measurement movement is rapidly dispelling this illusion.

It is the contention of curriculum experts that objectives are that part of the program which should be established, in advance, as the desirable goals or aims of education and classified into general and specific aspects so that the materials, which are to be used in the educational program, can be easily and definitely determined. According to this group, the outcomes are the actual and achieved results. The objectives and outcomes are synonymous only in the case of perfect teaching. In all other cases, the difference between objectives and outcomes enables us to estimate the effectiveness of the teacher and the teaching in a particular grade during a semester or year.

$$\frac{\text{Achievement Test} \quad \text{Outcomes Determined by} \quad \text{Objectives of}}{\text{Second Achievement Test} \quad \text{Course}}$$

First		
Achievement Test	Outcomes Determined by	Objectives of
	Second Achievement Test	Course

Teachers who follow this method of procedure will be in a position to validate their objectives and state them more accurately in terms of the children. The situation presented in the diagram above could represent poor teaching, but a particular class with a superior teacher might show outcomes as far removed from the objectives as this, if the objectives are not valid for the class or grade level. The problem of validating the specific objectives in the course of study is of paramount importance and will be discussed and analyzed later.

F. Core curriculum, constants, requireds. These terms have been developed to describe the common, integrating materials which have been accepted as fundamental in the education of American youth at all levels of the school system. In the first high school the core curriculum was the same as the curriculum, since every subject was constant and required for graduation. There were no variables or electives in the offering presented. To-day, there is a surprisingly large number of constants in the elementary, secondary, and collegiate levels of instruction.

The program of studies on pages 5 and 6 illustrates the meaning of these terms for the secondary school. The principles involved in this program of studies will hold, generally, for all levels of the educational system. The courses, other than electives, indicate the core curriculum of the particular curriculum. If the same required courses are found in all curricula, they represent the core curriculum of the entire school, in that they are the courses which every child must complete in order to secure a high-school diploma—the present insignium of a high-school education. In the program of studies reproduced here, they represent the common integrating experiences and activities that are considered fundamental in the development of American citizenship.

G. Variables. The reader has already noted that there is considerable variation between the core curriculum materials of different curricula, as, for example, the organization of constant materials in the scientific and commercial curricula. It is not unreasonable to suppose that the required materials in one curriculum might be of value and service to the student who is working in another organization of materials. When such a selection is made by the student, with the advice of a teacher or counselor, these constant materials which are taken over into the organized work of a student in another curriculum, in which they are not constant, are spoken of as variables. In most instances, these variables represent a real variation in the program of the child.

H. Electives. These organizations of educational experiences and activities in one curriculum can be core materials in another curriculum, but in most instances electives are included in the program of studies to enable students to select freely, according to their interests. They are often exploratory, since the student may find new and latent interests through these contacts and reorganize his major and minor fields, as a result of these new experiences and activities. They serve also as broadening courses by presenting opportunities for the students to build up cultural and esthetic backgrounds and avocational interests for their adult life.

I. Subject-matter, teaching materials, learning activities. These terms refer to the materials and experiences which are provided for the student and to processes which facilitate learning. They may be developed as the result of a great deal of study and research and organized into courses of study, curricula, and program of studies; or they may be organized extemporaneously by the student and the teacher, as a means of realizing the student's present interests in his environment. In either case, they are concerned with the development of the student's abilities in terms of doing, being, feeling, etc.

These learning activities are definitely determined by the specific objectives. It is essential, therefore, that one proceed from the specific objective to the subject-matter which shall be taught in the classroom. If, for example, in the health program of the school, medical authorities have determined, as a result of investigations of health or cleanliness, that it is important for the child to acquire the habit of brushing the teeth twice a day, administrative experts and health experts in the school can state the specific objective essential in this case. The learning activities essential in the mastery of this habit can be introduced, and the degree of proficiency attained by the pupils can be measured from time to time. This, also, constitutes a simple check upon the efficiency of teaching in the system and should be a part of every system of administration and supervision.

J. Fields of work or areas of learning. In the past, teachers have been concerned with subject-matter fields and have given little thought to integration of learning experiences which might eliminate many of the present subjects in the various curricula. The leadership in the development of fields of work has come from the activity school, although the organization of fields of work cannot be understood to be a consummation of their theory of education. In general, the activity people are experimenting with complete integration, while those who are concerned with revising and reorganizing the present program are considering integration through the development of fields of work. In actual practice, fields of work are being established in the following manner:

Social-science objectives demand the selection of materials from the old subject-matter fields of history, geography, economics, political science, sociology, and, in some instances, English.

Other fields of work which have been established are language, science, health, and mathematics. A consideration of any of them will indicate at once the organization of integrated fields of work and the elimination of large numbers of old subject-matter courses of study.

The curriculum maker or the committee in charge of course of study construction can begin at three different points, and all three of these points are being emphasized by one or more groups in the United States at this time. The interrelationship of these points can be illustrated by drawing an isosceles triangle and labeling each of the points to represent a possible beginning in curriculum construction.

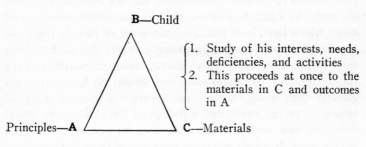

B—Child
1. Study of his interests, needs, deficiencies, and activities
2. This proceeds at once to the materials in C and outcomes in A

Principles—**A**　　　　　**C**—Materials

1. Develop general and specific objectives
2. Materials to realize objectives—C
3. Methods—B
4. Outcomes through measurement—B

1. Study of material in the school at the present time
2. Reorganization needed to meet principles in A
3. Development of new general and specific objectives in subject-matter field—A
4. Promotes study of child and development of new methods—B

1. *The group which emphasizes principles of life.* Greater emphasis is being placed upon the fact that tradition can be ignored in developing an educational program, and that more reliance can be placed upon acceptable principles of life and living. When these principles have been determined, general and specific objectives will enable the course of study committee to proceed with the problem of realizing them through improved materials, methods, and measurement of outcomes.

2. *The activity school or progressive education group* is stressing the importance of the child and the necessity of taking his interests, needs, and activities as the basis of the new educational program. Materials are used, and outcomes are achieved through this procedure, but the child and not the principles of education determines both the materials and the outcomes.

3. *Present materials of instruction* have been overemphasized in the past and receive too much attention to-day from committees interested in course of study construction. This procedure is based on the assumption that we must have courses of study in English, history, etc., in the public schools, and those which have been produced can serve as models for those required in other systems. However, granting that a start from this point in revision of curricula can mean stagnation and the continuation of the *status quo,* one should recognize that beginning with materials does not preclude a careful study of principles or the needs and activities of the child. New objectives and new methods can result from an investigation begun at this point. It is only when the scissors and paste pot constitute the tools or techniques that little or no progress is possible with this approach.

K. Method of teaching. This term has perhaps caused as much confusion as any other in the minds of educators. It is particularly important that persons interested in curriculum revision be capable of distinguishing between that which is curricular in nature and that which is concerned with method. They are closely related in that the progressive teacher, who is interested in curriculum revision, is likely to be a student of methodology. They can be developed separately and need not be related, except that the selection of a method in teaching naturally follows the selection of teaching materials. In those cases in which a particular method is used in a school, either because of administrative dictum or preferences of the teachers, there may be an interaction between curriculum construction and method, since the method may influence the selection and organization of materials.

The important place which method has assumed in education and in the thinking of educators is another example of tradition in this field. To give an example from a limited period of history, the transition from Herbart to Morrison has found the emphasis consistently upon the method of instruction rather than upon organization of content. It would be accurate also to point out that, in this period of history, the organization of content was made subsidiary to the development of method in educational writing and thinking. Much that has been called method in the past is nothing more or less than careful and pseudo-scientific organization of content. The Dalton Plan is an excellent example. This plan is selected since it represents a rather recent development and shows clearly the tendency of contemporary educators to subsume content under the heading of method.

The Dalton Plan is a method of teaching whereby the student works at his own rate of speed and determines his own progress in achieving objectives at the level selected by him. The assignment is general in the class, but the individual members adjust themselves to the various levels which have been organized within the unit being considered and proceed independently through conferences with the teacher. In most schools where the Dalton Plan is in use the entire program, which has been briefly outlined, is spoken of as method. The careful student will see at once the distinction between the organization of the materials of instruction into units and the individual method of assisting the student to master those units according to his own ability. Method has an important place in education, and the curriculum specialist would be the last to question its value and the first to add the most important results of recent investigations in that field to his organization of content for the guidance of the teacher. An illustration of the contribution of the scientific study of method to course of study construction is found in the results of the study of the teacher-demonstration versus the laboratory method in science classes. Valid results of experiments of this type can be used in organizing courses of study.

III. SUMMARY

It is so important that teachers who are interested in curriculum construction and course of study construction think clearly about these problems that this first chapter has been devoted to specific definitions and explanations which will serve as a basis for this type of work in the remainder of this book. There has been and still is so much confusion from misunderstandings in phraseology that the author is desirous of laying this definite groundwork in the first chapter. It will be well for the reader to refer to this chapter, from time to time, until the correct use of these terms has become habitual. It will be valuable also for the student to write, under each incorrectly used word in treatises on curriculum construction, the term agreed upon as a basis for our development in this field of professional endeavor.

From the preceding discussion of definitions, it is apparent that American education is relatively complex. The tasks which face the high-school administrative and teaching staffs cannot be analyzed as clearly and definitely as those appearing in the Public School of England or the Lycée of France.

One reason for this confusion is the rapid expansion of the school population in this country along with a corresponding expansion of teaching fields and educational opportunities of both academic and extracurricular classifications. The battle-cry of the schools has been stated in terms of training a vast heterogeneous mass of pupils in a wide, undefined area of experience. Citizenship in a democracy, ethical character, worthy home membership, vocational efficiency, etc., express indefinite challenges flung to educators in every State and city. Educators have responded to these challenges by expanding the various curricula and adding additional curricula. In few instances have programs of study been analyzed and curricula revised. Additions of new subjects, special teachers, and the development of a vast, unintelligible field of extra-curricular activities have served to indicate to the American people that the school people were actively and scientifically engaged in solving vocational and educational guidance. This guidance has been expected to function in adjusting millions of boys and girls in the secondary schools. At the same time the machine age was becoming a reality, technocracy was challenging readers of the better magazines, and the mystical "New Deal" for the forgotten man was receiving national approbation.

As soon as a subject or an activity has been admitted to the fold and interests have been developed in its retention, there is difficulty in removing it from the system. An illustration of this condition presented itself forcibly to educators during the depression. Music, art, physical education, and other "new" subjects were eliminated. Such action was not based on a scientific study of their merits as educational instruments, but rather upon the fact that they had entered the educational field late. Algebra and Latin were retained almost universally for exactly the opposite reason.

Training for the realization of ethical character has promoted the addition of new courses and new extracurricular activities. Recognition of the need for intelligent citizenship has stimulated the introduction of new courses and new activities. Demands for vocational efficiency have led to a tremendous expansion of curricula in all high schools. Many high schools are presenting more than thirty curricula.[2] These conditions show that the relationship of these various phases of education, which have been defined in this chapter, has not been understood. There is confusion about the relationship between procedure and philosophy in this country. The following plan on page 28 will indicate that analyses and studies are needed in the solution of this problem.

When educators make additions to curricula in terms of objectives that are related definitely to principles of life and living instead of merely adding individual subjects to the hodge-podge that already exists, much of the confusion will rapidly disappear from the educational system, and confidence in education will be restored. Indiscriminate additions of subject-matter fields and sublime confidence that new fields of knowledge will solve new

[2] Department of Superintendence, *Sixth Yearbook* (1928), pp. 59 ff.

PLAN II. AN ILLUSTRATION OF THE RELATIONSHIP OF THE PRINCIPLES
OF EDUCATION, THE PROGRAM OF STUDIES, CURRICULA, AND
COURSES OF STUDY

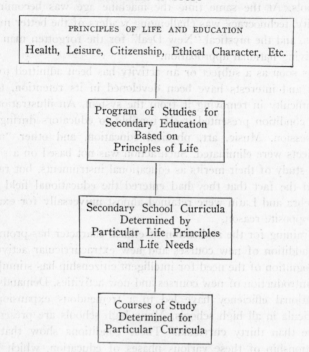

> PRINCIPLES OF LIFE AND EDUCATION
> Health, Leisure, Citizenship, Ethical Character, Etc.

> Program of Studies for
> Secondary Education
> Based on
> Principles of Life

> Secondary School Curricula
> Determined by
> Particular Life Principles
> and Life Needs

> Courses of Study
> Determined for
> Particular Curricula

and pertinent problems of living have tended to limit financial
support and undermine public confidence.

Only a few years ago a committee representing the Department of Superintendence and coöperating in gathering material
for the *Sixth Yearbook* found more than one hundred different
curricula in the high schools of this country. Even assuming a
great duplication in curricular materials organized under different titles, the situation still merits comment. The educator and
the layman are both ready to agree that little has been accomplished in stating educational goals and that curricula represent
a conglomeration of materials rather than carefully organized
goals and scientifically determined subject-matter for their
realization.

BIBLIOGRAHPY

ALMACK, J. C., "Curriculum Construction," *California Quarterly of Secondary Education* (January, 1933), Chap. VIII, pp. 143-147.

BOBBITT, F., *Curriculum Investigations* (The University of hicago Press, 1926).

———, *How to Make the Curriculum* (Houghton Mifflin Company, 1924).

———, *The Curriculum* (Houghton Mifflin Company, 1918).

BONSER, F. G., *The Elementary School Curriculum* (The Macmillan Company, 1920).

BRIGGS, T. H., *Curriculum Problems* (The Macmillan Company, 1926).

CHARTERS, W. W., *Curriculum Construction* (The Macmillan Company, 1923).

CLEMENT, J. A., *Curriculum Making in Secondary Schools* (Henry Holt and Company, 1926).

COCKING, W. D., *Administrative Procedures in Curriculum Making for Public Schools* (Bureau of Publications, Teachers College, Columbia University, 1928).

COUNTS, G. S., *The Senior High School Curriculum* (Department of Education, University of Chicago, 1926). Supplementary Monograph, No. 29.

COX, P. W. L., *Curricular Adjustment in the Secondary School* (J. B. Lippincott Company, 1925).

———, *The Junior High School and Its Curriculum* (Charles Scribner's Sons, 1929).

DAVIS, C. O., *Our Evolving High School Curriculum* (World Book Company, 1927).

Department of Superintendence of the National Education Association, "The Nation at Work on the Public School Curriculum," *Fourth Yearbook* (1926).

———, "The Junior High School Curriculum," *Fifth Yearbook* (1927).

———, "The Senior High School Curriculum," *Sixth Yearbook* (1928).

EELLS, W. C., *The Junior College* (Houghton Mifflin Company, 1931).

HARAP, Henry, *Economic Life and the Curriculum* (The Macmillan Company, 1927).

———, *The Technique of Curriculum Making* (The Macmillan Company, 1928).

HOPKINS, L. T., *Curriculum Principles and Practices* (Benjamin H. Sanborn and Company, 1929).

Lincoln Elementary School Staff, *Curriculum Making in an Elementary School* (Ginn and Company, 1930).

MCMURRY, C. A., *How to Organize the Curriculum* (The Macmillan Company, 1923).

National Education Association, "Creating a Curriculum for Adolescent Youth," *Research Bulletin,* Vol. VI, No. 1 (1928).

———, "Vitalizing the High School Curriculum," *Research Bulletin,* Vol. VII, No. 4 (1929).

———, "Keeping Pace with the Advancing Curriculum," *Research Bulletin,* Vol. III, Nos. 4 and 5 (1925).

National Society for the Study of Education, *Twenty-Sixth Yearbook,* "Curriculum Making: Past and Present and the Foundations of Curriculum Making" (Public School Publishing Company, 1927).

PETERS, C. C., *Objectives and Procedures in Civic Education* (Longmans, Green and Company, 1930).

PROCTOR, W. M., *The Junior College—Its Organization and Administration* (Stanford University Press, 1927).

SNEDDEN, David, *Sociological Determination of Objectives in Education* (J. B. Lippincott and Company, 1921).

STOUT, John E., *The Development of High School Curricula in the North Central States from 1860 to 1918* (Department of Education, University of Chicago, 1921).

STRATEMEYER, Florence, *The Effective Use of Curriculum Materials* (Bureau of Publications, Teachers College, Columbia University, 1931).

UHL, W. L., *Secondary School Curricula* (The Macmillan Company, 1927).

WILLIAMS, L. A., *The Making of High School Curricula* (Ginn and Company, 1928).

———, "Analysis Techniques in Curriculum Making," *School Review,* Vol. XLI, 437-443 (June, 1933).

CHAPTER II

Since the report of the Committee of Ten in 1893, there has been a gradual but consistent development: first, of the experimental attitude on the part of administrators and teachers; and second, in the organization of scientific techniques and procedures by research experts and professional leaders. The era of scientific determination of curricular materials has not arrived, but progress has been achieved in a relatively short period of time and the momentous problems which will be of vital concern in the immediate future are envisaged by American educators as never before. By 1910, the scientific movement in education was well defined, and its influence in curriculum building was apparent at once. The questionnaire had been used by Hall at Clark University for a number of years; the technique of the survey had been developed; statistics, as a tool, was being introduced into educational research; the reaction against faculty psychology had led to experimental studies in the learning of children, and these in turn promoted investigations concerning the size of classes, elimination and retardation of pupils, and measurement of achievement. The quantitative or fact-finding era was introduced, and it was influential in making available a vast amount of data.

The organization of these research studies stimulated educators to investigate the relationship among the goals of living, the principles which govern society as it is organized and functioning in the United States at the present time, and the education of present and prospective citizens. All problems of curriculum making are connected with an effort to synthesize these three aspects of life. A hiatus has been maintained between the educational program of the schools and society to such an extent that the practical business of living has been regarded as something apart from education. It is difficult to organize a dynamic educational system that will be effective and efficient in contributing to the dynamic social well-being of the nation.

Constant Revision Imperative

Living in the United States has become tremendously complicated. The simple pioneer life has given way to existence in a machine age, the significance of which is not apparent even to those who have produced it or now have a part in its direction. Education has given little evidence of being guided by those who have appreciated the evolution of society, and, as a people, American citizens have been dilatory in sensing the maladjustment which exists between their educational program and life as it is being lived in all sections of the country. Educators have not been stimulated by the parents of the children to make the schools function in training the youth to participate in society. Education is still regarded as providing an entrée to culture, which is thought of as being exemplified by past cultures, rather than as a preparation for the business of living in a society which is rapidly developing a new culture of its own. As education proceeds from its present status toward one that is more significant in the realization of the practical and social aspects of adjustment of individual members in society, it will be more apparent that constant reorganization and revision of teaching materials and methods of procedure are essential.

The Units of Instruction Must Be Defined

In the curriculum construction, which has been organized so far, it is evident that clear and concise definitions will have to be developed for the various units. An educational ladder has been constructed in this country without any clear thinking concerning the functions of the various administrative units.

They are still in the process of evolution, but the fundamental characteristics are becoming permanent in each unit. This enables one to characterize elementary, secondary, and collegiate levels of education.

A. Elementary education. To elementary education has been assigned the achievement of those skills, habits, attitudes, ideals, etc., which are basic in American civilization and required by every citizen. There is, in theory at least, no possibility of differentiation in achievement for the students in these fundamental essentials. There are only those who can attain basic standards and those who cannot. However, special schools or special programs are developed in most large cities for pupils who are unable to make suitable progress in the regular grades. The elementary school is a training ground for all in the fundamentals of American citizenship.

The dual purposes of the elementary school can be summarized as follows: first, to provide the common training which is the inherent right of every child, regardless of economic status, intellectual level, sex, race, creed, or special aptitudes; and, second, to produce an educated citizenry which has command of the essential skills, knowledges, and habits and similar basic attitudes and ideals. The future of American democracy is dependent, to some extent, on the integrated citizenship formulated and realized in the elementary school.

The succeeding chapters will discuss the approach made by educational societies and individuals during the present century to determine those basic facts, skills, attitudes, and ideals which are important enough to be included in the indoctrination program for every individual in the United States. As a result, many changes have appeared in the elementary curriculum. Many phases, which were considered important a short time ago, have disappeared; new conditions have been introduced both as the result of a prayerful aspiration on the part of educators and scientific research; old activities, which were a part of the differentiated program of the secondary school, have been reallocated to this level.

The failure of the various economic classifications in society to understand the position and objective of every other group has pointed clearly the need for a "new deal" in integrated education of the people. The problem of producing a like-minded citizenry will no doubt remain the goal of the elementary school for several decades at least. No faculty of any unit in American education has a greater responsibility.

Superintendent Herbert S. Weet stated the purposes of the elementary school as follows to the public in Rochester through the pages of the *Rochester Democrat and Chronicle* in 1926:

1. To read, write, and speak correctly the English language, and to know and use intelligently the elementary processes of arithmetic. By common consent these are the fundamentals without which neither the knowledge nor the training essential to the fullest enjoyment of life, to economic independence, and to satisfactory citizenship can be secured.

2. To know and observe the laws of physical health and well-being, and to appreciate the meaning of life and nature.

3. To know and to appreciate the geography and the history of his own community, state, the nation, and to some extent of the world at large; to sense his share in the social, civic, and industrial order of such a democracy as ours, and to meet to the full the obligations which such knowledge and appreciation should engender, to the end that justice, sympathy, and loyalty may characterize his personal and community life.

4. To share intelligently and appreciatively in the fine and useful arts through the pursuit of music, drawing, and literature; of manual training and the household arts as they are related to the three great universal needs of food, clothing, and shelter.[1]

B. Secondary education. In contrast with elementary education, secondary education is concerned primarily with the individual interests, and problems connected with the differentiation of the work of the school are paramount. In the first years of the secondary school, individual differences, abilities, aptitudes, and interests of students are explored; in the later years of this unit, those interests which have been definitely established are capitalized; and specialization is basic in the entire program by the conclusion of the junior college years. The selection of a life vocation by the pupil and training for effi-

[1] Department of Superintendence, *Fifth Yearbook* (1927) pp. 12-13.

ciency in the work of this field constitute one phase of the secondary program in this country. It begins as an exploratory program and extends through a period of rather intensive specialization.

Learning activities in the secondary school are concerned with adjusting the pupil to the world in which he is living and in which he will participate as a citizen. Since the world is constantly changing, it is essential that the objectives of secondary education be stated in terms of adjustment to a changing world. The culture of the past and present is used to develop a complete vision of an evolving culture and civilization and generate attitudes and ideals basic in an improving society. The secondary school is not for the purpose of teaching subject-matter as such, but for the purpose of educating pupils to adjust themselves to their social and physical environment through a study of the various subject-matter fields.

It is hoped that through these intellectual efforts the pupil will develop drives and interests which will stimulate him to continue his cultural interests in school and out of school. His ability to work definitely toward recognized goals will determine his approach to all intellectual, cultural, and moral problems in his later life.

C. Higher education. It has been pointed out in the last few years that the program presented in colleges and universities to-day is a confused jumble of secondary training and college and graduate work with the emphasis at all stages upon the arithmetical sum of the class hours completed rather than progress in securing an education. One of the great problems in this country is in developing a definition of higher education, or in redefining it through a reorganization of departments and courses.

The great increase in enrolments in institutions of higher education has made it necessary for college administrators and teachers to consider the problem of individual differences. This problem has affected the universities only recently, and halting, hesitating plans for meeting the situation are just being developed. Every unit in the educational system, beginning with the primary grades, has been made conscious of this problem in the present century, and particularly in the last decade.

The problem at the university level presents many complexing aspects. Entrance requirements, grades, credits, schemes of promotion, graduation, diplomas, honors, etc., are a few minor problems which cannot be solved until the major reorganization involving departments, colleges, and upper and lower division work has been completed.

Curriculum Making Must Function in Every School

At present, scientific curriculum study and revision are being carried on only in the larger cities such as Oakland, Cleveland, and Baltimore. This situation is due to the lack, in most cities, of financial resources and the trained technical direction needed to initiate and develop such a program. Even in the smaller schools, however, there is developing an appreciation of the fact that much remains to be done in the determination of teaching materials, and dissatisfaction with the *status quo* is pressing for the formulation of new programs. This has led administrators and teachers in the rural schools to seek advice and assistance from the larger towns. The demand for course of study bulletins has become so great that practically all these progressive school systems have been forced to take them off the free distribution list and gradually organize the business of publishing courses of study in various fields.

Every school system can, at a reasonable cost, become familiar with the extent of revision in any subject-matter field in the cities which are proceeding under the trained direction of a curriculum specialist. Securing courses of study from various cities and adapting them to the community or adapting the community to the teaching programs and methods found in these courses of study appear to be the procedure used in many communities at the present time. This adaptation of the community to imported courses of study has been called the "scissors and paste pot" method of organizing learning activities for the children. The values and limitations of this method are too apparent to merit discussion, but it is significant that thousands of communities are making an effort to reorganize and vitalize their educational program. This continuous effort, even in communities which are too small to hire trained experts or teachers who have had experience in this type of work, demonstrates that educators are recognizing that at least three important results are secured from this endeavor. First, the teacher who is engaged in this work is constantly becoming more and more professional since he must develop a philosophy of education as a basis for the program he is initiating and he automatically improves in his own teaching as he considers new teaching materials, new methods, new tests, etc. Second, the teacher and the supervisor can analyze the improvement in teaching in terms of objectives already agreed upon and of results which have been attained in the classroom. In a system in which the curriculum is being studied, supervision may be scientific rather than haphazard "snoopervision." Third, as results are secured in improving teaching and supervision, the child in his own community becomes more and more the center of curricular endeavor and research. It is necessary to keep in mind, however, that even in our larger cities, which are progressively minded, little progress has been made in establishing the child as the center of the curriculum-building program.

The small communities, which are without the services of a curriculum expert, may participate in curriculum construction and course of study making under the following conditions:

1. State courses of study are being developed in the more progressive states. In general, these are the results of teacher participation, and the teachers of the smaller communities may coöperate with the various committees and the state department. Committees in the various subject-matter fields are usually appointed by the state professional organization of teachers and are continuously studying the new data which have been reported as the result of investigation and research. All teachers attend these sessions and profit from the reports and discussions.

2. Research experts in curriculum construction may be se-

cured for larger units than the school district and the various districts participate in the expense of this phase of the program. Since the time element in course of study construction approaches two years, in most cases, such a director could efficiently supervise the organization and development of a number of courses in different communities simultaneously and coöperation between the committees of the various centers could be advantageously developed. A central library or meeting place would facilitate this.

3. The school system may be organized for professional work in this field without the services of a curriculum expert. This type of work necessitates the appointment, by the superintendent, of committees in the various subject-matter fields. A program of reading should be outlined, and the details of the reports which should be made to the entire faculty suggested. In general, these reports should represent at least a year's work by the committees and should adequately present and discuss:

a. Basic principles of education
b. General aims of the subject-matter field
c. Specific aims of the subject-matter field
d. Methods which are particularly desirable
e. Tests
   1. Standardized
   2. Those worked out by the committee
f. Grade placement of the subject-matter
g. Texts and materials essential for instructional purposes
h. Plans whereby the suggestions or certain phases of them may be incorporated into the school system
i. Comparison of these reports with similar reports and investigations carried on in towns of the same size, and with the formal reports of committees in the larger cities, where the program includes a curriculum expert.

The value of universal teaching participation in curriculum research may be stated in the words of W. J. Holloway. His conclusions, which were developed as the result of an investigation in the state of Maryland to determine experimentally the value of teacher participation in curriculum making in the supervisory program in the schools, were as follows:

1. True democracy in supervision requires that all teachers in service be encouraged to participate freely, and as fully as their abilities permit, in all activities that have to do with the improvement of classroom instruction.

2. A means of supervision upon which too little emphasis has generally been placed is the course of study itself. Administrative coöperation in the making of courses of study for all types of schools is a most effective means of securing (a) professional growth of teachers in service, (b) a broader understanding and a deeper sympathy between supervisors and the teaching force, and (c) an exercise of initiative, at present too little in evidence.

3. Every teacher may be expected to make some contribution to the curriculum, if only a unit of subject-matter, a lesson plan, or an intelligent criticism of the offerings of others. The extent and character of her contributions are determined by her natural endowments, her professional training, her desire for service, and the encouragement extended by the supervisor.

4. The final measure of the efficiency of any administrative or supervisory instrument is the extent to which it benefits the children. A course of study prepared by so-called experts with only incidental and unorganized assistance of the general staff of teachers, however excellent it may be from a theoretical standpoint, is a failure if it does not stimulate the intelligent and enthusiastic support of the average classroom teacher. The course of study most likely to be administered successfully is the one made through democratic coöperation between the superintendent and the supervisors and all the teachers working in the field under consideration. A committee will be satisfactory, provided its members are not all chosen primarily because of their abilities for this work; it is of major importance that types of teachers and all districts be represented.

5. A course of study made in accordance with the foregoing principles will stand the test of scientific scrutiny, considering (a) choice of material, (b) the best classroom procedure, and (c) the learning process.

6. The teachers and supervisory officials who participated in this study are practically unanimous in their belief that teacher participation in curriculum making tends to make such teachers more efficient as classroom instructors than if supervised in the "usual way." [2]

[2] W. J. Holloway, *Participation in Curriculum Making as a Means of Supervision* (Contributions to Education, Teachers College, Columbia University, No. 301), pp. 3-4.

The problems which are involved in making revision of the curriculum effective in every community can be summarized as follows:

1. Many states are organizing curriculum bureaus and taking the initiative in a program of course of study construction. Committees in the various subject-matter fields, such as the National Council of Teachers of English, National Council of Mathematics Teachers, etc., the Office of Education with its research staff, and national professional organizations, such as the Department of Superintendence and the Association of High-School Principals, are interested in the problem of organizing content in the course of study and correct grade placement of this material. Considerable activity has been in evidence, but little that can be used by the local committee has been forthcoming. Two general criticisms hold for most of the material that has been produced up to the present time. In the first place, much of the data secured as the result of these large surveys cannot be applied at once to the local situations. Local committees feel that they find little in these reports which is constructive in the sense that it is definite and specific enough to be applicable to their situation. Second, the reports of many of the large groups appear to be colored by the majority thinking of the group or the thinking of a small committee which makes a report for the group. Often, these reports appear to be organized with little understanding of the societal problems which are waiting for solution and with little or no concern about the remainder of the curriculum in relation to the material which is being stressed by the national organization.

2. The local situation cannot be improved by committees that are over-influenced by material which has been developed without due regard to social and educational tendencies. Furthermore, no scholarly committee will accept materials produced under such adverse conditions. Local committees, which are making real contributions, find it helpful to agree upon a philosophy of education and the place of their subject-matter field in realizing such a philosophy. Then all decisions of a controversial nature are settled in terms of this philosophy and the best advice avail-

able. This advice may come from national or state sources, or it may represent the scholarship of the local committee.

3. A survey of present-day curricula leads one to the conclusion that the greatest contributions for years to come will be made by the local committees. A scholarly local committee, familiar with all the research in the field and which has developed considerable research in policies, materials, and procedures in the local community, is in a better position than any outside agency to formulate the program for the local school system. The opposite of this situation is found in communities where the committee has lacked scholarship and has relied upon the curriculum work of Denver, Oakland, Cleveland, and other cities. These cities have been forced to publish courses of study on a commercial basis, because of the demands of other cities wishing to adopt their policies, materials, and the procedure by the "scissors and paste-pot" technique. There is no sound reason why the research of cities that have curriculum experts should not be available to every city in the United States for the purposes of comparing and evaluating the results obtained from local research, but it is adding little to the school system or the professional status of a faculty to produce a course that is only a combination or reorganization of the courses of several of the larger cities.

The results of the local committees' work can be evaluated not only in terms of the course of study produced, but also in terms of the effect of this work upon teaching efficiency in the school system. The course of study is, in a certain sense, a prepared lesson for the inexperienced or new teacher in the system, and it should include the pooling of teacher experiences and experimentation in adjusting teachers in the local situation.

4. The local course of study has the following advantages at the present time over the state or national program :

a. The teachers who participate on the committee and those who participate in the experimentation are re-educated in the content of the field and the new methods of teaching. All others gradually approximate the level of the participating groups.

b. A technique is developed among the teachers of that subject for the organization of any new group of learning experiences for pupils. Teacher initiative is developed along specific lines.

c. The work of the preceding and the succeeding units of the school system is understood, and the coördination of the work of all these units is provided.

d. A local course of study that really functions in the school system has within itself possibilities for the in-service training of teachers and a continuous program of subject-matter revision and reorganization.

PROBLEM IV

Curriculum Making Must Be Translated Into Better Teaching

Curriculum making and course of study construction are for the sole purpose of improving teaching and facilitating learning. Unless these goals are achieved, the time and effort as well as the money invested in the program have been wasted. It is unnecessary to emphasize the fact that many well-bound and beautifully printed courses of study have served only as an addition to the professional row of books which are on the teachers' desks.

In order that the course of study may be an instrument for the improvement of teaching, it must have the sympathetic understanding of the faculty and be the result of their intelligent coöperation. It must represent growth on the part of the faculty and contribute to further growth and professional development. It is imperative that the course of study be stimulating to the teachers, supervisors, and students in postulating objectives, suggesting interesting and valuable materials and experiences, presenting highly desirable methods, and prescribing an adequate and reliable checking and testing program. The course of study will be functional if it is organized according to these general standards and the supervision in the system is of the coöperative type.

PROBLEM V

Curriculum Making Must Proceed in Accordance with Certain Definite Limitations

Factors that determine the rapidity with which a curriculum program may be developed or factors that determine the comprehensiveness of such a program are in evidence in every community. The following list of forces that limit and determine the extent and effectiveness of course of study construction is composed of items not all of which are important in every community. In some cases probably only one or two of them are operative, while in other cities the complete list is of significance to the administrator who is outlining a revision program.

1. *Financial condition of the school system.* It is true that the courses of study may be reviewed and analyzed by a faculty without incurring any large financial outlays. It is also true, however, that a program operating under the direction of a curriculum specialist and necessitating the allocation of committee rooms, the development of a curriculum library, hiring substitute teachers in place of those who are engaged in active work in the revision, buying thousands of tests, etc., costs a great deal of money and must have a place in the budget and be allocated certain mileages in determining the school tax. It is therefore essential that the program receive the enthusiastic support of the people, so that additional funds may be voted and the district may be in a financial condition to support this new activity without undue financial strain.

2. *The size of the school plant.* Unless the building or buildings used for school purposes are adequate to permit the school to operate under the new organization, there is little likelihood that the objectives established in the revised fields will be translated in terms of student realizations. Lack of laboratory space, lack of physical-education facilities, overcrowded classes, heavy teaching loads, and lack of auditorium space are a few of the factors that must be considered in determining the possibilities of extensive curriculum revision.

3. *The amount of equipment in the school plant.* This factor is related definitely to the one discussed in the preceding paragraph. It may be illustrated by the school library. Many of the objectives of the newer courses in English cannot be realized unless there are adequate library facilities in the school or in the city. It is manifestly impossible to check the improvement of the students in the appreciation of literature, unless books,

magazines, and newspapers are available. It is not the contention
here that nothing should be done in order to improve present
conditions, if certain facilities are not available, but teachers who
are working under those conditions should realize the limitations
which are imposed.

4. *The professional training of the teaching staff.* The training and preparation of teachers for participation in the work
of revising the curriculum and courses of study will determine
the point of departure and the types of programs which can be
accomplished as well as the time element of each project. This
factor is so important in the ultimate success of this work that
many school systems organize regular training courses for those
teachers who have been selected as committee members or po-
tential leaders in this work.

5. *Community interests and aptitudes.* Lay opinion of the
community, particularly of those who are interested in education
and those who support the schools through the payment of taxes,
must be considered. Curriculum revision and reorganization is
more than an education of the faculty and students; its success
rests upon the ability of the school people to educate the people
of the community and secure their coöperation in the undertaking. Before any real work can be assigned to the various departments in the school, it is essential that a survey be made to
determine the limitations which are imposed by conditions in
the community. This survey should include an analysis of the
following facts:

    a. Local heritages, mores, and customs. These may be racial, or
    merely provincial, but they should be carefully studied.

    b. The cosmopolitan school. The results of recent surveys indi-
    cate that children will attend the nearest school even if their
    interests are not served by the curriculum. A study of the
    community will make possible a nice balance between cur-
    riculum and interests of students.

    c. Local opinions and beliefs. These may be deeply rooted, and
    only misfortune can develop from a radical and abrupt attempt
    to eradicate them through the educational system. The famous
    case of evolution in the State of Tennessee is an excellent
    illustration of this impasse!

d. The professional classes. These represent the educated clientele of the school, and their support is vital to the success of the reorganization. If they are well represented on the school board or are influential in educational matters, the program may be considerably accelerated.

e. Local societies, religious and patriotic, etc. It is difficult to proceed with revision unless these societies are in accord or at least neutral. A bias or a prejudice on the part of any organized group must not be stimulated.

f. Vocational opportunities. One of the important problems to be faced by any school system is the vocational placement. The vocational training that may be developed in the school system will depend, to a large extent, on the coöperation of vocational leaders and organized industrial groups.

6. *Types of students.* There are, at least, two aspects of this problem from the standpoint of the students themselves. The general level of intelligence among the students is a deciding factor in determining types of curricula. If very few students have ever entered institutions of higher learning and practically none will go from this year's senior class, this fact should be considered in organizing the program of studies. In the second place, the amount of mobility in the student body will be a significant factor. If there is little or no mobility in the student body, the problem of articulating the school with others need receive but slight consideration. Great mobility necessitates a program of studies in which incoming students may be adjusted without difficulty and one which enables outgoing students to articulate themselves in other school systems.

PROBLEM VI

Curriculum Making Must Recognize the Similarities as Well as the Differences Which Exist Between Communities

Communities vary as to basic industries and vocations, and therefore, such curricula as commercial, agricultural, trade training, horticultural, and college preparatory will be emphasized in one section of the country and possibly omitted entirely in another. This condition may differentiate also among the various high schools in the same city.

There are common features of the educational program, however, which persist even in the most dissimilar situations. English, science, art, music, foreign language, social studies, etc., may vary to some extent in response to peculiar community conditions, but are essentially and basically the same in every community. Local studies will have but little general significance except in cases where emphasis, enrichment, or special applications in these fields are studied.

The following differences must always be kept in mind: (1) size of building and equipment, (2) size, training, and professional outlook of staff, and (3) the philosophy and training of administrators.

PROBLEM VII

Curriculum Making Must Recognize the Significance of Articulating Units of Education

In colonial days the elementary school was not related to the secondary program, and so there were no problems of articulation between these units. A few courses, composed almost entirely of classical content, were offered in the Latin grammar school, and these were organized as definite preparatory courses for the work in the classical fields that was offered in the college. It might be said that they were parts of the same educational system, although they were not under the same administrative organization. The educational objectives in those days were stated for both units as follows: "the training of young men for the service of God in Church and Commonwealth." With this common objective, the curriculum of each institution was carefully articulated with the other, since the educational development of the young man was regarded as a continuous process although two different units made a contribution. The close relationship between the two schools is further explained by the following quotation from the Entrance Rule (Harvard University) of 1643:

When any Schollar is able to understand Tully [Cicero], or such like classical Author extempore, and to make and speake true Latine in Verse and Prose, *suo ut aiunt Marte* (without any help whatsoever): and decline perfectly the Paradiams of Nounes and Verbes in the Greek tongue; Let him then and not before be capable of admission into the Colledge.

The problem is no longer so simple. Through the years gradual changes have come in the educational scheme of the United States. In the eighteenth century the elementary school was established as a part of the educational ladder and articulated with the secondary school. At the same time the new secondary school (the academy) began to supplant the Latin grammar school. New curricula, preparing for business and general life opportunities, were introduced and emphasized in the early stages of this movement to the exclusion of the college preparatory ideal or objective. Later, academies became preparatory schools, and problems, latent in the articulation of several curricula and hundreds of courses to the college and university program, began to engage the attention of educators. Those problems have increased rather than diminished through the years of the remarkable development of the high school. In 1935 there were more than twenty-five thousand public high schools and more than seven million pupils in these institutions. These pupils are engaged in studying courses ranging from advanced mathematics (solid geometry and trigonometry, etc.) to auto mechanics and wood-working. Hundreds of courses are organized into various curricula with objectives as diverse as college preparation and efficiency in manual trades. Hundreds of thousands of these students are petitioning for college entrance into curricula as different as the humanistic training of the colleges of liberal arts and the vocational training of the numerous curricula of the colleges of business administration. No one can concentrate on these problems without being appalled at the number of studies and investigations that must be completed before any solution can be developed for high-school and college administrators.

At present, the determination of educational objectives, the reorganization of old teaching materials and the developing of new learning experiences are concerning teachers and educators in the separate units, but little has been done in the matter of articulating the activities of the elementary school, junior high school, senior high school, junior college, and university. Expressions such as "the revision of the junior-high-school course of study in English" give credence to the popular concept that the courses of the unit are not necessarily related to the preceding or following work. Many college faculties are engrossed in the reorganization of the curricula of their various schools and colleges, but few are considering seriously the preparation which their students receive in the secondary units. A few glaring examples of this are found in a large western university. In this institution, it is absolutely impossible for the girl who has pursued a course of home economics in the high school to be admitted into the college of science for the purpose of working for a degree in home economics. In the same school, professors of chemistry have been heard to make the statement that they preferred students in their department who had never received high-school credits for work in that field. A protest of high-school teachers of English brought about an investigation of the teaching of college English. This investigation showed that many bright students, after making excellent records in high-school English, were failing in the freshman course in English or doing very unsatisfactory work in that department. Examples might be multiplied, but these are sufficient to indicate the present disregard that teachers in one unit have for the work of those in another, and the present lack of appreciation of the importance of articulating the educational program of the child from the kindergarten or elementary years to its consummation.

This lack of understanding, on the part of the teachers, has been a factor in the development of prerequisites. The student is required to have completed one or more courses in order that he may be permitted to enter a department or enroll in a particular field. The result of this procedure has been to focalize the thinking of our teachers and administrators upon the number of credits a student has attained and the grades which he has secured, rather than upon the knowledge he has acquired, the skills he has perfected, the attitudes that govern his daily reactions to his fellow man, and the ideals that are basic in his philosophy of life. In general, credits and grades, which represent little beyond the fact that the student has contacted the material in the course, are accepted in lieu of more reliable evidence that enrolment in the course has been a profitable experience. The outstanding example of this faulty thinking is the university that, in its entrance requirements, demands that the prospective student present grades of a definite standard for matriculation, but makes no effort to establish the amount of knowledge that the student has in these fields as a background for his college work. The assumption that grades represent real attainment is the basic cause of much of our maladjustment, both in the case of the students who are admitted and those who are refused admission.

The prerequisite is a clumsy way of preparing for a course. This is evidenced by the fact that many of the prerequisites of the present day have developed, as subjects lost their popularity, in order that the enrolments might be maintained. There are subjects in the university and secondary school that could not be offered year after year on any other basis. One of the most difficult problems facing the administrator, who wishes to reorganize the curriculum, will be found in the study of the values of these fields as essential prerequisites because certain fields have acquired "inherited" or "vested" interests through the years. As an illustration of the method of the development of "vested" interests in the curriculum, the author participated in a meeting of college professors who were considering the reorganization of the required courses in their department. There were eight men in the department, and the result of their deliberations was eight required courses of elementary work in sequential order. That each instructor should have a reasonable enrolment appeared to be the first consideration, while the educational needs of the students were expressed only in terms of "I believe" and "I think" on the part of these educational leaders.

There are two evidences of a reaction against the prerequisite program as it affects the modern university. The first is found in the more general requirements that are being presented to faculties for the matriculation of students. The second is the development within the department, school, or college of general or comprehensive courses that present the work formerly required from other faculties. In the English department, for example, comprehensive surveys of modern literature and modern thought are replacing courses in sociology and economics, which were formerly considered prerequisite to the advanced courses.

The reader should note, in summarizing his thinking on this problem, that in many statements on curriculum construction and by the activities in many school systems it is implied that a course of study developed in a particular subject will be usable in all curricula offered in the school and in all ability levels that have been organized in the system. In reality, teachers are not considering the course of study in English for the senior high school, but the course of study in English for the brilliant pupils in the school who will or may enter institutions of higher education; they are considering a course of study in English from the first grade to the fourteenth, if the system includes a junior college, and one that articulates with higher education in any case. An explanation of the manner in which these problems enter into the plans of the curriculum builder will be helpful in classifying the definitions that have been given in the preceding section.

1. *Courses of study for all curricula.* We have said that the program of studies is developed in accordance with the philosophy of the educators, and that it represents the fundamental principles or tenets of that philosophy. A curriculum, however, is the organization of teaching fields to achieve certain general objectives that have been formulated in harmony with these philosophical principles. While all curricula may be subsumed under these general principles, the general objectives governing the organization of teaching materials within particular curricula may range from college preparatory to some type of trade training.

The problem that concerns all curriculum makers (this title, which is so often used incorrectly, is used advisedly here) is to determine the variation in the organization of teaching materials in a field according to curricula. Even though both of the curricula mentioned might fit into an integral part of an educational philosophy, do not their general objectives demand different student experiences and learning activities in many subject-matter fields? If the answer to this question should be affirmative, then course of study construction would become a much more significant task than it is at the present time. A course of study would have to be constructed in all subjects for every curriculum, although this does not necessitate the publication of separate courses. The variations can be provided for in the development of a single course. Practically all attempts in this direction, however, have been ineffective because the committees working with the courses of study have not seen all the implications involved in the relationship of the course of study to the curriculum.

2. *Courses of study for all ability levels.* This problem of ability levels becomes significant as soon as we consider the millions of pupils who are entering our educational institutions. It applies not only to the elementary school and the high school but also to the university.

The organization of curricula within the school should provide for differences in ability as well as for variations in interests. The rapid expanding of the secondary units particularly has indicated that, no matter how far this procedure of developing curricula may be carried, the program will never provide adequately for all the levels of ability present in the school. If the committee considering course of study construction for a school system finds that in particular schools ability levels in the curriculum in which this material will be used vary as much as 40 I.Q. points (80-120), it might be necessary to develop distinct courses for these ability levels. We cannot envisage the student with an I.Q. of 80 having the same educational objectives in terms of subject-matter as the student with an I.Q. of 120. Thus, the problem of course of study construction is not only a horizontal one in terms of curricula, but is also a vertical one in terms of ability levels.

3. *Articulation of the courses of study.* As we consider the organization of a course of study for a particular grade or unit of the school system, the entire educational program of the children must be included. The child has certain potentialities as he enters school, and they influence the organization of his work at all levels, but more particularly as he enters the differentiated work of the secondary school and university. The organization of teaching materials for a particular ability level in a particular grade predicates that those in charge must have a clear, concise understanding of the educational background of the pupils as this has been built up in previous years. Any new organization of materials must be in terms of reorganization of materials for all the preceding grades or units of the school system and for all succeeding grades of the children's educational work. The chart on pages 54-58 from the Seattle, Washington, course of study in English indicates the articulation of needs, attitudes, habits, and abilities.

Courses of study that are organized for a particular unit or grade without reference, or with only desultory reference, to preceding and succeeding units provide neither for the educational gaps that are bound to occur nor the duplications that necessarily creep into the new course.

Course of study construction is intimately related to the development of curricula in the program of studies, to the development of work for all ability levels in the school, and to the articulation of the educational experiences of the child.

PROBLEM VIII

Curriculum Making at All Levels of the School System Is No Longer an Academic Problem; It Is a Matter of Concern and Interest to American Citizens

Many forces in the United States at the present time are influencing curriculum construction. Reverberations of this national interest are heard on the one hand from college halls and on the other from the elementary schools. There are definite and specific reasons for this awakening among the school people and the lay citizens:

1. *Social and economic readjustment in society.* From the days of the early industrial revolution (1865) to the days of the later industrial revolution (1929), schools attempted to adjust their programs to the millions of newcomers within their walls. The programs of studies that these students could complete increased by hundreds of courses. Most of the old courses have been retained. The cost of education has increased geometrically rather than arithmetically as enrolments have grown.

Teachers and administrators have been forced to study the curricula of all levels, since, first, these new students must be satisfactorily adjusted, and, second, this must be done without increasing taxation on real estate and personal property beyond the limits of human endurance. Recent elections have indicated that taxation of real estate will be relieved without reference to the curtailment of curricula in elementary, secondary, and collegiate grades of work. Recent statements of newly elected officials that State universities should receive every high-school graduate who wishes to come will probably force these institutions to consider extensive revisions of their curricula.

2. *Non-citizenship attitudes of the masses.* Recent elections have shown that a national crisis is necessary to develop an interest on the part of a great mass of the people in their rights of suffrage. They have, also, indicated a tendency to vote a straight ticket that does not require an analysis or even a consideration, on the part of the voter, of national or local issues, or the character and caliber of the candidates of the various parties. The thinking citizen is concerned, as never before, with the objectives and achievements of education.

Laymen, as well as school teachers, have been impressed with the increase of educational costs and facilities and the increase of crime of all types—murder, racketeering, and bootlegging, as well as fraud and graft among government officials. The need of training in citizenship is profoundly recognized in every group interested in the success of our experiment in democracy.

Basic Needs, Attitudes, Habits, and Abilities at Each Grade Level

Kindergarten and First Grade	Second Grade	Third Grade	Fourth Grade	Fifth Grade	Sixth Grade
BASIC NEEDS OF THE CHILD AT EACH GRADE LEVEL					
Adequate social adjustments. Development of desirable attitudes and habits	Opportunity for continued practice of previously acquired attitudes and habits	Adequate opportunity to interpret what he has read. New language expressions presented in positive situations	Careful guarding of habits of expression acquired in earlier grades	Attention to new units of expression. Growth toward mastery of these units	Functional presentation of new language techniques. Presentation of names of *nouns, verbs* and *adjectives* as additions to *vocabulary*
Kindergarten. Stimulation of spontaneous expression as a result of environment	Free oral expression as basic to the new group activity — written expression	Major emphasis on oral expression. Use of textbook permitted to groups whose mastery of reading assures pleasure and profit	Careful planning of written work: *a.* Purposeful *b.* Preceded by oral preparation. Participation of each child in group secured	Conservation of spontaneity and originality. Attention to problems of integration	New opportunities for use of additions to vocabulary resulting from enlarged experiences
First Grade. Conservation of kindergarten attainments. Willingness to wait his turn to express his ideas					

Kindergarten and First Grade	Second Grade	Third Grade	Fourth Grade	Fifth Grade	Sixth Grade
		ATTITUDES, HABITS, AND ABILITIES ESTABLISHED AT EACH GRADE LEVEL			
Kindergarten The desire to: a. Share experiences b. Speak in approved ways Confidence in expressing himself The habit of: a. Free expression in group enterprise b. Listening to what others say First Grade The desire to see his ideas expressed in writing	Confidence in the ability to express ideas orally and in writing Appreciation of the fact that ideas may be expressed interestingly Ability to use correctly and effectively new forms of expression Pride in ability to use written forms approved by the group	Greater freedom in speaking to audience Audience addressed more directly More discrimination shown in use of material Increased consciousness of correct forms Greater pride in use of new and approved forms Willingness to practice difficult forms	Acute consciousness of group as listeners Desire to: a. Entertain the group b. Influence opinion c. Contribute desired information Pride in holding to standards The habit of: a. Learning new words b. Re-reading and checking written work Ability to contribute to:	Consciousness of the group manifested by: a. Increased care in preparation of work b. Pride in successful performance Habits of: a. Consideration of group b. Planning of work with less dependence upon teacher c. Attention to: 1. Language forms 2. Appropriateness of	Genuine interest in a. Language problems b. The need of an enlarged vocabulary Habits of re-reading, correcting and revising first drafts of written work Ability to: a. Plan work independently b. Help the class to set up and maintain correct standards Skill in conducting class meetings and club activities

BASIC NEEDS, ATTITUDES, HABITS, AND ABILITIES AT EACH GRADE LEVEL—(Continued)

Kindergarten and First Grade	Second Grade	Third Grade	Fourth Grade	Fifth Grade	Sixth Grade
ATTITUDES, HABITS, AND ABILITIES ESTABLISHED AT EACH GRADE LEVEL—(Continued)					
Consciousness of his listeners and of the need to direct his talk to them The tendency to use correct forms when his speech has been corrected Satisfaction in acquiring new expressions			a. Group composition b. Group plans for programs Ability to preside over committee meetings	contribution Ability: a. To act upon committees b. To act as chairman of committees	

Seventh Grade	Eighth Grade	Ninth Grade	Tenth Grade	Eleventh Grade	Twelfth Grade
BASIC NEEDS OF THE CHILD AT EACH GRADE LEVEL				Public Speaking	Senior Composition
More stress upon language techniques	Conscious application of standards and princi-	Alertness and readiness in making adjust-	Strengthening of foundations Discovery of spe-	The techniques of public speaking	The course in Senior Composition

Seventh Grade	Eighth Grade	Ninth Grade	Tenth Grade		
Recognition of parts of speech in material on grade level Unfailing employment of complete sentence in written work manifested by: a. Correct use of capitals b. Correct end-punctuation	ples learned in earlier grades Recognition of words and word groups as tools Knowledge of phrase and clause forms Mastery of classification of the parts of speech	ments Recognition of: a. New techniques b. Need of constant practice in them	cial aptitudes and tastes Practice along lines of aptitudes Intelligent choice of next course Intelligent use of time and opportunity in preparation for next course	require: a. A good vocabulary b. A clear voice c. Clearness and force d. Appreciation of great speeches The pupil should develop ability to: a. Make extempore speeches b. Organize knowledge for effective discussion c. Organize formal speeches Creative Writing Creative writing demands: a. Recognition of the value of the course	assumes a need of: a. Detailed practice in language forms b. Application of received principles and standards to new forms of expression c. Organization of knowledge on specific levels: 1. In preparation for college 2. In anticipation of the needs of business life The course should develop the ability to: a. Use words accurately and appropriately

ATTITUDES, HABITS, ABILITIES ESTABLISHED AT EACH GRADE LEVEL

Seventh Grade	Eighth Grade	Ninth Grade	Tenth Grade
The habit of: a. Using clear and effective English b. Using correct language forms c. Making additions to vocabulary	The habit of seeking the right word Pride in speaking well in all situations Skill in variation of sentence form by arrangement of	The habit of: a. Investigating problems b. Analyzing them c. Organizing knowledge d. Careful wording of solution	The habit of: a. Attending to detail b. Subordinating ideas c. Studying thought processes d. Searching for underly-

BASIC NEED, ATTITUDES, HABITS, AND ABILITIES AT EACH GRADE LEVEL—(Continued)

Seventh Grade	Eighth Grade	Ninth Grade	Tenth Grade	Eleventh Grade	Twelfth Grade
ATTITUDES, HABITS, ABILITIES ESTABLISHED AT EACH GRADE LEVEL—(Continued)					
d. Acquiring and using standards for the correction of own work	words and phrases The ability to use clear, forceful, and beautiful English	Skill in handling group situations Ability to relate content material to language work	ing principles Ability to interest the group in carefully prepared creative work Ability to establish truth in the minds of hearers	b. Desire to attain the outcomes Pupil should show growth in handling short story and essay	b. Prepare effective outlines c. Organize and develop expository paragraphs and essays d. Compose correct and effective business letters e. Organize reports in effective manner
				Journalism	
				Journalism requires: a. Recognition of the values of words b. Skill in sentence and paragraph construction c. Ability to write clearly and coherently d. Recognition of value of newspaper	

The last decade has witnessed an increasing interest, on the part of our citizens, in educational programs and policies. This important topic cannot be adequately presented here, but the reader may investigate any of the following fields for further information: (*a*) legislative acts passed since 1900 providing for the teaching of, or prohibiting the teaching of certain subjects in all units from the elementary school to the state university; (*b*) articles written on education and educational policies and published in leading magazines in the last few years; (*c*) resolutions offered by nationally known patriotic societies and professional societies in favor of or opposed to certain materials in the curriculum; (*d*) increase in membership in Parent-Teacher Associations, etc.; and (*e*) coöperation of laymen with professional school people in studying educational problems, i.e., a committee to survey conditions, determine objectives of a course of study, or determine an educational policy.

3. *Minority-group influence in curriculum construction.* A study of the activities of certain groups having religious and political associations indicates the influence that well-organized minorities have been able to exercise through political lobbies and publications.

PROBLEM IX

Curriculum Making Must Be Based upon the Available Scientific Investigations, Studies, and Reports

The curriculum committee must be familiar with the scientific work that has been done in the particular field. Numerous national societies, as well as local investigators, are constantly presenting new data. A few of these will be mentioned.

1. *Reports of committees organized to study the curriculum.* Since the report of the Committee of Ten in 1893, many committees have influenced the educators who have been studying this problem. Of general importance, the following reports should be mentioned: Committee of Fifteen, Committee on the Economy of Time in Education, Commission on the Reorgani-

zation of Secondary Education, committees appointed by Dr. Cooper (Office of Education, Department of Interior) to study education at all levels on a national scale.

There are other committees, representing particular subject-matter fields, which have exercised, through their reports, an influence in the reorganization of materials in these fields. Some of the more important are: (a) Report of the Committee on the Place and Function of English in American Life, (b) Report of the School and College Conference on English, (c) Report of Committees of the American Historical Association on the History and the Other Social Studies in the School, (d) Reports and Yearbooks of the National Council of Mathematics Teachers, (e) Reports and Yearbooks of the National Council for the Social Studies, and (f) Reports of Committees appointed by the National Society for the Study of Education to study specific subject-matter fields.

2. *Contributions of colleges of education and other teacher-training institutions.* In the last few years, courses in the technique of course of study construction, and organization of curricula have taken a prominent place in the offerings of these colleges. The influence of these practical courses that can be used as laboratories in which to attack the problems of particular schools cannot be overemphasized. In many instances, Bureaus of Curriculum Investigation have been developed which offer the services of their specialists and library facilities to the schools of the country. Western Reserve University and Columbia University may be mentioned as notable examples of this movement.

3. *Contributions of the larger cities with specialists in charge of the curricular program.* Many of these cities, such as Cleveland, Baltimore, Oakland, and Detroit, have well-organized curriculum departments as guides for the work of their committees. The influence of these school systems is national in scope and, on the whole, beneficial to our educational program. The "scissors and paste pot" technique, however, is only transitional and will pass away with the improvement of teacher training and teacher-in-service programs.

Curriculum Making Must Be Based on Individual Differences of Children

In the last quarter of the nineteenth century, the organization of pupils into groups for instruction purposes became the custom, and the individual was submerged in the class. The recognition of the individual pupil as the object or unit of instruction has stimulated the development of several types of individual instruction in the present century. It is not essential here to discuss these various types, but to emphasize that every unit in the educational ladder, from the kindergarten to the university, is facing the problem of organizing learning activities so that the greatest good for the greatest number can be realized.

As soon as one realizes that the intellectual possibilities of pupils at all of these levels vary from border-line cases to genius, it becomes imperative that the organization of learning materials should be developed so that each individual can progress at his optimum rate of speed toward objectives which have been formulated in terms of his abilities and aptitudes.

Educators cannot countenance the development of a course of study in a particular subject for a school system. The course of study must be functional in terms of the pupils. This type of organization demands that learning experiences be developed so that the course of study will contain:

1. *Functional centers of interest for each group of pupils or each individual pupil.*
2. *Learning experiences developed at several different levels.* This means that different sets of objectives and different activities should be outlined for each level of work. It does not mean that ability groups, in the generally accepted connotation of that term, must be organized in the school. Deviations within ability levels must be recognized and adjustments made for individuals in each classification. The number of levels depends on the size of the school and the size of particular classes, varying from two to eight.
3. *Classroom procedures, adapted to the pupils of the particular classification.* All learning is conditioned by the emotional set of the pupils toward the work. The particular method chosen by a

teacher or committee for use with a group or an individual should be considered carefully before being selected.

Curriculum Making Is Conditioned by Current Experimentation in the Integration of Units and Teaching Fields

This means that curriculum makers are formulating their programs in terms of functional materials rather than merely divisions of subject-matter. The activity of the pupil is receiving greater emphasis, and the time-worn phrase, "learn to do by doing," is recognized as a basic principle of the construction of the unit of work. The immediate effect of this general acceptance of the concept has been the breaking down of old subject-matter fields and the organization of new integrated units of work.

There have been related effects of this movement in that old subject-matter fields may be retained and the units of work organized so as to integrate with the needs, abilities, and activities of the pupils and the needs and conditions of society. A unit organized as a functional unit would have a different type of title from the old-type subject-matter unit. It will not be stated as a division of subject-matter but as an aspect of the function of society or the individuals who make up society.

Swindler presents an interesting discussion on this subject as it is related to the social-service field:

It is now pretty generally recognized, among the users of units of work, that the traditional unit in social science has been, essentially and too nearly exclusively, a subject-matter unit. This, of course, was to be expected, considering the nature of the materials: texts, references, teacher-training methods, content, etc., that were offered in recent years as the basis for teaching and study in the social studies field. In fact, most of the earlier research studies with which teachers and curriculum makers in this phase of high-school instruction come in contact were surveys and analyses of subject-matter from various sources. Illustrations of this method are Hocket and Billings surveys of the years 1927-1930 and the surveys of the recent past, of the contents of newspapers, periodicals, etc., with which studies most of you are somewhat familiar. These studies, and the results published, rendered a real service, too, in that they helped to fasten in our minds the essentials in the common core of subject-matter and the practical use to which these essentials might be put. But, as in the case of much of our past teaching, as well as the prevalent use of objective tests, they "smacked" too much of the practice of using *tools* or *means* of education as an end in themselves, or as the end of education. The present movement is concerned more with the building up of the type of activity or experience unit which is in conformity with the ultimate goals of education now pretty generally accepted in our country, and not with testing the mastery of subject-matter alone. Locally, the new units in civics and American problems illustrate this trend toward a more functional unit. The vocational civics and geography units also are fairly good examples of this type of unit. This tendency means, in practical terms, that the student is given an opportunity to perform in a larger degree the activities and to have the experience in school similar to those he meets with in his life outside the school.[3]

PROBLEM XII

Curriculum Making Is Dependent on (1) the Organization of a Program of Studies Which Will Function in the Community and Is Based on the American Philosophy of Education, (2) Making a Distinction Between That Which Is Important in the Administration of the School and That Which Is Educationally Significant in the Life of Each Pupil in the School, and (3) the Development of a Technique for Organizing Materials So That They Will Function in the Realization of Curricular Objectives

The program of studies is the educator's response to the needs of the clientele in a particular community balanced by an understanding of the tenets of American philosophy of education. The factors, such as laws, judicial decisions, demands of various societies, as affecting the curriculum, etc., must be considered, but the effectiveness of the educational program depends on the grasp which the administration of the school

[3] R. E. Swindler, *Current Trends in the Development of Units in Social Science,* University of Virginia Record Extension Series. Vol. XIX, No. 3 (Oct., 1934).

system in the community has of the basic principles of education and community conditions.

Every superintendent and principal is interested in having his school system or his particular school attain results in an effective manner and with as little friction and "jarring" as possible. This desire for a well-oiled program sometimes causes the administrator to emphasize the cataloguing of pupils into curricula rather than meeting the tantalizing and elusive problems of adjusting the work to each individual pupil. There has been a recent tendency among educators to make the titles of curricula functional. That is, a curricula would not be called "scientific," but "Scientific Preparation for the College of Science or the College of Engineering." This has practically eliminated the former practice of naming them in terms of emphasis of subject-matter content.

However, as soon as emphasis is placed upon the functional aspect of the curriculum, the administrator is forced to face the problem of making a functional curriculum for each pupil. This not only complicates the work in the office, but also necessitates a complete revision of courses of study included in the administration curricula of the school. It is apparent at once that no curriculum-making program can proceed effectively without an understanding and highly-trained guidance officer to initiate many of the important details and confer and advise with pupils and faculty and, at times, participate in directing the curricular development in terms of pupil adjustment.

The third aspect of the problem presents the controversial issue of the development of fields of subject-matter in various curricula to meet the needs and interests of boys and girls in terms of to-day in the school and to-morrow in society, versus the policy of organizing materials to-day in coöperation with the pupils in the hope that ever-widening interests will guarantee complete adjustment in society after school days are over. The first can be more or less scientifically determined and techniques have been developed to assist curriculum makers in this work; the second approach is not so scientific, nor can its results be easily evaluated. Of course, there is a third position, midway between these approaches to curriculum construction, which insures most of the values claimed by the adherents of both schools of thought. The problem is merely mentioned here; a complete presentation will be made in the later chapters of the book.

SUMMARY

While progress has been made in the scientific determination of teaching materials, the teacher and administrator should have definitely in mind the pressing problems in curriculum construction. Many of these problems are stimulating to the progressive teacher, while others tend to circumscribe the work which may be accomplished in this field. A careful analysis of these problems at this time and constant reference to them as the later aspects of the book develop will enable the reader to see the present situation in its true perspective. This chapter analyzes the present background of curriculum construction.

BIBLIOGRAPHY

BAGLEY, W. C., *Education, Crime and Social Progress* (The Macmillan Company, 1931).

BOBBITT, Franklin, "Difficulties to be Met in Local Curriculum-Making," *Elementary School Journal*, Vol. XXV (May, 1925), pp. 653-663.

BODE, B. H., "Determining Principles of Curriculum Construction," *Educational Administration and Supervision*, Vol. XII (April, 1926), pp. 217-228. An excellent discussion of essential principles.

——, *Modern Educational Theories* (The Macmillan Company, 1927). A very stimulating book.

BRIGGS, T. H., *Curriculum Problems* (The Macmillan Company, 1926).

BUCKINGHAM, B. R., "Scientific Curriculum Making," *Journal of Educational Research*, Vol. I (May, 1920), pp. 404-407.

CALDWELL, O. W., "Types and Principles of Curricular Development," *Teachers College Record*, Vol. XXIV (Sept. 1923), pp. 326-37.

COUNTS, G. S., *The Senior-High-School Curriculum* (University of Chicago Press, 1926). A status study of the program of studies.

"Curriculum Making in Current Practice," A Conference at Northwestern University (College of Education, Northwestern University, 1932). A Symposium on current practice by leaders in the field.

DAVIS, C. O., *Our Evolving High School Curriculum* (World Book Company, 1927).

Department of Superintendence, *Fourth Yearbook*, "The Nation at Work on the Public School Curriculum" (1926); *Fifth Yearbook*, "The Development of the Junior High School Curriculum" (1927); *Sixth*

Yearbook, "The Development of the Secondary School Curriculum" (1928); *Seventh Yearbook,* "The Articulation of the Units of American Education" (1929); *Eighth Yearbook,* "The Superintendent Surveys Supervision" (1930).

EELLS, W. C., The Junior College (Houghton Mifflin Company, 1931).

EVERETT, Samuel, and OTHERS, *A Challenge to Secondary Education* (D. Appleton-Century Company, 1935).

FLEXNER, Abraham, *Universities* (Oxford University Press, 1930). A stimulating discussion of current university problems.

GLASS, J. M., *Curriculum Practices in the Junior High School and Grades V and VI* (University of Chicago Press, 1924).

GRAY, W. S., *The Junior College Curriculum* (University of Chicago Press, 1929).

HALLOWAY, W. J., "Participation in Curriculum Making as a Means of Supervision" (Contributions to Education, Teachers College, Columbia University, No. 301).

HARRINGTON, H. L., *Program Making for Junior High Schools* (The Macmillan Company, 1930).

JUDD, C. H., "How Modern Business May Aid in Reconstructing the Curriculum," *School and Society,* Vol. XVII (March 17, 1923), pp. 281-87.

——, *Problems of Education in the United States* (McGraw-Hill Book Co., 1933).

KINNEMAN, J. A., *Society and Education* (The Macmillan Company, 1932).

National Education Association, "Keeping Pace with the Advancing Curriculum," *Research Bulletin,* Vol. III, Nos. 4 and 5 (Sept. and Nov. 1925); "Creating a Curriculum for Adolescent Youth," *Research Bulletin,* Vol. VI, No. 1 (January, 1928); "Vitalizing the High-School Curriculum," *Research Bulletin,* Vol. VII, No. 4 (Sept. 1929).

National Society for the Study of Education, Twenty-Sixth Yearbook, Parts I and II (Public School Publishing Company, 1927). Part I presents current problems and an excellent bibliography. Part II contains the basic principles of curriculum making.

NEWLON, J. H., "Practical Curriculum Revision in High School." *The North Central Association Quarterly,* Vol. I (Sept. 1926), pp. 254-263. The suggestions are based on the Denver plan.

PROCTOR, W. M., *The Junior College* (Stanford University Press, 1927).

THRELKELD, A. L., "Curriculum Revision: How a Particular City May Attack the Problem," *Elementary School Journal,* Vol. XXV (April, 1925), pp. 573-582.

UHL, W. L., *Secondary School Curricula* (The Macmillan Company, 1927). The best single source on current problems of curriculum making.

WITHERS, J. W., "Adapting the Curriculum to Individual and Community Needs," National Education Association: *Addresses and Proceedings,* Vol. LXIII (1925), pp. 815-826. A critical discussion and an attempt at evaluation.

PART II

PRINCIPLES AND OBJECTIVES
OF EDUCATION

CHAPTER III

RELATING CURRICULA TO LIFE

I. THE CURRICULUM AND LIFE GOALS

Since the course of study is a vital part of the curriculum, and since the curriculum is determined by life goals and educational principles, it is necessary to analyze these goals and principles carefully in order that the true relationship of the course of study and the curriculum to education may be apparent. The curriculum has been defined already in terms of the administration of the school and *school education* of the child. The realization of the child from his school experience is his *individual* school curriculum. A pupil's individual curriculum may be spoken of accurately as his growth through his school activities and experiences. The child's individual-life curriculum is much broader and, therefore, much more significant from the standpoint of society than his school curriculum.

In the life educational program, the school must play an important part in the symphony of experimental growth. Unless the school is in touch with contemporary life, it cannot function in harmonizing the school curriculum with the life curriculum. The school is not to prepare for life; nor is schooling identical with life. Both of these statements, which have received so much attention at various times in education, are incorrect. There is an element of truth in each, however, which has been instrumental in causing them to attract the attention of thinking men and women in the educational field.

In the first place, the native drives and interests of the individual must be merged with the interests of society. Unless the latter can become the conscious objective of the pupil, school and society cannot coöperate. The second problem that immediately springs to life, as soon as agreement is reached concerning the congruence of the goals of society and the individuals who make up that society, is concerned with the determination of desirable social objectives. While society must determine the general development of the individual, it is equally true that the pupil must be taken into account in the establishment of definite social goals. Educators and curriculum builders must realize that there is constant give and take, action and reaction, interdependence, between the individual and the society in which he lives.

It does not follow from the foregoing that the education of the individual is only a preparation for a fixed social state that has been determined by identifying the related objectives of the individual and the group. Since individual experiences are dynamic and society is dynamic, the educational process must prepare for a dynamic life. No list of objectives, however complete, can visualize the perfect adjustment of the individual in a society, for society is changing and the individual as he grows and becomes educated learns to appreciate new levels of attainment in that society. Instead of final goals to be attained by the individual, the educator needs to keep in mind higher levels of achievement within a constantly evolving society. The ultimate attainment of the individual will depend to a large extent on his ability to adjust himself to constantly higher degrees or levels. Education, then, will not be a matter of preparing for something that is definitely anticipated, but rather a growth through various levels or steps, each of value in itself and leading to ever higher standards of performance.

The life of the individual cannot be prepared for in any real sense; it can be lived by him, from day to day, as he responds to circumstances and situations arising in the conditioning influences of the school and of life that he is contacting outside of the school. But in a narrow sense he can prepare for life in that he can study a trade course in order to enter a trade, or he can study German in order to be able to speak or read German fluently. His work in the trade or his speaking of German is only one phase of his life, which is made up of countless activities other than these. An analysis of either of these attempts to improve pupils' conduct appears simple in comparison with improving pupils' citizenship for the multitudinous experiences in adult citizenship. It is far more difficult to evaluate success in improved citizenship than improvement in the use of the German language, and, yet, if improvement or development toward a definite goal cannot be measured, that particular goal is of no concern in our educational program. Prior to 1918, the emphasis was largely on scholarship in the various subject-matter fields. Teachers were interested in producing scholars in Latin, mathematics, English, history, etc. With the publication of the bulletin on the "Cardinal Principles of Secondary Education," educators began to visualize those principles as basic in the organization of an educational program. In a haphazard and general way, administrators and teachers began to talk of making good citizens, good parents, adequately prepared workers, appreciative consumers of leisure as well as creating a healthy citizenry and one which represented outstanding examples of ethical character.

The attempt to develop a quantity production of good citizens, excellent consumers of leisure, or adults trained to qualify under any of the other principles resulted in confusion where these principles were accepted as goals and followed blindly. Progress cannot result from any statement of general principles unless these principles are analyzed into their specific component parts. Otherwise, educators cannot state or appreciate the goals upon which they are constructing an educational program. Leaders in the educational profession have been slow to appreciate the significance of this challenge. It is much easier to revise a course, such as German or wood-working, than it is to begin with the principles of life and organize an educational program; it is much easier to stimulate teachers to render lip service to their philosophical ideals than it is to make possible the realization of an educational philosophy through the school system as a functioning instrument. The translation of a philosophy of education into the minds of the teachers so that the realization of these concepts can be attained through the school system, represents not only the educational problem of this age, but also the problem that has concerned professional teachers of all ages since the formal school program developed in society.

II. THE MEANING OF EDUCATION

Educational practice and educational thinking are, in part, the product of all the theories, practices, and principles that have been developed in the past. It is necessary for the curriculum builder to search back through the ages to orient himself to the task at hand. While it is doubtless true that educators to-day cannot subscribe completely to the program and educational principles of any one of these periods, it is helpful to realize that many of the present principles that we regard as new and a product of our own enlightened age were proposed and advocated in the past. Indeed, it is the good fortune of the present age to be in a position to develop a synthesis of these principles and create an educational system that is a result of the best thinking and most efficient practice of the preceding generations. It is true, of course, that new knowledge, which has been created through research in science, psychology, and sociology, has made possible new interpretations, integrations, and syntheses of the old principles of life and education that were not contemplated by the leaders in educational thought in preceding periods.

In general, it may be said that investigations in science have contributed a vast amount of the curricular material; research in psychology has given us a new meaning of education in terms of growth, principles of learning, the value of interest in the student, and the desirability of effort on the part of the learner; investigations in the social studies comprising sociology, economics, political science, and history have analyzed society and individual participation in social organizations, methods of organizing social groups, problems concerning group and individual responsibilities, the well-being of groups and individual members, and contributions of the various economic levels of society as a whole. Briefly, science has contributed additional teaching materials; psychology has presented new interpretations of method; and sociology has made possible the development of new and more valid aims and goals of education in terms of life itself.

The curriculum is organized in terms of the philosophy of the past and present, and for the purpose of shaping the thinking or philosophy of life of the individual in the school. It is the mass of carefully selected materials, experiences, and activities through and by which the student can develop a philosophy, can think accurately regarding situations as they arise, and can make rapid and happy adjustments in society. This raises the interesting question concerning the rights of the individual and the rights of society in the development of the curriculum. To what extent is it desirable to condition the student to the same behavior patterns, emotional attitudes, habits, ideals, etc., as his fellow pupils? To what extent shall the educator consider the student as an individual and allow him to grow according to his own interests? It is essential that society improve in the direction indicated by its ideals and values which constitute the essence of the good life. Therefore, the degree to which it is necessary to promote common training, common materials, and experiences in the formal school program must be accurately and definitely determined. There must be sufficient integrated training in order that society and the individual may move forward in harmony with each other.

If the school is to aid in improving the general welfare of society, educational theory and practice must be synchronized with the promise inherent in our rich natural endowment, in our advanced technology, and in our human resources for a richer, finer, freer, and more abundant life for every citizen. In other words, if the general welfare is to be advanced, education must be for life as it *might* and *should* be lived as well as for life as it *is being* lived. Though it places a great responsibility upon the school, there can be no escape from the conclusion that the school must guide the future development of American society. Education should not attempt to escape the responsibility.

The purpose of the school is to modify original human endowment through organizing experience and operating the laws of learning so that the aims and values of society will become those of the individual. If the individual is to contribute to the evolution of society, he must be brought up to a certain standard in order that he can effectively coöperate in that evolutionary process. There is no guarantee, of course, concerning what experience will develop in the individual or society. New complexities will constantly appear in the associated living of human beings, and these complexities will become more and more apparent as extensive studies are developed in the fields of social and moral adjustments. Ultimate adjustment will depend on a completely inter-related analysis and synthesis of the total field of human experience.

Only those who have deliberately or otherwise blinded themselves to the facts revealed by everyday observation deny that every important aspect of life to-day is profoundly affected by far-reaching changes. It seems equally apparent that even more rapid change is to characterize the years which lie ahead. Consequently, if the school is adequately to serve the needs of our people, it must accommodate both its theory and its practice to the fact of change. Never again, it appears, will the school be called upon to serve a relatively static society. Rather, changed and changing conditions with reference to the family, church, communication, transportation, recreation, economy, occupations, justice, government, and world relations are placing and will continue to place staggering burdens upon the school.

In the preceding paragraph it was postulated that education can be defined only in terms of society and the individual. In a general sense, it is organized in a formal way in order that society may consider its movements, both positive and negative, analyze the goals toward which it is moving, and state principles which are governing its advance. As these goals are determined and analyzed, it should be possible to formulate the objectives of education in terms of the improvement of conduct on the part of the individual who will fit not only in society as it exists at the present time, but who will be able also to advance with society as it progresses in the realization of its goals or principles of living.

Since this is true, it will be apparent, as the more minute and definite aspects of the problem of organizing this program for the individual student are considered, that course of study construction or field of study construction must be worked out in terms of the improvement of conduct on the part of the student. How does the student perform at the conclusion of the course of organized experiences and activities? That is the only criterion of progress in the curriculum of the student or in life as presented in his adjustment in society. For this reason, it is essential that the statement of the objectives of the course or field should be in terms of improvement of conduct. The practical aspects of this problem will receive attention in later chapters, but it will be helpful here to indicate that the improvement of the individual in his relationship to the desired evolutionary improvement in society can be stated in terms of conduct.

There are two phases to this educational program of the individual pupil: first, he must see life as it has developed down through the ages so that he can gain an appreciation of the best in literature, art, government, and science in the construction of his social inheritance; and, second, he must see the ramifications of present social, political, economic, and scientific adjustments in the society in which he will be an effective citizen. Thus, the approach in every field or subject should be in terms of the present lives of the pupils, and new or revised curricula must be predicated on learning from the past, living in the present and looking to the future. In this reorganization, traditional subjects may have to be eliminated as such and new materials developed from a study of current and predictable near future social problems in which there is common interest. Effective educational programs will use the past only as a tool in understanding and controlling the present and future.

III. PRINCIPLES OF LIFE AND OF EDUCATION

Every nation, society, people, or period of history has had its spokesman (philosopher or scientist) who has stated for it the basic principles of life, and, incidentally, the basic principles of its educational program. Every significant change that has come in the educational organization has been preceded by a new statement or a restatement of the goals of life. These goals of life, or of living, give direction to the program of the formal aspects of education. It is only when the educator can see the definite relationship between these life goals and the educational process that there is opportunity for progress. These goals or principles of life have to be more than mere statements or stimulating phrases if they are to affect the educational program. When the educational process of the group is articulated with the ideals of society, and synthesis is developed so that progress in one may be measured in terms of the other, advancement is possible. There are two absolutely sure methods by which the educator may fail in organizing his program: first, the selection of goals for the educational programs which are not basic principles in the lives of the people to be educated; and second, failure to synchronize the educational practices with principles which are valid goals of living.

The goals of society must be the goals of the school, if this institution is to mold efficiently the individual members of society toward the correct aims, values, and purposes. The aims and values of society must become the aims and values of the individuals who make up that society. If educators place proper emphasis upon the goals of society, the individual differences of children, and the most effective methods of developing new reactions in the individual according to the laws of learning, the school can select those materials and activities which are of paramount importance in articulating the evolution of the individual member of society with the evolution of the race, nation, and generation. Education will always present certain problems since the social life of any group is constantly changing. However, these changes are not usually kaleidoscopic, nor are they completed in any generation to such an extent that a complete reorganization of goals has to be definitely established within the period. It is, therefore, essential that educators attempt to keep their programs up to date in order that the lag between society and the schools shall be as small as possible. The fact, however, that this lag exists makes it necessary for those directing the educational program to study constantly the goals of society, and revise and reorganize the experiences and activities which are incorporated in the student's school life, so that he may function as a citizen in the society in which he is living.

The new education will be apparent in a life of action rather than a life of leisure. Society needs an immediate and concentrated attack by adults and secondary-school and college students on problems related to current personal and social maladjustments. In the organization of an educational program to provide an integrated training for those in school, educators must revise their concepts of culture. In the past, the ideals of the traditional cultured persons have been stated in college entrance requirements which emphasized foreign language, ancient history, early United States history, technical and specialized mathematics, highly specialized courses in science as chemistry and physics, and English which emphasized formal grammar. There is little possibility that these subject-matter fields can provide a background for the adjustment of prospective citizens in the chaotic conditions of modern society. The new secondary school will have to eliminate these leisure-class teaching materials of another historical period and consider social problems which are transforming not only the superstructure but the very foundations of society.

Every subject retained in the school will be given a social meaning. The social sciences will be taught not as a body of useful information, but as the basis of a finer culture and civilization, in which national resources will be regarded as the heritage of society and the means of improving the common weal rather than existing for personal aggrandizement and exploitation. Science will emphasize new discoveries and techniques which are vitally affecting modern civilization. Technology, which implies a social reorganization in terms of scientific development, will tend to adjust man more adequately and completely in his life-long struggle with natural forces. The implications of this attitude in other fields such as art, music, literature, etc., are apparent at once. All subjects of study will be organized in accordance with the most varied interests of the masses of society. Vocational preparation, as such, will be postponed until the later years of the secondary school or relegated to specialized schools that will follow the completion of the work of particular pupils at reasonable levels of attainment in the high school. This will enable the secondary school to emphasize friendships, family life, natural life, natural beauty, active and effective participation in community, state, and national affairs as well as an intelligent vicarious participation in world affairs.

Culture will not be based on the traditional fields in the thinking of the American people, but the development of a keen interest and personal concern in all ramifications of the social, political, and economic life of the country. The reason for the renaissance in education is the social, industrial, economic, and political evolution of society at the present time. Schools that were developed to meet the educational needs of one social order are now called upon at a moment's notice to meet the exigencies of a new social and economic order. This new social order is still inadequately defined by the leaders in economic and political activities since it is still evolving with dazzling rapidity. Even though the innovations and adjustments in society are not clearly defined and it is impossible to distinguish social or economic progress from paths which may lead to ultimate ruin, the schools can no longer ignore the corresponding demands upon the revision of the content or learning experiences of the program of studies.

These new social currents which are disturbing our economic system are creating staggering demands upon every level of our educational program. The profound changes in all phases of our national life must be incorporated into the learning activities of the school. Present-day conditions must be emphasized in order that a comparison of the "here" and "now" with the past will enable pupils to evaluate and determine progress in terms of the past and present conditions.

In order that the reader may fully comprehend and appreciate this problem from the standpoint of education, he should analyze it historically. A statement of educational goals has been made by every people in all ages or periods of history. The transition of the schools, from the earliest times to the present, has been in response to the principles which have been enunciated by the leaders in education and philosophy. These principles have represented the philosophical, sociological, political, and economic tendencies and beliefs of the country or people, and it has been the problem of the educational system of each country or period to prepare prospective members definitely and carefully for entrance to this particular society. The statement that education is experience is not acceptable to any organized society, since this society, to guarantee its continuance and development in the particular direction as expressed by its goals, must control and organize the experiences, in part at least, which are presented to the child. Progress demands that the educational system shall control and direct the experiences and learning activities of the pupils. Psychology has shown, however, that the pupil must be taken into account when attempts are made to guarantee the *status quo* and to make progress in the realization of the goals of society and in the understanding of the social purposes.

Indoctrination is important in a dynamic society; it would be sufficient, in itself, as an educational program, in a static society. The elusiveness of the educational goals in a dynamic society makes the interests of the child challenge the process of indoctrination. This challenge is one of the major problems in modern education.

The reader in his historical summary of the principles of education should note: first, the goals and principles upon which the learning experiences have been built for the development of efficient citizens in the particular society; second, the attitude of the educational leaders and thinkers toward the nature of the child and his possibilities in realizing the goals established; and third, the organization of experiences so that continuity and progress could be established in the group. Every people has been interested in four aspects of education—pupil endowment, aspirations and hopes of society, the organization of experience, and the methods of presentation to the child so that his life may be harmonized with that of social life in terms of his ability—and has organized an educational program which has been proposed as an effective procedure in the realization of their social aims.

It will be evident to the educator that the adjustment of the individual cannot be secured by merely hoping or depending on faith. Both the experience and the native ability of the learner and the nature and objectives of society must be taken into account. It should be emphasized that the education of the individual is not concerned with the attainment of a final and definite result, but is a continuous growth which involves a better and finer appreciation of previous experience and a more exact understanding of the evolution of society. To summarize: education can establish no final goal for the individual although the starting point and the general guide lines can be more or less definitely determined since they represent the social outcomes and purposes which are the essence of the life of the society. Education must be considered as a process of experience and type of modification through which the learner can adjust himself to the society in which he lives and, in turn, modify and advance that society. Modern education is a problem of *growth* in terms of the *native endowment* of the individual and also in terms of the *social purposes* of the nation or race to which he belongs.

Further, it should be pointed out that these goals are not static in the affairs of men, but are constantly changing in terms of the evolution of society. They are dynamic in the sense that the aims have different connotations from age to age and from generation to generation. An illustration of this is the principle of health in the individual and society. Social and personal health have changed, as educational principles since the "gay 'nineties," and many ramifications and modifications are contained in the present concomitant aspects of the situation. Education for the principle of health, as understood at that time or at any previous time, would defeat its own ends in our modern program, since the evolution of society has made necessary an evolution in the meaning of the term. It is apparent, of course, that as the principles are affected by the evolution of society, the materials of instruction or the experiences of the pupils will also change. Society is dynamic, the principles of education are dynamic, and to be of value, the essential experiences of the student must be dynamic also. Indoctrination of the students in the principles of education, without providing them with a clear understanding that these goals are constantly subject to change, cannot be tolerated. The statement that curriculum revision is a constant, continuous process and that the final course of study in any subject will and can never be written is absolutely sound.

In discussing the principles of education in the United States in 1935, it is essential that the reader visualize the educational process as a procedure on the part of a social or political group. It will be evident from any historical analysis that education is racial and national in character. It is specific and dynamic rather than general and static. The education of a particular people appears to fit their needs and the demands of their social environs. It is correct to say that the Latin grammar schools met the needs of the early Puritan colonists. It is evident at once to the student of history that this particular type of school could not function in the later rugged, democratic society of the frontier; a particular type of education may serve the cultural needs of a race or nation at one time and be wholly inadequate at a later time to meet new cultural needs and interests. Yet in that past educational program is much that is of value in the basic reorganization which is necessary to meet the dynamic situations of the present. To attempt to proceed without using the results of past experimentation and merely trusting to empiric judgments is not a philosophical or scientific method. The present culture of a society is based in part on the culture of the antecedents of that society, and since education is rooted in the needs and culture of the present society, it cannot be totally unrelated to previous education. This does not mean that educators should reverence the past, but rather that they should recognize the culture, philosophy, and education of previous editions of that society and that therefore education is a matter of evolution and not revolution.

A student of society in this country at the present time will recognize at once that the trend is away from the individualistic type of development, based on *laissez faire,* and toward a planned program for the nation. That the culture of American society will be different in the next decade is admitted by every one. The increased amount of leisure for all classes in society will be significant in the development of this new culture. Education will have to respond to these new cultural elements and formulate a relevant and effective educational philosophy which will be a safe guide in the inevitable evolution of objectives, learning experiences, methods, etc. Both youth and adults in the evolving society should be thoroughly trained for their new social responsibilities and for the realization of rich, cultural, and wholesome lives.

A study and analysis of the principles of education that have been developed by different people through the ages is not suggested in order to point directly to the contributions of any or all of these to the present educational program of this country. Educators cannot look to the past for guidance in the solution of the problems of to-day and to-morrow. The economic adjustment that is being made in American life and the resulting social adjustments find no counterpart in history. However, it will be significant for the reader to think of education as having a geographical and cultural location and as being a function of a nation or a state at a particular time in the development of western civilization. It is hoped that the reader can see the evolution of culture and philosophy through a hurried summary of the thinking of the educational leaders in particular periods and the resultant practices in the society of that time. The future which is of vital significance to every American citizen cannot be divorced completely from the philosophy and the practice of the past.

Herbert Spencer was the first modern scientist to attempt a

statement of educational principles. He outlined a program in preparation for complete living as follows:

1. To acquire knowledge that is essential in self-preservation. In many respects this corresponds to the present principle of health which is very much emphasized. He asserted that a knowledge of physics, chemistry, hygiene, and physiology is basic.

2. To acquire knowledge that is indirectly essential in self-preservation. In this principle he insists that the individual should have information concerning shelter, clothing, and food. Harap has emphasized this principle in his books and articles in the curriculum.

3. To acquire knowledge of the rearing of children. This has been included, in recent times, under the caption "worthy home membership."

4. To acquire knowledge of social and political life in order that the individual may be an intelligent and participating citizen.

5. To acquire a knowledge of literature, art, and music of our own country and foreign countries.

It is apparent that Spencer was concerned with what to teach, or, as he expressed it, "what knowledge is of most worth." He was not interested in the prosaic discussion of the Continent regarding the methods of the classroom. He thought of education in terms of complete living. This meant first, the selection of facts which were fundamental in the well-being of the individual and the race, and second, the development within the student of the ability to use this information. A glance at his principles will be sufficient to note the importance of science in their realization and the comparatively unimportant places occupied by the social sciences and cultural materials.

Spencer's position is opposed to the theory that had dominated education, that a subject lost its educational value as it attained vocational, practical, or utilitarian value. He was interested in bringing to every one the educational advantages that had been enjoyed by relatively few people, and for this reason, placed the cultural aspects of education in the last place in his list of principles. However, his program outlined an educational plan whereby every one would have an opportunity to explore the cultural as well as the utilitarian training. The cultural aspects were not reserved for the few, and the utilitarian phases were developed for the many.

IV. THE INFLUENCE OF JOHN DEWEY

In the period between 1850 and 1900 two principles developed in the consciousness of those who are interested in shaping the educational program. They were apparent in the educational theory of Rousseau, Pestalozzi, Herbart, Froebel, and others, and have become of prime importance in all of the leading nations in the recent period of economic and social reorganization. The principles are: first, the development of economic training in order that the individual may be efficient and independent; and second, the organization of social and political training in order that citizens may be effective and intelligent members of society. These principles postulate the realization of the improvement of society through the improvement of its individual citizens. It is not necessary to enumerate the various changes which have developed in the school systems of our own States in attempting to realize these principles.

With the opening of the twentieth century, the emphasis upon the individual pupil was enlarged rather than replaced by an emphasis upon society. The need of developing the citizen to take part in an ever changing society became the most important factor in education. The idea that the school should be an example of community life and that this principle govern all plans of school work—discipline, teaching, pupil activity, etc.—gained as a result of the thinking, writing, and speaking of John Dewey. He has been the most potent factor in formulating guiding principles, promoting curriculum revision, and organizing extracurricular activities. His principles relate closely to the self-activity theory of Froebel. Dewey has always stressed "coöperative and mutually helpful living" and has introduced the American people as well as other nations to the fundamental principles that should govern a modern educational program. As early as 1899, he visualized the new program as shown in the following pronouncement: "In this case the child becomes the sun about which the appliances of education revolve; he is the center about which they are organized." [1] Newlon says that the following principles, emphasized by Dewey, claim the attention of educators in considering new concepts and procedures:

1. Dewey focused the attention of teachers on the nature and needs of the child. He makes child growth rather than the demands of subject-matter the center of the school's activities, a distinction of the utmost importance.

2. Education is the process of experiencing. In *The Child and the Curriculum,* Dewey says, "The child is the starting-point, the center, and the end. His development, his growth, is the ideal. It alone furnishes the standard. To the growth of the child all studies are subservient; they are instruments valued as they serve the needs of growth. Personality, character, is more than subject-matter. Not knowledge or information, but self-realization is the goal. To possess all the world of knowledge and lose one's own self is as awful a fate in education as in religion. Moreover, subject-matter never can be got into the child from without. Learning is active. It involves reaching out of the mind. It involves organic assimilation starting from within. Literally, we must take our stand with the child and our departure from him. It is he and not the subject-matter which determines both quality and quantity of learning." [2]

3. The doctrine of interest and effort. This emphasizes the fact that teaching materials should be identical with pupil growth, and demanded by the learner in order to develop into himself. Newlon says that there was no problem of curriculum making until the doctrine of interest emphasized the need of selecting subject-matter that would appeal to the child. The identification of learning materials with the growing child is the problem of modern education.

4. The school is a social institution—a little community—in which the social processes are not different from those that go on outside the school. [3]

An excerpt from one of his books will illustrate his program of realizing adult needs, knowledges, and activities through training the child to meet childhood problems satisfactorily. Dewey says:

[1] John Dewey, *School and Society* (The University of Chicago Press, 1899), p. 51.

[2] John Dewey, *The Child and the Curriculum* (The University of Chicago Press, 1902), pp. 13-14.

[3] J. H. Newlon, and Others, *John Dewey—The Man and His Philosophy* (Harvard University Press, 1930), pp. 37-63.

If our education is to have any meaning for life, it must pass through an equally complete transformation. This transformation is not something to appear suddenly, to be executed in a day of conscious purpose. It is already in progress. Those modifications of our school system which often appear (even to those most actively concerned with them, to say nothing of their spectators) to be mere changes of detail, mere improvement within the school mechanism, are in reality signs and evidences of evolution. The introduction of active occupations, of nature study, of elementary science, of art, of history; the relegation of the merely symbolic and formal to a secondary position; the change in the moral school atmosphere, in the relation of pupils and teachers—of discipline; the introduction of more active, expressive, and self-directing factors—all these are not mere accidents, they are necessities of the larger social evolution. It remains but to organize all these factors, to appreciate them in their fullness of meaning, and to put the ideas and ideals involved into complete, uncompromising possession of our school system. To an embryonic community life, active with types of occupations that reflect the life of the larger society, and permeated throughout with the spirit of art, history, and science. When the school introduces and trains each child of society into membership within such a little community, saturating him with the spirit of service and providing him with the instruments of effective self-direction, we shall have the deepest and best guarantee of a larger society which is worthy, lovely, and harmonious.[4]

Cubberley has spoken of Dewey as the foremost American interpreter, in terms of the school, of the vast social and economic changes that have taken place. The following quotation from *An Introduction to the Study of Education* will illustrate his point of view:

The school, then, is a place where children are working rather than listening, learning life by living life, and becoming acquainted with social institutions and industrial processes by studying them. The virtues of the modern school, as Dewey points out, are learning by doing; the use of muscles, sight, and feeling, as well as hearing; and the employment of energy, originality, and initiative. The virtues of the school of the past were too much the colorless negative qualities of obedience, docility, and submission. These are but a poor preparation for social and industrial efficiency, or for democratic life and government. Responsibility for good government, under any democratic form of organization, rests with all, and the

[4] John Dewey, *op. cit.*, pp. 43-44.

school should give preparation for the political life of to-morrow by training its pupils to meet responsibilities, developing initiative, awakening social insight, and causing each to shoulder a fair share of the work of government in the school. That "the school should be life, not a preparation for living, are fundamental parts of Dewey's educational philosophy." [5]

An illustration of the application of these principles to a school program is found in *School and Society.*

In educational terms, this means that these occupations in the school shall not be mere practical devices or modes of routine employment, the gaining of better technical skill as cooks, seamstresses, or carpenters, but active centers of scientific insight into natural materials and processes, points of departure whence children shall be led out into a realization of the historic development of man. The actual significance of this can be told better through one illustration taken from actual school work than by general discourse.

There is nothing which strikes more oddly upon the average intelligent visitor than to see boys as well as girls of ten, twelve, and thirteen years of age engaged in sewing and weaving. If we look at this from the standpoint of preparation of the boys for sewing on buttons and making patches, we get a narrow and utilitarian conception—a basis that hardly justifies giving prominence to this sort of work in the school. But if we look at it from another side, we find that this work gives the point of departure from which the child can trace and follow the progress of mankind in history, getting an insight also into the materials used and the mechanical principles involved. In connection with these occupations, the historic development of man is recapitulated. For example, the children are first given the raw materials—the flax, the cotton plant, the wool as it comes from the back of the sheep (if we could take them to the place where the sheep are sheared, so much the better). Then a study is made of these materials from the standpoint of their adaptation to the uses to which they may be put. For instance, a comparison of the cotton fiber with wool fiber is made. I did not know until the children told, that the reason for the late development of the cotton industry as compared with the wool industry is, that the cotton fiber is so very difficult to free by hand from the seeds. The children in one group worked thirty minutes freeing cotton fibers from the boll and seeds, and succeeded in getting out less than one ounce. They could easily believe that one person could

[5] E. P. Cubberley, *An Introduction to the Study of Education* (Houghton Mifflin Co., 1925), pp. 158-159.

only gin one pound a day by hand and could easily understand why their ancestors wore woolen instead of cotton clothing. Among other things discovered as affecting their relative utilities, was the shortness of the cotton fiber as compared with that of wool, the former being one-tenth of an inch in length, while that of the latter is an inch in length; also that the fibers of cotton are smooth and do not cling together, while the wool has a certain roughness which makes the fibers stick, thus assisting the spinning. The children worked this out for themselves with the actual material, aided by questions and suggestions from the teacher.

Then followed the processes necessary for working the fibers up into cloth. They re-invented the first frame for carding the wool—a couple of boards with sharp pins in them for spinning the wool—a pierced stone or some other weight through which the wool is passed and which as it is twirled draws out the fiber; next the top, which was spun on the floor, while the children kept the wool in their hands until it was gradually drawn out and wound upon it. Then the children are introduced to the invention next in historic order, working it out experimentally, thus seeing its necessity, and tracing its effects, not only upon that particular industry, but upon modes of social life—in this way passing in review the entire process up to the present complete loom, and all that goes with the application of science in the use of our present available powers. I need not speak of the science involved in this—the study of fibers, of geographical features, the conditions under which raw materials are grown, the great centers of manufacture and distribution, the physics involved in the machinery of production; nor, again, of the historical side—the influence which these inventions have had upon humanity. You can concentrate the history of all mankind into the evolution of the flax, cotton, and wool fibers into clothing. I do not mean that this is the only, or the best, center. But it is true that certain very real and important avenues to the consideration of the history of the race are thus opened—that the mind is introduced to much more fundamental and controlling influences than usually appear in the political and chronological records that pass for history.[6]

It was not surprising in 1918 to find the Commission of the Reorganization of Secondary Education including Citizenship and Vocational Efficiency in their cardinal principles. Effective participation in government, economic independence, and social responsibility are the keystones of American education. The

[6] *Op. cit.*

problem of education is provision for their complete realization.

V. PROGRESS IN THE REALIZATION OF EDUCATIONAL PRINCIPLES

The principles which were suggested by the Commission of the Reorganization of Secondary Education have been outlined by different individuals throughout the ages. However, while we may use the same terms to-day, the evolution of society has made them assume new connotations. Citizenship does not mean the same relationship between the individual and society as it did to the ancient Greeks. Any society is constantly revising its principles or its goals in theory and in practice. Naturally, it is far easier to revise theory than it is to change the actual practices in situations which have been established throughout the centuries. It is only reasonable to expect that the schools, which have the formal training of young people in the performance of these skills, habits, knowledges, etc., would lag behind even the societal practices of life. Thus, we are faced in this country with the synchronizing of three ancient educational levels. The problem that education must face is the elimination of these three and the establishment of one level. The first level is that of the philosopher or frontier thinker who is interpreting the principles of education for society; the second level is that of society gradually readjusting itself to these principles; and the third level is that of the formal educational institutions heroically attempting to reorganize tradition, eliminate fallacies and bring the educational institutions into direct and harmonious relations with society. There are forces in our present civilization that are both hindering and assisting in eliminating this hiatus between society and the schools.

A brief discussion of these forces will clarify the problem which educators engaged in curriculum problems must solve.

1. *Forces which are hindering.* It is true that, in many instances, the associations and groups which are mentioned in this section are working strenuously for the well-being of the country and in the interests of patriotism and citizenship. One cannot question their aims, but their methods of approach have tended

often to prevent professional study of the educational problem of adjusting education and society.

a. Legislation on education. More than twenty-two hundred legislative acts passed by State legislatures have either compelled or prohibited the teaching of certain subjects in the elementary schools. Readjustments cannot be made rapidly or effectively by public-school people when such legislative enactments are encountered.

b. Demands of organized groups. More than fifty organized bodies in the United States are actively interested in the subject matter that is taught in the schools. Their reasons are usually patriotic, but their procedure is founded upon the assumption that the inclusion or the exclusion of this factual knowledge in the curriculum will guarantee individual conduct along desirable paths.

c. Textbook companies. Certain publishing houses have large investments in the maintenance of the *status quo* in education. As a consequence, high-powered salesmanship and other influences are brought to bear upon school people and others to avoid change. The attempt which is made to secure the contract of states and cities to long-time textbook contracts in conformity with state legislation is an illustration of this type of influence.

d. Conservatism of faculties, administrators, and school clientele. Evidence is apparent on every hand of the static influence of these groups. The basic reasons for the common attitude of these interested members of the school community are apparent, of course, but they have been allies in preventing change in the school curriculum. It is difficult to advance when the professional leaders hesitate.

(1) Faculties. This professional group has opposed extensive revision because many of them have devoted their lives to preparation for their tasks, and any revision that questioned the value of their particular subjects would jeopardize their positions. It is felt that any reorganization, in terms of the aims of education, would effect an unfavorable reaction toward the traditional teaching fields.

(2) Administrators. Those who have the responsibility for

the success of the school system, in terms of financial outlay and learning achievement, are slow to sponsor any movement which might produce an unfavorable reaction and cost them their positions. Reorganization in a particular subject-matter field can be carried on which will contribute to better teaching, more intelligent supervising, and receive little, if any, criticism. This type of revision creates as much favorable publicity as a complete and fundamental plan or reorganization, and has none of the inherent dangers. In the second place, subject-matter revision is not expensive and does not interfere with the ordinary routine of the school. These facts, together with the realization on the part of the administrators that there are no safe guideposts established at the present time in curriculum revision according to the aims of education, stimulate them to accept the situation as it is and undertake revisions and improvements in those subjects which are already presented.

Jesse H. Newlon made the following statement before the Department of Superintendence in Minneapolis, March 1, 1933:

In the last fifteen years, the curriculum has assumed increasing importance. Curriculum departments were established, teachers were drawn into the movement, yearbooks were issued, commissions created. We were more than justified in the assumption that the curriculum should be given more recognition in the administration of the schools. It is essential that schools set aside personnel and funds for keeping its educational offerings abreast of the best thought and practice. We were on firm ground in assigning a more important rôle to the teachers. The contribution of the teacher is indispensable, for the curriculum of the school is found in the way in which he conceives education.

The curriculum should be planned according to a considered philosophy of education. It is true that gains have been made in method, that subject-matter has been enriched, but there have been few far-reaching changes. In the high school hundreds of thousands of youth to-day are pursuing subjects which are utterly valueless to them and therefore to society. These courses set the pattern for teaching in all classes and limit experimentation on the part of the teacher. Thus education remains largely a process of "learning" subject-matter as an end in itself. The curriculum revision movement in the last twenty years has left the crucial problems in education untouched. A three-R curriculum is nothing short of a social

menace. We as teachers can no longer confine our attention to individuals, but we must become students of society. Youth must be
given a realistic understanding and critical appreciation of the
culture in which they live.[7]

(3) School clientele. The people of the community, who have
attended high school and college, are usually interested in the
subject-matter material in the school. They are familiar with
the old subject-matter fields and are inclined to be suspicious
of any extensive revision and reorganization. Any intimation
that a complete reorganization of the program should be undertaken, or that the educational value of particular subjects was
being questioned in terms of the goals of life would not be
received enthusiastically by the professional people of the community.

2. *Forces that are assisting in the adjustment of the schools
to goals of life and aiding in the revision of the educational
program in order that it may articulate with society.* The contributions of these forces have been mentioned in other sections
of the chapter and will be included here merely to give completeness to this section and to bring into direct relief those
forces that are opposing each other in harmonizing the goals
of life, society, and the educational program.

a. The philosophers. These thinkers are studying human experiences and are using facts, experimental research, and observation as the basis for proposing a program of life and
education that will enable the individual to realize his greatest
potentialities in the social order which is established.

b. The scientists. The investigations and the research of the
scientists are continually adding to the sum of human knowledge and are pointing to the needs of readjustment in our
educational system in order to permit the individual to adapt
himself happily in the ever changing social order.

c. The psychologists. The leaders in the various fields of
psychology are carrying on experiments which are contributing
to the solution of the problem of the mental development of

[7] *News Bulletin of the Society for Curriculum Study,* 1933: No. 3,
Part I, p. 3.

the individual and the easiest and most economical and effective methods of instruction.

d. The sociologists. The relatively new field of science, known as sociology, has made rapid strides in studying society and postulating new standards of culture and new and better ways of living. Society, as it is, and the possibilities of social development are vital factors in the problem of education.

e. The economists. A new economic order is in the process of being established. The new social and economic standards that are proposed as the result of the research of economists will have an important bearing upon the organization of society.

f. The political scientists. These groups are related to many of the others in that they are attempting to use the data produced by other investigators in proposing and developing new social groups and political organizations of society.

Other groups could be mentioned, but these indicate satisfactorily the scope and type of contributions that are being made in determining and promoting the well-being of society. The educator is attempting to harmonize the educational program and society in each decade and generation. The foundations upon which the educator can build are being established by these professional groups in their respective fields.

VI. DETERMINATION OF EDUCATIONAL PRINCIPLES

The preceding sections have indicated the interrelationship of society, educational principles, and the educational system of the race or nation. In the past these principles have been developed as the result of the thinking and pronouncements of educational philosophers and political leaders. Even a cursory survey of the history of any country will indicate the integration of the educational principles with the evolution of the social, economic, and political life of the people. Therefore, it is imperative that the determination of ultimate goals in education be made as scientific as possible rather than left to the philosopher or statesman. Neither of these should be ignored, but they should coöperate with the educators rather than dominate the evolution of education.

Since it is apparent to any student of education that the evolution of the schools lags behind the evolution of society, any attempt to make the schools a functioning part of societal change must begin with a careful and complete analysis of society. When this has been achieved, the philosopher and the frontier thinker can coöperate in a visualization of society as it will be in the immediate future. The schools should be concerned with prophecy and attempt to assist in the complete realization of future for the generation that will participate actively in the life of the next decade. If the schools accept only those principles of living that have been proved through the experiences of the race, the lag of the educational system will always be in evidence.

The determination of educational principles that will relate the curricula of the schools to life must proceed along the following lines and be based on the following types of investigations:

A. Analysis of society in the United States in 1935. In so far as this analysis has been completed, contemporary living in this country appears to have the following characteristics:

1. Economic life has become so highly industrialized that modern civilization can be spoken of as a machine civilization. Power development or energy release has modified the progress of society to such an extent that an era of human labor has been almost completely replaced by one of machine labor. In the short period of half a century, society has been transformed from an agrarian status to a highly industrialized one, and the center of this new life is the congested city rather than the rural sections.

2. Social life has been changed by innumerable discoveries and inventions which have modified living conditions and enlarged the individual's scientific horizon. The changes in industrial life—mass production, easy transfer of people, raw materials, and finished commodities over vast areas—accentuated the inevitable social changes in society.

3. The life of the individual has been changed by these new economic and social patterns. The decrease in the use of

human energy required for economic self-support has been attended by a proportionate increase in leisure. The intelligent use of leisure by the individual and the need of an educational program to further train the people in the realization of a wise use of leisure have become of paramount importance. However, educators must recognize that the life of a citizen presents many new opportunities for advancement through contacts with literature, newspapers, libraries, theaters, and the radio.

4. The political life of the American people is being rapidly transformed. It appears that a number of social and political institutions are in a process of decay or progressive transition. These new proposals and practices in relation to people, and social, as well as political institutions, have enabled the individual to formulate new attitudes and new ideals. A social and political philosophy, which was formally regarded as indicating heresy and treason on the part of the small minorities accepting it, is now emerging as a basic political and social theory of life.

Educators of the United States cannot afford to ignore the changes in economic life, social life, private life, and political life of the people. The school must make a transition from old, generally accepted, and highly dignified positions to new positions which are tentative in the evolution of society. Social development is being evaluated more and more by the criterion of group welfare rather than by the criterion of personal aggrandizement of material greeds through group exploitation. The recognition of the value of the individual member of society to an integrated society justifies the development of a new social philosophy based on the present complex social order. This new social philosophy will be based in part on (1) the right of the individual to have an opportunity to attain economic support for himself and his family, (2) the socialization of the outcomes of labor to such an extent that the general cultural level of society can be raised, and (3) the organization and management of production, distribution and consumption so that every member of society can be assured of the necessities of life which should include adequate food, clothing, shelter, medical care, education, and recreation.

B. Development of educational principles that will enable society to facilitate its normal evolutionary process. There are three interpretations of this obligation of education as evidenced in the national professional conclaves. First, there are those who would have our schools accept the principles of the past and present and endeavor to function as an agency for the maintenance of the best traditions. Second, many are advocates of the theory that the school should train for an impartial understanding of all fundamental problems and controversial issues in modern life. Third, a small number of educators are urging that the educators in charge of the schools participate in a program of planned social progress and no longer sit back as observers and analysts of contemporary life.

The procedures that would be followed by the first two groups in determining educational principles are apparent. An analysis of the past and the present would serve their purposes. In the case of the third group, which postulates the school as an active participant in the creation and direction of a new social order, education is not only a process of adjustment and socialization in terms of *what is* and *what will probably be in the future,* but socialization in terms of *what is* and *what ought to be in the future.*

Any attempt to determine the principles of education that will be significant in the socialization and adjustment of learners in a dynamic social order must take cognizance of the following aspects of life : first, the compilation of the basic attitudes, ideals, and appreciations with respect to social and political organizations and institutions, scientific knowledges and understandings essential in modern society, and understandings and appreciations essential in the creative and practical arts ; second, the determination of the principles which are fundamental in the formulation of generalizations concerning the economic and industrial, esthetic, social and economic, and scientific and natural phases of environment of members of society ; third, the determination of skills, abilities, knowledges, etc., that will enable the individual to meet, understand, and solve new and evolving problems that will arise in the future social order.

The school system should make provision for the pupils to apply these attitudes, ideals, generalizations, skills, etc., in the study and analysis of life situations. At least the evolution of society will be understood in terms of the present and apparent desirable future development.

The educational difficulties and problems of the present era can be generalized in the statement that the educators are really making an effort to adjust the school to life. There are problems in this country that are not in evidence in other sections of the world. The philosophy of a super-Germany under the former Kaiser and his forebears led to the institution of an educational system that would attain that philosophy in the attitudes and thinking of the people. There was a definite social and educational plan. The school was a fundamental item in the life of the German state and the life of its citizens in the nineteenth and early part of the twentieth centuries. At the present time, Germany, under Hitler, and Russia and Italy are striking examples of states that are planning for a definite type of citizenship and society. In those countries the schools have a definite program in the realization of the ideals of the state. Their objectives and their curricular offerings can be given in terms of the goals of the state.

The preceding paragraph has emphasized the ease of formulating an educational program in a state that has a definitely organized national policy and requires the schools to integrate that policy in the lives of the people. How different has been the situation in the United States! In the first place, no social pattern has been established in this country. The problem of relating the school life of the child to the life he will live outside the school is extremely difficult, as the answers to the following questions will indicate: To what extent can common, integrated materials be introduced into the schools without producing a uniformity, like-mindedness, and stability that will be unfortunate in solving the problems of a democratic state? How far dare education accept the principle of freedom as the basis of educational growth?

Unless movements now current are successful in establishing a planned society, there appears to be no chance for educators to work out a program of rigid adjustment in the United States. A school for a planned society would be relatively simple for the curriculum builder; but it is almost certain that the immediate future will still be challenging school people to construct a program sufficiently integrated to enable every one to work, play, and coöperate in essential social activities, and at the same time, promote the highest realization of the individual in terms of creative activity, initiative, and freedom.

The past has its contribution to make in the development of the principles of education, but the present and the future must be carefully evaluated by those who are planning for a society that has never been organized according to a design or plan. The challenge of a democratic society to curriculum makers is awe-inspiring in that it necessitates the relating of a tradition-bound education program to the evolution of new and undetermined social relationships and individual responsibilities.

Progress is dependent on the development of life goals or principles that are basic for an acceptable and understandable program of human and individual growth. An analysis of the forces that are hindering and assisting in the realization of present life goals will help the reader to appreciate the difficulties involved in determining and validating objectives in teaching fields.

As Finney states:

Institutions do evolve; and the collective intellect is constantly at work upon the enterprise of making this a better world in which to live. To be exact, therefore, the objectives of education are not merely the institutions as they are, but as they are becoming. And not merely either, as they are likely to be, but as they *ought* to be. It is not enough that the educational program anticipate the social order of the future; it must anticipate what *ought* to be; and thereby help create it. This is the telic function of education.[8]

[8] R. L. Finney, *A Sociological Philosophy of Education* (The Macmillan Co., 1928), p. 95.

BIBLIOGRAPHY

In order that the student can have access to the best materials relating to this age-long problem, an extensive bibliography is included.

ABBOT, Wilbur Cortez, *The Expansion of Europe.* A social and political history of the modern world, 1415-1789, Vol. I (Henry Holt & Co., 1929).

ADAMS, J. T., *Epic of America* (Little, Brown, and Company, 1931).

ADAMSON, J. W., *Pioneers of Modern Education* (Cambridge University Press, 1905). Contains references to the curricular suggestions advanced by pioneers.

———, *A Short History of Education* (Cambridge University Press, 1919).

ALLEN, P. S., "Sixteenth-Century School," *English Historical Review,* Vol. X (1895), pp. 738-744. This includes a reprint of a Latin manuscript dealing with customs and general regulations.

ARCHER, R. L., *Secondary Education in the Nineteenth Century* (Cambridge University Press, 1921). This is an excellent account of humanistic, realistic, and industrial education in England and Wales.

ARNOLD, Mathew, *Higher Schools and Universities in Germany* (The Macmillan Company, 1892). Published in 1869 as a report to the Schools Enquiry Commissioners.

———, *Thoughts on Education* (The Macmillan Company, 1912).

ASCHAM, Roger, *The Scholemaster* (1571). A progressive thinker deals with curricula.

AYER, F. C., "Major Purposes and Guiding Principles in the Curriculum Revision Program," *The Texas Outlook* (April, 1935).

BAGLEY, W. C., *Education and Emergent Man* (Thomas Nelson and Sons, 1934).

BARNARD, Henry, *Memoirs of Eminent Teachers and Educators in Germany* (Hartford, Brown and Gross, 1878).

BEARD, C. A., *A Charter for the Social Sciences* (Charles Scribner's Sons, 1934).

BENNETT, C. A., *History of Manual and Industrial Education, up to 1870* (The Manual Arts Press, 1926). Chapter II contains bibliography and source materials.

BRINSLEY, John, *Ludas Literarius or the Grammar School* (1612). This contains a discussion on what should be taught.

BROOME, E. C., *A Historical and Critical Discussion of College Admission Requirements* (Columbia University, 1902). Contains an account of the battle for the rights of secondary schools, in addition to information on curricula.

BROWN, E. E., *The Making of Our Middle Schools* (Longmans, Green and Company, 1903). This contains many interesting discussions on curriculum problems.

BUTTERWECK, G. S., and SEEGARS, G. C., *An Orientation Course in Education* (Houghton Mifflin Company, 1933).

Cambridge Modern History (The Macmillan Company, 1902). Chapter

XVII on "The Classical Renaissance," by R. C. Jebb, and Chapter XVIII on "The Christian Renaissance," by M. R. James.

Cardinal Principles of Secondary Education, Bulletin No. 35 (Bureau of Education, Department of the Interior, Washington, D. C., 1918).

CHERBURY, Lord Herbert, *Autobiography* (*c.* 1728). Contains curriculum suggestions and proposals.

CORCORAN, T., *Studies in the History of Classical Teaching* (Benziger Brothers, 1911). Deals with Irish and continental curricula from 1500 to 1700.

COUNTS, G. S., *Social Foundations of Education* (Charles Scribner's Sons, 1934).

CUBBERLEY, E. P., *An Introduction to the Study of Education* (Houghton Mifflin Company, 1925).

———, *Changing Conceptions of Education* (Houghton Mifflin Co., 1909). He discusses in this book the increasing acceptance of the sociological view.

DAVIDSON, Thomas, *A History of Education* (Charles Scribner's Sons, 1900).

DEFOE, Daniel, *The Compleat Gentleman* (*c.* 1728). Edited by Carl Bülbring (David Nutt, 1890). The Editor's introduction is excellent.

Department of Superintendence of the National Education Association, *Thirteenth Yearbook.*

———, *1935 Proceedings.*

DEWEY, John, *School and Society* (The University of Chicago Press, 1899).

———, *The Child and the Curriculum* (The University of Chicago Press, 1902).

DOUGHTON, Isaac, *Modern Public Education* (D. Appleton-Century Company, 1935). Introduction and Parts I, II and III.

DUGGAN, Stephen Pierce, *A Student's Textbook in the History of Education,* 2nd revised edition (D. Appleton-Century Co., 1936). Contains up-to-date discussions of the Russian, Italian, and German national systems.

ELIOT, C. W., *Educational Reform* (The Century Co., 1898). This includes some of the most striking addresses which led to reorganization in the twentieth century.

———, "What Has Been Gained in Uniformity of College Admission Requirements in the Past Twenty Years?" *School Review,* Vol. XI (1903), pp. 757-769. Discussions of this address follow to p. 781.

ELYOT, Thomas, *The Boke Called the Governour* (1531). A discussion on how the "governour" should be trained.

EMERTON, Ephraim, *Desiderius Erasmus* (G. P. Putnam's Sons, 1899).

ERASMUS, D., *Ciceronianus, or a Dialogue on the Best Style of Speaking.* Translated by Izora Scott (Columbia University, 1908). A satire on decadent humanism.

ERSKINE, G., *The American Scholar,* Vol. I, No. 1, (January, 1932). Published quarterly by Phi Beta Kappa.

EVERETT, Samuel, "The Changing Secondary School," *Progressive Education,* Vol. IX (March, 1932), pp. 207-214.

EVERETT, and Others, *A Challenge to Secondary Education* (D. Appleton-Century Company, 1935). Plans for the Reconstruction of the American High School.

FINNEY, R. L., *A Sociological Philosophy of Education* (The Macmillan Company, 1928).

GOODSELL, Willystine, "The Conflict of Naturalism and Humanism," *Teachers College Contributions to Education,* No. 33 (Columbia University, 1910).

GRAVES, F. P., *Peter Ramus* (The Macmillan Company, 1912). A description of an early modern example of content reorganization.

GUASTI, Cesare, *Intorno Alla Vita e all'Insegnamento di Vittorino da Feltra,* Lettere di Sassolo Pratese Volgarizzate (Firenze, 1869).

HALE, Edward E., and Others, *How I Was Educated.* (D. Appleton and Company, 1889). This is a series of articles on educational conditions in America during the early 19th century.

HANSEN, A. O., *Liberalism and American Education* (The Macmillan Company, 1926). A source book and exposition of such authors as Godwin, Ruch, Coram, and others.

HART, J. K., *A Social Interpretation of Education* (Henry Holt and Company, 1929).

———, *The Discovery of Intelligence* (The Century Co., 1924). Parts IV and V.

HASKINS, C. H., *Studies in the History of Mediaeval Science* (Harvard University, 1924). Contains an account of outstanding scholars and translators.

HENDERSON, Ernest F., *A Short History of Germany,* Vol. I (The Macmillan Co., 1902).

HERBART, J. F., *Outlines of Educational Doctrine.* Translated by A. F. Lange and Charles DeGarmo (The Macmillan Co., 1901).

HOOLE, Charles, *A New Discovery of the Old Art of Teaching* (1660). This treats of the curriculum.

HUGHES, R. E., *The Making of Citizens: A Study in Comparative Education* (Charles Scribner's Sons, 1912).

HUIZINGA, J., *Erasmus* (Charles Scribner's Sons, 1924). Edited by Edward W. Bok.

HUXLEY, T. H., Science and Education (New York, 1894). Makes an important plea for science.

HYMA, Albert, *A History of the Christian Renaissance: The Devotio Moderna* (University of Michigan dissertation; published at Grand Rapids, 1924).

ICKES, H. L., *The New Democracy* (W. W. Norton, 1934).

JACKSON, Samuel M., *Huldreich Zwingli* 1484-1531 (G. P. Putnam's Sons, 1903).

JANSSEN, *History of the German People at the Close of the Middle Ages,* Vol. I (Herder Book Collection, 1903).

JUDD, C. H., *Education and Social Progress* (Harcourt, Brace and Company, 1933.)

KEATINGE, M. W., *The Great Didactic of Comenius* (1632). (A. C. Black, 1896). Chs. XXX-XXXI.

KILPATRICK, W. H., *The Educational Frontier*. (D. Appleton-Century Company, 1935.)

———, *Source Book in the Philosophy of Education* (The Macmillan Co., 1924).

LaCROIX, Paul, *Science and Literature in the Middle Ages* (Bickers and Son, 1878). This includes an excellent discussion on curricula in medieval schools.

LAURIE, S. S., *Educational Opinion from the Renaissance* (Cambridge University Press, 1903). Contains a critical account of curriculum suggestions from leading educators.

LEACH, A. F., *The Schools of Medieval England* (Methuen and Company, Ltd., London, 1916).

LEARY, D. B., *Living and Learning* (Richard R. Smith, 1931).

LEVEN, *America's Capacity to Consume* (The Institute of Economics of the Brookings Institution. Publication No. 56, 1934).

LOCKE, John, *Some Thoughts Concerning Education* (1693). This has been one of the most influential books published during this period.

LOEB, Harold, and Associates, *The Chart of Plenty* (Viking Press, 1935).

LYMAN, R. L., *English Grammar in American Schools Before 1850*, Bulletin No. 21 (United States Bureau of Education, 1921). This is a critical study of sources.

MERIWETHER, Colyer, *Our Colonial Curriculum* (Capital Publishing Company, 1907). Out of print. This contains many illustrations of early school content.

MILTON, John, *Tractate on Education* (1644). An epitome of curriculum thought at the time as viewed by Milton.

MONROE, Paul, *Thomas Platter and the Educational Renaissance of the Sixteenth Century* (The Macmillan Company, 1904). This reviews curriculum construction during the period.

———, *A Text-Book in the History of Education* (The Macmillan Company, 1923).

MULCASTER, Richard, *Positions* (1581). Edited by R. H. Quick. (Longmans, Green and Company, 1888). Extensive suggestions for the curriculum are included.

MUNRO, D. C., "The Attitude of the Western Church toward the Study of the Latin Classics in the Early Middle Ages," *American Society of Church History*, Vol. VIII (1907).

MUNRO, D. C., and SELLERY, G. C., *Mediaeval Civilization* (The Century Company, 1904).

MUNRO, D. C., and SONTAG, R. J., *The Middle Ages* (The Century Company, 1928).

MURSELL, J. L., *Principles of Education* (W. W. Norton and Company, 1934), Chs. XIV, XVII, and XVIII.

NEWLON, J. H., and Others, *John Dewey—The Man and His Philosophy* (Harvard University Press, 1930).

NIGHTINGALE, A. F., "What Studies Should Predominate in Secondary Schools?" *School Review*, Vol. V (1897), pp. 321-331.

PAINTER, F. V. N., *Luther on Education* (Lutheran Publication Society,

1889). This contains a translation of Luther's most important educational writings.

PARRY, A. W., *Education in England in the Middle Ages* (W. B. Clive, 1920).

PEACHAM, Henry, *The Compleat Gentleman* (1634). Describes the curriculum needed by a prospective gentleman.

QUICK, Robert Herbert, *Essays on Educational Reformers* (D. Appleton and Company, 1928).

Recent Social Trends or *National Education Research Bulletin* on Recent Educational and Social Trends.

SANDYS, J. E., *A History of Classical Scholarship* (Second Edition, Cambridge University Press, 1906). Books III-IV.

SEYBOLDT, R. F., *Source Studies in American Colonial Education; the Private School* (University of Illinois, 1925). This deals with the teaching of modern languages, vocational subjects, mathematics, geography, and history in colonial America.

Sixth Yearbook: The Development of the High School Curriculum (Department of Superintendence, 1928).

Social Frontier (The Social Frontier, Incorporated, 66 West 88th Street, New York). A journal of educational criticisms and reconstructions.

SPENCER, Herbert, *Essays on Education* (D. Appleton and Company, 1860). Chapter I on "What Knowledge is of Most Worth?" is an excellent reference on the increasing interest in science in secondary schools.

SWIFT, Jonathan, *The Battle of the Books* (1704). This should be read in connection with d'Andeli's poem.

TEMPLE, Sir William, *Ancient and Modern Learning*. This essay is a seventeenth-century view of the relation of pedantry to learning.

TILLEY, Arthur, *The Dawn of the French Renaissance* (Cambridge University Press, 1918).

TOWNSEND, W. J., *The Great Schoolmen of the Middle Ages* (Hodder, 1881). Contains accounts of Abelard, Aquinas, and others.

UHL, W. L., *Secondary School Curricula* (The Macmillan Company, 1927).

WALKER, Williston, *The Reformation* (Charles Scribner's Sons, 1906).

WALSH, J. J., *The Thirteenth, the Greatest of Centuries* (Catholic Summer School Press, 1907).

WATSON, Foster, *The Beginnings of the Teaching of Modern Subjects in England* (Isaac Pitman Company, 1909). Out of print. This contains an especially valuable account of the early differentiation in curricula.

———, *The English Grammar School to 1660* (Cambridge University Press, 1908). An excellent history of English modern curricula.

———, *Vives: on Education (1531)*, (Cambridge University Press, 1913). This is one of the most progressive educational treatises in the sixteenth century.

WATTS, Isaac, *The Improvement of the Mind* (First published in 1753). This recommends a more comprehensive curriculum than Franklin did.

WEST, Andrew Fleming, *Alcuin and the Rise of the Christian Schools* (Charles Scribner's Sons, 1903).

White House Conference on Child Health and Protection (Century Company, 1932).

WOODWARD, W. H., *Education During the Renaissance* (Cambridge University Press, 1913). A critical account of the curriculum proposals.

———, *Erasmus Concerning Education* (Cambridge University Press, 1904). A critical account of the curriculum proposals of Erasmus.

———, *Vittorino da Feltre and other Humanist Educators* (Cambridge University Press, 1897). This contains an extended account of humanistic, realistic and industrial education in England and Wales.

CHAPTER IV

THE DETERMINING OF EDUCATIONAL OBJECTIVES
FROM PRIMARY SOURCES

I. INTRODUCTION

The previous chapters on educational principles and definitions that are basic in this field make an extended introductory statement unnecessary. These unrelated sections of previous chapters must be integrated, however, to make their correct relationships apparent. Otherwise, the reader might not grasp the need for the research that has been developed in the last decade or visualize the scope of the investigations that must be organized in the future, if education is to be a professional and scientific study.

It is essential that every community contemplating the revision of courses of study or the reorganization of curricula develop a philosophy of education. This is not an attempt to be pedantic in the matter. It is the only way in which consistent curriculum thinking can be attained by a group. Unless the social drives that are effecting changes in society are understood, unless the best that frontier thinkers and philosophers have produced in attempting to interpret the evolution of society to its individual members is appreciated, unless the professional school people have set forth the purposes of the school and the functions which it performs in modern society, it is impossible to make of curriculum building more than a perfunctory procedure, unrelated to social and institutional progress.

The problem that is of great significance to those interested in course of study construction is that of making the transition from the guiding principles of life to the learning activities and experiences of children in the school. In the past it has been left to the judgment of teachers to determine those experiences which will have significance in the realization of the goals of society. Ethical character was proposed by the Commission on the Reorganization of Secondary Education as a guiding principle of life, and the teacher was given the responsibility of determining whether or not it would be better practice to read the Bible for twenty minutes every day as a means of realizing this principle, discuss informally in class the merits of good citizenship in terms of mutual relationships, or establish a laboratory in which the students may practice social and moral relationships according to ethical standards. Is ethical character a matter of information and knowledge, or is it concerned with habits, attitudes, and ideals? The principles of life do not indicate what are essential in their realization. Educators are becoming more and more skeptical of the procedure of leaving this important matter to the judgment of the teacher, and they are attempting to fill in the gap between the statement of the principle and the basic activities and experiences developed *for,* and *with the coöperation of* the child in the school-room.

A great advance has been made in the last decade in eliminating this hiatus between the principles of life and the educational program of the child. The terms of *general* and *specific* objectives have been developed to indicate the method of procedure in scientifically organizing teaching materials in conformity with the principles of education. This point may be illustrated through the use of health as one of the fundamental principles of life. If it is found, as a result of analyzing this principle into its more and more specific aspects, that one definite and specific phase of health education is the development in the child of the habit of brushing the teeth twice a day, the educator may then first, determine the learning experiences and activities of the child; second, determine definite standards of achievement; third, evaluate teaching in a particular room, school, or system in terms of these standards which have been established; and fourth, take the child into his confidence in regard to the goals which are important in his advancement and work with him in checking his progress in the realization of those definite objectives.

It is probably unnecessary to point out that as soon as the

term *objective* had come into general use, as suggested in the preceding paragraph, many educators made use of it as an important phase of another type of course of study construction. In this procedure, the principles of education were ignored, and subject-matter specialists worked at the problem from the standpoint of the course which was already in existence. Thus, committees were appointed wholesale in various communities to study the revision of English or chemistry, in terms only of English or chemistry. The subject-matter was the important item, and the child, as a growing and developing individual in an evolving society, was of secondary concern. In a large and wealthy city in this country, voluminous and well-bound courses of study have been worked out by the teachers in the various subject-matter fields. It is significant to point out the use made of objectives in this vast expenditure of the taxpayers' money. On page *one* in each of the courses of study are five general objectives, and, strange as it may seem, these lists of objectives are identical in all the courses covering such unrelated fields as home economics and English. However, that inconsistency is as nothing compared with the fact that on page *two* in these courses of study are listed specific objectives, and these are the same again for all subjects in the program of studies. More strange than fiction, however, is the fact that in these courses all the specific objectives are word for word duplications of the general objectives. It may be observed that these objectives are in no way related to the learning experiences of the children or to good teaching. They are a mere formality and merely conform with the custom of having general and specific objectives at the beginning of the courses of study.

The reason for the rather general misuse of objectives in developing courses of study is the realization, on the part of educators, that objectives are difficult to determine and difficult to validate. Relatively little has been done in this field by research experts, and so the school system, which is in operation and wishes to revise its teaching materials, is either faced with years of research or is forced to proceed by using teacher opinion and the limited research which can be carried on in their system while the schools are in session. In the following pages of this chapter and in Chapter V, the sources of objectives and the techniques suggested for the determination of objectives will be discussed and analyzed. In so far as research results are available in any of these methods, they will be presented so that the teacher may have data at hand in the organization of the practical problems in the school system, and also, in order that the methods used in the investigations may be suggestive in setting up additional research projects.

II. RESEARCH IN OBJECTIVES BASED UPON THE ACTIVITIES AND INTERESTS OF CHILDREN

The determination of objectives and curricula through an analysis of the activities and interests of children dates back at least to Rousseau. It is not a procedure that has been invented or discovered recently as many of the activity school people would have educators believe. However, modern educational leaders interested in organizing teaching materials have developed two schools of thought concerning the emphasis that should be placed upon research in this field. Their programs and procedures may be defined as follows :

A. The activity school. Those who are interested actively or theoretically in this method of organizing subject-matter for these schools maintain that the school is concerned only with the growth and development of the child. Only such subject-matter as is definitely related to his interests, needs, and capacities will be used in this development or unfoldment of the personality of the individual child. The activity program takes the child where it finds him, considers his background or experiences, determines his innate capacity to grow or develop and his immediate needs in terms of these limitations, and sets up a natural, normal, and coöperative situation in which the child may acquire easily the knowledges, skills, habits, and appreciations which are essential in his further growth and development. This program is informal and is not intimately concerned with the problem of determining what the individual should acquire now in order that he may function as an efficient citizen in the society which will be in evidence ten or fifteen years later. Protagonists of the activity theory maintain that the child will have no difficulty in adjusting himself in society at that time, if he has been constantly growing and developing as an individual in happy, coöperative social relationships.

The activity school will be discussed in a later chapter, and this brief discussion is included only in order that the reader may distinguish, at this time, between the extreme point of view of the activists and those who are investigating children's interests to supplement studies which have been made in the social needs of children and adults. The true activist does not admit the need of establishing objectives in education, while those who claim to be more scientific in methods of procedure are using the results of their research to that end.

The activity school and many types of experimental schools are working on the assumption that the school and the teacher are not concerned with valid and specific objectives in the organization of the curriculum, but only with the outcomes that are observed from day to day and at the end of a unit, semester, or year. The child assists in the development of the courses of study in the school, and these can be organized only at the end of the term in the significant growth experiences of the child during the school year or term. In these schools, there is no point in publishing courses of study, since the one that has been followed need have no particular influence in determining those to be used in succeeding years. In the extreme types of these schools there has been a definite tendency to eliminate the formal school subjects and organize the work around one or more topics and develop these as the children's interests and aptitudes express themselves in the activities of the school.

The following statement from Rugg and Shumaker illustrates the point:

An outline of a year's work in the new school, such as any one of the samples presented in this chapter, can give merely the names of the growth experiences the children have had. It cannot portray their contents adequately, for they are as varied and broad as life itself. But such an overview of successive year-programs of a new school can indicate some outstanding characteristics of the work of the school as a whole. For this reason we are presenting, in greatly condensed form, a few representative year-programs—outlines of actual units of work and activities in which the children of given grades have taken part during the school year.

In presenting these illustrative year-programs we do not imply that they are the courses of study. The list of units of work as given for any one grade in a school does not necessarily give a complete picture of the entire work of that grade in one year. Our use of these year-programs, therefore, is merely illustrative. They are in no sense to be considered complete outlines of the curricula of the schools in which these units happened to be worked out. They are merely concise tabulations of units of work reported by these schools. We searched the published records of a number of progressive schools for descriptions of a complete year's work in each grade. We were able to find this in only one of the freer types of schools.

New schools do not publish so-called courses of study—in part because they do not have the records, and in part because they do not wish other schools to adopt verbatim, as authoritative, curricula which they regard as exceedingly tentative. Furthermore, the work of these grades often evolves from the spontaneous interests of children and hence does not lend itself easily to systematic classification. Such summary classifications as have been made by many new schools (always in retrospect) are regarded merely as a means of checking up the experiences that the pupils have had. They in no wise bind the next class to follow in similar steps. The new-school people hold that each class, according to its interests, capabilities, and needs, must develop its own units of experience. In the course of prolonged experimentation in many schools, however, the number of possible units is constantly being extended, and the opportunities for growth which those units provide are being determined. In this sense, then, a skeleton of the unit-experiences of a school year through the grades has value for comparative purposes.[1]

In actual practice, however, the outcomes of the previous classroom work are the bases upon which the programs for succeeding classes are developed. As soon as the teacher strives to achieve with a class the same outcomes which have been realized with preceding groups, objectives are established. In many of these schools, carefully prepared outlines of projects,

[1] Harold Rugg and Ann Shumaker, *The Child-Centered School* (World Book Co., 1928), pp. 74-76.

which are in reality excellent examples of units or divisions of the course of study as presented in the more advanced types of public schools, are retained from year to year to guide the teachers in the organization of the work for the students. In these cases it is evident that the teachers and directors of these schools have given thought and consideration to the problem of determining the objectives of education at particular levels, and of developing activities and experiences which could be tested as to their efficiency in realizing these objectives.

The activity school has made a great contribution in education in that it has emphasized the elimination of extreme formalism in organizing teaching materials and developing new teaching methods. Its greatest weakness is that its advocates have refused to use the standards of adult society and the possibility of measuring outcomes of education in terms of objectives which have previously been developed. Their position on objectives is becoming more and more difficult to defend, and it is probable that this term will find a place in these schools in the future. The student of course of study construction may be in a position now to point out the difficulties in securing coöperation among teachers and between teachers and administrators in a school that is operating without clearly stated and definitely understood objectives.

The emphasis upon outcomes by the experimental group is significant for educators. In the past there has been too much emphasis upon objectives and not enough upon the outcomes which should be compared with objectives. Experiments which have recently been developed have indicated that teachers have been striving in a particular class for objectives which were unobtainable. When the outcomes in a particular course indicate that only 25 per cent of the students are attaining the objectives, it is time that the objectives were studied in terms of these outcomes. In this way the analysis of outcomes will always be an important aspect of the problem of determining objectives in the public as well as in the experimental school.

B. The non-activity and semi-activity school. These groups maintain that there is danger in accepting, without reservation, the present activities and interests of children since these are not always desirable and useful. A curriculum constructed upon present practice, they assert, will perpetuate present practice, and this will be both desirable and undesirable. It is, however, an excellent point of departure and enables the teacher to suggest more important and valuable activities as well as wholesome interests. It is necessary to know the present before higher levels of attainment and performance can be determined. This group of thinkers does not divorce this type of investigation from supplementary investigations in the social needs of the learner in order that he may be completely adjusted in society as he matures and advances into the secondary levels of instruction.

Since the activity school will be discussed later in the text, the studies presented are of greater significance to those interested in the second school of thought. A comprehensive bibliography will be found at the end of Part II, but the following will indicate the type of research which is being carried on in this field:

LEHMAN, H. C., *Play Activities of Persons of Different Ages.* Chapter XIV in Curriculum Investigations, edited by Franklin Bobbitt, Supplementary Educational Monograph No. 31 (University of the Chicago Press, 1926). The play activities of 16,568 persons, ranging from eight to twenty-two years of age, are analyzed. A valuable study for any committee working in the field of health education which represents the type of work necessary before desirable curricular changes can be suggested.

HOPKINS, L. T., and KINYON, K. W., *Home Economics Research Monograph* Number 1 (Denver Public Schools, Denver, Colorado, 1925). Presents an analysis of the home economics activities of 5,106 junior high-school and senior high-school girls of Denver.

ELDER, V., and CARPENTER, H. S., "Reading Interests of High-School Girls." *Journal of Educational Research,* Vol. XIX (April 1929), pp. 276-282. A study of the reading interests of high-school girls. The data were secured through questionnaires submitted to 487 girls in the Julia Richmond High School in New York City. In addition, themes which the girls had written were studied and a careful check made of books selected by them for supplementary reading.

GRANT, E. B., and WHITE, M. L., "A Study of Children's Choices of Reading Materials." Teachers College Record, Vol. XXV (April 1925), pp. 671-678. Data were secured through a study of library withdrawals and interviews with students.

Investigations of this general type are valuable in that the starting point is indicated in the educational program of the child. It is important for the teacher to know that the child's free reading is the historical novel or the morbid love story. This information does not tell him what to do at once, but it indicates the scope of the work that confronts the teacher, and it gives him a starting point since it is essential to know first, that the child does actually read something, and second, the level of his present reading. Furthermore, investigations of this type are rather accurate checks upon the grade placement of teaching materials in the school. In literature, for example, the age-grade level of romance, adventure, etc., may be determined definitely enough to guide the committee or the teacher in the organization of the course of study.

A recent illustration of the use of this source was at Ohio State University during the years 1929-1932.

Under the direction of Dr. Charters, the Bureau of Educational Research of Ohio State University assisted the State Department of Education in the development of a curriculum in health for the secondary schools of the state. Four major ideas dominated that research: first, that the health interests of youth had not been given sufficient attention in current curriculums. To remedy this deficiency approximately 23,000 questions dealing with health problems were collected from high-school pupils, classified, and evaluated. Second, it was believed that finding and learning the answers to these problems was a major responsibility of the students. Chapter references to the best books in the field were therefore made for many of the problems. Opportunities were offered whereby additional sources of information not mentioned in the course of study might be utilized by the pupils. Third, it was believed that pupil's interest alone was not a completely valid standard for the selection of critical health problems. Therefore, the health problems which interested high-school boys and girls were supplemented by those important health problems in which they had shown slight or no interest. Fourth, reading activities were supplemented by a variety of other methods of gaining health experience, such as experiments, excursions, and discussions.[2]

---

[2] A complete discussion of the experiment and results will be found in the *Educational Research Bulletin*, Vol. XI, No. 7 (October, 1932).

III. RESEARCH IN OBJECTIVES BASED UPON THE NEEDS AND DEFICIENCIES OF CHILDREN

This research is particularly valuable as a means of checking the present status of the students as individuals and determining revision and reorganization programs in the courses of study. Such investigations are valuable as validating instruments of objectives as well as suggesting new objectives. It is necessary for educators to have standards by which needs, deficiencies, and difficulties can be definitely determined. There is emphasis, here, upon what the child needs to know, what deficiencies he has in his reactions according to standardized tests or adult standards, and what specific difficulties he is encountering in his work. It can be assumed, therefore, that these studies and research investigations will not report the child's natural behavior, but rather the present standards of performance of tasks in terms of desirable standards of performance. The standards which are generally used in these investigations are:

1. An acceptable scale of handwriting
2. Nationally accepted standards of performance in subject-matter fields as formal grammar, arithmetic, etc.
3. Adult levels of performance for any phase of subject-matter which is regarded as finished in any grade
4. Study of an advanced field of study to determine the amount of prerequisite training in a particular field
5. Standards established by experts as dentists, doctors, food experts, health experts, etc.
6. Standards of social life, manners, morals, etc., may be determined by a national authority or by a consensus of the faculty

The studies, which are presented with brief annotations in the following paragraph, will illustrate the sources of this type of investigation and the results which have been secured by those interested in such research:

OBERTEUFFER, D., *Personal Hygiene for College Students* (Teachers College, Columbia University, 1930). The determination of a course of study in personal hygiene for college students through consideration of students' questions on this subject.

JOHNSON, P. O., *Curricular Problems at the College Level* (University of Minnesota Press, 1930). This is a study to determine the extent to which an elementary required course in botany functions in later related courses.

HARAP, Henry, "The Most Common Grammatical Errors," *English Journal*, Vol. XIX (June, 1930), pp. 440-446. A composite of fifty-three investigations of written and oral errors made by pupils.

JOHNSON, R. I., *English Expression* (Public School Publishing Company, 1926). First, this is an analysis of the language activities of one hundred and four freshmen and their mothers. Second, it presents a comparison of one thousand business and social letters of college freshmen and high-school seniors with letters of recognized merit in order to determine deficiencies and needs.

IV. RESEARCH IN OBJECTIVES BASED UPON THE NEEDS AND DEFICIENCIES OF ADULT SOCIETY

It is the opinion of those who are interested in this type of research that the needs and deficiencies of adult society, exemplified in the general standards of life in this country, is a fertile field of investigation in determining objectives. If the needs or deficiencies of any economic or social group in society can be definitely stated, it will be possible for the curriculum builder to state the objectives of an educational program which will eliminate or minimize those aspects of living in the next generation. The standards used here may be, in part, a restatement of the standards suggested in the previous section which considered the needs and deficiencies of children. There is one other aspect of the problem of determining standards where the research is concerned exclusively with adult society. The investigator must realize that, in general, it is not sufficient to determine the *activities* of adults, but it is essential that the activities of those who represent high standards of living in each economic and social classification be studied in order that all people in the classification may be trained to perform their activities as efficiently as those who represent the higher levels of citizenship in that group. Progress is attained through raising the citizenship traits and attitudes of those who are average or below average to the level of performance of those who are above average or very good in comparison with others of the same social or economic level. If the objectives that are determined by this method are realized in society, each succeeding generation would represent higher levels of realization than were attained in the preceding generation.

This "case group" or "case type" technique, which has been developed by Snedden, has received considerable publicity, but it has been applied in only a limited number of localities. The assumption upon which the technique is based is that distinguishable groups in the population of each community can be determined and the needs and possibilities of each group analyzed in order that an educational program can be developed and organized for each group. It is the application of the technique of social case work to the problems of curriculum building.

Snedden has used the field of the social studies to illustrate the technique, and the only practical attempt to use the technique has been in the same subject-matter field.[3] It is, therefore, essential that the technique be illustrated by use of the social sciences and civic education. The development of a program through the use of this technique, may be suggested in the following steps:

Step one. In a distinguishable group in the community select one hundred men who have an age range from thirty to forty years. These men are ranked in order from one to one hundred according to the manner in which they exemplify good citizenship and civic virtues. The men who, in these qualifications in that particular group, are listed from 81-100 are called the *A* group. Those ranking 51-80 are classified as the *B* group. Those included in the ranking 21-50 are given the classification of *C,* and those in the last or lowest group, 1-20, are classified as *D* people.

Step two. The group which is designated as B (51-80) is the basis of the investigation. The cultural and civic qualities and virtues which these men possess are listed, as well as the civic deficiencies and social shortages of this group. The deficiencies and social shortages are restated as positive statements,

---

[3] Clyde Moore, *Civic Education, Its Objectives and Methods for a Specific Case Group* (Contributions to Education, Teachers College, Columbia University, 1924).

and these, combined with the positive qualities and virtues, make possible the organization of the objectives of education for the next generation. Society will be vastly improved by being raised to the standards of the B classification.

The following criticisms, which have been aimed at the technique, will explain certain phases of the program which may not appear to be sufficiently detailed in the two steps presented above:

1. The technique depends too much upon subjective opinion in the localities in which it has been employed. It is admitted, however, that scientific methods of organizing the research in determining the needs of the particular group, from the standpoint of living conditions, social life, economic life, intellectual life, etc., may be used rather than subjective opinion which has dominated the investigations up to the present time.

2. The technique should be successful in rural sections since there are only a few distinguishable groups, but it will never be a popular or scientific procedure in the large cities where a large number of groups exist. An educational program designed for a particular group in a large city would have to be instituted in all the schools of the city since the members of the group may live in any section of the community. Such a program, even if correctly determined, would be prohibitive because of the expense of installation. Only a frontier thinker with eyes seeing far into the future can visualize such a comprehensive educational program.

Harap makes the following pertinent comment on this technique:

The method has not as yet developed a complete and refined technique. Applications of this method have been made chiefly by students working directly under Dr. Snedden, resulting in the publication of a number of fragmentary studies and one extensive investigation. The latter was conducted by Mr. Clyde Moore to discover a program of civic education for mid-western farmers. He made a social analysis of this "case group" whose members were similar in many respects. This analysis included the geographic environment, intelligence, economic condition, home life, infant care, and so on. The civic shortages were listed, and the objectives of civic education were the positive elements of the program of which the civic shortages were the negative elements. The evaluation of the social habits of the group was entirely subjective.

This method assumes that the investigator will make a direct survey of the needs of a particular homogeneous group. It requires that one shall determine the abilities, characteristics, or traits of the good members of a particular group, that he shall discover the deficiencies of this group by a comparison with the desirable qualities of the good members and finally that he shall set up a program of training to correct the deficiencies. Such a method cannot escape a good deal of subjective thinking. However, it is possible to conceive of the investigator using sound objective data or reliable secondary data in analyzing a "case group." The validity, then, of the "case group" method depends entirely upon the specific techniques used in the study of the distinguishable group of persons. To carry out this method in certain of our large cities would require at least a dozen intensive curriculum studies because there is such a large variety of distinguishable groups.[4]

Snedden has presented a recent summary statement of this theory of the curriculum which is challenging enough to merit inclusion at this point:[5]

Schools (including thereunder all agencies created primarily to produce *learnings* in groups of persons coming together for that purpose) are supported at substantial expense to learners, parents, and communities, *not* to promote *all* learnings, but only those which meet two conditions, namely, they promise to be highly valuable learnings to the learners and to their societies, and they cannot well be given by non-school agencies.

But the values of such school-administered learnings are nearly always determined by their proximate or later *functionings* in one or more of the considerably compartmentalized areas of work, religious coöperations, civic coöperations, self-culturings, health conservations, superior pleasure seekings, family rearings and other areas in which civilized adults necessarily *function*—here called "careers."

Hence no scientifically balanced and functional courses of learnings can be procured by pupils through school until educational

---

[4] Henry Harap, *The Technique of Curriculum Making* (Macmillan Co., 1928), pp. 65-66.

[5] David Snedden, "A Summary Theory of the Curriculum," *News Bulletin of the Society for Curriculum Making,* Vol. 5, No. 4 (Western Reserve University, May 25, 1934), pp. 6-7.

administrators are somewhat agreed, not only on the *kinds* (qualitative) of school-fostered learnings which should be promoted through schools in each of the above (or more adequately differentiated) areas of optimum human functionings, but also are agreed on relative *amounts* or *intensities* or *depths* or *scopes* of such learnings (quantitative phases) which are likely to prove of optimum worth for specified types of learners in view of their expected optimum functionings.

It is obvious to any well-informed person that in our day the possible and even quite practicable "contents"—of knowledges, skills, attitudes, appreciations, and other distinguishable kinds of learning—which can be derived from the rich social inheritance—and including "plannings for the future and for social change"—toward higher competency in any one of the "career" fields are so extensive as far to transcend the learning powers and the available time of any school learners, including even the intellectually gifted.

Hence one set of crucial problems to-day confronting all educators who seriously share in responsibilities of making plans and specifications to assist teaching and other guidance of school learnings is that of "ranking" possible learning objectives in probable orders of relevancy and importance for specified classes of learners. But the "mechanisms" for this seem to be in a deplorable state of ineffectiveness at present and perhaps most so in areas of school learnings where progressive educators are striving desperately to be "off with the old" before knowing well how to organize the "on with the new"—thus creating in the minds of critical observers impressions that states of philosophical as well as administrative chaos prevail in most phases of curriculum construction outside of professional colleges.

Progress in the future towards scientific curriculum making for any level of schools will, therefore, require highly realistic employment of these procedures:

a. Determination of as many fairly homogeneous areas of expected "careers" or "life functionings"—a few of proximate high significance, the majority for deferred or adult expression—as practicable—even now as many as ten major "strands" and within some of them (e.g. the cultural) ten to thirty constituent strands.

b. Search for the "materials of learning"—that is, the readings, the excursions, the lectures, the laboratory practices, the "creative constructions," the games, the drills, the listenings, the pictures—which will best serve to produce learnings for expected functioning in particular areas.

c. Dissection and organization of expected learnings into "units" of large or small kinds which will permit their classification in "some order of importance" or as dictated by necessities imposed by the "law of diminishing returns."

d. In some situations, at least, adaptations of programs to the three or more "levels of ability" on the assumption that "values of learnings" in many areas are affected by the "abilities" of those making them.

e. And in some situations at least adaptations of programs so as to coördinate effectively on the one hand with favorable or unfavorable conditions or extra-school learnings and on the other hand with expected variations in types of expected optimum functionings.

Obviously such adaptations are of fundamental importance and lead in all fields of education toward vocational competencies.

But it is probable that beyond elementary grade levels they may also prove of considerable importance in areas of civic, health-conserving, and cultural educations.

Snedden has recently indicated that he would determine his "case types" in the following manner:

1. The pupils in a school can be ranked according to I.Q. with sufficient accuracy for this purpose. They can be allocated to groups or types as soon as this has been accomplished.

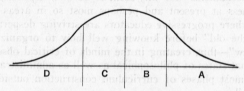

A = highest 25 per cent
B and C = middle 50 per cent
D = lowest 25 per cent

2. The same pupils can be grouped according to the wealth of their parents.

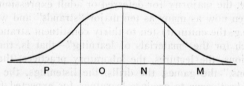

M = wealthiest 25 per cent of parents
N and O = middle 50 per cent of parents
P = poorest 25 per cent of parents

From these two groupings, it is apparent at once that pupils who can be grouped as *MA* (brilliant and having wealthy parents) are good college prospects, while pupils who can be grouped as *PD* (dull and having poor parents) are poor college prospects. The reader can build many other possibilities out of these two classifications.

Another form of "case-type" organization for educational purposes can be illustrated by the ignorant, benighted people of Louisiana who live in a malaria-infested portion of that state. They represent an educational group that can be identified for the purpose of determining its objectives.

The following studies illustrate the extensive use that is being made of this source of objectives:

BOBBITT, S. A., *Shortcomings in the Written English of Adults,* Supplementary Monograph No. 31 (University of Chicago Press, 1926). Chapter XII presents a study of 362 letters written to the open forum of the Chicago *Daily Tribune.* There were a total of 7,110 errors. This means that, on the average, twenty errors were made in every letter and that one error was made in approximately every fourteen words.

HERRIOTT, M. E., "Life Activities and the Physics Curriculum," *School Science and Mathematics,* Vol. XXIV (June, 1924), pp. 631-634. 576 activities, which include mechanics, heat, light, sound, magnetism, and electricity, are presented by six representative groups of citizens. These are catalogued by each group as (1) things that they do for themselves, (2) things that necessitate the assistance of experts, and (3) things that they think about.

MOORE, Clyde, *Civic Education, Its Objectives and Methods for a Specific Case Group* (Contributions to Education, Teachers College, Columbia University, 1924). A study was made of the social shortages of farmers of the Middle West based upon their environment, intelligence, economic condition, home life, infant care, etc. These shortages were then restated as positive objectives for a program of civic education.

An illustration of the use of this source is the determination of objectives for a course of study in health for high-school girls in Cleveland in 1932. The objectives were obtained from the following sources:

1. Data on most common diseases of women as recorded in half a dozen investigations
2. Most common minor ailments as recorded in two investigations
3. The most common physical defects as found in two investigations

4. Objectives of health education proposed by 155 high-school seniors
5. Objectives proposed by about 100 college students, over two years out of high school
6. Objectives proposed by the staff of the Cleveland Red Cross Teaching Center.

The objectives were organized under the following headings, which provided the units for the course:

I. Food and health	VII. Health and the mind
II. Health and cleanliness of the body	VIII. Health and sex
III. Clothing and health	IX. The care of infants
IV. Community health	X. The care of the sick
V. Prevention and treatment of diseases	XI. Prevention and treatment of minor injuries
VI. Health and the home	XII. Occupational health

V. RESEARCH IN OBJECTIVES BASED UPON THE ACTIVITIES OF ADULT SOCIETY

While this type of research is not so profound or difficult and usually is not so significant in its results as other types, it is being rather widely used. Its weakness lies in its usual failure to stimulate discrimination in the selection of activities. However, in certain fields of instruction this is not fundamental and, at times, in the other teaching fields, such investigations may make a contribution in determining various limited aspects of the work which should be presented.

While job analysis is concerned with the activities of the individual who will perform a definite and specific type of work, activity analysis proposes, in theory at least, a tabulation of all the activities of the human race, or of a national group. From this list, activities that are important in the improvement of the race can be determined, and certain aspects of the training program can be assigned to the public schools. If this system functioned completely at any time, the relationship of school education to the complete education of the people could be appreciated at once, and the integration of an educational philosophy could be understood by every one. This will be more and more apparent as the various steps in the technique are presented.

Step one. The constant study of the activities of a national group will indicate that all these can be classified under some ten or twenty generalizations or principles of living. The list need not be considered final at any one time, as further study may suggest greater refinement. Neither is it essential that every curriculum-making group have the same list. It is inconceivable, however, that lists developed by educational groups which are studying the same lists of activities will vary more than the statement of the seven cardinal principles of education and the classification of ten principles developed by Franklin Bobbitt, of the University of Chicago. These are presented that the significance of this point may be fully appreciated:

Seven Cardinal Principles
Health
Command of fundamental processes
Citizenship
Vocation
Worthy use of leisure time
Worthy home membership
Ethical character

Bobbitt's Classification
Language activities—social intercommunication
Health activities
Citizenship activities
General social activities—meeting and mingling with others
Spare-time activities—amusements, recreations
Keeping one's self mentally fit—analogous to health activities of keeping one's self physically fit
Religious activities
Parental activities—the upbringing of children and proper home life
Unspecialized or non-vocational activities
The labors of one's calling

Bobbitt's classification appears to have an advantage in that there are more items and that they lend themselves to the type of organization which is proposed in activity analysis. It would be difficult to use the following statement of general educational objectives which was developed by one of the committees coöperating in the production of the *Sixth Yearbook* of the Department of Superintendence.

1. To promote the development of an understanding and an adequate evaluation of the self
2. To promote the development of an understanding and an appreciation of the world of nature
3. To promote the development of an understanding and an appreciation of organized society
4. To promote the development of an appreciation of the force of law and of love that is operating universally

It is apparent also from a study of the three sets of generalizations that only one was developed as a result of the study of the activities of the American people, and the others represent the philosophical hopes and aspirations of a sincere group of educators.

Step two. As soon as the list of generalizations or principles has been completed, it is essential that each principle or generalization be subdivided until specific activities have been determined. The definite and specific activities will indicate to the curriculum group the child and adult activities which must be mastered in order that this generalization or principle of life may be realized in the life of the individual.

Step three. In order to secure the important activities which should be included under each generalization, it is essential that the experiences, acts, and doings of men and women, boys and girls, at all levels, be catalogued. Education is for the purpose of training every one to perform efficiently those activities which are fundamental in American life and civilization. Bobbitt, who is the chief exponent of this technique, says, that the determination of the actual activities of mankind "will be made on the basis of simple observation. This is all that is needed so long as there is virtual unanimity on the part of all objective-minded analysts of the situation. This will largely be the case with the major units and their larger subdivisions. As the analyses approach the units that are minute, numerous, and interrelated with each other, an accurate, quantitative definition demands careful and scientific assembling of facts. The activities once discovered, one can see the objectives of education. The latter are the *abilities* to perform, in proper ways, the activities. The two are cognate, but not identical." [6]

This step, in the technique of determining the activities, is important since, naturally, the curriculum maker is interested only in those activities which are performed by people representing a high standard of American life. The average is not the goal of this program; the determination of those activities of high standard, even though infrequently exemplified in our civilization, is absolutely essential. If these activities are to be determined by a study based on a frequency count of a mediocre society, then our educational system would be merely a means of perpetuating mediocrity. The problem raised here is merely one of validation. Out of the mass of activities which are secured, it will be necessary for the group, making the investigation, to formulate criteria by which they can segregate the activities which are important in improving the civilization of our people from those which are unimportant or undesirable.

Step four. The determination of the activities which are important and desirable enables the curriculum group to state the objectives of education immediately. These objectives will be just as definite and specific as the activities; they will be validated objectives since the activities from which they develop are validated. The activity will enable the group concerned with the problem to state the objectives in terms of ability, attitudes, appreciations, habits, skills, or knowledge. This step in the activity analysis is relatively simple and requires little, if any, discussion.

Step five. The specific activity restated in terms of a specific objective will indicate at once the learning experiences or teaching materials which should be instituted in order to realize these objectives. This would involve the determination of standards of performance that can reasonably be expected from different social, economic, and intellectual strata in society.

Step six. The preceding step indicates at once that, as soon

[6] Franklin Bobbitt, *How to Make a Curriculum* (Houghton-Mifflin Company, 1924), pp. 9 and 10.

as this stage has been reached, subject-matter fields may be considered. The allocation of certain objectives and activities to definite subject-matter fields means, of course, that course of study construction can proceed from that point.

It has been apparent in the discussion of this technique that the sources are (1) people who represent society in general or various classes of society, (2) expert opinion or a jury of leaders in a particular classification of society, and (3) items in newspapers, magazines, books, and other secondary sources of investigation. The technique which is known as activity analysis secures data from these sources in one of the following methods:

1. The use of the personal interview or questionnaire to secure either lay opinion or expert opinion.
2. The use of individuals or groups of individuals to observe and tabulate the actual daily performance of people in general or people of a particular social classification over a definite period of time.
3. Tabulation of items in newspapers and magazines and the topics treated in books.

The revision of the Dental School Curriculum for the American Association of Dentists, under the direction of Charters, is an example of activity analysis. The following summarization from the report to the Association will give the procedure and results:

The committee endeavored to find out from the public the kinds of services that dentistry should perform and in doing this has secured information from thousands of patients. It has likewise set up the objectives of dentistry with very great care and has secured a consensus of judgment of the leaders of the profession by correspondence, discussions, and interviews. It has made a collection of all the diseases, deficiencies, and conditions with which the dentist deals and the operations that are necessary in coping with them. With unusual care they have studied the economic and business activities and the ethical ideals of the profession and have reported thereon by a variety of methods which might be indicated.

After this phase of the study had been completed the Committee addressed itself to the assembling of information from all the fields of knowledge which are related to the detailed picture which has just been described. In doing this they had regard for the fundamental fact that they were concerned not so much with training a dentist as with training a man who would follow the profession of dentistry. This means that the curriculum presented provides for the general education of the dentist, the information and attitudes that he should have in order to live a broad and wholesome life beyond the practicing of his profession.

On the professional side it became apparent at an early date that the Committee should have to consider not only professional "dental" courses dealing with practices of dentistry, but also service courses or scientific courses which give reasons for the methods that the dentist uses in the office, such courses including chemistry for dentists, physiology for dentists and the like.

In the building of the service courses the Subcommittees waited until the "dental" courses had been completed and secured from those courses specifications of what the student should know in the service field before he began to study the "dental" courses.

The faculties of the dental schools participated in the formulating of objectives. The organization of each course was carried on ordinarily by three instructors who had their work checked and verified by large numbers of professors who did not participate in the tentative organization of the material. The specifications for the general courses were made by a committee composed of members of the dental teaching profession and of the field of general education.[7]

In concluding the discussion of this technique, one may note some of its limitations. These are staggering when one thinks of its application to activities on a national scale. It is evident that these limitations will seriously affect the work, even though the field is local or involves only one stratum in society. They can be summarized as follows: (1) the cost of conducting the investigations, (2) the length of time involved in conducting the vast numbers of separate investigations that would be essential in organizing a national program, and (3) if the technique is used in connection with local conditions or vocational activities, it can be termed job analysis, since it will differ so little from that technique.

The following type studies will indicate the limitations of the source of objectives as well as the contributions which may be expected from research in this field:

[7] "Revision of the Dental School Curriculum," *News Bulletin of the Society for the Study of Curriculum,* Vol. V, No. 7 (Nov. 28, 1934).

HASTIE, M. A., "The Home Survey for Curriculum Revision in Home Economics" (New York State Department of Education, 1928). The results of a questionnaire, which is submitted to adults to determine their household activities, is presented in this report.

HOPKINS, L. T., and WHITNEY, F. L., "Curriculum Revision Based on Social Needs," *Industrial Arts Magazine,* Vol. XIV (Nov., 1925), pp. 403-405. This article describes a study of repair and construction activities in homes in Denver.

Report of the Committee on Place and Function of English in American Life. *English Journal,* Vol. XV (Feb., 1926), pp. 110-134. This report presents a study which was made of the language activities of 2,615 people who were engaged in 253 occupations.

WILSON, G. M., *What Arithmetic Shall We Teach?* (Contributions to Education, Teachers College, Columbia University, 1919). This book contains important data regarding the arithmetical operations performed by adults.

BREED, F. S., "What Words Should Children Be Taught to Spell?" *Elementary School Journal,* Vol. XXV (Oct., 1925), pp. 118-131. Additional articles on the same subject are found in the November and December issues of that year. These present data from children's and adults' vocabularies as determining factors in organizing a spelling program in the schools.

VI. RESEARCH IN OBJECTIVES BASED UPON THE OCCUPATIONAL AND VOCATIONAL NEEDS OF INDIVIDUALS PREPARING FOR PARTICULAR VOCATIONS AND TRADES

Investigation in this field was limited universally to vocational and industrial education in the beginning, but as procedures have been refined, this source of objectives has been analyzed by universities, professional schools, and the public schools. A few years ago investigators in this field had not used the term *objectives* extensively, because they were working with specific operations in a trade or occupation and were satisfied with the mere statement of the skill, knowledge, or trait which must be acquired by the learner. There is no inherent reason, however, in the source itself or in the procedures that have been used in analyzing the source, for this failure to state specific objectives in the particular field. It may be observed that recent attempts to extend job analysis to civic education and the more general fields of education have resulted in the formulation of objectives.

The development of vocational and industrial curricula in the schools led to the selection of this technique as a means of determining the skills, knowledges, attitudes, etc., which will be needed by the worker in the trades, the manager in directing industry, or the professional man in the performance of his duties. It has developed rapidly along scientific lines and, for this reason, adaptations have been made of the technique so that it can be used in subject-matter fields other than those having a practical or vocational content.

It is true in the trades, as in other walks of life, that many of the tasks which are performed have become habitual and are carried on subconsciously rather than as a result of analytical thinking. However, if these various activities are to be taught to prospective workers, they must be definitely organized in the thinking of the teacher, and plans and methods carefully developed for their realization. The reliability of job analysis in accomplishing this result is the reason for the attempts being made at the present time to transfer the procedure to the study of citizenship and other more or less intangible fields.

There are several different methods of attacking the sources of objectives through the use of job analysis. It is essential that the list of duties and responsibilities that are secured shall be as complete as possible. Therefore, the investigator who is interested in the mental as well as the physical activities of the individual must realize the difficulties involved in making such an analysis and understand the possibilities of the several avenues of approach to these sources. It is infinitely more difficult to determine the mental operations and thinking processes of the individual than it is to observe and catalogue the basic and essential physical operations which are performed in the completion of a particular activity. It should be understood that, although each of these methods is presented and discussed separately, all are often used in connection with a particular investigation, either for the purpose of securing data, or for the purpose of checking and validating results which have been secured through the use of only one of the methods.

A. The questionnaire. This is the first method to be considered, since it has pioneered in the field and is still used to some extent. However, it is limited in certain respects which affect its reliability and usefulness. In the first place, the questionnaire, when it is well-organized and inclusive, is difficult for the worker to complete. Its length causes the interest of the one who is responding to it to wane rapidly, and inaccuracies, due to lack of attention and concentration, filter into the work. Second, while the questionnaire may be logically arranged, it may not follow the organization of the work, which the man performs daily, and is confusing to the individual who is endeavoring to fill out the required information. In the third place, the questionnaire may be clear, concise, and intelligible to those who are sending it out, and at the same time be unintelligible and confusing to those who are asked to collaborate in the work. This condition often leads to a misrepresentation of the facts. Lack of understanding on the part of the collaborator and too great haste in completing the work are the conditions which usually nullify the results of the investigation and produce results which are a mass of inaccurate statements. In the fourth place, the investigators cannot be sure that an adequate sampling will be secured, since a reduction in the expected returns will invalidate the report.

The chief value of the questionnaire, at the present time, is its use in securing data which are valuable in indicating the scope of the problem. It can open avenues of approaching the problem which are scientific and which will produce more reliable results.

B. Analysis of his job by the worker. This method involves having the worker think about his work and list all the significant duties which he performs in carrying out his daily routine. Naturally, more than one individual in each vocation would be asked to collaborate in this work so that the final list would constitute a composite sheet including every point of significance indicated by any member of the coöperating group. For example, a master list made from the introspection of one hundred carpenters would be more extensive, more accurate, and more valuable than the contributions of one carpenter. This method is probably not as accurate in attaining reliable results, or as economical, considering the time devoted to the investigation, as other methods of procedure which will be discussed in the ensuing paragraphs.

C. The interview. This method differs from the one which has just been presented in that the interviewer personally asks the men or women to give a complete list of the duties which they perform in their regular work. The one who is conducting the interview makes a hasty but sufficiently complete summary of this list. This list is later revised, typed, and then returned to the individual workers for corrections. A composite list is secured in exactly the same manner as described above, and this is also returned to all of the workers contributing to the investigation for a final check. It is important that this final revised list be submitted to a foreman, executive, or an employer who knows the work thoroughly in order that the list may be approved or that items which have been omitted can be included in the composite list. The great difficulty in using this method is in stimulating people, who are being interviewed, to recall those tasks which have become so much a part of their everyday lives that they are not conscious of their performance. It is helpful to ask the persons being interviewed to think of the difficulties they have overcome in the performance of their tasks. Such an approach often recalls duties which are not thought of in connection with the "regular line of duty" activities.

D. Analysis of the job by the investigator. In this method, the investigator must learn to perform all the duties in the particular job, with scant knowledge of the basic operations. It is probable that some one who is unfamiliar with the work has an advantage over a worker in attempting to determine the total list of duties which are essential in the performance of this work. None of these tasks will have become a part of the life of the investigator, performed from force of habit rather than because of conscious effort. It may be unnecessary to point out that this procedure necessitates a great amount of time, since the investigator must learn thoroughly the essential duties in a new job. Owing to this fact, the interview is preferred by most of those who are conducting investigations.

Smith writes:

In developing this proposed procedure we have given special recognition to the postulate advanced by others that the basis of a curriculum should be the *activities of persons*. Where others have secured a "list of activities" through the expensive and time-consuming job analysis of questionnaire methods, for purposes of efficiency and practicality, we proposed a group-conference method conducted with competent judges selected from the fields of industry, education, and organized labor. In place of using "frequency of occurrence" (often only a quantitative measure) as a criterion for evaluating each activity, we are proposing a checking technique which evaluates on a qualitative basis each activity on a one-hundred-point scale. And many other distinguishing features will be shown as we proceed in this investigation.[8]

An outline of his proposed technique is given in the following excerpt from his monograph:

The Six Steps in Building an Industrial Curriculum. Giving due recognition to established general principles of curriculum construction and customary methods of procedure in education and industry, we have evolved the following six steps into which we divide the actual process of industrial curriculum building:

1. To isolate a definite group of persons in industry for intensive study.

Industrial educators have agreed that best results in any industrial training program can be secured when given to a homogeneous group of students. Also the best industrial courses are those prepared for an especially selected homogeneous group. In keeping with these practices our first step calls for a process which will produce a group homogeneous in those values affected by an industrial education program.

2. To determine the ultimate objectives of the curriculum by:

a. Analyzing the activities of the selected group in actually meeting employment situations.

b. Discovering those activities in which these persons should be more efficient, in order to meet situations in a more creditable manner.

Education should approach the learner from the standpoint of his present condition and prepare him to meet new situations and added responsibilities. It is the purpose of this step to reveal the present

[8] Fred C. Smith, *Curriculum Problems in Industrial Education*, No. 16 (Harvard Bulletins in Education, Harvard University Press, Cambridge, Mass., 1930), p. 9.

behavior of his isolated group and to discover the new situations the learner will meet as he takes on added responsibility. The skills, attitudes, ideals, knowledge, and appreciations necessary to meet intelligently these new situations constitute the basis for the content of the curriculum. The ultimate objective of the curriculum is to give these values which result in the ability to meet intelligently these situations.

3. To arrange these determined values into groups or units convenient for organization into teaching material.

Before a body of knowledge can be presented through a teaching process it must be organized into comparable groups and all elements related. The purpose of this step is to arrange the values revealed through the application of 2-b into groups convenient for analysis as to technical content.

4. To select the actual content in each subject which will produce the desired values.

When the ultimate objectives of the curriculum have been established and expressed through the groups of values under 3 above, technical course content capable of producing these values must be selected. Such is the purpose of this step in our procedure.

5. To arrange subject matter in each group according to proper sequence and degree of difficulty of topics.

As each bit of new knowledge must relate itself to some knowledge already in possession of the learner, it is necessary to arrange subject-matter in logical sequence. This step purposes to secure such sequence and continuity.

6. To arrange courses into a curriculum according to the logical order of presentation and feasibility of administration and supervision.

As the proper sequence and continuity of material within a course is essential, so the order of presentation of separate courses within the curriculum is important. This step has two functions: (a) arranging separate courses in logical order of presentation, and (b) arranging course schedules from the standpoint of administration and supervision.

With these six steps as a working basis we propose to examine the field, determine the need, and evolve an adequate curriculum. In accordance with step one of the proposed procedure we purpose first to isolate a group of industrial workers for special study.[9]

The use of one or all of these types of analyses will enable the investigator to determine the jobs that must be mastered in learning the trade. When a complete list of jobs has been se-

[9] *Ibid.,* pp. 10-12.

cured, it will be possible for the investigator who is interested in constructing an education program for novices in the trade to undertake the arrangement of these jobs into units of work. These units are composed of jobs that require common skills, tools, knowledge, etc., and in which specific objectives, stated in terms of skills, abilities, etc., can be developed for the use of the student and the teacher. While little has been done on the development of specific objectives in job analysis, the block or unit of work, when developed, presents an excellent opportunity to state and validate specific objectives. These specific objectives enable the educator to determine the specific skills, information, and types of performance that should be mastered by the student. Testing the student to determine his degree of mastery or proficiency would be a simple matter then, and examinations could be developed for various levels within the block or unit. Those who have worked with this technique have spoken of the organization of the jobs into units as "blocking the trade," and the determination of points within the unit where the learner's proficiency can be tested as the establishment of "checking levels." The examination constructed for the checking level in the technical trades usually consists of completing a type job that includes many or all of the operations used in the training program to that point. This fact demands, of course, that the educator make an orderly arrangement of jobs within the unit according to difficulty of performance, psychological principles, and the principles of learning. The order of the jobs, as they occur in production or in industry, should be disregarded completely in the organization of the unit for instructional purposes.

As soon as the organization of each unit has been completed according to psychological and educational principles, the organization of the complete course of study should be attempted. This involves the determination of the correct order of the units. This order will be determined largely by the objectives that have been stated for the units as type jobs, and by the teaching materials which have been selected for these objectives from the previous work of the director or teacher.

Job analysis has made a great contribution to education in that it has stimulated the organization of teaching materials in every field. It has demonstrated to educators in other than vocational fields that the selection of valid content in courses must proceed from valid objectives. Many variations have been attempted from this technique, but the influence of job analysis will be found in all of the techniques used to-day. These variations from the procedure of job analysis have made many contributions and have extended the original scope of job analysis. Job analysis has been criticized because it did not emphasize, or even consider the attitudes and ideals that are important in the character of the good workman, or in the actual manipulations that he must learn in order to perform his tasks efficiently. There is no reason why attitudes and ideals, which are fundamental in the success of the workman, cannot be determined by job analysis and means for their realization included in the instructional program. It must be admitted that the validity of objectives relating to attitudes and ideals is not as high as in the case of those relating to the mechanical aspects of the instructional program. The work of developing techniques, which will be considered in this chapter, indicates, however, that noticeable progress has been made in this respect and the technique of job analysis has been broadened correspondingly.

The Denver course of study in Industrial Arts, published in 1928, is an excellent illustration of the use of job analysis in the public schools. The following method, which was used in securing the essential data, is presented in Chapter I of the course:

A questionnaire was developed by the committee. It contained lists of activities grouped under headings related to various types of hand and tool work that were being done, or that were likely to be done, in or about the home. These lists were then submitted to the teachers of industrial arts for suggestions of additional activities. With these additions the questionnaire was given to each boy in each of the junior and senior high schools of the city. He was asked to take it home, read it over with his parents or landlady, and underscore all of the work listed which he or they recalled as having

136   PRINCIPLES OF CURRICULUM MAKING

been done, or needed to be done, in their home or in any other home with which they were acquainted. He was also asked to write down any additional activities of this kind that were not listed. Three thousand three hundred and fourteen questionnaires were returned and used.[10]

The following table illustrates one phase of the results of the questionnaire:

NUMBER AND PERCENTAGE OF BOYS REPORTING VARIOUS HOME ACTIVITIES IN BRICK AND CEMENT WORK—RANKED ACCORDING TO TOTAL FREQUENCY OF MENTION [11]

Rank	Activity	Totals 3314 Cases		Junior High Schools 1937 Cases		Senior High Schools 1377 Cases	
		No.	Per Cent	No.	Per Cent	No.	Per Cent
1.	Repairing a walk	890	27	554	29	336	24
2.	Repairing an ash pit	824	25	501	26	323	23
3.	Laying brick for camp fireplace	776	23	509	26	267	19
4.	Making a new walk	675	20	424	22	251	18
5.	Repairing a basement floor	559	17	342	18	217	16
6.	Repairing a chimney	490	15	307	16	183	13
7.	Making a foot scraper	471	14	296	15	175	13
8.	Making an ash pit	390	12	251	13	139	10
9.	Repairing a flue	366	11	228	12	138	10
10.	Making a porch box	355	11	225	12	130	10
11.	Treating floors and walls to make them waterproof	269	8	163	9	106	8
12.	Cement-coating old brick foundations	268	8	159	8	109	8
13.	Making a bird-bath	262	8	162	8	100	7
14.	Putting in tile about a fireplace	247	7	152	8	95	7
15.	Setting fire brick in a furnace	198	6	123	6	75	6
16.	Making a cement curbing	169	5	109	6	60	4
17.	Setting tile in a bathroom	167	5	111	6	56	4
18.	Making a lawn seat	160	5	89	5	71	5

[10] Research Monograph No. 4, *Industrial Arts* (Public Schools, Denver, Colorado, 1928), p. 9.
[11] *Ibid.*, p. 12.

The types of processes involved in the activities presented in the home are indicated by the presentation of a part of the table presenting these data:

NUMBER OF DIFFERENT PROCESSES INVOLVED IN EACH OF 208 HOME INDUSTRIAL ARTS ACTIVITIES [12]

(*These activities are the ones most frequently mentioned in the survey*)

Rank of Activity	Activity	Number of Processes Involved	Rank of Process Complexity
1.	Sharpening Knives	4	178.5
2.	Washing a car........................	5	165
3.	Cleaning a spark plug..................	9	127
4.	Repairing a faucet.....................	10	116.5
5.	Gardening	5	165
12.	Repairing a bicycle.....................	2	202.5
12.	Repairing a tire (bicycle)..............	9	127
12.	Replacing a spoke (bicycle).............	6	153.5
12.	Truing a wheel (bicycle)..............	2	202.5
12.	Aligning the frame and wheels (bicycle).	4	178.5
12.	Repairing the chain (bicycle)...........	4	178.5
12.	Repairing the grips (bicycle)...........	2	202.5
12.	Adjusting the handle bars (bicycle)......	2	202.5
12.	Adjusting the seat (bicycle)............	3	192.5
12.	Replacing the mud guards (bicycle)....	3	192.5
12.	Adjusting the cones (bicycle)..........	5	165
12.	Adjusting the hangers (bicycle).........	2	192.5
21.	Repairing a baseball...................	7	145
22.	Repairing a fence......................	11	109
23.	Repairing an inner tube.................	10	116.5
24.	Painting the porch floor and ceiling......	8	137
25.	Repairing the garden hose..............	5	165
26.	Varnishing furniture	4	178.5
27.	Removing and replacing a tire..........	9	127
28.	Putting up a Christmas tree............	7	145
29.	Connecting batteries and cells...........	10	116.5
30.	Repairing and installing door-bells......	20	66.5
31.	Draining and filling the radiator, etc.	3	192.5

The steps involved in organizing the material are presented in the following quotation from the course of study:

[12] *Ibid.*, p. 18.

General technique employed in using the results of the survey

Several steps of procedure were followed in using the findings of the survey:

1. Make a list of desirable activities to be used in the course. These are determined by the frequency rank from the survey.
2. Make a list of desirable processes to be used in the course. These are determined by the frequency with which they appear in the analysis of these activities.
3. Make sure that the activities chosen contain the desirable processes.
4. Discard those activities which are impracticable on the basis of
   a. The difficulty of the job
   b. The lack of shop facilities

Supplementary technique used:

The survey material was found not to be entirely adequate as a basis for a course of study, and it was necessary to select and incorporate content which would supplement and make the activities more effective. This was done as follows:

1. Include additional activities where survey material is inadequate. Secure activities from various schools which the teachers are using as successful problems.
2. Analyze these school activities for processes involved.
3. Determine process rank correlation of processes derived from the home activities with those of school activities.
4. Arrange activities according to simplicity and convenience.
5. Develop related information as the material presents itself in carrying an activity to completion.[13]

The following quotation from the Commonwealth Teacher Training Study, conducted by Charters and Waples, presents an excellent illustration of the use of job analysis in teacher training:

Whether the curriculum constructor should begin with race experience and eliminate the facts not useful to teachers, or begin with activities and traits and select the related and useful items of race experience, is a question. Choice between the methods is partly a matter of individual background and temperament, and is partly

[13] *Ibid.*, p. 69.

determined by the scope of the course, the students' maturity, the time available for instruction, and various other obtainable facts. The more conventional method starts with available knowledge and uses the activities as a basis for selection; the alternative method, and as we believe the better one, begins with activities and selects useful methods and principles from the accumulation of race experience. Both of the methods, however, are illustrated in this study, and both should be applied whenever conditions permit—one method being used to supplement and check the validity of the other.

1. Adopting the latter method that proceeds from the activities and traits of teachers, we first ascertained the traits that characterize excellent teachers.

2. Turning our attention to the teachers' activities, we proceeded to collect the activities performed by teachers in service, all types of public day-school teachers: teachers in high schools, elementary schools, rural schools, and other types. To the activities performed by teachers of typical schools we took great pains to add those performed by teachers of experimental schools and still other activities which progressive educational thinkers believe *should* be performed. The activities thus obtained constitute a master-list of teachers' activities from the first grade to the twelfth, as shown in complete form.

3. By means of the master-list we have been able to discover what duties are performed by different types of teachers by the simple device of having a representative number of teachers of each type check the list for frequency of performance. The findings cover teachers representing schools of five main types—high school, junior high, intermediate, primary and rural—with numerous subtypes to represent typical communities, subjects, and other varieties.

4. In addition to the check for frequency we have asked teachers of each type to pass judgment on the activities according to three other criteria: importance, difficulty of learning, and value of pre-service training.

5. Recognizing that the judgments of teachers are not sufficiently inclusive, we have secured the judgment of superintendents, principals, professors of education, supervisors, and other experts according to the criteria that each is best qualified to apply.

6. When the activities have been thus evaluated, it becomes necessary to define the teachers' objectives in order to select appropriate methods of performing the activities. One tries to answer the question, "What has the teacher in mind, or what should he have in mind, as his aim in performing the activity?" This can be answered, of course, only in terms of individual judgment or synthetic judgments which are preferably based on an adequate philosophy of

education and of life. Objectives are not derived from activities by any scientific process, though in many cases the activities suggest objectives that are present but not otherwise called to mind. Since the objectives are always primary, the methods of performing activities are based upon objectives that lie beyond the activities.

For this reason no attempt has been made to formulate a list of objectives for teacher-training institutions at large. However, certain objectives are assumed wherever they are needed to illustrate procedures involved in constructing a given curriculum or course.

7. Knowing the teachers' activities and the objectives, the curriculum constructor is then obliged to explore the problems and difficulties implied in both. Some of the problems lie in the field of special methods, some in general methods, some in the fields of management and extra-curricular activities; but in whatever field they are classified, the problems and difficulties become the focus of instruction.

8. After the difficulties and problems have been determined the next step is to select efficient methods for their solution. If the activities are to be carried on and if students must be taught how to perform them, it is the function of the training curriculum to provide this information. Some of the methods can be secured from the literature, but many of them are found in unrecorded form in the classroom.

9. For an intelligent grasp of teaching methods, a knowledge of principles is indispensable. Therefore the principles and facts that validate the selected methods must be located and segregated in the underlying and related fields. These become the principles of education, whether they are classified as such or as educational psychology, philosophy of education, and other so-called fundamental subjects.

10. At this point we have accounted for the elements or raw materials from which a curriculum is derived. It still remains to organize the materials into courses of instruction and adapt them to the needs of the students concerned.

The procedures described thus far are based upon the activities of teachers. But courses of instruction may also be derived by proceeding from the alternative point of reference, namely, from the organized experiences of the race. We may first ask experts to secure the facts and principles from underlying and related fields that are believed pertinent to the teacher's work. Then one may select the facts and principles for a teacher-training curriculum by checking them against the known and evaluated activities. By this process or otherwise one decides "by inspection" which of the principles and facts may be omitted and which should be emphasized in greater or less degree in courses within the fundamental subjects.[14]

The following studies will indicate the possibilities of working with this source of objectives:

BARR, A. S., "An Analysis of the Duties and Functions of Instructional Supervisors," University of Wisconsin Bureau of Educational Research, Bulletin No. 7 (January, 1926). This is an exact and careful study of the specific duties and functions performed by supervisors.

CHARTERS, W. W., and WHITNEY, I. B., *Analysis of Secretarial Duties and Traits* (Williams and Wilkins, 1924). A definite and exacting study of the duties and traits of secretaries.

STRONG, E. K., "Job Analysis of the Manager in Industry," *School and Society,* Vol. XXII (April 16, 1921). This analysis of the manager involved six different types of approach: (1) duties of the position—what the executive did, (2) essential qualifications that the manager needed in order to perform these duties, (3) qualifications that are of value but not essential, such as information needed to improve his work on the job, (4) the route to the job which the manager had followed, (5) the probable line of promotion, (6) recommendations and notes of any sort.

VII. RESEARCH IN OBJECTIVES BASED ON THE ACTIVITIES AND IDEALS OF MEMBERS OF SOCIETY

This technique of analyzing activities and ideals, while similar in many respects to activity analysis and job analysis, is deserving of special treatment because of its emphasis upon ideals and its insistence that standards of performance are fully as important as performances. In the opinion of Charters,[15] the attitude of the individual toward the task, whether that task be living or making a living, and the ideals that govern the standards of performance for the person, are as important as determining the activities which the best members of society perform efficiently. Both are necessary standards in directing the younger generation in the attainment of a similar proficiency in these activities and attitudes. A statement of objectives attained by an analysis of the activities of outstanding citizens is not sufficient; objectives must be analyzed into both activity and ideal objectives. The

[14] W. W. Charters and Douglas Waples, *Commonwealth Teacher Training Study* (University of Chicago Press, 1928), pp. 3-6.

[15] W. W. Charters, *Curriculum Construction* (The Macmillan Co., 1923).

point emphasized by Charters is that in working for the improvement of citizenship, educators are concerned with objectives which should be stated in terms of the activities of the good citizen and the ideals of the good citizen. A man's attitude toward the responsibilities of citizenship are as significant as the duties and activities which he publicly performs. Otherwise, the technique is very similar to others which we have studied. A brief statement of the steps which are involved will make this clear.

Step one. There is no important difference in the first step from that proposed by Bobbitt in the organization of an activity analysis. Briefly, it is necessary in the beginning to determine the general or major objectives of life from a study of life and society. The methods discussed in connection with activity analysis will suffice here.

Step two. These general objectives are then analyzed into objectives which are concerned with ideals and those which are stated in terms of activities. This process of breaking down the more general statements into specific and definite statements is continued until working units are secured. The relative importance of these ideals and activities is determined as they are subsumed under their various general classifications.

Step three. This working list of specific and definite ideals and activities, classified under their respective general classifications, is then scrutinized carefully and reorganized in terms of the importance of the ideals and activities to children and adults. Those which have high value for children and low value for adults are given the most significant position in the training program. At the same time those which can be acquired outside the school are deleted from the list.

Some have listed seven steps as essential in using this technique. It seems hardly necessary to complicate the situation needlessly by introducing additional steps when these three are sufficient to enable the investigator to secure and organize objectives in education.

A possible criticism of this technique is that it is entirely subjective in character. The complete list of ideals and activities is secured by the investigators thinking about those which will naturally classify under the general objective which is being considered. However, the method is simplified and probably made more valid by listing the activities down the side of the page and the ideals across the top, so that suggestion of new ideals will accompany the inclusion of new activities, and the development of new ideals will motivate the organization of new activities through which they may be realized. This arrangement also simplifies the breaking down of both ideals and activities to working units, for which the selection of teaching materials can be made from a number of available sources. The following quotation will clarify the method of handling this technique:

An analysis chart. In order to clarify the relations between ideals and activities the familiar form of the graph can be used. What is needed in order to derive the curriculum from objectives is, as we have seen, an analysis of activities to the level where they may be handled efficiently. For instance, in the case of Herbart's objective we may say that the individual should lead a life "which is ethical." In this there are obviously two elements, ethical ideals and living a life. In living a life the individual performs series and groups of activities which are controlled by ethical ideals. It is necessary, then, to analyze ethical ideals on the one hand into such items as honesty, sympathy, etc., and similarly to analyze the activities involved in living a life.

AN ANALYSIS CHART

Activities	Ethical Ideals					Social Ideals, etc.		
	1	2	3	4	Etc.	1	2	Etc.
A								
1.								
(1)								
(a)								
i	x		x					
ii	x	x				x		

The resulting situation may be represented by a graph, along the top of which are run the ideals, while along the side are listed the activities, and in the squares are checked the ideals which dominate the performance of each activity. In the foregoing chart the ethical ideals are analyzed into five classes, let us say indicated by the figures from one to five. Other classes and subclasses of ideals extend to the right. The group of activities (A) is analyzed and subclassified as shown on the left. The checks indicate that in performing activity A 1 (1) (a) i, the ethical ideals 1 and 3 dominate, while in performing activity A 1 (1) (a) ii, the ethical ideals marked 1 and 2 and the social ideal, 1, control.

Considering the vertical column it will be found that an ideal along the top adheres to the many activities along the side. A housewife might conceivably seek to perform many actions in conformity with the ideal of neatness. She might wish to be neat in dressing in the morning, in preparing breakfast, in mixing a mash for the chickens, in clearing the table, in making beds, etc. Or if we consider an activity along the side, it may happen that one of these will be dominated by a number of ideals, not only ethical, but social, esthetic, etc. In serving breakfast, for instance, the housewife may be dominated by the ideals of neatness, health, and sociability. Viewed from either top or side we may either teach ideals through activities, or teach activities under the domination of ideals, depending on our philosophy of life.

The effect of adding other ideals is merely to increase the width of the graph. The activities do not change. They are determined by an analysis of the physical and mental experiences of the individual. This widening of the range of ideals would merely resume in the control of the activity by more ideals. In that case instead of the person's merely attempting to turn out an honest piece of work, he might also attempt to make it beautiful and perform it as a service to humanity.[16]

VIII. PRIMARY SOURCES USED BY CURRICULUM COMMITTEES

A number of courses of study have been analyzed in order that the techniques of determining objectives from primary sources would be apparent to the reader. These courses are all recent and represent the best current work in course of study construction. Since these techniques can be illustrated from any course of study, no attempt has been made to include all academic fields. The reader should note that occasionally techniques

[16] *Ibid.*, pp. 53-54.

of determining objectives from secondary sources are included in order that the distinctions between these two sources of objectives will be apparent.

SOCIAL STUDIES

1. *Kansas City, Missouri.* Grades 1—3. Date of publication, 1930.

A study was made of the interests and experiences of five thousand school children, in school and out, by means of a questionnaire. The questionnaire was sent to pupils in schools situated in different sections of the city. The questions were answered by the pupils themselves where maturity permitted; otherwise, the children were interviewed individually by the teacher. This information was tabulated and classified under the seven generally accepted divisions of life's major activities.

In order that the organization of such a questionnaire can be duplicated, if desirable, a copy of the one used in Kansas City is included.

QUESTIONNAIRE—PUPILS' EXPERIENCES AND INTERESTS

PART I. OUT-OF-SCHOOL

School............................. Grade......... Date...........

Sex...............   Age...............

1. What did you do last Saturday?
   (List here)
   Which thing did you like best?
   Which thing did you like least?
   What would you like to have done that you did not do?

2. What did you do last Sunday?
   What did you like best?
   What did you like least?
   What would you like to have done that you did not do?

3. What did you do after school last night?
   (From time you left school until you went to bed.)
   What thing did you like best?
   Which thing did you like least?
   What would you like to have done that you did not do?

4. What did you do before you came to school this morning?
   (From the time you got up.)
   Which thing did you like best?
   Which thing did you like least?
   What would you like to have done that you did not do?

5. What did you do last vacation?
    During the summer?
    During other vacations including holidays?
    Which thing did you like best?
    Which thing did you like least?
    What would you like to have done that you did not do?

PART II. IN SCHOOL

6. Of all the things you did last week in school which did you like best?
    Which did you like least?
    What would you like to have done that you did not do?

NUMBER OF CHILDREN RESPONDING TO QUESTIONNAIRE

Year	Boys	Girls
Kindergarten	213	189
First Grade	206	243
Second Grade	328	335
Third Grade	303	316
Fourth Grade	220	223
Fifth Grade	278	268
Sixth Grade	249	294
Seventh Grade	234	274
Freshman	129	165
Sophomore	131	143
Junior	141	153
Senior	124	170
Totals	2,556	2,746

The questions were answered by the pupils themselves where maturity permitted. In kindergarten and primary grades, children were interviewed individually by the teacher. The information was tabulated and classified into the generally accepted divisions of life's major activities, namely:

1. Physical life
2. Command of fundamental processes
3. Family life
4. Vocational life
5. Civic life
6. Recreational life
7. Ethical and religious life

ENGLISH

1. *Baltimore, Maryland.* Grades 7—12. Date of publication, 1932.
   a. A survey of the needs in English of pupils and of adults.
      (1) The results of a questionnaire to selected high-school students in Baltimore, in which they were invited to list situations in and out of school in which they needed to read, speak, or write English.
      (2) Teachers' statements of pupils' needs in English.
      (3) Occasions for reading, speaking, and writing contained in Baltimore courses of study.
      (4) A sampling of textbook "study helps."
      (5) Specimens of pupils' work in English.
      (6) Studies such as Johnson, *English Expressions* (Public School Publishing Company, 1926); Gray and Monroe, *Reading Interests and Habits of Adults* (Macmillan, 1929); Lyman, *Summary of Investigations in Language, Grammar, and Composition* (University of Chicago Press, 1929).
      (7) Courses of study published since Pendleton's survey in 1924.
      (8) Job analyses undertaken by the American Council on Education and other agencies.
      (9) What Baltimore employers say about public high-school graduates.
      (10) Textbooks based on an experimental study of pupils' needs, interests, or capacities.
   b. A study of the cumulative research and statistical data available in the Bureau of Research.
      (1) The 101st Annual Report of the Board of School Commissioners showing changes in the high-school population over the past ten years, the individual differences in interests, capacities, and future goals of students, and the longer time they are remaining in the secondary school.
      (2) Semi-annual reports of intelligence and of reading tests in elementary and in secondary schools.
      (3) Studies reported in the Baltimore Bulletin of Education.
   c. A study of several significant criticisms of secondary-school English:
      Consulted in this connection were such references as Counts, *Senior High School Curriculum* (University of Chicago Press, 1926); Department of Superintendence, *Sixth Year-*

book, *The Development of the High School Curriculum* (1928); Monroe and Herriott, *Reconstruction of the Secondary School Curriculum—Its Meaning and Trends,* University of Illinois *Bulletin,* Vol. XXV, No. 42 (1928).

d. Examination of all instructional materials:

As part of the general supervisory program in English, teachers were acquainting themselves with the new books and other instructional material as they became available. This procedure was carried forward as a continuous part of the curriculum program, with the additional feature of securing experimental data in the suitability of the materials for various types of pupils.

e. Analysis of research studies by chairman:

In order to acquaint teachers with the various techniques for studying curriculum programs, the chairman made a case analysis of the research studies already available. This analysis revealed techniques applicable to local problems and served to guide the procedures used by the teachers in their own research. A few titles are listed to indicate the scope of this phase of the program: Barton, *Outlining as a Study Procedure* (Teachers College, Columbia University, 1930); Broening, *Developing Appreciation through Teaching Literature* (Johns Hopkins Press, 1929); Carroll, *Spelling Difficulties of Bright and Dull Pupils* (Teachers College, Columbia University, 1927); Odell, *The Use of Scales for Rating Pupils' Answers to Thought Questions* (University of Illinois, 1929); Smith, *Class Size in High-School English* (University of Minnesota Press, 1931); Stephens, *Individual Instruction in English Composition* (Harvard University Press, 1928).

f. A summary of unpublished studies:

These were occasional studies made by Baltimore teachers for university classes and for departmental meetings and frequently served to supply immediate answers to specific curriculum problems.

g. A study of recent publications on the teaching of reading, literature, composition, spelling, etc.

These differed from the foregoing in being books of method and not research studies *per se.* An extensive bibliography of this nature is included in the course of study.

h. Preparation of instructional tests:

Individuals and groups of teachers prepared objective tests in reading and in technical English. These are included and discussed in the course of study.

HOME ECONOMICS

1. *Oakland, California.* Grades 7—9. Date of publication, 1929.
    a. A study was made of the surveys and analyses of home activities in which girls engage. (Five studies were used.)
    b. A sampling of the activities of high eighth-grade girls in the Oakland public schools was secured.
    c. Opinions of home-economics teachers.
    d. Study of newer tendencies in home economics.
2. *State of Idaho.* Grades 7—12. Date of publication, July, 1932.
    a. The committee, in charge of the work for the schools of the state of Idaho, formulated the following program:

> As a basis for revising the present state course of study it seemed advisable to secure information concerning the activities of school girls and of homemakers, the types of communities in which they live, their home conditions, and the approximate ages at which girls assume responsibilities of home making. The needed information was gained through means of questionnaires. Studies were made of recent courses of study and of text and reference books to determine present trends in home economics.

SUMMARY OF STUDIES

A. Aims
   The aims of the studies were:
   1. To determine the present responsibilities and activities of junior and senior high-school girls and homemakers as one means of deciding what kind of training is needed to prepare girls to better meet their present problems in home and school life and to become successful homemakers.
   2. To determine present trends in home economics in the secondary schools of the country.
B. Methods used
   1. Three main factors were considered in determining the type of training needed:
       a. The activities of girls from the seventh through the twelfth grades.
       b. The activities of present homemakers.
       c. The training which graduates feel would have helped them in solving problems they now have.
   2. Questionnaires were sent to one hundred girls in each of the six grades, seventh to twelfth inclusive, in different sections of Idaho to determine the:
       a. Duties of girls at home.

   b. Foods being prepared in the home.
   c. Clothing being made in the home and that purchased ready made.
   d. Use of labor-saving equipment in the home.
   e. Use of business methods in home finances.
   f. Recreational activities of the family.
3. Another questionnaire was prepared and copies sent to two hundred and fifty homemakers in Idaho homes, the questions covering the same type of activities as in the study of activities of school girls.
4. A third questionnaire was sent to girl students of the last ten years of twelve representative high schools of the state to ascertain:
   a. How long Idaho girls attend school.
   b. How soon after leaving secondary schools Idaho girls marry.
   c. What type of work they take up after leaving school.
   d. What type of school home economics they find of greatest actual value.
5. A different type of study was used to determine present trends in home economics in the secondary schools of the country:
   a. Analyses of course of study published since 1925.
   b. Analyses of home economics reference and text books published since 1928.

3. *Denver, Colorado.* Two courses, Grades 7—9 and 10—12. Date of publication 1927 and 1928.

These courses were based on a questionnaire study. The home economics activities of junior and senior high-school girls were determined through a questionnaire submitted to 5,106 pupils. The findings of the study were as follows:

Cleaning, going to the store, care of own room, laundry work, and help in preparation of meals are major activities in the relative order of importance. General care of the home, some form of which is engaged in by every girl in school, is predominant in the Saturday and Sunday activities. It is readily apparent that required work in junior high-school home economics must place less emphasis upon skill in cookery and clothing construction and more upon *care of the home and sanitation,* together with the care and repair of appliances to be used, household and personal laundry, and proper marketing methods.

In order to find out whether the topics now stressed in cookery were the important ones, pupils were asked to list those foods occurring once a day for five days per week and those occurring only three times per week. For the curriculum maker this had two points of significance.

First it shows those foods which are used most commonly in the home and preparation of which should be taught. Second, it shows those which are frequently used, but are undesirable from the standpoint of health. This means that the curriculum should include the development of such habits and knowledge as will increase the consumption of desirable foods, such as cooked cereals, fresh and cooked vegetables, salads, eggs, and soups; likewise, the development of such habits and knowledge as will decrease the consumption of less desirable foods, such as coffee, pancakes, fried meats, cake, and pie.

To find out what should be taught in the field of clothing, students were asked to list articles which were bought ready-made, those which were made at home, and those which were sometimes bought and sometimes made. This shows very clearly that the major problem in this field is one of clothing selection, as the garments which are bought ready-made in almost every instance greatly outnumber those made in the home. The findings showed that garment construction was confined to house dresses and simple undergarments; therefore, actual skill needs to be developed in the making of these.

The results on remodeling showed that outer garments of silk and wool are frequently made over, while outer garments of cotton and linen and undergarments are seldom remodeled. For the curriculum maker, this means that the remodeling of outer garments of the better quality of textiles should receive some emphasis in the home economics course.

In the social activities of students there is found a wealth of suggestion for teachers in tying up home economics instruction in school with outside social activities, as well as with social activities within the school.

If we are to prevent subject-matter from being isolated from situations requiring its use, then the teaching of home economics should be set to meet the time when these activities are participated in most frequently by the girl in her home. Those activities which are engaged in by the largest number of pupils should be placed in required subjects and at a period before many girls drop out of school. The remaining activities of lesser importance can be placed in elective courses and at a later date.

USE OF THE LIBRARY

1. *Denver, Colorado.* Grades 7—9. Date of publication, 1927.
   a. Based on "after-school" life of pupils.
   b. Experimentation. Children were given free play periods in which they might play as they chose. Their activities were listed by grades and according to frequencies.
   c. Results of experimentation elsewhere as in the Horace Mann School. Reported in Teachers College Record, Vol. XXIII, pp. 327-360.
   d. Interests of the junior high-school children determine objectives of instruction.

MATHEMATICS

1. *Lincoln, Nebraska,* Arithmetic. Grades 4—6. Date of publication, 1930.

    Study of the quantitative experiences of the elementary-school child and the need for training children to solve problems arising from these experiences.

2. *Kansas City, Missouri.* Grades 7—9. Date of publication, 1929.
    a. Information as to the mathematical experiences of junior high-school pupils was secured by means of the following questionnaire:
        (1) What did you do in the past week outside of school that relates to mathematics?
        (2) What did you see or hear that relates to mathematics?
        (3) What did you read about that relates to mathematics
    b. A study was made of the mathematical knowledges and skills needed by pupils in other school subjects and activities. This study and the preceding one were used extensively as a means of suggesting actual pupil needs and activities, especially for the first-year course.

KINDERGARTEN

1. *Berkeley, California.* Date of publication, 1931.
    a. Scientific investigation in the Berkeley schools.
    b. Consideration of the professional literature.
    c. Secured assistance of special supervisors in art, music, physical education, hygiene, nature study, and corrective speech.
2. *Kansas City, Missouri.* Date of publication, 1931.
    a. Study of the interests of children by the committee and the curriculum department.
    b. Study of the experiences of children by the committee and the curriculum department.

INDUSTRIAL ARTS

1. *Denver, Colorado.* Grades 7—12. Date of publication, 1928.

    The committee on curriculum revision in this field attempted to find out what activities of construction and repair are being carried on in homes. The list of activities found by the home survey did not, of itself, determine the content of the tentative course of study. While it would have been possible to select from these activities enough to constitute a course of study, it was found to be preferable to base the course on the tool processes required to perform these home tasks. To illustrate one type of difficulty in using the home activities directly as the course of study, the woodwork unit may be cited. Among the most frequently mentioned home activities were repairing a fence and repairing a screen door. Neither of these activities could well be used in the school shop. The eleven tool processes involved in repairing a screen door have been used along with the processes involved in other home activities in determining the suitability of proposed shop subjects. In other words, those shop projects that involved most nearly the same processes as the home activities most frequently mentioned have been selected for the course of study.

ACCOUNTING

1. *Cleveland, Ohio.* Grades 11 and 12. Date of publication, 1928-29.

The committee that prepared this course of study began its work by analyzing the commercial occupations surveys made by Nichols [17] and Barnhart [18] of the Federal Board for Vocational Education. The committee continued its work by coöperating with a committee of the Cleveland Schoolmasters Club, Roy W. LaDu, Chairman, which was making a study of commercial occupations in Cleveland.[19] On the basis of these studies, the committee recommended the following curriculum in general clerical service and elementary accounting:

Grade 10—General clerical service
Grade 11—Elementary accounting
Grade 12—Elementary accounting

The next work of the committee was to make a job analysis of the work of the bookkeeper in the Cleveland District and to set up

[17] F. G. Nichols, "Survey of Junior Commercial Occupations," *Bulletin No. 54* (Federal Board for Vocational Education, June, 1920).

[18] E. W. Barnhart, "Preliminary Report on the Senior Commercial Occupations Survey" (Federal Board for Vocational Education, Washington, D. C.).

[19] The Cleveland study revealed that only about 5 per cent of commercial workers gained bookkeeping or accounting positions during the first five years out of school; and only those who had acquired maturity and education equal to or in excess of the maturity and training of high-school graduates ever attained such positions. On the other hand, the study revealed that almost half of all commercial workers do general clerical work during the first five years out of school, and that these general clerks are the youngest and the least well-trained group in commercial work. See LaDu, Bulletin No. 174, 1924, B. E. R. Connor, "The Community Background of the Commercial Course and How to Understand It," University of Iowa Monographs in Education (July, 1926), pp. 136-144.

vocational objectives for a course of study. The committee also made analyses of (*a*) certain problems in teaching, and set up objectives and related activities and materials for realizing them, (*b*) certain social values in bookkeeping, and set up social objectives for them, (*c*) certain cultural values in bookkeeping, and set up objectives for them. The objectives obtained in this manner were then organized into a complete and logical outline.[20] This material was set up in such a manner that competent critics of it might easily express their opinions as to the value of each item and the place it belonged in the course of study.

The objectives thus set up were distributed to a great many persons, and a critical judgment was requested. The committee obtained the judgments of Cleveland teachers of elementary accounting, a number of outstanding teachers of elementary accounting outside of Cleveland, and a number of accountants and university teachers of accounting on the value of each objective, and on the order of the arrangement of the objectives and their grade placement in the course of study.

These judgments were studied statistically and a pedagogical arrangement of the material made on the basis of them. The committee then employed an accountant and the author of the textbook in elementary accounting adopted for use in the Cleveland schools to work with them in making a final check of the content and arrangement of the material.

The work described above required about three and one-half years. The course of study presented in this pamphlet is the result.[21]

IX. TECHNIQUE OF DETERMINING OBJECTIVES FROM PRIMARY
SOURCES AT THE COLLEGE LEVEL

The following statement by Charters outlines the plan of securing objectives and determining the teaching field at Stephens College.[22] His complete statement is included, because it is so significant in the college field.

The method commonly known as "activity analysis" was used in the major studies dealing with the functional objectives of the col-

---

[20] Bureau of Educational Research, Bulletin No. 24 (November, 1925).

[21] *Tentative Course of Study in Elementary Accounting,* Grades XI-XII (Cleveland Public Schools, 1928-1929).

[22] W. W. Charters, "The Stephens College Program for the Education of Women," News Bulletin, Society for the Study of Curriculum, Vol. V, No. 5 (Sept., 1934), pp. 2-4.

lege. The basic activities study was designed to reveal the specific fields of experience in which the special needs and interests of college women lie. Three hundred women, all college graduates, participated in the study by keeping careful "diary" records of activities growing out of their own personal needs. After listing and classifying more than 7,500 items, the investigators reported seven areas of experience in which the curriculum must provide subject matter for training, (1) communication, (2) physical health, (3) mental health, (4) civic relations—social, economic, and political problems, (5) esthetic appreciation—art, literature, music, (6) consumption-purchasing, getting the best for one's efforts, (7) an integrated philosophy of living. Thus a sevenfold objective is established which applies equally to all students of the college irrespective of probable vocations. Courses leading to competence in these fields may ultimately be required of all students. Vocational interests are met largely through elective preprofessional curricula. Whether or not the homemaking area should constitute a separate required unit is at present under consideration.

The next step was the providing of subject-matter in the seven fields. This involved the building of special courses or the rebuilding of courses already in the curriculum. Each course was developed experimentally with a small group of students and later made available to many or all of the students.

Communication. The activity of communication embraces approximately one-fourth of all the items recorded by the diarists who assisted in the basic study. In order to determine the types of expressional activity which might be called "functional" in daily life, an extended investigation was carried on by a member of the staff. This investigation resulted in defining the following types of oral and written expression as centers of organization for the curriculum in communication, (1) letter writing, (2) conversation, (3) story telling, (4) report making, (5) speech making, (6) personal memoranda, (7) round-table discussion, (8) giving directions, explanations, and instructions. These activities have become known as the "functional centers of expression" and have been widely adopted in English courses of study. At Stephens College they are the basic content of the course in communication—supplemented in special-interest groups by appropriate types of "creative writing."

To take care of the troublesome matter of mechanics, a system of English "hurdles" has been devised to permit students to demonstrate early in the course their mastery of usage. Each student takes each "hurdle" as rapidly as she can. Many different forms of each hurdle are available so the students who fail their first attempt may study and practice for the next form.

The work in communication is further supplemented by a plan of coöperative emphasis in the enforcement of good English practice in all class work and by a "voice clinic" in which substantially one-fourth of the students are given specific practice in the improvement of voice quality.

Social and *civic relations.* To secure material for a social problems course which would prepare the way for an active, intelligent interest in the social and civic affairs in after-college activity, an analysis of persistent major social problems as reported in periodical literature was made. This investigation was supplemented by a study of the activities of outstanding women leaders and of women's organizations. As a result a list of *economic, political,* and *social* problems was evolved which furnished the topics for the course.

The form of organization which has been developed for the college community offers a unique citizenship laboratory which provides first-hand contact with various problems and forms of community organization.

Physical health. The maintenance of health at a high level and the mastery of the techniques of relaxation are major objectives. Regular participation in physical-education activities is required of each student, the type of exercise being adapted to the individual student in accordance with the results of physical examination and diagnosis. Conspicuous among the plans to promote relaxation is the siesta, a rest period from one to two o'clock on Monday to Friday inclusive. Periodic evaluations of the siesta have resulted in its continuation by almost unanimous consensus. The hygiene unit of the science curriculum has been reorganized along functional lines to incorporate problems emerging in the basic activities study. As an extra-curricular activity in health promotion, a "scientific eating" program is sponsored in the autumn by the home economics department and is given recurrent emphasis throughout the year.

Mental health. The course in general psychology, it was felt, should lean toward clinical psychology rather than the usual laboratory psychology or systematic psychology. The major effort is as yet upon the modification of the conventional course to include the various types of problems classified as "mental hygiene" in the basic activities study. It has seemed to those in charge of the course that better results are to be obtained by definitely connecting the personal problems to be considered with the basic units of subject-matter necessary to an understanding of psychological principles involved.

Esthetic appreciation. It was clearly indicated in the original study that women derive deep and varied comforts from the informal appreciation of art, literature, music, and nature. The development of a unit of the curriculum designed primarily to promote esthetic appreciation was therefore undertaken. The materials for instruction were drawn from three fields, literature, music, and art, with a persistent and unifying emphasis upon the common elements of artistic production. While the emphasis in this unit is on appreciation rather than performance, much is done to stimulate students to do creative work in one or more of the fields of expression.

Consumption. One of the requirements for each student is a report each year (in the form of a "thrift book") on expenditures for all purposes while in college. This activity has elicited much favorable comment. The problems related to consumption, however, cover a much broader area than the wise expenditure of money. Women not only spend money to purchase things of value; they also spend effort to achieve accepted ends. Probably in the long run more training is needed in the field of effort than in the field of finance. A course is now being experimentally developed to meet problems arising in this area of experience.

Integration. The development of this unit in any systematic and formal manner is only beginning. A tentative technique has been formulated as follows: (1) selecting disturbing "conflicts" in experience; (2) assembling principles of ethics, philosophy, and religion that may be used in resolving these conflicts; (3) giving instruction at the student's level of experience through use of specific cases or problems. For the more thoughtful student, integration of learning will probably result from fortunate but informal contacts made in the normal course of experience. But the realization of this important objective cannot be left to the hazards of casual instruction.

After the discussion of the sevenfold objective as determined by the basic activities study, the author of the bulletin describes briefly the plans and purposes of the religious education department, the avenues which are utilized for "personality development," the vocational fields touched by the curriculum, extra-curricular activities, permanent leisure interests developed on campus, criteria for faculty selection, the work of the research division, and the major administrative policies in effect.

X. SUMMARY

Techniques, which can be used in determining objectives from primary sources, have been discussed in this chapter. In the discussion of each procedure, sufficient studies and investigations were presented to illustrate the extensive use which may be made of these sources. Further bibliographical references of research in this field may be found in:

DRAPER, E. M., and ROBERTS, A. C., *Study Guide in Secondary Education* (The Century Company, 1933).

HARAP, Henry, *Technique of Curriculum Building* (The Macmillan Company, 1928).

Annotated Bibliography of Investigations of Curriculum Objectives, Bulletin No. I (School of Education, Western Reserve University, 1932).

Annotated Bibliography, *Review of Educational Research*, Vol. IV, No. 2 (National Education Association, April, 1934).

An extensive bibliography of similar investigation organized according to subject-matter fields is included at the end of Part II.

CHAPTER V

THE DETERMINATION OF OBJECTIVES FROM SECONDARY SOURCES

I. INTRODUCTION

In general, investigations in primary sources of data will have to be exhaustive in character and extend over long periods of time. One curriculum expert has estimated that education is in need of five thousand completed research projects in primary sources before definite statements can be made regarding objectives or teaching materials. The time element and the necessity of using large numbers of people mean that the cost of working out the complicated techniques that have been devised for carrying on research in primary sources will be almost prohibitive to all except the largest school systems, and might well be initiated, to a large extent, by the Office of Education.

There are many secondary sources of data which can be investigated and which describe rather accurately the needs, deficiencies, activities, and interests of both children and adults. Most of these sources eliminate both the time element and the number of people needed to make the former type of experiment an adequate sampling. One person—the investigator—can usually organize and systematize for school people quantitative data of a secondary character which is already in existence. However, students of curriculum constrution should not fail to evaluate correctly this type of investigation. As is usually the case, the cheapest, or the easiest accomplished, is not always the most worthwhile. There is no comparison in value between a study indicating definitely the actual and specific needs, deficiencies, etc., of a case group in society and an investigation which summarizes the opinions stated by a relatively large number of competent people.

II. ORGANIZATION OF OBJECTIVES THROUGH INVESTIGATIONS OF MATERIAL IN NEWSPAPERS, MAGAZINES AND BOOKS

These investigations have been based on the assumption that publications of these types reflect accurately social conduct, social needs, deficiencies, and activities of the population. Two distinctly different types of valuable material are available in these sources.

The first is the writing of the editors, authors, and special writers in these publications. The problem, in this case, is to determine the amount and kind of an education which will enable the citizen to read understandingly and interpret correctly the facts presented in the items, articles, and manuscripts. Therefore, the investigators have proceeded to determine the vocabulary needed in the various subject-matter fields in order to read these publications intelligently and to determine and analyze the facts from science, social science, geography, arithmetic, and other subjects which are essential in the correct interpretation of the facts presented.

The second type of material investigated in these sources are the communications which are forwarded to these publications by subscribers and readers. Various opportunities are offered through contributors' columns, letters from readers, special editors on health, domestic science, etc., who request communications and questions from subscribers. These reflect the interests, activities, and needs of the people and in this limited sense the current publications are a mirror of life.

The extensive use which is made of these sources necessitates a consideration of the limitations which are imposed upon the investigator.

1. The publications must be carefully selected in order to avoid:
   a. Religious or political bias.
   b. Those which are poorly written and show inferior editorship.
   c. Those which stress sensationalism at the expense of intellectual and educational leadership.
   d. Those which do not touch certain fields of life or present inadequate treatments.

    e. Those which do not represent general community interest.

    f. Overemphasizing one period of history which might show a
       great interest in race clashes, economic depression, or a par-
       ticular adjustment of international relations.

2. The findings from these investigations should be considered as
   only supplementary to other research either in primary or secondary sources.

3. These publications may not always mirror life correctly and
   unless standards, such as were suggested in the study of primary
   objectives, are used for comparison peculiar and unsound results
   may be attained.

The following investigations will illustrate satisfactorily the
comprehensiveness of the data which may be secured and, in a
general way, the usable character of the results:

BOBBITT, Franklin, "Discovering the Objectives of Health Education."
Elementary School Journal, Vol. XXV (June, 1925), pp. 755-762. A
comprehensive study of health needs as indicated through inquiries to the
press.

————, "The Technique of Curriculum Making in Arithmetic," *Elementary School Journal,* Vol. XXV (Oct., 1924), pp. 127-143. Dr.
Bobbitt presents the results of a study made by H. W. Adams of the
mathematics occurring in the press.

PARTRIDGE, C. M., "Number Needs in Children's Reading Activities,"
Elementary School Journal, Vol. XXVI (Jan. 1926), pp. 357-366. The
study is made of a single issue of ten magazines to determine the numerical situations which are presented.

THORNDIKE, E. L., *The Psychology of Algebra* (Macmillan Company, 1924). In chapter two of this book, Dr. Thorndike presents an
analysis of forty-four texts in social science, science, biology, and practical arts and also a study of the references to mathematics in the first
two hundred pages of each of the twenty-eight volumes of the Encyclopedia Britannica.

BURKHART, O. E., "Concepts of Pupils in Secondary-School Science,"
The Teachers Journal and Abstract, Vol. V (May 1930), pp. 315-320.
This is a study of the most common concepts involved in the reading
of books and articles on popular science.

HOPKINS, L. T., "A Study of Magazines and Newspaper Science Articles with Relation to Courses in Science for High Schools," *School
Science and Mathematics,* Vol. XXIV (Nov. 1924), pp. 793-800. Presents a study of the scientific facts and principles which are required
in order to appreciate reading in these sources.

POWERS, S. R., "A Vocabulary of Scientific Terms for High-School
Students," *Teachers College Record,* Vol. XXVIII (Nov. 1926), pp.
220-245. A study of the most common scientific terms found in fifteen
science texts and fifty magazine articles.

III. ORGANIZATION OF OBJECTIVES THROUGH INVESTIGATIONS
OF NATIONAL AND COMMUNITY DOCUMENTS, STATISTICS,
RECORDS, SURVEYS, BOOKS, AND OTHER PUBLICATIONS

Educators have not been inclined, as a rule, to emphasize this source of information. In part, this is because they have not realized the value of the data presented through these materials, and, in part, perhaps, because they have recognized that some of the data are unreliable and must be carefully analyzed and checked against acceptable standards of living. There are, however, many agencies which are in a position to furnish valuable information and data concerning the activities and habits of the people in this country.

The Departments and Bureaus in the National government which publish such materials are The United States Bureau of Labor, The Department of Agriculture, The United States Geological Survey, The United States Bureau of Public Health, The United States Bureau of Standards, The United States Bureau of Domestic and Foreign Commerce, The United States Bureau of Mines, The Department of Commerce, The Department of the Interior—including the Office of Education, and many others. A complete list of these publications can be secured by writing to each department or bureau.

There are other sources which are national in scope, but not connected with the government, such as platforms of political parties, records and publications of national patriotic societies, records and publications of the Anti-Saloon League, the American Legion and auxiliary organizations, the Women's Christian Temperance Union, and the American Federation of Labor. The material secured from these sources must be carefully evaluated. Most of these organizations are interested in education and have exercised great influence in shaping the school curriculum in the past.

In the State and local community, many agencies and bureaus are carrying on investigations and publishing bulletins which are of significance to the educators interested in objectives. It is only necessary to mention a few examples from each of the outstanding classifications in order that these almost unlimited and yet rarely used sources of objectives may be realized and appreciated:

1. State departments of health, education, efficiency or statistics, labor or employment, etc., present extensive resources for the determination of objectives.

2. In the city, there are chambers of commerce, real-estate boards, retail and wholesale associations, credit associations, countless local units of the American Federation of Labor, labor colleges, social senates or councils, social agencies and various types of relief organizations, and experts or research bureaus in connection with city planning and development.

It will be apparent at once that an analysis of data of this type is not a study of life, but an investigation of descriptions of life and living conditions. It is because of this fact that extreme caution must be exercised in the use of this material. A peculiar bias, prejudice, hobby, or principle of a group of individuals must be given consideration in the use of any of the data published. In this connection it should be noted that many books are published by experts or specialists in these fields which present valuable data. Also, publications are available by others who have a militant interest in the work of a particular field, but who are neither experts nor specialists. That which merely represents opinion must be separated from that which consists of statistical evidence.

The technique advocated by Harap for the determination of the economic activities of the American people is more objective, hence more scientific, than those that have been considered in the field of civic education. His technique was used, primarily, to determine the habits, skills, knowledge, or attitudes which should be achieved in the improvement of standards for the consumption of food, shelter, fuel, and clothing.[1] Harap says:

It is a postulate of this study that, all things being equal, it is sounder to frame school policy on the best obtainable evidence than

[1] A recent study in this field is available for the student: L. V. Koos, "Consumer Education in the Secondary School," *School Review*, Vol. XLII (Dec., 1934), pp. 737-750.

on opinion. It is assumed also that the process of gathering data to form the basis of curriculum change will continue and that inadequate evidence will be replaced as rapidly as new and better evidence can be discovered. We may, therefore, anticipate that the data will be of varying degree of validity and scope, but that they will be of the best obtainable evidence of present practice checked up by the best data on standard practice.[2]

A discussion of the steps involved in the technique will illustrate this point.

Step one. The investigator making the analysis must determine the present economic habits of the American people. A direct study of the economic habits of a nation of one hundred and twenty-five millions would be an enormous task and require the coöperation of a vast army of assistants. However, studies that show what people actually do in the process of consuming food, clothing, shelter, and fuel have been completed by government agencies and public organizations. There are various kinds of secondary data, not in reality definite items of the economic habits of the American people, but items that reflect the standards attained by various groups in economic adjustment. These items are available for use in the investigation.

Data of these types are illustrated by the following:

a. Census Reports. The volume on manufacturing gives the quantitative data on the raw materials which are transformed into commodities to be consumed by the American people. The most important products of most industries are also included in this report.

b. Yearbooks of the Department of Agriculture. This gives excellent data concerning food consumption by the people of this country. The United States Bureau of Markets also publishes data indicating the production and consumption of food. The reports of the United States Food Administration published during the war have valuable information concerning the food habits of the people at that time.

c. United States Bureau of Labor Statistics. Data which are secured by this bureau and published in its *Monthly Labor Review* indicate housing conditions. These are further supplemented by

[2] Henry Harap, *The Education of the Consumer* (The Macmillan Co., 1924), p. 5.

reports published by the United States Housing Corporation, which operated during the war.

   d. *United States Bureau of Mines.* The fuels of the nation are best presented through the data published by this bureau. Supplementary data are submitted by the United States Geological Survey.

   e. *United States Federal Trade Commission.* Although the data submitted by the Census Report were adequate in giving information concerning the production and consumption of clothing, the United States Federal Trade Commission and the United States Tariff Commission are helpful in accumulating additional valuable data.

It would be possible to include several pages of societies and organizations which are functioning in the organization of data of similar types. Reference to the final chapter of *The Education of the Consumer* will enable the reader to secure a complete bibliography of the work which has been accomplished and the agencies which are contributing to this program.

Many of these studies, which are listed in the bibliography mentioned above, are direct studies of the habits of people in the consumption of food, clothing, fuel, and use of housing facilities. An example of a direct study of the habits of a large group of people is that conducted by the United States Bureau of Labor Statistics. This study contained data from more than twelve thousand families located in more than ninety-four communities in different sections of the country.

Step two. The investigator must secure the most scientific standards of consumption of food, clothing, and shelter. These standards may be secured from various sources:

   a. *Food.* Nutritive standards have been worked out by the Department of Agriculture and nationally-known dietary experts. Budgetary standards have been worked out by individuals and by bureaus of research, such as the Philadelphia Bureau of Municipal Research.

   b. *Housing.* The Bureau of Applied Economics and the National Industrial Conference Board have made convenient summaries of the standards which have been developed by the Department of Labor and other agencies.

   c. There are almost unlimited sources of data in the fields of clothing and fuel. Scientific law and scientific experimentation have established standards here to a large extent. For example, the heat values of fuels, norms of strength, quality, and utility of materials, as well as the strength and chemical structure of materials, have been determined and are made available by the Bureau of Standards and the Department of Agriculture and by many private and semi-private agencies.

d. It should be mentioned that certain standards of consumption have been established by law. There are national and local laws and codes which deal with standards of food consumption and organization of housing facilities.

Step three. It is now possible to compare the actual economic habits of the American people with standards of good living which have scientific support. Such comparisons will result in conclusions concerning the desirability of certain habits and standards of daily living and the undesirability of others. We will know that certain habits should be discontinued and that other habits should be developed as rapidly as possible. These statements of our economic needs and deficiencies become the objectives of economic living. Harap makes the following comment concerning the value of the data secured:

It is probable that at present the designer of the course of study in social science and household economy will find this book more useful than any other worker in education. He will find that certain content is definitely recommended because the evidence shows that it is vital to effective living. It should be remembered, however, that the recommendations proposed in this study are made on the theory that pupils *shall do things; that they shall form habits of living.* It may easily be construed that this work intends that pupils shall know new facts about living. This is in no sense the primary purpose of this study except when *to know* facts about living is necessary in order *to do* things in life.

Let us assume that the teacher of social studies wishes to include the fuel problem in his course. He is not certain whether his pupils should put greatest emphasis on coal, gas, kerosene, wood, or electricity. The section of this study on fuel consumption will furnish quantitatively the relative importance of these fuels. If he has neglected to consider gas, let us say, he will find that it is not much less important than coal as a fuel. And if he wishes to emphasize household consumption exclusively, he will find that gas is more important than coal. He will find that the particular problems which the utilization of coal presents are different from the particular problems which the utilization of gas presents. He should get some assistance in determining exactly what should be learned by his pupils with respect to the chief fuels.

Let us assume that a teacher wishes to ascertain in a general way what pupils should learn with respect to furniture in the home. On turning to the section on *Furniture* in the chapter on Household Materials he finds the best available data showing specifically what woods enter into furniture. He finds information concerning the relative importance of these woods. He discovers what species of wood enter into bookcases, kitchen cabinets, phonographs, and the like. He discovers the common methods of finishing woods to make them appear more expensive than they really are. He finds data giving the durability of the woods actually used in furniture. Following the presentation of such data, specific topics of study on furniture are recommended. For example, he discovers that pupils should learn to know the common furniture woods and their relative durability and costs, to distinguish birch from mahogany, to identify a veneer, to identify the print of quartered oak on cheaper woods, etc.[3]

A few examples of investigations in these secondary sources of objectives are presented to illustrate the points which have been emphasized in the preceding paragraphs:

ALDERMAN, G. H., "What the Iowa Layman Should Know About Courts and Law," *School Review,* Vol. XXXII (May, 1922), pp. 360-364.

BASSETT, B. B., "The Content of the Course of Study in Civics," *Seventeenth Yearbook* of the National Society for the Study of Education, Part I (Public School Publishing Company, 1918), pp. 63-80. The most significant political problems suggested by a study of party platforms are presented as the basis of such a course.

ESSERT, P. L., "Curriculum Content for Teaching Obedience and Respect for Law," *Teachers' Journal and Abstract,* Vol. VI (Jan., 1931), pp. 61-64. This study presents an analysis of the city ordinances of fourteen representative cities in order to determine, first, the most frequent municipal requirements, and, second, the reactions of citizens to these requirements.

BOBBITT, Franklin, "Curriculum Investigations," Supplementary Monograph, No. 31 (University of Chicago Press, 1926). In Chapter XI of this monograph, C. H. Lorenzen attempts to determine approved social behavior through an analysis of eleven books on social ethics, one hundred and twenty-three articles in the American Magazine on social ethics and six books dealing with etiquette.

[3] *Ibid.,* pp. 14-15.

LERRIGO, M. O., *Health Problem Sources* (Contributions to Education, Teachers College, Columbia University, 1926). This study indicates the use which may be made of mortality statistics, the publications of the United States Public Health Service, annual reports of the Surgeon-General of the United States, reports of public-health associations, textbooks by competent authorities and publications of life insurance companies.

IV. ORGANIZATION OF OBJECTIVES THROUGH INVESTIGATIONS OF THE OPINIONS OF COMPETENT PEOPLE, EXPERTS, AND "FRONTIER THINKERS"

This secondary source has been used extensively in the past. At present, however, the tendency appears to be to use this source for the purpose of supplementing other investigations, or as a check upon results which have been secured through research in other sources. This is because these opinions are often unreliable on account of the training which has made the individuals experts in their particular fields. The narrowness and intensiveness of the training that produces experts is likely to restrict the point of view of the individual so trained and develop prejudices.

People whose opinions are valuable may be subsumed under the three classifications suggested in the heading of this section. It may be helpful to the beginner to have a partial analysis of each classification.

1. Competent people.
   a. Leaders in the industrial, economic, and social life of the community.
   b. Teachers and professional classes.
   c. Successful business men and farmers.
2. Experts.
   a. Professional people in their own field, as the opinion of the doctor concerning the health program.
   b. Technical experts in their own fields, as the engineer or research worker.
3. "Frontier thinkers."
   a. Men and women who are careful students of society and social problems and who are in a position to present a prevision of society in which the children of to-day will function as adult citizens of to-morrow.

This "blue print" technique is the most highly developed plan for the determination of objectives from these sources. Dr. Peters, of Pennsylvania State College, has carried on many interesting and scientific investigations in the field of sociology, and, as might be expected by students interested in his work, his technique approximates, in many respects, that of his friend and teacher, Dr. Snedden. This will be apparent as the various steps in the blue print technique are analyzed and discussed in a later paragraph.

By way of introducing this technique, it should be pointed out that the author has in mind the determination of the attitudes, ideals, habits, and facts which are essential in the excellent citizen, and the construction of a blue print of this optimum citizen. This will be as valuable to the teacher and administrator who are assisting children, through the curriculum, to attain these ideals in a democracy, as the blue print of the house is to the carpenter who is responsible for its construction. Peters says:

Such procedure as we have described makes of education a kind of engineering. The engineer first plans the object he wishes to make —the house, the bridge, the electric transformer, the railroad bed. He sets up his plan in the form of a detailed blue-print and studies the adequacy of each of its parts from the standpoint of established theories. After he has perfected his blue-print in every detail, his next step is to have the plan embodied in concrete materials. Now precisely the same procedure characterizes the new education. Our first step is to get a blue-print of the individual of the society we want—a detailed picture of the good citizen, the man of culture, the vocationally efficient person, etc.—indicating the specific ideals, skills, bodies of information, attitudes of mind, prepared judgments, abilities to reason which are needed for getting on in his life. Our second step is, then, by using such instrumentalities as school subjects, discipline, and example as tools, to forge out individuals to conform to these blue-prints. In searching for means through which to attain clearly conceived ends, the educational engineer determines by scientific experiment which will most economically serve his purpose. When he is obliged to choose between a course in economics and one in history as a means of developing abilities needed in citizenship, he does not make his choice on the basis of tradition or of arm-chair philosophizing, but sets up an experiment in which he uses one kind of subject-matter with one group and the other with the other group, keeping all other conditions the same for the two contrasted groups, accurately measures his results from the two kinds of materials, and chooses for future uses the one which more largely achieves the ends he is seeking. Similarly he chooses between methods of handling his subject-matter—for example, between the project method of teaching economics and the logically organized, textbook method—not on the basis of a priori reasoning but on the measured outcome of scientifically controlled parallel-group experimentation. On the whole, there has been a considerable amount of this sort of scientific experimentation in the field of education, but unfortunately very little in the field of education for citizenship. Most of our questions there as to which of alternative procedures is better must still be answered on the basis of impression and of argumentation of a theoretical sort. But throughout the whole range of education we are moving toward the time when we shall have subjected to scientific tests all of our vital alternatives.[4]

From this blue print, the objectives of civic education are apparent at once, and they can be assigned to the various subject-matter fields in the curriculum. So far, no attempt has been made to extend the operation of this technique to other phases of good citizenship than that of efficient membership in organized society, particularly the responsibility of the individual as a member of a political group. Peters has pointed out that further research is essential in the field of citizenship in order to determine blue prints for good citizenship as far as personal culture, health, vocation, morality, and domestic relations are concerned.

In using this technique to determine the political qualifications of efficient citizenship, Peters has developed the following steps:

Step one. The coöperation of more than one thousand graduate students, many of whom were professional schoolmen, at various universities was secured. This large number was necessary in order that the blue print, which was based upon a composite list organized from the individual lists, would present a true picture.

[4] Charles C. Peters, *Objectives and Procedures in Civic Education* (Longmans, Green and Co., 1930), pp. 21-22.

Step two. Each of these students, who coöperated with Peters made a job analysis of good citizenship based upon his experience in living in association with other members of a political democracy. In order that the organization of each report might be as specific and definite as possible, every one was asked to think of the most efficient citizen in his community, and list all his activities that were related to good citizenship. Furthermore, these contributors were asked to think of some one who was regarded as a poor citizen, and list those traits, habits, and lack of abilities which appeared to be incorporated in his low standard of citizenship. These statements were then translated into positive descriptive terms and included in the first list.

Step three. A master list or composite picture of the excellent citizen was constructed from these individual lists. Peters states that after he had telescoped five hundred of the individual descriptions into the master list, no new items were observed, and he believes that the list which he presents in the book, *Objectives and Procedures in Civic Education,* is complete as far as the political efficiency of the citizen is concerned.

Step four. The investigator should understand that it will be necessary for him to break the general statements which are presented in the original lists, into specific statements so that their attainment may be stated clearly in terms of objectives. This step will facilitate the introduction of definite and correct learning experiences for the students.

Step five. Investigations may be carried on concerning the present standards of efficiency in certain type groups of citizens, in order that, first, reasonable standards of attainment may be developed in our educational program, and second, outstanding deficiencies in the achievements of these groups may indicate to educators the needed emphasis in the development of an educational program so that the general efficiency of the citizens may be increased. As Snedden and Peters have indicated, this problem of determining a reasonable level of attainment is significant. Educators should first work for reasonable and attain-

able standards rather than those which are so lofty and ideal
that they are representative of a very small percentage of
society. Peters elaborates this point of view in the following
quotation :

We have been speaking of educational engineering in the sense
of ascertaining what are the demands society makes upon the individual and then so using educational materials and methods as to
bring it about that the youth shall be sent out equipped to meet these
demands. But social engineering can go still further than that; it
can purposely remake society itself. We are at present, in respect
to our social institutions, as much the victims of undirected forces
as our grandfathers were in respect to their health and in respect
to the material processes with which they struggled. Our social
institutions have grown up haphazardly. They are the result of
accidental beginnings, which have been forged into shapes more or
less "fit" by the grim necessity of survival in the struggle for
existence. As might be expected, they contain many vestigial elements which have not yet been eliminated and which are the cause
of much present unhappiness. It is the function of social engineering to apply human purposes to the untangling of this knotted web,
and to the reweaving of parts of it into a social fabric that em-
bodies more consistently the legitimate aspirations of mankind. And
evidently our technique will be the same here as in the cases where
we wish to forge out individuals according to order. We shall
need, that is, first a blue-print of the institution that we want—
a blue-print for the organization of the state, the family, the
church, the community. Then we shall need to put into play agencies
for the realization of these plans. Our social engineers are our
economists, our sociologists, our political scientists, eugenists, and
constructive statesmen; our social mechanics, who must be expected
to embody in practical outcomes the plans made by constructive
leaders, are our teachers, preachers, newspaper editors, motion picture producers, voters, and politicians. If such engineering technique
can be applied to the improvement of our social institutions throughout the next century as the technique of mechanical engineering
was applied throughout the century just passed, it ought to increase
the spiritual wealth of mankind by as large a margin as other types
of scientific direction have increased the purity of our water supply, our control over yellow fever, the comfort of our homes, the
proper hygiene of our eyes and throats, our general health, and
our material wealth.[5]

5 *Ibid.,* pp. 23-24.

Students who are interested in this field may profitably spend considerable time in the study of Peters' technique and the results of his investigations up to the present time.

A brief discussion of several types of studies which have been developed through the use of these sources will indicate the possibilities in this field.

LEONARD, S. A., and MOFFETT, H. Y., "Current Definition Levels in English Usage," *English Journal,* Vol. XVI (May, 1927), pp. 345-359. This study secures the opinions of twenty-two linguists, authors, and editors on the correctness of 102 expressions.

PENDLETON, C. S., *The Social Objectives of English* (Published by the author, Peabody College for Teachers, 1924). In this study, 1581 social objectives of English were submitted to eighty teachers, who were doing graduate work at the University of Chicago, to be evaluated. They were ranked according to the combined judgments of the teachers.

SEARSON, J. W., "Determining a Language Program," *English Journal,* Vol. XIII (Feb., 1924), pp. 99-114. In this study 7752 competent people are consulted regarding the essential language skills.

American Classical Leagues, *The Classical Investigation,* Part I (Princeton University Press, 1925). The opinions of teachers of the classical languages are utilized extensively in securing the data for this report.

National Committee on Mathematics Requirements, *The Reorganization of Mathematics in Secondary Education* (1923), pp. 45-46. Certain items of mathematics, which are considered for the secondary level, are evaluated by prominent college teachers of mathematics.

HOCKETT, John, *America's Crucial Problems* (Contributions to Education, Teachers College, Columbia University, 1927). A study is made of frontier books in order to determine the most significant social problems.

RUGG, Harold, "Problems of Contemporary Life as the Basis for Curriculum Making in the Social Studies," *Twenty-second Yearbook* of the National Society for the Study of Education, Part II (Public School Publishing Company, 1923), pp. 260-273. This is an analysis of the writings of frontier thinkers in order that important social problems may be determined.

V. ORGANIZATION OF OBJECTIVES THROUGH INVESTIGATIONS OF TEXTBOOKS, COURSES OF STUDY, AND CURRICULUM RESEARCH

Work with these sources of objectives has developed through several stages. A study of the continual refinement of methods of securing objectives from these fields of research will illustrate the best methods of using these sources at the present time:

1. A decade or so ago it was common practice for the city interested in curriculum revision or course-of-study construction, to secure courses of study from educators in another city who had already completed a program of curriculum revision. These were compared with others that had already been secured, and, by the "scissors and paste-pot" procedure of copying objectives and learning activities from all of these, a new course was developed in the course of time. It is apparent that this method was not scientific and, as a result, the revisions were unsatisfactory.

2. As more courses of study were published, long lists of objectives became available which could be compared with textbooks and curriculum investigations. Teachers in a particular school system often secured the coöperation of other professional groups in selecting the most significant and the best from these lists.

3. Textbooks are of value as a means of checking a list of objectives, but several rather careful investigations have pointed out that the objectives cited in texts are not necessarily related to the materials of instruction which are included. These studies have made educators more or less skeptical concerning this source unless other sources are considered at the same time.

4. Bureaus of Curriculum Research, which have been established in many of the larger cities and in the leading colleges of education, have produced much material that is valuable and significant for those interested in organizing objectives. From these centers, criteria for the evaluation of courses of study are being formulated, correct methods of stating objectives are being studied, and methods of validating objectives are being determined, and the results are becoming available for teachers.

5. There have been several strictly curriculum studies organized and completed which are well worth the attention of educators interested in this field. It is perhaps sufficient at this time to mention the following which are well known:

GLASS, J. M., *Curriculum Practices in the Junior High School and Grades 5 and 6,* Supplementary Educational Monographs, No. 25 (The University of Chicago Press, 1924).

COUNTS, George S., *The Senior High School Curriculum,* Supplementary Educational Monographs, No. 29 (The University of Chicago Press, 1926).

FOSTER, William T., *Administration of the College Curriculum* (Houghton Mifflin Company, 1911).

HAWKES, H. E., HANFORD, A. C., AYDELOTTE, Frank, HOPKINS, L. B., and BOUCHER, C. S., *Five College Plans* (Columbia University Press, 1931).

The source materials here are almost unlimited, and space prevents the mention of many which deserve the attention and study of teachers working in this field. In passing, mention should be made of the publications of the National Society for the Study of Education, reports of various national committees representing subject-matter fields as the Classical Investigation, and the recent reports of the Office of Education covering the surveys and studies that were carried on under the direction of Dr. Koos.

Course of study analysis may concern itself with the consideration of the present course that is being taught in the particular community and the reorganization of these teaching materials in terms of community needs and expert opinion. Waples [6] has proposed a technique which may be used in a practical, every-day school program. The aim of the author is the development of a procedure that approximates as nearly as possible the more elaborate techniques and yet can be used by teachers who are not exprts in curriculum construction. The simplicity of the procedure makes it practicable to work on the courses of study while the schools are in session and at an expense that is not prohibitive in the smaller systems.

Step one. Make a detailed topical outline of the course as taught. All topics are to be included that require a treatment of two or more days in the present course.

Step two. List those topics (according to the teacher's judgment) in order of importance in achieving values in real life activities to students at present in the course.

---

[6] A complete discussion of this technique is found in an article by Douglas Waples in the *Journal of Educational Research,* Vol. XIII (January, 1926), pp. 6-7.

Step three. Make a parallel list of typical life situations in which each topic could be most usefully applied.

Step four. These lists should then be submitted first, to other successful teachers of the subject, second, to teachers of other subjects, and, third, to intelligent persons of affairs. These people should be asked to check them, indicating the life situations that are most important, most frequently met, and most difficult to meet successfully. All three groups should be asked to add life situations that would be valuable for this group of students.

Step five. Further rating of these situations can be secured from the social and occupational groups that the students are likely to enter. This may be carried on until the sampling appears to be complete.

Step six. All topics for which parallel situations can be checked as important, frequent, and difficult should be retained while all other topics of the original course should be eliminated unless they provide the necessary background for the new course.

Step seven. Considerable data should be available for the original course as a result of these investigations, and these materials should be arranged in the syllabus to enable the students to deal with additional situations.

Step eight. The selected situations can then be organized in proper instructional order and, if possible, in problem form.

Step nine. The selected situations should determine the organization of both the new and old material.

If all communities that do not have research experts or highly trained teachers would use this technique suggested by Waples and add one step, progress in course of study construction would be evidenced immediately. The tenth step would consist of checking this course of study which has been developed through Step Nine in the local setting with other fine courses of study developed in other communities to meet educational needs similar in part but different in many respects. If this tenth step can be added without a course of study from some important curriculum center being accepted as basic in the organization of the work, much good may come from the comparison of local results with those attained elsewhere.

The following annotated studies will illustrate the way in which these sources of objectives are being investigated by educators and curriculum specialists:

GOOD, C. V., "English Objectives and Constants in Secondary Schools," *Peabody Journal of Education,* Vol. VI (Jan., 1928), pp. 230-235. This study is based on courses of study secured from State departments of education and several of the largest city school systems.

GUILER, W. S., "Curriculum Building in Arithmetic," *Educational Research Bulletin* (Feb. 6, 1924), pp. 49-54. Presents the analysis and tabulation of items in thirty courses of study in arithmetic.

MUTHERSBAUGH, G. C., "Objectives of a Proposed Course of Study in Physics for Senior High Schools," *School Science and Mathematics,* Vol. XXIX (Dec., 1929), pp. 943-953. A study of the present objectives of physics using the following sources (1) courses of study, (2) textbooks, (3) treatises on the teaching of physics.

VI. TECHNIQUES USED BY CURRICULUM COMMITTEES IN DETERMINING OBJECTIVES FROM SECONDARY SOURCES

A number of courses of study have been analyzed in order that the techniques used by recent curriculum committees in the determination of objectives for secondary schools might be available for the reader. All the courses selected for this investigation were recent and represented the best work that had been done in these cities, according to the judgment of the director of curriculum or the superintendent of schools. While the investigation did not cover all fields represented in the program of studies, the results have been grouped according to subject-matter fields in order that the reader may refer at once to his own field or to fields related closely to his work. In every case, the source that was basic in developing objectives and content for the course is listed.

SOCIAL STUDIES

1. *Cleveland, Ohio.* Grades 7—9. Date of publication, 1927.
    a. Analysis of thirty-one recent courses in the social studies by the Department of Superintendence. (*Fifth Yearbook.*)
    b. Study of the results of investigations by graduate schools in the various universities.
    c. Opinions of three hundred teachers of the social studies.

2. *Denver, Colorado.* Grades 10—12. Date of publication, 1931.
   a. Study of all available research in the field of social science by the members of the committee.
   b. Results of scientific research by the Department of Research.
   c. Results of classroom experimentation and trial.
3. *Portland, Oregon.* Grades 7—8. Date of publication, 1928.
   a. Study of findings of national councils and organizations of social-science teachers and departments of research.
   b. Study of the results obtained in a number of experimental schools.
   c. A careful study of the children and the psychological aspects of the problem.
   d. Opinions of Portland teachers and principals obtained by interview.
4. *Lakewood, Ohio.* Grade 1. Date of publication, 1931.

Child interests have been utilized as the starting point of curriculum revision in the social-science field in the kindergarten and primary grades. All teachers in the kindergarten and first three grades were asked to canvas their children's interests by finding out from the children what they wanted to know. Each teacher prepared lists which were tabulated by the committee on revision.

ENGLISH

1. *Chicago, Illinois.* Grades 1—3. Date of publication, 1929.
   a. Results of research by specialists in the Bureau of Curriculum.
   b. Opinions of teachers of English.
   c. The educational needs of the children were studied by committees, chosen for experience, skill, and scholarship.
2. *Denver, Colorado.* Grades 7—9. Date of publication, 1931.
   a. Results of classroom experimentation and trial.
   b. Results of research by the Department of Curriculum.
   c. Study of professional literature and reports of investigations bearing on the problem.
   d. Opinions of junior-high and senior high-school teachers of English who comprised the committee.
   e. Opinions of other English teachers obtained by round-table discussions.
   f. Study of new courses of study in the field.
3. *New York City.* Grades 1—8. Date of publication, 1930.
   a. Scientific investigations of the interests of children.
   b. Analysis of other courses of study.
   c. Reading lists recommended by public libraries.

4. *Philadelphia, Pennsylvania.* Grades 4—6. Date of publication, 1930.
   a. Results of research by the research department.
   b. Opinions of successful elementary principals and teachers.
   c. Results of classroom experimentation.
   d. Study of special scientific investigations in the field of reading.
   e. Analysis of courses of study used in other progressive cities.
5. *Pittsburgh, Pennsylvania.* Grades 10—12. Date of publication, 1927.
   a. Conclusions presented in latest research studies in the field of English.
   b. Study of recent courses of study.
   c. Opinions of a specialist in English.
   d. Opinions of high-school teachers of English on the committee.
6. *Sacramento, California.* Grades 3—6. Date of publication, 1931.
   a. Opinions of leading authorities in the field of reading.
   b. Study of several excellent courses of study already in existence.
7. *San Diego, California.* Grades 1—6. Date of publication, 1928.
   a. Study of the large body of literature on the subject.
   b. Opinions of the teachers in the San Diego schools.
8. *Detroit, Michigan.* Grades 1—6. Date of publication, 1931.
   a. Study and observations of classroom situations.
   b. Opinions of teachers and supervisors. (Obtained by discussions developed in the Detroit College Extension classes.)

HEALTH EDUCATION

1. *Minneapolis, Minnesota.* Grades K—6. Date of publication, 1933.
   a. Revision of former health program.
   b. Suggestions and opinions of Minneapolis teachers.
2. *San Francisco, California.* Grades 4—6. Date of publication, 1931.
   a. Study of the courses of other cities.
   b. Study of the professional literature on the subject.
      (1) Wood and Lerrigo's *Health Behavior.*
      (2) The joint reports of the National Education Association and the American Medical Association.
      (3) Chicago Principals' *Yearbook* (1930).
      (4) Publications of the American Child Health Association and the National Committee on Mental Hygiene.
   c. Experience of the members of the committee.
   d. Study of research and practice in the field.

MUSIC

1. *Oakland, California.* Grades 5—6. Date of publication, 1931.
   a. Opinions of music teachers throughout the school system.
   b. Demonstrations conducted by the committee followed by conferences and discussions at an informal dinner.
2. *San Francisco, California.* Grades K—3. Date of Publication, 1931.
   a. Careful study of the best public school practice.
   b. Opinions of experts in the field of public-school music.
   c. Experiences of members of the committee.

USE OF THE LIBRARY

1. *Detroit, Michigan.* Grades 1—6. Date of publication, 1931.
   a. Opinions of specialists in library work.
   b. Opinions of leading librarians in the city.

PHYSICAL EDUCATION

1. *Oakland, California.* Grades 1—2. Date of publication, 1931.
   a. Results of classroom experimentation.
   b. Analysis of other courses of study.
   c. A comparative and comprehensive survey of the latest educational literature on physical education.
2. *Denver, Colorado.* Grades 10—12. Date of publication, 1932.
   a. Experimentation and practice in the schools of Denver.
   b. Analysis of courses of study from other schools.
   c. Writings of leaders in the field of physical education.

MATHEMATICS

1. *Pittsburgh, Pennsylvania.* Grades K—6. Date of publication, 1928.
   a. Courses of study of other cities.
   b. Articles in educational magazines.
   c. Books on mathematics.
   d. Textbooks.
   e. Recent researches on special subjects in mathematics.
   f. Experiences of teachers in the classroom.
   g. Suggestions from the administrative staff.
2. *Kansas City, Missouri.* Grades 1—6. Date of publication, 1928.
   a. Studied and evaluated all important research studies in the field of mathematics.
   b. Studied the experience of other progressive cities.
   c. Investigated courses of study which have been developed recently in this field.

    d. Surveyed present practice in the Kansas City schools.

    e. Studied the needs of the children in those grades.

3. *Lincoln, Nebraska.* Arithmetic 4—6. Date of publication, 1930.

    a. All important research studies made in arithmetic in recent years.

    b. Study of the psychology of the subject.

    c. Progress of curriculum revision throughout the country.

    d. Quantitative experiences of the elementary school child and need for training children to solve problems arising from these experiences.

4. *Kansas City, Missouri.* Grades 7—9. Date of publication, 1929.

    a. A careful study was made of all available literature and research dealing with the objectives, materials, methods, and psychology of junior-high-school mathematics.

    b. Local conditions and needs were carefully studied and considered.

    c. A critical examination was made of recent texts and courses of study.

    d. Information as to the mathematical experiences of junior-high-school pupils was secured by means of the following questionnaire:

        (1) What did you do in the best week outside of school that relates to mathematics?

        (2) What did you see or hear that relates to mathematics?

        (3) What did you read about that relates to mathematics?

    e. A study was made of the mathematical knowledges and skills needed by pupils in other school subjects and activities. This study and the preceding one were used extensively as a means of suggesting actual pupil needs and activities, especially for the first-year course.

SCIENCE

1. *Oakland, California.* Elementary Science. Date of publication, 1932.

    a. Extensive research in the field.

    b. Analysis of most important points suggested by different authorities in the field.

2. *Denver, Colorado.* Grades 7—9. Date of publication, 1931.

    a. All science teachers coöperated in an intensive study.

    b. Recommendations of the science teachers.

    c. Survey of science courses offered in other junior high schools.

    d. Survey of the newer science textbooks.

    e. Survey of current literature readable by the pupils.

    f. Writings and advice of curriculum experts.

3. *Kansas City, Missouri.* Grades 10—12 (Physics). Date of publication, 1933.
   a. Practical and cultural needs of the pupils.
   b. Chance variation of types of pupils from one class to another.
   c. Variation in laboratory equipment.
   d. Variation in administrative conditions under which the teachers work.
4. *Kansas City, Missouri.* Chemistry. Date of publication, 1933.
   a. Used the *Thirty-First Yearbook* of the National Society for the Study of Education, Part I, organized by the committee on the Teaching of Science to determine objectives from the following sources:
      (1) Needs, aptitudes, and aspirations of students.
      (2) Abilities of teachers of science.
      (3) General objectives consistent with plan of education in general.
5. *Lakewood, Ohio.* Chemistry. Date of publication, 1932.
   a. Effort made to have course conform with the recommendations and spirit of the *Thirty-First Yearbook.*

COMMERCIAL

1. *Long Beach, California.* Junior Business Training. Date of publication, 1932.
   a. Textbooks: ZuTavern, *Business Training,* and Miner, Elwell, and Trouton, *Business Arithmetic.*
   b.. *Fifth Yearbook,* Department of Superintendence, p. 433.
2. *Denver, Colorado.* Grades 10—12. Date of publication, 1932.
   a. Teachers of commercial subjects in the junior and senior high schools.
   b. Special committee of three members from each of these units.
   c. Outside specialists brought in for consultation.

VII. TECHNIQUES USED AT THE COLLEGE LEVEL IN DETERMIN-
ING OBJECTIVES FROM SECONDARY SOURCES

There are very few examples available of the use of sources of objectives in determining teaching fields and teaching materials. The following study which was developed recently in the College of Education at Ohio State University is significant and merits consideration.

Bennett indicates the reasons for the study being made and the development of sources and techniques.

The College of Education of the Ohio State University recently has been studying and reorganizing its courses and curriculums, both graduate and undergraduate, with a view to their greater effectiveness in the preparation of teachers and other educational workers. One of the major problems has been to determine what subject-matter actually is needed for the professional courses required in the curriculum for prospective high-school teachers. In the endeavor to solve this problem the *Commonwealth Teacher Training Study* by Charters and Waples has been used extensively—the Commonwealth list of teachers' activities having been reorganized for this purpose under an appropriate list of fifty-one topics.

The initial stop, naturally, in planning the curriculum reorganization program had been to set up the general educational objectives of the College. This was done through the usual procedure of formulation, revision, and adoption by committees and subsequent approval by the College faculty. While the general objectives of the College thus developed should be primary in curriculum making, such objectives do not indicate, directly, the details of subject-matter needed by the curriculum.

As bases for determining needed subject-matter, curriculum workers, in recent years, have used various types of data, such as the central tendencies of existing curriculums in a group of institutions, the judgments of alumni and teachers in service, or the actual analysis of teaching activity. Because of their greater objectivity, the data from activity analysis have been preferred by our Committee; and accordingly the second major step in the curriculum reorganization was to provide a statement of teachers' activities.

The Commonwealth list of teachers' activities, being the most comprehensive analysis of teaching available, was adopted by the Curriculum Committee as the basic list from which this selection of activities for curriculum treatment was to be made. In a preliminary phase of the curriculum investigation the Commonwealth list had been used as an instrument for checking the content of existing education courses. At this time, certain disadvantages in the organization of the list had appeared, which it seemed wise to overcome before proceeding with the more fundamental reorganization of the education courses. Accordingly, it was decided to undertake a reorganization of the Commonwealth list.[7]

An outline is presented of the program which was worked out at Ohio State University:

[7] R. A. Bennett, "A Basis for Selecting Content of Required Courses in Education," *Educational Research Bulletin,* Vol. XIII (May 16, 1934), pp. 113-119.

1. The Commonwealth list of teacher activities, being the most comprehensive analysis of teaching available, was made the basic list of activities.

   a. This had previously been found to be unsatisfactory in some respects in checking courses against it so a reorganization was made of the list.

   b. 1,001 activities of *Commonwealth* Study were grouped under fifty-one activity topics.

     (1) Defining and showing the implications of objectives.

     (2) Planning for classroom activities.

     (3) Selecting and organizing subject-matter.

     (4) Determining and providing for individual differences.

     (5) Guiding learning activities.

     (6) Evaluating pupil achievement.

     (7) Exhibiting useful teaching traits.

     (8) Planning and compiling records and reports concerning pupils.

     (9) Utilizing records and reports concerning pupils as a basis for improvement of teaching efficiency—including conducting investigations based upon records and reports.

  (10) Influencing and directing the personal conduct of pupils in relation to other pupils and teachers in the classroom and on school premises.

  (11) Influencing and directing pupil conduct in the performance of routine school activities.

  (12) Supervising pupil health and physical efficiency.

  (13) Counseling students in the planning of programs.

  (14) Conducting special exercises.

  (15) Grouping pupils for instructional purposes.

  (16) Adapting teaching procedures to size of classes.

  (17) Supervising the school and classroom library.

  (18) Supervising the school lunchroom.

  (19) Utilizing pupil assistants.

  (20) Taking precautions against fire.

  (21) Controlling tardiness and absence.

  (22) Administering intelligence tests.

  (23) Caring for special defects of pupils such as stammering, hysteria.

  (24) Maintaining informal personal contacts with pupils in matters not directly related to school activities.

  (25) Offering guidance to pupils in matters relating to (a) personal habits, (b) social contacts, (c) vocational and employment problems, and (d) financial problems.

(26) Supervising play and athletics.

(27) Supervising musical organizations.

(28) Supervising (a) pupils' dramatic activities, (b) pupils' publications, (c) pupils' forensic activities, and (d) departmental clubs.

(29) Supervising the unspecialized extra-classroom activities of pupils, (a) social activities of pupils, (b) school assemblies and special programs, (c) drives and campaigns, (d) coöperating with student self-government organizations, and (e) other types of pupil organizations, such as honor societies, girls' clubs, boys' clubs, Boy Scouts, Campfire Girls, and Hi Y.

(30) Maintaining coöperative relationships with administrative and supervisory officials such as state superintendent, local superintendent, local school board, county superintendent, assistant superintendent, principal, supervisor, department head, and dean of women.

(31) Maintaining coöperative relationships with business-department employees, especially the custodian of supplies and janitor.

(32) Maintaining coöperative relationships with school librarian.

(33) Maintaining coöperative relationships with school nurse, school physician, and visiting teacher.

(34) Maintaining coöperative relationships with colleagues, namely, other regular teachers and substitute teachers in a school system.

(35) Coöperating with individual parents in the interest of the individual child.

(36) Coöperating with parents through activity in organizations of parents and teachers, such as the parent-teacher association.

(37) Coöperating with (a) occupational groups, (b) social organizations, and (c) members of the community at large.

(38) Using the community as a source of material for the school curriculum.

(39) Growth of the teacher through participating actively in the social and cultural organizations of the community.

(40) Professional and personal growth and advancement of the teacher in service through engaging actively in the work of professional organizations.

(41) Professional and personal growth and advancement of the teacher in service by improving teaching skill.

(42) Professional and personal growth of the teacher in service through reading and engaging in advanced professional study.

(43) Professional and personal growth and advancement of the teacher in service through undertaking professional research and publication of the results of study.

(44) Qualifying for a higher type of certificate.

(45) Professional advancement of the teacher through obtaining appointment or promotion to teaching positions.

(46) Providing for personal financial welfare.

(47) Providing for health, recreation, and satisfactory social contacts.

(48) Regulating the heat, lighting and ventilation of the schoolroom.

(49) Maintaining attractiveness of school grounds, buildings, and rooms.

(50) Selecting textbooks, supplies, equipment, and floor space.

(51) Producing, ordering, maintaining, and organizing textbooks, supplies, equipment, and floor space.

All these activity topics must be consistent with approved general educational objectives.

These topics must be formulated with the view to their use as centers in the subsequent selection and organization of subject-matter for courses.

Objective data were used in grouping activities under topics. Studies of teachers indicate that sponsorship of certain activities is connected closely with teaching fields while others are not related at all.

 c. The fifty-one topics became centers for selecting the needed raw material for entire groups of required courses.

A complete topical outline became the first major step in determining, on the basis of teachers' needs, the subject-matter to be selected.

 d. Further problems involved:

(1) Selecting subject-matter to test each of the fifty-one topics in terms of approved objectives.

(2) Organizing and testing this material in tentative courses.

(3) Organizing experimental content into permanent courses.

(4) Present course organization will not hamper revisions needed.

VIII. SUMMARY

The problems involved in the determination of educational objectives from secondary sources have been presented in this chapter. The availability of the secondary source materials is apparent at once. This accounts for the fact that most of the investigations listed at the end of Part II are of this type.

The following books and monographs can be used as references by the reader who is interested in studying and evaluating recent curricular investigations:

DRAPER, E. M., and ROBERTS, A. C., *Study Guide in Secondary Education* (The Century Company, 1933).

HARAP, Henry, *Technique of Curriculum Building* (The Macmillan Co., 1928).

Annotated Bibliography of Investigations of Curriculum Objectives, *Bulletin No. I* (School of Education, Western Reserve University, 1932).

Annotated Bibliography, *Review of Educational Research,* Vol. IV, No. 2 (National Education Association, April, 1934).

CHAPTER VI

ORGANIZING OBJECTIVES FOR COURSE OF STUDY CONSTRUCTION

I. INTRODUCTION

The last two chapters have presented sources of objectives and methods of analyzing these sources in order that sound objectives may be secured. After the raw list of several hundred objectives has been found, there still remains the important problems of first, separating the valid ones from those that are invalid as far as a particular course is concerned, second, allocating these valid objectives in terms of child life rather than as teachers' goals or as methods of instruction; and, third, grouping the objectives so that the greatest economy and least duplication can be effected in the development of learning activities in the school system. These important problems will be analyzed in the present chapter. It is unnecessary to point out to the educator, who has read the preceding pages carefully, that the ultimate value of the course of study depends on the character of the work at this point. Later effort cannot completely compensate for unreliable, invalid results of studying and checking objectives, as they are determined directly from the sources.

II. VALIDATION OF OBJECTIVES

The importance of this step has been emphasized in previous chapters. To attempt to make progress with invalid objectives is almost as futile as to trust that an educational program can be achieved without objectives. Since this step is so significant in the development of the learning experiences, it is proposed to analyze the methods of validation extensively and thoroughly.

Practically every school system that has received recognition as a leader in curriculum construction uses one or more methods of validating its teaching materials. The author wrote to the curriculum departments of sixteen school systems that have received national recognition in course of study construction and asked for the courses of study that, in their judgment, represented their best and most scientific work. Forty-two courses of study were received as a result of this request. These have been carefully analyzed to determine the validating procedures which were employed. Validating procedures involve the use of the sources of the objectives, since they are significant in themselves as the means of validating the objectives which are secured.

If possible, the student should refer to these courses of study in order that the complete program involving (1) sources of objectives, (2) techniques of determining objectives, and (3) methods of validating objectives can be understood and appreciated. In the following analysis, the briefest possible statements are used to conserve space. A concise organization of data for all these cities was considered to have more value than a more extended statement from a few that might represent the best programs in the judgment of the author.

A. A study of current practices. An analysis of these forty-two courses of study from sixteen cities is presented on the following pages to determine and compare current practice in advanced curriculum centers in methods of validating objectives. The reader should note that techniques of determining objectives as well as sources of objectives are implied in many cases and often definitely stated.

SOCIAL STUDIES

1. *Baltimore, Maryland.* Grades 4—6. Date of publication, 1931. Objectives and materials submitted to classroom experimentation for one year.
2. *Cleveland, Ohio.* Grades 7—9. Date of publication, 1927.
   a. Opinions of competent people.
      (1) Submitted to one hundred and forty social studies teachers who were asked to evaluate the objectives by ranking them.
      (2) Opinions of outstanding editors, ministers, and social workers.

    b. Subjected to one year of experimental teaching.

    c. Compared with the *Fifth Yearbook* of the Department of Superintendence.

    d. Validated by selection from several authentic sources.

3. *Denver, Colorado.* Grades 10—12. Date of publication, 1931.

    a. Curriculum tests prepared, administered, and interpreted by the Department of Research. These tests were given to determine what the course accomplishes in comparison with the objectives which have been developed.

    b. Submitted to specialists in the field.

    c. Subjected to experimental teaching in the classroom.

4. *Kansas City, Missouri.* Grades 1—3. Date of publication, 1930. Objectives were determined by a questionnaire submitted to five thousand school children concerning their interests and experiences in and out of school. The replies were basic in the formulation of the course after they had been validated by a committee made up of specialists, teachers, supervisors, and principals according to the following criteria:

    a. Do they coincide with adult and racial experiences?

    b. Are they worthwhile in themselves?

    c. Have they leading-on qualities which will influence later work?

    d. Are they usable in connecting in-school and out-of-school life?

5. *Portland, Oregon.* Grades 7—8. Date of publication, 1928.

    a. Reports of National Committees and Departments of Research.

    b. Selection from several authentic sources.

6. *Lakewood, Ohio.* Grade 3. Date of publication, 1931.

    a. Child interests were indicated by questionnaires which were submitted to the students orally or in written form. The results were validated by the social-science-curriculum committee according to the following criteria:

        (1) All interests and activities not relating to social science were found to be in the field of science and were turned over to that committee.

        (2) All suggested topics which did not help the child to understand and adjust the world about him and lead him to ever larger interests were discarded.

        (3) Children's interests were not considered sacred, since the school must lead the child beyond his present interests. He must grow into the larger spheres and meanings of life.

        (4) Units must be rich in intellectual content, since the pres-

ent will be explained and understood in terms of the past. This will widen and stimulate interests.

ENGLISH

1. *Chicago, Illinois.* Grades 1—3. Date of publication, 1929.
    a. Subjected to experimental teaching.
    b. Compared with analysis of pupil activities.
2. *Denver, Colorado.* Grades 7—9. Date of publication, 1931.
    a. Submitted to six specialists outside the city of Denver.
    b. Submitted to eight committees of three teachers each (one each from the elementary school, junior high school, and senior high school).
    c. The fourteen ratings obtained from 1 and 2 were combined, and this compilation was used as the basis for the course.
    d. Compared also with analyses of new courses of study in the same field.
    e. Subjected to classroom experimentation.
    f. Several authentic sources were used in selecting objectives.
3. *New York, New York.* Grades 1—8. Date of publication, 1930.
    a. Opinions of educators and students of literature as expressed in:
        (1) Other courses of study in this field.
        (2) Reading lists recommended by public libraries.
    b. Further validated in connection with content of the course as follows:
        (1) Is the content within the comprehension of the children and true to human experiences?
        (2) Is the language suitable? Does it possess charm of style and beauty of words?
        (3) Is it varied as to experience? As to countries represented?
        (4) Is the subject-matter capable of developing correct attitudes toward life?
4. *Philadelphia, Pennsylvania.* Grades 4—6. Date of publication, 1930.
    a. Submitted to classroom trial and experimentation.
    b. Selected from several authentic sources.
    c. Comparisons were made of the analyses of several courses of study in the field.
5. *Detroit, Michigan.* Grades 1—6. Date of publication, 1931.
    a. Study and observation of classroom teaching for preliminary validation of objectives. These programs were then used for a period of one to three years and revised in terms of this

experimentation. Several hundred classroom teachers took part in this validation process.

b. Submitted to two district principals.

6. *Baltimore, Maryland.* Grades 7—12. Date of publication, 1932. The extensive list of sources which were used (see previous chapter) validated the objectives selected but the following criteria were also used:

a. Psychological facts of adolescence regarding interests and capacities of pupils.

b. Social demands reflected in good colloquial English expression and adult uses of literature as recreation.

c. Employers' requirements in oral and written English and in reading.

d. Frontier thinkers' statements as to what society is demanding of an educated citizen.

e. Entrance requirements of higher institutions.

f. Creative artists' description of what "creative consumers" and "creative craftsmen" experience.

g. Empirical evidence from Baltimore teachers including specimens of pupils' work.

h. Objective test data on the application of specific skills and methods of teaching and learning.

HEALTH EDUCATION

1. *Minneapolis, Minnesota.* Grades K—6. Date of publication, 1933.

a. Check list based upon *Health Behavior* by Wood and Lerrigo was sent to a group of thirty or more local physicians and others interested in health work.

b. List of health topics checked by a committee of school nurses and teachers.

c. Submitted to the teachers of the Bancroft and Schiller schools.

(1) Each teacher presented one or more of the topics in her classroom and kept a careful record of her work.

(2) At discussion meetings, materials were reported and appraised and revisions of the topics or units were made accordingly.

d. Course reviewed by a General Health Committee appointed by the Superintendent of Schools.

e. Course criticized by the General Curriculum Committee.

2. *San Francisco, California.* Grades 4—6. Date of publication, 1931.

a. Selected from several authentic sources.

b. Comparisons made with analyses of several courses of study from other cities.

1. *Oakland, California.* Grades 7—9. Date of publication, 1929.
   a. Classroom trial and experimentation for one year. Teachers' opinions were secured through a conference at the end of the trial. Revisions were made, and the course was submitted to another trial for a year.
   b. Study of surveys and analyses of activities in which girls engage.
   c. Objectives selected from several authentic sources.
2. *State of Idaho.* Grades 7—12. Date of publication, July, 1932.
   a. Submitted to experimentation in the classrooms of fifty teachers during the year 1931-32.
   b. Discussed by teachers of home economics in State conferences of vocational departments.
   c. Discussed at sectional meetings of the Idaho Educational Association.
   d. The work, generally organized under home economics, was then divided among committees of teachers and studied. These committees were representative of the State.
   e. The needs of children at the present time and as they go into their own homes were considered in the organization of the course.

1. *Oakland, California.* Grades 1—2. Date of publication, 1931.
   a. Classroom experimentation.
   b. Comparison with analyses of other courses of study.
   c. Use of several authentic sources.
2. *Denver, Colorado.* Grades 7—9. Date of publication, 1927.
   a. Experimentation in Denver.
   b. Results of experimentation carried on elsewhere were checked and continued.
   c. Interests of children and after-school life of people compared.
3. *Denver, Colorado.* Grades 10—12. Date of publication, 1932. Comparisons made from:
   a. Experimentation and practice in the Denver schools.
   b. Courses of study which had been developed in other schools.
   c. Experts and writers in the field of physical education.

MATHEMATICS

1. *Pittsburgh, Pennsylvania.* Grades K—6. Date of publication, 1928.
   a. Trial in eight selected schools for one semester.
   b. Opinions of teachers and principals.
   c. Selected from several authentic sources.
2. *Kansas City, Missouri.* Grades 7—9. Date of publication, 1929.
   a. Evaluated according to the underlying principles or the general objectives of education.
   b. Evaluated according to the objectives of junior-high-school mathematics.
   c. Evaluated in terms of effective teaching in junior-high-school mathematics.
   d. Practical and intrinsic values in mathematics.
   e. Social need of mathematics.
   f. General usage of mathematics.

SCIENCE

1. *Lakewood, Ohio.* Chemistry. Date of publication, 1932.
   As this course was tried during the school year 1932-33, teachers were urged to coöperate in the following ways and thus contribute to the building of the course:
   a. On the blank side of each page in this course, teacher reactions should be made to every division of each unit. Thus, criticisms will be written in the courses opposite to the part of the course to which they refer.
   b. Many of these tentative units are thin or weak in many parts. Therefore, valuable contributions can be made in the following ways:
      (1) Check time allotment.
      (2) Improve objectives.
      (3) Indicate better organization of the elements of the unit.
      (4) Check approaches used. Add others.
      (5) Check activities used and found to be profitable. Indicate those not so valuable. Add others.
      (6) Revise outcomes. Show those actually achieved.
      (7) All errors in tests should be recorded. Work out tests to measure other outcomes.
2. *Denver, Colorado.* Grades 7—9. Date of publication, 1931.
   a. Experimentation in the classroom.
   b. Comparison of five authentic sources of objectives.
3. *Kansas City, Missouri.* Chemistry. Date of publication, 1933.

The *Thirty-First Yearbook* of the National Society for the Study of Education, Part 1, which was organized by the Committee on the Teaching of Science.

4. *Kansas City, Missouri.* General Science. Date of publication, 1930. The validation of objectives and other phases of the course was placed in the hands of the teachers. They were asked to make the following contributions:

   a. Scope and content.

   (1) Do the units cover the field?

   (2) Does each particular unit cover its particular field?

   (3) What changes, additions, or eliminations are desirable?

   b. Organization.

   (1) Comment on the organization as a whole; on that of each particular unit.

   (2) What phases are most helpful?

   (3) What parts can be eliminated?

   c. Reference material and enrichment reading.

   (1) Note those that are especially helpful.

   (2) Add others that are valuable.

B. Standards by which objectives can be validated. The tabulation of these data from the leading curriculum centers makes possible the organization of sources of objectives and validating processes that have been used. Analysis will clarify many of these issues.

1. *Studies of sources.* These studies are usually concerned with the organization of the original or primary lists of objectives. In general, such investigations are concerned with primary sources, although secondary sources are also included. If more than one of these sources is investigated in connection with the same set of objectives, one of these investigations will serve to assist in validating the resulting list. In the material presented in the courses of study that have just been analyzed, the following four types of investigations were carried out.

a. Questionnaire studies. Kansas City sent a questionnaire to students to determine their interests and activities. To illustrate the scope of this questionnaire and the possibilities of using this method, the questionnaire has been included in the chapter on sources of objectives.

b. Analysis of pupil activities and interests. This source was used extensively by the curriculum departments of various cities in organizing their course of study for the kindergarten and lower grades.

c. Analysis of the social and vocational interests of adults. This source was used in only a few instances by any of the cities studied either as an original source or in validating objectives obtained from other sources. It is so important, however, that it should be listed here.

d. Investigations of the academic uses of the subject-matter in a particular field. Many of the cities made investigations of this character to determine the place of the materials in a particular subject in the various units and grades of the school system.

e. Investigations of the value of the material in the general or specific reading of children and adults. A study of the validating procedures will reveal emphasis upon these points.

2. *Analysis of textbooks.* While only one of the schools made use of this source, it is valuable enough to merit the attention of students interested in this work.

3. *Analyses of courses of study.* It is significant that ten of the courses of study considered used this source. The ease with which these courses can be secured from other cities probably influences curriculum committees to use them.

4. *Reports of national committees, national councils of teachers, etc.* It is difficult to understand why investigations and reports as important and valuable as these were used in only three instances. They should be extremely useful in determining sources and for purposes of validation.

5. *Submission of objectives to a competent jury for evaluation.* In the courses which were examined three types of juries were organized: first, specialists in the subject-matter field; second, professors of education and general education; and third, classroom teachers of the subject, principals, and superintendents. Objectives in thirty-nine of the forty-two courses were subjected to the scrutiny of such a selected group.

6. *Experimental classroom teaching.* Fifteen of the courses were used as the basis of experimental teaching programs in the various schools before they were accepted as valid for particular grades and groups of students.

7. *Selection from several authentic sources.* This method of selecting objectives has the advantage of partially validating

them at the time of selection. This would be true if each objective were checked to determine if it could be obtained from all or from a majority of the sources. Any objective meeting such standards could be accepted as more valid than an objective appearing in only one or two of the sources.

8. *Establishing a set of criteria and evaluating objectives in terms of those criteria.* This procedure was followed in one instance and suggests at once Schorling's [1] plan of validation. In fact, Schorling's plan has played such an important part in stimulating the development of validating processes that his technique is presented as a basis for comparison.

Schorling used the following sources for the determination of objectives in the field of junior high-school mathematics:

a. Indices of five standard arithmetics
b. Indices of five standard algebras
c. Indices of five sets of junior-high-school mathematics books
d. Objective studies in education dealing with the selection of mathematical materials
e. Judgment of seventy-five students in a special course
f. A few items were added by the two juries of general educators and teachers of mathematics.

When the list of objectives had been completed and apparently was inclusive of all of the objectives that could be secured from these sources, it was checked against the following criteria for purposes of validation:

a. The list of material suggested on pp. 21 and 27 and in Chapter II of the *Report of the National Committee on Mathematical Requirements.*
b. The contents of seven junior high school mathematical texts.
c. The combination of Guiler's inventory of courses of study in arithmetic and the results of Schorling's inventory of courses of study in ninth-grade algebra.
d. Objective studies in education having a bearing on the selection of teaching materials in mathematics.
e. Judgments of an educational jury and the judgments of a jury of competent mathematics teachers. Members of these juries had not participated in the determination of the objectives.

[1] Raleigh Schorling, *A Tentative List of Objectives with Investigations for Determining Their Validity* (George Wahr, 1925), p. 10.

Schorling established standards by which an objective in the original list had to meet three of the five conditions set forth in the criteria, if it were to be included in the list of essential objectives.

The truth of any conclusion depends on two things: first, the accuracy of the premises; and second, the rigor of the logical process by which the conclusions are reached. Philosophy has been criticized for considering only logic—deeming a conclusion verified if the logical process, the thought process, is defensible. Dewey,[2] in his *Reconstruction in Philosophy,* urges that, if philosophy is to continue to be of service in the solution of human problems, it must learn to demand the certainty of truth in its postulates. Two methods of checking the truth of postulates are available: first, the verification of the entire postulate body; and second, the method of science, the verification by the comparison of theorems or conclusions logically derived from the results of experimental observation. That is, assuming the logic to be rigorous, experimental validation of *all* theorems or conclusions will indicate the truth of the premises. The reader should note that this involves, first, the assumption of rigorous logic, and second, the necessity of experimentally proving the truth of all possible conclusions by the application of rigorous logic to the premises.

In the validation of objectives, it is obviously impracticable to verify experimentally all the possible conclusions, since an unavailable amount of time and expense would be required. The experimental attainment of all objectives would involve the perfection and application of valid tests, etc., and the determination of the contribution of these specific aims in the achievement of the general aim of education, in terms of which the validation of specific objectives is to be made. Of course, as education becomes more scientific, such scientific proof of the validity of objectives will appear or, in the case of invalid objectives, fail to appear. This final appearance or nonappearance will serve as the basis for permanent inclusion or exclusion of particular

[2] John Dewey, *Reconstruction in Philosophy* (Henry Holt and Co., 1920), Chap. I.

specifics in the body of objectives. Educators cannot wait for such validation; in fact, advancement will not be apparent until teachers have, at least hypothetically, accepted a set of objectives and started to work upon them.

There are, however, two other means of checking the validity of the aims: first, by verifying the premises; and, second, by insisting upon rigorously logical steps in arriving at conclusions. In the case of the specific objectives of any subject-matter field, the primary assumption is evidently that the general aim of education is improved living, and that the particular subject in question can contribute effectively and efficiently to this aim. The general objectives of this field constitute, in a sense, a secondary set of assumptions. A third set of assumptions would consist of such statements as the following:

1. The interests of children are a valid partial basis for a course of study.
2. An analysis of what adults do will indicate the needs of children.
3. The scientific attitude can be developed.
4. The deficiencies of children and adults can be determined.
5. The judgments which are secured from teachers, members of the community, parents, industrial and social groups in the validation of objectives will be based upon correct data and facts.
6. That throughout the process of validation the relationship of the specifics and generals can be distinguished. It must be possible for the course of study committee to work from generals to specifics and to eliminate at different stages of the investigation invalid specifics and valid specifics that do not relate definitely to the more general objectives.
7. Teachers are willing and capable of experimenting in their classrooms to enable the committee to determine accurately the outcomes of teaching in terms of the objectives which have been selected as valid enough for experimental teaching.
8. That judgments used in validating both procedures and objectives represent the best judgments available to the investigator, and that these judgments have not been biased by any personal interest or prejudice.

After the assumptions are validated, the logical process by which the conclusions are reached can be validated. The requisite

200 PRINCIPLES OF CURRICULUM MAKING

here is simply that the process be logical, that it follow the "rules of thought." Both of these methods of validation are philosophical rather than experimental and, as such, will probably produce the best results by means of a consensus of competent authority and surveys of current literature. The submission to recognized authorities of lists of assumptions and objectives, if practicable, is another method. Careful critical analysis by the individual of the premises assumed and the process of reaching conclusions is another. Obviously, any premise must appear valid in the light of the best information available, if it is to be included. Keyser [3] offers the following guide-posts in critical evaluation:

Confronted by a doctrine in any department of thought, Criticism demands answers to these questions: What is *assumed*—what are the *postulates?* What are the *undefined* or *variable* terms? What are the *theorems* or proved propositions and what are the *defined* or *constant* terms? *How* have the theorems been *deduced,* and the defined terms *defined?* What *meanings* have been *assigned* to the *variable* terms, and *how?* Upon these questions criticism, if it is to be criticism of thought is bound to insist—there is no alternative.

Final validation of specific objectives must wait upon actual tryout and check against the general objective of education. Pending this final scientific validation, educators can validate specific objectives, at least partially, by defining and verifying assumptions, and by criticizing the process by which conclusions are reached. Reference to competent opinion, and careful and rigid self-criticism are important at this point.

It may be stated, in summary, that, first, a continuous program of research and course of study construction is being carried on in many cities at the present time. It was true in every case selected for this study. Second, scientific research is being used to a considerable extent, in determining the original lists of objectives in the course of study. Third, in the courses studied, however, only four instances of scientific research as a means of validating objectives in the course of study were indicated. It is significant for the future that even 10 per cent

[3] Cassius J. Keyser, *Mathematical Philosophy* (E. P. Dutton and Company, 1922), p. 15.

of the committees included in the study used scientific methods of evaluating their original lists of objectives.

III. SELECTION OF OBJECTIVES BY SUBJECT-MATTER COMMITTEES

The final selection of objectives for a course of study will be made by a committee, consisting largely of the teachers of that subject-matter field in the school system. The selection of objectives for a particular course may be determined by the application of the following criteria:

A. Does the objective occur frequently in present life activities that fall within this subject-matter field? This involves, first, a study of present activities of adults and children; second, an analysis of the present objectives of the course as taught; and third, the validation of objectives proposed for inclusion in the new course of study.

B. Will these objectives occur frequently in the future life activities for which this subject-matter can adequately prepare students? The committee will have to consult the works of "frontier thinkers" in order to apply this criterion successfully to the objectives and materials with which they are working.

C. Has the objective a high degree of cruciality? Certain activities occur infrequently in life and yet are so important that life may depend on a mastery of these skills, knowledges, etc. These objectives should be realized in the program of studies and in the subject-matter field being considered by the committee, if the bureau of research, the administration, or the curriculum committee has allocated their achievement to this particular field.

D. Will the children be interested in realizing this particular objective? Can it be made stimulating to them and will it motivate their enthusiasm for the content of the course which has been developed? On this point, there is a great divergence of opinion as to the value of this criterion. Some advocate giving 100 per cent consideration to the interests of children and excluding everything which cannot meet this standard. However, there is some intrinsically important material that is not 100 per cent interesting to pupils. This material must be taught, even though uninteresting to children who cannot see the ultimate utility of these activities.

E. Can the objective be achieved by the students? This criterion becomes more important every year as increased enrolments are noted in every unit of our educational program. To take an example from the secondary unit, objectives are being stated in terms of groups and individuals rather than for the educational program within that unit. In one junior high school, seven ability levels have been organized. In the highest group, the I.Q.'s range from 135 up to genius, and in the lowest group the range is from 75 down to "border line" cases. Naturally, the same objectives cannot, in all cases, be included in all groups. The Dalton plan of constructing courses of study is another example of designating levels of objectives for individuals assigned to particular subject-matter fields.

The modern foreign-language study, which has been referred to in previous chapters, indicates the futility of striving to teach materials in this field to students who cannot comprehend or who attain grades at a very low level. The results of their extensive investigation indicate that students who finish a two-year course in these subjects and pass the work, but who rank in the lower 50 per cent of the class, are lacking in mastery of the subject in four important respects: first, they have only a limited vocabulary range; second, they do not know and cannot use the grammar of the language correctly; third, they possess a very limited reading knowledge of the language; and fourth, they are inaccurate in writing a composition or short essay in the language.

F. Should the school assume the responsibility for the realization of this objective? As the school is only one part of the educational program of the child, it must not assume too great a responsibility. Many objectives, which are not within the province of the school, should be eliminated at once.

The faculty committee must recognize also that certain objectives, proper in one school system, may be out of place and a source of embarrassment to the faculty in another locality. One could suggest that objectives in the fields of religion, sex, and evolution should not be developed in the school systems of certain communities.

G. Is the objective measurable? Are standards of achievement available for the proposed objective? It is a waste of time of both teacher and student to include objectives in which progress cannot be measured. If one cannot say that the child has attained mastery of the subject-matter or has arrived at a definite standard of proficiency, the educational program is being burdened with a group of high-sounding phrases.

H. Is the proposed objective most efficiently attained through the study of this subject? It is fundamental that the committee decide whether this objective is of primary or secondary concern in the teaching of this subject-matter. Such consideration forces the committee to think of the integration of subject-matter rather than differentiation of materials in the program of studies.

IV. ALLOCATION OF OBJECTIVES

After objectives have been subjected to the treatment suggested by the lists of criteria, they can be allocated to the various courses of study in the school and to the particular units within each course of study by means of which they will be realized. This is largely a problem of grade placement of learning experiences and activities. As yet, little has been accomplished in this field, and the criteria are largely of a subjective character. It should be of value, however, to consider in some detail the procedures used in actual school situations. As no definite and specific procedure is available, a survey of the factors considered will be presented.

A. Best judgment of those serving on the course of study committee. This is the most common practice and, while it is subjective, in part at least, much valuable work has been done by these committee members. The analysis, which has been made of children's activities and interests, indicates definitely the adequate placement of learning activities in certain types of subject-matter. In opening to children the rich field of literature, it is necessary to know their present likes and interests. If boys of a particular grade indicate that they like to read Blackmore, Cooper, Churchill, Henty, Kipling, and Stevenson and the girls prefer to read the works of Alcott, Lamb, Tennyson, and Shakespeare, the committee has valuable information upon which to base a decision.

Dr. W. B. Featherstone, Director of Research in the Los Angeles Schools, states in a letter to the author that:

... we decide as scientifically as we can whether it is worth while to give children in the fourth-grade experiences along a particular line. We then determine what kinds of activities are best adapted to their stage of development. By this device we might have a course such as you suggest in your letter, in social service in any one of a number of grades, the nature and content of course being considerably different from grade to grade.

We have as yet no very scientific method of deciding what general types of interests or activities are of greatest value at any particular grade level. I suspect that our criteria are largely subjective at the present time. But we are trying to make them as objective as we can.

B. Reports of national committees, organization of material in textbooks, courses of study, and scientific investigations which have been made outside of the school system. Scarely a school system fails to use supplementary material and data of these types. They are valuable, and when supplemented by local studies and results of experimentation, they can serve as a basis for grade placement.

Dr. W. W. Theisen, Assistant Superintendent of the Milwaukee schools, makes the following practical statement regarding grade placement in his school system:

... The determination of objectives is usually an outgrowth of committee analysis of the professional literature of the subject plus any evidence of our own which may suggest certain changes in emphasis. Any original work we have done in recent years has been confined to the fields of arithmetic and reading.

As to placement, the two most influential factors are the recommendations of various national committees and the textbooks in use. A third factor is the judgment of our local committees. All these are of course more or less arbitrary.

One of the difficulties we have always encountered in any attempt to determine a placement which differs from textbook or national committee recommendations is that students who desire to transfer either to or from a school having different grade allocations find themselves in difficulty.

Dr. I. Keith Tyler, Assistant Director of Curriculum at Oakland, California, made the following comments concerning grade placement in a letter to the author:

1. Does this material belong in the elementary or secondary field? This question would be answered by reference to our general objectives of the elementary school, the junior high school, and the senior high school drawn up as a result of careful study by a general curriculum committee. This might be called the philosophical placement of materials on the basis of the general purposes of the particular division of the school system.

2. Do the general objectives of the subject and research studies of the nature of children give any indications of the grade level at which this material would be most suitable? For example, if the objective of spelling be "to be able to spell the words he uses" a research study of the words used by fourth-grade boys and girls in

their school and out of school activities would give a rather clear indication of the spelling words to be taught at that level.

3. Are research studies available as to the best placement of this material in terms of the ability of children? Factors to be considered here would be the mental level of Oakland pupils and research findings as to the mental level at which this material is best taught.

Dyer [4] selected the one hundred best courses out of a group of 1,000 courses in home economics. She studied and analyzed these selected courses to determine the content and grade placement of the learning experiences and activities. Many other fields could be improved by similar studies of the best current practice in selecting content and determining grade placement.

C. Experimentation in the schools. In a number of schools the deciding factor is the experience of the teachers in working with the materials at various grade levels and with various ability levels. Tyler, who was quoted in the preceding paragraph, has this to say concerning experimentation:

Tentative allocation of material on grade levels would be checked experimentally by means of try-outs of material among a selected group of teachers including those teaching "x," "y," and "z" type youngsters.

As an example of grade placement, may I refer you to the recent supplement, "Supplement to the Tentative Outline of the Handbook in Science for Elementary Grades," in which, for the first time in our school system, elementary-science material has been tentatively allocated to grade levels. In this case, the objectives of the elementary school determine the type of science material to be taught in the elementary grades, the studies in the *Thirty-First Yearbook* of the N. S. S. E. and other studies gave help in a tentative location of materials, and the experience of several years of Oakland teachers was used in a further refinement. Revision of this chart will be based upon its use in the next year or two.

Miss Prudence Cutright, Director of Curriculum, Minneapolis, Minnesota, uses the following experimental technique in the Minneapolis schools:

The *placement of materials* is determined by experimentation. After the objectives of a course have been determined, the units of

---

[4] A. R. Dyer, *Placement of Curriculum Materials in Home Economics* (Bureau of Publications, Teachers College, Columbia University, 1927).

learning which seem contributory to those objectives are selected and outlined. Teachers in several different grades are then asked to try out these units and to make detailed reports on the reaction which they obtain. The materials are eventually placed on the basis of the teacher's experience in using them.

Dr. W. L. Connor, Director of Curriculum Research of the Cleveland Public Schools, uses a course in health education to illustrate the experimental work in determining teaching materials in the Cleveland schools:

Defects actually found in seventh-, eighth-, and ninth-grade pupils determined suitable health materials for their correction. The additional materials in the course have been based on pupil interest which was experimentally determined.

The goals that teachers seek in grade placement are optimum materials from the standpoints of student interest and difficulty. When teachers are guided merely by tradition and opinion, materials that could have been mastered in the fourth or fifth are found in the twelfth grade. This is pertinent criticism of the social-science field at the present time.

Unless the matter of grade placement is carefully and statistically studied by the committee, many annoying and ridiculous situations will arise. The school administrators of a large western city desired the development of a course in social science (community living) for the tenth-grade of the senior high school. A fine professional committee was appointed to develop the course and worked diligently for two years. At the conclusion of this work a highly organized course was presented to the city. But the committee had overlooked the repetition in the new course of many units of material included for several years in the junior high schools. Their course was a failure because it met neither of the criteria suggested. First, the pupils were not interested in materials that they had already studied, more or less successfully; and, second, material, which was appropriate for the junior high school, and which could have been mastered at the level, had no place in the senior high school. This failure could have been avoided by using the Buffalo plan. Dr. Berten

B. Bean, Director of Higher Elementary Grades, Buffalo, New York, summarized this plan as follows:

Our courses of study are based upon three factors: our own past practice, current research, and revision as a result of experimental evidence in our schools. Courses of study are in a continuous process of revision. Committees of teachers, supervisors, and administrators work together and determine the educational practice to be followed; the units are set up, tried out in the school, and revised to meet the needs of the children, the educational goals which are set up, and to provide for minimum and maximum essentials according to individual differences found within the various levels.

On the next page is presented a summary sheet for the convenience of course of study committees in selecting and allocating objectives. As soon as an objective has been rated according to these criteria, a satisfactory tentative grade placement can be made. It will be found valuable by administrators, directors of research, and curriculum committees as a check upon the scientific character of the investigations of life or subject-matter that is being considered.

V. HOW SHALL OBJECTIVES BE STATED?

A decade or so ago, it was customary to state objectives as teaching objectives. The problem of the teacher was to secure evidence of having taught certain subject-matter to the students. Recently, however, it has been realized that teachers' objectives must ultimately be translated into pupils' objectives. Cities in which the most advanced type of curriculum work is being developed present subject-matter objectives in terms of pupil goals.

The difference between the two statements of objectives can be illustrated as follows:

Teachers' goal: To present or teach the knowledges, skills, habits, attitudes, ideals, etc., that are basic in the course.

Pupils' goals:
    (1) To know the multiplication tables
    (2) Ability to construct a blue print
    (3) To brush the teeth twice daily
    (4) To coöperate with fellow students.

TECHNIQUE FOR SELECTING AND ALLOCATING OBJECTIVES
(Grade Placement)

OBJECTIVES	1. Frequency in present	2. Frequency in future	3. Cruciality	4. Interest to learner	5. Difficulty (statistical)	6. Attained outside of school	7. Measurable	8. Responsibility of the subject-matter field	CHECKED BY A. Opinion of committee	B. Reports of national committees	C. Other courses of study	D. Scientific investigations	E. Experimentation	F. Experimental or try-out teaching	TOTAL SCORE
1.															
2.															
3.															
4.															
5.															
6.															

Scoring

Column 1. Rating 1-10
  " 2. " 1-10
  " 3. " 1-10
  " 4. " 1-10
  " 5. Grade levels, 7-8 or 11-12
  " 6. Yes or No
  " 7. Yes or No
  " 8. Rating 1-10

Column A. Grade level, Majority vote
  " B. " " " number
  " C. " " " "
  " D. " " " "
  " E. Grades included, as 7-9
        Best results as 8
  " F. Grades included—results, as
        7-9, 8a, etc.

7.
8.
9.
10.
11.
12.
13.

There is no reason why the student should not know what objectives are to be realized by himself in a particular course. Definite, specific statements enable students, under the guidance of the teacher, to achieve these objectives. The curriculum committee has not performed its function until objectives are stated in terms of pupils' goals and are specific enough so that both pupils and teachers can check the realization of them.

The following criteria will enable the committee to determine the correct statement of objectives:

A. Does each statement contain one objective only?
B. Is the proposed objective stated in objective terms?
C. Is the proposed objective stated in specific terms?
D. Is the proposed objective so stated that it may be understood by both teachers and pupils?
E. Is the proposed objective stated in terms of pupils' goals, not teachers' goals?
F. Are the statements of objectives extensive enough to realize pupil needs in the particular grade or subject-matter field?

VI. GROUPING OBJECTIVES

After the final list of objectives has been secured by treating the original list to the processes previously discussed in this chapter, it is necessary to group them for purposes of economy and efficiency. This grouping prevents duplication that would result if the content of the courses (learning experiences and activities) were selected for individual and isolated objectives. It also simplifies the organization of units of work, contracts, problems, projects, laboratory work, etc., that will be discussed in later chapters. It is essential, furthermore, that objectives be organized in groups so that they can be assigned to subject-matter fields and to committees of teachers interested in developing in greater detail the refinement of statement and scope.

At this point, it will be more profitable to the student to have examples rather than an extended discussion of this problem. For clarity, the first example will be analyzed in reverse order, *i.e.,* from the unit back to the objectives. In a course in home economics, a *unit of work* should be given to the planning, preparing, and serving a breakfast in attractive fashion. This large unit is organized as a result of the development of the following sub-units:

1. Information necessary in order to plan a breakfast that will promote health
2. A knowledge of the effects of fruit upon health
3. Knowledge of milk as a healthful food
4. The value of beverages in the diet
5. The food value of different kinds of toast
6. Influence on the family of properly arranged table and attractively served meals
7. Health value of cereals to the growing child
8. Value of eggs in the diet and their correct preparation for breakfast
9. Quick breads that can be used for breakfast and their preparation

These sub-units are developed by grouping the more specific and definite objectives and learning experiences in this field. Suppose we consider sub-unit 2, which represents a grouping of all objectives concerning fruit as an important phase of the diet. The following subheads could be developed under which can be subsumed still more specific and definite objectives:

1. Why should fruit be used for breakfast?
2. Why should all fruit be washed before using?
3. If fresh fruit is not available what substitutes can be used?

These subheads immediately suggest further refinement of statement to the reader. Let us select number one of the preceding grouping:

1. Why should fruit be used for breakfast?
   A. Need
      1. Gives bulk to diet
      2. Contains acid
      3. Contains mineral salts
      4. Contains vitamins
   B. Use for breakfast
      1. Stimulate the appetite
      2. Acts as a laxative

C. Selection
   1. Season
   2. Quality
   3. Quantity
   4. Cost

The problem of relating and grouping objectives has been approached from the standpoint of the complete unit to indicate a logical system of grouping the subdivisions of a determined teaching unit. However, if the most refined and specific statements, as 1, 2, 3, and 4 under *Need,* were stated in terms of valid objectives derived from child and adult needs, one can visualize the organization of objectives into groupings which would determine sub-units and units of the course. In order that this operation of proceeding from objectives to units may be clearly understood by the reader, an organization of objectives is suggested as a means of developing units in a course in safety education in the elementary grades.

1. To be willing to observe and obey traffic regulations
2. To understand how easily fires are started
3. To develop habits of correct and just playground conduct
4. To become acquainted with dangerous intersections near the school
5. To understand how fires can be prevented
6. To develop a sense of responsibility for the safety of others
7. To respond immediately and correctly to given signals
8. To appreciate the fireman as a safety worker
9. To appreciate fair play in community and school relationships
10. To appreciate the services of the traffic officer
11. To know what to do in case of fire
12. To know safe places for recreation on and off the school grounds
13. To understand necessary precautions to be observed in the neighborhood
14. To be able to use a clear and intelligent safety vocabulary
15. To obey fire-drill regulations
16. To be able to turn in fire alarms correctly and efficiently.

These can be grouped into units in the course as follows:

A. To develop habits of conduct which will aid in safety in traffic

 1. To be willing to observe and obey traffic regulations
 2. To become acquainted with dangerous intersections near the school
 3. To respond immediately and correctly to given signals
 4. To appreciate the services of the traffic officer
 5. To understand necessary precautions to be observed in the neighborhood
 6. To be able to use an intelligent safety vocabulary

B. To understand the importance of preventing fires
 1. To understand how easily fires are started
 2. To understand how fires can be prevented
 3. To appreciate the fireman as a safety worker
 4. To know what to do in case of fire
 5. To obey fire-drill regulations
 6. To be able to turn in a fire alarm correctly and efficiently

C. To conduct oneself so as to contribute to greater safety on school grounds
 1. To develop habits of correct and just playground conduct
 2. To develop a sense of responsibility for the safety of others
 3. To appreciate fair play in community and school relationships
 4. To know safe places for recreation on and off the school grounds

It will be noted that, no matter what sources and techniques are used, objectives are likely to develop as a heterogeneous mass. It is essential for the committee to proceed, as has been indicated in the preceding paragraphs, and organize them under headings that will probably be incorporated into the course of study as units of work. This step is important, since objectives will rarely be handled beyond this point as individual goals, but will be treated as organized fields or units. These units can then be assigned to sub-committees and individuals for further analysis and experimentation.

It should be emphasized at this point that the organization of the course of study begins with the objectives and not with some preconceived idea of the general organization of the course. It will be far easier to organize the headings of the course and work down to objectives as we did in the organization of the material in home economics. It is only after long hours of study and consultation that a valid, teachable plan will begin to emerge, if the attack begins with a valid list of objectives that the committee has secured from its investigations.

VII. SUMMARY

This chapter has undertaken an intensive analysis of the tasks which face the course of study committee after the objectives have been attained and before they are acceptable for inclusion in the course of study. To be of value to the committee, the objectives must be validated; criteria must be developed for selecting and allocating objectives to subject-matter fields; the objectives must be stated in terms of the pupil and not as goals of the teacher; the objectives must be grouped, after careful study and experimentation, into proposed units of work.

Grade placement must be carefully studied to eliminate duplication and overlapping. Years can be wasted in course of study construction unless a procedure has been worked out for the correct placement of objectives in the school system. A chart has been included in this chapter to enable a course of study committee or the administration of the school system to formulate a procedure by which objectives can be correctly placed in the educational program.

BIBLIOGRAPHY FOR PART II

READING

BEINHART, Freida, "My Leisure Time," *Training School Bulletin*, Vol. XXVII (Vineland, N. J., February, 1931), pp. 161-166. This study indicates that mentally retarded boys choose literature far below their chronological-age levels.

BELSER, D. "The Reading Interest of Boys," *Elementary English Review*, Vol. III (November, 1926), pp. 292-296. A survey of the reading interests of German, French, and Italian children.

CAIN, William R., and BROWN, Francis J., "An Evaluation of the Outside Reading Interests of a Group of Senior High-School Pupils," *Journal of Educational Sociology*, Vol. V (March, 1932), pp. 437-442. They found that more than half of the books read by senior high-school pupils were of literary merit, and that the percentage of harmful literature was small.

CHARTERS, W. W., "The Books Boys Read," *The Library Journal,* Vol. LIII (June 1, 1928), pp. 481-483. Popular books for boys in the opinion of librarians from twenty-four cities.

DANFORTH, Marie Lusk, "Purposes in the Selection and Arrangement of Material in Supplementary Readers," *Elementary School Journal,* Vol. XXXIII (Feb., 1933), pp. 427-433. She verified the conclusion that recent readers have been affected by current objectives of teaching reading after studying the reasons given in supplementary readers for selection and arrangement of material. The results showed that the two main trends are a consideration of children's interests and the value of material to children.

DOWELL, Pattie S., and GARRISON, K. C., "A Study of Reading Interests of Third Grade Subjects," *Peabody Journal of Education,* Vol. VIII (Jan., 1931), pp. 202-206. They determined by analysis the most popular interest elements after locating the most popular selections in third-grade readers.

ECKHER, M. H., "Children's Choices of Poems," *Elementary English Review,* Vol. V (June, 1928), pp. 182-185. A comparison of poems in anthologies made by children in grades 1, 2, 3.

ELDER, V., and CARPENTER, H. S., "Reading Interests of High School Girls," *Journal of Educational Research,* Vol. XIX (April, 1929), pp. 276-282. A study of the reading interests of high-school girls made by questionnaires, themes, and records of books read for supplementary reading.

GARRISON, S. C., and HACKWORTH, Lector, "A Comparison of Ten Book Lists for Children's Reading," *Peabody Journal of Education,* Vol. IX (Sept., 1931), pp. 102-111. They presented a graded book-list after studying and comparing ten book-lists, which reflected the judgment of previous studies.

GATES, A. I., "The Construction of a Reading Vocabulary for the Primary Grades," *Teachers College Record,* Vol. XVIII (May, 1926), pp. 625-642. The selection of a vocabulary based on several factors such as utility and interest.

————, *Interest and Ability in Reading* (The Macmillan Co., 1930). He found the general characteristics of reading materials which are most interesting to primary children to be surprise, liveliness, conversation, humor, and plot.

GATES, A. I., PEARSDON, Celeste C., and SARTORIUS, Ina C., "Studies of Children's Interests in Reading," *Elementary School Journal,* Vol. XXXI (May, 1931), pp. 656-670. In this study concerning kinds of material primary grades prefer, they found work and play exercises, narratives, and informational selections were chosen in the order given above.

HUBER, M. B., "Children's Interests in Poetry," *Teachers College Record,* Vol. XVIII (Oct., 1926), pp. 93-104. A study of choices of poetry by 50,000 children in grades one to nine.

HUBER, M. B., BRUNER, H. B., and CURRY, C. M., *Children's Interests in Poetry* (Rand, McNally and Co., 1927). They made an analytical study of grade placements in poetry.

HUBER, M. B., and CHAPPELEAR, C. S., "Children's Magazine Reading," *Journal of Educational Method,* Vol. VI (Dec., 1926). pp. 145-149. A study of the magazine reading of children of several schools.

IDE, Alice M., and OBERG, Walda, "The Content of Present-Day School Readers as Compared with Children's Interests and Reading Objectives," *Elementary English Review,* Vol. VIII (March, 1931), pp. 64-68. They suggest an answer to the consideration of interest and educational and cultural value by comparing the content of present-day readers with children's interests and reading objectives.

JENNINGS, Joe, "Leisure Reading of Junior High School Boys and Girls," *Peabody Journal of Education,* Vol. VI (May, 1929), pp. 333-348. A study of the out-of-school reading of 880 children in two junior high schools.

KEALY, Sister Mary Eugenia, "An Empirical Study of Children's Interests in Spiritual Reading," Catholic University of America, *Educational Research Bulletin,* Vol. V, No. 4 (Washington, D. C. Catholic Education Press, 1930). She found that children like spiritual reading provided it contains the same elements which make other subject-matter attractive.

LANCASTER, J. J., "A Study of the Voluntary Reading of Pupils in Grades," *Elementary School Journal,* Vol. XXVIII (March, 1928), pp. 525-537. A study of the voluntary reading of 4,469 children in grades four to eight.

LEWERENZ, A. S., "An Experiment in Evaluating Books Read and Enjoyed by School Children," *Educational Research Bulletin,* Los Angeles City Schools (Sept., 1929). This study is based upon 259 titles and 2,349 reports from school children.

MILLER, G. T., *Story Telling to Live-Wire Boys* (E. P. Dutton and Co., 1930). Chapter III is a study of the reading interests of boys between the ages of eight and seventeen.

NESMITH, M. E., *An Objective Determination of Stories and Poems for the Primary Grades* (Teachers College, 1927). Sixteen experts evaluate certain existing practices in the first three grades.

RHINEHART, Anne Campbell, "What Pittsburgh Junior High School Pupils Read," *School Betterment Studies,* Vol. III, No. 1 (Henry C. Frick Educational Commission, 1931). This study indicates that junior high-school pupils find an enjoyment primarily in fiction, more especially short stories, books of travel, and biography.

SHUTTLEWORTH, Frank K., "A Critical Study of Two Lists of Best Books for Children," *Genetic Psychology Monographs,* Vol. XI, No. 4 (Clark University Press, 1932). He compared the grade placement and the relative worth and interest value of books as given in the "Winnetka Graded Book List" and "A Guide to Literature for Character Training."

SMITH, F. O., "Pupils' Voluntary Reading," *Pedagogical Seminary,* Vol. XXXIV (June, 1927), pp. 208-222. A study of the voluntary reading of 2,199 pupils in grades six to twelve.

SMITH, Nila Banton, "Successive Emphases in American Reading Instruction," *Teachers College Record,* Vol. XXXIV (Dec. 1932), pp. 188-203. In this study the problem of successive emphases in reading content is studied, and the author identifies five successive periods of emphasis.

————, "The Construction of First Grade Reading Material," *Journal of Educational Research,* Vol. XIX (February, 1928), pp. 79-89. Describes a procedure including choice of vocabulary and stories.

STAATS, Pauline, "A Vocabulary Study of First-Grade Poetry," *Childhood Education,* Vol. IX (Dec., 1932), pp. 127-128. Evidence to support the conclusions of Stone is found in studying eighty-seven poems recommended for first-grade children. The results show that the vocabulary used far exceeds most first-grade lists.

STONE, Clarence R., "Grading Reading Selections on the Basis of Interest," *Educational Method,* Vol. X (Jan., 1931), pp. 225-230. He concluded that interest appeal should be supplemented by other considerations such as vocabulary burden, sentence structure, and comprehension tests by the pupils as criteria in grade location of reading selections.

TERMAN, L. M., and LIMA, M., *Children's Reading* (D. Appleton and Company, 1926). Reports the results of a study of 10,000 recorded readings of children.

UHL, W. L., "Scientific Determination of the Content of the Elementary School Course in Reading," *University of Wisconsin Studies in the Social Sciences and History,* No. 4. Also in UHL, W. L., *The Material for Reading,* Chapters IV-V (Silver, Burdett and Co., 1924). A study of selection of reading material based on teachers' and pupils reactions.

WHEELER, H. E., and HOWELL, Emma A., "A First Grade Vocabulary Study," *The Elementary School Journal,* Vol. XXX (Sept., 1930), pp. 52-60. A study of the vocabularies of ten primers and ten first readers published since 1922.

WITTY, Paul A., and LEHMAN, Harvey C., "A Study of the Reading and Reading Interests of Gifted Children," *Pedagogical Seminary and Journal of Genetic Psychology,* Vol. XL (June, 1932), pp. 473-485.

HANDWRITING

ARNOLD, Esther Whitacre, "The Transition from Manuscript to Cursive Writing," *Elementary School Journal,* Vol. XXXIII (April, 1933), pp. 616-620. The transition from manuscript to cursive writing should be made at the beginning of the fourth grade according to the evidence based on observations.

CRIDER, Blake, "The Adaptability of Pupils to Manuscript Writing," *Elementary School Journal,* Vol. XXXII (April, 1932), pp. 617-622. He showed that a late transfer tends to establish the new form in from six months to a year.

EASON, Joshua L., "Diagnostic Study of Technical Incorrectness in Writing of Graduates of Tennessee County High School," *Contributions to Education,* No. LXIV (George Peabody College, 1927).

HARAP, Henry, "Making a Handwriting Course of Study," *Educational*

Method, Vol. XI (Jan., 1932), pp. 202-209. This article, which classifies the curriculum problems in handwriting, serves as a guide to past investigations in the field, and presents the problems which require further investigation.

KIRK, J. G., "Handwriting Standards to Determine Finishing Standards for the Philadelphia Public Schools," *The Journal of Educational Research,* Vol. XIII (March and April, 1926), p. 259. A study of handwriting of employees to determine the standard to be attained in school.

NEWLAND, T. E., "A Study of the Specific Illegibilities Found in the Writing of Arabic Numerals," *The Journal of Educational Research,* Vol. XXI (March, 1930), pp. 177-185. Analysis of 135,000 digits written by 1,127 pupils and adults.

PRESSEY, L. C., and PRESSEY, L. L., "Analysis of Three Thousand Illegibilities in Writings of Children and Adults," *Educational Research Bulletin,* Vol. VI (Sept. 28, 1927), pp. 270-273, 285. A study of the illegibilities in 450 papers of children in grades three to eight.

WAHLERT, Jennie, "Manuscript Writing," *Childhood Education,* Vol. VIII (June, 1932), pp. 517-519.

WEST, Paul V., *Changing Practices in Handwriting Instruction* (Public School Publishing Company, Bloomington, Illinois, March, 1927). Suggestions and discussions based upon a survey of present practices and problems.

SCIENCE

CURTIS, F. D., *A Synthesis and Evaluation of Subject-Matter Topics in General Science* (Ginn and Co., 1929). A study of the topics in general science found in curriculum investigations, textbooks, and courses of study—eighteen sources in all.

DOWNING, E. R., "Does Science Teach Scientific Thinking?" *Science Education,* Vol. XVII (April, 1933), pp. 87-89. Tests were given to 2,500 pupils in grades eight to twelve, dividing the group into those who had studied science and those who had not. He concluded that a course in science skills in high school does not necessarily develop a scientific thought process.

EDMISTON, R. W., "Instructional Implications from a Study of Overlappings in Science," *Journal of Educational Research,* Vol. XXVI (March, 1933), pp. 501-507. He concluded that if overlapping in general science and biology were eliminated, a semester could be saved.

HIMES, H. E., "What Biology Functions Most Largely in Giving Pleasures of Recognition," National Society for the Study of Educational Sociology, *Second Yearbook* (1929), pp. 118-128. The opinions of 245 high-school pupils and former students of biology concerning the usefulness and interest of 108 biological facts.

HUNTER, George William, "Sequence of Science in the Junior and Senior High School," *Science Education,* Vol. XVI (Dec., 1931), pp. 103-115. He reported on curriculum trends as he observed them in a selected list of schools which he studied in 1908 and again in 1923.

HUNTER, G. W., and KNAPP, Roy, "Science Objectives at the Junior and Senior High School Level," *Science Education*, Vol. XVI (Oct., 1932), pp. 407-416. A questionnaire study of the objectives of junior- and senior-high-school science based upon 393 replies. These were from every state in the Union, with the exception of West Virginia.

HURD, A. W., *Coöperative Experimentation in Materials and Methods in Secondary School Physics* (Columbia University Press, 1933). He presents conclusions which he developed after making a series of extensive and significant investigations in the reorganization of content to suit the needs of pupils enrolled in secondary-school physics classes.

MONROE, W. S., HINDMAN, S. A., and LUNDIN, R. S., "Two Illustrations of Curriculum Making," *University of Illinois Bulletin*, Vol. XXV, No. 26 (Feb. 28, 1928). *Bureau of Educational Research Bulletin*, No. 39, Chap 3. Gives objectives and activities in horticulture for high-school pupils.

NETTELS, Charles H., "Scientific Interests of Junior High School Pupils," *Science Education*, Vol. XV (May, 1931), pp. 219-225. He made a survey of boys' and girls' scientific interests in grades seven, eight, and nine, finding 178 different interests in these grades in Los Angeles.

PERSING, Ellis C., "Present Objectives in Biology," *Science Education*, Vol. XVII (Feb., 1933), pp. 24-34. He analyzed five curriculum studies, five courses of study, and six textbooks in an investigation of subject-matter objectives which revealed 440 objectives.

PERSING, K. M., "Present Specific Objectives in High School Chemistry," *Journal of Chemical Education*, Vol. VI (Nov., 1929), pp. 1959-1978. Specific objectives of high-school chemistry for three curriculum investigations, six textbooks, and six courses of study. Shows 235 specific objectives.

POWERS, S. R., "A Vocabulary of Scientific Terms for High School Students," *Teachers College Record*, Vol. XVIII (Nov., 1926), pp. 220-245. A study of the most common words found in fifteen science textbooks and fifty magazine articles.

PRUITT, C. M., "Status of General Science as Revealed Through State and City Courses of Study," *General Science Quarterly*, Vol. XIII (Jan., 1928), pp. 367-381. Gives aims and general objectives for city and state courses of study.

RODEAN, William A., "Overlapping of Content in Textbooks in General Science and Biology," *School Science and Mathematics*, Vol. XXXII (June, 1932), pp. 605-613. He analyzed five general-science textbooks and four biology textbooks, and revealed an overlapping of material in the two courses.

SEARLE, A. H., and RUCH, G. M., "A Study of Science Articles in Magazines," *School Science and Mathematics*, Vol. XXVI (April, 1926), pp. 389-396. A study of the scientific information in eleven magazines for a ten-year period to discover the principal subjects considered.

STEVENS, C. P., "The New Courses in High-School Chemistry," *School Science and Mathematics,* Vol. XXXII (March, 1932), pp. 244, 249. An investigation based on the examination of professional literature and replies from queries sent to 235 high schools of the U. S.

STEVENSON, Elms N., "Children's Nature Interests," *Elementary School Journal,* Vol. XXXI (Dec., 1931), pp. 276-284. Analysis of nature interests of 119 children in grades 4 to 6 by means of a check list, the asking of questions, and the writing of compositions by the children.

WELLER, Florence, "Attitudes and Skills in Elementary Science," *Science Education,* Vol. XVII (April, 1933), pp. 90-97. She made a study of sixth-grade children to determine the value of elementary training in science as a base for developing desirable attitudes and skills in problem solving.

WELLER, Florence, and CALDWELL, Otis W., "The Nature Study and Elementary Science Movement," *School Science and Mathematics,* Vol. XXXIII (Oct., 1933), pp. 730-740. They sought the opinion of thirty-seven college biologists on a list of topics which they compiled from a study of eleven textbooks in high-school biology.

MATHEMATICS

BEÑTHACK, Emil, "Standards for the Selection of Arithmetic Textbooks," *Educational Research Record,* University of Nebraska, Vol. I (Feb., 1929), pp. 85-90. Gives standards for the selection of arithmetic textbooks based both on research and opinion.

BILLETT, Roy O., "Provisions for Individual Differences, Marking and Promotion," United States Department of the Interior, Office of Education, *Bulletin* No. 17 (1932). *National Survey of Secondary Education,* Monograph No. 13, Washington, D. C. (Government Printing Office, 1933). He reported a consideration of the provisions for individual pupil differences, showing the need and extent of grouping from grades seven through twelve.

BOWDEN, A. O., *Consumer's Use of Arithmetic* (Teachers College, 1929). A study of the uses of arithmetic by parents and sixth-grade children by means of check lists.

BRESLICH, E. R., "Measuring the Development of Functional Thinking in Algebra," National Council of Teachers of Mathematics, *Seventh Yearbook* (Teachers College, Columbia University, 1932), pp. 93-118. He discusses functional thinking, its attainment and uses, and reports his findings on a test given to 901 pupils in grades 9 through 12. He reveals a tendency to increase in ability in functional thinking.

BRUECKNER, L. J., "Analysis of Difficulties in Decimals," *Elementary School Journal,* Vol. XXVIII (Sept., 1928). A study of pupil difficulties in decimals.

BRUECKNER, L. J., and IRVING, James A., "A Technique for Comparing the Difficulty of Problems in Textbooks in Arithmetic," *Elementary School Journal,* Vol. XXXII (Dec., 1932), pp. 283-285. In studying ten fifth-grade arithmetic books, they found a large difference in the average difficulty of problems. The average percentage of correct solutions of problems selected at random being sometimes less than 40 percent.

BUSWELL, G. T., and JOHN, L., "Diagnostic Studies in Arithmetic," *Supplementary Educational Monograph*, No. XXX (University of Chicago, 1926). A study of errors made by 400 pupils.

——, "The Vocabulary of Arithmetic," *Supplementary Educational Monographs*, No. XXXVIII (University of Chicago Press, 1931). They studied the development of the arithmetic vocabulary and number concepts in the first six grades.

BUTLER, Charles Henry, "Mastery of Certain Mathematical Concepts by Pupils at the Junior High School Level," *Mathematics Teacher*, Vol. XXV (March, 1932), pp. 117-172. He made an investigation by means of the test method to measure the mastery of sixty-three concepts listed by Schorling in his study of objectives in teaching mathematics, and found that while the median seventh grader has mastered only one-third of the sixty-three, progress is uniform and by the end of the ninth grade, he has mastered two-thirds of them.

Cleveland, Ohio, Public Schools, *Arithmetic Activities* (1931). Description of arithmetic activities conducted at Gordon School, formerly curriculum center for arithmetic.

CONGDON, A. R., "Training in High School Mathematics Essential for Success in Certain College Subjects," *Contribution to Education*, No. 403 (Teachers College, 1930). A study of physics texts to discover the mathematical facts, concepts and skills necessary for success in the field.

DALE, E., "Economics for Children," *Educational Research Bulletin* Vol. IX (Oct., 1930), pp. 381-384. Data secured from 106 children by an investigator stationed in a grocery store to note purchases made.

DAVIS, David R. (Mrs.), "A Comparative Study of Textbooks in Junior High School Mathematics," *High School*, Vol. VIII (Feb., 1931), pp. 103-114. Ten series of mathematics books compared as to aims, subject-matter, problems, methods of presentation, and methods of motivation.

Denver Public Schools "Arithmetic, Elementary School," *Research Monograph*, No. II (1926). Analysis of arithmetic into its detached steps.

FREEMAN, Ellen M., "Textbook Trends in Plane Geometry," *School Review*, Vol. XL (April, 1932), pp. 282-294. Ten textbooks, published between 1896 and 1901, ten books in use in 1928, and five recent ones published since 1925 were analyzed. She found that trends were toward making geometry more practical, and geometry was being correlated with other subjects, and adjusted to individual students.

FULLER, Florence D., *Scientific Evaluation of Textbooks* (Houghton, Mifflin Co., 1928). A detailed explanation of a coöperative plan by which textbooks in junior high-school mathematics were selected.

GEORGES, J. S., "A Study of Procedures Used in the Determination of Objectives in the Teaching of Mathematics," *Mathematics Teacher,* Vol. XXII (March, 1929), pp. 156-165. Teachers of mathematics evaluate six methods of determining objectives in mathematics.

GILLETT, H. O., "The Placement of Arithmetic Topics," *Journal of the National Educational Association,* Vol. XX (June, 1931), pp. 199-200. This study deals with subject-matter placement from a purely computational aspect.

GRUBER, W. S., *Objectives and Activities in Arithmetic* (Rand, McNally, and Co., 1926). Part I contains objectives arranged by grades. These were obtained from an analysis of thirty courses of study.

HEILMAN, J. D., "What Should and Should Not Be Taught in Elementary Arithmetic," *The Teachers Journal and Abstract,* Vol. I (Sept., 1926), pp. 460-469. Summary of several investigations.

HIZER, I. S., and HARAP, Henry. "The Learning of Fundamentals in an Arithmetic Activity Course," *Journal of Educational Method,* Vol. XI (June, 1932), pp. 536-539. A survey of the steps necessary for learning decimals and the practice secured on these steps in an activity program.

IRWIN, E., "How Much Wood Can a Woodchuck Chuck if He Doesn't Chuck All Day Long," *Progressive Education,* Vol. V (April, May, June, 1928), pp. 104-107. Children with I.Q.'s from 100 to 135 learned as much in arithmetic, although they began one to one and one half years later and spent less than one third as much time daily, as did children who spent full time for six years.

LIDE, Edwin S., "Instruction in Mathematics," U. S. Department of the Interior, Office of Education, Bulletin, 1932, No. XVII, National Survey of Secondary Education, Monograph No. 23 (Government Printing Office, 1933). He investigated and analyzed courses of study in seventy-nine schools and systems throughout the country, and presented the conclusions he drew from this study.

LOCKERLY, Florence, "Banking," *Teachers' Lesson Unit Series,* Vol. XXVIII (Teachers College, Columbia University). She reported on the development of curriculum topics by experiment for grade levels.

MACLATCHY, J. H., "Another Measure of the Difficulty of Addition Combinations," *Educational Research Bulletin,* Vol. XII (Ohio State University, March 8, 1933), pp. 57-61. He investigated young children's number ideas, and the types of their information on arithmetic.

National Committee on Mathematics Requirements, *Report of the National Committee on Mathematical Requirements* (Houghton Mifflin, 1927).

National Society for the Study of Education, *Twenty-ninth Yearbook,* Societies Committee on Arithmetic, "Report of the Societies Committee on Arithmetic," Part II (1930) Ch. IV.

NOREM, F., and KNIGHT, F. B., "The Learning of One Hundred Multiplication Combinations," *Twenty-Ninth Yearbook of N.S.S.E.* (1930), Ch. VII. A study of the relative learning of the basic multiplication combinations.

PARTRIDGE, C. M., "Number Needs in Children's Reading Activities," *Elementary School Journal,* Vol. XXVI (Jan., 1926), pp. 357-366. A study of the numerical situations in a single issue of ten magazines.

PRESSEY, L. C., and ELAM, M. K., "The Fundamental Vocabulary of Elementary-School Arithmetic," *Elementary School Journal,* Vol. XXXIII (Sept., 1932), pp. 46-50. A list of 117 essential terms in arithmetic is presented. Criteria for selection were frequency of use, importance, and social usefulness.

PRESSEY, L. C., and MOORE, W. S., "The Growth of Mathematical Vocabulary from the Third Grade Through High School," *School Review,* Vol. XL (June, 1932), pp. 449-54. They found, by giving a series of tests in the vocabulary of arithmetic, algebra, and geometry to pupils in grades 3 through 12, that there is a low median vocabulary in both algebra and geometry, which, they conclude, accounts for the difficulty encountered by people of all ages in dealing with mathematics.

RATHS, L. E., "Grade Placements of Addition and Subtraction of Fractions," *Educational Research Bulletin,* Vol. XI (Jan. 20, 1932), pp. 29-38.

SCARF, R. C., "The Mathematics Used in Popular Mechanics," Bobbitt, F., *Curriculum Investigations* (1926). An analysis of the Science articles in a random sampling of five general magazines and three books of popular science.

SCHORLING, Raleigh, Chairman, "Report of Committee on Individual Differences," *Mathematics Teacher,* Vol. XXVI (Oct., 1933), pp. 350-365. They reported a study of teaching mathematics to slow pupils, revealing a tendency for slow pupils to show a high level of achievement in learning academic tasks, and to remember a thing once it has been mastered.

———, "Report of Sub-Committee on Junior High-School Mathematics," *North Central Association Quarterly* (March, 1928), pp. 396-419. Contains objectives for seventh, eighth, and ninth grades.

SMITH, D. E., and REEVE, W. D., "Objectives in Teaching Junior-High-School Mathematics," *Second Yearbook,* National Council of Teachers of Mathematics (1927), pp. 173-227. Chapter III contains the objectives to be obtained and the first chapter describes how they were obtained.

STORM, H. C., "Grade Placement in Arithmetic," *Illinois Teacher,* Vol. XX (Dec., 1931), pp. 113-114.

VOORHEES, M., "New Methods in Arithmetic," *Progressive Education,* Vol. V (Apr., May, June, 1928), pp. 125-130. Gives principles underlying arithmetic activities.

WAPLES, D., and STONE, C. A., *The Teaching Unit a Type Study* (Appleton, 1929). Describes steps in constructing a typical unit for the course in junior high-school mathematics, according to the Morrison plan.

WASHBURNE, Carleton, W., "The Grade Placement of Arithmetic," National Society for Study of Education, *Twenty-Ninth Year-Book*

(1930). This is a study to determine the mental age and skill essential in the prerequisite topics which are necessary for the satisfactory learning and retention of certain arithmetic topics.

——, "Mental Age and Arithmetic Curriculum," *Journal of Educational Research,* Vol. XXIII (March, 1931), pp. 210-231. A summary grade placement investigations of the committee of seven.

WHITECRAFT, Leslie Harper, "Some Influences of the Requirements and Examinations of the College Entrance Examination Board on Mathematics in Secondary Schools of the United States," *Contributions to Education,* No. 557 (Teachers College, Columbia University, 1933). He investigated the extent to which the college Entrance Examination Board has influenced mathematics in secondary schools through a study of enrolment figures, textbooks, courses of study, and opinions of teachers and superintendents.

WOODY, Clifford, "Achievement in Counting by Children in the Primary Grades," *Childhood Education,* Vol. VII (March, 1931), pp. 339-345. In this study he confirms earlier reports on children's ideas and information in the arithmetic field, which showed that young children acquire a much larger background in arithmetic than was previously thought possible.

ART

CARROLL, Herbert A., and EURICH, Alvin C., "Abstract Intelligence and Art Appreciation," *Journal of Educational Psychology,* Vol. XXIII (March, 1932), pp. 214-20. They reported that abstract intelligence has little to do with critical ability in art at the college level, and general abstract ability affects art judgment only in the extremes.

ENG, Helga, *Psychology of Children's Drawings from the First Stroke to the Coloured Drawing* (Harcourt, Brace and Co., 1931). She observed, in examining psychologically the drawings of one child from the age of 10 months to 8 years, that there was an automatic synthesis from the beginning, based on personal observation, mental images, feelings, will, etc.

GOOD, C. V., "The Objectives and Status of Art Education in Secondary School," *Journal of Educational Method,* Vol. VII (February, 1928), pp. 209-213. Analyses of courses of study.

KINTER, Madaline, *The Measurement of Artistic Abilities.* Prepared for the Carnegie Corporation by the Psychological Corporation, under the supervision of Paul S. Achilles. (February, 1933). She presented an extensive survey of studies relating to measurement of abilities and interests.

KNAUBER, Alma J., "A Study of the Art Ability Found in Very Young Children." *Child Development,* Vol. II (March, 1931), pp. 66-71. She found that children's interests as reflected in voluntary drawing were stimulated by new and interesting factors of environment without regard for particular patterns.

LARSON, Minnie E., "An Analytical Investigation of Courses of Study in Art, Education for the Elementary School," Master's Thesis

(University of Chicago, 1931). She examined courses of study and other materials dealing with art curriculum for elementary schools.

McLANDRESS, Helen, "The Relation of Elements and Principles of Art to Everyday Life Objects," Master's Thesis (University of Chicago, 1932). She found, on investigation of the relation of art principles to everyday life, that color was the most frequently mentioned element, and home materials the most frequently mentioned objects.

MEBANE, Eleanor V., "Art Education in the Junior and Senior High School," Master's Thesis (George Peabody College for Teachers, 1931). She studied the art curriculum and materials for junior and senior high schools.

MENDENHALL, James, and MENDENHALL, Marcia E., *The Influence of Familiarity upon Children's Preferences for Pictures and Poems* (New York, Teachers College, Columbia University, 1933). They tested junior high-school pupils' preferences for pictures, finding that repeated exposures to these materials developed distinct preferences or dislikes.

MOORE, Lucy Hunt, "Educational Principles and Art Practices in Progressive Schools," Master's Thesis (George Peabody College for Teachers, 1932). She treats of courses of study and art curriculum materials for progressive schools.

MULLINS, Vernon H., "Survey of Junior College Curricula with Regard to Vocational Opportunity in Art," Master's Thesis (University of Southern California, 1932). He examined curricula and courses of study for junior colleges.

Parent-Teacher Association of Lincoln School, *Spend Your Time; New York Resources for the Use of Leisure* (Teachers College, Columbia University, 1933). The association edited this volume, which included, along with other resources for the use of leisure time, a section on art activities with specific information as to sources.

PEARSON, Ralph M., "Creative Arts in Community Life," *Progressive Education,* Vol. IX (April, 1932), pp. 319-322. He analyzed the dominance of the profit motive in modern industry as it affects the creative instinct in art education and art production, and recommended the extension and encouragement of creative practice in every phase of pupil life.

SKILLMAN, H. C., "American Art from the College Campus; a Year's Activities in the Nation's Art Departments," *Parnassus,* Vol. V (May, 1933), pp. 27-34. He investigated courses of study and curriculum materials for all colleges.

SMITH, J. B., "Trends of Thought in Art Education," *School Review,* Vol. XLI (April, 1933), pp. 266-277. He analyzed objectives evident in courses of study in art for the past 40 years, and concluded that visual training, development of graphic vocabulary, and esthetic appreciation have showed throughout as major aims, while free expression, application of art to daily life, and the use of tests have appeared recently.

TAYLOR, Herma Madge, "Children's Interests as Revealed by Their Drawings in Three Grades," master's thesis (George Peabody College for Teachers, 1932). After a study of the drawings of primary children, she specified interests in trees and buildings as basic.

WALL, Ernest A., "Aesthetic Sense and Education," doctor's thesis (New York University, 1931). An investigation of the status of esthetic tastes by means of a questionnaire submitted to 758 pupils. He concluded that esthetic taste is intuitive, native, and universal, and can be divided chronologically into three categories: birth to 8 years, 8 to 12 years, and 12 to 16 years.

WAYMACK, Eunice H., and HENDRICKSON, Gordon, "Children's Reactions as a Basis for Teaching Picture Appreciation," *Elementary School Journal,* Vol. XXXIII (December, 1930), pp. 268-276. They arrived at the conclusion that elementary-school pupils reacted to pictures on the basis of art fundamentals after definite instruction whereas, previously, their interest in people, scenery, etc., had been a criterion.

WHITE, Roberta, and JOHNSON, B., "Children's Classes in Modern Art," *Child Development,* Vol. I (December, 1930), pp. 347-349. They reported a greater amount of discriminatory taste in pictures on the part of pupils who had had definite instruction.

WHITFORD, William G., "Changing Objectives and Trends in Art Education," *School Arts Magazine,* Vol. XXXII (April, 1933), pp. 459-461, ix-xi. He attributed the recent sharp decline in art instruction to the failure of art educators to emphasize sufficiently the value of art education in schools.

———, and Others, "Report of Sub-committee on Art Education," *North Central Association Quarterly,* Vol. I (March, 1927), pp. 479-503. Contains objectives for secondary schools.

FOREIGN LANGUAGES

American Classical League, *The Classical Investigation,* Part I, General Report (Princeton University Press, 1924). The curriculum studies involved in this investigation are based upon present practice and the opinion of teachers.

ARNOLD, H. H., "List of Graded Vocabularies and a Method of Grading," *Modern Language Journal,* Vol. XVI (May, 1932), pp. 644-655. His study of six Spanish authors as to vocabulary shows a high frequency of idioms.

———, "Tense Frequency in the Spanish Novel and Drama," *Modern Language Journal,* Vol. XIV (Dec., 1929), pp. 234-235. He listed the verb forms in order of frequency as he found them in five Spanish plays and five novels.

BAKER, Florence M., "A Tentative Vocabulary for First Year French Students," *Journal of Educational Research,* Vol. XVIII (Dec., 1928), pp. 369-377. She compiled a tentative vocabulary list for first-year French Students, basing her study on two other word books.

BLACKBURN, Margaret, "An Analysis of the Vocabulary of Two Recent French Grammars," *Modern Language Journal,* Vol. XIV (March,

1930), pp. 431-441. She examined French grammars, studying them in regard to size of vocabulary, and lack of agreement with one another.

BRECKHEIMER, J. P., "The Kind and Frequency of Typical Errors in Written French," *Modern Language Forum,* Vol. XII (June, 1927), pp. 5-7. He analyzed errors in French compositions and translations made by high-school students, finding the same classes of errors persistent throughout. The highest percentage of error was in spelling.

BUCHANAN, M. A., A Spanish Word Book (University of Toronto Press, 1927). The most common words in current written discourse.

COLE, Robert D., "Selecting French Readers," *Modern Language Forum,* Vol. XVII (April, 1932), pp. 42-45. He studied the percentage of words in ungraded texts supplied by the first 2,000 words in the *French Word Book.*

CRIDER, Blake, "An Analysis and Interpretation of Errors Made in Translating Spanish Prose," *Modern Language Journal,* Vol. XV (Nov., 1930), pp. 123-126. He found that in translating from Spanish into English 65 per cent of the errors were in vocabulary, and the remainder in form.

ENGEL, E. F., "The Use of a Standardized Vocabulary in Beginning German," *Modern Language Journal,* Vol. XV (Jan., 1931), pp. 281-291. A report of vocabulary study showing that about 1,450 German words are learned by his college students during the first semester.

FLANAGAN, Sister Wilbrod, *Verb Syntax in Modern French Literature,* summarized in: Coleman, Algernon, *An Analytical Bibliography of Modern Language Teaching,* 1927-1932 (University of Chicago Press, 1933), pp. 155-157. She tabulated cases of verb usage in two French readers. The findings indicated that the present tense was used frequently in narrative.

FOTOS, John T., "Word and Idiom Frequency Counts in French and Their Value," *Modern Language Journal,* Vol. XV (Feb., 1931), pp. 344-353. He presented a tabulated vocabulary list of nine beginners' texts containing approximately 4,000 items.

GARCIA, Edward C., "Reading Method and Culture Study," *Modern Language Forum,* Vol. XVI (April, 1931), pp. 60-61. The maximum vocabulary of second year Spanish students was determined and the amount of vocabulary progress which can be made each year was suggested.

HATHAWAY, Lillie V., "A German Error Count—an Experimental Study," *Modern Language Journal,* Vol. XIII (April, 1929), pp. 512-533. She studied and classified student errors in versions of German exercises.

HAUCH, Edward F., German Idiom List (The Macmillan Co., 1929). Selected on the basis of frequency and range of occurrence.

HAYGOOD, J. D., "The Amount and Composition of a Minimum Essential French Reading Vocabulary," *Modern Language Journal,* Vol. XVIII (Dec., 1933), pp. 177-189. A sampling technique was used studying French literary works for vocabulary. The *French Word Book* was selected as a reference.

HILLIS, E. C., "Spanish Words of High Frequency," *Hispania,* Vol. XIV (Nov., 1931), pp. 338-340. He subjected the assumed high frequency group of idioms set forth in the *Graded Spanish Word Book* to a test, and found that four of them occurred too infrequently in twenty-one plays which he examined to be included in the list.

HILLS, E. C., and ANDERSON, J. O., "Frequency of Moods and Tenses of Verbs in Recent Spanish Plays," *Hispania,* Vol. XII (Dec., 1929), pp. 604-606. They presented results of an investigation of verb forms and tenses in Spanish plays.

———, "Relative Frequency of Spanish Personal Pronouns," *Hispania,* Vol. XIV (Nov., 1931), pp. 335-337. They studied the relative frequency of Spanish personal pronouns, and listed them in order of frequency.

KNEASE, Tacie Mary, *An Italian Word List from Literary Sources* (University of Toronto Press, 1933). She listed 2,100 Italian words which she compiled after studying forty recent literary sources.

MILLER, John F., *A Vocabulary Study of Ten French Reading Texts Based on the Vander Beke French Word Book,* summarized in: Coleman, Algernon, *An Analytical Bibliography of Modern Language Teaching* (University of Chicago Press, 1933), pp. 144-146.

MORGAN, B. Q., and OBERDECK, Lydia M., "Active and Passive Vocabulary," *Studies in Modern Language Teaching,* Publications of the American and Canadian Committees on Modern Languages, Vol. XVII, Ch. 6 (Macmillan Co., 1930), pp. 213-221. They presented conclusions concerning the "active" and "passive" vocabulary.

MORGAN, B. Q., and PURIN, C. M., *A German Word Book* (The Macmillan Co., 1927). A word list based on a previous study of over ten million words.

North Central Association, "Report of Sub-Committee on Latin," *North Central Association Quarterly,* Vol. II (March, 1927), pp. 483-504. The subject-matter of Latin in the opinion of a Committee.

O'SHEA, M. V., "The Reading of Foreign Modern Languages," *United States Bureau of Education Bulletin,* No. XVI (1927). A study of the utilization of modern foreign languages by high-school and college graduates.

PURIN, C. M., *A Standard German Vocabulary of 2,000 Words and Idioms* (University of Chicago Press, 1931). He based his vocabulary study on the labor of three other men, and on personal judgment. A list of German words suitable for a standard vocabulary is presented.

RYAN, H. H., and Others, "Report of Sub-Committee on First-Year Spanish and First Year German," *North Central Association Quarterly,* Vol. III (March, 1928), pp. 445-461. Contains a list of objectives.

SANDAL, Caroline, "Difficulties in the Learning of French in the High Schools," *Bulletin of High Points,* Vol. XII (June, 1930), pp. 13-22.

Her analysis of errors in French made by high-school students raises the question of whether the curriculum should be changed, or most students should be denied admittance to foreign language classes.

SCHINNERER, O. P., and WENDT, H. G., "A Suggested List of 1,000 Active German Words," *German Quarterly*, Vol. VI (March, 1930), pp. 77-90. They presented a list of 1,000 German words of "active" use, basing their study on existing lists.

SEARS, Edith K., "The Vocabularies of Two Direct-Method French Grammars for Beginners," *Modern Language Journal*, Vol. XV (May, 1931), pp. 599-606. She studied two recent French grammars, and showed the extent of the vocabularies, their disagreement, and lack of repetition.

WEST, Michael P., "Speaking Vocabulary in a Foreign Language (1,000 words)," *Modern Language Journal*, Vol. XIV (April, 1930), pp. 509-521. He tried to establish a basis for choosing the first 1,000 items of a speech vocabulary.

SPELLING

FITZGERALD, James A., "Words Misspelled Most Frequently by Children of the Fourth-, Fifth-, and Sixth-Grade Levels in Life Outside the School," *Journal of Educational Research*, Vol. XXVI (Nov., 1932), pp. 213-218. He reported some important new data after analyzing friendly letters of children in the fourth, fifth, and sixth grades for frequency of misspelled words.

HORN, Ernest, "A Basic Writing Vocabulary," University of Iowa, *Monograph in Education*, No. IV (April, 1926). A list of 10,000 words most commonly used in writing.

KRAMER, Grace A., "What Words Do Adults Misspell?" *Baltimore Bulletin of Education*, Vol. X (May, 1932), pp. 190-191. A significant original research in the field of adult writing.

SELZER, Charles A., "Lateral Dominance and Visual Fusion; Their Application to Difficulties in Reading, Writing, Spelling, and Speech," *Harvard Monograph in Education*, No. XII, (Harvard University Free Press, 1933). He decided that spelling disabilities were an indication of lateral cerebral dominance.

SHAMBAUGH, C. G., and SHAMBAUGH, O. L., "A Core Vocabulary for Elementary School-Pupils," *Journal of Educational Research*, Vol. XIX (Jan., 1929), pp. 39-46. A core vocabulary of 1,309 words obtained by responses to 400 stimulus words made by fifty pupils in grades one to eight.

WICKEY, Rose, and LAMADER, May B., *The Teaching of Spelling* (Webster Publishing Co., 1932). Among recent investigations dealing with the diagnosis and treatment of spelling disability, theirs is a statistical study of types of errors and causes of misspelling.

WILLIAMSON, Edmund G., "The Relation of Learning to Spelling Ability," *Journal of Educational Psychology*, Vol. XXIV (April, 1933), pp. 257-265. Rejecting the idea of spelling disabilities, he concluded that spelling ability is directly related to intelligence.

HEALTH AND PHYSICAL EDUCATION

BRAMMELL, P. Roy, "Health Word and Physical Education," U. S. Department of the Interior, Office of Education, Bulletin No. 17 (1932), *National Survey of Secondary Education,* Monograph No. 28 (Government Printing Office, 1933). He pointed out certain trends in modern health education which he had observed in a survey of 460 secondary schools.

BURKARD, Wm. E., *An Analysis of Educational Objectives and Outcomes in the Field of Health Education* (University of Pennsylvania Press, 1927). A study based on the analysis of thirty-four texts, fifteen courses of study, curriculum investigations and certain other miscellaneous sources.

CLEVETT, Melvin A., "An Experiment in Physical Education Activities Related to the Teaching of Honesty and Motor Skills," *Research Quarterly of the American Physical Education Association,* Vol. III (March, 1932), pp. 121-127. He reported a three months' experiment in testing the effectiveness of various types of physical activities in developing skills and moral and social values, especially honesty.

COOPS, Helen Leslie, *High School Standards in Girls' Athletics in the State of Ohio* (Teachers College, Columbia University, 1933). She discussed objectives in physical education, and treated types of activities with reference to student enjoyment.

CRAPSER, A. Lester, "National Physical Achievement Standards," *Journal of Health and Physical Education,* Vol. I (Jan., 1930), pp. 14-16, 56. He reported a study of standards and criteria for the selection and organization of activities for different situations in physical-education programs.

EASTWOOD, Floyd R., "A Study of Subject-Matter, Materials, and Methods in Health," *Journal of Educational Sociology,* Vol. III (May, 1930), pp. 536-545. He considered materials and methods in relation to the changing social needs of a child, and suggested means of stimulating interest in health practices.

FORMAN, W. O., "Use Made of Leisure Time by Junior High-School Pupils," *Elementary School Journal,* Vol. XXVII (June, 1926), pp. 771-774. A questionnaire study to determine the leisure time activities of 175 boys.

FRANZEN, Raymond H., "Influence of Social and Economic Factors on the Health of the School Child," *School Health Research Monographs,* No. 4 (American Child Health Association, 1932). He reported on the influence of social and economic factors on the health of school children.

HARAP, H., "Disease Data Determine Emphasis in Health Course," *The Nation's Health,* Vol. VIII (Oct., 1926), pp. 665-667. A study of statistical data describing the condition of health of girls and women. States about thirty objectives.

HEAGAN, Rena, "Principles Underlying the School Health Program," *Journal of Health and Physical Education,* Vol. III (Feb., 1932), pp. 10-12+. Outlines methods of realizing a program in practice.

JAMESON, E. D., *Physical Education for the Preparation of Elementary School Teachers* (Teachers College, Columbia University, 1930). A study of content and requirements in courses of physical education in twenty-two state teachers colleges and normals during 1926-1927.

LAPORTE, William R., Chairman, "Report of the Committee on Curriculum Research," *Research Quarterly of the American Physical Education Association,* Vol. I (May, 1930), pp. 15-40. He showed by a series of comparative charts the values of various activities in a physical-education program for boys.

LEE, Mabel, "The Case for and against Intercollegiate Athletics for Women and the Situation since 1923," *Research Quarterly of the American Physical Education Association,* Vol. II (May, 1931), pp. 93-127. She studied the fundamental and general educational principles applied to teaching methods in each technical field.

LERRIGO, M. O., *Health Problem Sources* (Teachers College, Columbia University, 1926). An analysis of mortality statistics using United States reports, life insurance company reports, and textbooks by competent authorities.

NEILSON, N. P., chairman, "Report of the Committee of the American Physical-Education Association on Teacher-Training in Physical Education in the United States," *Research Quarterly of the American Physical Education Association,* Vol. IV (March, 1933), pp. 51-67. He presented a standard curriculum in physical education for elementary schools.

OBERTEUFFER, Delbert, "Personal Hygiene for College Students," *Contributions to Education,* No. 407 (Teachers College, Columbia University, 1930). He presented a series of questions raised by students as a guide to their interests. These are suggested as a basic guide to the selection of health-education-program items.

PHALEN, Annette M., *A Study of School Health Standards* (Teachers College, Columbia University, 1933). She treated health· education and its emphasis in the modern curriculum on the basis of statistical findings.

STURTEVANT, Sarah, and STRANG, Ruth, "Activities of High School Girls," *Teachers College Record,* Vol. XXX (March, 1929), pp. 562-571. One thousand daily records secured through 152 deans of high-school girls.

VAN ALSTYNE, Dorothy, *Play Behaviour and Choice of Play Material of Pre-School Children* (University of Chicago Press, 1932). A careful study of the reactions of 112 pre-school children to play materials.

WHITMAN, W. G., "General Science and Hygiene in the Junior High Schools of Massachusetts," *Science Education,* Vol. XV (May, 1931), pp. 215-218. He studied general science as a contributing subject in the health-education program.

SOCIAL SCIENCE

AITCHISON, Alison E., "Torrid, Temperate and Frigid Zones—Sources of Error in Children's Thinking," *The Teaching of Geography,*

Thirty-Second Yearbook, National Society for the Study of Education, Bloomington, Ill. (Public School Publishing Co., 1933), pp. 483-485. She studied the errors of pupils in learning the geographic zones.

BAGLEY, W. C., and KYTE, G. C., *The California Curriculum Study* (University of California Press, 1926), pp. 164-169. Summarizes the results of six studies of the relatively important places.

BARR, A. S., and GIFFORD, C. W., "The Vocabulary of American History," *Journal of Educational Research,* Vol. XX (Sept., 1929), pp. 103-121. A list of 1,899 words which occur most frequently in eight representative senior high-school texts in American History.

BIXLER, G. K., "Social Problems of the Labor Group," In F. Bobbitt, *Curriculum Investigations,* Ch. IX (1926). Analysis of ten widely used books and several periodicals which deal with labor problems.

BLYTHE, Irene T., "The Textbooks and the New Discoveries, Emphases, and Viewpoints in American History," *Historical Outlook,* Vol. XXIII (Dec., 1932), pp. 393-402. Her study of textbooks published between 1893 and 1928 revealed an unfortunate neglect on the part of textbook authors to incorporate new viewpoints in their books.

BOBBITT, Franklin, "Social Value of Junior High Curriculum," *School Executive Magazine,* Vol. LII (Jan., 1933), pp. 179-181. A discussion of social studies in relation to mastery of techniques and the distribution of program time.

BROOKS, Alice R., "The Integration of Library Instruction with the High-School Social Studies," *Social Library Yearbook,* No. V (American Library Association, 1932), pp. 121-124. To find the library knowledge and material needed in high-school social studies, she analyzed twelve courses of study in a "library job analysis."

BRUNER, H. B., "Curriculum Planning for Changing Society," *Childhood Education,* Vol. IX (Jan., 1932), pp. 171-176. A vital discussion of the problems which face the curriculum maker to-day.

CAREY, Alice E., HANNA, Paul R., and MERIAM, J. L., *Catalog: Units of Work, Activities, Projects, etc. to 1932* (Teachers College, Columbia University, 1932). They presented, in catalogue form, a study of units which have been used and reported by elementary-school teachers.

CARMICHAEL, A. M., "Primary Children's Comprehension of a Social Situation," *Bulletin of School of Education,* Indiana University, Vol. IX, No. 1 (Sept., 1932), pp. 102-124. This investigation endeavors to ascertain the growing ability of primary children to apprehend or conceive certain intellectual aspects of a situation in which a child is defeated by his playmates.

CARROTHERS, George E., "High School Curriculum Revisions and Innovations," *Junior High School Clearing House,* Vol. VI (Jan., 1932), pp. 262-270. He presented conclusions which he drew from an analysis of department enrolments, changes in courses of study, and curriculum changes.

CARTER, Thyra, "Racial Elements in American History Textbooks," *Historical Outlook,* Vol. XXII (April, 1931), pp. 147-151. She found a tendency to minimize the importance of foreign countries and to create an unfavorable attitude toward certain countries in various senior-high-school textbooks which she examined.

CLOGSTON, E. B., "Setting up Aims for the Social Studies," *Historical Outlook,* Vol. XX (March, 1929), pp. 115-116. Committee of nine from three high schools in Terre Haute, Indiana, make up a *list of aims* for social studies.

CLUCAS, Charles, "The Problem of Dates in the Teaching of History and in Measurement," *Journal of Educational Research,* Vol. XXVI (October, 1932), pp. 90-96. He found that the "date load" in most American history textbooks ran from 685 to 1,356 mentions, which he considered far too heavy, and presented a list of the twenty-six most important dates.

CRAMER, John Francis, "Relative Difficulty of Junior High School Social Studies Texts," *Journal of Educational Research,* Vol. XXVI (Feb., 1933), pp. 425-428. In an experiment he determined that the Rugg social-science books gave adequate coverage of material, and offered less reading difficulty than the state textbooks which they replaced.

FISH, O. C., "The Aims and Content of Junior High School Geography," *The Journal of Geography,* Vol. XXVI (Nov., 1927), pp. 313-321. Investigation to determine the aims of teaching geography as set forth by expert opinion.

FITZGERALD, J. A., "Situation in Which Children Write Letters in Life Outside of the School," *Educational Method,* Vol. XII (Jan., 1933), pp. 223-231. An analysis of 3,184 letters written by children in grades 4, 5, 6.

FLOYD, Oliver R., "Overlapping Between the Senior High School Courses in Problems of Democracy and American History," *Historical Outlook,* Vol. XXIII (Oct., 1932), pp. 296-302. He found overlapping in high-school texts in American history and problems of democracy, and suggested reorganization of the two courses.

GOLUB, Jay, and SWAHN, Alfred D., "Do American History Students Change Their Attitudes After One Term's Work?" *Historical Outlook,* Vol. XXIII (Jan., 1932), pp. 7-21. They attempted to differentiate between factual knowledge and understanding of ideas as results of history courses.

HARCOURT, John, "The World War in French, German, English, and American Secondary School Textbooks," *First Yearbook, National Council for the Social Studies* (McKinley Publishing Co., 1931), pp. 54-117. He carefully analyzed German, French, English, and American textbooks as to their treatment of the World War, and determined that it is evident that pupils in each of the different countries will have conflicting viewpoints on the war.

HART, Isabelle K., "A Classification of Common Errors in Geography Made by Teachers and Pupils," *The Teaching of Geography, Thirty-second Yearbook,* National Society for the Study of Education (Public School Publishing Co., 1933), pp. 479-482. In collecting and classifying common errors made by teachers and pupils in geography, she found a close relationship between the two classifications.

HATCH, R. W., *Training in Citizenship* (Scribners, 1926). Chap. 15 gives specific objectives brought about by student activity.

HATCH, R. W., and STULL, E., *The Social Studies in the Horace Mann Junior High School* (Teachers College, Bureau of Publications, 1926).

HERRIOTT, M. E., "How to Make a Course of Study in Social Studies," *University of Illinois Bulletin,* Vol. XXIV, No. 5 (1926).

——, "Objectives in U. S. History," *School Review,* Vol. XXXVII (Feb., 1929), pp. 107-116. A list of names and dates to be learned by children, submitted by a group of elementary teachers and checked for grade placement by high-school teachers.

HOCKETT, John, *America's Crucial Problems* (Teachers College, Bureau of Publications, 1927). A study of frontier books to discover the most significant social problems.

HOPKINS, L. Thomas, "Constructing a Character Curriculum," *Journal of Educational Sociology,* Vol. IV (Dec., 1930), pp. 206-211. Recognition of character situations and development of wholesome attitudes toward a situation and its solution. Discussion of correct solution of specific character problems. Practice remedial treatment with individual help and guidance. Define the relationship of character education to the total processes of education.

HOWE, George F., "A Study of the Ability of Elementary School Pupils to Read Maps," *The Teaching of Geography, Thirty-Second Yearbook,* National Society for the Study of Education (Public School Publishing Co., 1933), pp. 486-492. His study of ability in map reading in elementary schools led him to conclude that more study and attention to the development of such skills was necessary.

JOHNSON, Laura Terrell, "Changing Objectives in Geography," *Classroom and Administrative Problems in the Teaching of the Social Studies, Second Yearbook,* National Council for the Social Studies (McKinley Publishing Co., 1932), pp. 175-180. She studied courses and objectives since 1900 to determine present tendencies.

KIMMEL, William G., "Instruction in the Social Studies," U. S. Department of the Interior, Office of Education, Bulletin No. 17 (1932), *National Survey of Secondary Education,* Monograph No. 21. (Government Printing Office, 1933). His study revealed that there was greater uniformity in the courses of study in grade seven than in grade eight, and that there was sometimes a differentiation made between students who expected to go to college, and those who did not.

LACEY, Joy M., "Social Studies Concepts of Children in the First Three Grades," *Contributions to Education,* No. 548 (Teachers College, Columbia University, 1932). She studied carefully the social science concepts of elementary-school children and found that while they possessed considerable information, much of it was entangled with misconception. The study reveals a need for more careful teaching and testing of the results of teaching in the social studies.

LEE, Baldwin, "Issues in Social Studies," *Social Science Monographs,*

No. 3, 183 (The Lincoln School of Teachers College, 1928). An analysis of major issues of social studies by a study of textbooks and other treatises in this field.

LIMBERT, Paul M., "What Children Think About War," *Progressive Education*, Vol. X (Feb., 1933), pp. 67-71. A study of attitudes of students in grades six through twelve toward war and peace. The author expressed a conviction that teaching of the subject should be more realistic.

MAEDER, H. G., *Educational Outcomes Unique in the Teaching of Ancient History* (U. of Penn., 1927). The objectives were determined by a study of textbooks, courses of study, and educational works.

MARKS, Florence Pool, "The Social Studies in Grades 9-12 in Reorganized and Un-reorganized Schools," *School Review*, Vol. XLI (May, 1933), pp. 347-355. She presented information which she gathered concerning changes in courses of study in reorganized junior and senior high schools as compared with four-year high schools.

NASON, J. M., "International Relations as Revealed by Editorials, Cartoons and Textbooks in American History," Department of Superintendence, *Fifth Yearbook* (1927), pp. 230-231. An analysis of 124 editorial pages, 1,057 cartoons, and 7 textbooks.

National Committee on High-School Geography, "Geography in the Junior High School," *Journal of Geography* (Sept., 1927), pp. 207-220. Report of the committee on what the aims of geography should be.

National Society for the Study of Education, *The Teaching of Geography, Thirty-Second Yearbook* (Public School Publishing Co., 1933). This study contains three articles on difficulties and errors.

NEVILLE, C. E., *A Study of the Outcomes in Education through Geography Teaching* (University of Pennsylvania, 1927). Determining certain general objectives of a study of existing curriculum investigations, courses of study and textbooks.

OBRIEN, F. P., and WATKINS, G. E., "Objectives of History Teachers in High Schools of Kansas," *University of Kansas Bulletin of Education*, Vol. III (Oct., 1931), pp. 6-9. They made a particular study of objectives used by Kansas City classroom teachers of history.

PENNINGROTH, Paul W., *A Study of Public Opinion on International Relations in Certain Communities* (Florida Grower Press, 1932). From a study of two communities, he tried to discover (1) the identity of the generators of public opinion, and (2) the scope of attitudes on international affairs.

PIERCE, Bessie Louise, "Citizens' Organization and the Civic Training of Youth," *Report of the Commission on Social Studies* of the American Historical Association, Part III (Charles Scribner's Sons, 1933). She made a study of the aims and programs of 200 organizations which have tried to influence civic education since the war, and reported impartially on the purposes and methods of the more significant ones.

PRESSEY, L. C., "The Needs of College Students in History," *Historical Outlook*, Vol. XXI (May, 1930), pp. 218-223. Analysis of history texts, periodicals to discover essential dates, persons, etc., for freshman history.

PRESSEY, L. C., and FISCHER, R., "The Geographical Background Necessary for the Study of History," *Educational Research Bulletin*, Vol. XI (Ohio State University, April, 1932), pp. 234-238. They examined history books to discover what items of place geography seemed most important.

REED, Mary M., and WRIGHT, Lula E., *The Beginnings of the Social Sciences* (Charles Scribner's Sons, 1932). They studied the interests of primary children, and presented them in outline form.

ROBBINS, Floy, "Can Geography Contribute to an Interest in, and an Understanding of, Current Magazine Articles?" *The Teaching of Geography, Thirty-Second Yearbook*, National Society for the Study of Education (Public School Publishing Co., 1933), pp. 561-565. By analyzing magazine articles he found that a knowledge of geography should tend to increase interest in literature.

ROSENBLOOM, Minnie, "Men Mentioned in Five Junior High School American History Textbooks," *Historical Outlook*, Vol. XXII (Jan., 1931), pp. 26-27. She studied the names of men mentioned in various junior high-school textbooks, finding only a small percentage common to all.

RUGG, E., "An Analysis of Social Science Textbooks," *Third Yearbook*, Department of Superintendence (Feb., 1925), pp. 256-261. A study of persons and topics in widely used social-science textbooks.

SCHERF, Charles H., "The Social Studies in Fifty Typical Junior Colleges in the United States," *Historical Outlook*, Vol. XXII (Jan., 1931), pp. 7-17.

SHIELDS, H. G., "School and College Courses in Economics," *Journal of Educational Sociology*, Vol. IV (Nov., 1930), pp. 154-162. He made a detailed investigation of the status of courses in economics in high school and college, and analyzed time, topics, and textbooks.

SHILLING, D. C., "Legal Requirements for the Teaching of Civics," *Historical Outlook*, Vol. XXIV (April, 1933), pp. 181-186. He set forth legal requirements for the teaching of civics, the Constitution, and patriotism.

SNEDDEN, David, *Civic Education* (World Book Co., 1927). The latter part of the book contains a number of studies of case groups.

STEVENSON, Elmo N., "Children's Nature Interests," *The Elementary School Journal*, Vol. XXXII (Dec., 1931), pp. 276-284. Analysis of nature interests of 119 children in grades 4 to 6 by means of check list, the asking of questions and writing of compositions by children.

STEVENSON, Orlando, "The Special Vocabulary of Civics," *Journal of Educational Research*, Vol. XVIII (Nov., 1928), pp. 297-304. A study of vocabulary found in ten civics textbooks.

SYMONDS, Clare, "The Status of Geography in the Senior High School," *The Teaching of Geography, Thirty-Second Yearbook*, National Society for the Study of Education (Public School Publishing Co.,

1933), pp. 545-546. He found geography a senior high-school subject in 70 per cent of the schools studied.

THOMAS, Katheryne Colvin, "The Ability of Children to Interpret Graphs," *The Teaching of Geography, Thirty-Second Yearbook,* National Society for the Study of Education (Public Schools Publishing Co., 1933), pp. 492-494. She found ability to read simple graphs as early as the fourth grade.

THORP, Mary Tucker, "Studies of the Ability of Pupils in Grades Four to Eight to Use Geographic Tools," *The Teaching of Geography, Thirty-Second Yearbook,* National Society for the Study of Education (Public Schools Publishing Co., 1933), pp. 495-506. After a study of pupil capacity to use such geographical materials as maps, globes, picture graphs, etc., she concluded that more attention should be given to the grade placement of these skills.

THRALLS, Zoe, "Some General Curricular Principles and Their Applications," *The Teaching of Geography, Thirty-Second Yearbook,* National Society for the Study of Education (Public Schools Publishing Co., 1933), pp. 201-218. She analyzed several courses of study in geography, finding the modified one-cycle method of organization becoming dominant.

TYLER, R. W., "Improving Test Materials in Social Studies," *Educational Research Bulletin,* Vol. XI (Nov. 9, 1932), pp. 373-379. Test materials in social studies are concerned largely with informational objectives. It is important to set up tests for habits, attitudes, and ideals required for socially effective citizens.

VAN DYKE, George E., "Trends in the Development of the High-School Offering," *School Review,* Vol. XXXIX (Nov., Dec., 1931), pp. 657-664, 737-747. He reported a marked increase in social-science study in the high school after examining the courses of thirty-five high schools.

WELLS, C. O., "The Political Science of Everyday Life as Revealed by an Analysis of Newspapers and Periodicals," *Fifth Yearbook,* Department of Superintendence (1927), pp. 232-235. A study of political activities as revealed in 104 issues of newspapers and other sources.

WILSON, Ella M., "Difficulties in Using Geography Texts," *The Teaching of Geography, Thirty-Second Yearbook,* National Society for the Study of Education (Public Schools Publishing Co., 1933), pp. 475-479. She prepared a check list of difficulties in using geography texts, and submitted it to several teachers and supervisors. The conclusions were many texts fail (1) in emphasizing geographic relations, (2) in realizing objectives for children, and (3) in stimulating pupil coöperation.

WILSON, H. E., and ERB, B. P., "A Survey of Social Studies Courses in 301 Junior High Schools," *School Review,* Vol. XXXIX (Sept., 1931), pp. 497-507. Basing their conclusions on a study of thirty courses of study, they found a new spirit and interest in civic education, and a disagreement as to what should be taught in grades 7, 8, and 9.

ZINK, Norah E., "Eighty-Two Studies in the Teaching of Geography

Classified by Content and Technique, with Selected Summaries," *The Teaching of Geography, Thirty-Second Yearbook,* National Society for the Study of Education (Public Schools Publishing Co., 1933), pp. 431-473. She listed and classified eighty-two studies in geography, reported in the past thirty years.

ENGLISH LANGUAGE AND GRAMMAR

ALVEY, Edward, Jr., "Organizing Units around Functional Centers," *English Journal,* Vol. XXII (Feb., 1933), pp. 119-127. In this study he gives his solution of the difficult problem of the determination of suitable centers of organization for composition activities. Functional centers of work are included.

BARDWELL, Richard, "The New Emphasis in Language Teaching," *Elementary School Journal,* Vol. XXXIV (Oct., 1933), pp. 95-105. In his report on curriculum study of elementary English, he insists on encouragement of speech opportunities through natural activities. Error correction is not stressed.

BARNES, Walter, "Language as Behavior," *Elementary English Review,* Vol. VII (Dec., 1930), pp. 241-245; Vol. VIII (Jan., Feb., 1931), pp. 14-17, 24, 44-46. He analyzed the behavior factors in development of speaking and writing.

CLAPP, F. L., "A Test for Habits in English," *Elementary English Review,* Vol. III (Feb., 1926), pp. 42-46. Contains a list of most common errors made on a comprehensive test designed by the author.

COPE, Pauline, "Developing a Usage Conscience through Coöperation," *English Journal* (H. S. Ed.), Vol. XXII (May, 1933), pp. 399-405).

DAWSON, M. A., "Traditional Versus Progressive Practices in Teaching Language Usage," *The Elementary English Review,* Vol. IX (March, 1932), pp. 53-56, 79. The emphasis of this discussion is on diagnosis, individual instruction, coördination, and life situations.

DE BUSK, B. W., "The Persistence of Language Errors among School Children," *University of Oregon Publication,* Vol. II, No. 4 (1930). A study of frequency types and the persistence of grammatical errors for grades three to ten.

DEYER, C. A., "The Placement of Poems in the Grades," In F. Bobbitt, *Curriculum Investigations,* Ch. XV (1925). Grade placement based upon practices in 150 courses of study.

FITZGERALD, J. A., "Situations in which Children Write Letters in Life Outside of the School," *Educational Method,* Vol. XII (Jan., 1933), pp. 223-231. An analysis of 3,184 letters written by children in grades 4, 5, and 6.

GUILER, W. S., "Analysis of Children's Writings as a Basis for Instruction in English," *Journal of Educational Methods,* Vol. XII (Feb., 1926), pp. 259-264. A study of errors in punctuation and capitalization in 1,731 children's themes.

HARAP, H., "The Most Common Grammatical Errors," *English Journal,* Vol. XIX (June, 1930), pp. 440-446. A composite of thirty-three investigations of written and oral errors made by pupils.

HATFIELD, W. Wilbur, "Social Changes and English," *English Journal,* Vol. XXII (Sept., 1933), pp. 536-541. The adaptation of the English course of study to a changing world. The reports of a questionnaire investigation are reported.

HAVEN, Ruth M., and ANDRUS, Ruth, "Desirable Literature for Children of Kindergarten Age," Pedagogical Seminary, Vol. XXXVII (Sept., 1929), pp. 390-414. A study of the literary interests of nineteen children.

HINCHMAN, Florence M., "Teaching the Dull Freshman," *English Journal* (H. S. Edition), Vol. XXII (Dec., 1933), pp. 830-834. A new experiment in teaching retarded pupils in the secondary school.

KOOS, Leonard V., "The National Survey of Secondary Education: Its Implications for Teachers of English," *English Journal* (H. S. Edition), Vol. XXII (April, 1933), pp. 303-313. He discusses the implications of the national survey of education in secondary schools for secondary English teachers.

LEONARD, J. Paul, "Functional Grammar: What and Where?" *English Journal* (H. S. Edition), Vol. XXII (Nov., 1933), pp. 729-735. The tendency in popular use is more liberal than that taught in schools.

LEONARD, S. A., "The Wisconsin Tests of Grammatical Correctness," *English Journal,* Vol. XV (June, 1926), pp. 418-432. Contains a list of thirty-one most common errors made by pupils in a comprehensive test designed by the author.

LYMAN, R. L., "A Summary of Investigations Relating to Grammar, Language, and Composition," *Supplementary Education Monographs,* No. 6 (University of Chicago, 1929). Contains a summary of curriculum investigations, including grammar and composition; also a summary of investigations in methods of teaching.

PRESSEY, S. L., "A Statistical Study of Usage and of Children's Errors in Capitalization," *English Journal,* Vol. XIII (Dec., 1924), pp. 727-731. An analysis of letters, magazines, and newspapers to discover what capitalization is most frequently used.

———, "A Statistical Study of Children's Errors in Sentence Structure," *English Journal,* Vol. XIV (Sept., 1925), pp. 530-535. A study of the types of errors in sentence-structure based on a total of 980 papers written by pupils of grades seven to twelve.

PRESSEY, S. L., and CAMPBELL, Pera, "The Causes of Children's Errors in Capitalization," *English Journal,* Vol. XXII (March, 1933), pp. 197-201. They investigated capitalization errors in children's writing.

PULLIAM, Roscoe, "Should Formal Grammar Be Discarded?" *English Journal* (H. S. Edition), Vol. XX (Oct., 1931), pp. 654-661. By summarizing research reports on the problem, he attempted to answer the question as to whether or not formal grammar should be discarded.

RIVLIN, Harry N., "Functional Grammar," *Contributions to Education* No. 435 (Teachers College, Columbia University, 1930). A study of functional grammar based on study of textbooks and urban and rural teachers' ratings.

SMITH, Dora V., "Instruction in English," U. S. Department of the

Interior, *Office of Education, Bulletin* (1932), No. 17. *National Survey of Secondary Education,* Monograph No. 20 (Government Printing Office, 1933). She surveyed the condition of secondary English in the United States, revealing analyses of courses of study, curriculum trends, time allotments, and specific trends in various phases of English in secondary schools.

TERMAN, L. M., and LIMA, M., *Children's Reading* (Appleton, 1929). Reports the results of the study of 10,000 readings of children.

THORNDIKE and Others, "An Inventory of English Constructions with Measures of Their Importance," *Teachers College Record,* Vol. XIX (Feb., 1927), pp. 580-610. A study of constructions found in pupils' compositions, encyclopedias, textbooks, and fiction.

TRESSLER, J. C., "What Conventions Shall We Teach? How?" *English Journal,* Vol. XXI (March, 1932), pp. 200-204. He dealt with the conventions of language, selection of those to be taught, and the grade placement of these conventions.

WASHBURNE, C., and VOGEL, M., *Winnetka Graded Book List* (American Library Association, 1926). A study of the choices of 36,750 children, chiefly in grades five to eight, yielding a list of 700 books.

WISWALL, Z. E., "A Study of Sentence Structure in Eighth Grade Composition," *Elementary School Journal,* Vol. XXVII (Feb., 1926) pp. 441-448. An analysis of 800 compositions to discover defects in sentence structure.

ZYVE, Claire T., "Conversation Among Children," *Teachers College Record,* Vol. XIX (Oct., 1927), pp. 46-61. The topics which third-grade children discuss spontaneously.

MUSIC

BANNAN, Mary Frances, "A Comparison and Evaluation of Six Elementary Music Courses," Master's Thesis (George Peabody College for Teachers, 1930). After evaluating 6 elementary-school courses of study in music, she concluded that no one of the six methods supplied all the needs of musical education.

BOARD, Lorraine, M. A., "A Musical Survey Based on an Intensive Analysis of the Thomas Jefferson Platoon School, Glendale, California," Master's Thesis (University of Southern California, 1930). She analyzed the results of a test given to the school for the purpose of finding a basis for making a musical education program for the school.

CAMERON, Donald O., "An Experiment to Determine the Value of Technical Analysis in Teaching an Appreciation of Music," Master's Thesis (Pennsylvania State College, 1932). He showed that technical analysis in music teaching brings forth greater ability in music appreciation.

EARHART, Will, and GATTO, Frank M., "An Experimental Study of Creative Work in Public School Music," *Pittsburgh Schools,* Vol. VIII (November-December, 1933), pp. 44-56. They accord the creative approach a much superior rating, on the basis of tests of sight-reading, taste, musical knowledge, and musical performance.

HARAP, H., "Reading Music Programs Intelligently," *Journal of Educational Sociology,* Vol. II (March, 1929), pp. 419-423. A study of terms found in 210 musical programs collected by one person from 1917-1927.

HAVESON, Sophia, "Musical Ability of Sixth Grade Pupils in Minneapolis," master's thesis (University of Minnesota, 1930). She studied the music ability of sixth-grade children in Minneapolis, finding more correlation between factual knowledge and performance than that between intelligence ratings and school marks.

PIERCE, Anne E., "Music," *Instruction in Music and Art,* U. S. Dept. of the Interior, Office of Education, *Bulletin No. 17* (1932); *National Survey of Secondary Education,* Monograph No. 25, Part I, Washington, D. C. (Government Printing Office, 1933), pp. 1-43. Her report shows that (1) a general music course is almost always required in the seventh and eighth grades, (2) from that time on music being placed on an elective basis, and (3) that music educators agree on objectives but disagree on means of attaining them.

SEASHORE, Carl E., "What Is Musical Ability?" *Child Study,* Vol. IX (September, 1931), p. 11. He answered the question of what musical ability is by presenting an analysis of the hierarchy of traits and capacities which constitute musical talent.

WEINSTEIN, Max, "The Development of Individual Powers, Talents, and Aptitudes in the Public Schools of the City of New York," *Brooklyn Teacher,* Vol. XI (September, 1931), pp. 10-12. He reported the discovery of talented young musicians in New York City, and reviewed their training during and after school.

WOLNER, Manuel, and PYLE, W. H., "An Experiment in Individual Training of Pitch-Deficient Children," *Journal of Educational Psychology,* Vol. XXIV (November, 1933), pp. 602-608. They reported that even children with deficient ear-mechanisms can be taught to distinguish pitch.

WRIGHT, J. C., and EARHART, Will, "The Vocational Value of Music to High-School Pupils," *Curriculum Study and Educational Research Bulletin* (November-December, 1929). A survey of musical activities of 16,260 junior and senior high-school pupils of Pittsburgh.

COMMERCIAL

BOWMAN, C. E., "Bookkeeping in Teacher Training Institutions," Eastern Commercial Teachers Association, *Second Yearbook* (1929), pp. 293-297. A study of the topics included in the course in bookkeeping in 37 commercial teacher-training courses.

CONNOR, W. L., and JONES, L. L., *Scientific Study in Curriculum Making for Junior Courses in Business Education* (Gregg, 1929).

COOPER, Edward L., "A Survey of the Effects of Single and Double Periods in Bookkeeping," *Research Studies in Commercial Education* V, University of Iowa Studies in Education, Vol. VIII, No. III, Monographs in Education, No. 12 (University of Iowa, 1932), pp. 75-92. He made an experimental study of the relative value of double- and single-period classes in bookkeeping, and found the single-period more efficient.

FISHER, John Edwin, "Community Needs as the Basis for a High School Commercial Course," Master's Thesis (University of Chicago, 1931). He studied community needs as a basis for forming a high-school commercial education course.

GRAY, Ruth A., compiler, *Bibliography of Research Studies in Education, 1931-1932,* U. S. Dept. of the Interior, Office of Education, Bulletin No. 6 (Government Printing Office, 1933), pp. 217-222. This is a bibliography of various unpublished doctors' and masters' theses, including Morrisey on home-business activities, Peterson on business spelling, Check and Norton on teacher personnel, etc.

————, compiler, *Bibliography of Research Studies in Education, 1932-1933,* U. S. Dept. of the Interior, Office of Education, to be published (1934) as a bulletin. This is a bibliography of various studies such as that of Oak on commercial education in Negro colleges, Petrie and Tonne on social-business subjects, Thompson on business education in Presbyterian colleges, Cox on commercial geography, Kliotz on retail selling, Brogdon on student personnel, etc.

KING, W. Harry, *Commercial Subjects in Rural High Schools* (Government Printing Office, 1933). Address delivered before the American Vocational Association, December 8, 1932. This report reveals the fact that rural commercial-education programs emulate the city programs.

KYKER, B. F., "The Construction of a Commercial Curriculum by Job Analysis," *Balance Sheet,* Vol. XI (March, 1930), pp. 199-202. A job analysis of 450 business concerns.

MERRILL, F. E., "The Formulation of Criteria for the Evaluation of Typing Textbooks and a Comparison of Current Typewriting Texts According to the Criteria," master's thesis (New York University, 1931). A study of the collection of typewriting texts in the office of the Department of Business Education of New York University.

NICHOLS, F. G., "A New Conception of Office Practice," *Harvard Bulletins in Education,* No. XII (Harvard University Press, 1927). A study by questionnaire to discover the work done by clerical workers in large offices.

NYQUIST, R. E., "A Job Analysis of Bookkeepers' Duties," *Research Studies in Commercial Education,* Vol. II, University of Iowa, Monographs in Education, First Series, No. 8 (January 1, 1928). A job analysis of bookkeeping in Mason City, Iowa.

TYRELL, Doris, "An Activity Analysis of Secretarial Duties as a Basis for an Office Practice Course," *Journal of Experimental Education,* Vol. I (June, 1933), pp. 323-340. She considered the problem of making use of the results of job analyses once the analyses have been completed on the junior-college level.

WRIGHT, Edith A., compiler, *Bibliography of Research Studies in Education, 1930-1931,* U. S. Dept. of the Interior, Office of Education, Bulletin No. 16 (Government Printing Office, 1932), pp. 351-360. This bibliography contains references to such material as McAlmon's survey of needs of commercial education at the junior-college level. Milley on business skills and information necessary to a complete understanding of a selected list of magazines, Croasdale on procedures for analysis of vocational activities, etc.

Young, Bessie A., "The Relative Efficiency of Single and Double Periods in Typewriting," *Research Studies in Commercial Education V*, University of Iowa Studies in Education, Vol. VIII, No. III, Monographs in Education, No. 12 (University of Iowa, 1932), pp. 136-148. She reported that a single period of typing was relatively more efficient than a double period.

HOME ECONOMICS

Adams, Lucy, "Objectives in Teaching Family Relationships," *Journal of Home Economics,* Vol. XXIV (February, 1932), pp. 121-125. "Master farm homemakers" agreed, after checking objectives in family relations compiled from courses of study, that most of them should be included in the school curriculum.

Amidon, Edna P., "The Teaching of Science Related to the Home," *Federal Board for Vocational Education* Bulletin, No. 158 (Government Printing Office, 1931). A study of the general-science needs of high-school home-economics pupils.

Beeman, Mary, "A Brief Study of the Interests of High School Girls in Home Activities," *Journal of Home Economics,* Vol. XXI (December, 1929), pp. 900-904. Pupil interests as expressed by themselves, and as expressed by their teachers were found to differ in some important particulars. The girls' interests were found to change from year to year.

Charters, W. W., "Traits of Homemakers," *Journal of Home Economics,* Vol. XVIII (December, 1926), pp. 673-685. Fifty persons check and add to a list of forty-two traits which were determined by a preliminary study of twelve homes.

Child, Alice M., Niles, Kathryn B., and Kolshorn, Agnes, *Food Preparation Studies* (John Wiley and Sons, 1932). They indicate some principles in food preparation essential in home economics.

Cook, Rosamond C., "Money Management and the Home-Economics Curriculum," *Journal of Home Economics,* Vol. XXIII (April, 1931), pp. 333-336. She reports on a survey of courses of study for analysis of the extent of money-management teaching.

Coon, Beulah I., "What Shall We Teach? Selection of Subject Matter in Relation to Activities of Pupils," *Home Economics News,* Vol. II (August, 1931), p. 73. She compared course of study content with home activities in one locality, finding little correlation between the school achievement and the home responsibilities of pupils. This was especially true where the course content was almost entirely theoretical.

Dyer, A. R., *The Placement of Home Economics Content in Junior and Senior High School* (Teachers College, Columbia University, 1927). Based upon the occurrence of topics in present courses of study.

Fresno Public Schools, "Vocational Survey," Department of Superintendence *Fifth Yearbook* (1927), pp. 372-373. A study of the home activities of 300 junior high-school girls.

Good, C. V., "The High School Curriculum in Home Economics," *Journal of Home Economics*, Vol. XIX (December, 1927), pp. 686-690. Analysis of courses of study of the five largest cities in each state.

Hadley, Laura B., "Objectives in Teaching Family Relationships," *Journal of Home Economics,* Vol. XXIV (February, 1932), pp. 125-128. After interviews with 83 mothers, she determined the difficulties in child development and training on which they need help before assuming the obligations of parenthood.

Hastie, M., and Gorton, G., "What Shall We Teach Regarding Clothing and Laundry Problems?" *Journal of Home Economics,* Vol. XVIII (March, 1926), pp. 127-133. A study of the actual sewing and laundry problems in over 4,000 rural and urban homes.

Herrington, Evelyn M., *Homemaking* (D. Appleton-Century Co., 1935). An integrated teaching program.

Humphrey, Alice W., "A Study of Certain Leisure Time Activities and Financial Practices in the Homes of Minnesota High-School Girls," *Abstracts of Unpublished Masters' Theses in the Field of Secondary School Administration,* Bulletin No. 47, Department of Secondary School Principals, National Education Association (March, 1933), pp. 21-23. She found some evidence to justify the assumption that training in home economics produces an interest in home activities.

Kneeland, Hildegarde, "Leisure of Home-Makers Studied for Light on Standards of Living," *Yearbook of Agriculture* (Government Printing Office, 1932), pp. 562-564. From records of adult activities in the home, she compiled a list of activities which go to make up a working week of from 52½ to 61½ hours.

Leighton, F. H., "A Basis for Building a Course in Economics of the Home," *Contributions to Education,* No. 459 (Teachers College, Columbia University, 1931). By means of personal interviews with 75 families, the errors of consumption were determined.

Lindquist, Ruth, *The Family in the Present Social Order* (University of North Carolina Press, 1931). The greatest causes of fatigue, in the opinion of 306 "successful" homemakers, were child development, laundering, and care of the house. Caring for the house, children's training, and maintaining a satisfactory standard of living on an inadequate income were the chief causes of worry.

Maclary, Dorothy, "A Study of Curricula in Thirty-two Representative Institutions to Determine Typical Courses, Curricular Practices, and Methods of Teaching in the Education of Home Economics Teachers," unpublished thesis (University of Minnesota, 1933). A study of curricula in thirty-two teacher training institutions in home economics.

Nofsker, Julia F., "Home Economics Objectives as Shown in a Survey of Educational Literature," *Journal of Home Economics,* Vol. XXIV

(April, 1932), pp. 353-364. Personal values rank first in importance, family and homemaking values second, and general social values are considered least important as objectives for home-economics courses as expressed in educational books and periodicals, government bulletins, and reports and yearbooks from educational organizations.

PETERS, C. C., "The Objectives of Education for Worthy Home Membership," National Society for the Study of Educational Sociology, *Second Yearbook* (1929), pp. 136-147. The author collected the qualities and actions of an efficient husband or wife from 100 graduate students.

PHILLIPS, Velma, "Evidence of the Need of Education for Efficient Purchasing." *Contributions to Education,* No. 447 (Teachers College, Columbia University, 1931). She found much evidence that homemakers need training for efficient purchasing.

President's Research Committee on Social Trends, *Recent Social Trends in the United States* (McGraw-Hill Book Co., 1933), Chs. III, IV, VIII, XIII, XV, XVIII, XXIV. The committee summarized several trends dealing with the family and its functions, people as consumers, childhood and youth, new inventions, etc.

RHYAN, Ivah M., "Home Problems for Boys," *Journal of Home Economics,* Vol. XXII (March, 1930), pp. 191-196. She found that reports from representative men in business and from boys differed but little in their ideas of what phases of home economics would be most valuable to them.

SHERBON, Florence B., and FERRIS, Emily, "The Experience and Opinions of 350 Married Women Graduates of the University of Kansas," *Kansas Studies in Education,* Vol. II, No. 2 (University of Kansas, 1931). A study of graduates of the University of Kansas showed the feeling that the University would have proved a greater aid to the home if it had given more assistance on establishment and management of the home, and on other kindred problems of health and relationships.

TURNER, Marcia E., and HALL, Mabel M., "Objectives for High-School Courses in Home Relationships," *Journal of Home Economics,* Vol. XXIII (March, 1931), pp. 238-242. They surveyed courses, and compiled a list of course objectives in home-relationships teaching.

WHITCOMB, E. S., "Progress in Home Economics Education," United States Bureau of Education Bulletin, No. 4 (1926). Leading educators state the general objectives of home economics.

WILSON, Mary A., "A Study of Homemaking Activities of Girls in Rural Mississippi," State Board for Vocational Education, Bulletin No. 65 (1931). She found that ninth-grade girls in rural Mississippi, who had had no courses in home economics, failed to utilize even meager labor-saving devices.

WOODHOUSE, Chase Going, "Study of 250 Successful Families," *Social Forces,* Vol. VIII (June, 1930), pp. 511-532. She set up some of the characteristics of family success as found in 250 successful families, emphasizing those concerned with economics.

INDUSTRIAL ARTS

ALBERTY, Luman H., "Analytical Selection and Evaluation of Auto Related Subject-Matter for Auto Trade Classes," Master's Thesis (University of Wisconsin, 1931). He obtained information from eighty-one teachers and tradesmen throughout the country, and listed teaching aids, methods of selection of subject-matter, and common teaching practices in related subjects.

ALDERSON, Glenn A., "Trends in the Industrial Arts Teacher-Training Curricula for the Past Ten Years," Master's Thesis (Iowa State College, 1932). He tried to determine and indicate trends in industrial arts teacher-training courses after studying the curricula of twenty institutions.

American Vocational Association, Committee on Standards, *Standards of Attainment in Industrial-Arts Teaching* (1931). A list of things which junior high-school pupils should be able to know and do at the end of their junior high-school term, according to judgment of the committee and interested persons who were solicited to aid in the project.

BAUERSFELD, Albert, "Industrial Arts Education in Large City High Schools," *Education,* Vol. LII (June, 1932), pp. 587-589. After studying graduates of four-year technical high schools, he concluded that a technical education is excellent preparation for all avenues of life, and that a four-year technical education pays dividends as a preparation for the future productive period of a worker.

BOTTENSLOG, Fred G., "Home Mechanics Based on Home Repairs in Asheville, N. C.," Master's Thesis (George Peabody College for Teachers, 1931). He analyzed home jobs being done by members of Asheville, N. C., families or outside workmen and grouped them arbitrarily, outlining one job in each to illustrate the kinds of material which might aid in making instruction sheets and in teaching.

CASWELL, William E., "Selecting the Units for the Secondary School Industrial Arts Program," master's thesis (Ohio State University, 1932). From a study of the literature for valuable criteria in selection of units which should be included in industrial-arts programs in secondary school, he presented the major outcomes as a means of focusing attention upon the size of the problem rather than on solution. He concluded that the general shop course gives a better understanding of the interdependence of industries.

CHRISTOPHERSON, Clarence H., "State Courses in the Industrial Arts," master's thesis (University of Minnesota, 1933). He made an analytical study of state industrial-arts courses as to policies and instruments for promotion and supervision.

ELLINGSON, Mark, "Activity Analysis as a Basis for Course Content," *Personnel Journal,* Vol. XII (June, 1933), pp. 12-15. The most difficult task in building a curriculum is selecting the materials which should go into the course.

ERICSON, Emanuel E., *Teaching Problems in Industrial Arts* (Manual Arts Press, 1930), pp. 291-294. Gives five objectives with nineteen subdivisions.

FINK, Charles, "Judgments of Alumni Concerning the Vocational Value of the Courses Offered by Three Technical High Schools in Chicago," master's thesis (Northwestern University, 1932). By means of a questionnaire submitted to 577 graduates of technical schools, he attempted to determine the value of technical training in high schools.

FLEMING, Ralph, "Industrial Arts Practice in Nine Large Cities," *Industrial Education Magazine,* Vol. XXXV (July, 1933), p. 9. In attempting to determine modern trends in industrial arts, he studied the subject in typical American cities. He found interest in general shopwork as keen as that in unit shopwork, though the quality was not so high, due to the shorter amount of time devoted to each particular type of work.

HALE, William P., "Mechanical-Drawing Content Based on Consumers' Needs," Master's Thesis (Iowa State College, 1932). He analyzed various kinds of drawings found in newspapers, magazines, advertisements and circulars, and textbooks for mechanical drawing. His suggestions are based on the consumers' needs.

HARTMAN, Harry V., "Organization and Content of Courses in Auto Mechanics for Junior and Senior High Schools," Master's Thesis (Iowa State College, 1931). He analyzed the auto-mechanics trade. and organized courses of study for junior and senior high school.

JACKEY, David F., "An Evaluation of the Basic Curriculum of Vocational Teacher-Training in Trade and Industrial Education in the State of California," Doctor's Thesis (University of Pittsburgh, 1933). In a survey to evaluate the basic curriculum of vocational teacher-training in trade and industrial education in California, he studied various sources, and recommended tentative changes on the basis of present inadequacies which he found.

JENNINGS, Royal F., "Current Changes in Automotive Service Occupations," master's thesis (University of Minnesota, 1932). He suggests that modern trends in automotive service occupations be used as a basis for curriculum construction.

NEWKIRK, Louis V., "The General Shop," *Education,* Vol. LII (June, 1932), pp. 596-600. Mentions several objectives of industrial arts for adults.

Pittsburgh Public Schools, Department of Curriculum Study, *Courses of Study for Experimentation, 1931-1933.* The details and workings of an experiment with courses of study for mechanical drawing, metal work and wood work is the subject of this review.

PREBBLE, Fred, "Organized Material for Curricula in Home Economics for Boys," master's thesis (Iowa State College, 1933). He obtained material from homes of eighth- and ninth-grade pupils, teachers, principals, superintendents, college professors, and persons who have written magazine articles on the subject, and outlined courses in home mechanics for boys.

ROBERTS, W. E., "Progress and Accomplishment in Manual Arts Teaching," *Education,* Vol. LII, pp. 590-591. Gives concise statement of objectives.

248   PRINCIPLES OF CURRICULUM MAKING

Schweickhard, Dean M., "Comparative Objectives of Industrial Arts Education," *Education,* Vol. LII (June, 1932), pp. 569-573. General aims of industrial arts from elementary through high school, as seen by the Assistant Superintendent of Minneapolis.

Smith, Homer J., "The Industrial Arts Teachers' Responsibility," *Education,* Vol. LII (June, 1932), pp. 605-607. Enumerates six proposed objectives.

Smith, Lester C., "Developing a General Shop Course," *Industrial Arts and Vocational Education,* Vol. XXII, p. 104. A study of the one hundred most frequent male occupations to determine what basic aids may be given in industrial arts.

Snedden and Warner, *Reconstruction of Industrial Arts Courses* (Bureau of Publications, Teachers College, Columbia University, 1927).

Strube, Paul E., "A Study of Content for High School Farm-Shops," Master's Thesis (Ohio State University, 1932). He surveyed the "know" and "do" requirements for high-school farm-shop students as presented by Master Farmers and county agents in Kansas, and reported an analysis of jobs to determine difficulty, range, and importance of skills and information.

Vocational Education Survey of Minneapolis, United States Department of Labor, Bureau of Labor Statistics, *Vocational Education Series,* No. 1 (1916). Technique explained and findings shown in Appendix B.

Voth, John J., "An Analysis of Mechanical-Drawing Textbooks Used in Iowa High Schools for the Purpose of Determining a Reading Vocabulary for Mechanical Drawing," Master's Thesis, (Iowa State College, 1933). A vocabulary study, based on selection from 102,000 running words in currently used mechanical-drawing textbooks, of 1,425 words, which he presents in order of frequency as well as alphabetically.

Warner, William E., *Policies in Industrial Arts Education* (Ohio State University Press, 1928). On page 8 is a tabulation of the trend of change in objectives. On pages 33-45 is a report of the findings of a jury of sixty industrial-arts professors and teachers concerning proper objectives.

Yager, Sylvan A., "Objectives of the General Shop," *Industrial Arts Magazine,* Vol. XXXIV, p. 152. Mentions seven objectives of the general shop in particular and of industrial arts in general.

PART III
THE UNIT OF WORK

CHAPTER VII

LEARNING ACTIVITIES AND TEACHING MATERIALS

Throughout the country there appears to be a woeful unawareness of the seriousness of the problem of selecting learning activities and of the techniques essential for its satisfactory solution. While teachers and administrators are generally interested in checking the grade placement of teaching materials, they apparently rely almost entirely on the judgment of a group of teachers or of a single teacher. In many cases, content is being selected and varied according to the nature of the class or the ability of a majority of the students, without consideration of the necessity for selecting and varying the objectives according to the grade or ability of all the students. Any procedure which does not integrate objectives and content cannot be justified in terms of the complete reorganization of a learning program and, when carried out in a haphazard and piece-meal fashion, it usually serves only to confuse the instructors and disintegrate educational work.

A method has been developed in the last few years in which the establishment of standards or criteria for the selection of content is basic, and by which it is possible to insure a synthesis of content with the validated objectives. In establishing such standards, attention must be centered first, upon pupil activities which are essential as integrating materials, and, second, upon learning experiences which are introduced as differentiating aspects of the program of studies. While the same standards can be used in both cases, integration and differentiation materials must be weighted differently by the committee. The scale of weight must be determined by the use that is to be made of the prospective content.

251

I. CRITERIA FOR THE SELECTION OF CONTENT WHEN TEACHING
MATERIALS ARE ORGANIZED IN ADVANCE

In this section, attention will be centered upon both objectives and content, since these two aspects of the course of study are fundamental when preparation is being made in advance for the education of children. It has been stated from time to time that these aspects are so intimately related that one cannot be studied adequately without making a careful analysis of the other.

In many school systems at the present time—and this was almost universally true in the past—content is being selected without reference to any list of standards or criteria. Even as late as the beginning of the twentieth century, difficulty and logical organization of content were satisfactory criteria for those who believed in faculty psychology. A student's wits would be sufficiently sharpened and his powers of reasoning, memory, imagination, etc., definitely improved by any content that was difficult and carefully organized. In addition, it was regarded as highly satisfactory if the student happened to dislike this difficult material, although this condition can hardly be dignified by being called a criterion.

With the passing of faculty psychology, the responsibility for selecting content has been relegated to classroom teachers and writers of textbooks. Both have presented at least one weakness in fulfilling the requirements for an organizer of content. First, the teacher has to use his own judgment in selecting content that will represent educational experiences for pupils of a particular level of ability. While all educators and administrative officers are working on grade placement and ability placement, few data are available for the classroom teacher. Second, while it must be admitted that many recent textbooks show the influence of scientific data regarding the suitability of teaching materials, many other textbooks still in use were published before these data were known. The importance of this statement is apparent when one realizes that any book published as early as the beginning of the last decade could not have been based upon scientific studies of teaching materials for particular grade levels. Unfortunately, there are two significant reasons for the retention of an out-of-date book in a school system. First, the school district may have purchased a large number of these books and economy may demand that they be worn out on the children. Second, textbook companies have been able in some cases to exert enough political and personal power to retain the adoption of an out-of-date book in a city, county, or state.

In order to select content, the curriculum or course of study committee should set up criteria or standards by which activities, experiences, information, etc., can be judged. Otherwise, they may find that there is little, if any, relationship between the specific objectives and the learning activities of the pupils. The following criteria will be of value to the committee when it has reached the point of determining the content of the course:

Criterion 1. Can pupils at this particular grade level attain mastery of these facts, activities, etc.?

Two problems are implied in this criterion. The first has to do with grade placement, the importance of which depends on whether the materials are a part of the core curriculum or of merely elective courses.

The second problem is concerned with the degree of mastery that can be attained by a particular ability group at a given grade level in a given time. If mastery cannot be achieved at the grade level or in the ability group under consideration, it is foolhardy to anticipate growth and educational progress through use of this material. Mastery must be thought of in terms of the students, and the levels of mastery should be established through an ability grouping program or through differentiation in the classroom. Brilliant students can easily and enthusiastically attain success in handling materials which demand reasoning and the development of logical conclusions, while those who are in the lower levels have difficulty in attaining the basic skills and essential information.

The capacity of the class level for which the material is intended must be carefully studied. Any other procedure is as unfair as to send a heterogeneous group out into an orchard to pick fruit. The tall children would fill their baskets, the short ones would secure little, if any, of the fruit. However, the ones who are short in stature could have devoted their time and energies profitably to picking gooseberries or blackberries. Each would attain results, although of different nature, if given appropriate opportunity. The basic elements of good citizenship can be taught to all, barring the feeble-minded, just as the essential techniques of picking fruit can be mastered by every one. Differentiation in the class or grade necessitates the careful evaluation of the material introduced to meet the needs of particular groups and individuals.

Average ability, or better, is required for the successful completion of a commercial course and the rendering of efficient service in the business world. However, Miss Wilson, principal of the South Philadelphia High School for Girls, has demonstrated that girls with low ability ratings can attain a high level of performance in a few specific duties in the commercial field. The same girls could never make a credit in the regular commercial course, but the business men of Philadelphia find them acceptably trained to do one or more specific and definite duties in their offices. This is a remarkable example of the adjustment of content to the ability of the pupils, rather than attempting to adjust the pupils to the content.

There is great need in all school systems for scientific studies of the difficulty of content. A few cities have undertaken such studies, and in some instances outstanding results have been secured. It is highly significant to find that materials, as organized in a particular course, are suited to the ability of 50 per cent of the pupils in the class. How immeasurably such studies must assist the teacher and students in those classes in securing a reorganization of the program!

Burch [1] found that a course in literature, which was in use in the classes of the junior and senior high school, was suited

[1] Mary C. Burch, *Determination of a Content of a Course in Literature of Suitable Difficulty for Junior and Senior High School Students*, Genetic Psychological Monographs, Vol. X (September, 1928), pp. 170-332.

to the ability of only 50 per cent of the students in those classes. Her problem is so significant and so scientifically worked out that a careful analysis is presented here for the guidance of the reader.

A. Problems which concerned Miss Burch:
1. To what extent do the selections deemed suitable for literature differ from one another in difficulty?
2. To what extent do the students in the secondary-school grades (7—12) differ in their ability to understand these selections?
3. What degree of difficulty in literature constitutes optimum material for a group of students having a given amount of comprehension ability?

B. The solution of these problems:
Step 1. She found the objectives of English as presented by various committees and commissions.
Step 2. She determined how nearly the school was presenting the material suggested for the realization of their objectives. Material was listed under the names of the authors, rather than by individual books. Thus, the name of Cooper was used in place of the titles of any of his books, as *The Last of the Mohicans* or *The Deerslayer*.
Step 3. Samples were selected from these books which were representative of the difficulty of the book. The judgment of the author was used here exclusively.
Step 4. Questions were prepared on the samples. These were of the multiple-choice form. Two tests of the same material were arranged to be given on different days in order that the reliability might be checked.
Step 5. To eliminate the embarrassing fact that a student might have read one book and not another and, in his answers, make one book appear easier than another, obscure books by the same author and of approximately the same difficulty were included in the test.
Step 6. (a) Tests were submitted to experts in order to arrange the questions in order of difficulty. (b) A vote of six out of seven experts was required in order to determine the validity of the questions.
Step 7. There was a preliminary trial of the material on students in order to check difficulty, order of questions, and amount of time required for the test.
Step 8. Evaluation of the test in terms of the reaction of good and poor students to the questions. Any question was chal-

lenged which did not show better scores by higher groups of students.

Step 9. The reliability of the tests was determined by giving A and B sections of each test to all grades to be considered.

Step 10. The tests were given to the students and graded.

C. The results of the study indicated:

1. Fifty per cent of each grade (7 to 12 inclusive) were studying material unsuited to their needs.

2. Each grade should be divided into ability groups and content built up for each group.

Criterion 2. Can the content be made of interest to the students? The objectives of the unit or course indicate the lines along which the pupil is to advance, while the content suggested represents the experiences which are to make these projected hopes and plans a reality to the student. It has been noted that the objectives should be interesting to the student; that is, the student must be interested in achieving the goal. Teachers have been assured in many instances that if the students were interested in attaining the particular goals included they would automatically be interested in the content provided for that purpose. This does not follow in all subject-matter materials. An objective may be interesting and stimulating to the student; the content introduced for the realization of this objective may be void of both characteristics.

In checking content according to this criterion, it is important to have in mind that there are two types of pupil interest. In the first place, the interest that is inherent in the student must be considered. There are certain interests which are a vital part of his existence, and the educational problem is to present opportunities for the fruition of these intrinsic interests. Such interests are of primary importance in selecting content. Second, there are interests which are extrinsic, if known at all. They are apparently extraneous to the life of students, and the organization of material to realize extrinsic objectives may well be questioned. They will never be of value, and so they deserve little consideration unless it can be pointed out clearly that the development of an interest far removed from the present life of the student may have the effect of making other material of intrinsic importance. It may thus become a part of his life and of vital significance.

For example, two boys are taking a course in physiology. The first boy has determined already to be a physician and surgeon and has an intrinsic interest in the subject. The other is not interested in the subject, but loves to play football and engage in all the athletic activities of the school. He has a vital interest in the development of athletic prowess, skill, and proficiency. This interest may be the means of developing an intrinsic interest in the subject-matter of physiology. However, his achievement will not be great unless his interest in physiology becomes, of itself, an intrinsic part of his educational program.

Pollack [2] has studied the intrinsic interests of children in the organization of materials for a course in general science. A survey of this type presents data which are of incalculable worth in analyzing present interests and determining the possibilities of developing desirable interests. He says:

The content of what we teach is to take root in the everyday life of the child. Obviously then we must determine the pupil's environment if we would know what content to teach.

He suggests three methods of determining this environment:

1. Canvass students' science environment through home, street, and camp, etc.
2. Organize science hunts. Divide students into groups, each following a previously determined course, and have them bring back long lists of science items which they would like to have discussed.
3. Each student to present five carefully thought out questions which he wishes to have answered in science study.

He decided further not to allow the text to determine the course but to base the work upon the interest of the child himself. He decided also to make use of any texts and other readings which would help.

[2] C. A. Pollack, "Children's Interests as the Basis of General Science," *Educational Research Bulletin*, Vol. III, No. 1 (Ohio State University, January 9, 1924).

Criterion 3. Does the content under consideration have a high degree of utility in present social activities? Those materials which provide a training in the basic systems of conduct are the core curricular subject-matter. As we proceed outward from this central core of the curriculum, we have materials that are relatively less important in current living. This process continues until a summary of all materials which are found only on the fringes as far as utility is concerned enables the curriculum builder to differentiate between those having high utility to-day and those having less and less present worth.

Watson[3] found that much of the old content of physics was not considered valuable by the parents of the children in school, while much material in the subject-matter field, which was not included, was considered very valuable by these adults.

Herriott[4] determined the elements of the physics course of study entering into daily activities of six representative groups of people. He organized three categories, which includes a total of 576 activities, involving mechanics, heat, light, sound, magnetism, electricity, and invisible radiation. The categories were:

a. Those things which people do for themselves.
b. Those things which people have others do for them.
c. Those things which people think about.

This criterion has become more important as society has entered into a highly specialized era. There are more facilities and techniques available in the twentieth century, and the results of scientific investigations that will establish valid teaching materials according to this criterion are becoming available. There are still many difficulties involved in the application of the criterion, but its importance in determining teaching content demands that it be employed by every committee.

In one sense, two criteria are suggested in this section. These are (1) the social value of the material to-day, and (2) the

[3] C. H. Watson, "A Critical Study of the Content of High School Physics with Respect to Its Social Value," *School Review,* Vol. XXXIV (November, 1926), pp. 688-697.

[4] M. E. Herriott, "Life Activities and the Physics Curriculum," *School Science and Mathematics,* Vol. XXIV (June, 1924), pp. 631-34.

social significance of the material for the future. However, since life and education are continuous processes and the activities of to-day are intimately related to those of to-morrow, it is safe to assume that high utility in the present will have great significance in the future. The use of this criterion will depend on the assistance of "frontier thinkers" when political and social issues are being considered. Highly-trained scientists in the laboratories will contribute the probable trends in scientific development in the immediate future which are of educational interest now.

This criterion is fundamental in all content which is introduced for integrating purposes. The high frequency of certain skills, facts, activities, etc., in modern life demands a basic training in them. It is important that outcomes for this type of content be expressed in terms of like-mindedness.

Criterion 4. Will the content have a high degree of utility in the future lives of the students? If this criterion were not used and those which have been previously mentioned were accepted by the committee, society would develop very slowly, to say the least. It was pointed out in the chapter on Principles that frontier thinkers would have to suggest to us desirable trends in society in the immediate future. Workers in sociology, political science, philosophy, psychology, and all fields of science who qualify as men of vision can render a service to the curriculum maker at this point.

Several examples may be cited of the values accruing to a program which is far-seeing:

1. The direct election of United States senators by the people became a reality when the generation which had learned of the evils of the old system became eligible to vote. The remedy for the situation was found as soon as the younger generation had reached the voting age.
2. The campaign for woman's suffrage centered in the schools. Little progress was made until students who had been trained to think liberally of the status of the sexes were admitted to suffrage.
3. By way of comparison, we are witnessing in the administration of President Roosevelt changes in theories and practices of production and consumption which would have required another

generation, at least, to realize through educational programs. It is possible that an educational program would have required fifty years in order to achieve effectively the eradication of child labor. One of the fortunate results of the exigencies of the depression was its immediate abolition.

Criterion 5. Will these activities or learning experiences contribute definitely to the achievement of the objective? In the past the tendency in both textbooks and courses of study has been to organize a set of objectives and then ignore them to a large extent as far as the development of the content was concerned. The problem presented by this criterion is the determination of the value of present content as compared with other available content in the realization of the goal of the course.

Hopkins and Paul [5] showed that writers of mathematics textbooks for junior high-school pupils varied greatly in objectives and material for the realization of common objectives. As soon as lists of objectives became more extensive, greater difficulty in organizing material was observed.

The validation of the objectives in the course and the rigid checking of every item of content against these objectives would do much for most courses of study at the present time. Some teachers refuse to follow the course and emphasize for a month or more aspects of the course in which they are interested, but which may merit a treatment of only a few days in terms of student objectives. An ever-extending introduction to a course is another subterfuge which teachers use to include extraneous material in the course of study.

In view of these facts, teaching materials should be evaluated by scientific studies, using in many instances a statistical organization of the data. The study by Burch, which was previously mentioned, is an example of a scientific procedure which was used in organizing the content for a course in literature for the junior and senior high school. This criterion can be stated as follows : *Content must be developed directly and specifically from validated objectives.*

[5] L. T. Hopkins and F. S. Paul, "Analysis of Thirteen Sets of Junior-High-School Mathematics," *Fifth Yearbook,* Department of Superintendence (1927), pp. 202-207.

As soon as the objectives have been obtained, validated, and grouped, the content can be developed as the next logical step in the construction of the course of study. This applies to all sections of the course that can be standardized and made to serve a general purpose for a number of individual students. Again it should be emphasized that indirect and intrinsic aspects of the content can be introduced from day to day as the life situations, needs, and interests of the pupils dictate. Since it is impossible to determine these daily specific needs and interests of children, adjustments must be made daily to adapt the classwork to the pupils. The superior teacher has the insight and understanding to make adequate provision for these emergencies.

It is opportune to mention the position taken by those educators who maintain that neither objectives nor content should be determined in advance of the teaching situations. These teachers and administrators maintain that only objectives and content which are established daily will have a sufficient correlation with pupil experience to promote worthwhile incentives for learning on the part of the pupils. Since pupil participation in the learning situation is the *sine qua non* of the classroom, it is essential that only such content be introduced as is related specifically to the present experiences and interests of the learner. Any other procedure, according to the extreme activity group, encourages passive learning or "inactive" activity. This is another way of saying that results will probably be negligible or negative, unless pupil participation is given paramount consideration.

The curriculum committee which overlooks the value of the principles of these activity groups will be very unwise. That part of the program which develops from pupil-teacher co-operation from day to day is significant. However, the extreme claim that the curriculum should be organized solely in terms of child interests and experiences contains a number of fallacies. All the objectives and the content for their realization cannot be organized by the pupils and the teacher to meet daily life situations. The following quotation from Kilpatrick is a moderate statement of the position of the activity group:

Many are the proposed plans of attack upon curriculum making. Most of these assume, naïvely it would seem, that we must first make a curriculum, then teach it. Such an assumption is by no means necessary; in fact it may be as wrong as it would be to say that a tennis player must fix in advance the order of his strokes. It may be, who knows, that a curriculum can no more be contrived in advance than can the succession of strokes in a tennis match. In both cases thinking should look as far into the future as it can, and prepare as adequately as feasible for what is foreseen; but the teacher's thinking can never take the place of what the children only can supply.[6]

The Educational Creed of the Curriculum Committee of the social-science teachers of the Ann Arbor, Michigan, public schools presents, in part, an excellent statement of a defensible position in this long controversy concerning the time of organizing teaching materials:

We Believe: That the CURRICULUM should be organized in terms of experience.

That these experiences integrate subject-matter and eliminate sharply drawn distinctions between the conventional school subjects.

That such a curriculum is based upon the assumption that subjects of study, as organized bodies of information, should be the end point and not the beginning of an educative experience.

That within certain limits teachers and pupils should be given a large degree of freedom in choosing and organizing the particular unit experiences which will enter into any grade.

That these experiences should be so chosen and arranged that participation in life on increasingly higher levels of achievement is possible.[7]

These statements have emphasized the importance of pupil-teacher coöperation in the organization of teaching materials. It is essential, at this point, that the necessity of determining

---

[6] W. H. Kilpatrick, "Illustrations in English work in the Junior High School" (Bureau of Publications, Teachers College, Columbia University, 1925). Foreword.

[7] G. Robert Koopman, and Others, "Helping Children Experience the Realities of the Social Order" (Board of Education, Ann Arbor, Michigan, 1933), p. 5.

validated objectives and content, in advance of the participation of the students in the activities of the classroom, be emphasized, since it effects and modifies the part to be played by both the teachers and the pupils. The problem is stated in the fourth paragraph of the Creed, which is quoted above, *i.e.,* "That within certain limits the teachers and pupils. . . ." It is imperative that these limits be defined and that those materials which can be organized "on the spot" be compared with those which must be organized in advance.

Criterion 6. Will the content selected have propædeutic values for other courses in later or higher education? In the past this criterion has been overemphasized. It has a place in the consideration of the committee but does not merit consideration which is likely to develop a malformed course in terms of student objectives.

It has been noted in previous chapters that college entrance requirements have played a great part in stimulating the close attention of secondary schools to this criterion. In college, the prerequisite complex has promoted sequential organizations which have little justification other than guaranteeing that all courses shall secure at least a minimum of students. Most of the studies of the essential features of prerequisite courses, which have been considered as a fundamental background before matriculation in advanced courses is available, have shown little validity in these assumptions.

For an effective integration program, it is apparent to every student interested in course of study construction, that every organization of subject-matter probably contains material that is essential for further learning in the field, and in pursuing other fields, as well as offering an opportunity to develop proficiency in several basic skills, habits, etc. This type of material is selected not in accordance with the criterion of interest, but according to needs. The teacher's place in the program is that of educational guide. Often, material which cannot be justified because of intrinsic interests can be made stimulating through extrinsic interests. As an illustration, the multiplication tables cannot be of intrinsic interest, and they may test the ingenuity of the teachers to develop satisfactory extrinsic interests in them. However, if the student is to develop proficiency in many phases of the school and of life activities, these tables represent a necessary and essential phase of the integrating program of the elementary school.

Powers and Uhl have summarized the types and characteristics of mental functions as follows:

Six general types of mental functions have been implied in the preceding sections: (1) problem solving; (2) acquisition of knowledge; (3) acquisition of skill; (4) social competence; (5) creative activity; and (6) esthetic experiencing.

All progressive conduct, *i.e.*, all educative activity, consists of improved adjustment of the individual to the external world and to the conditions which exist within himself. This improved adjustment consists of the development of modes of indirect responses to stimuli. Excepting cases in which this improved adjustment is due to chance, it is, at least in part, a product of problem solving, and, in part, a product of the acceptance of some one else's solutions of problems. In this sense all six of the mental functions just named are fundamentally processes of adjustment and, therefore, in part, problem solving. The other five are in this sense special applications or subdivisions of the first function. A relatively unanalytical or complacent pupil may be unable to state clearly the life problem which confronts him as he acquires knowledge or skill. Ordinarily, however, his training is planned so that he acquires knowledge, as in science or history, for the purpose of solving a problem or avoiding a problem by acquiring some one else's solutions and thus improving his adjustment to this world. In social life also, one may find that certain reactions yield desired results; such a discovery through problem solving often leads to further problems which involve social competence. A pupil's mathematics or music or any other subject may be used by any resourceful teacher to suggest activity that, to the pupil, is original or, in a sense, creative. A problem in creative activity may thus arise. This problem may, in turn, as in the "creation" of geometrical designs, contribute to the pupil's esthetic experience.[8]

The academic work of the junior college contains some integrating materials, and these increase rapidly in relative importance as one surveys the preceding units: senior high school,

    [8] F. F. Powers and W. L. Uhl, *Psychological Principles of Education* (The Century Company, 1933), pp. 78-79.

junior high school, grammar grades, primary grades, and kindergarten. The diagram on page 266 illustrates the place of integrating and differentiating materials in the school system up to the university level.

A glance at this diagram will indicate clearly the importance of this criterion in the determination of content. Every student studies a basic content which is essential in his preparation for further education and for ultimate citizenship. If the material can meet this criterion during the first fourteen grades of the school program, it must be given a place in the content of some course. However, the committee must be ever zealous and cautious in admitting that certain content fulfils this standard. This criterion has been overemphasized in the past to the detriment of the training of the children. As soon as teaching material or subject-matter fields have ceased to have justifiable objectives, an immediate move is made by their adherents to demand that this content be included because of its propædeutic values. To-day, thousands upon thousands of high-school students are preparing for colleges and universities which they never will enter. Much light would be thrown upon the American school system if all teaching materials were checked carefully against this standard.

Criterion 7. Does the content articulate with materials that have been presented in the lower units of the school system and with more advanced materials which will be presented to the students in this or in other subject-matter fields in later grades? This criterion, as well as a similar one in educational objectives, will do much to prevent the deadening effect of having to repeat material from course to course and year to year. This does not mean that the same topic cannot be treated in successive grades. It does mean, however, that in case the material is introduced more than once in the educational experiences of the child it must (1) be presented in relation to other material which is new and which gives insight into the wider and more extensive use of the material, (2) be presented to realize an entirely new set of objectives from those emphasized in previous grades, which will add to the comprehension of the student, and (3) be presented

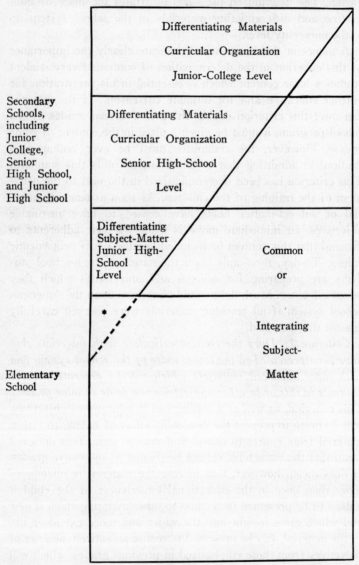

* An insignificant amount of differentiating subject-matter.

for the realization of a more highly refined set of objectives which involves standards of attainment not contemplated in the previous contacts with the material.

There is also the problem of articulating or correlating teaching materials which are allocated to different subject-matter fields in the same unit of the school system. There has been a tendency to organize material into fields of study rather than subject-matter fields. Connor made the following report at the Atlantic City meeting of the Department of Secondary-School Principals in 1930: [9]

One example of collecting scattered courses under one head is the new social-science course in which history, geography, civics, occupational information, and current events are organized as one unified course taught to all pupils one period every day or five times a week. Tests and measurements reveal the fact that achievements are higher; and financial accounting, that expenditures for teaching are lower.

The full effect of the improvement in instruction and savings may not be felt for some years to come. However, results to date are encouraging and administrative persistence is bringing the reward: a little more education for a little less money.

Criterion 8. Does the content present the breadth and possibilities of intensive training necessary to meet the fundamental and basic career needs of the pupils?

A glance at the diagram on page 266 indicates that an increasing amount of the content beginning with the junior high-school grades is differentiating in character and provides for the organization of individual and administrative curricula. The objectives of these curricula represent educational, career, and life needs of these pupils. It is apparent at once that materials introduced for purposes of differentiation must meet the requirements of this standard satisfactorily.

The committee can well afford to give serious consideration to this criterion. Every year, as the enrolment in the educational institutions increases, the career needs of a larger percentage

[9] W. L. Connor, *Bulletin* of the Department of Secondary-School Principals (Published by the Department, March, 1930), pp. 99-129.

are being more or less satisfactorily met. Educators have only begun to study the problem of differentiating programs for pupils.

Criterion 9. The development of the content should be for extended periods (kindergarten to senior high school) and should proceed from "concrete" to "abstract." This principle must be applied at every level in order that the content may be related to some basic and fundamental phase of the pupils' activities and interests. Otherwise the educational growth will be haphazard and disjointed.

Comenius contended that the elements of all subjects should be begun early and gradually widened in their extent and complexity. In the transition from unit to unit in the school system, the pupil proceeds through many subjects in a spiral fashion. United States history is studied in the elementary grades, the junior high school, the senior high school, junior college, and the university. There is danger that the pupil will devote too much time to a field and will be bored by extended or intensive treatment after the introductory work has been completed. However, it is apparent that such a system provides excellent reviews and makes it impossible for permanent misunderstandings to develop as a result of the initial treatment.

Herbert Spencer emphasized the fact that teachers are too apt to begin with principles rather than particulars. The inference is that in all cases it is more difficult for the child to understand rules, abstractions, and generalizations than it is to attain mastery of facts and processes. While in general one is inclined to accept Spencer's position that the generalization must be developed in the learner's mind and grow out of his experiences and activities, yet it must be recognized that in many instances abstractions are really easier to learn than concrete facts. Powers and Uhl assert that it is possible to overemphasize this criterion in the selection of subject-matter. The following statement by them will clarify the problem of inducting the pupil into materials and activities in a field of work: [10]

Object teaching has been refined for use at all levels of instruction. In the nursery, toys which will attract the child and lead to

[10] F. F. Powers and W. L. Uhl, *op. cit.*, pp. 323-24.

some form of manipulative or constructive activity with them are used. Fully made, complicated toys are often rejected, for they are alleged not only to bewilder the child, but also to leave nothing further for the child to do save to operate them in their completed form. Formal kindergarten materials, as cubes, cylinders, spheres, have been rejected, except when supplied in sufficient quantity to allow the child to construct something for himself. The forms, as symbols, are difficult and without significance; but the objects, as construction blocks, are easy and significant for the child. In science laboratories, apparatus is effectively used upon the same basis: simply constructed apparatus is useful as object teaching, if it leads the child to obtain significant data; but apparatus that is complicated may be either unintelligible or so difficult as to prevent the pupil's seeing a relationship between the apparatus and the problem which confronts him. The apparatus used in determining the coefficient of the expansion of heat, together with the mathematics of the problem, is, for example, often overcomplicated, fruitless object teaching for many pupils. The use of technical slides in biology is another example of proceeding too abruptly from the objects that can be used without involved analysis to representations which can be understood only by the pupil who has previously experienced the objects in a simpler form. Complicated object teaching of this sort has progressed to such a point in secondary schools and colleges that attempts to show the relative value of individual laboratory work by pupils and lecture demonstrations by teachers have often shown an apparent advantage of the latter. This difficulty of showing the advantage of direct object teaching when pupils manipulate the objects is probably due to the technical difficulties presented by the objects. The teacher as lecture-demonstrator probably reduces these difficulties by his running account and by pointing to the significant, functional aspects of the apparatus. This point will be discussed later in connection with the presentation of the psychology of curricula.

However, mental growth is always related to a vital life problem and must be initiated with real, genuine experiences. The subject-matter in the school will never be effective in the education of the child until it is related to the activities in which he is participating. This means that the new curriculum of the child will be less formal and will be based on life interests and achievements of the learner.

II. A CURRENT STUDY OF CRITERIA FOR THE SELECTION OF CONTENT

In order that the reader may evaluate the work which is being done in the public schools in solving the problem of selecting content, it is proposed to present a survey of the criteria found in courses recommended by leading cities in curriculum construction. It will be remembered that the courses were selected first, by choosing only cities that had received some recognition for their work in course of study construction, and second, by asking either the superintendent or the director of research to send a recent course which in his opinion represented the finest example of scientific research that his system had produced.

These courses (forty-two in number) were analyzed to determine the criteria used by the various committees in selecting content. As the data accumulated, it became evident that it would be interesting and valuable to present two organizations of these criteria: (1) general criteria for selection of content which are applicable to all courses of study, and (2) criteria for the selection of content which appeared to have special significance in the various subject-matter fields. The latter were organized so that comparisons could be made between the criteria used by various cities in the same subject-matter fields.

A. General criteria for the selection of content. Since various criteria for the selection of content have been analyzed in this chapter, it is not necessary to present here the relative merits of these standards. They are organized so that the reader can see at a glance the frequency of use of these criteria. The forty-two carefully selected courses of study yielded seven criteria which were rather generally used and fifteen others which received scattering votes. The twelve criteria that were most frequently used have been included in the table following.

CRITERIA FOUND IN FORTY-TWO CAREFULLY SELECTED COURSES OF
STUDY FOR SELECTION OF CONTENT APPLICABLE
TO ALL SUBJECTS

1. Must be capable of yielding desirable outcomes in attitudes, appreciations, and ideals, as well as knowledge and skills .... ///// ///// ///// ///// / (21)

2. Should allow for the use of judgment and initiative on the part of the teacher...... ///// ///// ///// ///// (20)

3. Must be adapted to the abilities, physiological tendencies, and different age levels of the pupils .... ///// ///// ///// / (16)

4. Must be based on present needs of the pupil, grow out of life experiences and acquired interests of the pupil ///// ///// ///// (15)

5. Must be true to human experiences .... ///// ///// // (12)

6. Must be justified by one or more of the major objectives of education .... ///// //// (9)

7. Must be interesting and attractive, carry its own motivation .... ///// // (7)

8. Must come from a variety of sources, from widely diverse fields .... //// (4)

9. Scientific methods must be used in its selection........ /// (3)

10. Should permit of modification in order to provide adequately for individual differences .... /// (3)

11. Must be of value in meeting the basic needs of a possible future career .... /// (3)

12. Must be consistent with the abilities of the teacher in service, must be of value to the experienced teacher as well as to the inexperienced teacher .... ///   (3)

B. Criteria of selecting content organized according to subject-matter fields and course of study committees. In this section of the chapter the reader is given an opportunity to compare criteria which were selected by various committees in the same subject-matter fields in different cities, and also to evaluate these subject-matter criteria by general criteria which would be applicable to subject-matter in any field.

The data are organized in the following pages to enable the reader to make direct comparisons for himself of current criteria. The fields of learning are grouped so that the investigator who is interested in a particular subject may turn at once to the data which are available.

HOME ECONOMICS

1. *Idaho State.* Grades 7—12. Date of publication, 1932.
    a. Should be based on present needs of pupils and needs and activities of future homemakers.
    b. Must lead to worthy home membership.
    c. Allow for the use of initiative and judgment by the teacher.

2. *Oakland, California.* Grades 7—9. Date of publication, 1929.
    a. Meet the needs of pre-adolescent girls. The girl has been considered as home-helper, with emphasis upon immediate rather than deferred values.
    b. Should lead to worthy home membership.
    c. Allow use of initiative and judgment by the teacher.

3. *Oakland, California.* Grades 10—12. Date of publication, 1932.
    a. Lead to worthy home membership.
    b. Make possible the wise use of leisure time.
    c. Subject-matter should be organized around problems which grow out of the life experiences of students in the class.

READING

1. *Detroit, Michigan.* Grades 1—6. Date of publication, 1931.
    a. Material must be suited to the abilities of pupils.

    b. Reading must be developed both as a skill and as an art.

    c. Should allow for the use of initiative and judgment by the teacher.

2. *Philadelphia, Pennsylvania.* Grades 4—6. Date of publication, 1930.

    a. Material should have a variety of sources; should come from widely diverse fields.

    b. Suited to the abilities of the pupils.

    c. Interesting to pupils.

    d. Lead to attainment of reading objectives.

    e. Lead to appreciation of literature, as well as developing skill.

    f. Allow for the use of initiative and judgment by the teacher.

3. *Sacramento, California.* Grades 3—6. Date of publication, 1931.

    a. Suited to the interests and abilities of pupils.

    b. Should come from widely diverse fields.

    c. Should lead to appreciation of literature, stimulate thinking, etc., as well as develop skill and knowledge.

4. *San Diego, California.* Grades 1—6. Date of publication, 1928.

    a. Develop attitudes, appreciations, and ideals as well as skill in reading.

    b. Material, procedure, etc., must develop all types of reading abilities.

GEOGRAPHY

1. *Baltimore, Maryland.* Grades 4—6. Date of publication, 1931.

    a. Should be true to human experience.

    b. Indicate relationship between human and natural elements; emphasize the idea of man's adjustment to his natural environment.

    c. Content graded according to the degree of complexity of the geographical relationship involved. (Adjustment to mental maturity.)

2. *New York City.* Grades 4—8. Date of publication, 1928.

    a. Should indicate the relations between human activities and the physical environment.

    b. The value of geography in developing correct attitudes and ideals is emphasized although this is not given among the criteria by which subject-matter was selected.

    c. Should be within the comprehension of the child.

    d. Should be true to human experience.

3. *District of Columbia.* Grades K—6. Date of publication, 1931.

    a. Yield desirable outcomes in attitudes and appreciations, habits, and skills.

    b. Allow for the use of initiative and judgment by the teacher.

4. *Nashville, Tennessee.* Grades 4—9. Date of publication, 1928.
    a. "Should recognize that the human and the physical side of geography are closely related."
    b. Emphasis should be given to facts relating to the life and activities of man, later to the influence of causes in the development of industrial and commercial relations.
    c. Must be within the comprehension of the child. "Children are interested, primarily, in life."
    d. Allow for the use of initiative and judgment by the teacher.

HISTORY

1. *Baltimore, Maryland.* Grades 4—6. Date of publication, 1931.
    a. Subject-matter organized for the "development of an attitude of worldmindedness."
    b. Must emphasize human rather than political aspects and interpretations.
    c. Allow for the use of initiative and judgment by the teacher.

2. *New York City.* Grades 1—8. Date of publication, 1930.
    a. Must emphasize the present results of past events.
    b. Material and content should show realization that any particular event is part of a larger historical movement.
    c. Constitute a vital part of our American tradition.
    d. Develop right attitudes and ideals; must have ethical significance.
    e. Realize relationships between geographical factors and historical events.
    f. Material should be selected that is adapted to the age and understanding of the pupils.
    g. Allow for the use of initiative and judgment by the teacher.

3. *District of Columbia.* Grades 4—6. Date of publication, 1931.
    a. Content and material must emphasize the interaction between external environment and human experience.
    b. Should allow use of initiative and judgment by the teacher.

4. *Omaha, Nebraska.* Grades 1—8. Date of publication, 1923.
    a. Should lead the child to know and appreciate his historical inheritance.
    b. Bring the past within the child's own experience.

5. *Portland, Oregon.* Grades 7—8. Date of publication, 1928.
    a. "Suit the material of instruction to the capability of the child."
    b. Bring the past within the child's own experience.

1. *Portland, Oregon.* Grades 7—8. Date of publication, 1928.
   a. Content should be confined to those aspects of life not touched upon by other subjects.
   b. This simplified content must be presented so that it becomes an actual part of the experience of the pupil.
   c. Allow for the use of initiative and judgment by the teacher.

SOCIAL STUDIES

1. *Denver, Colorado.* Grades 10—12. Date of publication, 1931.
   a. Must be capable of developing correct attitudes toward life.
   b. Should provide for actual social-civic participation on the part of pupils so that the lessons learned will function in their lives.

2. *Kansas City, Missouri.* Grades 1—5. Date of publication, 1930.
   a. Basis underlying the nature of subject-matter.
      (1) Subject-matter should consist of such suggestive lists of pupil experiences and problems as will enable the child to achieve the objective set up.
      (2) It should be in accord with the capacities and with the psychological and physiological tendencies at different age-levels.
      (3) It should form a part of normal child activities and be related to the child's instinctive tendencies and acquired interests.
      (4) It should utilize the immediate interests and purposes of the child and appeal to him as material that is worth while.
      (5) It should furnish opportunity for the development of individuality.
      (6) It should include a general content core which prevails throughout the nation and also additional material adapted to individual and community needs.
      (7) It should give practice in the habits and attitudes necessary for physical and mental health and promote active participation in group life on increasingly high levels.
   b. Basis underlying the selection and organization of subject-matter.
      (1) Subject-matter should be derived through a study of the child, of society, and of the accumulating experience of the race.
      (2) It must be justified by one or more of the seven general

objectives of education set up for the Kansas City schools.

(3) It should be selected in so far as practical from those materials and activities which will serve in the greatest number of life situations.

(4) It should permit of big problems and the unifying, correlating, and tying together of content materials.

(5) It should be so organized as to provide opportunity for both individual and group projects.

(6) Should permit of modification in order to provide adequately for individual differences in capacities, aptitudes, and ambitions.

(7) Should be selected and organized in accord with the following outstanding contributions of modern educacational theory.

1. General transfer is not automatic and inevitable.
2. There is no desirable "discipline" in doing what is merely difficult or distasteful.

3. *Sacramento, California.* Grades 2—5. Date of publication, 1931.

   a. Subject-matter should be capable of developing correct attitudes and ideals. Through it the pupil should be brought to a sympathetic understanding of the conditions and problems of other peoples and of how their present difficulties came about.

   b. Should provide for participation in community and citizenship activities.

   c. Approach must be from the near to the remote, from the known to the unknown.

   d. Content must provide for the varying abilities of children.

   e. Must allow use of initiative and judgment by the teacher.

4. *Cleveland, Ohio.* Grades 7—9. Date of publication, 1928.

   a. Materials should be useful in the development of better human relations.

   b. Must be within the comprehension of the child and true to human experience.

   c. Specific objectives set up in terms of the behavior sought in pupils to-day and in citizens to-morrow. Content and subject-matter selected in the light of the objectives.

   d. Material should carry its own drive.

   e. Material must be attractive and suitable for pupil's use, in contrast to the old condensed and crowded outlines.

   f. Scientific methods should be applied to the solution of the specific objectives and the materials and activities used to realize these objectives.

g. Subject-matter must be capable of developing correct attitudes toward life.

h. Content selected with the idea that no available textbook, even when supplemented by the richest collection of materials in the library, would be adequate to the needs of the course.

MATHEMATICS

1. *Boston, Massachusetts.* Grades 7—10. Date of publication, 1930.
   a. Materials should be within the pupil's powers of comprehension.
   b. Content should be useful and valuable for pupils in any career they follow.

2. *Pittsburgh, Pennsylvania.* K—6. Date of publication, 1928.
   a. Content selected in terms of aims that were set up.
   b. Have utilitarian values.
   c. Selected on a basis of scientific research.
   d. Must allow for the use of initiative and judgment on the part of the teacher.

3. *Iowa State.* Grades 9—12. Date of publication, 1932.
   a. Based upon the cardinal objectives.
   b. Adaptable to classroom situations.
   c. Develop proper attitudes, ideals, habits, and skills.
   d. Considered in relation to textbooks.
   e. There should appear those teacher procedures of known value which make learning desirable, economical, and permanent.
   f. Scientific methods should be used in the selection of procedures, activities, etc.
   g. Pupil difficulties which have been discovered through research should be mentioned and methods of proven value for meeting these difficulties should be included.
   h. Suggested ways of utilizing pupils' experiences should be made.
   i. Material should include means of motivation.

ENGLISH

1. *Chicago, Illinois.* Grades 1—3. Date of publication, 1929.
   a. Based on children's needs and interests.
   b. Material should be within the comprehension of the child and toned to human experience.

  c. In composition only those facts and principles should be taught which are necessary for rendering thought and communication more effective.

  d. Have human interest and imaginative appeal.

2. *Denver, Colorado.* Grades 7—9. Date of publication, 1931.

  a. Selected in terms of worthy objectives.

  b. Meet the present needs of pupils of all abilities.

  c. Be capable of developing correct attitudes toward life.

3. *Sacramento, California.* Grades 10—12. Date of publication, 1930.

  a. Must be within the child's understanding and ability.

  b. Should be based on real life situations.

  c. Place emphasis on student activity rather than on teacher activity.

  d. Be capable of developing an ethical attitude toward human relations.

  e. Allow for initiative and judgment on the part of the teacher.

4. *Denver, Colorado. Expression.* Grades 3—6. Date of publication, 1931.

  a. Should be within the child's understanding and ability.

  b. Must be based on real life situations.

  c. Place emphasis on student activity rather than teacher activity.

  d. Be capable of developing an ethical attitude toward human relations.

  e. Allow for initiative and judgment on the part of the teacher.

5. *New York City. Composition.* Grades 1—8. Date of publication, 1928.

  a. Must appeal to the child's interest.

  b. Should include real life situations.

6. *New York City. Literature.* Grades 1—8. Date of publication, 1928.

  a. Must be within the comprehension of the child and toned to human experience.

  b. Is the language suitable? Does it possess charm of style and beauty of words?

  c. Is the subject-matter in the course varied as to experience? As to countries represented?

  d. Is the subject-matter capable of developing correct attitudes toward life?

  e. Allow for initiative and judgment on the part of the teacher.

1. *Oakland, California. Chemistry.* Grades 11—12. Date of publication, 1931.
   a. Must include a wide range of activities.
   b. Allow for initiative and judgment on the part of the teacher.

2. *Oakland, California. General Science.* Grades 10—12. Date of publication, 1933.
   a. Leaves choice of subjects to the discretion of the teacher.
   b. The appeal to the student should be through the senses and through enjoyment.
   c. Elementary-science courses are to encompass elementary but basic instruction and experience in a well-balanced selection from all major scientific fields.
   d. Should enable pupils to gain a scientific attitude and method.
   e. Supplementary materials must have intrinsic value to the pupils and teacher.
   f. Must be adaptable to the school's environment and the interests of the class.

3. *Kansas City, Missouri. Chemistry.* Grades 10—12. Date of publication, 1933.
   a. Program must be consistent with the abilities of the teachers in service.
   b. Should meet the needs, aptitudes, and aspirations of the pupils.
   c. Lead to attainment of general aims of education and special aims of science.
   d. Develop correct attitudes and appreciations.

4. *Kansas City, Missouri. Physics.* Grades 10—12. Date of publication, 1933.
   a. Content should meet the individual differences of teachers as well as of pupils.
   b. Consider the practical and cultural needs of pupils.

1. *Oakland, California.* Grades 5—6. Date of publication, 1931.
   a. Music education should minimize the importance of technique and drill, and provide situations in which the creative attitude may be developed.
   b. It should at all times emphasize the unity of art and ally itself with a wide range of culture.
   c. Should utilize the children's interests and motives.

HEALTH AND PHYSICAL EDUCATION

1. *San Francisco, California*. Grades 4—6. Date of publication, 1931.
   a. The approach to the subject should be a positive, joyous one, emphasizing well-being, vigor, and the joy of health. The child should be oriented to think of health as "the quality of life that enables the individual to live most and serve best."
   b. The subject-content must be suited to the capacities, interests, processes of learning, and emotions of the age period under consideration. The child of this age is not interested in health *per se;* therefore, scientific details of structure and function have no place in the curriculum.
   c. Must develop desirable health habits which are the specific objectives of the course.
   d. Selected in view of the fact that health is more than a school subject; it is a major objective of education. As such it is not an isolated subject, to be taught by itself; its motives and practices should be woven into every part of the school work.
   e. Must allow for initiative and judgment on the part of the teacher.

2. *Minneapolis, Minnesota*. Grades K—6. Date of publication, 1932-33.
   a. Develop desirable habits in health and safety.
   b. Meet the requirements of the pupils at various levels of mental maturity.
   c. Every effort should be made to select activities and materials which will develop confidence and poise rather than uncertainty, timidity, and self-consciousness.
   d. Based upon pupils' needs and interests.
   e. Should allow for initiative and judgment on the part of the teacher.

3. *Oakland, California*. Grades 1—2. Date of publication, 1931.
   a. Based upon desirable child experiences.
   b. Based on large-muscle activities.
   c. Should provide opportunity to express in rhythmic and dramatic form the child's own concepts.
   d. Should provide opportunity for self-expression and use of creative power.
   e. Stimulate an appreciation and love for good music and wholesome forms of rhythmic expression.

f. Provide the opportunity to live the play instincts of the child's age-period.

g. Provide opportunity to play harmoniously as a member of a group.

h. Provide relief from prolonged work requiring fixed positions, such as writing and drawing, and from similar schoolroom fatigues.

i. Provide for "satisfaction in accomplishment" (as in stunts) and for development in skills, muscular strength, and good posture.

j. Provide occasions for practice of self-control, honesty, coöperation, courtesy, kindness, initiative, and alertness.

PENMANSHIP

1. *St. Louis, Missouri.* Grades 1—6. Date of publication, 1930.

a. Handwriting is a means to an end; it should not be made an end.

b. Movement is the foundation of writing.

c. Course planned to give the child the means of expressing his ideas through writing and to satisfy his desire for written expression in situations of real interest to him.

d. Must lead to desirable outcomes set-up.

III. IMPORTANCE OF SELECTING CONTENT

The realization of both specific and general objectives depends on the accurate and correct selection of content. Objectives and content are interdependent. In the same way that valid objectives are stalemated by poor content, excellent content is devitalized when used in attempting to achieve invalid objectives.

This problem is so basic in organizing the course of study that the fundamental philosophy of education, which is accepted by the administrator and the faculty, governs the policy in a particular system. Although this has been implied in the chapter on sources of objectives, it merits the attention of the reader at this time. Two diametrically different philosophies of education have produced two schools of thought and procedure in connection with the determination of content.

A. **Those who would select content in advance.** These educators believe that the general objectives, specific objectives, and content or subject-matter which will be reasonably uniform in attaining these objectives should be in the hands of teachers preceding the registration of students in a course. They admit that modifications will have to be made to fit local conditions in the community or residential section of the city, and that daily life situations and interests for which specific needs of the class may be secured will have to be provided for in the daily organization of the work. They are decidedly unwilling, however, to allow any daily inventory of the interests and moods of the class to determine the major aspects of the work for the semester or year.

B. Those who would select content in terms of the interests, moods, and reactions of the class from day to day. Extremists of this school of thought advocate an educational program which is organized "on the spot." What shall constitute the program depends on the students. The skilful teacher, appreciating the educational possibilities of these daily interests, leads the children in building an educational program, through stimulating them to search out data and acquire fundamental facts and processes as they work out the ramifications of their interests.

C. A third group select content in advance, basing this content upon the known interests of children. Most of the "activity group" come under this classification, although the voluminous writing in the field of the activity or experimental school often gives the impression that true and undefiled education is represented only by those who invoice the interests of children from day to day. There is no question but that material can be prepared in advance and still appear to grow out of the interests of the children. If the teacher is talented, even the pupils may accept that point of view and believe that content is molded to their interests.

If the unit of work is carefully prepared in advance as a result of previous experimentation, the geography of China can be learned by a class without its being conscious that it is studying the geography of China. The children's interest can be aroused by the opportunity to suggest that they give a Chinese dinner. This will involve learning all the essential facts concerning food, clothing, manners, customs, agricultural and manufacturing products of various sections of the country, etc.

Such units of work, when they have been completely organized for the guidance of teachers of future classes, usually meet the most important criteria of a course of study. It is a handicap to education that the two extreme groups cannot meet on this common ground.

IV. SUMMARY

The discussion has pointed out six generalizations which can be stated as a summary of this chapter. The reader should study the material in this field carefully and become either a proponent or opponent of these generalizations before proceeding to the task of actually organizing a unit of work.

1. Materials and learning experiences which have no significance in the actual living adjustments of pupils should not be included. Instructional materials should be selected because of their bearing on present problems and experiences of the group. This position demands that present learning activities be related to past learning experiences.

2. Basic and core materials should be determined by experts in curricular psychology and subject-matter. The teacher has a place in curriculum making, but it is indeed unfortunate when the available research in methods, objectives, and content materials are overlooked and ignored by professional people. Their task is primarily that of providing the approach and organizing applications of material already determined by experts. A distinction should be made between learning experiences having proved value and those of passing or temporary interest.

3. Content must be significant to the learner, but it is also essential that it be learned in a life-like situation. It must be more than appreciated and significant; it must be vital to the pupil because it relates to the life he is living at the present time. Learning materials should lead to an understanding of basic concepts and principles which enable the individual to meet new situations.

4. The organization of learning experiences for the student

is very important in terms of the transfer of training. The pupil should not be confronted with the problem of relating activities and experiences from isolated situations, but the educational life of the child should be related as parts of an integrated program. The development of a scientific attitude and mastery of the scientific procedure so that they will be fundamental in the adjustment of the pupil to life situations is an illustration of the significance of this point. The coöperation of the pupils in the selection and organization of learning materials will promote the ability to choose and select after careful evaluation.

5. Education demands that the learner be able to proceed from particulars to generalizations and from generalizations to particulars. The life of the individual may not be affected by isolated items of information; generalizations may have no significance unless they can be analyzed into specific aspects so that the·individual can adjust himself to a particular situation. Thus learning materials must be within the range of comprehension of the class; they must be selected from real life and be in accord with the interests and needs of the group.

6. The selection of learning materials should be determined by the individual differences in abilities, interests, and needs of the class. These experiences should provide for the continuing growth and development of every child.

BIBLIOGRAPHY

ADAMS, Mary A., "City-Wide Experimentation in the Intermediate Curriculum Program in Geography and History," *Baltimore Bulletin of Education,* Vol. IX (April, 1931), pp. 172-177. She described city-wide participation of teachers in an experiment in intermediate-school social-studies curricula.

ALVEY, Edward, Jr., "Organizing Units Around Functional Centers," *English Journal,* Vol. XXII (February, 1933), pp. 119-127. In this study he gives his solution of the difficult problem of determination of suitable centers of organization for composition activities, and chooses functional centers.

BARNES, Emily A., and YOUNG, Bess M., *A Unit of Work: Children and Architecture* (Teachers College, Columbia University, 1932). They reported on some experimental development of curriculum units for various grade levels.

BERGSTROM, John A., "Correlative Constants in the Major Fields of Woodwork," Master's Thesis (Iowa State College, 1933). He listed the common processes and operations of cabinet-making, carpentry, and pattern-making courses to provide a basis for more widely functioning exploratory courses.

BLYTHE, Irene T., "The Textbooks and the New Discoveries, Emphases, and Viewpoints in American History," *Historical Outlook,* Vol. XXIII (December, 1932), pp. 393-402. Her study of textbooks published between 1893 and 1928 revealed an unfortunate neglect on the part of textbook authors to incorporate into their works new viewpoints.

BRUECKNER, Leo J., "Social Problems as a Basis for Vitalized Arithmetic Curriculum," *Journal of Experimental Education,* Vol. I (June, 1933), pp. 320-323. He suggested as one basis for curriculum building the social problems dealing with quantitative aspects of units taught in arithmetic classes.

BRUECKNER, Leo J., and LAUMAN, G. S., "The Measurement of Accuracy of Judgments of the Difficulty of Arithmetic Problems," *Educational Method,* Vol. XII (March, 1933), pp. 338-345. They suggested that, since they proved that estimates of difficulty of problems on the basis of a scale of known value yielded reliable estimates of difficulty, this technic might well be used by committees comparing textbooks.

BRYSON, W. M., and HUTSON, P. W., "The General Curriculum," *School Review,* Vol. XLIII (Jan., 1935), pp. 17-27.

CALDWELL, Otis W., and LUNDEEN, Gerhard E., "Changing Unfounded Beliefs: a Unit in Biology," *School Science and Mathematics,* Vol. XXXIII (April, 1933), pp. 394-413. In this study they present their findings on problems of unfounded belief in science.

CASWELL, William E., "Selecting the Units for the Secondary-School Industrial-Arts Program," Master's Thesis (Ohio State University, 1932). From a study of the literature for valuable criteria in selection of units which should be included in industrial-arts programs in secondary school, he presented the major outcome as a focusing of attention upon the size of the problem rather than on solution, and he concluded that a general shop gives a better understanding of the interdependence of industries.

COOPER, Ruby, "Overlapping of Content in Elementary Readers," *Elementary School Journal,* Vol. XXXII (March, 1932), pp. 542-545. To determine recent trends in reader content, she studied sixteen sets of recently published readers, and compared her results with those of other studies.

CRAMER, John Francis, "Relative Difficulty of Junior High-School Social-Studies Texts," *Journal of Educational Research,* Vol. XXVI (February, 1933), pp. 425-428. In an experiment he determined that the Rugg social-science books gave adequate coverage of material and offered less reading difficulty than the state textbooks which they replaced.

CURTIS, Francis D., "The Teaching of Science in Secondary Schools," *North Central Association Quarterly,* Vol. VI (March, 1932), pp. 433-74. He made a study of the teaching of science in 1,802 secondary schools of the North Central Association, revealing that two years of biology is offered in 2.2 per cent of the schools in the association.

DANFORTH, Marie Lusk, "Purposes in the Selection and Arrangement of Material in Supplementary Readers," *Elementary School Journal,* Vol. XXXIII (February, 1933), pp. 427-433. She verified the conclusion that recent readers have been affected by current objectives of teaching reading after studying the reasons given in supplementary readers for selection and arrangement of material, finding that the two main trends are a consideration of children's interests and the value of material to children.

ENGEL, E. F., "The Use of a Standardized Vocabulary in Beginning German," *Modern Language Journal,* Vol. XV (January, 1931), pp. 281-291. He presented a report of vocabulary study showing that about 1,450 German words are learned by his college students during the first semester.

FARNUM, Royal Bailey, "Art Education," *Biennial Survey of Education,* 1928-1930. Vol. I. U. S. Dept. of the Interior, Office of Education, Bulletin No. 20 (1931), Ch. VIII (Government Printing Office, 1932), pp. 297-322. In this study and two others he presents his conclusions as to the trend of art as to wide extension of activities and professional quality of work.

FREEMAN, Ellen M., "Textbook Trends in Plane Geometry," *School Review,* Vol. XL (April, 1932), pp. 282-294. She analyzed ten textbooks, published between 1896 and 1901, ten books in use in 1928, and five recent ones, published since 1925, to find the trends were towards making geometry more practical, and a wider attention being given to correlation of geometry with other subjects, and to individual students.

GATES, Arthur I., PEARDON, Celeste C., and SARTORIUS, Ina C., "Studies of Children's Interests in Reading," *Elementary School Journal,* Vol. XXXI (May, 1931), pp. 656-670. In this study concerning kinds of material primary grades prefer, they found work and play exercises, narratives, and informational selections designated first choices in the order above given.

GILSON, John G., "Content for a Course in Related Science for Woodworkers," Master's Thesis (Iowa State College, 1933). He analyzed textbooks in woodworking science for the purpose of determining the science items needed for an adequate understanding of woodworking.

GOODRICH, T. V., "Is the Work-Book a Necessity or a Luxury?" *School Executives Magazine,* Vol. L (April, 1931), pp. 359-361, 396. He summarized reports from 245 schools using work-books and concluded that while the work-book is not a necessity, neither is it a luxury, but may be considered as a tool that enables the skilled workman to turn out a better job.

GRAY, William Henry, "An Experimental Comparison of the Movements in Manuscript Writing and Cursive Writing," *Journal of Educational Psychology,* Vol. XXI (April, 1930), pp. 259-272. In a laboratory study he found that the two types of handwriting encourage different types of movement.

GUNDERSON, Agnes G., "Geographical Materials Contained in Readers for the First Three Grades," *Elementary School Journal,* Vol. XXXIII (April, 1933), pp. 608-615. In studying readers for the first three grades, she found geographical material formed only a small part of the total amount of material, but that the amount increased from grade to grade, a fact which indicates that the amount of material from the content fields included in readers is insufficient to give young children the needed understanding in modern life.

HARRING, Sydney, "What Primer Shall I Use Next?" *Elementary School Journal,* Vol. XXXII (November, 1931), pp. 207-213. He was concerned with selecting the most approriate primers to supplement a basal text and, to secure the information, made an analysis of fifteen primers.

HEISS, Elwood D., *An Investigation of Content and Mastery of High School General Science Courses* (East Stroudsburg, Pa., 1932). By an analysis of modern textbooks of general science, he found the subject-matter to be grouped under unit headings which were each concerned with a field of science.

HILPERT, Robert S., "Art," *Instruction in Music and Art,* United States Department of the Interior, Office of Education. Bulletin No. 17 (1932), National Survey of Secondary Education Monograph No. 25, Part II (Government Printing Office, 1933), pp. 45-68. He reported the trends in art to be toward more extensive esthetic appreciation education, more encouragement of creative expression, and greater correlation with other subjects.

HUGHES, A. W., *A Unit of Work: Carrying the Mail, a Second Grade's Experiences* (Teachers College, Columbia University, 1933). His is a report on experimentation in work units in the elementary field.

HURD, A. W., *Coöperative Experimentation in Materials and Methods in Secondary School Physics* (Teachers College, Columbia University, 1933). He presented conclusions which he drew after making a series of extensive and significant investigations in the reorganization of content to suit the needs of pupils enrolled in secondary-school physics classes.

IDE, Alice M., and OBERG, Walda, "The Content of Present-Day School Readers as Compared with Children's Interests and Reading Objectives," *Elementary English Review,* Vol. VIII (March, 1931), pp. 64-68. They suggested an answer to the consideration of interest and educational and cultural value by comparing the content of present-day readers with children's interests and reading objectives.

JACKEY, David F., "An Evaluation of the Basic Curriculum of Vocational Teacher-Training in Trade and Industrial Education in the State of California," Doctor's Thesis (University of Pittsburgh, 1933). In a survey to evaluate the basic curriculum of vocational teacher-training in trade and industrial education in California, he studied various sources and recommended tentative changes on the basis of present inadequacies which he found.

JAMES, H. W., "The Effect of Handwriting on Grading," *English Journal,* Vol. XVI (March, 1927), pp. 181-185. He also studied the effect of handwriting quality on grades.

KELLEY, T. L., "A Communication Concerning the Difficulty of Achievement Test Items," *Journal of Education Research,* Vol. XXII (November, 1930), pp. 309-314. He emphasized the discriminating quality of test words.

KEPPEL, Frederick P., and DUFFUS, R. L., *The Arts in American Life,* Recent Social Trends Monograph (New York, McGraw-Hill Book Co., 1933). They presented a statistical report of the increase in numbers of art teachers, art pupils, and schools offering an art course, and discussed the closer relation of art education to everyday life.

KIMMEL, William G., *Instruction in the Social Studies,* United States Dept. of the Interior, Office of Education, Bulletin No. 17 (1932), National Survey of Secondary Education, Monograph No. 21 (Government Printing Office, 1933). His study revealed that there was greater uniformity in the courses of study in grade 7 than in 8, and that there was sometimes a differentiation made between students who expected to go to college, and those who did not.

KLAR, Walter H., WINSLOW, Leon L., and KIRBY, C. V., *Art Education in Principle and Practice* (Springfield, Massachusetts, Milton Bradley Co., 1933). Recommendations in curriculum making.

Koos, Leonard V., "Trends in Secondary-School Programs of Studies," *School Review,* Vol. XLI (September, 1933), pp. 497-507. In an investigation of the dynamic tendencies in secondary-school curricula, he found that schematic arrangements of courses designed to suit the needs of particular groups of pupils are increasing, and in the academic subjects social studies show the only increase.

LACEY, Joy Muchmore, "What Effect Has the Emphasis on Social Studies Had on the Content of Readers?" *Educational Method,* Vol. X (June, 1931), pp. 532-537. To determine the extent to which reader content has been influenced by other subject-matter, she studied representative primers and first, second, and third readers for the purpose of finding the extent to which the social studies have affected reader content. She concluded that because the material was simple and thin, readers supply only a small amount of information in that field.

LARSON, Minnie E., "An Analytical Investigation of Courses of Study in Art Education for the Elementary School," Master's Thesis (University of Chicago, 1931). She examined courses of study and other materials dealing with art curriculum for elementary schools.

LOCKERLY, Florence, "Banking," Teachers' Lesson Unit Series, No. 28 (Teachers College, Columbia University). She reported on the development of curriculum topics by experiment for grade levels.

LONG, H. H., and MAYER, W. C., "Printing versus Cursive Writing in Beginning Reading Instruction," *Journal of Educational Research,*

Vol. XXIV (December, 1931), pp. 350-355. In a minor experiment, they found manuscript writing an aid in learning to read.

LYMAN, R. L., *The Enrichment of the English Curriculum,* Supplementary Educational Monographs, No. 39 (University of Chicago Press, 1932). He presented a bibliographical study of all the research work in English. Particular attention is given to language and composition, and to the relation of English to other school subjects.

MEBANE, Eleanor V., "Art Education in the Junior and Senior High School," Master's Thesis (George Peabody College for Teachers, 1931). She studied art curriculum and materials for junior and senior high schools.

MONAHAN, A. C., "Science and Its Recognition in the High School Curriculum," *School Science and Mathematics,* Vol. XXX (November, 1930), pp. 875-880. He made a study of the enrolment in science classes as shown by the figures of the Bureau of Education for 1915, 1922, and 1928.

MOORE, Lucy Hunt, "Educational Principles and Art Practices in Progressive Schools," Master's Thesis (George Peabody College for Teachers, 1932). She treats of courses of study and art curriculum materials for progressive schools.

MULLINS, Vernon H., "Survey of Junior-College Curricula with Regard to Vocational Opportunity in Art," Master's Thesis (University of Southern California, 1932). He examined curricula and courses of study materials for junior colleges.

MURSELL, G. L., *Human Values in Music* (Silver, Burdett & Co., 1934).

National Education Association, Department of Supervisors and Directors of Instruction. *Eighth Year Book* (1935). Materials of Instruction.

POOLEY, Robert C., "Eighteenth Century Ghosts in Twentieth-Century Textbooks," *Elementary English Review,* Vol. X (March, 1933), pp. 71-73, 78. He analyzed rules for good usage as found in currently used textbooks, finding that they preserve distinctions not found in current use.

PREHM, Hazel, "Developing a Spelling Morale," *Elementary English Review,* Vol. VIII (January, 1931), pp. 10-13. She obtained an unusual amount of improvement in both spelling efficiency and morale by using a combined group and individual method.

PRESSEY, S. L., PRESSEY, L. C., and ZOOK, R. C., "The Essential Technical Vocabulary of Plane Geometry," *School Science and Mathematics,* Vol. XXXII (May, 1932), pp. 487-489. They attempted to determine a "core" vocabulary for use in three standard tests, and they present a list of seventy-seven terms which survived the checking of classroom teachers.

PULLIM, Roscoe, "Should Formal Grammar Be Discarded?" *English Journal* (H. S. Edition), Vol. XX (October, 1931), pp. 654-661. By summarizing research reports on the problem, he attempted to answer the question as to whether or not formal grammar should be discarded.

290   PRINCIPLES OF CURRICULUM MAKING

PURIN, C. M., *A Standard German Vocabulary of 2,000 Words and Idioms* (University of Chicago Press, 1931). He based his vocabulary study on the labor of three other men, and on personal judgment, presenting a list of German words suitable for a standard vocabulary.

ROBINSON, R. R., *Two Centuries of Change in the Content of School Readers,* Contributions to Education, No. 59 (George Peabody College for Teachers, 1930). After studying the content of school readers published during the past 150 years or more, he classified them into five periods each with a different objective, which corresponded closely with those of Smith.

ROSENBLOOM, Minnie, "Men Mentioned in Five Junior High School American-History Textbooks," *Historical Outlook,* Vol. XXII (January, 1931), pp. 26-27. She studied the names of men mentioned in various junior high-school textbooks, finding only a small percentage common to all.

SHEPHERD, Everett M., "The Effect of the Quality of Penmanship on Grades," *Journal of Educational Research,* Vol. XIX (February, 1929), pp. 102-105. He dealt with the effect of handwriting quality on teachers' estimates of English composition merit.

SHILLING, D. C., "Legal Requirements for the Teaching of Civics," *Historical Outlook,* Vol. XXIV (April, 1933), pp. 181-186. He set forth legal requirements for the teaching of civics, the Constitution, and patriotism.

SISSON, Edward O. "Statistical Determination of the Social-Science Curriculum," *Journal of Educational Research,* Vol. XXVII (September, 1933), pp. 41-45. He showed some of the dangers and limitations in trying to determine the social-science curriculum by strictly statistical and objective methods.

SKILLMAN, H. C., "American Art from the College Campus; a Year's Activities in the Nation's Art Departments," *Parnassus,* Vol. V (May, 1933), pp. 27-34. He investigated courses of study and curriculum materials for all colleges.

STRUBE, Paul E., "A Study of Content for High-School Farm-Shops," Master's Thesis (Ohio State University, 1932). He surveyed the "know" and "do" requirements for high-school farm-shop students as presented by Master Farmers and county agents in Kansas, and reported an analysis of jobs to determine difficulty, range, and importance of skills and information.

STULL, DeForest, "The Nature and Quantity of the Geographic Content of Social-Studies Courses," The Teaching of Geography, National Society for the Study of Education, *Thirty-second Yearbook* (Public School Publishing Co., 1933), pp. 566-571. He reported more attention being given to history and civics than to geography in the junior and senior high schools.

SWEENEY, Frances G., BARRY, Emily F., and SCHOELKOPF, Alice E., *Western Youth Meets Eastern Culture; a Study in the Integration of Social Studies, English, and Art in the Junior High School* (Teachers College, Columbia University, 1932). They described an experiment with the integrated course in the study of the Far East in junior high school.

SWINDLER, R. E., "The High School Library and Reading Problems in the Social Studies," *Historical Outlook*, Vol. XXII (December, 1931), pp. 407-416. Basing his conclusions on an extensive survey of school libraries, he decided that social-science material is neglected in the libraries, and made a list of criteria for selection of such material.

THRALLS, Zoë, "Some General Curricular Principles and Their Application," *The Teaching of Geography*, National Society for the Study of Education, *Thirty-second Yearbook* (Public Schools Publishing Co., 1933), pp. 201-218. She analyzed quite a good many courses of study in geography, finding the modified one-cycle method of organization becoming dominant.

TORGERSON, Roland, "Unit Operations in Junior High School Woodwork," Master's Thesis (University of Minnesota, 1931). He studied the selection and ranking for importance, time, difficulty, and necessary drill of units of work in junior high-school woodworking.

VAN BIDDER, Lena C., "An Exploratory Study of Specific Classroom Difficulties in the Teaching of History and other Social Studies," *Classroom and Administrative Problems in the Teaching of the Social Sciences*, National Council for the Social Studies, *Second Yearbook* (McKinley Publishing Co., 1932). She reported teaching difficulties resulting both from method and curriculum after making a detailed investigation of the subject by studying magazine articles, questionnaires, and addresses.

VOORHIS, Thelma G., *The Relative Merits of Cursive and Manuscript Writing* (Teachers College, Columbia University, 1931). She found in an extensive experiment that manuscript writing facilitates learning to read.

WESLEY, Edgar B., and MURRA, Wilbur F., "Social Science Reference Books in Fifty-Eight Minnesota High School Libraries," *Historical Outlook*, Vol. XXIII (December, 1932), pp. 403-407. They presented a list of books found most frequently on school library shelves, and revealed that libraries are slow in acquiring new books, and that teachers do not make adequate use of material at hand.

WHITFORD, William G., "Analysis of the Art Curriculum," *School Arts Magazine*, Vol. XXXII (June, 1933), pp. 582-589, x-xi. He suggested that the art curriculum be divided into three sections of objectives—social, vocational, and leisure time.

WILSON, G. M., "A Reply to Dr. Kelley's Communication," *Journal of Educational Research*, Vol. XXII (November, 1930), pp. 315-316. He contended that words in a spelling test must be justified by their warranted appearance in the course of study for spelling.

WIRTH, Fremont P., "Classroom Difficulties in the Teaching of History," *Historical Outlook*, Vol. XXII (March, 1931), pp. 115-117. He listed seventy-one common difficulties in history teaching, both in method and curriculum.

WOODY, Clifford, "The Nature and Amount of Arithmetic in Types and

PRINCIPLES OF CURRICULUM MAKING

Reading Material for the Elementary Schools," *Educational Outlook,* Vol. VI (May, 1932), pp. 199-217. He analyzed reading material to determine the nature and amount of arithmetic with which pupils come into contact in other school subjects.

WRAY, R. P., *The Relative Importance of Items of Chemical Information for General Education,* Penn State Studies in Education, No. 6 (1934).

ZINK, Norah E., "Eighty-two Studies in the Teaching of Geography Classified by Content and Technique, with Selected Summaries," The Teaching of Geography, National Society for the Study of Education, *Thirty-second Yearbook* (Public Schools Publishing Co., 1933), pp. 431-473. She listed and classified eighty-two studies in geography, reported in the past thirty years.

ZINN, Mary C., "A Study of Originality in Children's Drawings," master's thesis (Pennsylvania State College, 1932). She investigated originality in children's drawings, finding a direct correlation with age and experience, the boys showing superior results, and concluded that originality is a special skill.

CHAPTER VIII

COURSE OF STUDY UNITS OF WORK

I. INTRODUCTION

The term *unit of work* has become more popular than any of the other titles applied to techniques of organizing content for presentation to students. As a matter of fact, many of the activists have laid claim to this title as descriptive of the organization of their content materials and experiences. Since the adoption of this term is so general among educators, it is necessary to study the various kinds of units of work which can be developed and note their characteristics. The inexperienced as well as the experienced teacher will recognize the variations which are imperative in constructing units in the different subject-matter fields.

Wilson makes the following comment:

> Very few words appear more frequently in the educational literature of the last decade than does the term "unit." The little word has become a sort of educational football—for some a password into the mysterious realms where curricula are made, and for others an educational excrescence either to be scorned or to be attacked with true quixotic ardor. Like many another shibboleth, in education and in other fields, this one has suffered from excessive popularity. It has become a catch-all in educational theorizing, and, in educational practice, no more a clue to progress than a blanket to cover a multitude of sins. Textbooks, courses of study, and even curriculum makers use the word more liberally than meaningfully. Sometimes "unit" is a synonym for "chapter," sometimes for "section"; sometimes it is identified with fusion, and sometimes it refers to a type of correlation. One textbook has been so bold as to label one of its parts "Miscellaneous Unit," and the contradiction between adjective and noun has seemed to bother many readers of the book no more than it did the publishers and author.

One is forced to fear, by the inconsistencies of its use, that the word "unit" is well on its way towards death at the hands of its erstwhile friends. Yet in its original sense the term stood for an educational idea of significance, and that idea should survive, whatever the fate of the label. Like any other concept, this one should be frequently redefined. Only by trying repeatedly to state with increased clarity the meaning of the term can its life be preserved. Without such analysis and reanalysis the term becomes an empty husk—a symbol of an attempt to translate into a mechanical formula an organic, living idea which dies when mechanized.

In the direct sense of the term, as it is used in reference to the curriculum, a unit is a body of subject-matter, every item of which is related to a central core of thought. The central core of thought is a unifying agency and the distinctive mark of a unit; it is an interpretation of the subject-matter clustered about it. The unit idea, or central core of thought, is a generalization, comprehensible through the data grouped about it, and the data themselves acquire full meaning only when they are in direct focus on the generalization. For illustration, items of information concerning the number of commercial treaties negotiated by the United States each year since 1789, concerning our annual totals of exports and imports, concerning the Monroe Doctrine, Spanish-American War, and World War acquire their educational significance only when seen in focus on a generalization deducible from them, such as "the United States has become a world power." In an American history course where information about our foreign relations, both political and economic, is sandwiched in among data of purely domestic concern, there is not a unit on "the United States as a world power," though there may be, of course, units of a different nature. The encyclopedia does not have ideational unity, except within its separate articles. The textbook which treats the quarrel over slavery and the slave trade in the Constitutional Convention on page 100, the Missouri Compromise on page 140, abolition on page 175, and which has a chapter on "Life and Literature in the 1850's" between the chapters on "Expansion and Slavery" and "The Civil War" does not have a unit of material on "the slavery controversy." The data are all in the book, but they are not focused. A basic effort in education of the last generation was to get, not away from but *beyond*, straight, undigested factual material. The unit, the embodiment of an idea which arises from but transcends raw data, is an outgrowth of the effort to bring meanings and ideas into a curriculum which is too frequently, for pupils, an uncharted, pathless wilderness rather than a series of insights into the meaning of human experiences.[1]

[1] H. E. Wilson, "The Unit in the Social Studies," *Junior-Senior High-School Clearing House,* Vol. IX (Sept., 1934), pp. 29-31.

It should be pointed out that the use of the term "unit" by those who prepare materials in advance does not necessarily imply a particular form of organization. Units vary greatly in scope and form of organization. There is no type unit which can be used satisfactorily in all fields or even in one field. The unit has developed so that facts may be related to the essential generalizations. Otherwise, the trees and not the forest are represented in the educational growth of the child. This means that the unit must be teachable and placed at the correct learning level of the child. The variations that are noted in units appear as a means of realizing teaching goals at different levels. The unit organization used in one course of study in a particular field by one group of teachers may have essential differences from units organized in other fields or in the same field by other groups. Even though the same criteria are used by teachers of home economics and social sciences in the organization of their respective courses of study, the units of work for such courses can be very different in regard to form and method of presentation.

According to Morrison, a unit is a comprehensive and significant aspect of the environment or of an organized science capable of being understood rather than merely remembered. He amplifies this statement as follows:

Now the whole process of education, of adjustment to the objective conditions of life, is made up of unit learnings each of which must be mastered or else no adaptation is made. These unit learnings cannot be measured but they can all of them be evidenced by symptoms or signs revealed in the learner's behavior. Some symptoms are plainly manifest if we observe thoughtfully; others can be detected only by tests designed to bring them out; others still can be observed only by the methods and it may be only with the help of the instruments, of the skilled psychologist. Whatever the test, its purpose is to throw light on the question, Has the pupil learned or has he not?

It follows that the course material which we find in the curriculum is valuable in education only as it is analyzed into significant units of learning which generate adaptations in the pupil and in that way contribute to his adjustment. It is meaningless to prescribe a course in arithmetic or English or grammar or French, and let it go at that. The issue is not learning any of these but rather the mastery of certain significant units in arithmetic or English or grammar or French. The most learned of scholars would hesitate to say that he had mastered any of these fields. But the child of nine years can indisputably learn to add and to identify situations in which adding is the appropriate process. When he has done so, he has mastered that unit and will never know how to add arithmetically any more truly than he does now, albeit he can improve almost indefinitely in the skill and accuracy and acumen with which he applies the process. Similarly, the boy in junior high school can indisputably learn to read French, that is, he can learn how to use the printed page in the manner which has the characteristic symptoms of reading. He masters the unit of learning which we may define as the reading adaptation in French. In brief, while it is idle to speak of mastering a given field of knowledge, at least in the secondary school, it is not only entirely possible to master important units within that field, but no less attainment constitutes learning in the educational sense at all.[2]

This significant statement by Morrison serves to emphasize the importance of specific objectives in the development of the unit. Probably no more conclusive argument has ever been offered for the clear analysis of objectives and the organization of units of learning experiences and activities to realize those specifics which are appropriate for the age and grade of the pupil.

In order that the reader will not think exclusively of habits, information, and skills developed through materials, experiences, and activities which have been organized into units of instruction for classroom use, it is imperative that the social significance of the unit be emphasized at this point. It is intimately related to social welfare and progress and is representative of life situations for the pupils. The staff at the Lincoln School has presented an excellent statement of the relationship of the activities of the unit to the life of the school and to adult life:

A unit of work which provides opportunity only for acquiring more information would be thought undesirable. Each unit must

[2] H. C. Morrison, *The Practice of Teaching in the Secondary School* (The University of Chicago Press, 1926), pp. 36-37.

give the child a chance to grow in the habits which are going to be most helpful to him in his own child life as well as in the life of adult society. He must find in the unit possibilities for growth in personal and group responsibility, initiative, coöperation, good judgment in proportion to experience, economical methods of study and work, power to plan ahead, intellectual interests, open-mindedness, fair play, courage in self-expression, creativeness, self-direction, and sympathy and kindliness.... It seems safe to say, however, that where a thing is largely practiced some increase in its fixation as habit will result.[3]

In this school, the emphasis appears to be on the large unit or project which draws on many forms of experience and includes a variety of subject-matter. The units are developed in terms of growth and real life situations which appeal to the children. If any criticism can be made, it is that child interest rather than the objectives of education receive the major emphasis. Special drills are organized outside the units for the acquisition of the fundamentals which the child must master as a background for his interests.

This brings us to one of the greatest faults of unit construction. Too often, the teacher or the committee feel that the primary criterion is the logical organization of subject-matter. So a block of learning experiences which are intimately related is selected and developed as a unit. It should be constantly in the minds of the teachers that the unifying principle in the unit is derived from the general objectives and their subsidiary specifics which determine the growth of the individual. The subject-matter can be as diverse as day and night if the goals are achieved.

In planning the organization of a unit of work, it is fundamental that the teacher recognize the unit as representing a situation which is important in the life of the pupils (present life interests can be emphasized, but considerations of later life interests should receive attention also). The objectives will indicate the organization of the unit, or if the life situation is determined the objectives essential in its realization can be

[3] Staff of the Elementary Division of the Lincoln School, *Curriculum Making in an Elementary School* (Ginn and Company, 1927), p. 41.

formulated. For example, in high-school English the need of acquiring the ability to write a correct business letter will be apparent either from the study of objectives or of life situations.

If the habits, skills, knowledge, and attitudes and ideals that are important in the teaching of the pupil have not been determined previously, they can be enumerated as the specific objectives of the unit. They will naturally be concerned with capitalization, punctuation, etc. However, the reader must note at this point that the capitalization and punctuation are not ends in themselves; they are only aspects of the correctly organized business letter. The unit is not made up of a number of phases of writing, but the unit is for teaching (teacher aspect) and learning (pupil aspect) how to write a correct and engaging business letter.

How can the child acquire these abilities? Activities must be selected and allocated to a unit that offers opportunities to attain these objectives. These learning activities are for the purpose of guaranteeing the desired products. They have little value in themselves, but, as an integrating aspect of a unit of closely related learning, essential in the mastery of a life situation, they are all-important.

The *learning unit* is made up of objectives, which are understood by the pupil, and activities which the pupil performs until mastery is attained. The *teaching unit* includes the learning unit and the methods which are adapted to the unit, suggestions for adapting the work to various levels of ability, and a testing program. The learning unit considers only the first two phases of the unit of work while the teaching unit is a significant title for the entire unit. The learning unit is a learning device, and the teaching unit is prepared for the benefit of the teacher. This distinction will be made clear in the chapters devoted to units, contracts, projects, problems, and activities for the pupils and the chapters considering general and specific methods and tests which are of interest to the teacher. The unit of work includes both pupil and teacher sections.

II. A COMPARISON OF COURSE OF STUDY UNITS OF WORK

In this and the following chapter, various types of *units* of work will be defined and illustrated by examples from courses of study developed in cities which are outstanding in curriculum revision. This procedure will be criticized in some quarters, since it may appear to stimulate course of study revision based almost entirely upon a comparison of current courses of study. There is no justification for a "cutting and pasting" technique in course of study construction, but much can be said in favor of using present courses of study as references. The best of them are produced from scientific research, classroom experimentation, and years of experience in studying the educational growth of children.

There can be little doubt that adaptations which are made from carefully chosen courses of study will be as satisfactory, in many cases, as objectives and learning experiences developed by a more original procedure in a school system which does not have a curriculum director and which is limited in finances and necessary school equipment. Those phases, which can be adapted, have already undergone years of experiment in grade placement and organization. For this reason they will be suggestive to the unsupervised teacher in a small system and essential as a check upon the results attained in the larger system which is conducting research in the field. The use of courses of study for these purposes deserves the same consideration as the use of expert opinion in other educational activities. The opinions of many professional people, based in many instances on scientific research, are represented in the course of study.

The reader should accept the illustrations given in the following chapters as illustrative of a principle in the construction and organization of a course of study and not as perfected phases of a course which can be adapted to any school system in any community.

A. The unit may be a large division of work. The following unit—*Home Geography and History* from the "Social Studies for Primary Grades" developed in the public school of

Kansas City, Missouri—illustrates this type which is commonly used in the elementary school. It represents a large division of work, based upon the known interests of the pupils, and incorporating into the learning activities all the essential work of the formal subjects taught in that grade.

HOW AND WHY KANSAS CITY HAS GROWN AND DEVELOPED

Objectives

To develop some understanding and appreciation of individual responsibility toward the welfare of home, school, and city.

To give the child a better understanding of the problems involved in securing food, clothing, and shelter, through a study of Kansas City: its early settlement, its growth, and present condition.

To help the child understand how climate, soil, and geographical location affect the basic needs of man, and how they have influenced the growth and development of Kansas City.

To develop, through observation of the seasonal and weather conditions, the ability to draw simple conclusions of their effects upon life.

To develop correct concepts of simple local land and water forms.

To establish a sense of direction through reference to natural objects.

To help the child put meaning into pictures, maps, written material, and other forms of symbolic representation.

Unit Experiences in School Which Utilize or Approximate Real Life Experiences and Interests

Geography and history:

Reading stories of Indian and pioneer life to see how the early settlers secured food, clothing, and shelter.

Looking at slides of early Kansas City and comparing life of the Indian and pioneer with that of modern man.

Making a collection of pictures describing early Kansas City and Kansas City to-day.

Interpreting pictures of geographical nature.

Using blue-print map of early Kansas City to locate rivers, important streets, and places of interest.

Using recent maps of Kansas City to name and locate rivers, public buildings, important industrial plants, parks, and boulevards.

Discussing kinds and sources of food in pioneer days as compared with those of to-day.

Discussing clothing, as:
   Kinds and materials used in pioneer days and present time
   How skins and furs are secured
   From what source cotton material comes
   What kind of climate is required for flax
   How cotton clothing differs from silk clothing
   Why heavier dresses and wraps are needed in winter
Comparing shelter of pioneer days with shelter of to-day as
   regards types, materials, methods of heating, and reasons for
   differences.
Comparing covered wagon, stage-coach, and boat travel of
   pioneer days with ways of transportation in Kansas City
   to-day.
Discussing progress in ways of communication; air mail, tele-
   phone, telegram, ocean cable, radio.
Making an excursion,[4] e.g.:
Visiting the boat landing at the foot of Main Street to see
   where the Kaw flows into the Missouri River, and to find out
   how the river gives us food and water.
Visiting the city market or dairy plant.
Visiting Swope Park to find out about the animals or to ob-
   serve land and water forms.
Going to Penn Valley Park to see Scout, Pioneer Mother, Santa
   Fe Markers, and to observe land and water forms.
Going to Cliff Drive, Independence, Missouri; museums, art gal-
   leries, Union Station, memorials.

Language:
   Making plans for excursions.
   Discussing and making oral reports about important experi-
      ences of the excursion.
   Writing coöperative stories about early Kansas City to Kansas
      City to-day.
   Making or writing original stories or poems from pictures col-
      lected.
   Making booklets, *e.g.:*
      Food—Food used by pioneers and by people to-day
      Dress—Indian, pioneer, colonial, and present-day
      Homes—Various types used in early days and at present time
      Transportation and Communication—Development in methods
         of traveling and communicating.

   [4] Some teachers will find it convenient to take more than one excursion, according to the location of the school and the needs of the pupils.
However, all teachers should take advantage of the rich opportunities
afforded by experiences derived from excursions.

Writing letters to absent classmates, telling about some of the interesting things being studied or about a pleasant trip taken.

Dramatizing suitable stories or writing original dramatizations about life in early Kansas City.

Reading:

Finding and reading suitable material in text and library books.

Reading news items units and units on charts about Indian and pioneer life and about important events in Kansas City to-day.

Reading descriptive material on slides and pictures.

Reading stories and poems written for booklets.

Making a bibliography of interesting stories and poems.

Making, interpreting, and checking informal reading tests.

Going to public library for books.

Art and handwork:

Making illustrations and cut paper poster compositions showing:
    Fruit and vegetable market
    Early experiences of pioneers
    Activities in pioneer home life
    Present-day city life

Making a pioneer living-room with furniture and articles of household use, constructed of heavy paper, wood, and clay.

Designing and making from study of pioneer quilts, a pieced-quilt block for pillow top or other use.

Illustrating booklets, original stories, and poems.

Lettering titles for booklets.

Illustrating changes of weather: rainy day scene, ice skating, sled riding, picnicking.

Spelling and writing:

Spelling and writing words needed for booklets, original stories, and poems.

Practicing capital and small letters and figures needed.

Arithmetic:

Using inches in measuring illustrations and pictures for booklets and posters and in making simple charts and maps.

Using quarts, gallons, pounds, and ounces in making and weighing butter.

Using such terms as block, mile, length, height, etc.

Making original problems involving fundamental processes.

Music:

Singing old favorite songs enjoyed in pioneer days.

Learning new appropriate songs.

Making original songs.

Enjoying and interpreting march, waltz, and other records.

Physical education:

Participating in games and dances enjoyed by children of pioneer days.

> Games: Drop the Handkerchief
> Blindman's Buff
> London Bridge
> Looby Loo
> Mulberry Bush, etc.
>
> Dances: Grand March
> Virginia Reel
> Waltz, etc.

Related activities:

Making candles.

Churning butter.

Parching or popping corn.

Weaving mats or rugs.

Having an old-fashioned spelling bee.

Having a singing school.

Playing games typical of early life and life at the present time.

Having a Thanksgiving feast.

Making a visit to the Harris Home to see relics of pioneer life.

Taking a bus trip through certain sections of the city.

Taking an excursion to observe geographical facts.

Taking a trip to fur, wool, and hide warehouse.

Keeping a weather chart.

Reading thermometer daily or reporting weather conditions from newspaper or radio.

Making a room museum.

Preparing a Thanksgiving program.

Other possible unit experiences:

Kaw Indian tepee

Fur trading post

Pageant showing development of Kansas City

Original play

Progress in transportation

Radio program

Newspaper

Library

Specific Values to be Derived from Experiences Involving the Study of Kansas City

Better realization of the fact that Kansas City becomes a better place, as each of its citizens grows in health, character, and worthy attitudes.

Deepening respect for law and for those entrusted with its enforcement; in home, school, city.

Growing ability of coöperating with others in solving problems.

Knowledge of the simple story of Kansas City's history.

Knowledge of the life and customs of Kansas City's early pioneers: their food, dress, dwellings, transportation and communication.

Knowledge and appreciation of the changes and progress in life and customs—food, dress, dwellings, transportation, and communication—that have developed since pioneer days.

Growing understanding of the effect that climate, soil, and natural location have had on the early settlement, the growth, and the development of Kansas City.

Greater enjoyment of the beauties of Kansas City: natural scenery, parks, boulevards, works of art, public buildings, etc., and a growing sense of responsibility for their care and protection.

Ability to make simple conclusions, based on observation, of seasonal and weather effects on food, clothing, shelter, transportation, communication, and recreation.

Growing ability to tell direction from natural objects.

Better concepts of land and water forms: hill, cliff, bluff, valley, island, creek, river, bank, mouth, falls, lake, and spring.

Ability to interpret simple map symbols, through making diagrams or charts of special interest and through using blueprint map of Kansas City.

Improved work habits through practice in purposing, planning, organizing, and checking progress.

Realization that there are many sources of information: nature, people, books, periodicals, pictures, maps, charts, etc.

MATERIALS—HOME GEOGRAPHY AND HISTORY

I. BIBLIOGRAPHY

For Pupils

ALLEN, Nellie B., *How and Where We Live* (Ginn and Co., 1924).

BAILEY, Carolyn S., *Boys and Girls of Colonial Days* (A. Flanagan Co., 1928).

———, *Boys and Girls of Pioneer Days* (A. Flanagan Co., 1928).

BASS, Florence, *Stories of Pioneer Life* (D. C. Heath, 1900).
"Lincoln's Journey to Indiana"
"Daniel Boone"
"A Journey to the New Home"
"Clearing Land and Raising Corn"

"Schools"
"Clothing"
"Money"

BRANOM, F. K., and GANEY, Helen M., *Home Land and Other Lands* (William H. Sadlier, Inc., 1928).

CARPENTER, Frank, *Foods We Eat* (American Book Co., 1925).

———, *Clothes We Wear* (American Book Co., 1926).

———, *Houses We Live In* (American Book Co., 1926).

CARPENTER, Frances, *Ourselves and Our City* (American Book Co., 1928).

———, *The Ways We Travel* (American Book Co., 1929).

DAVIDSON and ANDERSON, *The Lincoln Readers,* Third Reader (Laurel Book Co., 1922).

"Storing Food in Colonial Days"
"Two Brass Kettles"

EARLE, Alice Morse, *Child Life in Colonial Days* (The Macmillan Co., 1922).

HARDY, Marjorie, *Best Stories, Third Reader* (Wheeler Publishing Co., 1926).

"Daniel Boone"
"Indian Travel"
"Pioneer Travel"
"Travel by Stage-coach"
"The Pony Express"
"The First Railroad"
"The Telegraph"
"The Telephone"

HORN and McBROOM, *Learn to Study Readers, Book Three* (Ginn and Co., 1922).

"A Brave Pioneer"
"Soap Making in Pioneer Days"

KNOWLTON, Philip A., *First Lessons in Geography* (The Macmillan Co., 1924).

LITTLE, Charles, *Life and Literature Readers, Third Reader* (Pioneer Publishing Co., 1911).

MAGOWAN, Ellen B., *Soap Bubbles* (The Macmillan Co., 1929).

"Soap Two Hundred Years Ago"

PERKINS, Lucy Fitch, *Pioneer Twins* (Houghton Mifflin Co., 1927).

SERL, Emma, *The Story of Kansas City, Book One* (Board of Education, Kansas City, Missouri, 1924).

SHEPHERD, Edith P., *Geography for Beginners, Book One* (Rand, McNally and Co., 1927).

SHILIG, Elnora E., *The Four Wonders* (Rand, McNally and Co., 1913).

THOMPSON, Ruth, *Type Stories of the World for Little Folk,* Part I and Part II (Harr Wagner, 1922).

WARREN, Maude R., *Little Pioneers* (Rand, McNally and Co., 1916).

WAYLAND, John, *History Stories for Primary Grades* (The Macmillan Co., 1925).

For Teachers

BLAISDELL and BALL, *Log Cabin Days* (Pioneer Publishing Co., 1928).
Book of Knowledge
Classroom Teacher (The Classroom Teacher, Inc.), Vols. 3 and 5.
EARLE, Alice, *Home Life in Colonial Days* (The Macmillan Co., 1923).
McMURRY, Charles A., *Pioneers of the Mississippi Valley* (The Macmillan Co., 1904).
NIDA, S. H., *Letters of Polly the Pioneer* (The Macmillan Co., 1924).
NIDA, William L., *Following the Frontier* (The Macmillan Co., 1924).
　　"The American Pioneer"
　　"The Hunter—Pioneers"
　　"Life of Kentucky and Tennessee Hunters"
　　"The Cabin and Its Furniture"
　　"Pioneer Food and Cooking"
　　"The Clothing of Frontier Settlers"
　　"Other Activities of Pioneer Life"
　　"Travel by Water"
　　"The Overland Journey"
　　"Yankee Farmer on the Prairies"
　　"The Pony Express"
　　"The Telegraph and Telephone"
Teachers College, *Scout—Civic Art in Kansas City* (Teachers College Kansas City, Missouri, January, 1930).
The World Book

For Pupils and Teacher

Poems
　　"City Houses," *Short Poems for Short People*, Alice Aspinwall.
　　"Skyscrapers," *The Pointed People*, Rachel L. Field.
　　"The Old Coach Road," *Taxis and Toadstools*, Rachel L. Field.
　　"The Sampler," *The Pointed People*, Rachel L. Field.
　　"The Gate to the West," Albert E. Shirling, *The Story of Kansas City*, Book Three, Emma Serl.
　　"The Kansas City Spirit," Clara V. Townsend, *The Story of Kansas City*, Book Three, Emma Serl.
　　"I Go A-Traveling" (entire Selection), James S. Tippett.
　　"Apartment Houses," *I Live in a City*, James S. Tippett.
　　"In the City," *I Live in a City*, James S. Tippett.
　　"The Park," *I Live in a City*, James S. Tippett.
　　"Park Play," *I Live in a City*, James S. Tippett.
　　"From a Railway Carriage," *A Child's Garden of Verses*, Robert Louis Stevenson.

II. ART—PICTURES FOR APPRECIATION

Pictures and art objects:
　　The Santa Fe Trail, Young-Hunter
　　Taos Indian Roasting Corn, Couse
　　Apache Bag, Couse

The Solemn Pledge, Walter Ufer
The Vegetable Stall, Richmond
Pictures, *First Families of the Southwest,* Fred Hervey Co.
Pictures and text, *Official Guide Book of Missouri State Capitol,*
    pp. 64, 90, 92, 96, 106, 122
Indian Symbols in Design, *School Arts Magazine,* February 1927
Plates in color of pottery, weaving, basketry, etc.

III. VISUAL INSTRUCTION

Lantern-slide sets on:
    Early history of Kansas City
    Parks and boulevards
    Some Kansas City buildings

Sets with notes prepared especially for Grade Three on:
    Dairying
    Meat foods
    Grains
    Fruits and vegetables
    Clothing from animals
    Clothing from plants
    Homes
    Transportation
    Indians
    Land forms
    Water forms
    Seasons

IV. MUSIC

Songs:
    The Pioneers' Song, "Songs for Children," p. 14 [5]

Other courses of study which contain excellent units developed according to this criterion are:

1. Course of Study in Arithmetic for Grades 1—6 (Board of Education, Greensboro, N. C., 1932).
2. Course of Study in Social Studies for Grades 1—3 (Board of Education, Kansas City, Mo., 1930).
3. Course of Study in English for Grades 1—6 (Board of Education, Kansas City, Mo., 1932).
4. Course of Study in Kindergarten (Board of Education, Berkeley, California, 1931).
5. Course of Study in Kindergarten (Board of Education, Kansas City, Missouri, 1931).
6. Course of Study in Nature Study and Elementary Science (Board of Education, Kansas City, Missouri, 1930).

[5] *Social Studies for Primary Grades, Kansas City, Missouri* (1930), pp. 199-207.

7. Course of Study in Character Education (Board of Education, Kansas City, Missouri, 1931).

8. Course of Study in Physical Education (Board of Education, Oakland, California, 1931).

B. A unit may be a sub-division of the work for the year or semester. The second type of unit, which is an adaptation of the first, is produced by taking the semester's or year's work and dividing it into large phases, units, or divisions of the course. An illustration has been selected from the social-science course of study for grades 10 to 12 in the Denver schools. In the first semester of the tenth grade, World History is divided into the following problems: Contributions of Primitive and Early Civilizations, Contributions of the period of Transition from Medieval to Modern Times. The first unit, which outlines the work for the first three weeks of the semester, is presented in its complete organization.[6]

CONTRIBUTIONS OF PRIMITIVE AND EARLY CIVILIZATIONS

(Time, three weeks)

Understandings to be developed. This is a period of beginnings in all phases of life. The time differs with different peoples. A period of primitive development with an African tribe is perhaps contemporary with higher civilization in Europe. Unit I deals with primitive man up to the time he learned to write; Unit II with oriental civilizations. The Egyptians and Babylonians were people whose geographical environment made living conditions easy enough to permit time for the development of architecture, science, literature, and law; with the Hebrews comes the monotheistic idea in religion; with the Phœnicians, the evolution of a sea-going commercial navy; with the Chinese, Japanese, and Indians (Aryans), different kinds of art and architecture, elaborate and ceremonious governments, and new theories of philosophy and religion; with the Persians, the imperial idea of government which was overthrown by the western democratic Greeks at Marathon.

Unit III is optional. It covers the early civilizations of people who once inhabited the Americas, the Cliff Dwellers, the Mayas, and Aztecs; their occupations, systems of government, and Arts. Brilliant civilizations arose in Mexico, Central America, and Peru,

[6] Course of Study Monograph No. 19 in Social Science, Grades 10, 11, and 12 (Denver Public Schools, 1931), pp. 28-34.

where splendid cities, temples, and palaces showed skill rivaling that of the Egyptians. The Toltecs learned from the Mayans, and the Aztecs were heirs to both the Mayan and Toltec civilizations. The Incas had able rulers, wise laws, and great wealth. The world is indebted to the American Indians for domesticating valuable food plants and herbs.

Teaching suggestions. Pupils can be encouraged to become familiar with Hebrew literature from the Bible, as a source book, by being asked to write in class a short account based on the readings listed in the syllabus.

In connection with the time line, compare the suggestions in *Text,* p. 3, and in Wells' *Outline of History,* pp. 14 and 60. Note also stair-step plan in Hillyer's *Child's History of the World.*

Teachers are urged to choose from among the less frequently taught of the early civilizations.

A study of archeology and its contributions may be an optional exercise. A visit to the State Historical Museum at Fourteenth and Sherman Streets, Denver, will give access to the finest collection of prehistoric relics in America. The following references may be helpful in this study:

BOYLE, Mary E., *Man Before History*
CHAPMAN, Arthur, *Story of Colorado,* pp. 63-74
THOMPSON, *The Civilization of the Mayas*

Things about which to think. The attention of the teacher is called to two distinct values of the interest question: first, to create interest in the pupil as a motive for attack on his part—the answers to be developed during the term; second, to explore the pupils' knowledge —the teacher basing his approach to the new work on what he discovers of the pupils' previous knowledge. The teacher may, if he wishes, give an exploratory test to guide him in the selection of units.[7]

1. How many countries can you name where relics of primitive man are found?
2. How far had primitive men advanced before they learned to write?
3. What do the Mesa Verde ruins show us of ancient peoples? (See Chapman, *Story of Colorado,* pp. 63-74.)
4. How do Egyptians live in a country which is covered with twenty-five to thirty feet of water every spring? How do you suppose they irrigate in the season of low water?

[7] See Monroe and Carter, *The Use of Different Types of Thought Questions.*

5. Why did the Egyptians build pyramids? Was the purpose of the Egyptians the same as that of the Toltecs?
6. What is the origin of the names: Saturday, Sunday, and Monday? *Text*, p. 19.
7. What year is this according to the Jewish calendar?
8. Why is the religion of Zoroaster considered one of the great religions of the world?
9. Why has Chinese civilization influenced America so little?
10. What is the "caste" system?
11. What is the origin of the American Indian?
12. Why did the Amerindians of South and Central America become civilized while those of North America remained in a semi-civilized state?
13. What do you know about: Confucius, Rig-Veda, Pan-Hu, Jimmu Tenno, Dravidians, transmigration of souls?

Map work. The teacher will provide direction for the use of the desk outline maps purchased by the pupils, and of the wall outline maps obtained on requisition by the principal. The wall outline maps are especially adapted for projects made by the whole class.

Guidance outline. The following points are suggestive of the development of the subject-matter:

Unit I (*Required*). What does the development of primitive man contribute toward modern civilization?

1. In government: family, patriarchal, tribal
2. In their ways of living: occupations—hunting and fishing, herding, agriculture; family life; social life; education
3. In religion: nature worship; polytheism
4. In art: pottery; weaving; drawing on walls of caves; carving on bone; megaliths—Stonehenge
5. In music: vocal; formation of instruments (Optional)
6. In written literature: Discuss *historic* and *prehistoric*

REFERENCES

Text, Ch. I.
BAILIE, *Peeps at Men of the Old Stone Age.*
BEARD and BAGLEY, *Our Old World Background* (for limited groups).
BOYLE, *Man Before History.*
BREASTED, *Ancient Times,* Ch. I.
HAMILTON, *Outline of Music History,* pp. 4-6.
HAMLIN, *History of Architecture,* Ch. I.
HAYES and MOON, *Ancient and Medieval History,* Chs. I and II.
OSBORN, *The Hall of the Age of Man.*
OSGOOD, *History of Industry,* Chs. I and II.
PARSONS, *The Stream of History.*
REINACH, *Apollo,* Chs. I and II.
SAWTELL and TREAT, *Primitive Hearths in the Pyrenees.*

SEIGNOBOS, *History of Ancient Civilization,* Ch. I.
SMITH, *Posters on Primitive Man.*
THOMPSON, *Civilization of the Mayas.*
VAN DYKE, *History of Painting,* Introduction.
VAN LOON, *The Story of Mankind,* pp. 3-15.
WATERLOO, *Story of Ab* (Fiction).
WELLS, *A Short History of the World,* Chs. IX-XIV.

Unit II (*Required*). What was the advance of Oriental peoples
over primitive man?
Oriental civilizations: Egyptian, Babylonian, Hebrew, Phœnician,
Persian, Chinese, Indian (Aryan). Choose two or more countries
according to the explanatory test and the abilities of the class. It is
suggested that the Far-Eastern Orient be considered.

1. In their ways of living: agriculture—study of climate and
   geographical conditions; handicrafts; trade, commerce, business; civil and military service; family and social life;
   education; industries; religions
2. In government: (type studies) patriarchy—Abraham, Isaac,
   Moses; monarchy—Hammurabi, Pharaohs, David, Solomon,
   Nebuchadnezzar Chou; dynasty—Asoka; empire—Cyrus,
   Darius, Jimmu Tenno, "Son of Heaven"
3. In science: surveying; irrigation; architectural engineering; mathematics; astronomy; the calendar; writing and
   writing material
4. In religion: future life—Hebrews, Egyptians, Persians, Indians (Aryans); ancestor-worship of China; Monotheism—
   Hebrews, Chinese, upper-class Egyptians; leaders—Confucius, Buddha, Zoroaster
5. In literature: Egyptians—Book of the Dead, Rosetta Stone;
   Babylonia—Code of Hammurabi; Hebrews—Old Testament;
   Indians—Rig-Veda; Chinese—Wu-King (five canons),
   Confucius; Persia—Zend-Avesta; Phœnicians, alphabet
6. In arts and music: Egyptians—painting, especially mural,
   sculpture; Chinese—water colors; Assyrians—glazed brick;
   musical instruments; handicrafts—metal, ivory, glass
7. In architecture: pyramids, sphinxes, obelisks, temples, tombs,
   Great Wall of China

REFERENCES

Text, Chs. II and III. Also use index.
BEARD and BAGLEY, *Our Old World Background.*
Bible, The Book of Genesis: Exodus 20:1-7, 21:1-20 and 28-36; Ezekiel
27:1-25.
BREASTED, *Ancient Times,* Chs. II-VII. The teacher should use para-
graph headings for portions wanted, also the index.

Current History, June, 1924.
DAVIS, *Readings in Ancient History: Greece and the East*, Chs. I-III; note especially pp. 35-38.
Encyclopædia Britannica. See *Egypt*.
HAMILTON, *Outlines of Music History*, pp. 6-19.
HAMLIN, *History of Architecture*, Chs. II-V.
HAYES and MOON, *Ancient and Medieval History*, Chs. III, IV, XII. See paragraph headings and index.
HERRICK, *History of Commerce and Industry*, Chs. II and III.
National Geographic Magazine, May, 1923.
OSGOOD, *History of Industry*, Chs. III and IV.
PARSONS, *The Stream of History*.
REINACH, *Apollo*, Ch. III.
RICHARDSON and OWEN, *Literature of the World*, pp. 5-59.
SEIGNOBOS, *History of Ancient Civilization*, Chs. II-VIII.
STEIGER, BEYER, BENITEZ, *A History of the Orient*, See table of contents.
VAN DYKE, *History of Painting*, Chs. I and II.
WELLS, *A Short History of the World*, Chs. XV, XXII, XXVIII-XXX.

Unit III (*Optional*). What have other early civilizations contributed to modern man?

Cliff dwellers, Mayans, Toltecs, Aztecs, Incas, American Indians: agriculture, arts, governments, temples, cities, domestication of plants.

REFERENCES

Carnegie Institute of Washington, *News Service Bulletins.*
CHAPMAN, *Story of Colorado*, pp. 63-74.
HAYES and MOON, *Ancient and Medieval History*, p. 12.
National Geographic Magazine, December, 1929.
PRESCOTT, *Conquest of Peru.*
———, *History of the Conquest of Mexico.*
THOMPSON, *Civilization of Mayas.*
State Historical Museum collection of relics.

Summary. The pupil should make an organized summary review of the topics studied.

Suggested activities. Class projects may be carried on as follows:
1. Keep a bulletin board using articles, pictures, clippings relative to the period studied.
2. Make a collection, originals or imitations, of ornaments and implements.
3. Start a museum of relics.
4. Make a parallel time chart. See Hayes and Moon, *Ancient and Medieval History*, p. 94.
Individual projects may interest the pupils.
1. Construct a date line, 1000 years to the half-inch, repre-

senting the time from 5000 B.C. to the present. Place at the proper points the dates suggested below:

Cir. 3400 B.C.—Menes
Cir. 2000 B.C.—Abraham, Hammurabi
Cir. 1500 B.C.—Moses
Cir. 1000 B.C.—David, Solomon
Cir. 1200-1000 B.C.—Rig-Veda. Oldest Indo-European literature
1122-249 B.C.—Chou Dynasty
776 B.C.—First Olympiad. Accurate chronology begins with this date.
660 B.C.—Jimmu Tenno
Cir. 560-483 B.C.—Buddha
551-479 B.C.—Confucius
264-227 B.C.—Asoka
214 B.C.—Great Wall of China begun

2. Write and illustrate the biography of some leader of your choice.
3. Make a model of a Phœnician ship or an Egyptian pyramid.
4. Write and illustrate a diary of your life as a member of one of the ancient nations.
5. Read an historical novel, such as: Waterloo, *The Story of Ab;* Crump, *Og, Son of Fire;* or Kingsley, *Hypatia.*
6. Make a map on which are indicated the important physical features and locations of countries and places which have been studied.
7. Make a word list of important people studied.

The following courses of study will be of value to the reader in his further investigation of this type of unit organization:

1. Courses of Study in Social Studies for Cleveland, Ohio. Grades 7—9, 1928.
2. Course of Study in Social Studies for Denver Public Schools. Grades 7—9, 1931.

C. A unit may be a section or major topic in the subject-matter field. A subject-matter field may be divided into units representing important sections, topics, or phases of the course. In each of the units the learning activities of the pupils are carefully and thoroughly organized, in order that complete mastery can be indicated for the teacher and pupils and attainments of the pupils can be accurately and definitely measured.

In the Tentative Course of Study in English for the 7A grade of the Lakewood, Ohio, schools are excellent examples of units of this character. Seven units are organized under the Language and Composition work which is to be taught in that grade. They are as follows:

Unit 1. Writing anecdotes for the school paper
Unit 2. Writing letters
Unit 3. Writing minutes of meetings, announcements and notices
Unit 4. Making outlines for reports
Unit 5. Writing news stories
Unit 6. Writing accounts of personal experiences
Unit 7. Creative expression: writing original verse and stories

Unit No. 5 has been selected as an illustration of the organization of a unit of this type: [8]

UNIT 5. WRITING NEWS STORIES

I. *Objectives*
  A. To learn to write a conventional news story in an accurate and readable way.
  B. To read more intelligently news stories in daily newspapers.

II. *Elements of This Unit*
  A. Definitions of news:
    1. "News . . . is anything that happens in which people are interested. The best news is that which carries the most interest, significance, and importance for the greatest number."
        —H. F. Harrington, *Writing for Print*, p. 4.
    2. "News is anything that happens that will interest a number of students, provided the authorities agree that it should be printed."
        —Bessie M. Huff, *How to Publish a School Paper*, p. 32.
    3. "News is a record of timely facts of interest to a large number of readers."
        —Harrington, *The Newspaper Club*, p. 90.
    4. "News may be defined as any accurate fact or idea that will interest a large number of readers; and of two

[8] *A Tentative Course of Study in English for the 7A Grade* (Board of Education, Lakewood, Ohio, 1933), pp. 52-58.

stories the more accurate one that interests the greater number of people is the better."

—M. Lyle Spencer, *News Writing,* p. 26.

B. Differences between a news story and a literary account.
  1. In order to give the most information in the quickest way, the news story is built in the inverted pyramid style, playing up, or featuring the items of greatest interest and working down to the least important fact.
  2. In American newspapers the reporter is not permitted to comment on or indicate his own emotions with regard to the facts that he is recording, as the author of a literary account usually does. Any reactions which the reporter includes must be those of the people about whom he is writing.

C. Parts of a news story.
  1. Summary lead:
    a. The summary lead gives in the first few words the most important fact of the story by telling *who, what, where, when, why,* and sometimes *how.*
    b. The lead should be so complete in itself that it might be printed alone.
    c. It features by placing at the beginning the detail that will best catch the interest of readers. Whether *why, who, when, where, what,* or *how* shall be answered first depends upon the nature of the facts to be presented.
    d. Unless the article concerns matters of routine interest containing little or no tone, the lead sets the tone for the news story by striking the keynote of pathos, humor, or tragedy.
    e. The lead should be written without regard for headline; that will be written later.
    f. Variety in leads may be obtained either through variety of thought or of grammatical construction. It is recommended that in some 7A classes the emphasis be upon thought, although in some sections the simplest differences in grammatical construction, such as subject leads and prepositions; phrase leads, may be pointed out.
    g. *A, an,* and *the* should be used very sparingly to begin leads.
  2. Body of the news story:
    a. Here the facts are placed in their natural order.

    b. The opening paragraph of the body should make it clear that the story is reverting to the beginning.

    c. Paragraphs should be shorter than in literary articles. No printed paragraph should be of more than fifteen to twenty lines. About 140 words is the length limit. Paragraphs of two or three sentences are common.

    d. Each new paragraph, as well as the lead, should feature an interesting fact.

    e. The style should be simple, avoiding superlatives. Direct and indirect quotations supply variety.

    f. Each paragraph should be written to meet the "cut-off" test made necessary by space limitations. Have the important details been given as soon as possible? Could the reader stop at the end of every paragraph, feeling that the story is complete?

    g. Above everything, the story should be accurate. The reporter should check facts and names and spelling.

D. Essentials of journalistic style.
  1. Accuracy
  2. Clarity
  3. Terseness
  4. Interest

E. Preparation of copy.
  1. The story should be carefully checked for accuracy.
  2. Only one side of the paper and every other line should be used.
  3. A wide margin should be left at either side of the page as well as an inch at the top and at the bottom of the paper.
  4. The reporter should follow the style book in such matters as spelling, capitalization, abbreviations, and punctuation.
  5. Each page of a story should be clearly numbered and the end of the article indicated by the sign of completion agreed upon.

III. *Procedure—Activities*
  A. Suggested approaches.
    1. The lesson may be planned for the day following an issue of the school paper. Let pupil subscribers bring their copies to class, and borrow additional copies for use by the non-subscribers. Conduct a discussion on:
      a. The meaning of news.
      b. Various kinds of stories in a newspaper.

    c. The arrangement of news by pages.

    d. Places of feature in a newspaper:

       (1) On the front page the most important article is printed in the upper right-hand corner. The article next in importance is in the upper left corner, and the headlines of all other important news stories appear above the fold.

       (2) On inside pages the upper left corner is of most importance.

    e. Why use headlines?

    f. The difference between the story of the "Wreck of the Golden Mary," for example, as told by Charles Dickens, and by a newspaper reporter. As a result of this discussion the children, when asked what questions they expect to find answered in the first sentence of a news story, will be able to give the five W's.

2. Let the children bring a city newspaper to class. Conduct a discussion as with the school paper.

3. If any members of the class have taken part in a recent assembly program, or in any other activity of interest to the whole school, secure the coöperation of the adviser of the school paper in the form of a request from him that the class write the account of the assembly for the next issue of the paper. Now conduct a discussion on the characteristics of a news story, illustrating the points made by reference to city and school papers.

4. After reading a selection in the literature book, such as one of the stories from *Grandfather's Chair,* or *The Legend of Sleepy Hollow,* or *The Winner Who Did Not Play,* conduct a discussion on the difference in the way this story would be told in a newspaper. The discussion should terminate in the listing of the five W's by the pupils.

B. Suggested activities.

  1. Explain the term "lead." Pupils are to learn the five W's. They may be interested in Kipling's rime:

> "I keep six honest serving-men;
>   They taught me all I knew;
> Their names are What? and Why? and When?
>   And How? and Where? and Who?"

  2. Explain "feature." Let the pupils decide what W is featured in each of the following leads:

a. Flashing his red-nosed plane, "Bumblebee," full throttle up and down the speed course in front of the Air Race grand stands in the eerie light that marked the height of the partial eclipse of the sun late yesterday afternoon, Major James H. Doolittle established a new unofficial world's landplane speed record of 292.195 miles per hour.

b. In an apartment at 2034 East 83d Street lives Rudolph de Bourbon, who believes the impoverished nobleman, Prince Edgard de Bourbon, whose murder in Paris was recorded in Associated Press dispatches early yesterday, was his father.

c. For the first time since its founding in 1894, the Cuyahoga Fair at Berea will not be held this year, trustees of the Cuyahoga County Agricultural Association decided at a special meeting last night in the Berea City Hall.

d. Joseph F. Rock, famous plant explorer and leader of the National Geographic Society's Yunnan Expedition, whose narrow escapes from bandits along the China-Thibet frontier were reported in cable dispatches a few months ago, arrived in Washington recently.

e. One of the new plane maneuvers invented since the World War was demonstrated yesterday at the National Air Races by Lieut. Andrea Zotti, 25-year-old commander of the Escadrille Folle, at Udine, Italy.

f. That a new building is to be erected to house the activities of the State Society for the Prevention of Cruelty to Animals was the announcement of Dr. R. A. Brown, president of the society, in his monthly report which was made public yesterday.

g. Among the 350 boys and girls who poured into Cleveland yesterday for the eighth annual Ohio Junior Live-Stock Exhibition opening at the Equestrium, 6800 Denison Avenue S.W., Carole McIlroy of Peoria, Union County, is outstanding.

h. Dr. J. C. Placak, president of the anti-Tuberculosis League, told yesterday in an address at Severance Hall of the development by a professor in the Pasteur Institute in Paris of a vaccine "that may prove of value in the immunization of children against tuberculosis."

i. LONDON, Oct. 18 ... (AP) ... Sir Henry Fielding Dickens, last surviving son of Charles Dickens, retired to-day after fifteen years as the common sergeant of London at the famous Old Bailey Court.

j. BERLIN, June 20 ... Laws of physics and chemistry have been toppled, five atoms split and an almost unimaginable volume of electrical voltage released in experiments conducted here by Dr. Fritz Lange and Dr. Arno Brash, it was revealed to-day.

k. Because he permitted his 15-year-old son to go joy-riding in the family automobile, John H. Jones, 1214 S Homan Avenue, was held by a coroner's jury yesterday on a charge of having been an accessory to manslaughter.

3. Assignment: Mount on theme paper three news stories clipped from the newspaper. The lead of each story is to feature a different W. Draw a line beside the lead. Under each clipping list the five W's, and then write the answer to each question from information given in the lead. (It is recommended that for slower sections this assignment be simplified to mounting and analyzing three news leads, without requiring that each feature a different W.)

4. Let the pupils rewrite the following stories. Each pupil should check his own work carefully to be sure that he has answered each of the five W's, and that he has featured the most interesting fact.

   a. Last Monday afternoon at 3:30 the Girl Reserves held a meeting in Room 115. Miss Bowman was present at the meeting which was conducted by the president, Irene Tandow. It was decided that the club fill ten Christmas baskets for needy families this year. Each girl's contribution is to represent some sacrifice on her part.

   b. This summer Mary Ann Evans, 9B, 106, enjoyed a trip to Yellowstone National Park. Having ambitions of becoming a geologist some day, Mary Ann found the geysers particularly interesting. A lesson in natural history which was not so pleasant was given her by a peevish bear which scratched her arms badly in his attempt to secure a sandwich which she had refused him.

5. Assignment: Strike out needless words and substitute

others in the following sentences. If you think best, re-write the sentences entirely.

  a. Director Jones was present at the meeting and made a few appropriate remarks.

  b. When the Girl Reserves finally came to the place, they found the building closed and locked.

  c. A meeting of the committee was held last Friday afternoon to discuss features of the coming presentation of the operetta.

  d. The entire proceeds of the pageant, amounting in all to $300, will be used to pay for the new talkie machine.

  e. The fire was first discovered by the alert night watchman, John Crosby, who excitedly sounded the alarm.

6. Assignment: From the following sentences take out expressions of personal opinion and all unnecessary words.

  a. The talk on television was interesting and it is too bad the crowd was so small.

  b. The Parent-Teachers Association is planting beautiful and much needed shrubs on the front campus.

  c. We are glad to welcome Robert Owen, our famous alumnus, back to the best little school on earth.

  d. *Captain Applejack* is a splendid play given by a fine cast, and is sure to be enjoyed by every one.

  e. Every one should have come to the music festival last Friday, for it was the best one ever held in the school. More than 400 people were in attendance.

  f. Arthur Walters, representing our school in the county oratorical contest, really deserved first place. Every one thought his oration, "Eyes That See," the best, in spite of the decision of the judges.

  g. Our basketball team is now county champion. The entire student body extends its appreciation to Coach Winters for his excellent work with the team this season.

7. Assignment: A reporter on a high-school paper gathered the following notes. Arrange the material in answers to the five W's, decide which fact should be featured most effectively, and write the news story. Hand in your analysis of the notes with your finished story.

  a. Robert Freeman is captain of the Glenville High School football team.

He was hurt in a practice scrimmage yesterday.

Dr. John McNally said last night the injury was slight.

To-day it was found that Freeman's collar bone was broken.

This means that Captain Freeman will be out of the big Thanksgiving game with East.

Glenville players are pessimistic.

—Leo A. Borah, *News Writing for High Schools,* p. 120.

8. Assignment: Interview a schoolmate on some experience or activity which you think would be of interest to the whole school. Take your notes in the form of answers to the five W's. Underline the fact which you think will be the best feature. Now write your story. Here are some questions to ask yourself after you have finished:

   a. Is every detail accurate?

   b. Have I spelled the names and other words correctly?

   c. Does the lead give the answers to each of the five W's?

   d. Is the feature well chosen?

   e. Does the lead attract and hold interest?

   f. Is the meaning of each sentence clear, or might the reader interpret a line?

   g. Have I made mistakes in grammar or punctuation?

   h. Have I included the first names of all persons mentioned, and given the homeroom number and grade of every student mentioned?

   i. Have I expressed my own opinion?

   j. Are there any unnecessary words?

9. Let pupils write news stories based on literature read recently in class. The following topics offer possibilities:

   a. *The Legend of Sleepy Hollow*

      The Van Tassel's quilting frolic

      The Disappearance of Ichabod Crane

      The wedding of Katrina Van Tassel and Brom Bones

      News brought by an old farmer of Ichabod Crane's success in New York

   b. *Grandfather's Chair*

      Betsy Hull's wedding, the gift of the pine-tree shilling

      First news of the Stamp Act to reach Boston

      The hanging in effigy of the Earl of Bute and of

Andrew Oliver on Liberty Tree as a protest against the Stamp Act

Stationing of British soldiers in Boston

An affray between the British soldiers and young Bostonians in front of the customs-house or the State House

The Boston Massacre

c. *Tales of a Grandfather*

The reunion of Robert the Bruce and James Douglas in the woods on the island of Arran

The taking of Edinburgh Castle

The taking of the Castle of Lithgow

The battle of Bannockburn

10. Divide the class into groups. To each group assign one school news source, such as the librarian, the office secretary, the manager of the cafeteria, the chairman of assembly programs, etc. Each member of the group may use the same material if necessary. Interest can be increased by securing from the faculty adviser of the school paper permission to print the best stories.

IV. *References*

A. Teacher references.

BLEYER, W. G., *Types of News Writing* (Houghton Mifflin).

BORAH, L. A., *News Writing for High Schools* (Allyn and Bacon).

CLARK and Others, *The Highway to English* (Winston).

DILLON, Charles, *Journalism for High Schools* (Noble).

GREENAWALT, Lambert, *School Press Management and Style* (McGraw, Hill).

HARRINGTON, H. F., *Writing for Print* (D. C. Heath).

———, *Essentials in Journalism* (Ginn).

HARRINGTON, H. and E., *The Newspaper Club* (D. C. Heath).

HUFF, Bessie M., *How to Publish a School Paper* (Mentzer, Bush).

HYDE, Grant M., *A Course in Journalistic Writing* (Appleton).

———, *A Handbook for Newspaper Workers* (Appleton).

Knickerbocker and Others, *Thinking, Speaking, and Writing*, Book III (Silver, Burdett).

MILLER, C. G., *High School Reporting and Editing* (McGraw, Hill).

OTTO, William, *Journalism for High Schools* (Harcourt, Brace).

SPENCER, M. Lyle, *News Writing* (D. C. Heath).

WELLS, G. C., *Student Publications* (Barnes).

V. *Desired outcomes*

  A. Knowledge and understanding of the following:
  1. The make-up of a newspaper
  2. What constitutes news
  3. Sources of news stories
  4. How to read a news story intelligently
  5. Essentials of conventional news story composition

  B. Habits and skills.
  1. Checking one's own work for completeness, clearness, and accuracy
  2. Keeping the reader in mind while writing
  3. Planning before writing
  4. Analyzing material to find items of greatest importance and interest
  5. Discarding the nonessential and irrelevant
  6. Expressing one's self clearly, simply and accurately

  C. Attitudes and appreciations
  1. Reading the news stories in daily papers
  2. Grammar, spelling, and punctuation because of greater appreciation of their practical value

The following courses of study present further illustrations of this method of organizing units of work:

  1. Course of Study in Safety and Health Education, Minneapolis, Minnesota. Kindergarten to sixth grade, 1932-1933.
  2. Course of Study in Art, Long Beach, California. Grades 4—6, 1931.
  3. Course of Study in the Use of the Library, Detroit, Michigan. Grades 1—6, 1931.
  4. Course of Study in Art, Long Beach, California. Grades 10—12, 1932.
  5. Course of Study in Art, Oakland, California. Grades 7—12, 1931.

  D. A unit may be a sub-division of a major topic or section in the course of study. The term "unit" can also be applied to a subdivision or component of a major topic. The larger organization of subject-matter has been determined upon and the unit represents a logical, rather than a psychological, development of the treatment which will be accorded the material in the particular grade. The following discussion of the unit in mathematics is pertinent here since it clarifies this point:

There are really two types of units in mathematics, namely: units of understanding and drill units. The outcome of a unit of understanding is an understanding which is mastered or not mastered. The product of a drill unit is skill which may or may not stay with an individual. Two types of teaching are required for these two different units. The following characteristics are pertinent to a unit of understanding in mathematics:

1. It is a body of closely related facts and principles so organized as to contribute to the understanding of an important aspect of the work.

2. It must be possible to present the unit, as a whole, in a form so concise as to give the learner a clearer conception of it before he undertakes to study it.

3. The objectives must be so definitely stated that they are clear not only to the teacher but also to the pupil. The learning products must be known.

4. All pupils properly qualified to take the course must be able to master the minimum essentials necessary and sufficient to attain complete understanding of the unit. In addition to this minimum, the unit must contain supplementary material to allow freedom in adapting the work to the individual differences of the pupils.

5. It must be possible to devise tests which secure objective evidence of the understanding of the unit.

A unit that has been properly selected presents a comprehensive aspect of the subject, and the teaching of it demands, upon the part of the instructor, an overhead view which enables him to give fuller meaning to the entire course than is possible under the page by page teaching.

The unit is a significant and important aspect of the world of well nigh every individual who lives in a civilized society. It is inclusive of the whole aspect and not a fragment.[9]

In the Health and Physical Education course of study of San Francisco, California, one of the major topics for grade V

[9] Breslich, E. R., "The Unit in Mathematics," *Junior-Senior High School Clearing House,* Vol. V (February, 1931), pp. 321-326. The author has used freedom in selecting outstanding items from this valuable article.

is The Healthful Organism. There is a logical organization of sixteen units of work under this topic, as follows: Nutrition, Sleep and Rest, Fresh Air and Sunshine, Care of the Skin, Care of the Teeth and Mouth, Care of the Nose and Throat, Care of the Eyes, Care of the Ears, Hair and Scalp, Care of the Hands and Nails, Care of the Feet, Elimination, Clothing and its Care, Posture, Height and Weight, Big Muscle Activities. The complete unit on nutrition is presented in order to illustrate this type of organization.[10]

The following courses are excellent illustrations of this type of unit organization which can be used by the student:

1. Course of Study in Mathematics for Grades 9—12. State of Iowa, 1932.
2. Tentative Course of Study in Mathematics for Grades 7—8. Lakewood Public Schools, 1931.
3. Tentative Outline of Course of Study in Biology. Kansas City, Missouri, September, 1932.
4. Tentative Outline of Course of Study in Chemistry for the Senior High School. Kansas City, Missouri, September, 1932.
5. Tentative Outline of a Course of Study in Physiography for the Senior High School. Kansas City, Missouri, September, 1932.
6. Tentative Outline in General Science for Grades 9—12. Kansas City, Missouri, 1930.
7. Tentative Outline of a Hand-book in Science for Elementary Grades. Oakland, California, 1932.
8. Course of Study in Mathematics Revised, Grades 7—10. School Document No. 2, 1930, Boston Public Schools.

III. CRITERIA ESSENTIAL IN THE DEVELOPMENT OF COURSE-OF-STUDY UNITS OF WORK

The outstanding examples of the several types of units have been analyzed and illustrated, and it is important that the teacher or the committee formulate definite standards by which to undertake the organization of the unit. The following criteria will not only serve as a guide in the development of the teaching

[10] *Health and Physical Education* (Board of Education, San Francisco, California, 1931), grades IV, V, and VI, pp. 42-44.

THE HEALTHFUL ORGANISM

GRADE FIVE

A. Nutrition

Habits	Knowledge	Attitudes	Suggested Activities	Correlations	References
Milk					
Drinks at least one quart daily	Milk is the almost perfect food	Desires to eat proper kinds of foods regularly	Adopt class motto	Art-Language	Andress and Evans, *Health and Success*; Chs. IV and V, pp. 26-41; Chs. VIII-XII, pp. 60-103
Drinks milk slowly	Whole milk aids growth		Construct posters which illustrate energy-giving foods; body-building foods; regulating foods	Art	
	Milk should be kept clean, cool, and covered	Maintains a cheerful attitude at meal times	Show on a map of the United States where grain, vegetables, fruits, and dairy products used in daily menus are obtained	Geography	Bigelow and Broadhurst, *Health for Every Day*, Ch. IV, pp. 84-114
					Burkhard, Chambers and Maroney, *Health Habits*, Book I, Chs. IX and X, pp. 186-236; 261-264
					California Dairy Council pamphlets
Water					
Drinks at least four glasses a day, be-	Two-thirds to three-fourths of the		Plan a balanced menu for one day for the		Newmayer and Broome, *The Way to Keep*

Habit	Reason	Activity	Subject	Reference
fore meals and when thirsty	body weight is made up of water. The body loses three quarts daily, which must be replaced	average fifth grade child. (Use various devices as charts and posters)		*Well*, Ch. XV, Ch. XVI, pp. 136-171
Uses only individual drinking cups, or a drinking fountain		Build a definition of food	Language	Turner and Collins, *Health*, Chs. VII-XIII, pp. 44-100
Uses drinking fountain correctly	The drinking of water aids digestion and elimination	Collect food labels and paste them in the state which furnished the product (from sample cans, if possible)	Geography	Turner and Pinckney, *In Training for Health*, Ch. IV, pp. 38-48
Does not drink with food in the mouth				
Fruits, Vegetables and Cereals				Williams and Dansdill, *Health and Control*, Chs. IV, VI, pp. 37-80
Eats two green vegetables daily	Fruits and vegetables supply the needed minerals, natural sugar and water. They aid in elimination	Contrast the food problem of Byrd's expedition with that of Magellan's	History	
Eats fresh fruit daily				Winslow and Hahn, *The New Healthy Living*, Book I, Chs. IV, VIII, pp. 29-78
Eats a cereal (preferably cooked) each day	Cereals furnish heat and energy	On a map of the world have pictures of ships carrying healthful foods from our de-	Geography	*Note:* Armour's Food Products Map is especially helpful in this grade

THE HEALTHFUL ORGANISM—*Continued*

GRADE FIVE

A. *Nutrition*

Habits	Knowledge	Attitudes	Suggested Activities	Correlations	References
	The body needs building foods, energy (fuel) foods, and regulating foods		pendencies to the United States		The following readers contain additional information:
			Indicate the products by samples or pictures connected to the ship by streamers		*Thought Study Reader*, Book V "Bread for Everybody," pp. 101-109 "How to Fold a Paper Cup," p. 110 "A Story about Tapioca Pudding," pp. 211-213
Hygienic Habits of Eating Chews food well	Chewing food well aids digestion		Start a Health Scrap-Book in which may be placed original songs, rhymes, and drawings or cut-outs illustrating the topics under discussion	Language Music Writing	
Eats regularly	Eating between meals overworks the stomach				"What Our Dependencies Bring Us," pp. 333-340
Is cheerful at meal times	Digestion begins in the mouth (teeth, saliva)				*Child Story* V "Fresh Food for Everybody," pp. 307-312
Washes hands be-					"Raising Poultry," pp. 339-344

		"America's Sweet Tooth," pp. 345-352 "A Food of the Gods," pp. 352-358 "Bananas! Bananas!" pp. 370-375
fore eating or handling food		
Eats candy and sweets only after meals and in moderation	Digestion prepares the food so that it can be used by the body	
Is temperate in eating	Eating sweets between meals destroys the appetite for more wholesome foods	

unit, but will also constitute a gauge by which the completed unit can be evaluated:

1. The objectives must be clearly stated, so that both the teacher and the pupils can understand them and work together for their realization.

2. The unit must have coherence, that is, it must form a natural transition from real life activities, which have been experienced by the pupils, to the achievements established by the aims of the present unit, and carry on to future realizations.

3. The unit should provide for the participation of the pupils. They should have the opportunity to plan, originate, and direct any phases of the unit which are to be worked out extemporaneously in the classroom.

4. The unit should be organized so that it is practicable in the particular community and school system. Materials and facilities in both will determine the limitations of the educational program.

5. The unit should challenge the pupils at the particular grade level, but should contain minimum essentials which are within the pupils' ability to achieve mastery.

6. The unit should reproduce real life situations and should make use of activities, experiences, and materials which occur in the life of the community and state. However, it will be noted that some exceptions were listed among the illustrations. Henry Harap makes the following statement concerning this criterion: [11]

What are some reasonable exceptions to organizing units based on life situations? Teachers who find it difficult to organize their courses on the basis of life situations are likely to become impatient with these notes because they cannot apply them completely to their subjects. There are certain reasonable exceptions to such an organization which will be given below. In any case, if the curriculum maker wishes to organize a course on the basis of topics or processes, or principles, he need only to state his objectives in terms of the mastery of these, and proceed with the building of units on that basis. For example, in the field of language, one may set up

[11] Henry Harap, *Curriculum Laboratory Bulletin,* No. 17 (School of Education, Western Reserve University, November 30, 1931), p. 6.

the objective, to form the past tense of the most common irregular verbs, and proceed to build a unit which will result in the accomplishment of the goal.

Contact with various school people has demonstrated these reasonable exceptions to our proposed organization of units: (1) Some teachers or administrative officers conscientiously believe that a series of graded steps, as in arithmetic, arranged for coherence, for progressive difficulty, and for systematic distribution of practice, is the best organization for economical learning and for effective living. (2) Some conventional subjects, like algebra, which have to be taught bear little relationship to life. (3) Some subjects, like penmanship, do not have a rich enough body of source materials to guide the average teacher in the necessary reorganization. Only the ingenious and studious teacher may be expected to create the new materials which the new adjustment requires.

7. The unit should be interesting if it is based on intrinsic materials; the objectives of the unit should be especially stressed as interesting and valuable to the pupil if the unit is made up of extrinsic material to any appreciable degree. If the student is not directly interested, he must be satisfied as to the value of the outcome of the work.

8. All phases of the teaching unit—objectives, content, methods, supplementary materials, tests, etc., should be so clearly and definitely organized that a new teacher or a substitute teacher can efficiently organize and conduct the work with the coöperation of the pupils.

9. The unit should proceed usually from the known to the unknown; from the concrete to the abstract; from the particular toward the generalization. The information should be accurate and the activities true to life so that the pupils can have the opportunity to judge, evaluate, and discriminate as they make progress.

10. The unit should designate the materials which will be of value to the pupils and to the teacher. Any bibliographical data should be complete and exact whether for teachers or pupils.

11. The unit of work must provide for individual differences. This can be done by building the unit for a particular ability level or by indicating levels of achievement within the unit.

The following excerpt from the course of study in the social sciences for the junior high schools of Ann Arbor, Michigan, will illustrate professional work involved in the construction of the unit of work:

The teachers in developing the unit outline were also very conscious that the teacher's task is an arduous one. Consequently every attempt was made to prepare the teacher's lesson for him to the extent that it was wise and possible. It was thought that the several sections devoted to actual suggestions concerning activities and materials might serve as either direct suggestions or as stimulating materials for both the teachers and pupils.

DIRECTIONS FOR WRITING UP UNIT

Please observe the following directions in writing up a unit:
1. Fill in every topic and sub-topic heading.
2. Be as concise and at the same time be as clear as possible.
3. Do not hand in the unit until you have taught it and revised your original plan. We want this to represent your best judgment of what would be most helpful in teaching this unit.
4. Be careful of your sentence structure. *Have your work in such form that you would be glad to have it published with your name attached.*

UNIT OUTLINE
(Title)

(Sub-title: The predominant purpose of the unit stated in a *single, short* sentence.

I. *Introduction*
   A. Delimitation and definition
   B. Social justification for the unit
   C. Curriculum integration
      1. Relation of this unit to courses in the elementary and senior high school
      2. Relation of this unit to related junior high-school courses
      3. Relation of this unit to other social-studies units, especially those studied in the same semester
   D. Peculiar local considerations
   E. Major facts and hypotheses which aid in attacking problems involved in the unit

II. *Professional Literature*
   The references listed here have been found to be helpful in

teacher-preparation on this unit. No doubt there are other useful books to be had, and current literature should be under examination at all times.

III. *Fields of Experience Peculiar and in Most Cases Fundamental to This Unit*
So-called specific aims should always be interpreted in terms of fundamental changes to be made in the child. The teacher's effort should not be to *teach* but rather to help the child to experience so completely and so deeply that his attitudes and consequently his future actions will be those of an individual who is making his *fullest contribution* to society and at the same time making the most satisfactory personal adjustment. The fields of experience in this unit are indicated by the following phrases:

IV. *Solving the Problem*
   A. Suggested approach activities
   B. Several statements of the general problem as derived from pupils
   C. Suggested activities which may be used in the solution of the problem

V. *Experiences in Planning and Social Action*
Out of the various solution activities naturally come group and individual interests so intense and pointed that they may easily carry over into social action. For the school to withhold its guidance at this point is to emasculate the entire proceedings. Certain "next steps" implying social action by the children well within their range of execution may be allowed to mature as a part of the work of the unit.
Note: The following suggestions for social action have been used: making posters and placing them where they will do the most good; joining an existing group or forming a new group whose aims are those of the child (this group may be a continuous study or discussion group); writing and distributing pamphlets to the student body or the public; distributing printed materials obtained from organizations carrying on a clean-up campaign; actually reforesting some area, however small; petitioning the proper body for some reform; writing letters to officials to influence action; joining organizations representing national movements.
Suggestions for this unit:

VI. *Materials for the Pupils*
   A. Visual materials
   B. Reading references and materials in the building
   C. Reading references and materials not in the building

VII. *Suggested Time Allotment*
VIII. *Authorship*

IV. PERTINENT QUESTIONS FOR THE TEACHER OR COMMITTEE

The teacher or the committee which is considering the completion of the unit of work should not proceed to present it to the Superintendent or Director of Research until the following questions have been answered satisfactorily:

1. Are the general and specific objectives or the purpose of this unit definitely stated? Unless this has been done, confusion may arise as to the goals which are to be achieved by the pupils; the time and place of the unit in the course of study may be misunderstood; and much material and activities which have no place in this unit may be included to the detriment of the course as a whole.

2. Has the teacher or committee selected or developed a set of criteria which will serve to direct the development of the unit? They should be used at every step in order that each phase may be carefully checked.

3. If only the purpose of the unit has been stated and the specifics have not been worked out, many problems will arise concerning the sub-divisions of the unit. How can these be efficiently evaluated, organized, and allocated as sections of the unit?

4. Have all of the available sources been included in the standards used in evaluating the sections of the unit? The following should be considered essential:

1. Past experiences of the committee members in teaching the subject or field.
2. Consult specialists or leaders in the activity or field.
3. Consult books and documents which are authoritative.
4. Visit other schools, and consult courses of study developed in other cities.
5. Have the unit tried out in your own system by special teachers and confer with colleagues in other school systems. Study and evaluate these criticisms as a basis of adding to, eliminating from, or modifying the product of the committee.

BIBLIOGRAPHY

ALVEY, Edward, "Current Developments in the Unit Method of Teaching," *University of Virginia Record,* Vol. XIX, No. 3 (October, 1934).

———, "Current Trends in the Development of the Unit in English," *University of Virginia Record,* Vol. XIX, No. 3 (October, 1934).

BAILEY, O. C., *An Approach to American History: Students' Guide Sheets* (University of Chicago Press, 1927). An examination of the Morrison unit plan.

BAMESBERGER, V. C., *An Appraisal of a Social Studies Course* (Bureau of Publications, Teachers College, Columbia University, 1928).

BAXTER, T., "Some Techniques and Principles Used in Selecting and Teaching a Unit of Work," *Teachers College Record,* Vol. XXX (November, 1929), pp. 148-160.

BRESLICH, E. R., "The Unit in Mathematics," *Junior-Senior High School Clearing House,* Vol. V (February, 1931), pp. 321-326.

BRUCE, G. V., "Some Essentials of an Elementary Science Unit," *Journal of Chemical Education,* Vol. X (August, 1933), pp. 484-486. The essential elements of the elementary-science unit are discussed.

BURTON, W. H., "The Unit Concept in Learning: An Attempt at a Simple Explanation," *Educational Outlook,* Vol. VII (May, 1933), pp. 206-213.

COLLINGS, E., "Social Foundations of Project Teaching," *Journal of Educational Sociology,* Vol. V (September, 1931), pp. 35-42.

Curriculum Making in an Elementary School, Lincoln Elementary School Staff (Ginn and Company, 1927), Ch. III.

Curriculum Making in Current Practice, Conference at Northwestern University (School of Education, Northwestern University, 1932). Contains a number of discussions of units in general and units in particular subject-matter fields.

GECK, E. E., "The Large Unit in History," *High School Teacher,* Vol. VI (January, 1930), pp. 31-32.

GRAHAM, R. C., "Administrative Aspects of the Unit Method of Teaching," *University of Virginia Record,* Vol. XIX, No. 3 (October, 1934).

GRINSTEAD, N. B., "The Learning Situation Afforded by Industrial Arts," *Industrial Arts Magazine,* Vol. XIX (February, 1930), pp. 291-293.

HARAP, Henry, *The Technique of Curriculum Making* (The Macmillan Company, 1928). Parts VI and VII should be read.

HOPKINS, L. T., *Curriculum Principles and Practices* (Benjamin Sanborn and Company, 1929), pp. 464-471.

LANKFORD, F. G., "Current Trends in the Development of the Unit in Mathematics," *University of Virginia Record,* Vol. XIX, No. 3 October, 1934).

LAUGHLIN, B., "The Unit Method in Junior High School Mathematics," *Junior-Senior High School Clearing House,* Vol. V (February, 1931), pp. 326-328.

Montgomery County, Maryland, *Professional Yearbook* 1931. This is devoted to a discussion of units of work.

MORRISON, H. C., *The Practice of Teaching in Secondary Schools* (University of Chicago Press, 1933). This book may be called the parent of the unit movement and should be read by every one engaged in the construction of units.

PHIPPINS, C. H., "Recent Trends in Instructional Procedures for Individualizing Instruction," *University of Virginia Record,* Vol. XIX, No. 3 (October, 1934).

Raleigh Public Schools, "Statement of the Aims and Educational Program of the Raleigh Public Schools," *Curriculum Bulletin* No. 2, pp. 37-38 and 61-67.

REEDER, E. H., "What are Life Situations." *Teachers College Record,* Vol. XXIX, (February, 1928), pp. 409-416.

Research Bulletin of the National Education Association, Vol. II, "Keeping Pace with the Advancing Curriculum," Nos. 4 and 5 (September, 1925), pp. 179-181.

RUGG, H., and MENDENHALL, J. E., *Teacher's Guide for an Introduction to American Civilization* (Ginn and Company, 1929). In Chapter I, ten psychological principles are stated which form the basis of the theory underlying each unit of work.

SHELTON, A. L., "An Experimental Study of the Daily Recitation Versus the Unit Plan," *School Review,* Vol. XXXVIII (November, 1930), pp. 694-699.

SIMPSON, Mabel E., "Theory of the Kindergarten Primary Unit," *Childhood Education* (November, 1929), pp. 110-114.

SMITH, E. T., *A New Approach to European History: Teachers' Manual* (University of Chicago Press, 1929).

STEVENS, M. P., *The Activities Curriculum in the Primary Grades* (D. C. Heath and Co., 1921), pp. 299-300.

SWINDLER, R. E., "Current Trends in the Development of the Unit in Social Science," *University of Virginia Record,* Vol. XIX, No. 3 (October, 1934).

———, "The Unit System of Instruction." (This excellent statement is found in his book, *Social Studies Instruction in the Secondary Schools,* published by Prentice-Hall, Inc., 1933, pp. 177-256.) A thorough treatment of the unit system. Some experimental evidence has been included in discussing the pros and cons of certain questions.

THAYER, V. T., *The Passing of the Recitation* (D. C. Heath and Co., 1928), Chs. XVIII and XIX. Chapter XIX discusses the nature of the teaching unit.

THRALLS, Z. A., "The Teaching Unit in Geography," *Journal of the National Education Association,* Vol. XXII (May, 1933), pp. 153-154.

TIPPETT, J. S., and Others, *Curriculum Making in an Elementary School* (Ginn and Company, 1927). In Chapter III, criteria for the selection of units of work are presented.

"The Unit Method of Teaching," *University of Virginia Record,* Vol. XIV, No. 9 (March, 1930). An Exposition of the Unit Plan with illustrations from English, mathematics, social studies, and science.

WAPLES, D., and STONE, C. A., *The Teaching Unit: A Type Study* (D. Appleton and Company, 1929). A typical unit for a course in junior-high-school mathematics according to the Morrison plan.

WEAVER, R. B., and HILL, H. C., *United States History by Units.* Parts I and II (W. F. Quarrie and Company, 1933). Part I deals with the development of the unit and teaching procedures, while Part II contains actual units with objectives, references, questions, and pupil activities.

WHITFORD, W. G., "The Unit Conception of Teaching Applied Art," *School Review,* Vol. XLI (June, 1933), pp. 443-449.

WYNNE, J. P., *The Learning-Teaching Unit (Farmville Herald,* Farmville, Va., 1934). These eighty-six pages of lectures consider the nature of the unit, criteria for evaluating the unit, etc.

CHAPTER IX

UNITS AS CENTERS OF INTEREST

The units analyzed and illustrated in this chapter represent complete educational experiences for the child or large centers of interests for the pupils. In these respects they are similar to each other and different from any of those considered in Chapter XIV. However, both of these types are common in up-to-date public-school systems.

I. A UNIT MAY BE A COMPLETE EDUCATIONAL EXPERIENCE FOR THE CHILD

A unit of work—such as the construction of a dress of wool—may be a complete educational experience for the pupils in which they achieve mastery of all of the objectives essential in the attainment of this goal. An illustration has been selected from the Tentative Course of study in Home Making for Junior and Senior High Schools published by the Kansas City Schools. In the second year of the senior high school, the following work is outlined for the first semester.[1]

		Weeks
Unit 1.	Introduction	1
Unit 2.	Income and expenditure	1
Unit 3.	Construction of a wool dress	16
	a. Study of wool: fiber and fabric	1
	b. Color in dress	1
	c. Figure and line study	1
	d. Selection and purchase of fabric and pattern	1
	e. The process	12
	f. Margin of time	2

[1] *Tentative Course of Study in Home Making for Junior and Senior High Schools* (Board of Education, Kansas City, Missouri, 1933), pp. 145-153.

UNIT III. CONSTRUCTION OF A WOOL DRESS

Objectives

To give guidance in the making of a wool dress which gives satisfaction and meets approved standards of workmanship and of taste.

To give opportunity for the expression of individuality through choice of fabric and construction of one's own dress.

To develop practical understanding of the economic, esthetic, and hygienic aspects of dress.

To give a knowledge of the principles underlying the choice of fabrics and patterns.

A. A STUDY OF WOOL; FIBER AND FABRIC

Content and Pupil Activities	Teaching Suggestions
Sources and production of raw material Making reports on topics such as the following: Animals furnishing wool Countries producing wool Care of sheep, washing and shearing	As an approach, show films portraying the wool industry from the raising of wool-producing animals to the weaving of woolen fabrics The use of process cases provides visual aid, also
Manufacture of raw product into yarn Reporting of factory processes: sorting, scouring, drying, blending, preparing yarn, finishing	Show and discuss pictures that illustrate factory processes
Adulteration of wool Discussing the various substitutes for wool Bringing samples of woolens from home for testing and checking ability to recognize adulterated wool	Discuss and demonstrate chemical and physical tests to determine whether or not a fabric is adulterated. Microscopic tests show better than any other means the kind and quality of fiber in fabrics under observation

Content and Pupil Activities | Teaching Suggestions

Difference between woolens and worsteds

Furnishing samples of woolens and worsteds

Studying and listing characteristics of each fabric

Manufacture of wool into fabric

Giving reports on: weaving, finishing processes, Jacquard loom

Make use of materials brought into class for construction as a means of checking ability to distinguish between woolens and worsteds

Discuss advantages of woolens and worsteds and uses for each

Show and discuss pictures of Jacquard loom

Use samples of damask to show how design is developed by use of Jacquard loom

Characteristics of wool

Noting the difference between the characteristics of wool and cotton

Have girls list characteristics of wool:
Is the warmest fiber
Is very absorbent
Soils easily
Is a poor conductor of heat
Tends to shrink when washed

Wool products

Discussing and listing finished wool products

Making special reports on Gobelin tapestry

Oriental and domestic rugs

Listening to talks by connoisseurs on Oriental rug-making

Make use of colored prints of Oriental rugs to develop an appreciation for color combinations and design and to help in the identification of rugs. If possible, visit a store where Oriental and domestic rugs may be compared

B. COLOR IN DRESS

Color in the life of the girl

Discussing the following topics:
Favorite colors and color combinations
Reasons for choice of various colors

Through discussion find out from the girls their tastes, preferences, and practices in connection with color. Use the information thus obtained as a basis for the actual work

Content and Pupil Activities	Teaching Suggestions
Colors that attract attention Joyousness of color Effect of color on one's mental state Relation of color to youth	which follows and also for the improvement of standards and practices Give varied experiences in arranging the combining colors through the use of flowers, pottery, and textiles
Colors and their effects Discussing the effect of the primary colors with disregard for complexion types Deciding which one of the primary colors is most pleasing on all types Noting the effect of black, white, and gray on all types	Discuss choice of colors for all types, stressing these points: Appropriateness to one's age Color, when worn next to the face, of medium value and intensity Avoidance of too many contrasts Enhancement of one's best features or improvement of less desirable ones
Colors and complexion types Deciding on characteristics of the various types Listing colors best suited to blond, brunette, and Titian types Using color samples to test the becomingness of colors to types	Explain the reasons for using draped material for testing colors to types Discuss the manner in which daylight and lamplight affect color, also the effect of texture on color
Colors and costumes Discussing appropriate colors for costumes to be worn: At home On the street For afternoon For evening Considering colors suitable for garment decoration Deciding on colors that are harmonious to the eye Discussing the hat as part of	Emphasize the importance of: Cheerful, colorful, but not glaring colors for house costumes Deep, rich colors for street costumes Light, to high light colors, for afternoon and evening costumes Color in hose, gloves, shoes, to harmonize with costume

Content and Pupil Activities	Teaching Suggestions
the costume, its color and trimming Noting how color in hats adds interest to an otherwise uninteresting costume	Remind girls that texture as well as colors should harmonize when two materials are used in a garment. Remind girls that, if only one hat may be had, it should combine with all costumes Suggest how the beret, made from scraps, permits a hat for each costume

Colors and undergarments

Considering such questions as the following:
  Best colors to use for undergarments
  When the deeper colors may be used
  When all color is to be avoided
  When bright colors and conspicuous designs do not conform with the principles of good taste
	Remind girls that white is the most satisfactory color for underwear that must be worn with many costumes
	Explain that one's admiration for deeper colors may be expressed through her negligee

Color and costume jewelry

Discussing points to consider when selecting rings, clips, necklace, bracelet; e.g., color, use, design, size, appropriateness	Suggest that color accent may be repeated in a costume ring, a modest clip, or ornament for the neck. All accessories should be planned with a definite aim in view, to insure a harmonizing of the entire ensemble

Color and size

Considering the effect of color on the size of the figure Discussing the colors that seem to increase or diminish size Offering for class discussion and evaluation color preferences of individuals	Present for discussion questions such as the following: How do light and dark colors affect the silhouette? What is the effect of dull and bright colors on the silhouette? Warm and cool colors? What is the effect of shiny and dull textures? Heavy and transparent textures?

C. FIGURE AND LINE STUDY

Content and Pupil Activities	Teaching Suggestions
Study of the human figure	Explain that the paramount purpose of clothing is to protect and adorn the body and to conserve its heat
Discussing such points as the following:	
Marks of beauty in girl	
Figures and carriage	
Possible irregularities in girl figures:	Lead the girl to understand that many irregularities of the figure may be improved or entirely overcome by one's mode of living and by will power. Beauty of carriage is free to all
Round shoulders	
Prominent abdomen	
Large hips	
Large upper arm	
Full bust	
Hollow chest	Suggest that well-fitting garments do not restrict the movements of the wearer and, if well chosen and cared for, can be forgotten
Narrow shoulders	
Improvement through corrective measures	
Discussing healthful living	Discuss with the girls points of graceful carriage; for example:
Exercise	Head and chest up
Rest	Abdomen in
Food	Shoulders up and back
Mental state	Chest high
	Feet close to each other
	Arms relaxed and near the body
Improvement through attention to lines in clothing	
Discussing effect of	Make use of trial models of cambric to note the effect of various neck lines
Cape and bolero	
Direction of the shoulder line	Warn against the use of raglan or kimono sleeve for round shoulders
Flaring and straight lines	
Broad and narrow brims	
Perpendicular and horizontal lines in fabric and garment	Remind girls that the belt which is too wide and too tight emphasizes the bust and the abdomen
Round, V, or square neck	

Content and Pupil Activities	Teaching Suggestions
Raglan and kimono sleeve Solid colors and prints Hem line and belt line	Show the effect of a sagging hem line on the appearance of posture

D. SELECTION AND PURCHASE OF FABRIC AND PATTERN

Plan for shopping
Discussing previous shopping experiences
Discussing such questions as the following:
Where shall I shop?
What should influence my choice of shops?
When shall I shop?
With whom shall I shop?
What should influence my choice of fabric and color?
What should be my attitude toward salespeople?
When should I purchase?
Formulating simple principles underlying the etiquette of shopping.

Make sure that the girl has in mind:
Shops dealing in woolens
Amount of material needed
Kind and amount of trimmings
Number, size, and make of pattern
Point out the disadvantages of adulterated wool
Emphasize the importance of an early discussion of plans
Discuss the advantages and disadvantages of sales, also popular colors and fabrics with relation to types
Demonstrate pleasing color combinations by use of samples and color charts
Encourage the girl to make choices in the light of her own knowledge instead of through influence of clerk and friends
Review characteristics of woolens and worsteds with purpose of dress in mind

Purpose of the dress
Considering questions such as the following:
Where the dress is to be worn
What style will be most appriate
What fabrics to use

Stress the fact that the dress must be suited to the use to which it is to be put. For persons with limited income the dress should serve more than one season. The type of the dress should be in keeping

Content and Pupil Activities

What trimmings to use
Esthetic requirements

Teaching Suggestions

with the social position of the
wearer. If a business dress, it
should be tailored in type and
should be easily cleansed
Make sure the dress will satisfy
the love of beauty as well as
the laws of fitness

Amount allowed for purchases
Discussing such points as:
The price one may expect to
pay for wool that will
give satisfaction
Comparison of price and
width, also width and
amount of fabric
The price of pattern
The amount specified in
budget for dress

Give definite idea of price and
quality of wool, using samples
sent from shops
Stress the economic value of the
better commercial patterns
Demonstrate the economy of
fifty-four inch wool and make
plain the comparison of width
and price from the economic
standpoint.

E. THE PROCESS

The material
Sponging:
Discussing reasons for
sponging: water spotting,
shrinkage, pressing
Straightening:
Making ends straight by:
tearing, cutting by woven
design or on a drawn
thread
Pulling material into shape
so that warp and woof
threads are right angles

Discourage the sponging of wool
in the home. It is done more
efficiently and cheaply at the
shop
Show by demonstration materials
that should be straightened by
tearing, by cutting, by drawn
thread
Discuss the necessity for having
warp and woof threads at
right angles before cutting
garment. Use a woven plaid
to illustrate

The pattern
Making use of the counter
books in selecting a pattern
for the woolen dress
Studying direction sheet to determine how pattern is put

Suggest that each girl choose at
least three designs for the
dress, then help her with the
final selection. This plan avoids
the choice of a pattern with

Content and Pupil Activities	Teaching Suggestions
together and how it is placed on material	phases that will be too difficult
Preparing to test the pattern	Encourage use of direction sheet and explain, by group instruction, how to interpret it
Pinning all the parts together making seam allowances, darts, tucks, and pleats in accordance with pattern directions	Lead girls to understand the necessity for testing the pattern before purchasing materials or cutting dress. It is possible to make alterations on the pattern and save serious mistakes, e.g., length of sleeve, length of skirt, position of waist line, amount of material required for one garment. This practice gives the girl an understanding of the way the dress is put together before she is ready to baste
Placing only those parts to be used in the selected view of pattern	
Placing pins in material to hold the pattern flat to fabric	
Marking with tailors' chalk: seam allowances, right side of material, any changes to be made before cutting	
Accurately cutting the garment, following edge of pattern or chalk line indicating necessary changes	Demonstrate how changes in pattern are made.
	Stress the importance of good pins by demonstrating ways in which dull tarnished pins injure the fabric
	Emphasize the importance of marking right side of wool material before the garment is cut. This practice does away with two sleeves for one arm, gores placed wrong side out, and indecision as to right and wrong side of material
	Discuss the necessity for a smooth edge when cutting, and warn against danger of following pattern instead of chalk line when allowances have been made
The marks	
Marking, by use of tailor's tack, all notches, perfora-	Show pupils the disadvantages of cutting notches and mark-

Content and Pupil Activities

Teaching Suggestions

tions, and pleat lines that have to do with putting the garment together

Marking center front and back of garment with running stitch, also notches indicating how sleeve is set to arm-scye

ing notches with pencil, and the advantages of the use of the running stitch in marking notches indicating the position of the sleeve in the arm-scye

The basted dress

Assembling and basting all parts of the front, all parts of the back, and the sleeve

Fitting basted dress and making necessary changes, noting position of waist line, size and length of sleeve, shoulder and neck line, hip line, width of hem, armscye

Turning and basting hem in the dress, determining length of dress in relation to the proportions of the figure and prevailing fashion

Setting and basting sleeve to arm-scye, keeping in mind the various trends and finishes of the modern sleeve

Review essential points in pinning and basting parts of garment. Show how fitting is simplified by basting all parts of the back, leaving the underarm seam to be basted when front and back are complete

Demonstrate way of turning hem in wool dress with pleats

Show how to avoid making two sleeves for one arm and demonstrate the placing of the sleeve to the arm-scye. Stress proper length of sleeve and the effect of a sleeve that exposes the large bone at the wrist

The finished dress

Pressing parts of garment as they are finished

Completing the finishes at the neck, the hand, the hem line, the waist line

Discussing the finishes used on wool and comparing them with those used on cotton garments

Impress the fact that, with a wool dress, the pressing is done as the parts are assembled instead of waiting until the garment is completed

Demonstrate the effect of heat and steam on wool, the use of the press cloth, sleeve board, and cuff pad

Stress the importance of skill in finishings on the dress of wool

Content and Pupil Activities

Teaching Suggestions

Criteria

Formulating standards for rating the dress, e.g.,

Is the dress becoming?

Is it comfortable?

Does it fit well?

Can it be easily cleansed?

Is it appropriate?

Does it cover or accentuate any irregularities of the figure?

Will the style permit the dress to be worn a second season?

Does any part of the workmanship detract from the beauty of the dress?

Will parents feel the investment for material has been worth while?

Have the girl stand before the class wearing the dress she has made. Be sure that she understands why comment is invited: to help her to repeat those phases that add charm and individuality and to discard those that detract from her personality and attractiveness. This plan affords opportunity to show how color may brighten or dull the eyes and hair, clear the skin, add glow to the cheeks, and affect the mental state of the individual. This is an excellent time also to commend girls who have good posture and to point out the effect of posture on the costume

Evidences of Desirable Progress

Pride and satisfaction in the completion and wearing of a garment that meets with approved standards

Improved personal appearance and greater care of clothing

Greater ability and self-confidence in choosing design, color, and fabric

Acquired knowledge and skill put to practical use in the making of garments in the home

Use of acquired knowledge and skill in vocational activities

MATERIALS FOR UNIT III

Bibliography for Teacher

Section A

DENNY, Guldena, *Fabrics and How to Know Them* (J. B. Lippincott, 1923).

DYER, Elizabeth, *Textile Fabrics* (Houghton Mifflin, 1927).

RATHBONE and TARPLEY, *Fabrics and Dress* (Houghton Mifflin, 1931), Ch. VII.

Sections B, C, D, and E

BUTH and WELBOURNE, *Design*, Unit II (Little, Brown, 1932), Ch. I
BUTTERICK, Helen G.,   *Principles of Clothing Selection* (Macmillan, 1923), Ch. V.
FRIEND, Mata R., *Earning and Spending the Family Income*, Unit VI (D. Appleton, 1930), p. 253.
GILLUM, Lulu W., *Color and Design*. Chs. II, IV.
RATHBONE and TARPLEY, *Fabrics and Dress* (Houghton Mifflin, 1931), Chs. V, VI.

Bibliography for Student

BALDT and HARKNESS, *Clothing for the High School Girl* (J. B. Lippincott, 1931), Chs. VIII, IX.
DENNY, Guldena, *Fabrics and How to Know Them* (J. B. Lippincott, 1923).
FRIEND, Mata R., *Earning and Spending the Family Income* (D. Appleton, 1930).
HEMPSTEAD, Laurence, *Color and Line in Dress* (Prentice-Hall, 1932).
MCGOWAN and WAITE, *Textiles and Clothing* (Macmillan, 1931), Chs. I, III, VI, VIII, X.

Visual Aids
Slides and Photographs:
  Clothing and Its Sources
  Sources of Wool
Films:
  Spinning and Weaving
Case showing wool processes

The following courses also present excellent units organized according to this standard:

1. Course of Study in Practical Arts, Little Rock, Arkansas. Grades 7—9, 1930-1931.
2. Course of Study in Home Economics, Idaho State. Grades 7—12, 1932.
3. Course of Study in Home Economics, Oakland, California. Grades 7—9, 1929.
4. Course of Study in Commercial Education, Minnesota State. Senior High School, 1932.

II. A UNIT MAY BE A LARGE CENTER OF INTEREST

The learning unit may be a large center of interest for the children and the learning activities of an entire grade can be organized around a number of interests which are known as units, problems, and projects. In most schools using this form of unit organization, the conventional school subjects are completely ignored. Several plans of organizing teaching materials will be illustrated briefly in order that the characteristics and peculiarities of these types of interests can be compared with other types of units.

A.   The project-problem type of unit. The literature on the project-problem and interest unit is so voluminous that it will be necessary to define the exact limits of this discussion. In the first place, no attempt will be made at this point to evaluate the problem, project, or interest unit as a system of methodology; they will be analyzed only as a method of organizing content (learning experiences) in the course of study. This approach is contrary to the general concept of these terms, since they are regarded by most writers merely as methods of classroom procedure. In the second place, no attempt will be made in this section to deal with either of these as a technique by which children may develop their own courses of study "on the spot." That problem will be taken up in a later chapter. Under the present topic, only those aspects will be presented which indicate that pupils and teachers can work together to develop learning and teaching materials, organized in this fashion, for weeks, months, and years in advance of the actual classroom situations in which the children will contact these experiences. Naturally such a position does not discriminate against any suggestions, contributions, or innovations which may be made by the children during their classroom experience or at any time during which the problem or the project is being organized for the particular individual or class.

1.. *Definition of the project.* The project was introduced into school work in the first place by those interested in agriculture and other practical courses. It was proposed to supplement the work in the classroom with projects which could be worked out at home and which would permit an application of the principles developed in class. This is far from the position assumed by many advocates of the "project method" to-day, for a number of reasons: First, the project came into education as the final phase of a learning situation, that is, as an illustration of principles developed in the classroom rather than as the beginning of the learning experience out of which principles are to be developed. Second, in the early days of the project, nothing was said of method since it was rightly regarded as merely the organization of practical content by which pupils could arrive at a clearer understanding and appreciation of the principles which had been expounded. It appears that the transition here involves the following stages: (1) The project was regarded as an organization of practical materials; (2) it began to be spoken of as a "method" or organization of content materials, and then, (3) the "project method" came to be accepted as a method of classroom procedure. There are methods of classroom instruction which need to be taken up in connection with the use of the project, but these are scarcely different from any of the socialized procedures which are recognized by methodologists. Third, the project has now been developed in many school systems as the beginning of the learning experience, and the principles have been developed from the practical data secured from the investigations of pupils, construction of plans, etc.

2. *Illustration of the project.* The following projects will illustrate the organization of content according to this plan:

MAKING A HEALTH MAGAZINE

Approach

Among the new books on the library table were several attractive ones about health. Several children reported upon them during opening exercises and exhibited original illustrations.

A boy who had brought to the library table a magazine made in another school showed it to the class. The group liked it so much that they wished to make a magazine of their own. Since they were already interested in health, they decided that their magazine should be devoted chiefly to health.

Development of the Activity

Early discussions should center about the form of the magazine and the type of material it should contain. As several children had had experience in helping to operate the school mimeograph, the group decided to make use of it for their magazine. The following types of content were decided upon and were listed on the board:

News articles
  Dental corrections
  Purchase of new glasses
  Games
  Interviews with nurse, doctor, traffic officer
Editorials
  Cleanliness
  Posture
  Food
Original stories and poems
Book reviews

An editorial staff, consisting of an editor-in-chief and five associates, was elected. A committee of five was appointed to find reading materials. This committee not only made a conscientious examination of readers, geographies, and supplementary books in their own room, but, with the teacher, examined the contents of the general book room. They also made a tour of the building, borrowing from third-, fourth-, and fifth-grade rooms whatever materials on health could be spared.

Since the morning inspection and discussion for the past weeks had centered about cleanliness and posture and the special reports had dealt with foods, these three subjects were the ones emphasized in the first issue of the magazine.

Contribution of Subject Fields

Reading periods for a week were devoted to the intensive study of foods. The following questions were formulated and served as guides in assembling reading materials:

What foods should we eat every day?
What foods help us to grow?
What foods give us strength for work and play?
What foods help us to have good teeth?
Why is milk so important a food?
Where do we get our fresh fruits and vegetables? our meats? our cereals?
What rules about eating should we observe every day?
What are the food habits of different countries and why are they different from ours?

The class had been divided into three groups on the basis of reading abilities. After reading materials on health were assembled, they were apportioned among the groups according to difficulty of content. The first group, which was able to read, enjoy, and present to the class a more detailed and scientific study of foods, was given material of strictly informational type. They worked out the following outline which was placed upon the board and discussed by the entire group:

Foods that build tissue (proteins):
  Milk, butter, cheese, eggs, meat, fish, beans, peas
Foods that furnish energy (fats, sugars, starches):
  Milk, butter, cheese, breads, potatoes, macaroni, spaghetti, fruit, honey
Foods that regulate body processes:
  Water, fruits, leafy vegetables, dark breads
Foods that contain vitamins:
  Milk, butter, cream, cheese, green vegetables, coarse cereals, egg yolks, oranges, tomatoes
Foods that contain iron:
  Carrots, spinach, lettuce, celery, apples, oranges, prunes, raisins, egg yolks, molasses, liver, beef, veal, oysters
Foods that build bone (calcium):
  Milk, cauliflower, lettuce, spinach

The second group was given material of narrative or story type, which dealt with the food habits of different peoples. They made reports to the class on the following subjects:

Foods that people in the cold lands eat
Foods that people in the jungle eat
Foods that people in the desert eat

The third group, whose reading abilities were limited, read the more simple material that centered about milk and habits of eating. They formulated a set of rules regarding wholesome food practices and wrote a short coöperative story, "Why I Drink Milk."

Since the study was to culminate in a magazine, much of the work was done in the language period. Reports on dental corrections and new glasses purchased after visits to the oculist were written as coöperative compositions. Stories, poems, and special articles written during the regular language periods were submitted to the editorial staff for correction and approval. The young editors were prone to pass over papers carelessly prepared and poorly written. This tendency served as a strong motive for correct spelling, good sentence structure, and legible penmanship, since every one hoped to have something of his own published in the magazine.

Stress was laid upon the importance of accuracy and truthfulness in preparing statements. As one boy remarked, "If you are going to print a thing, it's got to be right."

The children on many occasions consulted special reference books and more difficult texts, in their efforts to verify or disprove statements that had been made. One little girl made a special trip to her family dentist to consult him regarding the worth of a homemade mouth wash that had been recommended.

Some of the stories and poems centered about the knowledge of foods that had been gained. Others, such as "How I Get Ready for School," "How I Get Ready for Bed," "My Trip to the Dentist," embodied actual experiences of the children. In addition to the short editorial regarding posture, stories were written about people or groups whom the children had observed as being attractive because of their good posture.

One little girl, who possessed unusual literary ability, volunteered to write a serial story to be published in three instalments.

Several children made small, individual magazines during their leisure time. Two little girls collaborated in making such a magazine and did it so creditably that they were awarded special honors in their Camp Fire Group.

Values of the Activity

The results of the activity were gratifying from several standpoints. The children gained a more accurate knowledge of foods and their uses and of the importance of cleanliness and good posture.

The group had more dental corrections to its credit than any other group in the school.

Parents became interested. One little girl reported, "My mother says that, if I ever fuss again about eating the right things, she will know it's because I am naughty and not because I don't know better—but I won't fuss."

Skills in language, penmanship, and spelling improved.

The result of working together busily and enthusiastically toward a common goal was a happier, more wholesome *esprit de corps.*

Interest in health study continued to the extent of making plans for subsequent issues of the magazine which would deal with problems of clothing, shelter, sports, transportation, and their relations to health and safety.

Illustrations from the Magazine

NEWS ARTICLES

DENTAL CORRECTIONS

The dentist is a good friend. He helps us to keep well by cleaning our teeth and filling any cavities which he finds in them. These children from Room One have been to the dentist and have had all necessary corrections made.

Meredity	Helen	Yetta	Leroy
Minerva	Mamie	Jack	Robb
Marion	Annie	Laura	Betty

THREE CHILDREN SECURE GLASSES

Sometimes we need to go to an eye doctor to have our eyes examined. If a child tires easily or has frequent headaches, it may be that he needs to wear glasses. These children have been to the eye doctor and are wearing glasses that he prescribed for them.

Howard   Jane   Henry

EDITORIALS

ARE YOU READY FOR SCHOOL?

Do you jump up from bed cheerfully when your mother calls you? Do you wash your face, hands, neck, and ears with soap and warm water? Do you put on clean underclothes and a clean dress if you need them? Do you eat the good, wholesome food that your mother has prepared for you? Do you go to school cheerfully?

If you do these things, you are a healthy child and are ready for school.

ORIGINAL REPORTS AND POEMS

POSTURE AT THE MILITARY SCHOOL

When we were riding one day, we passed a military school. The boys were out walking. I was very much surprised to find that the boys, even when they were not drilling, walked with their backs very, very straight. They had the best posture of any boys I have ever seen.

—Maxine

THE SOLDIERS AT THE CIRCUS

One time when I was at a circus, some soldiers came down the street. Then they marched around in an open space in the tent. Their shoulders were straight, and they walked straight. They marched for a long time and followed commands carefully, and they still walked straight. Everybody clapped for them.

—Maurice

MY BREAKFAST

When I go down to breakfast,
  I always smile and say
"Good morning, everybody,
  What's good to eat to-day?"

And mother says, "Here's milk to drink
  And cream for oatmeal too,
And oranges and buttered toast—
  Do they sound good to you?"

And so I eat the lovely things,
  That she has made for me,
And I am cheerful all day long—
  I start out right, you see.
    —The Class

THE APPLE

I'm an apple
  Rosy to see,
I'll make your cheeks
Look quite like me.
                —Betty Jo

MY CEREAL

When I go down to breakfast,
  I'm always glad to see
That nice big bowl of cereal
All steaming hot for me.
                —Mamie May

MILK

I don't like coffee
I don't like tea.
But I do like milk,
And milk likes me.
                —Francis

MILK

For breakfast I like milk and toast,
  But never tea;
Milk makes me happy, strong, and
    well.
It's good for me.
                —Maxine [2]

A CAFETERIA

Because of the number of underweight children in the class, the teacher of the 2A grade, Barbee School, was anxious that the children should become interested in a unit of work which would give her an opportunity to lay special emphasis on proper food and proper habits of eating. Early in the fall some of the members of the class decided that they would like to build a play house on the school grounds. On account of lack of lumber and bad weather, they were unable to start on the house so boxes and boards were brought by the children and work was started on the furniture. A table was made first. The children enjoyed so much sitting at this table when eating their lunch that other tables were built. Chairs were made, also.

The children enthusiastically accepted the teacher's suggestion that they give up, for the time being, the idea of a playhouse out-of-doors, and build a cafeteria in the corner of the classroom. The project immediately became their own. They took the responsibility of collecting materials, bringing in boards, boxes, crates, thread, cloth, needles, rags for rugs, leather for hinges, clay from the bank of the stream, hammers and saws.

The children decided what furniture should be made. Every day new problems arose. Often the teacher made suggestions and gave help, but many times the children were able to work things out for themselves. One boy, for example, who had assumed the responsibility for making the top part of a cabinet, had difficulty in making the shelves steady enough to hold clay dishes. One morning he hurried into the schoolroom with the announcement that he knew how he was going to brace the shelves. He had gotten a practical idea from some shelves he had seen. Orange and egg crates were covered by the children with heavy

[2] *Health in the Curriculum,* Elementary Grades I-VI (Board of Education, Kansas City Public Schools, 1933), pp. 119-123.

brown paper to serve as building blocks for the walls of the cafeteria. Openings were left for a door and window.

The furnishings consisted of tables, chairs, a counter with shelves under it and a money drawer, a cabinet for dishes, cushions for chairs, table cloths, curtains for the cabinet and for the window, clay dishes, paper money, posters and signs, a window-box for flowers, and a rag rug, woven on a box loom.

The completed cafeteria was crude, but it brought so much satisfaction to the children that a month after its completion they were unwilling to give it up, or, at the suggestion of the teacher, change it into a grocery store or a market. Even while working on an entirely different activity, they still ate and played in the cafeteria, cleaned it up, washed and ironed the table cloths, mended the furniture, made new dishes and covers, brought in empty raisin boxes, tended the flowers in the window box, and arranged flowers in the clay bowls on the tables.

OUTCOMES

Language (Oral)

At the close of the activity period, which lasted from eight-thirty until nine o'clock, there was a conference period in which the children reported on what they had done and on what they had expected to accomplish. At this time they criticized each child's work and offered suggestions for improvement. Because they were interested, they had much to talk about, and because they were dealing with concrete materials, their conversation was definite. The timid child often forgot himself in his interest in his work.

At the lunch period each day groups of children ate in the cafeteria. At this time the teacher encouraged them to carry on pleasant, natural conversation in well-modulated voices.

Language (Written)

A letter was written to a manufacturer of breakfast foods asking for samples.

On account of the interest of the sixth grade in this activity and because they were to be transferred to another school, the second-grade group decided to give a party to celebrate the completion of the cafeteria, and invitations were written to each member of the sixth grade.

Sentences were composed by the children and whispered to the teacher. These were written on the board to serve as reading lessons for the other members of the class. The children gained through this a better idea of a sentence and learned to give a series of connected sentences. For example:

> Thomas brought an egg crate this morning.
> He covered it with brown paper.
> It will make part of the cafeteria wall.

Reading

At the close of the activity and conference periods each day, there was a period of blackboard reading. At this time items of interest to the class were written on the board. These usually told of some accomplishment or plan for the cafeteria, as:

> Evelyn finished her chair to-day.
> The class does not think it is strong enough.
> She says she can brace it more.
> —Dictated by a child.

Silent reading lessons based on the children's activities were at first made by the teacher and written on the board. Later the children made these for other members of the class. This was written by one of the children:

> Draw a big brown basket.
> Fill it with fruit.
> Put a cross over the kind of fruit you buy in the cafeteria.
> Draw two other things you get in the cafeteria.
> Put two lines under the one you like best.

Arithmetic

The activities in connection with the building and furnishing of the cafeteria gave opportunity for measuring and for estimating the cost of materials. Simple problems were made by the children for the group to solve, as:

> We made sixty cents at the candy sale.
> We bought some paint for thirty cents.
> We bought two brushes for twenty cents.
> How much did we have left?

In playing in the cafeteria the children had practice in making change. Such problems as these were written by the children:

> Hallie had seventy-five cents.
> She bought a bowl of soup.
> She bought a glass of milk.
> She bought an apple.
> How much did she have left?

Spelling

While writing problems, letters, and sentences, the children at first asked the teacher how to spell words. One boy started keeping a list of words he needed in the back of his tablet. Out of this idea grew the cafeteria spelling book which each child made. These were kept in their desks and were consulted daily, at first. Later, certain words became so familiar to them that they did not need to look them up. The most familiar words were:

apple	counter	left	red
ate	cups	many	sandwich
bag	dime	milk	some
bottle	dollar	money	soup
bought	drink	much	sugar
box	eat	nickel	table
butter	fed	orange	two
cabbage	feed	paint	under
cabinet	fruit	peach	vegetables
cafeteria	good	pear	very
chair	have	penny	water
cocoa	hot	piece	window

Fine Arts

A milk poster sent out by a cereal company was given to the class. From this the children got the idea of making posters. Such signs as "Eat Fruit," "Drink This Milk," "Try a Good Hearty Soup," were made and, when they met the approval of the class, were put on the cafeteria wall.

Clay dishes were made and painted.

Colors were selected for cushions for chairs, for curtains, and for rugs.

Place cards for the party were made and covers for spelling books.

Through these activities the children gained an appreciation of proper arrangement and spacing
combination of colors
the value of neatness in pasting.

The following masterpieces were placed one by one on the bulletin board. The children discussed these informally and became familiar with them:

"The Blessing," by Chardin
"The Mowers," by Dupre
"The Gleaners," by Millet
"Woman Churning," by Millet
"Feeding the Hens," by Millet
"Feeding Her Birds," by Millet

Health

Cleanliness. There was an improvement in the children's standards for cleanliness. After eating and playing in the cafeteria for a time, they became more particular about the cleanliness of the floor, the dishes, the table-covers, and their hands when eating. One boy suggested that the cafeteria should be screened. No plan was worked out for screening it, but the suggestion brought forth much discussion on the subject of flies.

Kinds of food. Through their activities they became interested in talks made to them on the proper kinds of food. They made menus and were careful to include the four kinds of food which they need—cereals, fruit, milk and vegetables.

Habits of eating. Such habits as these were emphasized:

1. Washing hands before eating
2. Eating slowly
3. Conversing pleasantly while eating
4. Courtesy at the table
5. Resting after eating

Ideals, Attitudes, Habits

1. Personal and group responsibility
2. Initiative
3. Self-reliance
4. Resourcefulness in acquiring material and adapting it to suit needs
5. Care of materials
6. Care of tools
7. Honesty and fair play
8. Courtesy
9. Respect for the opinions of others
10. The habit of completing tasks undertaken
11. Cleanliness of food; of hands when eating; of the cafeteria
12. A realization of the importance of the right kinds of food; of well-prepared food
13. Certain habits of eating.[3]

3. *Criteria by which projects can be developed.* There is danger in the development of the projects that much time of the pupils and teacher may be wasted effort. To avoid this, the committee or the teacher should follow definite standards and demand an organization which includes at least the following characteristics:

a. The course of study is made up of a number of projects, and while these are independent and unrelated, they should be progressively difficult and should be selected in terms of the interest of pupils, their worth in promoting educational interests,

[3] *Teaching in Grades 2 and 3,* Curriculum Bulletin No. 4 (Board of Education, Raleigh Public Schools, Raleigh, N. C., 1931), pp. 56-64.

and their value in achieving the objectives of the grade or subject-matter field.

b. The particular project in the course of study must conform with reasonable standards governing that activity in life situations. This criterion should never be ignored even though regular subject-matter fields have to be broken up or eliminated. However, in the extended project, which necessitates the elimination of subject-matter fields, as arithmetic, grammar, etc., provision should be made to indicate how these materials can be handled through the project and through careful organization of projects within projects for that purpose.

c. The project must be organized in such a way that the approach will be indirect rather than direct as in the case of the regular course of study. The essence of the project is that the student feels that the activity has been selected and organized by himself and his classmates and represents self-imposed tasks rather than teacher-imposed activities.

d. The project must have definite, specific, and clearly-stated goals which are interesting to the child, attainable by him, and, in part at least, selected by him. The participation of the children has really little influence in the development of the project, but the feeling that they are making a contribution stimulates their interest and motivates the completion of the project.

e. The nature of the project makes it relatively simple to introduce objective standards of measuring the results of children's activity. It is imperative that the project outline the means of checking the results so that the children can evaluate their own work.

4. *Definition of the problem.* Many writers in methodology have struggled with the difficulty of distinguishing between project and problem. While many words have been wasted on this needless controversy, it can be pointed out briefly in passing that, in general, the project has to do with a larger or longer series of activities than the problem, and the project is carried out in a natural and lifelike environment while the problem may be on the mental or thinking plane only. It is usual to find that any extended project includes a number of problems. The

development or organization of problems is nothing more than extending to pupils challenges which are worth while and worthy of solution from the standpoint of the child and of society. The complete organization of the problem involves the references, materials, etc., which are essential in its solution. The teacher merely guides the pupil in handling and organizing these materials, and assists in checking conclusions which are accepted by the pupil or the class at various stages of the solution of the problem.

5. *Illustration of the problem.* The following problem, selected from an outstanding course of study, will serve to illustrate the use of the problem in education and forms of organization of material according to this plan. This is particularly valuable as an illustration, since it shows clearly the relationship of the problem to the project or unit of instruction.

GRADE 1A
Unit 1
HOW THE FARMER HELPS US
Time: 8 to 10 weeks

I. **Objectives**
   A. To know something about life on a farm
   B. To have a realization how we depend upon the farmer for our food

II. **Major problem: What do we get from the farm?**

Elements of This Unit
Attack 1

A. *What is the work of the farmer and his boys?*
   1. Plowing, planting, cultivating, harvesting, caring for animals, hauling products to the city, keeping bees
   2. Work of the farmer at different seasons of the year
B. *What is the work of the farmer's wife and her girls?*
   1. Making butter, cheese, caring for milk
   2. Raising chickens, ducks, geese, gathering eggs
   3. Housekeeping
   4. Making apple-butter, cider, vinegar
   5. Gathering apples, berries, vegetables

C. *What do we get from the animals on the farm?*
   1. Fowls: chickens, ducks, turkeys
      a. Food
      b. Care
   2. Animals: cows, sheep, pigs, horses
      a. Food
      b. Care
D. *What machinery is used by the farmer?*
   1. Plow, harrow, tractor, reaper, threshing machine, corn-sheller, planter, drill, cultivator
   2. Milking machine, cream-separator, windmill
E. *What does the farmer need from the city?*
   1. Clothing, furniture
   2. Machines, books, papers, etc.
   3. Food: salt, tea, sugar, coffee, spices
F. *What products do city people get from the farm?*
G. *How does the farmer communicate with the city?*
   1. Telephone
   2. Radio
   3. Postman
H. *What recreation does the farmer and his children have?*
   1. Social life: threshing, picking apples, making apple butter, quilting bee, etc.
   2. Swimming, climbing trees, fishing, wading, riding horses, etc.

Attack 2

The unit may be divided into sub-units to suit the community as follows:

A. *How does the truck-farm supply some of our needs?*
   1. Hotbeds, greenhouses
   2. Soils, vegetables, implements, fertilizers
   3. Care, harvesting
   4. Work of farm, rain, sun, late frost, heavy wind
B. *What work is done on a fruit-farm?*
   1. Orchards: peach, apple, pear
   2. Small fruits: berries
   3. Vineyards
C. *What do we get from the chicken- or poultry-farm?*
   1. Houses, feeding, care, eggs
   2. Hatching, incubators, brooders
D. *What do we get from farms which engage in general farming?* (See Attack 1)
E. *What do we get from farms which emphasize stock raising?*

III. **Procedure—Activities**

A. *Suggested approaches:*

1. Experiences on farms related by pupils
2. Display on bulletin board of pictures relating to farm life
3. Excursion to a farm—truck-farm, fruit-farm, poultry-farm, general farm
4. Drive through country, observing farm buildings, crops, radio aërials, telephone lines, mail boxes, and products offered for sale at roadside stands
5. Trip to grocery
   Topic of discussion: Where does food come from?
6. Visit a fruit and vegetable market. Discuss where the products come from.
7. Children may see trucks loaded with vegetables passing the school building.

B. *Suggested activities:*

1. Orientation activities to get new experiences
   a. Observation
      (1) Look at books and pictures pertaining to farm life
      (2) Lantern slides or movie films showing farm scenes.
   b. Reading of prose and poetry
      (1) Listening to farm stories read by teacher, such as Perkins' "The Farm Twins"
      (2) Listening to poems about farm life
      (3) Pupils read simple books pertaining to farm life and look at illustrations
   c. Listening to and singing songs about farm animals
   d. Playing games such as "The Farmer Sows His Seed," "The Farmer in the Dell," "The Ducks"
   e. Rhythms descriptive of hoeing, planting, picking fruit, etc.: duck walk, trotting, galloping
   f. The teacher should read to or tell pupils about many farm activities such as
      (1) Plowing, planting, cultivating
      (2) Cutting hay, threshing
      (3) Caring for animals, bees
      (4) Making garden
      (5) Getting vegetables ready for market
      (6) Taking produce to the city
      (7) Milking, caring for milk, making butter

(8) Caring for bees

(9) Feeding chickens, gathering eggs, etc.

2. Research activities

   a. Pictures are brought by children and grouped on bulletin board or pasted into community booklets or charts. Suggested subjects for reference booklets or charts: farm products; farm machinery; things made from grain, as cereals, baked goods, etc.; things the farmer needs from outside

   b. Collections of farm grains, vegetables, or fruits for charts

   c. Collection of toys, as tractors, trucks, garden implements, toy animals

   d. Experiments

   Plant gardens

   Seed germinated on damp cotton or blotters

3. Group discussion activities to use experiences

   a. Discuss each element of unit.

   b. Discuss plans for construction activities.

   c. Discuss plans for party, assembly, or play.

   d. Discuss health values of vegetables and fruits.

4. Practice activities

   a. Make lists of farm animals, machinery, things needed for construction work.

   b. Dramatize stories and activities, as planting seeds, butter making, caring for animals.

   c. Summary activities

   Plan a party or assembly for another room using dramatizations, oral talks, rhythms, songs, poems, and display and explanation of creative work.

   d. Community language lessons illustrated and used as reading lessons.

   e. Stories and illustrations prepared for school newspaper.

   f. Making butter in large Mason jar or small churn. Have a tea party.

   g. From time to time list the following and print charts of the same for reading purposes:

   (1) Animals on the farm

   (2) What grows on the farm—later to classify as follows: vegetables, farm products, fruits

   (3) The work of the farmer

   (4) What the farmer's wife does

   (5) What the farmer's children do

h. Reading
  (1) Charts suggested above
  (2) Informal tests
  (3) Silent reading from flash cards such as: Call the chickens, Feed the pigs, etc.
i. Pantomime—each child may pantomime some farm activity or farm animal. Other children may guess the activity
j. Dramatize the work of the farmer's wife, good times on the farm, Farm activities such as harvesting, corn husking, storing crops, etc.
k. Coöperative letters and invitations to another class asking them to attend farm assembly
l. The children will enjoy making riddles similar to the following depicting the various phases of farm life.

> It grows very tall.
> Horses eat it.
> Flour is made from it.
> What is it?

> They are white and brown.
> Hens lay them?
> What are they?

m. Individual farm booklets serve as a means of organizing the pupils' experiences. These booklets may contain the children's drawings, cuttings, printed or written coöperative stories, and poems.
n. Make vegetable soup. Can or preserve fruit.
o. Vocabulary to be developed: loam, soil, cultivate, plow, harrow, roots, stalks, stems, hotbeds, weeds, hoe, rake, turnip, onion, etc.
p. Spelling: use in spelling words taken from this unit.
5. Construction and original creative activities to express experiences
  a. Construct a miniature farm with buildings, fields, fences, animals, farm machinery. House, barns, silo, chicken houses, etc., made of large corrugated boxes and painted. Make the farmer's machinery of boxes and pasteboard.
  b. Sand-tables
    Different phases of farm life may be worked up in paper or in natural clay: chicken yard, corn field, garden.

c. Art
  (1) Friezes of farm animals, farm activities, such as apple picking scene, how vegetables grow above and below ground
  (2) Frieze such as farmer working in field, farmer's wife milking cow, and child feeding poultry
  (3) Frieze showing farm scene: buildings, fields, trees, etc.
  (4) Illustrations of good times on the farm
  (5) Illustrations of farm machinery, methods of harvesting crops
  (6) Individual drawing and modeling of farm animals and of vegetables and fruits
  (7) Illustrations of roadside stand with people in autos stopping to buy fruit and vegetables
  (8) Poster showing hen in coop with little chickens running about
  (9) Poster of rural mail carrier putting mail into box

d. English
Coöperative stories and rimes which the children dictate to the teacher, on such topics as:

> What grows on the farm
> Grains that grow on the farm
> Vegetables that grow on the farm
> Animals that live on the farm
> What we get from the farm
> Farmer's care of the cow
> The story of bread
> Zepherine's dress
> Making butter
> The story of wheat
> The story of corn
> The story of tobacco
> Work of the farmer
> Use of animals on the farm
> Fruits that grow on the farm
> Making apple butter
> Butchering day

e. Music
Make original songs (words and melodies) about farm animals, animal calls

IV. References

MATERIALS

A. **Teacher**
PITKIN, *Seeing America; Farm and Field.*
WELLS, *An American Farm.*
MANN, *Beginning in Agriculture.*

Bees

TAPPAN, *The Farmer and His Friends,* p. **75.**

Poultry

Ironclad Incubator Company, Racine, Wisconsin.
TAPPAN, *The Farmer and His Friends,* p. 66 (hens).
Bulletin 1067, United States Department of Agriculture, "Feeding
    Hens for Production"; Bulletin 957, "Important Poultry Dis-
    eases"; Bulletin 1040, "Poultry Primer"; Bulletin 801, "Mites
    and Lice on Poultry."
BLAICH, *Three Industrial Nations,* p. 236.
FABRE, *Our Humble Helpers,* International Harvester Company, Agri-
    culture Extension Department, Harvester Building, Chicago, Illi-
    nois. "Poultry for the Farm Home"; "Poultry is Profitable";
    "Preserved Eggs for Winter."
NIDA, *Farm Animals and Farm Crops.*

Corn

CARPENTER, *North America,* pp. 164-172.
Industries of Man, pp. 23-29.
BLAICH, *Three Industrial Nations,* Ch. 13.
ALLEN, *Industrial Studies of United States,* Ch. 10.
WINSLOW, *The Earth and Its People,* pp. 63-65; *The United States,*
    p. 13.

Commercial Raw Materials

International Harvester Pamphlets: "Seed Corn," "Do You Know
    That It Will Grow?" "Growing Prize Corn," "Harvest Corn
    Before It Freezes."
Department of Public Instruction, Springfield, Illinois, *Corn Day
    Annual.*
Cottrell Rock Island Lines, Chicago, *How to Double the Corn Crop.*
    American Steel and Wire Company, Chicago, *Kafir, the Coming
    Cereal.*
CARPENTER, *How the World is Fed.*
MERRILL, *Our Country,* Bk. IV, pp. 110-113.
TAPPAN, *The Farmer and His Friends,* p. 28.

Fertilizers

German Kali Work, Chicago, *Experiments with Fertilizers.*
American Steel and Wire Company, Chicago, *Farmyard Manure,* 1913.

Fruit

National Lead Company, Chicago, *Saving Fruit Trees,* 1911.
Greening Nursery Company, Monroe, Michigan, *Fruit Culture.*
Industries of Man, pp. 54-60 (apples, peaches).
WINSLOW, *The Earth and Its People,* p. 83.
TAPPAN, *The Farmer and His Friends,* pp. 45, 51.

Hogs

BLAICH, *Three Industrial Nations,* Ch. 16, p. 230.
Industries of Man (pork).
COMSTOCK, *Pet Book.*
WINSLOW, *United States,* pp. 139-143.
Commercial Raw Materials.

Horses

COMSTOCK, *Pet Book.*
WINSLOW, *United States,* pp. 139-143.
BLAICH, *Three Industrial Nations,* p. 59.
CARTER, *Story of the Horse.*

Irrigation

WINSLOW, *The Earth and Its People,* p. 75.

Silos

International Harvester Pamphlets, Chicago, "Home-Made Silo";
    "Silo Campaign"; "A Silo on Every Farm."
Universal Portland Cement Company, Chicago, *Concrete Silos,* 1911.
Association American Portland Cement Manufacturers, Philadelphia,
    Concrete Silos.

Vegetables, Gardening

What, Where, When and How to Plant, 1914, School Garden Asso-
    ciation of America, New York.
International Harvester Company, Chicago, "Storing Sweet Pota-
    toes"; "Grow a Vegetable Garden"; "Spraying"; "Potatoes";
    "Weed Charts."
IVINS, *Garden Crops.*
BLAICH, *Three Industrial Nations,* Ch. 14.
Industries of Man, pp. 47-54.
United States School-Garden Army, Department of Interior, Bureau
    of Education, Washington, D. C., *Garden Annual for South-
    western Region.*

TAPPAN, *The Farmer and His Friends,* p. 9.
CHAMBERLAIN, *How We Are Fed,* pp. 32-38.
CARPENTER, *How the World is Fed.*

Canning, Drying, Preserving

"Cold-Pack Canning"; "Home Drying of Fruit and Vegetables"; "Grow a Vegetable Garden"; "Spraying," International Harvester Company, Agriculture Division, Chicago.

Machines

HILL, *Wonder Book of Knowledge,* "The Story of an Up-to-Date Farm."
FORMAN, *Stories of Useful Inventions,* plow and reaper.
CLARKE, "Electric Giants and Modern Marvels," *The Modern Agriculturist.*
COLLINS, *Birdseye View of Inventions,* thresher, plow, harrow, grain-drill, reaper, binder.
DARROW, *Boy's Own Book of Great Inventions; A Century of Cultural Progress.*
SMITH, *Farm Machinery and Equipment* (Cleveland Library).
Miniature Implements, Cleveland, Ohio, International Harvester Company, Cleveland Branch.

B. Children

Many of these references should be read to the children.

ORTON, *Bobby of Cloverfield Farm; Prince and Rover of Cloverfield Farm; Queenie, Story of a Cow; The Little Lost Pig.*
HANTHORN, *Billy Boy on the Farm.*
PERKINS, *The Farm Twins.*
CLARKE, *Work and Play on Belle River Farm; Stories of Belle River Farm.*
TIPPETT, *The Singing Farmer.*
DIETZ, *Good Times on the Farm.*
READ, *Grandfather's Farm.*
ZIRBES and KELIHER, *The Book of Pets.*

Picture Books such as:

SMITH, *The Country Book, The Farm Book, Buttercup Farm, Farm-yard Animals, The Chicken World.*
Hardy, *Best Stories* (meat, grains, milk, vegetables), *New Stories* (rural postman).
KENT, *Puppy Dog Tales.*
ADAMS, *Five Little Friends.*
KOS, *Just Horses.*
MINOR, *Fun at Sunnyside Farm.*
PENNELL and CUSACK, *Happy Children Reader, Bk. I* (farm babies), *Children's Own Reader, Bk. I* (in the barnyard), *Bk. II* (milking, going for the cow).

HOPKINS, *The Sandman's Farm Stories*.
LUCIA, *Peter and Polly in Spring*.
GATES and HUBER, *The Work Play Readers*.
PERSING and PEEPLES, *Elementary-Science, Bk. 2* "A Trip to Market," "The Turkey," "Outdoor Gardens."
FREEMAN and Others, *Child Story Reader, Bk. 1* "At the Farm," "In the Hay," "Jack and Jane Make Butter," "Little Black Hen," "The Ducklings," "Jack and Donald Ride the Calves."
GECK, Story and Study Primer.

C. Poetry

ALDIS, Dorothy, *Anything and Everything*, "Nice Mr. Carrot."
ROBERTS, Elizabeth M., *Under the Tree*, "The Chicken," "The Cornfield," "Milking Time."
THOMPSON, Blanche, *Silver Pennies*, "Water Noises," "The Hens," "The Pasture," "Baby Seed Song."
HUBER-BRUNER, Poetry Book I. "Dame Duck," "The Clucking Hen," "Swimming," "The Dog, the Cat, the Duck and the Rat."
DE LA MARE, Walter, Stuff and Nonsense, "Horses," "Bah."
STEVENSON, "The Friendly Cow," "The Hayloft," "Farewell to the Farm."
RILEY, "The Moo Cow Moo."
FOLLEN, "The Three Little Kittens."
TAYLOR, "The Little Pussy."
Mother Goose, "Baa, Baa, Black Sheep," "Mary, Mary," "Little Bo-Peep," "Little Boy Blue," "Higgledy Piggledy My Black Hen," "Come, Come, Butter Come," "Bow-wow-wow," "This Little Pig Went to Market," "I Have a Little Pony," "Pussy Cat, Pussy Cat," "Ride a Cock Horse."

D. Visual Aids

1. Pictures showing every phase of farm life, collected and mounted. Interesting pictures may be obtained from such magazines as *Country Gentleman, Country Life, Breeders' Magazine*, poultry and seed catalogues.

   Lakewood Library, pictures of farm activities and implements:
   a. Starting the plowing season
   b. Disc-harrowing with mules
   c. Plowing, harrowing, pulverizing
   d. Making a good seed-bed
   e. Smooth harrow with riding attachment
   f. Manure-spreader. Manure-spreader in operation. Fertilizing a ten-foot strip
   g. Operating disc-harrows with an oil tractor
   h. Pictures of vegetables in color: tomato, pepper, cucumber, asparagus, cabbage, lettuce, beans, peas, radishes
   i. Tomatoes growing in the garden
   j. Pictures of farm implements used in truck farming—obtained from the Charles M. Ingersoll Company Warehouse, Linda Street, Rocky River

2. Lantern slides and stereopticon views—Keystone View Company, Meadville, Pa.

p 230 (26398) A home garden
p 46 (16659) Tomatoes growing in gardens
p 272 (26400) An American truck-farm
p 151 (23108) Riding plows drawn by horses
p 164 (26374) Furrowing an orchard with a tractor
p 193 (V26366) Irrigating newly-planted fields
p 47 (6715) Harvesting onions on a truck-farm
p 48 (6716) Digging poatoes on a truck-farm
p 137 (V26386) Washing lettuce before packing
p 222 (26395) Loading the truck with vegetables for market
p 233 (26397) Public city market from the outside
p 232 (26399) A public city market close up
p 170 (18267) Buying, selling, and delivering groceries

E. **Songs**

NEIDLINGER, Small Songs, "The Chicken," "The Bee," "The Kitten and the Bow-wow," "Mr. Duck and Mr. Turkey."

Childland, "Piggywig."

Progressive I, "Kitty Mine."

Introductory Music, "Little White Chicken," "Apples," "Cherry Red," "Mr. Rooster," "The Wise Bee," "Honey Bee."

The Music Hour First Book, "Playing Horse," "The Bee," "Apple Man," "Where We Get Our Bread."

Music Hour for Kindergarten and First Grade, "Bow-wow-wow," "Baa, Baa, Black Sheep," "Gray Pony," "My Hen," "Piggy Wig and Piggy Wee."

Dann First Year Music, "My Garden, "Can You Plant the Seeds?" Tone calls: toma-toes, pota-toes, cabbages, cucumbers, radishes.

F. **Games**

Did you ever see a lassie? into Did you ever see a farmer?
The farmer in the dell
The farmer plants the seed
Oats, peas, beans, and barley grow
New Orleans—using farm activities to dramatize [4]

The organization of this teaching material for ten weeks represents a unit or project. The major problem for the children is to determine what foods and materials are secured from the farm. This problem is made up of a number of minor problems such as A, B, C, etc., which are subsumed under the main problem. In a like manner the project and the unit are

[4] *Social Sciences—A Tentative Course of Study for the First Grade* (Board of Education, Lakewood Public Schools, Lakewood, Ohio), pp. 63-71.

usually made up of a number of problems. However, if the reader will refer to the discussion of the definitions of project and problem, the distinction between a project and the major problem in this week's work will be apparent at once.

6. *Criteria by which problems can be developed for the classroom.* It should be recognized at once that the problem plan of organizing materials cannot be adapted to every subject-matter field and can hardly be made use of in every phase of any subject-matter field. The success of the problem plan of organization depends entirely on the material to be taught and the ends to be achieved. The following standards should help the teacher in determining the form of organization to be used in case the problem is being considered as one of a number of possible types.

a. The problem should be used only when it is desirable to have children face issues which are before the people at the present time and which may change for both individuals and the nation. It is not a means of teaching hard and fast facts so much as a plan by which students may be kept up to date and made aware of significant issues in political, economic, and social life.

b. Any material which is controversial in character and which is introduced in order to develop open-mindedness in the pupils often lends itself to this type of organization. When this material is organized as problems, it tends to stimulate discussion and the search for facts to justify the positions taken by pupils.

c. Problems must challenge the interest of the pupils and stimulate intensive work and study. Facts and decisions have more meaning for the pupils when they are arrived at through such investigations and research.

d. Problems should be organized so that the children will appreciate the relationships which exist between various phases of the work. The illustration above shows how this can be accomplished. Organization of material which promotes guessing on the part of pupils should be ruled out at once.

e. The steps in the solution of the problem should be carefully checked, since it is easy to spend too much time in the development of all phases of the problem. It is often a waste of time to provide for the pupils' investigation and discovery of all the facts needed in the solution of the activity. The experimental try-out of the problem will usually indicate these "waste" points.

f. The problem must be worth while in itself and the solution of the problem must have a vital significance in the education and development of the pupil. Extensive investigation cannot be justified merely as an exercise—the results as well as the effects of the work must be considered.

g. The problem must be carefully checked by the achievement standards of the grade in which it is to be included. It is easy to introduce problems which are out of range of the students. These may develop excessive activity on the part of pupils but minimize their intellectual growth.

B. A tentative course of study in the social sciences for the second grade of the Lakewood, Ohio, schools contains units which are developed around large centers of interest. The following unit provides from four to six weeks' work early in the grade.[5]

THE DOMESTICATION OF CERTAIN WILD ANIMALS
(Cow, Sheep, Goat, Horse, Cat, Pig, and Dog)

General Theme: Man's increasing control over nature
Aspect of the Theme: Man's first attempts to use animals to help him work

   I. **Objectives**
      A. To know how certain animals have helped man
      B. To learn how we should care for and treat these animals
  II. **Major Problems:** How has man domesticated and used certain wild animals to help him work?
                          How should we care for these animals?

Elements of This Unit

   A. *How has man used the cow?*
      1. For food: butter, milk, meat
      2. For work

   [5] *Tentative Course of Study in the Social Sciences* (Board of Education, Lakewood, Ohio, 1931), Grade II, pp. 21-28.

B. *How has man domesticated and used sheep and goats?*
   1. For clothing
   2. For food
   3. Miscellaneous uses
C. *How has the hog helped man?*
D. *How has the horse been one of man's most valued helpers and friends?*
   1. Wild horses and their domestication
   2. Work done by horses
E. *How has the dog served man?*
   1. Pets
   2. To carry loads
   3. Soldier dogs
   4. Policemen
   5. Shepherds
   6. Guides for the blind and lost
   7. Hunting
   8. Arctic explorations
F. *How has the cat helped man?*
G. *What other animals has man tamed to help him work?*
H. *What do we know about the ancestors of these animals?*
 I. *What part did environment play in the development of these animals?*

III. **Procedure—Activities**
   A. *Suggested approaches:*
      1. Display on bulletin board pictures of animals who are man's helpers: dogs, cats, horses, cows, pigs, goats, sheep
      2. Discuss what we know about these animals and what we want to know about them. Make a list of the questions the children want answered about man's use of the wild animals
      3. Read "Taming the Animals" by Nida
      4. Have a dog and a cat show at school. Make tickets. Give ribbons for littlest pet, smartest pet, best trained pet, etc.
   B. *Suggested activities:*
      1. Orienting activities to get new experiences
         a. Visit a farm to see the farm animals
         b. Children may tell of summer vacation experiences with wild animals at the farm
         c. Teacher tell experiences with domesticated animals
         d. Visit the butcher shop to see uses made of sheep, cows, lambs, pigs, for meat

      e. Tell parts of *Robinson Crusoe* which tell how he domesticated his animals and how they in turn helped him

      f. Visit the Parker Ranch to learn about horses

      g. Invite some excellent horseman to talk to the children

      h. Visit a pet shop to see the dogs and cats

      i. Teacher tell how cats were worshiped in Egypt, how used by the Egyptian government

2. Research activities to use experiences

      a. Children may read books to gain information. See references such as "Queenie, the Cow" by Orton

      b. Collect materials for a chart showing what sheep give us: leather (morocco), tallow candles, musical instruments, fertilizers, clothing

      c. Make a chart showing the evolution of the horse

      d. Make chart showing different kinds of cats, dogs

      e. Pupils may prepare simple reports upon various domesticated animals

3. Group discussion activities to use experiences

      a. Discuss why man wanted to domesticate the dog, horse, cat, etc.

      b. Discuss how man domesticated each animal—methods used

      c. Discuss characteristics of each domestic animal and how they respond to the right kind of care and treatment

      d. Discuss how these various domestic animals vary as to intelligence and ease with which they learn. What can the horse, cow, dog, cat, pig, etc., be taught to do?

4. Practice activities to assimilate experiences

      a. Group stories similar to the following may be written:

            What We Know About Wild Cows
            How Dogs Work For Man
            Wild Horses
            What Sheep Give Us
            Horses of Long Ago

      b. Dramatize Æsop's fable "The Shepherd Boy" Dramatize stories from Nida's "Taming the Animals."

      c. List the new words learned, such as: male—billy or

buck; female—nanny goat; kids, wild, tame, ox, ewe, colt, ancestor

d. Dramatize the "Bell of Atri"

Dramatize any dog story the children like

e. Pupils may tell how they have taught their own domesticated animals

f. List different kinds of horses and ways in which they are used: draft, ponies, race, etc.

g. Listen to galloping records in music

h. Make cat, horse, dog books containing stories, riddles, and pictures, or make composite book on domesticated animals

i. Give an assembly for another room or parents as a culminating activity for this unit. The program might include the following suggested work:

Animal songs, sung and played on instruments

Animal books made for the library

Group charts, animal stories read

Picture charts, shown and explained

Animals winning prizes at pet show

Museum—what the animals give us—shown and explained

5. Construction and original creative activities to express ideas

a. Make a movie entitled "All About Horses"

b. Model in soap or clay: horses, cows, sheep, goats, hogs, dogs, cats

c. Paint pictures of a flock of sheep, shepherd, and dog, for class booklet

d. Write rimes about the domestic animals for the class book

e. Write original individual stories about these animals and their usefulness to man

f. Make a frieze entitled "The Work Done by Dogs"

g. Construct cages for animals for pet show

h. Make signs for the dog show.

IV. References

MATERIALS

A. **Teacher**

LYMAN and HILL, Literature and Living, Book II, Section C, pp. 70-86.

ELSON and KELLY. Child Library Readers, Book VI, "Horses," pp. 13-51.

CHASE, *Domestic Animals.*

FABRE, *Our Humble Helpers.*

NIDA, *Farm Animals and Farm Crops; Taming the Animals; Wild Animals.*

TAPPAN, *The Farmer and His Friends.*

BAYNES, *Polaris.*

DARLING, *Baldy of Nome.*

DERIEUX, *Animal Personalities.*

HILL, *Peter Spots, Fireman.*

JOHONEET, *Cat and Dog Book.*

TERHUNE, *Lad, a Dog.*

ATKINSON, *Greyfriars Bobby.*

WOOD, *Animals, Their Relation to Men.*

B. **Children**

CLARK, Bertha, *Work and Play on Belle River Farm* (Rand, McNally).

EIFRIG, C. W., *Our Great Outdoors* (Rand, McNally, 1928).

GASK, Lillian, *All About Animals from A to Z* (Thomas Crowell Co.), "True Stories of Dogs."

GECKS, Mathilde and WITHERS, John, *Friend to Man* (Johnson Publishing Company, 1928).

HANTHORNE, Ann, *Billy Boy on the Farm* (Benjamin H. Sanborn Co., 1930).

HERVEY, Walter, and HIY, Melvin, *Friends on the Farm* (Longmans, Green, 1929).

KNIGHT, *Animals of the World* (Fred. A. Stokes Co., 1908).

NIDA, William, *Taming the Animals* (Laidlaw Bros., 1930).

NIDA, William and Stella, *Trailing Our Animal Friends* (D. C. Heath, 1928).

———, *Our Pets* (D. C. Heath, 1928).

ORTON, Helen, *The Little Lost Pig* (Fred. A. Stokes Co., 1925); *Queenie, the Story of a Cow* (1929).

PARKER, *Bow-wow and Mew-mew.*

SLOANE, *Animal Pets from Far and Near* (Beckley Cardy Co., 1927).

TROXELL, Eleanor, *Pammy and His Friends* (Charles Scribner's Sons, 1928).

WOOD, Carolyn D., *Animals, Their Relation to Men* (Ginn and Co., 1917).

ZIRBES, Laura, and KELIHER, Alice, *The Book of Pets* (Keystone View Co., Meadville, Pa., 1928).

Bobbs-Merrill Second Reader, "The Bell of Atri."

C. **Pictures**

National Geographic

Animal Picture Books

Library collections

Perry Picture Company

The following unit from A Study of Language Expression in the Elementary School (Raleigh, N. C.) [6] will further illustrate this type of unit organization.

The following activities for language are suggested for the third grade:

1. Telling original stories of personal experiences
2. Relating a particular incident
3. Choosing titles for the different parts of a story
4. Preparing a talk
5. Presenting an oral composition
6. Listening to oral compositions of others
7. Criticizing the oral compositions of others, keeping in mind:
   a. Posture
   b. Manner of speaking
   c. Interest
   d. Logical sequence
   e. Unnecessary repetition of words
   f. Vocabulary
8. Reading to gain vicarious experiences
9. Naming characters in a picture
10. Answering questions about a picture
11. Selecting a title for a picture
12. Telling a story about a picture
13. Retelling a picture story in improved form
14. Bringing pictures to class
15. Reproducing:
    a. Fairy stories
    b. Fables
    c. Legends
    d. Anecdotes
    e. Stories of adventure
    f. Stories of heroes
16. Listening to stories told by teacher
17. Reproducing and dramatizing the story in part or as a whole
18. Dramatizing character sketches
19. Guessing what character is being dramatized
20. Telling how to make and do things
21. Making and guessing riddles
22. Listing new words

[6] "A Study of Language Expression in the Elementary School," *Second Yearbook* (Raleigh Public Schools, Raleigh, N. C., 1932, Raleigh Elementary Education Council), pp. 96-100.

23. Telling and guessing riddles
24. Reproducing memory selections
    a. Poems
    b. Songs
25. Expressing original thoughts, with or without rimes
26. Playing language games
    a. Play
        (1) Free play (quiet and active)
        (2) Apparatus
        (3) Stunts
        (4) Sports
        (5) Games
        (6) Puzzles
        (7) Representative (dramatic) play
    b. Free conversation, discussion, deciding daily problems; class meetings
    c. Creative expression, making use of:
       Paint, crayon, clay, paper cutting, rhythm, dancing, orchestra, original songs, puppet shows, pantomimes, poems, nonsense rimes, stories, records of experiences, class magazine
    d. School-room chores and responsibilities
    e. Handwork, or manual work, making things, needed or wanted
        (1) Tops and games
        (2) Costumes
        (3) Presents to others
        (4) Food to eat
            Activities include
        (1) Cooking
        (2) Sewing
        (3) Making baskets
        (4) Weaning
        (5) Cutting and pasting
        (6) Woodworking
    f. Miscellaneous activities:
        (1) Excursions
        (2) Parties
        (3) Assemblies
        (4) Nature work
            (a) Bulbs
            (b) School-room plants
            (c) Gardening
            (d) Study of wild flowers

- (e) Tree study
- (f) Bird study
- (g) The aquarium
- (h) Study of animals
- (i) Study of bees
- (j) The keeping of pets
- (k) Rocks and stones
- (l) Weather
- (m) Stars
- (n) Orientation and map making
- g. Learning and singing rote songs
- h. Look and listen activities
  - (1) Poetry
  - (2) Stories
  - (3) Talks
  - (4) Music
  - (5) Movies
  - (6) Entertainment by other groups of children
  - (7) Pictures
  - (8) Bulletin board
  - (9) Concrete materials to handle
- i. Tool Subjects
  - (1) Reading
  - (2) Spelling
  - (3) Handwriting
  - (4) Speech
  - (5) Arithmetic
- j. Literature
  - (1) Reading and telling of stories
  - (2) Reading books for information
  - (3) Poetry appreciation, with some memory work
- k. Social studies
  - (1) Environmental studies
    - (a) Neighborhood and community life
    - (b) Holidays and special days
    - (c) Appropriate current events
    - (d) The home
    - (e) The farm
    - (f) The child's own town, or city
    - (g) Present day activities (with such allied activities as play city, store-keeping, the postman)
  - (2) Industrial arts studies
    - (a) Food
    - (b) Clothing and textiles

        (c) Shelter
        (d) Dishes and other utensils
        (e) Lighting
        (f) Means of communication
        (g) Transportation
    (3) History studies
        (a) Primitive life in reference to the Indians and Eskimos
        (b) Pastoral life
        (c) The Vikings
        (d) Colonial life
        (e) Migration and pioneer life
    (4) Study of a country
        (a) Holland
        (b) Japan
        (c) Switzerland
        (d) Scotland
        (e) China and others
    (5) Colonial life
        (a) Candle and soap making
        (b) Drying apples, canning
        (c) Piecing a quilt
        (d) Dyeing cloth with vegetable dye
        (e) Stories of colonial life
        (f) A colonial play

The following courses will be helpful to the student in organizing units according to this standard:

1. Course of Study in Kindergarten, Kansas City, Missouri, 1931.
2. Course of Study in Kindergarten, Berkeley, California, 1931.

BIBLIOGRAPHY

BRANOM, M. E., The Project Method in Education (Gorham Press, 1919). Chapter II can be read profitably.

CAREY, A. E., HANNA, P. R., and MERIAM, J. L., *Catalogue of Units of Work, Activities, Projects,* etc. (Bureau of Publications, Teachers College, Columbia University, 1932). Contains an extended list of projects and information on how and where to secure them.

CHARTERS, W. W., "The Limitations of the Project Method," *Vocational Guidance Magazine,* Vol. I (April, 1923), pp. 568-70.

COLLINGS, E., *An Experiment with a Project Curriculum* (The Macmillan Company, 1923). An excellent book which should be read by every student.

———, "Social Foundations of Project Teaching," *Journal of Educational Sociology*, Vol. V (Sept., 1931), pp. 35-42.

———, *Project Teaching in the Elementary School* (The Century Company, 1928).

———, "Learning the Fundamentals in the Activity Curriculum," *Journal of Experimental Education*, Vol. I (June, 1933), pp. 309-15.

CROWLEY, J. A., "Socialization of the School Program," *Journal of Educational Method*, Vol. III, pp. 381-388.

DOUGLASS, H. R., *Modern Methods in High-School Teaching* (Houghton Mifflin Company, 1926). An excellent annotated bibliography is included in Chapter XI.

HEACOX, A. E., *Project Lessons in Orchestration* (Oliver Ditson Company, 1928).

HORN, E., "Criteria for Judging the Project," *Educational Review*, Vol. LXIII (February, 1921), pp. 93-101.

HOSIC, J. F., and CHASE, S. E., *Brief Guide to the Project Method* (The World Book Company, 1924). Ch. II.

———, "What is the Project Method?" *Journal of Educational Method*, Vol. II (Sept. and Oct., 1922), pp. 23-28, 65-67.

HOTCHKISS, E. A., *The Project Method in Classroom Work* (Ginn and Company, 1924).

KILPATRICK, W. H., *Foundations of Method* (The Macmillan Company, 1931). Chs. XIII and XXI.

———, *The Project Method, Teachers College Bulletin*, Series 10, No. 3 (October 12, 1918).

LANCASTER, T. J., "Project Teaching," *Education*, Vol. LI (January, 1931), pp. 310-313.

LULL, H. G., and WILSON, H. B., *Redirection of High School Instruction* (J. B. Lippincott and Company, 1921), Ch. IV.

PEARSON, F. B., "Projects in English," *High School Teacher*, Vol. V (December, 1929), p. 344.

PERRY, R. C., "The Project Method," *High School Teacher*, Vol. VI (February, 1930), pp. 59-60, 90.

STEVENSON, J. A., *The Project Method of Teaching* (The Macmillan Company, 1921), Ch. III.

STORMZAND, M. J., *Progressive Methods of Teaching* (Houghton Mifflin Company, 1924), pp. 164-70.

STOTT, Leila V., *Eight Year Old Merchants, Record of Group VIII* (E. P. Dutton, 1928). An account of the project of running a store.

WELLS, M. E., *A Project Curriculum* (J. B. Lippincott and Company, 1921). Outlines the projects developed in the first three grades of the Training School of the State Normal School, at Trenton, N. J.

WEISEND, W. F., "The Problem Method Applied to History," *Education*, Vol. XV (June, 1920), pp. 601-605.

CHAPTER X

UNITS OF WORK FOR INDIVIDUALIZED LEARNING

I. INTRODUCTION

These plans have many characteristics of the units which have been considered in the preceding chapters. There are significant differences, however, which make it imperative that these be analyzed as distinct types of subject-matter organization rather than as a phase of unit construction.

These methods of organizing content were developed in response to the demand for the individualization of instruction and, therefore, have common elements. Nevertheless, they are sufficiently distinct and individual in character to merit a separate treatment. The following sections of this chapter will formulate a program of organizing content or teaching materials to meet individual and class needs according to the philosophy underlying the Dalton and Winnetka plans.

II. THE CONTRACT PLAN OF ORGANIZATION

The contract plan, which is spoken of as the Dalton Plan in many schools, is predicated on the theory that the unit or contract should be developed for the child rather than for the teacher. The emphasis is placed definitely upon the individual child, since the contract can be adjusted to his ability and the pupil enters into an agreement to take the contract and complete the work at his level of attainment. In many schools which use the Dalton Plan this laboratory method of instruction has proved of value, as it permits both individualization and socialization. These are among the important reasons for considering the contract as a separate method of organizing divisions of work in advance rather than as a phase or special type of unit organization.

The discussion in this chapter will consider only those aspects of the contract which is related to the development of teaching materials or learning experiences and activities. A later chapter on general methods of teaching will include those features which are concerned with teaching procedure. Unfortunately for the immediate purpose of this chapter, this term has come to mean a type of teaching procedure to many people, and this connotation complicates the presentation of descriptive material which, otherwise, would be relatively commonplace. In reality there are both teaching materials and teaching procedures involved in this plan. Both phases—materials of teaching and methods of teaching—will be considered, but in different chapters, in order that their relationship may be apparent.

A brief historical background may be helpful here in understanding the development of this plan. Dr. Frederick Burk, late president of the San Francisco State Teachers College, originated some phases of the plan when he abandoned the daily assignment and recitation and produced sections of the courses of study which could be placed in the hands of the student teachers and make possible an extended assignment covering several days or weeks. The idea proved to be stimulating to the pupils as well as to student teachers, and the faculty of the college became enthusiastic over this method of organizing subject-matter. The next development at the San Francisco Training School was that of a series of units which were supposed to be self-instructive to the pupil and to permit him to proceed at his normal rate of speed. With the death of Dr. Burk and the recent development of the school under the direction of President Roberts, little emphasis is now given to this system of organizing content by the faculty of this college. The idea and practice are being carried forward, however, by former members of Dr. Burk's staff and are now spoken of as the Dalton Plan, the Winnetka Plan, etc.

Since the contract is developed in order that it may be placed in the hands of the student, it is necessary that a great amount of care and skill, based upon years of experience, an understanding of the laws of learning, and common sense, be exercised in its preparation. Since these contracts are developed by the various departments of the faculty, the same opportunity for professional growth exists as in the school system where course-of-study construction is continuous. Better teaching and scientific supervision are inherent in any program which is constantly seeking to evaluate, revise, and recheck the educational diet of the pupil.

Miss Lucy L. W. Wilson, principal of the South Philadelphia High School for Girls, makes the following statement concerning the professionalization of teaching under the Dalton program:

> May I say a word here in reference to the so-called contract, job-sheet, assignment, plan, or, as we prefer to call it, guide-sheet? It is individualized mechanically by placing in the hands of the pupil a mimeographed copy of each plan in each subject. Any one who has taught even a single month can see the very great advantage of this device to the pupil, enabling him to overcome difficulties due to a short memory span, or absence, or different abilities, or different speeds, or a substitute teacher. But, mere mechanical individualization of the plan of work is not enough. Behind and before its composition, the teacher or teachers concerned must see not only the natural units, but also the minimum core of each of these units. By minimum core we mean the minimum information, skills, abilities, attitudes *et al.*, which must be *mastered* before attacking the maxima, or electives, along the same general line, or before attacking the minimum core of the next unit. Of course, no teacher has been able to do this in her first attempt, but equally, of course, the groups of teachers who are attempting it and watching the effects on different groups of children are rapidly accumulating a wealth of understanding which, sometime, will help in the creation of a new curriculum with new courses of study. Now these observations and understandings are functioning in the enrichment of essentials, and the development of methods that mean constantly better applications of the laboratory idea and of Morrison's *Mastery Formula.*[1]

A. Samples of contracts. The following contracts, which were presented to the author by Miss Wilson at the time of his

---

[1] Lucy L. W. Wilson, "A Method of Training Teachers in Service, The Dalton Laboratory Plan," *Educational Administration and Supervision,* Vol. XIV (February, 1928), pp. 117-122.

visit to the South Philadelphia High School, will illustrate the essential features of this plan of organizing content:

12A. SOCIAL SCIENCE

BIBLIOGRAPHY

Texts
ASHLEY, *The New Civics*
BARNARD and EVANS, *Citizenship in Philadelphia*
BIRCH and PATTERSON, *American Social Problems*
GREENAN and MEREDITH, *American Democracy*
HUGHES, *Problems of American Democracy*
MAGRUDER, *American Government*
SMALL, *Legislative Handbook*
TOWNE, *Social Problems*
WILLIAMSON, *Problems of American Democracy* and *Readings*
WOODBURN and MORAN, *The Citizen and the Republic*

Magazines
Annuals of the American Academy, Atlantic Monthly, Current History, Literary Digest, Survey, World's Work

Pamphlets
Penal Affairs, and others

So far we have studied the technical process by which a law is made. Let us devote our attention next to the part that we, the people, may take in it and why we fail to do so.

Unit I. **The Legislature**—The share of the people in it. (3 days).
REFERENCES: Hughes, pp. 453-458; 540-541; Ashley, pp. 125-131; Magruder, pp. 288-290.
A. Make a list of all possible ways in which the people may influence legislation. Be able to explain each one clearly.
B. (1) Do the people interest themselves in laws being made? Why?
   (2) Can you suggest any laws or amendments in which the people have recently interested themselves? Was this before or after they were passed?
   (3) What can you suggest to make people more interested? Does it make any difference whether they are or not? Give references to definite laws or instances in discussing this.
   (4) What arguments can you give in favor and what against direct legislation such as initiative, referendum, and recall?

Through our representatives, we, the people, make the laws and enforce them. Yet, in spite of this, we need some institution to settle disputes that arise among us, to punish those of us who fail to observe our own laws and to safeguard our rights. This institution is the judiciary, the organization and work of which we shall investigate part of this month, since most of our contact is with the courts having jurisdiction over violations of such laws.

Our third problem this term will be crime and law enforcement. Our aim will be to discover how adequately the courts function in the control of crime and the criminal.

Unit II. Courts

A. 1. Pennsylvania Courts—kinds, cases tried by each, judges (method of choice, term, salaries, duties)
   2. Philadelphia courts, names, kinds, cases tried.
B. 1. Would you like to see the magistrates' courts abolished? Why?

REFERENCES: Barnard and Evans (old) pp. 290-302; or (new) 385-398; Ashley, p. 143; Small, see index for constitution of Pennsylvania.

ELECTIVES: (1) The work of Judge Ben Lindsey (See *Readers' Guide* for references.)
   (2) Traffic Courts

Unit III. Court Procedure and Reform

A. 1. Juries—kinds, manner of selection, duties, procedure
   2. Juries—defects of system and suggested reform
B. 1. Would you prefer to be tried by a jury or a judge? Why?
   2. What reforms in court procedure can you suggest?

REFERENCES: Barnard and Evans, pp. 292-295; Woodburn and Moran, pp. 169-171; Ashley, pp. 144-148 (particularly the footnotes); Magruder, pp. 314-316; Hughes, pp. 488-502.

SUGGESTED REFERENCES: Barnard and Evans, 297; Woodburn and Moran, 191-192.

ELECTIVES: (1) Reforms suggested, Greenau and Meredity, pp. 87-94.
   (2) New measures for crime prevention and criminal reform, Williamson, pp. 195-203.

Unit IV. Crime

It is well to remember that a criminal is an individual unadjusted to his environment. There is no such thing as the "criminal type." All of us have potentialities for good as well as for evil. Remember the old Scotch proverb, "There is so much good..." etc.

GENERAL REFERENCES: Birch and Patterson, Chs. XVIII-XIX; Towne, Ch. XI; Williamson, Ch. XXI; Ellwood, Ch. XIV;

Hughes, pp. 115-121; and *Annals,* May, 1925, March, 1928; *Survey,* March 1, 1928.

A. Definitions: Crime, legal and social; criminals; classification. Towne, Ch. XI, and Ellwood, Ch. XIV, or Birch and Patterson, Ch. XVIII.

B. Extent and cost
   Towne, Ch. XI, or Ellwood, Ch. XIV. Suggested: *Literary Digest,* Aug. 15, 1925.

C. Causes, hereditary and environmental.
   Birch and Patterson, Chap. XVIII or Towne, Chap. XI or Ellwood, Chap. XIV.

D. Punishment
   1. Motives: revenge, protection, reform, prevention, Birch and Patterson, Chap. XIX. Suggested: *Current History,* Dec., 1924, p. 369; *Survey,* March 1, 1926, p. 605.
   2. Defects in criminal procedure. *Survey,* March 1, 1925, p. 602; April 15, 1927.
   3. Defects in our prison system (Note especially the woman prisoner). "Penal Affairs"—pamphlets and *Atlantic Monthly,* April and May, 1925. Suggested: *Survey,* January 15, 1927, p. 490.
   4. Probation and Parole. Towne, Ch. XI; Birch and Patterson, Ch. XVIII, and "Penal Affairs." Suggested: *World's Work,* March, 1927, pp. 548-555; Williamson, *Readings,* pp. 587-591; *Survey,* January 15, 1927, pp. 488.
   5. Juvenile Court. Towne, pp. 229-231; Williamson, *Readings,* pp. 285-287. Suggested: *Survey,* June 1, 1925, pp. 227-231; *Annals,* Sept., 1925, pp. 60-69; May, 1926, pp. 68-78; January, 1923, pp. 229-242.

Electives (One necessary for credit)
   1. Evolution of the Juvenile Court and Juvenile Probation. *Annals,* January, 1923, pp. 213-228.
   2. Prison labor. Towne, Chap. XI; *Penal Affairs,* recent regulation, and digest of Pennsylvania social legislation.
   3. Legal Aid Bureaus. *Annals,* March, 1926, Part I, p. 1-15 and any article in Part I.
   4. The Public Defender. *Annals,* March, 1928, Part IV, pp. 119-129 and pp. 146-152.
   5. The Relation of the Police and Courts to the Crime Problem. See pamphlet of that name.
   6. European Methods and Ideas of Penal Treatment. See pamphlet of that name.

These three books are of interest in connection with this unit. If read and reported upon they may count for maximum. Perhaps you can suggest some others that might be approved in their stead. Why not consult the *Atlantic Monthly* for articles?

My Life in Prison, Donald Lowrie
My Life out of Prison, Donald Lowrie
The Revolt of Modern Youth, Ben Lindsey

ALGEBRA IV

TEXT: Milne-Downey, *Second Course in Algebra*

Unit I. **Quadratic Equations**

A. *Review of quadratic equations containing one unknown* (10 days)
1. Incomplete quadratic equations
   Study Ex. 1, p. 213. Work Exs. 3, 6, 9, etc., on p. 213.
2. Complete quadratic equations.
   a. Solution by factoring
      Study Ex. 1, p. 213. Work Exs. 3, 6, 9, etc., on p. 215.
   b. Solution by completing the square.
      Study Ex. 1, on p. 216. Follow the rule on p. 216 very carefully in working examples on pp. 216, 217.
   c. Solution by formula.
      Learn the formula on p. 217. Use the formula to solve Exs. 2, 4, 6, etc., on p. 218.
   If you need more practice, work examples on p. 219.
B. *Literal quadratic equations* (2 days)
   Solve by the method best adapted. On p. 227, work Ex. 2, 3, 4, 5, 10, 12, 17. If you need more practice your teacher will assign additional examples.
C. *Formulas* (1 day)
   Formulas are literal quadratic equations, some incomplete and some complete. Solve Exs. 1-6, p. 225.
D. *Problems* (2 days)
   The equations for these problems are quadratic. On pp. 220-224, solve Exs. 1, 4, 7, 13, 26, 27, 41.
E. *Maximum assignment*
1. Work Exs. 33-40, p. 220.
2. Radical equations involving quadratics. Work on p. 229, Exs. 3, 4, 8, 10, 15, 16, 17.
3. Equations in quadratic form. You will need a conference on this work. On pp. 230-231. Work Exs. 3, 5, 6, 8, 10, 11, 13, 14, 16, 19, 20, 21, 23, 24.

F. *Systems of equations involving quadratics* (10 days)
  1. One equation is of the first and the other of higher degree. Method of solution—substitution.
     Study the illustrated example on p. 238 and work Exs. 1, 4, 7, etc., on pp. 238, 239, omitting 22. Under *Problems* work Exs. 1, 4, 5, 6, p. 239.
  2. Both equations are symmetric.
     Study the definition of a symmetric equation and read carefully p. 240. Work Exs. 4, 7, 10, etc., p. 240.
  3. Special Devices.
     Read carefully pp. 240-241, 242 and solve Exs. 7, 10, 13, etc., on p. 243. Be sure to consult your teacher if there is anything on pp. 240-243 that you do not understand.

G. *Summary of systems of quadratic equations* (5 days)
  1. Study pp. 243 and 244 and work Exs. 1, 5, 6, 7, 13, 18, 22, 25, 35, 38, p. 245.
  2. Under *Problems,* p. 245, work Exs. 4, 8, 12, 15, 18, 19, 24, 25, 33.

H. *Graphs of quadratic equations*
     These graphs are either parabolas, circles, ellipses, or hyperbolas. These curves are called conic sections. Do you know why?
  1. Study pp. 209, 210, 211. Ask your teacher for a conference if there is anything you do not understand.
  2. On p. 212, solve graphically Exs. 1, 4, 7, etc.
  3. Study carefully pp. 231-235. Note the type equation for each curve. (Circle 2) p. 232; parabola, p. 233; ellipse, p. 234; hyperbola (2) p. 235.
  4. On pp. 231-235 solve graphically Exs. 2, 3, 5, 7, 9, 10, 12.
  5. Systems of equations involving quadratic equations. Read carefully pp. 236, 237 and learn the rules in italics on p. 237.
  6. Solve graphically Exs. 7, 9, 10, 13, 15, 17, p. 237.
  7. Be sure to consult your teacher if you have any difficulty understanding the work on graphs.

9A. TECHNICAL ENGLISH

Your next work will be concerned with the writing of personal letters.

  1. Read Chapter X, *Visiting by Mail,* in *Practical English for High Schools,* by Lewis and Hosic. Note particularly the six parts of the letter, the appearance of the letter, and the appearance of the envelope.

2. Conference.

3. Write a truly interesting letter to an out-of-town friend telling him of your plans for the summer vacation.

   Make sure that your letter sounds very natural. Make sure that every sentence shows that you know something about sentence structure.

   For spelling, use your dictionary. For punctuation, consult rules in *Grammar to Use*.

4. Many girls hand very carelessly written excuse notes to their record teachers. The following is a clear, simple note. Study it.

2103 Ritner St.,
Philadelphia, Pa.
May 1, 1929

Dear Miss Winton:

   Please excuse my daughter Ruth at the end of the seventh period today. She is needed at home because of her mother's illness.

Very truly yours,
David Smith

   Pretend the postal announcing your absence yesterday has not arrived. Write a note to your record teacher asking her to excuse the absence. Have one of your parents sign it.

5. In order to make you think about your sentence structure and to help you to improve it, we have very carefully limited everything you have said or written up to date. You probably feel you could be much more interesting than we have given you a chance to be.

   Your opportunity is here now. You are going to prepare to tell us interesting stories you have heard from others. Make these story hours thrilling. There must be some exciting or amusing tales that are told regularly in your family. Your mother, or father, or perhaps your grandfather tell of things that happened long ago. Come to conference prepared to tell us the tale you have always loved to listen to. You might start your story in the following way: "One of the stories my father likes to tell is about..." After you have told your story, the girls will tell you what they think of it. Work hard for the answers you would like to the following questions:

   A. Was the story interesting in itself?
   B. Did the teller's manner add to or take from the interest?
   C. Was she vitally interested and enthusiastic?

D. Did she use well-built sentences?

E. Was her sentence structure natural or bookish?

F. Was her voice conversational and chummy?

6. Look up the word *idiom* in the dictionary, and then see what Lewis and Lynch, in *Grammar to Use,* have to say about it (pp. 201 and 202).

Make yourself familiar with the idiomatic expressions on pages 203 and 204 before your next conference.

Maximum: If your teacher gives you permission to do maximum work, read *Little Women, Rebecca of Sunnybrook Farm, The Covered Wagon, The Perfect Tribute,* or one of the books on the 9A-9B Vacation Reading List, and prepare either an oral or written report on your reading. Before preparing this report, have a conference with your teacher to find out just what should be included in a good book report.

11A. ENGLISH

Central Objective: The ability to discover possibilities of getting satisfaction out of life:

1. Through certain jobs
2. Through certain hobbies
3. Through certain relations with people

This requires:

1. An understanding of our situation at present
2. The recognition of what we need to meet life successfully
3. Ability to recognize the problems we face in the situations which we must meet
4. Ability to secure adequate information to help in solving problems
5. Ability to communicate effectively

A. *Ability to communicate effectively* (review)
   1. Factors involved in communicating clearly are
      a. Clear organization: outline, topic and ending sentences, transitions
      b. Clearness in sentence structure
   2. Review of outlining. Do this work quickly and carefully.
      a. Make outlines of the sentences on page 290 in Hitchcock's *Composition and Grammar,* making parallel items parallel in structure. Also exercise 4, page 291.
      b. Outline exercise 6, page 56. Write a topic and an ending sentence for it.

   c. Make an outline and a topic and an ending sentence for a theme from 3 *c.*

 3. Review of sentence structure. We are going to review only certain items, mistakes which label you in your conversation as plainly and as unpleasantly as eating onions labels you at a party. Each mistake (in English or in onions) points out clearly, "That girl doesn't know any better. Isn't it too bad!" Do whichever exercises your teacher suggests.

   a. Many of you make bad mistakes in using verbs.

    (1) Study the tenses of verbs so that you are sure you know how to use verbs correctly.

    (2) Do exercise in *Ways to Better English,* p. 225.

   b. Most of you have no conception of being consistent in your point of view. Do not change the subject or the tense in your sentences unless you have a reason for it. Avoid the passive voice.

    (1) Do Supplementary B on p. 223, in *Ways to Better English.*

    (2) Tell briefly the story of some movie you have seen or some book you have read lately. Explain what qualities the hero or the heroine illustrated. Write this roughly, but clearly enough for you to read without stumbling. Your work will be criticized for consistency and for parallel structure.

   c. People are judged by what other people see them do or hear them say. Most of you are very good to look at, but very uninteresting to listen to when you talk in a group or when you write. What ideas have you on some of the following?

    (1) The rich and the poor

    (2) Partners

    (3) Artists in living

    (4) Ignorance

    (5) "I got cheated"

    (6) Electives

    (7) Self-government

   Make an outline with topic and ending sentences for one of these topics.

   d. Test theme in which you will show your ability to write themes with interesting ideas expressed clearly without errors in tense or consistency.

 B. *Understanding our situation at present*

  1. List reasons for going to school.

2. List conditions you are up against in life. What would you need to meet each?

3. List what you can get out of school to help meet these conditions. Work in groups with chairman handing in the report with names of all in the group.

4. Panel discussion on reports of chairman.

5. Test theme in class, "Why go to school?"

C. Ability to understand problems we are up against in every situation

1. Situation: John has asked me to go to the early show at the movies.

   Problem: How can I get out of the dishes and so go?

   Analyze this situation into the factors that must be considered in any solution—facts, attitudes of different persons, difficulties.

2. Frequently one needs to look up information in connection with meeting a situation. Select a situation, and analyze it into (*a*) a problem, (*b*) facts you must look up, (*c*) opinions and attitudes you must recognize.

Suggestions

(1) You have been asked to recommend a book for a certain girl.

(2) You have been offered five dollars for a biography of Doctor Wilson.

(3) Much time is spent in trying to train children to select books wisely.

(4) You have been offered a part-time job after school hours for which you will receive a dollar a week. Your mother says, "Why bother?"

(5) You have made new friends this summer, several of whom live not far from your home.

3. Is group work worth while? Give reasons for your verdict.

11A. LIBRARY LESSONS

Aim: *To train you in the use of books and libraries.*

LESSON I

Before you finally decide upon the topic for your essay, browse around among the books and magazines in the library. To do this intelligently you must be familiar with the arrangement of the books. You must know how to make use of the card-catalogue and the *Readers' Guide to Periodical Literature.*

A list of suggested topics has been given you. It will be well to have some idea of the topic you wish to use before you go very far in your library lessons. You should keep your topic in mind as you look over the books.

Arrangement of a library. All modern libraries use the same system in arranging their books. This is known as the *Dewey Decimal Classification*. It was originated by Mr. Melvil Dewey. It is called a decimal classification because it consists of ten main classes which are divided and subdivided and carried down to decimals. Memorize the ten main classes of the Dewey Decimal Classification. Go to the shelves, and look over the books in each class. This will help to impress on your mind the numbers of each class.

Card-Catalogue. You should know the following:

How the card-catalogue is arranged

The number of headings under which you will find the same book

The difference between an author and a subject-card

The meaning of a call-number

Where the call-number is found on the catalogue-card

Where the call-number is found on the book

Remember, in looking up a topic, that the card-catalogue does not take the place of the index of a book. You may be interested in Submarines. You will not find this heading in the card-catalogue and yet you will find a chapter on Submarines in the book called *Modern Inventions*. A history of England may include chapters on the customs of the people or the literature of the country. The book itself will be entered in the card-catalogue under the heading: "England—History." The card-catalogue gives only the general heading for a book. The topic you select may not be entered in the catalogue, and yet you may find a great deal of material on your subject in the books. Look over the books on the shelves for books on your subject and also on related subjects. Your knowledge of the Dewey Decimal Classification should help you here.

LESSON II

Reference Books. Two kinds:

General encyclopedias

Reference books on special subjects

General encyclopedias

These contain information on all subjects and are arranged alphabetically like a dictionary. An encyclopedia will give you some information on your subjects. It will also direct you to other articles in the same book on allied subjects; this is known as a cross-reference. At the end of each article is given a list of books on the subject. This is called a bibliography.

Reference books on special subjects

These are classified according to the Dewey Decimal Classification, just as are the other books. Look over these books carefully, and make a note of the kind of information in each.

LESSON III

Browsing. By this time you have decided upon the topic for your essay. This lesson will be devoted to browsing among the books in the library. As you look over the books keep your topic in mind and make a note of any which will help you. Before the next lesson make a list of all books including reference books in which you found information on your topic. Give first the name of the book with its author and call-number; then the chapter heading and paging of the material of use to you. This will be the beginning of the bibliography of your subject.

LESSON IV

Magazines contain a wealth of material which would be inaccessible if it were not for a valuable reference book, known as the *Readers' Guide to Periodical Literature*. This indexes magazines and government reports from 1900 to date. Back numbers will be distributed in class. Look these over carefully and note the following points:

1. Published monthly
   Cumulates:
   > Every few months
   > Yearly
   > Every three years
2. Arrangement of entries
   Alphabetically like a card-catalogue
   > Author
   > Title
   > Subject
3. Meaning of entries
   Author and title of article
   Name of magazine abbreviated
   Volume; paging
   Date of magazine
   > *e. g.*, Curry, John F. "Man Who Makes the Tiger Smile," *Literary Digest*, Vol. 101, May 11, 1929, pp. 45-46.
4. List of abbreviations in the front of each volume

Your bibliography should now be complete as far as the books are concerned. Before your fifth lesson add to your bibliography the magazine articles that will help you. To do this properly you should:

> First consult all the volumes of the *Readers' Guide.*
>
> Make a list in your note-book of all the references to your subject, copying carefully author's name and title of the article, name of the magazine with volume, paging, and date.
>
> Consult the posted list of magazines to see if the magazine is in this library.
>
> Go to the shelves, find the magazine, look over the article carefully to see if it will be of use to you.
>
> Check the titles that you wish to add to your bibliography.
>
> Cross off the titles of articles you have examined and found of no use.
>
> Be sure to put back each magazine in the right box or bundle. Some one else may wish to use the same magazine.
>
> Complete your bibliography, and be ready to hand it in at the next lesson.

LESSON V

This lesson will be devoted to browsing among the magazines. You will be given topics to look up in magazines. Each girl will be supposed to read the article and give an oral report in class, with a description of the magazine itself. The completed bibliographies will be collected at this lesson.

B. Organization of contracts. Inasmuch as the illustrations have come from the South Philadelphia High School, it will be helpful to utilize teaching experiences in that school in discussing this problem. Miss Mildred Baird made the following report on the organization of guide-sheets in history to the general faculty of the school on November 22, 1928:

I am presenting a resumé of the history-department's work on assignment, the purpose of which is to secure from children real thought and understanding rather than a return of the words of the book.

In the assignments for younger girls the emphasis is laid upon fact and organization of fact. Consequently they are more or less in outline form—partially planned. The training in thinking comes through thought questions asked in conference.

Beginning with 10B we make an attempt through the assignment, as well as in conference, to stimulate thought. Miss Hazzard has developed the 10B assignments in the following form: Each unit is divided into A, B, and C. *A* concerns itself with required reading of the period or problem studied, *B* is a series of suggestive questions, *C* is electives. With the last my remarks have nothing to do.

A must be thoroughly prepared during laboratory periods at which time the teacher is available for consultation. It may be tested during the conference period in a written check-up or, more frequently perhaps, it is tested orally by a series of questions designed to discover the understanding of the pupils and to be sure that the material is thoroughly and properly organized. The emphasis in the first part of the conference then is on understanding of fact and text and on organization. In the latter, the children are lamentably weak. The rest of the conference is given over to a discussion of the suggested questions which the children are presumed to have done some thinking on before they come to conference.

The following is an illustration from the 10B assignment for November. In the 12A contracts, where for the first time we encounter real problems and controversial material, where the tendency to argue, to have opinions backed by a few facts, must be checked in order to stimulate thinking. Each unit is divided into A and B parts. Let me quote from the first assignment.

Let me tell you what the division of each unit into Parts A and B means. Part A trains your abilities in memory, accuracy and definiteness. It may be tested at the beginning of conference period. Part B "suggestive questions" trains you in initiative, logic, and constructive thinking. It may be tested by your contribution to conference discussions.

Since it may be tested, and in the early part of the term frequently is, to promote good habits at once, it must be prepared before coming to conference. This insures frequently almost uninterrupted use of the teacher in laboratory periods. Very few fact questions are saved till conference, especially since it is the practice if they are asked for one of the girls or the teacher to reply by telling where the answer may be found, not what it is. Thus there is considerably less use of the phrase "I don't understand" and more honest "I don't know." Conference and test questions, moreover, are attempts at least to presuppose a knowledge of facts and to develop use of those facts. For example when a study was made of the work of the executive departments among which the duties of the weather bureau came under discussion the question asked was "The effects of a recent disaster were lessened by the work of one of the National executive departments. What was the Bureau and department?" The Florida hurricane was filling the newspapers then.

Or again, we were studying about democracy, its benefits and disadvantages. The author listed as a disadvantage "popular indifference." The question asked was "What undesirable trait often characteristic of democracy was conspicuously absent during the campaign and at the last election?" Again, "What undesirable trait was present?' (Intolerance.)

One whole conference period recently was spent discussing the question, "Is voting a right or a privilege?" Incidentally, in the discussion all the facts which Part A had required the pupils to know came out. The girls seemed utterly unconscious that the teacher had secured a good test of their knowledge of facts, their accuracy and definiteness, as well as their ability in logic and constructive thinking. The question under discussion had been one of those asked in conference.

Another device used in the 12A contracts to stimulate thinking is the conference in laboratory periods, conference and criticisms of tests to the main aims of the course and their relative importance. These aims are presented to pupils at the beginning of the term.

Aims:

1. To become intelligently aware of the problems, largely political, of the world of which you are soon to become an active member.
2. To learn to appreciate all sides of a problem, to weigh and evaluate, to become more tolerant of another's point of view.
3. To become acquainted with a wealth of material sources and to make them your books of knowledge.
4. To acquire information.

One last device to stimulate thinking which is not on the assignment, but which has become a habit with the girls is the list of suggestive questions posted on the bulletin board in the room. These turn the girls' thoughts in more directions than is possible within the limits of the quiz or conference. The girls discuss them among themselves and outside and often bring them to the teacher for a positive settlement.

In the 12B contracts the division into A and B is abandoned. Facts come as a basis for discussion of problems which are so alive, so vital, that little stimulus to thought is needed; here much direction as to logical, unembittered judgments, to the attainment of an impersonal point of view, is the paramount necessity. In the 12A assignments the sequence of problems is varied from term to term so that the material under discussion as far as possible coincides with what is agitating the community; for example, the choice of an executive was the topic of September work this year, ballots, primaries, campaigns, etc., of November work. Another term the order may vary.

Test questions asked in connection with study of various units on 12A assignments for September-December, 1928.

September
Unit II. *The work of the executive*
1. May the governor pardon a man who has violated the Sherman Anti-Trust Act?
2. In what ways has the governor's power been limited over that given to the president?
3. In what way is the president's legislative power limited?
4. May the president pardon his secretary of state if he has been impeached ?
5. May the president pardon a soldier who has been court-martialed for sleeping while on duty?

October
Unit I. *The legislature—its composition*
1. Was the people's attitude toward the Stamp Tax typical or non-typical of their attitude toward law? Give the reason.
2. Name three laws the people are talking about now.

October
Unit III. *The legislature—the share of the people in it*
1. Is the rider an effective method of coercing the governor of Pennsylvania?
2. Do you think filibustering fair or unfair? Give the reason.
3. Is reading a man out of his party "fair or unfair"? Give the reason.
4. Why is recall of judicial decisions regarded by many as especially undesirable?
5. How does regulation of lobbyists control their actions?

September
Unit III. *Assistants to the executive*
1. Are the heads of the executive departments subject to summons by the legislature?
2. To what bureau in what department would a man who had invented a new type of oil can appeal if he wished to be safeguarded in his rights?
3. The effects of a recent disaster in the United States were investigated by the work of a bureau in the National Government. What was the bureau?

4. The work of what executive bureau affects the composition of Congress?
5. What bureau supplies the data necessary for engineers who plan extensions to our transcontinental railroads?
6. What bureau in what department would recommend to Congress an embargo on diseased Dutch bulbs?

November

Unit I. *The force of government*

1. Why was the United States not a democracy in 1776?
2. Name a country in which to-day monarchy exists in theory and democracy in fact.
3. Name an agency of government which protects your health.
4. Name a country which to-day has apparently given up democracy and returned to autocracy.

November

Unit IV. *Nominations and campaigns*

1. Are campaign funds for primary elections supervised by the National government?
2. Is enrolment necessary with an open primary?

ELECTIVES

All girls with a grade of G or better are allowed to do maximum or electives. We give a great variety of electives so that each girl may choose that kind which best suits her need.

Many girls like electives that round out the minimum topic and help them get a better pre-conference understanding, *e.g.,* an elective on free silver from an economic history was appreciated by some 11B girls.

Then there is the girl interested in reading. Personalities and new points appeal to her. She is no doubt interested in social movements and in the humaneness of history. For this type of 9A or B we offer myths and stories; some novels, notably the Spartan Biographies are used. These range all the way from juvenile biographies for 10A to Ludwig's *Bismarck* and McElroy's *Cleveland*. Magazine articles on historical and social questions as well as quasi-popular works, *e.g.,* Sullivan's *Our Times,* are used in the upper forms. We hope our girls will get the habit of this type of reading. In order to facilitate this we are going to use the English department's idea of giving summer reading lists in upper forms.

For G plus and E girls who are very much interested in history, we have monthly and term topics on phases of history and current events. These are first offered in 10B because they require and also aim to develop skill in hunting and organizing material and in weighing evidence. It is here that our girls get a passing acquaintance with source material and standard historians. And, also, others get training in group work. Occasionally a very good piece of work is produced—last year an 11B produced a very creditable paper on the bituminous coal strike.

For the girl whose interest first is in another subject, correlated electives are offered. The 12B social science and hygiene teachers coöperated in offering maximum showing relationship between heredity and defect. In 9B, art and history have correlated. This is a splendid type of maximum, but unfortunately it cannot be used in all forms.

The usual-minded girl may produce original maps and charts; the subtle girl who is good in art has her chance to hand in cartoons.

Our girls may formulate original electives, provided, of course, that they submit their preference to the teacher and get her approval of it. The most unusual case of the kind was that of a 9B who asked me whether she might read Dante's *Inferno* instead of doing the Renaissance electives.

Girls of much the same ability may differ greatly in their reactions to a given elective. One 11B this term was so impressed by "From Immigrant to Inventor" that she asked to be allowed to give a resumé of it to her class; another told me she started to read it three times but had to give it up as it was so dull.

Many of our girls are "free lancers." They will do an elective that provides a background this week, a magazine article next week, and so forth. They do the ones that suit them and seem to get profit and enjoyment from them.

For checking electives in our lower forms the conference for the group is sometimes centered about the electives. Each girl contributes the salient points of her elective. This only happens where you have a homogeneous group, in the upper forms where conferences on maxima have more thorough work and consequently lead to more discussion. Elective work is managed by giving short elective tests or by having resumés handed in.

All electives are not of equal value; the quantity and quality of the elective is taken into consideration in weighing it. Each elective states whether it is a week or two weeks or a term assignment. Likewise in marking it the difficulty of the work needs to be taken into consideration.

C. Criteria for the organization of content according to the Dalton Plan. The examples which have been presented undoubtedly have suggested a number of criteria for the development of contracts. The following list of criteria, while not exhaustive, will do much to assist any one interested in writing contracts in making progress with the work.

1. Contracts should be organized for definite periods of time, such as a month, and should be developed only after careful study of the year's course. The contract itself should then be divided into units, each covering a day's work or that of a slightly longer period. These smaller units will be determined by the nature of the course and character of the work at that point.

2. Each statement must be in simple, clear English and must be sufficiently detailed to guarantee complete comprehension on the part of pupils. This is of great importance since the pupil must have a clear understanding of the directions before he can make progress. In general, it may be stated that sentences should be short rather than long and that care should be exercised in the selection of words. The teacher must recognize that the assignment is being prepared for the *child* and not for the *faculty*.

3. The contract should be suitable both to the grade and the ability level of pupils. The individual differences of pupils can be met by developing two contracts for the same class or by providing for minimum and maximum assignments in the same contract. In the first instance, the two groups of students may do work which is entirely different in character, while in the second case, all students will complete the minima and those who have high ability and have learned how to study will complete additional and more difficult work.

4. The contract must be interestingly written and stimulating to the pupil. Since he is to use the contract as a personal guide-sheet, it is important, not only that the instructions be clear, but also that they motivate his enthusiastic mastery of the material.

5. Both discussion and questions should be included in the organization of the contract in order that thinking may be stimulated and a thoughtful attitude toward problems developed in the pupil.

6. The organization of the contract should provide for individual work, group consultations, and library work which can

be organized either on an individual basis or into committee assignments.

7. The contract should contain tests which will enable the student to check his progress from time to time and evaluate his own attainments. These results will give him the opportunity to determine whether he has achieved the proficiency necessary to complete remaining sections of the unit and satisfactorily meet the standards placed at the conclusion of the contract. The following test is the first check which the pupil has an opportunity to apply to his work in a class in 11A American history in the South Philadelphia High School:

11A AMERICAN HISTORY TEST No. 1

I. To test your sense of time sequence, put a "1" in the parentheses before the event which occurred first, a "2" before that which occurred second, etc.
   ( ) Mayflower Compact
   ( ) Papal Bull of Demarcation
   ( ) First representative assembly in America
   ( ) Discovery of America by Columbus
   ( ) Puritan Revolution in England
   ( ) English absorb New Netherlands
   ( ) Discovery of North America by John Cabot
   ( ) Founding of Virginia

II. To test your sense of direction and ability to locate accurately:
   A. Fill each blank with correct answer:
      1. The Atlantic Coastal Plain is in the ———— (eastern or western) part of the United States.
      2. The Mississippi River flows in a ———— (southerly or northerly) direction.
      3. Savannah is located in ————.
      4. The Great Lakes belong to ———— (St. Lawrence, Arctic, Mississippi) River System.
      5. The Mohawk Valley is located in ————.
      6. The mountain chains in the United States run ———— (east to west, north to south).
      7. The country north of the United States is ———— (Canada or Mexico), and the ocean west of it is ———— (Atlantic or Pacific).
      8. Hartford is located in ————.
      9. The Great Central Plain lies ———— (east, west, or south) of the Appalachian Mountain chain.

10. West New Jersey was near the colonies of —————— and ——————.

B. To test your ability to use the wall map, name the place indicated on the wall map by your teacher.

III. To test your ability to see the development of effect from cause, place in the parentheses the number which corresponds to the numbered causes in the left-hand column:

1. Wars of Louis XIV	( ) Lack of plantations in New England
2. New England's hatred of the Navigation Acts	( ) Georgia a buffer colony
3. Glacial soil of New England	( ) Formation of New England Federation
4. Quaker resentment of authority	( ) Necessity for strict government
5. Widening of the coastal plain in the South	( ) Coming of Germans to Pennsylvania
6. Lucrative fishing of New England	( ) Rise of the feudal system in New Netherlands
7. Union of French and Indians	( ) Belief in the separation of Church and State
8. Indian and Spanish attacks on the South	( ) Rise of commercial pursuits
9. Enticements offered by West India Company to Hollanders	( ) Resort to smuggling
10. Close settlement of New England population	( ) Development of agriculture

IV. To test your ability to discriminate between true and false information, place a T before the true statement, an F before the false, and a P before one partly true and partly false:

1. Jacques Cartier explored what is now the southwestern United States and so strengthened the French claim to North America.

2. The English possessed the Appalachian Mountain passes and were thus able later to seize the Central Plain.

3. Through their possession of the greater part of the Atlantic Coastal Plain, the English absorbed the Spanish in Florida.

4. In the sixteenth century southern Europe was believed to be in a position of advantage in regard to the best route of approach to North America.

5. The economic life of the Southern Colonies developed a leisure planter class which used its time in strictly regulating the life of the community.

V. To test your ability to organize in clear, correct English, discuss *one* of the following:
1. Physical features of the United States
2. Economic contrast between New England and the South
3. A century of exploration
4. The three governmental types of colonies planted by England in America

III. SUMMARY

A survey of the units produced by Daltonized schools indicate that the learning activities and experiences of the pupils are organized with great detail. This permits the learner to make progress outside of regular classroom supervision and permits him to adopt his entire program to his individual needs since he can spend as much or as little time as he feels necessary on the work of a particular unit or contract in a particular subject-matter field.

Teachers from all subject-matter fields in a particular grade coöperate in the preparation of the contracts so that the educational program of the pupil is an integrated one. That is, the contracts in English and history for grade X are correlated and are developed as the result of conferences and investigations on the part of the English and history teachers. For this reason most schools using contracts have a regular promotion system. Since the work in the various subject-matter fields of the particular grades is integrated, pupils cannot be advanced in one subject while remaining at another level in another study.

The contract is a course of study for the pupil and is placed in his hands to guide his educational progress. Herein lies the greatest contribution of the contract: the recognition that the pupil has a right to know the goals which are desirable for him and the avenues through which they can be attained.

IV: BIBLIOGRAPHY: THE DALTON PLAN

ANGELS, Sister Mary, "The Dalton Plan—A New Departure in Education," *National Catholic Welfare Congress Bulletin IX* (Jan., 1928), pp. 26-28.

BAIRD, Janet, "Restoration Assignments in English: A Modification of the Dalton Plan," *School Review,* Vol. XXXIV (Nov., 1926), pp. 702-706.

BARROWS, R. P., "Problems of American Democracy," *School Review,* Vol. XXXIV (June, 1926), pp. 422-425.

COOK, A. R., "The Contract Plan: Its Working," *Educational Review,* Vol. LXXIII (Feb., 1927), pp. 109-111.

DE FRANCESCO, I. L., "Art Education under the Dalton Plan," *School Arts Magazine,* Vol. XXVII (Jan., 1928), pp. 273-274.

DEWEY, Evelyn, *The Dalton Laboratory Plan* (E. P. Dutton and Co., 1922).

EASON, V. E., and COLE, R. D., "The Effectiveness of the Contract Method as Compared with the Ordinary Method of Teaching," *School Review,* Vol. XXXVII (April, 1929), pp. 272-281.

FLOM, F. J., "The Contract Method in Bookkeeping," *Balance Sheet,* Vol. IX (May, 1928), pp. 33-36.

FUNK, M. N., "A Comparative Study of the Results Obtained by the Method of Mastery Technique and the Method of Daily Recitation and Assignment," *School Review,* Vol. XXXVI (May, 1928), pp. 338-346.

GOUGLITZ, E. T., "French on the Dalton Plan," *School and Home,* Vol. X (Nov., 1926), pp. 24-28.

HARDY, R. C., "The Dalton Plan in Operation," *Bulletin of High Points,* Vol. VII (Jan., 1925), pp. 3-5.

IRWIN, M. E., and ODIUM, E. C., "Building English Contracts for the Dalton Plan," *The Elementary School Journal,* Vol. XXXI (Oct., 1930), pp. 136-141.

NORTON, H. C., "The Dalton Plan in Stenography," *Journal of Commercial Education,* Vol. LXVI (Feb., 1927), pp. 44-48.

PARKHURST, Helen, "The Dalton Laboratory Plan," *Twenty-fourth Yearbook,* National Society for the Study of Education, Part II 1925), pp. 83-94.

RICHMOND, J. E., "Home Economics under the Dalton Plan," *Journal of Home Economics,* Vol. XVIII (Aug., 1926), pp. 458-461.

SHELTON, A. A., "An Experimental Study of the Daily Recitation Versus the Unit Plan," *School Review,* Vol. XXXVIII (Nov., 1930), pp. 694-699.

SHERIDAN, M. C., "An Evaluation of the Dalton Laboratory Plan," *English Journal,* Vol. XV (Sept., 1926), pp. 507-514.

ULLMAN, R. N., "Dalton Plan Awakens Desired Interest in Study of Literature," *Education,* Vol. XLVII (June, 1926), pp. 606-611.

WALKER, U. D., "The Dalton Plan Applied to Manual Arts," *Industrial Arts Magazine,* Vol. XVI (Aug., 1927), pp. 283-286.

WALTER, M. M., "Individualized Instruction," *Industrial Arts Magazine,* Vol. XV (Feb., 1926), pp. 30-44.

WANGER, R., "World History under the Dalton Plan," *Historical Outlook,* Vol. XVIII (Dec., 1927), pp. 383-390.

WEBER, L., "The Use of the Unit-Contract System in Teaching Biology," *School Science and Mathematics,* Vol. XXVIII (April, 1928), pp. 399-413.

WILSON, H. E., "Systematic Teaching of High-School History," *Historical Outlook,* Vol. XIX (March, 1928), p. 121.

WILSON, L. L., "The Dalton Plan," *Progressive Education,* Vol. II (Sept., 1925), pp. 155-159.

——, *Educating for Responsibility* (The Macmillan Company, 1926).

——, "The Dalton Plan in an American Tax-supported Secondary School," *New Era,* Vol. XXVII (July, 1926), pp. 132-134.

——, "A New Road to Freedom in Education," National Association of Secondary-School Principals, *Proceedings, Bulletin* XI (Feb., 1926), pp. 90-100.

——, "Use of the Library Increased Threefold under the Dalton Plan," *School Life,* Vol. XXII (Nov., 1926), p. 49.

V. THE WINNETKA PLAN

A brief summary of the reorganization of the curriculum of the individual child as proposed and developed in the Winnetka schools is included because this plan differs in several important steps from the Dalton plan. While both of these plans emphasize the individual child in the development of the curriculum and learning materials in the courses of study each has its own characteristics and peculiarities. It is probable that a discussion of these two types present most of the essential steps in building individual courses of study. There are individualized programs which are not copied from the Dalton or Winnetka plans, but they present little that is essentially different in so far as the organization of teaching materials is concerned.

It is assumed at Winnetka that the complete development of the pupil is secured through a mastery of the common essentials, expressing himself freely in various channels and by practising coöperation in the life activities of the school. The latter are highly important, but are not analyzed into objectives of knowledges, skills, etc., which are needed by every child in the school. The learning activities in these fields promote coöperation and expose pupils to the best in literature and art. No one will question the value of these phases of individualizing the work of the pupil, but the command of the common essentials will be emphasized in this illustrative material since more definite and scientific organizations of subject-matter are found in this phase of the program.

The Winnetka plan assumes that there are certain knowledges

and skills which are essential in the life of every pupil. These are isolated through analysis and stated in very definite terms. A test is then organized which will measure the degree of mastery attained by the pupil. These tests are built to measure the mastery or lack of mastery of every specific objective or essential phase of every topic and is therefore diagnostic and indicates any weakness the pupil may have in this work.

The work is either organized in texts or is presented to the pupil as bound mimeographed sheets of assignment material. These mimeographed sheets either supplement a text or are used independently of any text.

The following quotation from the Washburne Individual Arithmetic by Dr. Washburne, Superintendent of Schools at Winnetka, and Miss Carswell illustrates the organization of material for the individual pupil.[2]

To the Pupil

You can teach yourself with this book. You can correct all your own work. You can test yourself and find out whether you understand what you have been doing. When you make mistakes in your tests, you can tell just what kind of practice you need.

The work is divided into steps. Each step has just one new thing to learn. At the beginning of some new steps there is an explanation. Always read this very carefully. Have your pencil in your hand, and work each part of the examples that are worked for you in the explanation. Be sure you understand what you are doing—you can if you read carefully and do the work.

At the beginning of each new step there are three examples all worked for you. Copy the examples, but not the work. Try to work the first one—while you are working it, look at the book if you need to. See whether your work is just like that in the book. Work the second one. Compare your work with the work in the book. See if you can work the third without any help from the book; then see if your work is right.

Then do all the examples under the letter A. Work neatly—untidy work causes mistakes. When you have finished the A examples, turn to the answer page. See whether you have made any mistakes. If every one of your answers is right, you may skip the examples marked B and C and D and go right on to the next step. But if you

[2] Carleton Washburne and Marion Carswell, *Washburne Individual Arithmetic,* Book Seven (World Book Company, 1928), pp. 1-2.

have made even one mistake in A, go back and work the wrong example over to see where you made your mistake. Try to correct it yourself. If you have trouble, go back to the worked-out examples at the top of the page, or to the explanation, and see if you can find out what you have done wrong. Then do all of B. Again turn to the answer page and correct your work. If you have made no mistakes this time, skip C and D and go right on to the next step. Do C if you have made any mistakes in B. If you still make mistakes in C, ask your teacher for help before you try D.

Always be sure that you have one step mastered—that you can do it perfectly before you go on to the next.

Ask your teacher or another child for help only if you cannot possibly master a step without help. But it is much better to get help than to go on to the next step without thoroughly understanding the step you are doing.

If you master each step, the next will not be hard. When you come to tests, you will be able to do them with very little trouble. You will be able to use your arithmetic in solving real problems.

Each step or goal in the attainment of the objectives is organized so that the pupil can proceed alone. There is no need for group consultations which are common in the Dalton plan. Each pupil carries on his work without reference to any other member of the school. The following example of arithmetic will illustrate this point:

LONG DIVISION

Explanation for Step 1

When we divide by small numbers (like $6\overline{)197}$), we can do much of the work in our heads. But when our divisor is big (like $63\overline{)197}$), we have to write down our work.

Let us get ready for big divisors by writing down our work even when the divisor is small. Take: $3\overline{)18}$. First think "3 in 18?" Write

$$\begin{array}{r} 6 \\ 3\overline{)18} \end{array}$$

6 over the 8. Now multiply 6×3. Write the answer under

$$\begin{array}{r} 6 \\ 3\overline{)18} \\ 18 \end{array}$$

18. Draw a line under the last number, 18, and subtract. 18

from 18 is 0. Write 0. The 0 shows that there is no remainder.

$$\begin{array}{r} 6 \\ 3\overline{)18} \\ \underline{18} \\ 0 \end{array}$$

Try another: 9)72. Think "9 in 72?" Write 8 over the 2. $\dfrac{8}{9)72}$

Think "8 × 9." Write the answer 72. $\begin{array}{r} 8 \\ 9)\overline{72} \\ 72 \end{array}$ Draw a line under

the last number, 72, and subtract. 72 from 72 is 0. Write 0. $\begin{array}{r} 8 \\ 9)\overline{72} \\ 72 \\ \hline 0 \end{array}$

Try this example: 6)18. Then look at the second example at the top of page 5 to see if your work is right.

Work this one: 4)24. Then look at the second example at the top of page 5 to see if your work is right.

Work this one: 7)35. Then look at the third example.

Work A on page 5 the long way. Compare your answers and your work with the answers on page 9. Remember if you get all the examples under A correct, you do not have to do B. If you miss any in A, you must do B.

LONG DIVISION—STEP 1

$\begin{array}{r} 3 \\ 6)\overline{18} \\ 18 \\ \hline 0 \end{array}$
$\begin{array}{r} 6 \\ 4)\overline{24} \\ 24 \\ \hline 0 \end{array}$
$\begin{array}{r} 5 \\ 7)\overline{35} \\ 35 \\ \hline 0 \end{array}$

A

4)36   6)54   8)48   8)56   8)64

8)72   9)54   9)63   2)18   3)18

B

3)24   3)27   9)18   8)40   7)28

C

You do not have to do C if you made no mistake in B.

9)72   6)30   8)32   7)42   5)30

D

D is only for children who made mistakes in C.

$9\overline{)81}$ $8\overline{)64}$ $5\overline{)20}$ $6\overline{)18}$ $7\overline{)49}$

The pupil is given the opportunity to check his progress by taking practice tests at the completion of his work. These preliminary tests cover every phase of the units of work and are usually divided into a number of parts. If the child completes the first part of practice test satisfactorily, he can turn at once to the real test and write on this examination. If he fails on any part of the practice test, he works additional sections. The child is allowed to look at the answers, and it will be noted that under each answer is included the page of the test or mimeographed material which will provide additional practice.

The following practice test and answers from the unit on long division is included as an illustration.

LONG DIVISION—STEPS 1 TO 8

Practice Test

Form 1

$20\overline{)80}$ $98\overline{)396}$ $98\overline{)3530}$ $97\overline{)8739}$

$81\overline{)89}$ $86\overline{)6020}$ $85\overline{)7140}$

Compare your answers with the answers on page 30. If your work is correct, ask your teacher for a real test.

Form 2

You do not have to work Form 2 unless you made mistakes in Form 1.

$99\overline{)894}$ $97\overline{)5825}$ $21\overline{)84}$ $96\overline{)7010}$

$43\overline{)3870}$ $71\overline{)4544}$ $91\overline{)96}$

Form 3

Form 3 does not have to be worked unless you made mistakes in Forms 1 and 2.

$$82\overline{)5498} \qquad 35\overline{)39} \qquad 96\overline{)388} \qquad 63\overline{)5858}$$

$$31\overline{)1674} \qquad 31\overline{)62} \qquad 95\overline{)6650}$$

For answers see page 30 (text).

LONG DIVISION—STEPS 1 TO 8

Practice Test

Answers for page 29

Form 1

Suppose you did not get 4 for your first answer. The (111) under the 4 tells you to turn to page 111 in your Correction Book. Work 5 examples there. When you have corrected your work, you may take Form 2 of the Practice Test.

4
(111)

4_{r4}
(114)

36_{r2}
(117)

90_{r9}
(119)

1_{r8}
(113)

70
(118)

84
(115)

Form 2

9_{r3}
(114)

60_{r5}
(119)

4
(111)

73_{r2}
(117)

90
(118)

64
(115)

1_{r5}
(113)

Form 3

67_{r4}
(117)

1_{r4}
(113)

4_{r4}
(114)

90_{r8}
(119)

54
(115)

2
(111)

70
(118)

Washburne contends that any text or course of study in social science can be adapted to the procedure used at Winnetka. He summarizes the essential steps in developing the individual approach in the construction of social-science units in his recent book.[3]

1. Select those facts which it is necessary for every child to master. Do this if possible in terms of the investigations that have been carried forward. But if the results of these investigations are not available, do it in consultation with other teachers or even just on the basis of your own common sense. Specify only those facts which you want every single child to master—which no child can omit. Specify them first by writing them for your own use in your notebook as definite statements—not in outline form, but in the form of fact statements like this: "Every child must know that (a) Columbus discovered America, (b) he was trying to find a short route to the Indies, (c) he was financed by Queen Isabella, (d) he sailed in 1492"—as definite and as detailed as that. Attempts to shortcut this process by using such general outline forms as "The Discovery of America—tell why and by whom" are fatal to clear thinking and good assignments.

2. Prepare a set of questions to be placed in the hands of each child to guide him toward the securing of the knowledge which you have specified. They can be and probably should be somewhat general. They might take such a form as the following: "Who discovered America? Why did he set forth from Spain? How was he financed? When did he set sail?"

These questions and definite instructions as to where the child will find the information, what pages of the textbook he is to read, what supplementary reading he is to do, what maps he is to prepare, if any, and how he is to prepare them, should if possible be mimeographed. If they are mimeographed, they can be used over and over in different years. If they are not mimeographed, they might be hectographed, or even in a pinch written on the blackboard. The trouble with writing them on the blackboard is that they have to be rewritten every year. They also are harder for the children to see, and they take up a great deal of space. Assignment sheets that can be placed in the hands of the children are much more satisfactory.

3. Let the children proceed through their unit of work during their social-studies study period strictly as individuals, each child

[3] Carleton Washburne, *Adapting the School to the Child* (World Book Company, 1932), pp. 117-120.

using his assignment sheet to guide him in his study of the given topic.

4. Prepare a test based upon your original set of statements as to what each child must know. This test should be of the most objective type. It might, for example be in the following form:

I. The Italian who discovered America was ———.

II. His voyage of discovery was paid for by:
   1. The merchants of Genoa
   2. The king of England
   3. Queen Isabella of Spain
   4. The scientists who wanted him to prove that the world was round

III. When he set forth from Spain he did so:
   1. To find a short route to the Indies
   2. To conquer India
   3. To find a new continent
   4. To find the fountain of youth

IV. The year in which he discovered America was ———.

There is only one possible right answer to each of these questions. If the child has made a mistake in any one of them, it is a simple matter for the teacher to see it, to assign additional reading to him, and to require him to make either an oral or a written report to her upon the element missed.

5. Use for discussions of debatable questions and for group and creative activities of the kind described in the next chapter the time that would ordinarily be used for recitations and for oral assignments.

The discussion of debatable questions will differ radically from recitations. There will be no right or wrong, there will be no marking, there will be no attempt to see whether the child has studied his lesson. There will simply be a vigorous give-and-take on such a question as to whether the South had a right to secede from the North, whether there should be government ownership of railroads, or whether we have a right to hold the Philippines.

In such discussions the teacher will scrupulously avoid molding the children's opinions to hers or even to those of the community or nation. Her one object will be to help the children to think their problems through scientifically and in the light of facts and logic.

By saving the time wasted through the usual class methods of instruction in the social studies, one can gain time for these life-giving activities. By clearly seeing the difference between those objectives which are definite and measurable and which concern themselves largely with the learning of certain essential facts, and those objectives which are desirable outcomes which we hope will result from certain types of activity and exposure, it is possible to combine the values of the individual with those of the group method of instruction.

Let us individualize those phases of the social studies which have to do with the mastery of factual material and which therefore are going to be tested and used as a basis for promotion. Having individualized these, let us use our saved time in a whole-hearted endeavor to get from the social studies those rich values which, though we cannot measure them as yet, are among the most socially valuable in our entire school curriculum.

VI. SUMMARY

The reader should note that both the teaching materials and the procedures developed at Winnetka are more individualized than is possible in many phases of the contract used in the Dalton plan. At Winnetka, the pupil can be in several different grade levels as far as the basic essentials are concerned. Since the units are organized on an individual basis, a pupil can be in the fifth grade and carry some work in the sixth grade. It is not even necessary for him to meet with the sixth-grade pupils in order to undertake and complete the work for that grade.

BIBLIOGRAPHY

Any one interested in the procedures used at Winnetka should write to Carleton Washburne for details and illustrative units. Reference has been made to Superintendent Washburne's recent book.

CHAPTER XI

CHILD-CENTERED UNITS OF WORK

I. INTRODUCTION

So much is being written about the unusual character and phenomenal success of the activity program of the "child-centered" school that its theory and practice need to be evaluated in so far as they are pertinent to a discussion of the organization of teaching materials. The claims of many educators of this group that they are not interested in aims or organized-learning activities for the realization of values merits the careful and unbiased consideration of every one working in this field. A comparison of the claims or theoretical expositions of educators with the practice in activity or experimental schools will improve the reader's ability to discriminate between intriguing phraseology and sound educational practice.

There are three systems of organizing teaching materials at the present time. Confusion arises from the general assumption that only two—the activity school and the formal organization of old subject-matter—are being emphasized. The third type may be called the new subject-matter program in that the results can be used in old subject-matter fields or may lead to the development of new fields of work. "Progressive" education, which emphasized child activity, and the new scientific attitude, which emphasizes the need of aims, evaluation of results of teaching, etc., represent two developments of the same decade. Both were opposed to the old textbook system of daily lesson assignment that placed the responsibility of educational progress upon the author of the textbook and the classroom teacher. Both were vitally interested in relating education to life and making the interests and activities of children a basic part of the determination of teaching materials. They differed in that the scientific group proposed to use adult standards as a check upon child activities and interests, while the activity group insisted that the interests and activities of to-day are sufficient guides for the educational program of to-morrow and the future. In the discussion which has followed, the scientific groups have accepted that which is sound educational doctrine in the program of the activists, but the activists, failing to appreciate the values inherent in the scientific procedure, have classified the new subject-matter group with adherents to the old textbook organization.

Owing to this attitude of "progressive" educators, an anomalous situation has arisen in many experimental schools. While visiting a well-known experimental school, the author was told that the term *objectives* was obnoxious to the faculty of the school. Those in charge further stated that they did not believe in the preparation of teaching materials in advance of the class period. But before leaving the school the author was presented with a large sheaf of outlines of projects that had been allocated to grade and ability levels. These outlines were completely organized and left little to the initiative of the teacher or the students. Methods of presenting the new project were indicated, and methods of motivating pupils to participate in the complete organization of the work for the project were specified. The outlines were similar to excellent courses except for the use of the terms "objectives" and "teaching materials," which are always included in those developed by scientific educators and consistently omitted from outlines of "progressive" educators. In actual practice there is little difference between the so-called "progressive" educational programs and those developed by scientific methods. This fact will be apparent as some of the outstanding programs which have been organized in "progressive" and "experimental" schools are studied and compared with those which have previously been presented.

The reader should realize that there is great divergence of opinion among the activists concerning the development of teaching materials. Here again is the extremist who advocates a program growing out of the activities and interests of the class as it is assembled. At the other extreme in this group are found those who hold that present programs should be based largely upon those "activity" materials which have been very successful in the past. Again a middle group accepts that which is good in previous classroom experiences and makes use of every indication of special interest of the class which has educational significance for the present.

There are three ways of developing a unit of work according to the "activity school" technique. First, the teacher can take the immediate interests and activities of the children as the basis of the work. Second, the staff can organize research pertaining to the previous work of a particular class, the work of previous classes in this subject at a definite grade level, and the social interests and experiences of children of this age, in order to develop an educational program that will provide broad experiences and rich contacts and also be within the comprehension and interest area of the pupils. Third, the staff can assume that the interests of children of a certain age or grade lie in particular areas and that all units in these areas, which have educational merit, will be satisfactory.

This does not mean that the unit as originally developed will be satisfactory. A continuous revision and reorganization of the original activity unit is necessary, since new materials, new activities, and new methods of procedure are constantly being presented to the progressive teacher. The final unit will probably be very different from the initial effort of the teacher. Hopkins presents the following plan for the development of units of work at the Lincoln School. His analysis of the procedure is so complete that the teacher or staff committee can afford to give it careful consideration before undertaking the organization of an activity unit.

Each teacher in Lincoln School keeps a full record of her unit from the beginning of the process of selection to the date when it is being prepared for publication. The initial planning, the first preview, the subsequent plans, the orienting activities, the exceptional work of individual pupils, the treatment of the unadjusted child, the ideas and leads brought out in the group discussion periods, the numerous questions and problems raised by individuals, the specific content ordinarily classified as subject-matter, the narrative daily account of the development of the group interest and the activities which go on outside of the unit, are all a matter of record. The form of record varies with the preference of the individual teacher and the nature of the unit.

The chief characteristics of curriculum making in the Lincoln Elementary School are: first, the curriculum is organized around units of work based upon genuine interests of children; second, the major responsibility for the selection, organization, development, and teaching of the units rests with the classroom teacher; third, the unit is planned in broad general outlines previous to the teaching; fourth, the process of planning is continuous until the unit is completed; fifth, a record of development of the unit is made; sixth, the teachers of special subjects act as counselors and advisers to the classroom teacher; seventh, the curriculum research staff offers aid throughout the entire process, and in addition, locates and studies special curriculum problems.[1]

II. A STUDY OF TEACHER-PUPIL COÖPERATION IN PREPARING CLASS ACTIVITIES

One of the best statements of the purposes and organization of the activity school is found in the *Introduction to the Major Units in the Social Studies,* which outlines the program for the elementary training school at the University of California at Los Angeles. This statement by Dr. Waddell, Director of the Training Department, is as follows:

The activity school aims primarily at the growth and development of children. It starts with the child as he is. It considers his interests, his needs and capacities. It respects the individuality of the child as a priceless asset which needs, not repression or elimination, but unfoldment and development. It gives freedom from unnatural and unnecessary restraint. It aims to teach children to use freedom effectively, with due regard to the normal checks which life itself imposes. It attempts to build upon the nature, the experience and the needs of boys and girls. It uses such subject-matter and such standards as contribute definitely to pupil growth. It is of necessity dominated by informality. It encourages natural activity, initiative, self-direction, self-control, self-judgment, self-mastery. It attempts to establish, in the schoolroom and on the playground, normal so-

[1] L. T. Hopkins, "Curriculum Revision at Lincoln School," excerpt from an address before the Department of Supervisors and Directors of Instruction at Washington, D. C., February 24, 1932.

cial relations, and encourages helpful intercourse and communication very much as these relationships function in real life. It aims at normal, friendly, helpful, coöperative relations in natural life-situations. It attempts to keep the whole child alive and at work at worth-while enterprises. It seems to provide situations in which the child acquires the knowledge, the skills, the habits, the appreciations and the methods of work he needs in the furtherance of his growth and of his education. It seeks to provide the setting in which these ends are attained naturally and in relations to their use in worth-while enterprises which are childlike and therefore interesting and profitable here and now. It attempts to find the conditions under which study and learning naturally and necessarily take place. It focuses the attention of children on doing, under conditions which make learning a necessary and inevitable result. It puts a premium on thinking, on self-judgment, on self-criticism and on the evaluation of one's contribution to the good of the group with which one works, as well as to one's own satisfaction. By all these aims and the procedures they inevitably require, it seeks to fit the child to live now in a dynamic, changing social order and, through them, to prepare him to live effectively in such a social order at any later period.

With such aims and objectives it is obvious that the criteria of success must be quite different and quite other than those which have commonly been used in judging the outcome of the traditional or "stalwart" school and its work. We have too long been content to judge of success in terms of the acquirement of knowledge and of a few fundamental skills. It is not strange that there is, at present, a dearth of reliable measures for the more imponderable but much more significant values at which the activity school primarily aims. We need much more exact measures for such things as capacity for creative self-expression; growth in capacity for wise use of freedom; improvement in social helpfulness; development in ability to plan, to execute and to judge one's own accomplishments; improvement in ability to think clearly and to the point; growth in the whole group of character qualities which constitute so large a part of real education. We have faith to believe that our need will be met. Our experts in educational measurement will undertake to make the difficult but immensely valuable contribution of supplying our need just as soon as they are convinced that such measures are in real demand and will be used. When they have finished the task, and not until then, shall we be able to evaluate truly the real accomplishments of the activity procedures in elementary education.[2]

[2] C. W. Waddell, C. A. Seeds and N. White, *Major Units in the Social Studies* (The John Day Company, 1932), pp. 5-7.

The plans by which this program can be put into effect are given here to enable the reader to check with the best practice of activity schools and of regular public schools that have developed activity programs. In the first place, it should be noted that teachers, responsible for guiding pupils toward educational goals, expressed in terms of successful living and growing out of activities which were planned and directed largely by the learners, must constantly carry on research in subject-matter, the integration of teaching fields, and methods of motivating pupil interest and achievement. As soon as the direction and the probable scope of pupils' interests have been determined, it is essential that a preview of the learning situations be developed in order that continuity and systematic progress be attained. Otherwise, objectives for the educational program will not be in evidence either in the planning of the teacher or the work of the pupils. The directors and faculty of the elementary school at the University of California at Los Angeles have adopted the following procedure in guiding the development of activities in their school:

I. Name of the study around which the activity of the children will probably center.

II. List the past experience and present needs of the children which would seem to make this continuing and integrated series of enterprises interesting, challenging and worth while to them at this time.

III. Outline richly and in detail the subject-matter possibilities of this proposed study.

IV. List the possible enterprises or experiences which it is hoped may arise and be interesting, feasible and worth while to the children in terms of:

   a. Experiences of a creative nature where ideas are expressed concretely, including expression in any field of endeavor, be it constructing with wood, notes, words or rhythmic steps. (Producer's enterprise—Kilpatrick.)

   b. Enterprise of an appreciative nature. (Consumer's enterprise—Kilpatrick.)

   c. Experiences in solving intellectual difficulties. (Problem-solving enterprise—Kilpatrick.)

   d. Experiences in the acquisition of knowledge, habits and skills. (Specific-learning enterprise—Kilpatrick.)

V. List possible approaches to the study as a whole which may stimulate the children to purpose further activity in that direction.

VI. Work through in detail at least one approach, showing how the teacher hopes to arrange the environment and guide the responses of the children into worth-while initial purposing which sets the activity going with zest. Be specific. State in detail what concrete materials and what materials which lead to vicarious experiences you will use; what excursions you will take and the conversation which you believe will occur under teacher-guidance.

VII. Outline briefly the anticipated sequence as one enterprise leads into another.

VIII. List ways of terminating the unit which might be desirable, probable and feasible and which would cause a reorganization of the children's experiences.

IX. Anticipated outcomes of this study in terms of:
   a. Knowledge
   b. Habits and skills
   c. Attitudes
   d. Leads into new interests [3]

In the second place, the teacher who has launched an activity program with a group of pupils should prepare an outline of the work based on the progress which has been made in comparison with the goals which were tentatively established, the contribution of each day's work as it modifies the proposed plan, and the outcomes which are apparent as the result of the related activities. The staff at the elementary school at the University of California at Los Angeles has formulated an outline for the guidance of the teacher in summarizing the progress and results or outcomes of the unit of work. The following quotation indicates the scope of the summary:

I. The situation out of which the activity arose (or the genesis), showing who and what started it.

II. What the children under guidance of the teacher purposed to do.

III. How the children and teacher planned together and through careful execution with continuous judging carried the activity to a successful termination. (This should include a description of all the enterprises carried on, showing how each led into the next, thus forming an integrated related study.)

[3] *Ibid.*, pp. 21-22.

IV. The specific outcomes of the activity in terms of:
  a. Knowledge
  b. Habits
  c. Attitudes
  d. Leads into new interests

It can be seen that once the enterprise is launched this anticipatory plan will change and grow as the daily needs of the group are met.[4]

In the third place, the teacher should have an overview of the work and be able to see each day's work as it is related to the complete unit or project. If this optimum situation is to develop, the teacher must prepare for each day's activities in advance and guide the pupils so that the previous work forms the background for their activities and guarantees that these activities will be valuable in promoting the desired outcomes for every child. The staff of the elementary school at the University of California at Los Angeles has made the following preliminary plan for the organization of the daily work, which is based on the procedure suggested by Mossman[5] in her book:

I. Brief statement of the relation of this lesson to the preceding one and to the study as a whole.
II. Purpose of the anticipated work.
III. Sequence of lesson procedure.

Things the teacher thinks will happen, showing how she expects to make provision for *readiness, exercise,* and *effect* on the part of the children.	Subject-matter needed, including skills in processes, etc	Illustrative material —references, etc.

A live narrative account of what actually transpired, noting any irregularities, unanticipated questions, leads, etc., including also a statement as to what should be the natural outgrowth of this day's work.[6]

Adams, in a study of the initiation of an activity program into the public schools, makes an analysis of the data secured

[4] *Ibid.,* pp. 22-23.
[5] Lois C. Mossman, *Changing Conception Relative to the Planning of Lessons* (Bureau of Publications, Teachers College, Columbia University, 1924).
[6] C. W. Waddell, C. A. Leeds, and N. White, *op. cit.,* pp. 23 and 25.

from 27 specialists, 660 teachers, 94 supervisors, 60 student-teachers, 70 administrators, and 38 university professors. One of the major problems considered was that of learning how to select and develop an activity in the school room. The results indicated that the following procedures were desirable in the order of mention.

A. *Excellent Solutions*
   b. Visit progressive teachers and observe the activities in progress ....
   i. Visit demonstration rooms ....
B. *Good Solutions*
   a. Read descriptions and records of activities ....
   d. Consult teachers experienced in activity work ....
   e. Analyze up-to-date courses of study ....
   f. Consult the supervisor ....
   h. Enroll in methods courses dealing with activities ....
   k. Study the interests and needs of the children ....
   l. Study the facilities of the school and the community......
   m. Analyze one's own experience ....
C. *Solutions Having Some Merit*
   c. Attend exhibits of pupil work ....
   g. Attend lectures on child development ....
   j. Read discussions of philosophy and psychology ....
D. *Solutions Having Little Merit*
   n. Read discussions of current social problems ....
E. *Undesirable Solutions*
   None ....[7]

The teacher should be able to see the probable results and outcomes of the unit in terms of the class and the individual students. There are problems which will have to be solved by individuals or by the class from time to time, and these must be envisaged by the teacher and prepared for through individual reports or class discussions. In many instances, these will appear to be the natural development of a particular class period, but the teacher should have prepared in advance for these contributions by the group and individual pupils.

[7] Fay Adams, *The Initiation of an Activity Program Into a Public School.* Contributions to Education, No. 598 (Bureau of Publications, Teachers College, Columbia University, 1934), p. 30.

It is significant that the analysis of up-to-date courses of study ranks high in the possible solutions to the problem. This was true in the estimation of each of the five professional groups consulted. A study of the activity units presented in this chapter can serve as a guide to work in this field if the teacher will use the other important sources of information (listed under A above) in the study by Adams.

It is hoped that this discussion and the illustrations will serve to acquaint the reader with some of the professional responsibilities of the teacher in the activity school. They are not only extensive in scope, but they are of great significance in realizations secured in the activity school. Subject-matter which has been improvised by the teacher and pupils in the classroom as they work and play together is likely to lack continuity and educational value.

The difficulties which are likely to ensue when a school system is reorganized on the activity basis are indicated by Firman:

To my mind, many teachers who are attempting progressive education have accomplished so little because they have attempted so much. They have tried to "go progressive" all at once. Doubtless they have done this because they have failed to realize the magnitude of the task they were undertaking. Perhaps they have also failed to realize that the one change from traditional education to progressive education is greater than the combined changes that have been made in our system of education since the dawn of the century. All of the previous changes have been changes in means to the same end. We have kept the same objectives and have only tried to find better ways of reaching them. But in progressive education, we have thrown down the old gods and have set up new.

Among the objectives of progressive education are the development of initiative and the power to think and act independently, and preparation for social living. In striving for these, the pupils will acquire most of the academic skills that have been the objectives of traditional education; but they will acquire them in a new way. These will no longer be the prime objectives of education, however. They will be secondary to others. When Mrs. Ruggles of *The Birds' Christmas Carol* said to her children, "It ain't so much what you say, as how you say it," she uttered truth which for education may be paraphrased as "It is not so much what the pupils do, as how they do it. The doing is more important than the product."

There is altogether too general a belief among parents and teachers that a school which has an activity program is giving progressive education, even though the activities bear little relation to the subject-matter of the curriculum. In many classrooms this has produced a kind of "Dr. Jekyll and Mr. Hyde" type of education. The philosophy of progressive education pervades activities and the philosophy of formal education prevails in subject-matter.

There can be little doubt that activities lend themselves very readily to developing the initiative of the pupils. Every class should have an abundance of them, and they should be as "free" as possible; but the subject-matter of the curriculum should also be presented in such a way as to realize the aims of progressive education. Many activities are purely individualistic. Only class- or group-activities can give the pupils as much preparation for social living as can be given in helping them to learn the subject-matter of the curriculum in a thoroughly socialized way.[8]

In order that the reader can appreciate the part played by the children and the teacher in the organization of teaching materials, a part of the unit, "Life of the Early Hebrews," which was developed in the third grade of the elementary school at the University of California at Los Angeles, is included at this point. Lack of space prevents our including more than the introduction and the first section, which outlines how the study was developed by the children. However, enough is presented to enable one to see the relative responsibility of the teacher and the pupils in the organization of learning experiences.

LIFE OF THE EARLY HEBREWS

INTRODUCTION

The unit of work, *The Early Hebrews,* had been selected for the third grade to see how the children would react to the simple experiences of a group of people who lived in the early stages of civilization. Suggestions may be found at the end of Part C for the application of this unit to other grades. Various units had been tried with Grade III with success during previous semesters, such as:

A Study of Milk
The Study of Primitive Peoples
Early and Later Cave Men
Early Sea People

[8] Sidney G. Firman, "Taking the First Steps in Progressive Education," *Progressive Education,* Vol. XII (Jan., 1935), pp. 30-31.

The Study of Boats
The Western Indian
Life in Africa

The *Early Hebrew* unit was chosen because the Hebrews were adventurous, were primitive, and their lives portrayed the struggle with and constant readaptation of a race to its environment. Since it is assumed that subject-matter is not present until it is created in the mind of the child, this study offered much opportunity for worth-while activities in industrial arts and rhythms. Although the unit was selected before the children assembled the first day after vacation, there were countless choices within the unit which were freely made by the pupils. This will be more clearly brought out in the account which follows this introduction.

By referring to Part B, also, one can determine for oneself the value of the concomitant learning, the problems involved, the skills acquired, the knowledge gained, the habits and attitudes formed and developed, and the appreciations that just "grew up."

The unit of work was for the most part confined to the morning, the afternoon having been given over to the acquisition of certain skills in number and reading mechanics, and to other interests such as the Nature Club, the Book Club, and the Newspaper Club. The morning program was extremely flexible, and although all subjects fell within the range of a unit, and all types of enterprises were carried on as needs for each arose (producer's type, problem-solving, consumer's work, and specific learning) no special time was set aside wherein a certain thing had to be done in a certain way.

Teacher and pupil found it more convenient to have the work-period (consisting predominantly of industrial arts) at nine o'clock, as materials could easily be assembled before school. Besides, the children often wished to begin to work as soon as they came on the school grounds. The class average was about three work periods a week. Individual talks with the teacher and group discussions were held almost daily to estimate the progress made and to aid each child in solving difficulties. Assemblies were held whenever an interesting phase of work or unit of subject-matter had been finished. Problem-solving lessons were taught when a worthwhile problem arose. Drill lessons were given whenever some phase of learning or some special skill needed to be fixed. Several times a week regular spelling lessons were given to meet the demands of the new vocabulary. The class average for written language lessons was two a week. Frequently stories were read or told by the children or teacher for appreciation. Rhythms, music, and art found a place as the need arose. Time was often given for free play and dramatization. The entire class was not always busy with the same task. Often a group of children would be working with tools, while another group would be absorbed in looking at pictures or reading books to gather information to further their purposes, while still another group might be engaged in a dramatization. In general, the program organization was loose and flexible, according to traditional standards, but did not lack organization and pattern, since it was shaped by the demands of the enterprise as it grew.

Part A

Narrative Account as the Study was Developed by the Children

THE PROBLEMS FORMULATED

After summer vacation the boys and girls were anxious to tell of their summer experiences. The pupils told of trips taken by boat to Seattle, Hawaii, Alaska, Catalina Island, and of trips by train to the East. Some traveled by auto to near-by points. Some hiked in the mountains; others visited relatives who lived on ranches. One child brought pictures of his trip to Hawaii. Then the teacher showed pictures of travel, including travel in caravans. The children immediately became interested in camels and pointed out places (with the help of the teacher) on the map where camels were the only "trains." Other pictures of early Hebrew life were shown. The class was especially interested in the shepherds. Those who had been on ranches during the summer wanted to tell about cattle, sheep, hogs, and chickens. Some one asked if there were shepherds to tend the flocks to-day. The discussion which followed brought the class back to early days when flocks were led instead of driven. Some one had seen a picture of Jesus as the Good Shepherd. Some one else mentioned that camels were used in the time of Christ, too; he had learned about the Three Wise Men in Sunday School. Jesus' home was located on the map. The teacher brought out the number of years that had passed since that time. The children were interested in A.D. and B.C., many of them dating their papers 1929 A.D. throughout the term. Other children began to "make connections" with Sunday School. Some told of David as a shepherd boy. The teacher then asked them if they would like to hear a story about the Hebrew people who wanted to leave the city just as they had done during the summer, only the Hebrews had a very important reason for leaving the city of Ur. The children all wanted the story. The teacher read "The Caravan Starts" in Mrs. Bonser's, *How the Early Hebrews Lived and Learned*. The children enjoyed the story and discovered that Abram led his people out of Ur because he was tired of making and worshiping images—he wished to worship as he pleased. He wished to start a new nation, so he went in search of new lands and green pastures. The following questions arose and were listed on the board by the teacher:

1. What was the Hebrew religion like?
2. How did they travel?
3. Which direction did they go?
4. Where did Abram finally settle down?
5. Did it take them long to get there?
6. Were they robbed on the way?
7. Did any wild animals attack them?
8. What did they eat?
9. Where did they get their clothes?
10. Where were they sheltered?
11. Did Abram start a new nation?

THE CHILDREN MAKE PLANS

Faced with these problems the children decided to start on a journey with Abram, and as the journey progressed find out how Abram and his people worked out these problems. Under the guidance of the teacher the children decided:

1. To make a tent for shelter
2. To furnish the tent with mats and dishes
3. To make costumes
4. To prepare and eat "Hebrew food"
5. To make weapons
6. To make scrolls and write on them
7. To make a map so the journey could be traced
8. To make the mud houses of the city
9. To read stories of Abram, Joseph, Isaac, and others.[9]

The participation of the children in developing the work of the class is indicated in the outline of the procedures followed during the work periods. The following quotation analyzes the coöperation of the teacher and the pupils during this period.

PROCEDURE FOLLOWED DURING WORK PERIODS

A definite procedure was also followed during the work periods. When a large unit of work was started, such as making a paper plan for the outdoor map, making pottery, making mud houses, etc., the teacher and pupils planned together to carry out their purposes. The

[9] Gertrude Maloney, *Life of the Early Hebrews,* Teachers' Lesson Unit Series, No. 49 (Bureau of Publications, Teachers College, Columbia University, 1932), pp. 1-4.

blackboard was filled with ideas for executing with lists of materials and tools, etc. Important suggestions were transferred with black crayola on large sheets of brown wrapping paper so that the blackboard could be erased without loss of the results of the planning. These sheets were referred to and added to continually as the work progressed. Before the class started to work on any of the industrial arts phases of the activity, the entire group met and discussed the plans for the day. Enough time was allowed at the end of the period for another discussion group. Then they passed judgment on the work accomplished for the day, brought up new problems and made plans for the next work period. These discussion periods were most valuable in the developing of attitudes toward work, in developing responsibility to the group, coöperation, promptness, etc. They were also the most interesting and alive oral English lessons of the term. About once in two weeks assemblies were held. Grade IIIB was invited in, and each class was given the opportunity to describe its unit of work to the other. This encouraged free discussion, dramatization, and demonstration, was a summary of work accomplished, and served as a starting point for the development of new ideas and concomitant interests.

Each child kept a written record of the activity. Large scrapbooks were made and written work of merit was mounted and pasted in them. The books were illustrated with original drawings and with articles and pictures bearing on the project. The books varied in thickness according to each child's writing ability and his interest in the project. Some of the stories were only one paragraph in length; others were written in chapters; sometimes a thought was expressed in poetry. To encourage the latter, the teacher took down bits of fine prose uttered unconsciously by the children during the subtly supervised free-play periods and industrial-arts periods. For instance when the children were working with wool several were discussing the bad odor of the sheepskin which they had sheared. and the dirt in the wool. One child who did not find these things objectionable said, "But baby lambs are clean. I've never seen a dirty one. They are all fluffy and curly and white with a pink nose at one end and a tiny tail at the other." This was read back to the child who had spoken it a few days later. By a slight rearrangement of lines he made a poem for his scrap-book.

> An old sheep may be dirty,
> But have you ever seen a baby lamb?
> Its wool fluffy and curly and white
> With a pink nose at one end
> And a tiny tail at the other.
> I guess it's kept clean by its mother.

Some children preferred to make scrolls instead of scrap-books. They had read about the scrolls of the Hebrews. Imitation parchment was made by sprinkling finely shaven paraffin and beeswax over wrapping paper and pressing with a hot iron. The paper was pressed again to remove all superfluous paraffin. The children brought poles fourteen inches in length which they had cut from broomsticks, bamboo, curtain poles, etc., to which the paper was attached. A space of eleven inches was allowed for each article written. A few children who wished to "write straight" ruled paper that could be placed underneath the "parchment." They also learned how real parchment is made. A sample was brought in from a sixth-grade class which had been studying the history of records. The sixth grade also showed the class clay tablets and papyrus. A few of the children made some clay tablets themselves.[10]

In the early grades and the kindergarten, many valuable learning experiences have been developed by the children under the guidance of the teacher. Such a unit as "Building a Playhouse," which was organized in the first grade of the elementary school at the University of California at Los Angeles, illustrates adequately the significant contributions of the pupils.

BUILDING A PLAYHOUSE

Growth of the Plan of the House
The children began playing with the five large packing boxes which had been placed in the room. A "family" lived in each box. There was much visiting back and forth. Bobby and William claimed one for their own. "We got it first," said Bobby, and began pounding more nails where other nails were. There was no plan to this hammering, nor could they give any acceptable reason for the nailing. Randolph said to them, "Let us have this box for a house." But the two boys shook their heads and Randolph went to beg a home from another group who lived in a box. This "family" adopted him, and also Nancy with her doll, Mary Ann. The visiting of the groups continued for two or three days. The personnel of the family would change from day to day.

One day Frederick, who was quite uncomfortable in his box house, suggested a change. "I can't stand up straight, I bump my head." He was invited to try all the houses but found them to be the same height. "I know, let's take the top off," said Richard. All of the "families" thought this a good plan. Hammers began to be

[10] *Ibid.,* pp. 10-11.

used; the tops were difficult to pull off, but there were plenty of "laborers" now, even Bobby and William joined in. Soon one family was helping another to remove the *roofs*. ("Roofs" now substituted as a better term.)

While this coöperative, helpful feeling was permeating the group, the teacher joined in the work, pulling a nail here, loosening a difficult board there. After this work period when all tools were put away, the group sat on the floor gazing at their sorry looking houses. "They do not look much like houses, do they?" said Patricia. "How could we make them look like a house?" said the teacher. "I can fix them," said Richard. He began pushing them together. Two other boys caught his idea of making all of the boxes into one house, and began helping. After much arrangement and suggestions from the group the boxes were arranged in a square.

"But we need a big house."

"Yes, we must have a bed room."

"And a living room and a kitchen"—and so on, naming all the rooms from cellar to garret.

"We can nail boards on the sides and have a big house."

This met with approval. It was now "our house."

The next morning Bobby, whose new home was under construction, came into the room holding tightly to a paper on which his mother had written the one word "architect." "This," holding the paper so all could see the written word, "is what you have to get before you can build a house." He could not recall the word, but when the teacher read it and the term was understood, the children began to ask him many questions.

"How many rooms has your house?"

"Will you have a garage?"

"What kind of a house is it?"

He gave quite a graphic picture of the house, and in his effort to clear up some points he took the chalk to demonstrate. This led to a desire on the part of each child to make a picture of his own house. These pictures created much pleasure in the sharing of home experiences. Many of the children added window boxes and gardens, explaining the different kinds of flowers, fruit and vegetables grown. Their drawings were labeled "My house ——— (name of child) by the teacher, at the suggestion of one of the girls as she hunted through the box of drawings for her own. Some children were able to print their own names, others learned to do so; the teacher signed for others, who were not satisfied with their own efforts at writing. The looks and comments of those who put their names on "by themselves" stimulated greater effort on the part of others. One boy who had great difficulty in writing learned how to print his initials and proudly displayed them on all his work. These drawings were bound together in a book and Margaret's title was used—"Our Houses." Every day some one would add something to his picture as: a vine, fence, flowers, window curtains, etc.

At last when the tops were off of all the boxes, many questions arose:

"How many rooms shall we have?"

"Where will we get the boards for the side of the house?"

"These tops will make good tables."

"How high shall the house be?"

"How many doors? Where will we put the doors?"

"How many windows do we need?"

"Where shall we put them?"

"How can we keep the boards from falling?'

"Too many are pounding at once. What shall we do?"

"I think we should have the house as tall as Frederick," said Barbara Jean, "because he is the tallest boy in the room."

"No, Richard and Billy are as tall," said another.

The children stood back to back. Still there were disagreements. So measuring-rods, yardsticks and twelve-inch rulers were used. Some succeeded rather well in measuring the other fellow, but on the whole there were few who could use the ruler accurately. At last Nancy placed herself against the blackboard and had Mary *hold the place* until she could measure, after which she said, "I am three rulers high." This caused some to laugh, but created quite an interest in "feet," "inches," and "yards." Every one wanted to know his height; the ledge of the blackboard prevented accurate measuring, so the teacher secured a long board twelve inches wide and on this board the height of each child was marked off and his name written.

Frederick was found to be the tallest; measured by the yardstick he was one yard and twenty inches tall. To find how many feet he measured, he put the board on the floor and placed twelve-inch rulers from the lower end of the board to his mark. "He is four rulers and eight inches," said Richard. "This ruler is a foot. I am four feet and eight inches," said Frederick. They measured with the yardstick and said he was fifty-six inches tall. The teacher said it would be better to say fifty-six inches, or four feet and eight inches. They liked fifty-six inches better.

So the walls were to be fifty-six inches high.

Richard, who helped arrange the boxes, now showed how only the two outer sides of each box were needed and that these boards could be used for joining them.

"But they split when we knock them off," said one. The teacher showed them how to hold one board over the one to be knocked off; striking it prevented the board underneath from breaking. Two boys for each box were named as the committee to knock off the boards. Their names were written on the board under the word *Carpenters*.

"How many rooms shall we have?"

After much discussion, it was decided to have three rooms, but there was considerable disagreement on the number and position of windows and doors. Bobby said, "We must draw the plan; the planner" ("architect," corrected Evelyn,) "puts them in." "What does this plan look like, Bobby?" asked the teacher.

The next day two girls brought blue prints to school. Both were quite intricate but they could see the spaces marked for windows and doors.

"I'm going to be an architect," said Evelyn, and she took a large piece of unprinted newspaper and went to work. Many became "architects" and soon there were ten acceptable plans submitted. Some were very elaborate but others had caught the idea. The plan made by Rosemary was voted the best. It consisted of a living room, bedroom, and kitchen. Heavy black lines indicated the place for doors. "There are not nearly enough windows," they said, so two more were added.

This plan was pasted to the tag board with the record below:

> This is our plan.
> Rosemary made it.

Another chart contained this story:

> We are making a playhouse.
> It is going to have three rooms.[11]

This unit is carried on in successive weeks through such additional activities as determining the furniture for the house, dishes, curtains, sun porch, etc., in which pupils participate as they did in the first section of the unit. How public schools approach this problem of pupil participation in the development of learning activities in the classroom is illustrated in the excellent account given in the preface of the "Tentative Course of Study in the Social Sciences for the Kindergarten." To enable the reader to study the various steps in the solution of

[11] Clayton Burrow, *Building a Playhouse*, Teachers' Lesson Unit Series, No. 10 (Bureau of Publications, Teachers College, Columbia University, 1932), pp. 1-4.

this problem as participated in by pupils, teachers, and directors, extensive excerpts will be included from this course of study.

BASES OF SELECTION OF UNITS

Child interests have been utilized as the starting-point of curriculum revision in the social sciences in the kindergarten and primary grades. All teachers in the kindergarten and first three grades were asked to canvass their children's interests by finding out from the children themselves what they wanted to know. In order to have uniformity in procedure, a curriculum research bulletin was sent out to teachers.

CURRICULUM RESEARCH BULLETIN No. 1

TEACHERS OF SOCIAL SCIENCES—KINDERGARTEN—GRADES 1, 2, 3

In order to determine children's interests the social-science curriculum committee is desirous of ascertaining first-hand information concerning the things in which children are interested. Will you please use one social-science period next week to ask pupils those things about which they want to know and return this list to the Administration Building by Wednesday, December third?

Please star (*) first, second, third, and fourth choices of the entire class.

METHOD OF PROCEDURE

The teacher should ask her pupils: "Is there anything about which you would like to know which you have never found out about in school or out of school?" Examples: Airplanes, cowboys, how candy is made, etc. Make a list on the blackboard as the children suggest. After the point of diminishing returns has been reached, ask the class the following question: "If you could find out about only one of these interesting things at a time, which would you rather learn about first?" In this way obtain the children's first, second, third, and fourth choices.

1.
2.
3.
4.

School ....   Teacher ....

Grade ....   Number of Pupils ....

When the social-science committee began to tabulate, the results seemed to fall into two categories, namely, those topics pertaining to elementary science and those things pertaining to social sciences. Those topics pertaining to elementary science were turned over to that curriculum committee.

In selecting the final list of units of understanding, those topics which did not help the child to understand and adjust to the world about him and lead him out into larger interests, meanings, and experiences of life, were discarded. Nor were the children's interests considered sacred; for the problem of teaching is to use those interests, which are usually restricted to those things which intimately concern his welfare, in leading the child out into larger spheres and meanings of life. It is our obligation to lead the child beyond his present interests.

Units of understanding must be rich in intellectual content and help the child to understand how man has met and is meeting major problems in the progress of civilization. Units must open to the child such fields of knowledge as science, history, geography, literature, art, and help him to understand their relation to his present social environment. By this means the present is explained and understood in terms of the past, and the children's interests greatly widened and stimulated.

With regard to grade placement of the several units the following factors were considered:

1. Progressive degrees of difficulty of units as concerns construction work involved, and relative ability for children to profit from work
2. Interests of the children
3. Previous experience of the children
4. Practicability under school conditions

More units are suggested for each grade level than any teacher will use. The order of taking up the units for each grade has no significance except for the first two units on the kindergarten level. A teacher will select units appropriate for her level, in which her children are most interested.

Dewey has said, "In every school there should be some significant subject-matters undergoing consistent growth and formulation." In recognition of this idea the experimental units have been set up as required units on every level. These experimental units may be based upon the interests of each particular class. In selecting these experimental units the teacher should not infringe upon nor duplicate the work which has been set up for succeeding grades. However, if her class is interested in a unit which has been set up for a lower grade, the teacher may choose and develop that unit, provided the children have not already experienced it.

Through these experimental units we shall undoubtedly accumulate valuable information as to what types of units offer greatest possibilities for growth of children at certain school levels. Thus, each teacher can contribute to the building of a new course of study designed to grow and change as life situations demand.

ACTIVITIES

A clear understanding of an activity program is needed. Activity is not merely an end in itself, but a means of growth. By the term "activity program" is meant a school curriculum which provides a series of well-selected activities for different levels of growth, directed to some definite worth while end.

SOME CRITERIA FOR EVALUATING THE ACTIVITIES USED IN A UNIT OF UNDERSTANDING

It is suggested that activities employed in units of understanding in the social sciences be balanced in the three following ways:

1. Mental, physical, emotional activities should be closely correlated and provision made for all three types to function in a unit of understanding so as to permit the child's all-round development.

    Experiences for developing appreciations, points of view, emotional outcomes have been given rather indirectly in the past. In view of their importance the school curriculum, whenever possible, should be organized to make them direct outcomes.

    Vicarious reading is a mode of experience, and of normal living. Pupils should read to see the world. This collateral reading should be "concrete, vividly emotional, where one is simply luxuriating in human experiences."

    Because of the rich visual imagery of details pictures should be used in far greater abundance. Pictures is a term used to include all available kinds and afford a means of observing things distant and inaccessible to direct observation.

2. Group and individual activities should be provided in every unit of the social sciences. Children working together in a group are furnished with many contacts which call for coöperation in sharing suggestions and materials, for tolerance of another's efforts, for tact in giving constructive criticism of others' work and receiving criticism of their own, and for observance of others' rights.

3. Any unit of understanding should provide for a variety of endeavors or activities which require different procedures in working them out. Thus are opportunities offered to children for a variety of experiences through which they would learn to select and apply methods of thinking and acting useful to them in life situations. Again, many kinds of activities provide for individual differences in interests and abilities.

The following classification of activities represents a combination and modification of the plans proposed by Hopkins, Bobbitt, and

Rugg. They are set forth with some thought to the approximate order in which they will be likely to function in carrying out a unit of understanding.

1. *Orientation activities* to get new experiences; first-hand, contact experiences and activities are needed for orientation purposes.
   Observation is a mode of living. Continuous observation is one of man's normal reactions in the presence of environment. It is the nature of man to observe not only with his eyes; but to explore with his hands in lifting, feeling, examining; and to listen, to taste, to smell. Some of these forms of observation and exploration can take place inside the school plant, but most of them must be experienced individually outside the school. Homes, woods, farms, factories, the environment will be the laboratories. The technique of developing normal observational experiences outside the school is much undeveloped. The curriculum maker should augment it in amount and make it thoroughly effective. Whenever possible, the kindergarten and first three grades should begin a unit of understanding with an excursion.

2. *Research activities* demand that the pupil go to sources for information mastery. This preliminary mastery of information must often precede the understanding of the unit itself.

3. *Group discussion activities* with one's associates are important for prolonging, repeating, and intensifying one's experiences. Pupils will repeat them in imagination, retell them to others, and thus relive them. Pupils will give reports and listen to reports by associates, lecturers, parents, friends, members of committees, travelers, and others. There is vividness in this form of presentation. Therefore, for the earlier years of education there should probably be a considerable quantity of listening to oral reports of the experiences and observation of others.

4. *Practice or skill activities* should provide for progress in such tool subjects as contribute to the unit of understanding. As a skill activity problem solving individually and in class discussion will be made a major type of pupil experience. One is ever dealing with problems in life. Decisions have to be made, conclusions have to be reached. Pupils will be meeting problems at every turn of the road which require originating, planning, directing, evaluating.
   Generalization activities come without thought or effort where observations are frequent. One cannot help classifying and generalizing.

5. *Construction and original creative activities* provide opportunities for self-expression of experience.

INDIVIDUAL INTERESTS

Usually each child will have a particular individual interest in each big unit of understanding. The teacher should be ever watchful for these interests and should help to carry out his purpose, provided it has possibilities for growth and is sufficiently within the range of accomplishment of the learner to insure a satisfactory degree of success.

SIMULTANEOUS UNITS

A unit in social science and a more or less closely related unit in elementary science may be carried on simultaneously. For example, the children in Grade 1B may be working out the zoo or circus in the social sciences and wild animals in elementary science at one and the same time.

PROCEDURE

The procedure and activities indicated in this tentative course of study are suggestive rather than mandatory. It is highly desirable that teachers develop original methods of procedure, if the methods so developed stand the tests of good teaching and accomplish the outcomes desired. It is not intended that a teacher should work out all the units set up for her particular grade. She should select enough units to make up fifteen weeks of work. The remaining four weeks of each semester should be devoted to an experimental unit.

TIME ALLOTMENT

A flexible time allotment, commensurate with the available time for all units, has been suggested for each unit. In arriving at this minimum and maximum period the wide experience of teachers has been considered in the attempt to ascertain the benefits children will derive from the unit.

The following schedule shows the time allotted in minutes per week to social sciences in the respective grades.

TIME ALLOTMENT SCHEDULE

Subject	Grades			
	1B	1A	2	3
Social sciences	100	125	150	150
Thrift and banking (20 minutes weekly)				
Natural sciences	20	20	30	30
Art	80	80	90	90

In the first three grades art and the social sciences usually follow each other on the daily schedule since each contributes so much to the other and since they are so closely interwoven in development.[12]

The committee in charge of the organization of this course at Lakewood faced with the necessity of determining early the parts of the course that were to be organized in advance and those to be left to the interests of the pupils. The following statement indicates their position on this question:

COURSE OF STUDY PLANNED IN ADVANCE

A school is justified in planning in advance the general outline of a course of study in the social sciences as in other subjects. Thus, "sequential arrangement of material within each year and through successive years will be provided, resulting in a continuous acquisition of ideas and meanings and a constantly growing understanding and appreciation of human life and social relationships."

In no other way can great waste due to repetition be eliminated in a public school. This tentative course is presented *not* for the purpose of formalizing procedures or teaching a mass of facts, or advocating formal lessons; but it has been prepared to assist each teacher more adequately to provide situations through which children may learn some of the fundamental conceptions of life around about them, and extend their social understanding.

Many of the simple elements of geography and history are present in this social-science curriculum. This does not mean that the subjects of geography and history as such are formally taught during this period of the child's experience. Elements of arithmetic, spelling, reading, language, music, art, plays, and games, literature, appear to advantage in the development of each unit building up a background of enriched experience. While these units of understanding often call for experience and expression in other fields, such as music, art, et cetera, they cannot supply all the needed training and experience in these fields.

CRITICISM NOTES BY THE TEACHER

In order that curriculum building may be coöperative, in which every teacher has a part, this preliminary or tentative course is issued. Criticisms, additions, and eliminations are invited. As this

---

[12] *Tentative Course of Study in the Social Sciences for Kindergarten* (Board of Education, Lakewood, Ohio, 1931), pp. 4-8.

COURSES OF STUDY FOR KINDERGARTEN [13]

General Theme and Aspect to be Developed	Units of Understanding	Suggested Time in Weeks
	Kindergarten	
Theme: The increasing interdependence of one group upon another	1. Our home	3 to 5
	2. Our school	2 to 3
	3. How the grocer helps the family	2 to 3
	4. The market	3 to 4
	5. The baker	2 to 3
Aspect: How the community helps the family	6. The iceman	2 to 3
	7. The department store	3 to 4
	8. The florist and the greenhouse	3 to 4
	9. The policeman	2 to 3
	10. The fireman	3 to 5
	11. The postman	2 to 3
	12. The pet shop	3 to 4
	13. Maple sugar	2 to 3

	14. How we travel in our city
	   a. Street cars
	   b. Busses
	   c. Trucks
	   d. Horses—wagons
	   e. Automobiles
		6 to 8

	15. An experimental unit based upon the interests of each class may be worked out. In selecting these experimental units the teacher should not infringe upon or duplicate the work which has been set up for succeeding grades. However, if her class is interested in a unit which has been set up for a lower grade, the teacher may choose and develop that unit, provided the children have not already experienced it.	3 to 4

[13] *Ibid.*, p. 10.

course is tried out during the school year 1931-32, teachers are urged to coöperate in the following ways and thus contribute to the building of the course.

1. On the blank side of each page in this course teacher reactions should be made to every division of each unit. Thus, criticisms will be written just opposite to the part of the course to which they refer.
2. Many of these tentative units are "thin" or weak in many parts. Therefore, some most valuable contributions can be made in the following ways:
   a. Check time allotment
   b. Improve objectives
   c. Indicate better organization of the elements of the unit
   d. Check approaches used. Add others
   e. Check activities used and found to be profitable. Indicate those not so valuable. Add others
   f. Correct and add to the references. Indicate those references which are most valuable to the unit. Add more poems, songs, games, etc.
   g. Revise outcomes. Show those actually achieved
   h. All errors in tests should be recorded. Work out tests to measure other outcomes [14]

In the tentative course of study for the kindergarten, the following units of understanding were established for the guidance of the teacher in formulating the work in the classroom:

The first unit of understanding in this series is given in full for the guidance of those interested in this particular problem:

GENERAL THEME: The increasing interdependence of one group upon another

ASPECT OF THE THEME: How the community helps the family

OUR HOME

Time: 3 to 5 weeks

I. *Objectives*
   A. To learn about houses
   B. To build a house
   C. To work with tools
   D. To learn about the work of the family

II. *Major Problem:* How may a child be helped in the school to be a more worthy member of his home?

[14] *Ibid.,* p. 9.

ELEMENTS OF THIS UNIT

A. What should we know about our houses?
   1. Types of homes: apartments, courts, bungalows, duplex, singles, etc.
   2. Rooms in the home: dining-room, kitchen, living-room, bedroom, bathroom, nursery, basement
B. What materials are needed for a house and its furnishings?
   1. The various materials needed and their uses
   2. Proper selection of tools for different types of work
   3. Correct manipulation of tools
   4. Conservation of materials through planning before going to work
C. Who lives in the house and what do they do?
   1. Duties of each member of the family
   2. Ways in which members of a family help each other
   3. Activities in the home and care of the house
   4. Needs of a family
      a. Cleanliness, fresh air, sunshine, rest, play
      b. Proper food and clothing

III. *Procedure—Activities*
A. Suggested approaches
   1. Excursion to a house under construction
   2. Show pictures of houses, home life, babies, home activities, etc.
   3. Read a story about a house, stories of family life
   4. A trip to see a steam shovel operating
   5. How one unit started: One day Harry brought a pig made from a lemon. While looking at it, Jack said, "I know a story about a pig—Tom, Tom, the Piper's son..." etc. Lucille said, "I know one, too—This little pig..." etc. Junior: "There is a book in our library about *The Three Pigs*." He went to the library and brought the book. After hearing the story Mary said, "The brick house was the strongest." A conversation about houses followed, which ended in the suggestion that we build a larger and better house to play in in kindergarten.
   6. Children tell of home experiences such as work of various members of the family.
   7. Children play in playhouse.
B. Suggested activities
   1. Orienting activities to get new experiences
      a. Look at pictures on bulletin board, magazines, books

from library, to find different kinds of homes, house furnishings, different workmen to help build houses

b. Excursions

A walk to look at many kinds of houses under construction

Notice roofs, doors, chimneys; look for pretty gardens around homes

A trip to the grocery store for crates and cartons

A trip to a lumber-yard

A trip to a department store for furnishings for inside of the house, cambric, etc.

A trip to a building near by for sand and cement for use in our fireplace

A trip to a paper store for ideas for designs and curtain material

A trip to a plumber, ideas for sink, stove and iceless refrigerator

Investigate the inside of a house, looking at basement, kitchen, bedroom, bathroom, etc.

c. Reading of story by teacher: Maud Lindsay, "How the Home was Built" from *Mother Stories*

d. Harry told about his father's cottage under construction. Mary brought a shingle and told about her aunt's house being shingled.

e. A carpenter (a child's father) came over with his tools.

f. Sing songs listed under references.

g. Games: "Round the Mulberry Bush"; "I Went to Visit a Friend One Day"

h. Simple dramatization: cutting and sawing logs; hauling on train to lumber yard; playing family in the house, and the different helpers, as postman, grocer, etc., coming to serve them.

2. Research activities to get new experiences

a. Children bring in pictures of houses and various rooms in the house, also of work being done in and out of the home.

b. Children bring in brick, slate, shingles, stone, wood, cut from tree with bark on, plaster.

c. Collections of pictures and objects to clarify: family members, homes, furnishings, plumbing, mother's duties, father's duties, gardening, plastering, etc.

3. Group discussion activities to use experiences

a. Discuss how to build the house, materials for house

—crates, cartons, large sheets of cardboard and brown paper.

b. Discuss what is needed in a house
   (1) Wall-paper
   (2) Rugs
   (3) Furniture suitable to the rooms

c. Discuss plans for trips to get needed material
   (1) Measuring floor space
   (2) How many rooms
   (3) How separate the rooms (partition)
   (4) Plan for doors and windows
   (5) What house stands on (foundation)
   (6) Yard about house

d. Discuss possible sources of information for a problem to be solved in building the house:
   (1) Talk with mother, father, sister, brother
   (2) Talk with carpenter, plasterer, electrician, etc.
   (3) Visit homes looking for definite information, as kinds of roofs, kinds of windows, etc.

e. Discuss what the following workers do in the construction of a home: *carpenter, plasterer, electrician, paper-hanger, plumber, roofer, tinner*

f. Discuss beautifying the home surroundings

g. Discuss how to make rugs, furniture, dolls, how to paint the house, put in plumbing, make rooms, etc.

h. Discuss what part each child wishes to work on. Form committees to work on outside of house, certain rooms, dolls, etc.

i. After working period discuss individual work and how to improve it

j. Discuss family behavior in the house and care of the house, care of clothing

k. Discuss duties of the various members of the family, responsibility for the pleasure of others, needs of the family: food, clothing, play, rest, cleanliness, etc.

4. Practice activities to assimilate experiences
   a. Playhouse in the home built. Spontaneous play with the objects the children have made is a very important means of organizing information they have been gathering and of clarifying new meanings.
   b. Add new words to vocabulary through conversation, group-discussion, stories. In the development of this

unit the following words may be emphasized and clarified:

basement	electrician	slate	cement	roof
partition	sewing-table	lumber	shingle	carpenter
chimney	steam shovel	drapes	architect	log
plumber	frame	excavate	framework	plasterer
sawmill	brick	attic	foundation	plans

    c. Make jelly or soup. Pop corn
    d. Listen to original (Pupil) stories of family activities and fun.
    e. Dramatize "Little chick that did not want to go to bed" by Deihl (Samuel Gabriel and Sons, N. Y.)
    f. Rhythms: rocking baby, walking, running, skipping
5. Construction and original creative activities to express experiences
    a. Each child may draw a plan of the house to show how he wants his house to look. These pictures can be made into a class book.
    b. Measure and lay out house on the floor. Build the house large enough to keep house in. Paper the house.
    c. Make furniture large enough to use. Make furnishings for the house, such as curtains, rugs, awnings, flower-boxes, dolls, beds, bedclothes, etc.
    d. Children may plan patterns and make aprons to protect their clothing when they paint.
    e. Make stove, sink, piano, davenport, iceless refrigerator, of crates and boxes; rugs, curtains, drapes, bed-clothes, from cloth. Make dishes of clay.
    f. Make things for the mother of the home, such as dust cloths, vase of flowers, stove, pillow, doilies.
    g. Make things for the father of the house: ash-tray, shoe-shiner, inkstand, book-ends, paper-weight, calendar and blotters, etc.
    h. Make things for the baby of the house: net covering for the baby carriage, kitty, dolly, rattle, doll bed.
    i. Make father, mother, sister, brother, and baby dolls.
    j. Make books for house.
    k. Draw pictures of different types of houses.
    l. Large poster on blackboard of house, yard, using white and colored chalk
    m. Drawing and painting of houses, toys, members of family, home activities, ways families work and play

n. Designs (original) for wall-paper, rugs, walks in yards, bed cover, lamp shades

o. Clay—candle sticks

p. Picture books from drawings, showing home activities

q. Make a scrap-book of homes and furnishings

r. Make pictures for house

s. Tell original stories for the recreation of the school family

t. Make original games for the recreation of the school family

In all the above activities, aim to stimulate thought rather than fine workmanship [15]

The relationship of the course of study to an educational program based primarily on the activities of children is admirably stated in the introduction to the curriculum bulletin for the kindergarten of the Kansas City Public Schools. The purpose of the course is indicated in the following quotation:

The chief purpose of this Kindergarten Course of Study is to influence the activities of children so as to develop in them right habits and worthy attitudes. It recognizes the fact that the subject-matter of the kindergarten program is never static and that it must be supplied by both teacher and children from those activities, interests, and experiences which will help the child's life both to *be* and to *become* as rich and effective as possible. It does not intend therefore to lay down authoritatively precise lines of procedure, definite time limits, fixed content, and limited scope of equipment and material. Rather it purposes to suggest activities, methods and processes, desirable outcomes, and valuable sources of material and help, chiefly with the hope of guiding the teacher's planning and of inspiring initiative, alertness, progress, and above all, consideration of the child's welfare.[16]

A unit is selected from this course to illustrate the accomplishment of the committee in combining the activity principle with course-of-study construction. The work is developed from studies of children's tendencies and experiences. Outcomes

[15] *Ibid.,* pp. 15-20.

[16] *Kindergarten,* Curriculum Bulletin Number Nine (Kansas City Public Schools, Kansas City, Missouri, 1931), p. 19.

which can be derived from these experiences are suggested for the teacher, whose coöperation in the development of the unit is carefully organized.

USE OF CLAY

Child tendencies
  Physical
    Pounds
    Pats
    Handles
    Kneads
    Experiments: making balls, patties, snakes
  Mental and Emotional
    Seeks to express himself through new material
    Tries to make something useful to play with
    Desires to make something beautiful
  Social
    Seeks to make something useful or beautiful for group or teacher approval

Child experiences
  Pounding and kneading
  Patting and fingering
  Handling clay freely
  Experimenting aimlessly
  Making a crude form accidentally and giving it a name
  Planning to make simple forms: balls, snakes, pies, cakes
  Modeling objects to be used in play
    For the playhouse: dishes, dresser sets, vases, flower pots
    For the store: fruits, vegetables, meats, sign-standards
    For the bakery: pies, cakes, bread, cookies, candy
    For the farm: animals, troughs, pumps, fences
    For Halloween: pumpkins, cats
    For Thanksgiving: turkeys, fruits
    For Christmas: paper-weights, bill-files, pin-trays, candlesticks, match holders, vases
    For Easter: rabbits, chickens, eggs, nests
    Miscellaneous: beads, marbles
    Decorating and beautifying, with paint and clear shellac, the objects made

Educative outcomes to be derived from experiences with clay
  Pleasure in the activity of using clay

Gradual knowledge of the possibilities and uses of clay

Growing habit of trying many times in order to get a satisfactory result

Growing habit of protecting clothing, furniture, and floor

Growing knowledge that work is better if made from one piece of clay

Greater skill in molding clay to improve object

Growing knowledge that clay must be dry before it is painted

Increased ability to paint evenly and to choose appropriate colors for objects made

Growing ability to purpose and carry out ideas

Increased ability to take and use suggestions

Ability to understand and use such terms as *round, oval, oblong, square, height, width, length, size, shape, shallow, decorate, design, vases, statues*

Growing desire to tell about work so that others will enjoy listening

Growing respect for the rights of others

Suggestions to teachers

Keep clay always accessible and in good working condition

Appreciate the child's first efforts

Remember that the first interest in the use of clay lies in the activity, not in its uses as a means of expression. This manipulative stage is followed by the symbolic stage in which the child freely expresses his ideas in more or less crude form

Recognize the importance of the symbolic stage in the development of the artistic process, and do not impose technique before there is a need for it

Never destroy an object in the child's presence, as he may lose respect for his own creative efforts

Show the possibilities of the material and arouse the desire to experiment. When demonstrating, work quickly from the bulk, squeezing the mass into different forms. Then destroy, for the forms should not be used as models

Place emphasis on dominant characteristics rather than on technique, *e.g.*,

> Animals—head, ears, legs, arms
> Fruits and vegetables—shape, size
> Vases and flower pots—form, proportion

Take the child about the building and into classrooms where work with clay is being carried on

Plan excursions to see works of art

Help the child appreciate beauty of form in his surroundings

Provide suitable material with which to work; *e.g.,*
   Clay in unshaped pieces
   Oilcloth or newspaper to protect tables
   Aprons [17]

Many opportunities arise for the development of an educational program out of the interests of the pupils. The alert teacher makes immediate use of other interests in the organization of the content of the course. In the first year that the interests of children are used as the basis of classroom work, education can be identified, in part, with the natural activities of the pupils; but in succeeding years these successful experiments are carefully organized for the guidance of teachers who may wish to make capital out of the same or similar interests in the work of a particular level or grade. The work that was organized in the course in nature study and elementary science in Kansas City illustrates the development of the unit from the interests of the children to the outcome which may serve as objectives for teachers in the field. The course is summarized as follows:

I. Objectives obtained through an activity program. Topics are set up for each grade and taught in the appropriate season. In each grade, the subject-matter of the course is selected with a view to child interests and abilities and with a thread of continuity running throughout the school life. In the lower grades, more attention is given to animate nature. As the upper grades are reached an increasing amount of time is given to inanimate phases of science, including simple chemical experiments and mechanical operations, and to more advanced study of animate nature as involved in projects dealing with the yard and garden, and simple landscape work.

A questionnaire showed that the children had preference for flowers, stars, birds, and wild animals (mammals) as topics of study. More interest was manifested in wild than in domestic animals and in the woods than in gardens. Most children preferred going to the woods to going to the movies.

II. Illustrative material. Some items of nature study and elementary science can be presented successfully by means of models, pictures, diagrams, and experiments. Every school should strive to have a good picture collection as a part of its library equipment.

[17] *Ibid.,* pp. 36-37.

It should have also, if possible, a nature or science room equipped with apparatus and such illustrative material as can be used from year to year.

A. *Specimens and apparatus.* Somewhere in each building there should be cases and space for keeping specimens of various kinds and equipment for science teaching. Preferably each school should have a science room with abundant space for the display or storage of such material.

The specimens may include such collections as:

Old birds' nests, including cavities, houses, etc.
Rocks and minerals
Butterflies and other insects in Riker specimen mounts
Samples of hand-work illustrative of nature topics and correlated
    with science, such as leaf-prints and plaster-casts
Collection of fungi, galls, etc.
Collection of seeds, fruits, nuts, etc.
Museum specimens of reptiles, lizards, frogs, etc.
Wood samples

A minimum supply of apparatus should include the following:

Iron stand or support
Clamp, test-tube style
Clamp, ring style
Flasks, at least two, (500 cc.)
Funnel (10 mm.)
Lamp globes (3)
Test-tubes (half dozen) 6 in.
Glass tubing, ⅛ in., ¼ in. (about 18 in. of each)
Test-tube brushes (3)
Rubber tubing ³⁄₁₆ in. (about 2 ft.)
Corks, 1 doz. (assorted)
Rubber stoppers, one and two holes (test-tube size)
Wide mouthed bottles (4)
Bunsen burner (1)
Magnets: horseshoe (1), bar (2)
Magnetic needle
Magnetic compass
Iron filings
Battery jar
Insulated wire
Strips of copper and zinc
Door bell
Insulated wire
Beakers (2), 500 cc.
Alum
Ammonium hydroxide
Alcohol

Hydrochloric acid
Manganese dioxide
Potassium chlorate
Copper sulfate (4 oz.)
Sulphur (1 oz.)
Litmus paper (1 oz.)
Filter paper (1 pkg.)
Marble chips (broken oyster shells will do)
Phenolphthalein
Sulphuric acid
Frame for blue printing (may be made by pupils)

NOTE: The total cost of these items is about five dollars.

B. *Living things:*

1. Living things may be studied in their environment.

   a. In the school-yard and immediate neighborhood. An inventory of the trees, shrubs, vines, birds, flowers, and interesting insects to be found within a block of the school premises will yield surprising results. In this connection the school garden affords great opportunities.

   b. In convenient parks or vacant territory overgrown with trees and shrubs. Pupils may take field to the woods and parks. Usually it is best to take only a part of the class at a time. Groups may be made up of volunteers, or the class may be divided into groups which go according to regular turn or schedule.

   c. At feeding stations and bird bath.

   d. In the school garden.

2. Living things may be studied in the classroom. To facilitate this type of observational work each classroom in the school should have an aquarium, a terrarium, or cage in which insects and small animals may be kept for a time, and one or more window boxes.

   a. The aquarium. An aquarium with straight sides is better than one in the form of a globe. If possible have several smaller aquaria so that a greater assortment of life may be kept. Even common clear-glass fruit jars will do.

   b. The terrarium, or live specimen cage. Children are continually finding various small animals, insects, etc. and bringing them to school. These may be kept for a few days in the terrarium where they may be observed and perhaps gently handled.

   Every effort should be made to impress upon children the kind of care and attention that should be given these creatures. Keep the cage clean. Provide water and suitable food. Do not needlessly frighten the animals. Approach the cage gently, put your hand in slowly. Do not pound or shake the cage. Leave the creature undisturbed as much as possible. Pets, small wild animals, and insects are suitable for the terrarium.

 c. The window box.

C. Pictures. Through coöperation of the teachers, a splendid picture collection can quickly and cheaply be assembled and filed in the school library or in the supply room for use in the school.

Pictures should be mounted on good, durable cardboard cut to uniform size. Nine by eleven inches is suggested as convenient. They should be indexed and filed by subjects; as birds, flowers, trees, insects, animals.

 D. *Lantern slides and motion pictures.* Most schools are now equipped with one or more lantern-slide machines. These should be used frequently as a part of the regular class exercises, but not as a "picture show."

 E. *Field trips.* Field trips furnish a valuable means of enlarging children's experiences about matters pertaining to the life in their immediate neighborhood. They are fraught with difficulty and responsibility, however, and should be carefully planned and conducted in order that the results may be both safe and worth while. It is very essential that the teacher be familiar with the possibilities of the school surroundings and always know beforehand the ground to be covered. The pupils should have a part in deciding upon the trip, in planning for it, and in conducting it.

The following specific suggestions are offered:

 1. Preparation

  a. Be sure there is a definite reason for taking the trip, both for the teacher and for the pupils

  b. Build on the children's previous experiences

  c. With the help of the children

   (1) List the things to be looked for

   (2) List the things to be collected

   (3) Decide what to take

   (4) Decide how to get to the place

  d. Discuss standards of conduct; *e.g.,*

   (1) Be courteous and helpful

   (2) Respect the rights and property of others

   (3) Observe traffic and park rules and regulations

   (4) Refrain from disorderly conduct or boisterous talking and laughing

   (5) Keep within hearing distance of the teacher

   (6) Respond promptly to the teacher's signal

  e. Discuss good habits of observation; *e.g.,*

   (1) Keep ever in mind the purpose of the trip or the problem to be solved

(2) Adopt some motto, as "Learn to Look, to Listen, and to Wonder"

(3) Be accurate

(4) Notice relationships

(5) Take brief notes and make sketches (older children)

2. The trip

a. As far as practicable, make observations and collections as planned

b. See that all children have opportunity to make observations

c. Be constantly on the look-out for surprises; that is, for items not on the list of expected observations. It frequently happens that intended observations cannot be made and that others may be found to take their place. This is especially true with regard to bird study.

3. The next class meeting

a. Check the results of the trip

b. Engage in discussion of the more important items of the trip

c. Verify the accuracy of impressions and correct wrong impressions

d. Continue the study of certain more important or interesting phases of the study through drawing, construction, modeling, English expression, or extended activity

4. General hints

a. Cut flowers with stems long enough to look well in bouquets. Gather green foliage to go with the colors. Keep the flowers fresh by wrapping them well in damp paper or by putting them into a box with damp paper or bits of ice. When they are placed in a vase, have the stems immersed in water.

b. In all of the studies try to inculcate ideas of conservation and of kindness to all living creatures. Try to show that kind, humane treatment of wild animals pays: first, because animals as well as people suffer mental and physical pain; second, because with kind, careful treatment they become less fearful of man and thus give a better opportunity to learn of their interesting habits and behavior.

F. *Additional suggested procedures.* Encourage children to ask questions. Keep a list of those that are asked spontaneously from time to time. Some of these questions cannot be answered, even by scientists; many of them, however, can be utilized as approaches to worthwhile activities and as means of maintaining interest. An unfamiliar plant or animal placed in the room without comment will evoke enough questions to start and guide a most valuable study.

Utilize as the subject of the morning conversation or as the basis of the language lesson a specimen chosen from materials that the children delight in bringing to school. The following make interesting subjects: praying mantis, a spray of leaves, a thistle flower, bird's nest, mole, cicada, wasp's nest, tree cricket or katydid, turtle, cocoon, oak leaf. Provide the same kind of specimen for each member of the class. Direct observation by means of questions. Specimens of the following are easily available: bag-worm, May beetle, hickory leaf, elm twig in winter, dandelion, piece of granite, limestone and sandstone, crayfish, sunflower, block of wood.

Tell a story about some object not available for direct observation and follow with questions. Use pictures also. Interesting stories may be told about the opossum, the dragon-fly, snakes, fishing for crawdads, squirrels, rabbits.

Choose problems or definite questions for outdoor observation. A few suggested subjects are: autumn colors, English sparrows, evening insect concert, the grasshopper, the moon and stars, colors in a weed-patch, heat, air.

Decide with the pupils on some special problem for study. Spend several days or weeks on the problem. Report observations and discuss phases of the problem from day to day. Suggested problems are the following:

What birds are spending the winter in Kansas City?

How may we know the oaks of Kansas City?

How do animals spend the winter?

How can you tell a cricket from a katydid?

What weed seeds may be found in November?

Organize a Nature Club with committees or groups, each group responsible for a particular line of activity; as, Committee on trees, committee on birds, committee on electricity, committee on insects.

Elaborate on the various nature references in reading, geography, and history.

METHODS

Engage in extended class activities involving several or all subjects of the curriculum; *e.g.,*

Making a census of the trees of Kansas City

Making a Swope Park Zoo or a small city park

Making a May Day list of birds

Making and caring for an aquarium

Making an animal or tree booklet

Making a dream home

Giving a Thanksgiving dinner to the wild folks of the woods

Giving a flower show or a harvest picnic

Making a flower store or seed store
Making case of mounted insects
Collecting autumn leaves and making prints and casts
Writing and illustrating the life history of a bean plant.

Provide opportunities for the development of individual interests through suggesting activities of various types. Encourage each pupil to keep a record of his own nature activities, studies, observations, etc. Following are a great many activities from which a list could be made of various types of appeal.

Miscellaneous activities:

Keeping a well-organized, topically arranged "Naturalist's Scrap Book"

Making a collection of mounted pictures or diagrams on some important naturalistic topic

Drawing or painting good pictures of animals, birds, etc.

Making a map of two square blocks in the city and placing and identifying the trees on it

Preparing a balanced aquarium at home

Caring for classroom aquarium and plants

Making and identifying a collection of rocks and minerals

Making a serving tray of milkweed or cotton with moths, butterflies, flowers, etc.

Knowing the fish and game laws and game preserves in Missouri

Assuming leadership of some club or organization engaged in nature work

Reading a book of natural history—John Burroughs, Mabie, Thoreau, or others

Keeping a well-arranged, up-to-date nature calendar for one month

Knowing the names of ten great scientists, especially biologists and naturalists; knowing for what reasons they are famous

Preparing a paper of five hundred words or more upon any of these topics:

> Conservation of our native trees in Kansas City
> Our bird neighbors
> Reptiles and amphibians of Jackson County
> Our battle with bugs (related to agriculture)
> Our vacant lot

Keeping a daily weather chart for one month
Tree activities:

Giving evidence of recognition beyond question of certain trees in summer and winter

Collecting, pressing or printing, mounting, and identifying tree leaves, fruit, and woods

Making a scrap book collection of articles, diagrams, pictures, etc., about trees worthy of class attention

Knowing common tree pests and how they may be eradicated; as bag worm, web worm, etc.

Insect activities:

Making a carefully arranged and named insect collection

Showing life history of garden pests and how to eradicate them (May be arranged as poster display case, plaster paris, etc.)

Plant and flower activities:

Identifying weeds by pressing, by drawing, by blue prints, etc.

Collecting winter bouquet or table basket. Plants used must be identified.

Identifying ferns

Identifying grasses

Identifying wild flowers

Identifying mushrooms

Making for display a poster on conservation of wild flowers.

Bird activities:

Identifying birds

Making and erecting a bird box

Keeping a winter lunch counter for birds

Having a bird bath used by at least four kinds of birds

Keeping a chart of birds' migration; *i.e.*, list and dates of all kinds of birds seen in one season's migration.

Recording from personal observation the food and feeding of at least five birds

Making a Christmas census of not fewer than ten species

Photographing birds

Recognizing songs and calls of different birds

Making and displaying a poster for protection of birds

Animal activities:

Knowing description, habits, habitation, and food of native wild animals

Making for display a poster for conservation of wild animals

Making a wild-animal scrap-book—pictures, clippings, poems, etc.

Reptiles and amphibians:

Identifying reptiles

Identifying and learning habits of amphibia

Garden activities:

Growing a tomato from seed to fruit

Growing a geranium from cutting to flowering

Making and caring for a porch box throughout the season

Planting and successfully caring for a garden not less than fifteen by twenty-five feet, with not fewer than five kinds of plants.

A unit of work which illustrates the incorporation of the activity principle into the preconceived organization of content can be selected from the Fine and Practical Arts Course of Study for Kindergarten and Grades 1, 2, and 3 of the Long Beach, California, Public Schools. In this case the course has been developed completely for the grades and the interests of the pupils have been used only in the development of the course of study before the meeting of the class. Naturally, the interests of pupils have been studied as a basis for the preparation of the course, but only a limited amount of leeway is given the teacher.

WOOD

OBJECTIVE: To carry the child through the manipulative stage in working with wood, to the place where he puts meanings into the things he makes. To develop some feeling in the child for beauty in the objects he makes.

Activities

Beauty in any project involving the use of hammer, saw, nails, paint, etc., as in constructing and furnishing a store, a greenhouse, etc. Projects suggested under Social Studies.

Method

No course of study can state the needs that may arise.

When project has been decided upon by the group and the procedure followed as outlined in the Social Studies Course of Study, it will be found that the materials used will be largely discarded materials brought from home, contributed by the lumber-yard, stores, etc. Such as is necessary is furnished by the Board of Education.

Teach pupils to hold hammer firmly with the hand near the end of the handle, when hammering, and to look at the nail when striking.

Teach pupils to hold saw in hand with pressure on down stroke, taking long strokes.

Teach pupils to hold a yardstick when drawing a line on wood.

It is impossible to give a complete method of approach here as even the furniture should be the result of the child's plan.

Tables, chairs, and beds are easily made from boxes; walls may be made from heavy papers which come by the roll. Spools may be glued to boards for legs of stools.

Discarded materials of all types are used to construct toys—oatmeal boxes, spools from film, tin cans, etc.

Lead pupils to select pleasing colors for project use. They may use colors that blend (related) for all schemes.

Attainments

Ability to work with others in a joint project, sharing tools and materials.

Knowledge of tools used, where they are kept, and habit of returning them after using.

Habit of protecting clothes while working with wood, paint, etc.

Some ability to judge when a tool is working right.

Some feeling that they want beautiful objects—beauty of proportion and color.

Ability to saw easily, without twisting or leaning on saw.

Ability to choose a small nail for thin wood and a large nail for thick wood.

References

MATHIAS, *The Beginnings of Art in the Public School,* pp. 29-35.[18]

In the course of study in science for the kindergarten and the first six grades of the Oakland schools are excellent illustrations of the development of various types of activity units. A brief summary of this course is presented for the purpose of illustrating additional features of this difficult type of course of study construction.[19]

I. **Unit Organization**

Five types of units are suggested for organizing and presenting science material:

    A. Activity units
    B. Problem units
    C. Excursion units
    D. Casual units
    E. Subject-content units

[18] *Fine and Practical Arts for Kindergarten and Grades One, Two, and Three* (Long Beach City Schools, Long Beach, California, 1930), p. 16.

[19] *Science for Kindergarten and Grades One to Six* (Oakland Public Schools, Oakland, Calif., 1932).

The following are illustrations of each type:

A. *Activity unit:* A Garden
  1. Experiences:
     a. Gather seeds. Germinate in room
     b. Take walks to observe gardens
     c. Collect pictures
  2. Class discussion:
     a. Tell about gardens pupils have seen
     b. Plan the garden
  3. Handwork and construction:
     a. Make posters and gardens
     b. Make baskets for flowers
     c. Draw pictures of flowers
     d. Make sticks to measure distance in setting out plants
  4. Poems (references given)
  5. Stories (references given)
  6. Songs (sources given)
  7. Rhythms:
     Make up dances to victrola records, etc.
  8. Dramatization:
     a. Flowers in a garden. Impersonate bees, butterflies, wind, rain, etc.
     b. Buying and selling flowers in store
  9. Health
     (Suggestions for correlation with health education)
  10. Games

B. *Problem unit:* "The dog—man's oldest and most faithful friend"
  1. Problem:
     What natural equipment has he to fit him to be useful and companionable to man?
  2. Suggested approach:
     a. Pupils tell why they like their own dogs
     b. Create an interest by stories
     c. Show pictures
     d. Bring a dog to the room to illustrate points covered
  3. Suggested content:
     a. Natural equipment of the dog, fitting him to be a friend of man
     b. Use man has made of his equipment
     c. Character study of dogs
  4. Suggested activities:
     a. Draw and exhibit dog pictures

     b. Discuss personality of dogs

     c. Classify dogs on the basis of adaptability to climate, etc.

   5. References

C. *Excursion unit:* "A visit to Lake Merritt to discover why it was set aside as a game preserve"

   1. Organization:

     Divide the class into small groups so that the teacher can pass from group to group giving informal suggestions to keep the observation active and continuous. State questions in a challenging form so that each member of the group will enjoy finding answers or making estimates and comparisons as they walk along.

   2. Questions:

     List the things to be found out

   3. Observation at feeding ground:

     a. Locate the groups at vantage points to observe the activities and mannerisms of the birds

   4. Study of individual birds (Questions, etc., for each kind of bird are given in detail)

   5. General observations:

     a. List the several species of ducks, etc.

   6. Kinds of birds on Lake Merritt

   7. Classroom activities for follow-up after the excursion:

     a. Make maps showing where the ducks breed and where they winter

     b. Trace migration routes on maps

     c. Make a bird bath and feeding tray

     d. Collect pictures

     e. Drawing and painting birds

     f. Make a sand-table representation of the lake

   8. References

D. *Casual unit:* "A garden spider brought to school"

   Time: One science period

   1. Subject: A large garden spider brought to school in a glass jar by a pupil

   2. Aims of lesson:

     a. To give classroom recognition to a nature subject of sufficient interest to an individual child to cause him to bring it to school for the class to study and see

   3. Class procedure:

   Discussion of different phases of the subject: the usefulness of spiders, their conservation, poisonous species, etc. Study of the spinning of the web

E. *Subject-content unit:* "Seed making, the purpose of the flower"

Aim: To build up an understanding of the reasons for the existence of flowers—seed production

1. Approach: through appreciation, legends, and stories of flowers
2. Core thoughts:
    a. The use of the flower to the plant is to make a good seed
    b. Each part of the flower has a part to play
3. Insect visitors
4. Partnership of flowers and insects
5. Activities and lesson helps:
    Outlined in parallel columns
        Include discussions, reports, trips, collections, chart making, etc.

III. AN EVALUATION OF THE ACTIVITY PROGRAM IN THE ORGANIZATION OF LEARNING EXPERIENCES

The basic principle that life is activity is sound. Life in general and also any particular life are dynamic, ever adjusting to new situations and consequently ever-changing in terms of past experiences and present environment. The school must recognize that education is for the purpose of providing rich experiences in order that children may participate in activities that are meaningful for them and that make for a perfect adjustment in society to-day and in the future.

The problem facing every administrator and teacher is the determination of the extent to which the present interests of the child shall be allowed to weigh in the determination of learning activities and how these interests shall be tabulated, evaluated, and selected for use in the classroom. Even in the activity school of the extreme type, such tabulation, evaluation, and selection are fundamental in the organization of the work. Otherwise, a unified program would be an impossibility. Related to this problem is the determination of the amount of emphasis which shall be allocated to adjustment in present and future societal relations.

The Committee on Reports and Records of the Progressive

Education Association's Eight-Year Experimental Study states as its procedure in developing a plan for evaluating the movement:

> The first step, which will serve to direct effort, is for each school to formulate in a clear and understandable fashion the purposes or objectives which it is trying to realize. This proceeds on the assumption that education is a means of bringing about changes in young people and that these purposes or objectives represent a statement of the kinds of changes in its pupils which the school hopes it may help to bring about. These objectives will indicate the variety of aspects of pupil development which needs to be considered in a satisfactory program of evaluation. This statement of purposes will probably include statements of certain understandings to be developed, certain attitudes to be acquired, certain skills and habits to be realized. Together, they should represent major changes in young people toward which the effort of the school is directed.[20]

No brief can be made for the school system which proposes to organize learning materials and activities completely in advance and which employs dictator-teachers to "teach" such courses of study. Neither can the disconnected, unrelated educational experiences which result from improvising activities for apparent student interests be condoned. True education is a continuous movement or growth, not a jerky, spasmodic effort which follows both longitudinal and latitudinal lines according to ephemeral interests which are catered to from day to day. The teacher is employed neither to dictate a program to the pupils nor to be led on will-of-the-wisp trails toward educational mirages by immature interests and imaginations. The real teacher is a guide, counselor, and friend; she is a mainstay to which pupils may go for advice; she stimulates and motivates self-initiated and self-directed efforts toward goals which are valid and by paths which have proved effective in the past. The teacher must have sufficient freedom to select units of work, organize approaches to these units, and utilize intrinsic interests of pupils.

[20] R. W. Tyler, "Evaluation: a Challenge to Progressive Education," *Educational Research Bulletin,* Vol. XIV (Jan. 16, 1935), p. 13.

Education is *being,* and the interests of the pupils are paramount in the determining of the activities; education is also for the purpose of *becoming,* and society has the prerogative of determining the extent to which child interests can and should be modified in order to insure desirable habits, attitudes, and ideals. The life of the future citizen should *be* and *become* as rich, wholesome, and effective as possible. The school must determine and validate as accurately as possible the objectives and organize a general outline of the activities to be engaged in by pupils. The sequential and continuous development of the program gives the pupil the opportunity to acquire, gradually and definitely, essential data and understandings essential in appreciating life and living in a democracy.

The Committee on Reports and Records of the Progressive Education Association's Eight-Year Experimental Study suggests the following types of studies as being significant in evaluating the achievement of the pupils in realizing the objectives:

Undoubtedly, there will be certain kinds of evidence needed by several schools. A dozen schools perhaps might be concerned with ways of determining the degree to which their pupils were developing the habit of assuming responsibility in the social group. Many schools may be concerned with the development of a scientific attitude; that is, a tendency to look for evidence with reference to an important problem rather than jumping to an immediate conclusion. At these points where there are common needs for practicable methods of obtaining evidence of pupil progress, we can organize a coöperative attack upon the common problems. A committee of interested teachers, for example, may be working upon methods for determining the development of the habit of social responsibility; another committee may be concerned with means for discovering growth in social attitudes; a third committee, with methods for determining pupils' interests. Each committee will be attacking an important problem in the development of instruments for evaluating progressive education.[21]

The course of study in the modern school is for the purpose of suggesting objectives, activities, teaching procedures, and helps for both teacher and pupils. Administrators who appre-

[21] *Ibid.,* p. 14.

ciate the contributions of the activity schools are working toward this goal. The old course of study, which contained formal lessons, definite teaching procedures, and exact content and which defined outcomes in terms of a single standard of values, has no place at any level of American education. The "progressive" education movement, which accepts objectives, content, and other phases of course of study construction, but refuses to recognize formalism and tradition, has given to educators a concept that has revolutionized course of study organization and made it possible for the course of study to attain a dignity which it has long sought.

The activity movement can justly claim to have stimulated interest in the development of intelligent self-direction on the part of the pupil. There is nothing new about this concept of education, but teachers in general are more interested and have a clearer understanding of the meaning of the term. However, this widespread interest is also due, in part, to the recent developments in psychology. These have supported the idea that the child is a dynamic and purposing being rather than merely a receiving and responding organism. The growth of the individual in an intellectual sense is determined by the creative potentialities of the nervous system. If the essence of learning is discovery of something new by the individual, then education must become less and less a mass program and be based on the creativeness of the learner.

The statement of the Committee on Reports and Records of the Progressive Education Association's Eight-Year Experimental Study concerning the validation of the objectives in education is so comprehensive and significant to teachers in every type of school that the following quotation is included.

The first problem is to get some evidence with reference to these so-called "intangible" objectives. A later problem is to refine this evidence and make it more exact. There is no use to attack the second problem first. We cannot develop refined measures until we have first devised ways of collecting some objective evidence, even though they are crude. One reason for believing that a coöperative attack is likely to be fruitful is that a clarification of educational purposes, stated in terms of changes which we hope will take place in boys and girls, directs the attention of the teacher and parent in a way that makes intangible changes more and more tangible. That is, clarifying our own purposes makes it more easily possible to recognize the desired changes in young people when they are evidenced. Another reason for hope that practicable methods may be developed is due to the possibility of sampling. By a careful study of boys and girls and a record of their behavior in a variety of situations, it is often possible to discover a few indicative situations in which one may get a clear picture of the development of that boy or girl without having to study him in all the possible situations of life. Binet, for example, in devising a test of the general mental development of young children, found certain situations which he used that were especially indicative of the mental reactions of children in a wide variety of life situations. As a part of the coöperative attempt to develop needed instruments, we shall make some careful studies in an effort to locate indicative situations which would enable us to judge the changes taking place in boys and girls without having to follow them around with camera, dictaphone, or notebook all day long.[22]

It is evident that this eight-year program is being engineered by those leaders of the progressive movement who have their feet on the ground and are actuated by professional interests and willing to abide by results attained by scientific methods. The statement by Tyler concerning the immediate goals of the study is very significant:

Through the clarification of objectives, through the careful study of boys and girls in terms of these objectives, through the search for indicative behavior, through the trial of indexes, through wider community coöperation, I think it is very possible to develop instruments appropriate for at least four or five major purposes, for which we do not now have practical means of measurement. Each succeeding year might well result in similar expansion of our facilities for evaluation. This development of new instruments is possible and of tremendous significance. It is not a technical problem alone. The continuing improvement of progressive education depends upon the development of means for evaluating each promising effort of progressive schools in terms of its major, important purposes.[23]

[22] Ibid., p. 15.
[23] Ibid., p. 16.

IV. CRITERIA FOR ORGANIZING UNITS OF WORK IN WHICH
THE PUPIL IN THE CLASSROOM PARTICIPATES IN DEVELOPING
IMPORTANT PHASES "ON THE SPOT" TO MEET HIS INTERESTS
AND CORRELATE WITH HIS ACTIVITIES

As these units will be worked out by pupils and the teacher
in classroom situations, it is important that standards be established for the guidance of the teacher in motivating the work.
It has been pointed out that in most instances little is left to
the imagination of the teacher and pupils, but in so far as that
is true, they will need criteria by which the daily activities may
be worked into or made to correlate with the prepared and
prearranged outline of the course of study. Some of the important criteria are suggested here, and it is probable that this
list may be helpful to the teacher in determining which activities
shall be stressed among those observable in the classroom.

Criterion 1. The course of study will outline completely units
which have been selected from real life situation and which will
probably meet the interests and needs of the class. There must
be two types of flexibility in each unit. First, group and individual interests must be envisaged by the teacher. Group interests will be met in the main by the course of study, but the
individual interests will demand adjustments which can be
made only at the time the work is undertaken. Second, the
course of study must be so arranged and the instructions to the
teacher so clear and definite that there can be no mistake concerning the development of an attitude in the child when he
has had a part in the organization of the unit and his own
personal interests have dominated the organization of the work
in the class.

Criterion 2. The unit, project, or problem, which has been
developed in advance and which will be further organized by
the teacher and pupils in the classroom, must offer as many
activities and endeavors as possible in order that the pupils can
have a wide range of experiences in completing the work. They
should learn to select, classify, organize, compare, note like-
nesses, and gradually become aware of the essentials of scien-

tific thinking, which will then function in normal living and can be carried over into normal later life.

Criterion 3. The completed work of the classroom must lead definitely and directly to other units which are to be completed in successive months or years. This does not mean that the subject-matter of two successive units need be similar, but rather that the expanding interests of the pupils in one unit will offer greater possibilities in more advanced units for realization. In other words, the outcomes of one unit should stimulate an interest on the part of the pupil in the objectives of the next or succeeding ones.

Criterion 4. Each project, unit, or problem must be related to society as well as to the interests of the child. Otherwise, little that is worth while of the cultural, historical, or economic backgrounds of the human race will be made available to the pupils. This material can be introduced only as an orderly, consistent part of the work if it is planned in advance and constitutes the major part of the course of study which the teacher takes into the classroom with her. If all of this material which is so vitally important is to be improvised by the teacher to fit into the interest-determined program as it develops, the work of the grade will be disorganized at times and incoherent. The work should integrate the interest-determined type with that determined by the social life of the race. There is not so much danger that this important social material will be left out of the program in the "activity" school as there is that it will be repeated so often from grade to grade that it will be no longer stimulating and educative.

Criterion 5. The work should provide a considerable amount of free activity and informal association on the part of pupils. This means that the pupils should have the opportunity to direct, to follow the directions of other pupils, and to plan and originate many of the forms of activity and social relationships growing out of the program.

Criterion 6. No unit should be considered unless it provides for rich and varied experiences in the lives of pupils. If the work conforms with this criterion, it will stimulate activity in the so-called tool and information subjects and skills sufficient for the grade level of experiences which the pupil is enjoying.

Criterion 7. The unit of work must take into account the out-of-school life of pupils as well as the in-school life. Often, better learning situations are developed through a study of their experiences outside the school rather than in the class-room or on the play field. Many highly desirable social and work habits will be suggested in such a study and incorporated into the class program. Any modification of the out-of-school life will indicate the efficiency and worthwhileness of the unit of work.

BIBLIOGRAPHY

BONSER, F. G., *Life Needs and Education* (Bureau of Publications, Teachers College, Columbia University, 1932).

BURKE, A., and OTHERS, *A Conduct Curriculum for the Kindergarten and First Grade* (Charles Scribner's Sons, 1923). An outline of the work as developed in the Horace Mann School of Teachers College.

California Curriculum Commission—A Teachers' Guide to Child Development (U. S. Office of Education, Bulletin 1930, No. 26).

CAREY, A. E., HANNA, P. R., and MERIAM, J. L., *Catalogue of Units of Work, Activities, Projects, etc.* (Bureau of Publications, Teachers College, Columbia University, 1932). This is valuable since it gives titles, and indicates where and how to secure these materials.

CLOUSER, L. W., ROBINSON, W. J., NEELY, D. L., *Educative Experiences Through Activity Units* (Lyons and Carnahan, 1932).

CLOUSER, L. W., and MILLIKAN, C. E., *Kindergarten-Primary Activities Based on Community Life* (The Macmillan Company, 1929).

COLLINGS, E., "Social Foundations of Project Teaching," *The Journal of Educational Sociology,* Vol. V (Sept., 1931), pp. 35-42. Five different types of projects are described.

———, *Project Teaching in the Elementary Schools* (The Century Company, 1928). A good source of suggestions.

———, *An Experiment with a Project Curriculum* (The Macmillan Company, 1923). An interesting and stimulating discussion of a con-trolled experiment to compare the project organization of materials with the regular classroom program.

———, "Learning the Fundamentals in the Activity Curriculum," *Journal of Experimental Education,* Vol. I (June, 1933), pp. 309-315. An interesting comparison of the grades made by pupils in the tra-ditional school with those in the activity environment.

Curriculum Bulletin Number One—A Suggestive Course of Study for the First Grade (Board of Education, Public Schools, Dayton, Ohio, 1931). This is compiled as the result of three years of experimentation.

Curriculum Bulletin Number Two contains the material developed in the same way for the Second Grade at Dayton, Ohio.

Curriculum Records of the Children's School, Members of the Staff of the National College of Education, Evanston, Illinois (Bureau of Publications, National College of Education, 1932).

HOPKINS, L. T., "Learning Essentials in an Activity Curriculum," *Journal of Experimental Education,* Vol. I (June, 1933), pp. 298-303. The Stanford Achievement Tests are used to check the progress of the pupils in the Lincoln School.

KEELER, Katherine, and SWEET, Mayme, *Indian Life and the Dutch-Colonial Settlement* (Bureau of Publication, Teachers College, Columbia University, 1931). These two units are developed for the third grade.

Kindergarten Activities in the Pittsburgh Public Schools. Published in Pittsburgh Schools, Vol. VIII (January-February, 1934), pp. 112-164.

Lincoln Elementary School Staff, *Curriculum Making in an Elementary School* (Ginn and Company, 1927). An excellent treatment of developing criteria and selecting units of work in an experimental school.

MERIAM, J. L., *Child Life and the Curriculum* (The World Book Company, 1921). Learning experiences based upon the present activities and interests of the children. The work was carried on at the University Elementary School at the University of Missouri.

MINOR, Ruby, *Pupil Activities in the Elementary Grades* (J. B. Lippincott Company, 1929). Presents a series of natural learning activities for the first six grades of the elementary school.

MOSSMAN, L. C., "The Activity Movement," *The Thirty-Third Yearbook* of the National Society for the Study of Education (Public School Publishing Company, 1934). Part II.

PORTER, Martha P., *The Teacher in the New School* (The World Book Company, 1930). A teacher's account and evaluation of teacher-pupil activity in the classroom.

RUGG, Harold, and SHUMAKER, Ann, *The Child-Centered School* (The World Book Company, 1928). An excellent critical analysis of the activity movement.

SALISBURY, E. I., *An Activity Curriculum* (Harr Wagner, 1924). A curriculum developed from the activities of the pupils in the Elementary School of the University of California at Los Angeles.

SMITH, L. W., "A Quantitative Study of an Activity Program," *Elementary School Journal,* Vol. XXXIII (May, 1933), pp. 669-677. A questionnaire study is used in attempting to evaluate the activity program.

STEVENS, Marion P., *The Activities Curriculum in the Primary Grades* (D. C. Heath and Co., 1931).

TIPPETT, J. S., and OTHERS, *Curriculum Making in an Elementary School* (Ginn and Company, 1927). A discussion of the work in Lincoln School after ten years of experimentation.

WADDELL, C. W., SEEDS, C. A., and WHITE, N., *Major Units in the*

Social Studies (The John Day Co., 1932). Every teacher who is interested in activity curricula should have a copy of this book. It is based on the program of the Training School at the University of California at Los Angeles.

WELLS, M. E., *A Project Curriculum* (J. B. Lippincott and Company, 1921). An outline of the activities used by the author in the Training School of the State Normal School at Trenton, N. J.

CHAPTER XII

PROCEDURES FOR UNITS OF WORK

I. INTRODUCTION

Reference has been made in previous chapters to the interesting controversy that has developed between the methodologist and the curriculum builder. During this debate, method has been defined so comprehensively in some quarters as to include teaching materials, organization of teaching materials, and even education itself. Although it is valuable for the reader to understand the salient points in this controversy, the debate itself is not of sufficient significance to merit an extended discussion in this book.

For our purpose, the term *teaching procedure* will be defined to show at once the relationship between method and teaching materials. In the case of teaching materials, the educator is concerned, of course, with the activities of children. It is a problem of doing, being, becoming, and developing in terms of the objectives that have been established for the pupils. Since the objectives are stated in terms of the pupils, the teaching materials are pupil activities which are essential in the realization of the objectives. In the case of teaching procedures, the educator is concerned with effective methods and means of developing pupil efficiency in these activities. Teaching materials present a problem of realizing objectives through student activity, while the means of stimulating and motivating student interest in achieving the objectives through these activities is method of instruction. In this discussion of teaching procedures we shall be concerned merely with the effective methods of teachers in assisting students to achieve progress in a field of work. It is *way of doing* in a particular subject as compared with other methods of approach to the problem rather than the *actual activity* of the pupils. It is a *way of getting things done* rather than the *checking of the results of teaching.*

In comparing method and content, again, it should be pointed out that the content must be organized in some fashion as a result of the determination of the objectives before the method need be considered. Any number of different methods can then be introduced in the same unit, project, or contract in order to stimulate effective teaching and learning at various points in the development of the work. Method does not emphasize the organization of content, but is concerned with the relationship of the pupil and the teaching materials. How can the pupil attain mastery of the objectives? The answer involves adjusting the child to the educational program (objectives and content) and is vitally concerned with the following adjustments: first, effectively introducing the child to the objectives and the content so that he is interested in them and motivated toward his own realization of the objectives through a mastery of the content; handling the content in such a way that the pupils are constantly achieving at maximum efficiency; thinking constantly of the individual child and adjusting the work in terms of his individual program both within and without the school as he makes his approach into various phases of the course of study; and planning both for the child and his educational program in terms of the content which has been previously developed as the course of study and also in terms of the content which will be developed from day to day as progress is made in the organized work of the course.

If the student of curriculum building will read the literature in the field with this point of view in mind, the great ocean of conflict which appears to exist between the positions of Bobbitt on the one hand and Kilpatrick and Bode on the other vanishes as a mirage. Neither group would maintain that an education program can be preordained completely for the child and nothing developed from the interests and reactions of the child in the classroom. This represents the old regimen in which the textbook (content) and the recitation (method) constituted the school education of the child. It will be granted readily by both parties that much of the school education must be developed "on the spot" and be based almost entirely upon the interests and activities of the pupils. The difference lies in the fact that the one school of thought maintains that because these activities are developed by the teacher in the classroom they should be classified under "methods" and such terms as the "project method," the "problem method," etc., were developed to indicate not only the activities of children but also the ways and means of directing these activities. These were, in reality, merely titles of a philosophy of education, rather than a discussion of methods of teaching. The other school of thought maintains that activities are content and includes the activities of the children, whether they are developed in the classroom or outside of school and previous to the opening of school for the current year. No problem, other than that of terminology, is involved in the controversy, since the preceding chapters in this section have indicated that American education is far from the textbook and recitation stage.

II. THE FUNCTION OF METHOD

Educators should realize that method is functional only. So much time in the past has been devoted to the structural aspects of method that little emphasis has been placed upon the strictly functional character of this phase of the course of study. This is not written to disparage the importance of method, but rather to indicate its true place in education. It is self-evident that merely developing a content and bringing the child into contact with it does not guarantee an educated product. Equally important in the result of the educational experiment of bringing the child into contact with educational experiences is the method of presentation, which usually provides for, first, stimulating the pupil to understand and evaluate the objectives of the course, second, generating self-activities in working with the content, third, taking into account the educational level of the child and the class and proceeding from the concrete to the abstract and from the psychological to the logical, fourth, integrating the content of the course with the life of the pupil, both within and without the school, and, fifth, encouraging the pupil to be not only an activist and participant in working with the content of the course, but also to be interested in checking carefully his progress and evaluating the results of these activities in his social adjustment. Again it can be said that method is a way of doing, a means by which results are to be achieved; it is not and never can be a process which can be constructed for use by all teachers in all fields under diverse and sundry conditions.

In the past many methods of teaching have been developed and fostered by educators in the hope that a plan might be organized which would inevitably result in perfect achievement on the part of all students under the direction of any and all teachers. The Herbartian method, the project method, the problem method, the contract plan, the unit plan, and the activity plan have all been devised for that purpose. Like all schemes for the attainment of perpetual motion, these panaceas of educational method have never been completely successful. All have made contributions to educational practice, but each has failed to develop teaching procedure to a point where it is or ever can be more than one phase of the education of children. There is no such thing in teaching as an absolute and final process or procedure. One is safe in the assumption, however, that the textbook, as content, and the recitation, as teaching procedure, have disappeared almost completely from America's educational program.

III. GENERAL METHODS

In the discussion in this chapter, general methods, rather than specific methods applicable to particular subject-matter fields, have been considered. Specific methods are very important in the construction of the course of study and will be taken up in later chapters. At this point, it is proposed to take up various types of general method for the purpose of analyzing the successive steps in each and of noting the place of general method in education. It should be pointed out that the teacher usually has a type of general method which governs the presentation of the work in a particular course and may make use of a number of specific methods during the year in developing certain phases of the course with the class. It is essential, therefore, in the consideration of the problems in the field of method that a study and analysis be made of the general methods which are in existence and available for the course of study committee.

A. Herbartian steps. This procedure can be designated as the influence which determined the first departure from the old textbook and recitation method in the United States. Its place in education was marked a generation ago and its effect upon educational thinking to-day can be appreciated if one recognizes that several modern methods are merely adaptations of the five formal steps of the Herbartian program. It should be said in favor of Herbart that he did not advocate the formalization of education. He was interested in the problem of directing the *learning* of children, but his followers established from his psychological approach a formal set of steps which did much to regulate and formalize the *teaching* of children. From his writing [1] on interest and apperception, the following steps, which dominated teacher training and classroom teaching in the early years of the present century, were developed:

Step One.   Preparation of the student for the work which is to be taken up, by review of previous work and by pointing out the relationship of the aims of the lesson to follow with previous lessons.

Step Two.   Presentation of the facts to the pupils through textbooks, lectures, observation, visual aids, etc., and at the same time stressing the relationship of this new material to that which has been acquired previously by them.

Step Three. Comparison and abstraction. The pupils are guided in comparing the new material with the old facts. Facts which are unrelated to past experiences of the student are ignored and those which are similar are "abstracted" in preparation for the next step.

[1] In reality, Herbart formulated the first four of these steps and his friends have since added the fifth step. Reference can be made to his books: *Science of Education and Outline of Educational Doctrine.*

Step Four. Generalization. From the consideration of all these facts a law, rule, or formula is developed and learned by the pupils.

Step Five. Application. This stage involves the testing of new facts and materials according to the law, rule, or formula which has been worked out by the class.

This method of organizing the work in the classroom has been the foundation of much of the recent development of methodology. Where it has been followed in spirit and as a philosophy, teachers have profited much from this plan of organizing their work for class presentation. However, the tendency on the part of teachers and teacher-training institutions to formalize and standardize their procedure in steps, as a result of coming in contact with this technique, has been a weakness in many modern plans of teaching which cannot be overcome.

B. The Morrison steps. Another highly organized procedure has been developed by Morrison of the University of Chicago. There is much in his procedure that resembles the steps which have been presented in the previous section. The formalization of his procedure [2] by teachers in the field has

[2] *Note:* H. C. Morrison, *The Practice of Teaching in Secondary Schools,* Revised (University of Chicago Press, 1931), Chapters XIV and XV. If the reader will consider some of the earlier chapters in this book, he will be impressed with the emphatic denial by Professor Morrison that a formalized method can or should be developed. He has continually warned teachers not to stereotype or formalize his procedure. The following quotation (pp. 220-221) will clarify his position on this point:

"Teachers in schools of education and normal schools, superintendents and their staff officers in city-school systems, are frequently in receipt of letters inquiring what method is used for the teaching of reading or writing or science or perhaps modern language. There are sometimes enumerated in the writer's thought such vaguely descriptive phrases as the 'work-and-sentence method,' the 'phonetic method,' the 'blank system of penmanship,' the 'heuristic method,' the 'direct method,' the 'natural method,' the 'grammatical method,' the 'supervised study method,' the 'socialized recitation method,' and so on at great length. Pedagogical history is full of ephemeral methods attached to the names of places in which they have flourished or to textbooks which have 'swept the country.' Not infrequently the question is made a political issue and communities are caused the attention of educators to be centered upon these steps rather than upon the psychological principles involved in the procedure. He emphasizes the fact that the learning cycle is based upon the stimulation of the individual, the association of new facts with previously learned data which are already organized and used by the individual and involves the learner in making a response in which the new data are used in connection with previously acquired materials. The five steps which were developed by Morrison presented a method of approach in arriving at student mastery of the essential content materials. Involved in the five steps are most of the modern socialized techniques of teaching as well as the unit plan of the organization of content. Draper and Roberts state "The essential contribution of Morrison's book is the utilization of modern socialized techniques in mastering large units of work in all high-school subjects, including supervised study, pupil self-direction, use of all teaching helps such as visual materials, modern equipment, library aids, etc., and the teacher in the rôle of expert consultant rather than leader and director of class activities." [3] The five steps which make possible the attainment of this philosophy of mastery on the part of the pupil are as follows:

agitated by the ridiculous question, 'Shall we allow such and such a "method" to be used in our schools?' As if the matter could be settled wisely by popular vote! Or the writer of such letters may have a mind which is blank on the subject of methods, but convinced that if somebody will name a method all will be well.

"Now, this general attitude toward the problem of teaching is evidence of another mental stereotype like the ground-to-be-covered and time-to-be-spent stereotypes. This one we may call the 'method-to-be-followed stereotype.' Its essence is in the notion that if the teacher can find the specifications for the right method he can follow it in his teaching and nothing remains to be done but to grade the pupils according to their success in achieving the appointed tasks. The logic of the matter is that, if ground-to-be-covered and time-to-be-spent are lawfully determined and the method-to-be-followed is properly appraised, educational results must follow in proportion to the inherent and unmodifiable general ability of the pupil. Nothing could be more remote from a sound educational point of view."

[3] E. M. Draper and A. C. Roberts, *The Principles of American Secondary Education* (The Century Company, 1932), p. 455.

1. *Exploration.* This involves pre-testing of the pupils in order that the teacher can determine the previous preparation of the students for the unit of work.

2. *Presentation.* The unit is presented to the pupils so that they grasp the general scope of the work and can see the relationship of this work to the units which have preceded. It also gives the teacher the opportunity to justify the inclusion of this unit and stimulate interest in the pupil activities of the immediate future.

3. *Assimilation.* At this stage the pupil works out the problems, projects, challenges, etc., which are involved in attaining mastery of the unit, under the guidance of the teacher. It is in this phase of the work that the various facts are secured and the habits acquired which make possible the generalizations concerning the work which after all is the real basis of learning. In many fields the learning situations are as much a part of the lives of the pupils as those in the activity schools. A glance at the steps which have been discussed so far will indicate at once the ease with which this technique can be adapted to the activity program. If the pupils were permitted to participate in the selection of the unit of work, this plan of mastery could be adapted to any modern activity school.

4. *Organization.* At this stage the student makes a systematic and careful organization of the material which has been covered in the assimilation period. Tests and examinations are made a part of the work at this time to assist the pupil in grasping the essential points, developing a synthesis from the results of the various investigations, and attaining mastery of the facts, skills, habits, etc.

5. *Recitation.* The facts and materials which have been organized and mastered by the pupils are here presented as a part of the group discussions. Any differences of opinion are thought through on the basis of the facts which have been secured in the investigations. The goal at this time is complete mastery by the pupils.

The steps have been presented here as if learning in all fields led to the same kind of outcomes and permitted of the same method of approach. No one is more keenly alert to the difficulties in this situation than Professor Morrison, who makes the following statement on this point: "Most theories of teaching have been founded on the assumption that all teaching is one, that a theory of technique can be found which is equally applicable to all subjects found in the school. In a sense this is true, for there are certain laws which apply in one form or another to all forms of learning. Among these are the principle of apperceptive approach, the principle of motivation, the law of initial diffuse movement, the canon of the concrete before the abstract. In the theory which we here advocate, we make large use of the principle that all real learning, except the learning of skills, is in the form of adaptations in the individual. Nevertheless, a workable theory of teaching must take into account the fact that the psychology of the learning process, the nature of the essential objectives sought, and consequently the teaching process itself, all differ in important details as we go from one subject to another in the secondary school. We can, however, group all the subjects taught in the field of general education, and indeed in the field of vocational education so long as it is at the secondary level, into five different types, which characteristically differ among themselves in the nature of their objectives and in the psychology of the learning process." [4] These five types of learning can be summarized as follows:

1. *The science type.* "The objectives here are adaptations which are in form understandings of principles or processes in the relation of cause and effect. The method of learning is a process of reflection and rationalization——the product is an intelligent attitude toward some aspect of the environment or of a science." He further states that this type of learning applies to any field "in which the learning units are primarily understanding or rationalization." [5]

2. *The appreciation type.* "The learning units here are in the form of adaptations in terms of which are valued those products

[4] Morrison, *op. cit.*, p. 89.
[5] *Ibid.*, p. 89.

of civilization which are and have been contributed by the fine arts, religion, and by the best examples of moral behavior.——— Psychologically, the type is concerned with the effective side of man's nature." [6] It is pointed out that as soon as literature or religion is studied analytically and rationalization developed, it cannot be taught under the appreciation type and belongs under the science type.

3. *The practical-arts type.* "The objectives here are adaptations which lead to the intelligent manipulation of appliances and molding of materials." [7] It is recognized, of course, that certain phases of the practical arts must be taught as science types of learning and other aspects as appreciation types, while laboratory work in the sciences will be taught according to the practical-arts type of learning.

4. *The language-arts type.* "It is the type through which the use of spoken and written discourse is learned, but it is far from being limited to the learning of language. In general, it applies to the learning of any method of receiving or expressing thought or feeling in the form of continuous discourse." [8] However, it must be kept in mind that the learning of the techniques of language is not of this type, as the fundamental element in the type is running discourse on the part of the learner.

5. *The pure practice type.* "In the pure practice type, however, there is no thought content whatever included in the learning process itself, although the objectives may, in some cases, be the automatizing of certain products of learning which are in themselves content in the mind." [9] In all the preceding types mental content is of primary importance, although they may have practice with materials also. Morrison suggests three subtypes of the pure practice method: first, the improvement of special ability by pure practice as basic neuro-muscular development as in walking, finger movements in piano playing,

[6] *Ibid.,* p. 90.
[7] *Ibid.,* p. 90.
[8] *Ibid.,* p. 92.
[9] *Ibid.,* p. 93.

etc.; second, the fixing in the mind of those elements of learning which are constant in character such as spelling and memorizing the multiplication tables; and third, the learning of rules and formulæ which are used frequently, where the principles governing them have been acquired through other types of learning.

These types of learning have been in the field of specific methods. They have been included at this point because it was necessary to introduce them in order to indicate the scope of the Morrison plan or method. These and other types of specific method will be discussed more fully in later sections.

C. The Miller steps. The method which has been introduced by Miller in his stimulating book, "Creative Learning and Teaching," [10] is presented here for two reasons: it is an excellent method for committees to consider in the final organization of the course of study, and it suggests an eclectic method in the course of study, since Miller frankly admits that his procedure is an adaptation of the Herbartian and Morrisonian approaches and uses the contract plan of organizing teaching materials. It is important that course of study committees and teachers develop this point of view. Methods are not introduced in the course of study for the purpose of stereotyping the approach of the teacher to the problem of stimulating the learning of pupils. Their sole purpose is to suggest procedures which have been successful in the teaching of others and to make possible adaptations which will enable a particular teacher, with a personality of his own, to make the best possible adjustments for a group of pupils, each with his own peculiar personality and character. This does not mean that the teacher in the classroom will make absolute and final decisions concerning the methods which he will use in the classroom. The adaptations which will be permitted will be adopted after it has been demonstrated that they have value for a particular situation. The antecedents of the Miller program will be apparent at once in the following steps:

[10] Harry L. Miller, *Creative Learning and Teaching* (Charles Scribner's Sons, 1927), Chs. i, ii.

1. *Problem-raising movement.* Miller places great emphasis upon the fact that this first step is not an *overview* but a *problem-raising movement.* He makes the distinction that in the overview the teacher presents most of the material which the student should acquire for himself as a result of his investigating the sources which are available, whereas this phase of the study of the pupils should merely raise problems which will challenge them to definite and enthusiastic endeavor. Miller makes the following statement concerning this point:

In the problem-raising movement the teacher seeks to present a challenge. From the teacher's point of view the new unit of work is a sort of prescribed temptation. The brief period of twenty minutes is not to be devoted to teacher-talk and some ethical injunctions, nor to that much-abused, much-written-about term called motivation. By judicious questioning a good statement may be made. "Prohibition, boys and girls! Have you any suggestions, convictions or ideas about it?" Up jumps a little girl, displaying the fervor of an evangel. "I think people ought to have their personal liberty...." (And you know what her father thinks about the business.) Something is doing. Others are on their feet, *pro* and *con.* It would be easy to spend the hour in chattering on personal liberty. "Is there any other angle to the question of *Prohibition?*" A boy whose father's political faith may not be in doubt rises to the bait. "I think it was a big mistake for the national government to undertake the control of the liquor traffic." These are merely hints to indicate a possible direction. Out of this ferment two guide-lines emerge. The teacher sees to it that they are written under the first movement.

a. Individual liberty versus social constraint
b. National control versus state rights

The guide-lines are (*a*) and (*b*). They constitute the organizing principles by which intelligent study of the contract is to be launched and guided. These two guide-lines are the *common essentials* in the challenge. A remark may have been made about each in the first movement. In fact, a youngster did puncture the argument of the defenders of "personal liberty" by pointing to practices in sanitation, control of epidemics, traffic regulations. "We don't do as we please in such matters, do we?" We are ready at this stage, after casting up the guide-lines, to begin the second movement, *Directing Study.* (These guide-lines may not always appear as early in the contract.

Frequently they may not begin to clarify until the pupils are well under way in the second movement.) [11]

2. *Directing study movement.* In this step, the pupil works as an individual investigating that particular part of the challenge which appeals to him. Each pupil has a problem within the major problem, but it is essential that the activity of each student make a contribution toward the solution of the unit or contract which has been undertaken by the class. Miller states:

A unity is assured, never a uniformity. Every chart that is produced will have a direct bearing on the central problem. A basis is laid for the interrelating and sharing of various contributions. No upper limit is prescribed for any member of the group, either by setting a minimum or by prohibition of home study. No pupil is limited to a single phase of the unit of work. Stimulation to a single quantitative production will be avoided. Opportunities for enrichment will be cultivated.[12]

The work under the directing study movement takes about two-thirds or three-fourths of the total time devoted to the unit or contract. Throughout this period the pupil is constantly guided toward an ever-increasing individualism, although his problem must be a part of the major unit and make its contribution to the thinking of the group. Miller does not believe in giving the student a contract, however, and requiring him to work out quantitative reports which will be checked by the teacher from time to time and graded at the conclusion of the month's work. Rather it is a gradual development of the individual problem through conferences with the teacher concerning sources, methods of approach, and scope of the work in the relation to the unit under consideration. At times in this step, the contribution of an individual student can be brought to the attention of the class for discussion and further stimulation of the entire group in terms of the findings reported by the pupil. Miller's analysis of the duties of the teacher during this period is illuminating:

[11] *Ibid.,* pp. 34-35.
[12] *Ibid.,* p. 38.

The teacher has been active in checking results, in guiding study, in acting as a consulting expert, and in general management of pupils at work in various forms. It would be perfectly easy to describe what the new teacher is not doing in this stage of the second movement. He is not hearing lessons recited. He is not talking too much. He is not sitting at his desk looking over post mortems (examination papers of dead yesterdays). He is not criticizing the finished product of the pupils except in so far as testing for mastery is begun. He is not doing police duty in a mechanically driven type of supervised study.... The talking teacher will indulge in pedagogical chattering, making it quite impossible for any productive work to be done. All of these suggestions are intended to be partial descriptions of a varied procedure, the details of which can never be catalogued.[13]

The last phase of this movement is concerned with the testing for mastery. This examination is essential before the final organization of the material. It will usually be a test of understanding the principles involved rather than the remembering of information. There will be an evaluating of results, a comparing of results, and a preliminary analysis and checking of data in preparation for the final stage of the work of the unit.

3. *Organizing movement.* The last step in the Miller plan is devoted to the sharing of the results which have been attained or secured by various members of the class. There are various ways of developing this summarization of the work. A few of them are suggested by Miller in the following quotation:

In this third movement, the conclusion of the matter in an art class would be a display of the productions and a study of them, perhaps a scoring of them, or some appraisal to bring out pupil self-criticism of their own work. In mathematics the contract might culminate in a spirited demonstration of board work in which speed and accuracy, and a searching gripping of principles are emphasized. It is amazing to see what can be done in one of the *organizing, unifying* days when every pupil is "on his mark" doing his part in a coöperative drive for a comprehensive result. The activity may resemble the old-fashioned recitation. The point to be made clear is the fact that the last day or two of the contract is a culminating movement, and that pupils have worked up something which they may recite superbly. They see relations in perspective.[14]

[13] *Ibid.,* pp. 43-44.
[14] *Ibid.,* pp. 48-49.

D. The contract method of teaching. While the contract has been mentioned in the preceding section which considered the Miller steps, it is proposed at this point to discuss those methods or procedures which are fundamental in the Dalton plan. The contract, as an organization of content, has been analyzed in a previous chapter. Only those procedures which are effective in making the contract a useful instrument in the classroom will be considered here.

1. The development of the contract itself is a preliminary step in most Daltonized schools, *i.e.,* the content and the scope of the activities of the pupils are determined by the teacher in advance. This content, which usually provides four weeks of work for the pupil, is carefully and attractively written out and copies mimeographed or multigraphed for the entire class. The topics included permit the designation of minimum requirements and elective maximums in order that individual differences can be satisfactorily adjusted.

2. After the child has received the assignment, he can be allowed considerable freedom to work out the contract. He is free to use the study hall, library, vacant classrooms, or his own classroom, and his choice will depend upon his specific needs at that time. Much of his reference work will take him to the library, but there are certain types of reference materials and equipment which will be found only in the classroom.

3. As a result of steps 1 and 2, the class normally divides itself into small groups. However, certain phases of the work can be individualized, and this is insisted upon by the teacher when it appears that one pupil or a number will be benefited by this individual work.

4. Conferences are held regularly during the month and can be held at any time suitable to the convenience of the pupil and the teacher. If it should be a laboratory assignment, a check-up and short conference can be held at the end of the pupils' work period. In view of the fact that the work is individual and that every classroom is a laboratory for work, these conferences may be class discussions, group discussions, or talks with individual students. Conferences and intensive

study may be carried on in the same room at the same time. It may be that the conference is for the purpose of checking over the work which has been assigned to the class for completion at a particular time. In this case those who are not prepared are not permitted to attend, since they would have the opportunity of copying the work of the other students and saving themselves all the labor involved in the preparation of the contract to that point.

In most of the Daltonized schools the conferences naturally divide themselves into two types depending entirely upon the age, grade, and mental ability of the students. In general, it can be stated that younger children and those who are mentally slower require more teacher initiative in the conference. The questions will be framed by the teacher rather than by the students, and the teacher will have to check over the work of each student in order to determine his difficulties, since pupils who are young and bright as well as those who are old and slow mentally have difficulty in analyzing their perplexities or asking intelligent questions concerning the problems they are facing. The bright pupils at the secondary level will usually congregate in the same conference, and can be taught by placing great responsibility on them to analyze carefully the assignment, to appreciate the problems they are facing in completing the work, and to ask questions which will clear the way for mastery of the objectives.

Since provision has been made in the contract for maximum and minimum assignments, the classes are expected to divide themselves into at least two groups. Unfortunately, in many cases, classes will automatically separate into three or four levels of work, and the conference work becomes very great for the teacher of that subject. In such cases, conferences will have to be held after school if they are to meet the individual and group needs of the class.

5. The work of the class is checked by monthly examinations and by tests given during the conference periods throughout the month. If the intervening tests given during the period of the contract can be graded by the student, much valuable

insight into the scope of the work, the significance of part contracts, and the possibilities of the work in the future can be secured by the pupil. This check-up by the students of their own work will require close supervision by the teacher and should be done during one of the conference periods when she is present to guide them in their endeavors. These tests have an additional value in that they enable the teacher to evaluate the status of the individual members of the class, to stimulate those who are lazy, inefficient or slow in performance and low in mentality, in order that the work can be completed on schedule, and, if necessary, make-up classes can be organized for those who will do the contract again rather than proceed with the class to the work for the following month.

The Dalton Plan has much in common with both the Morrison and Miller procedures. In all of them, the major emphasis is upon that period in which the student works with the assignment. Making the assignment and checking the results occupy relatively short periods as compared with that phase of the work which centers upon child activity, in which the child contacts materials and carries on investigations. This important period has been designated in the three systems as (1) *Assimilation and organization,* (2) *Directing Study Movement,* and (3) *Conference.*

Miss Amy L. Clapp, writing of the modified Dalton Plan which is used in the mathematics department of the South Philadelphia High School for Girls, makes the following analysis of the conference period in her field:

Types of conferences. (1) Class conferences—three kinds. There are three types of conferences to which the entire class may be called. First, the group may be called, often in the beginning of the week, for a bird's-eye view of a new topic, for explanation of a new process, and sufficient drill in it to enable the pupils to continue independently; this type of conference is seen most frequently in arithmetic or algebra. Second, the group may be called, often just before the test day, for the purpose of summarizing the work just completed, of explaining the difficulties encountered, or of clinching the facts learned or processes acquired; this type of conference is seen generally in geometry. Third, the entire class sometimes has to be summoned to conference as a penalty for lack of faithfulness, *e.g.,* commercial arithmetic classes, who may not be of scholarly material, must often be summoned every day for ten minutes to ensure daily practice of rapid calculation.

(2) Special group conferences. Conferences of special groups may also be called. Those trying the maximum may be summoned—often to an informal discussion around the teacher's desk; as also may be slower girls. These last may be selected in various ways; they may be those who failed a certain test and who need more help before the second test; or they may be those whose past failures show them chronically weak or lazy; or they may be those who come voluntarily.

Technique of handling the conference. No definite rule can be given as to the technique of handling conferences; the teacher must keep clearly before her the aim in such work—to use the method that will best help the pupil to learn certain facts or points of view or to acquire certain abilities. The teacher may conduct the conference in the form of supervised study, or of an oral recitation or oral drill, or of a discussion carefully guided by well-chosen questions, or, rarely, she may prefer herself to present the work—a method desirable only if the presentation is brief, suggestive, and attention-arresting.

Obviously, the teacher in all conferences avoids giving unnecessary help and so handles any conference that is in the nature of a summary or review that her help is of no value to those pupils who have come unprepared. For instance, it is often wise to refuse, in a general conference, to solve a problem completely; help can be given over the difficult places and the remainder left for the industrious pupil to finish. Of course, this in no sense implies that adequate help should not be given to those whose work shows honest and unsuccessful effort—the teacher must always discriminate between faithful slowness and laziness disguised as mental slowness, and must help the deserving ones, often individually.

Then, too, conferences should be suited to the ability of the girls involved; for instance, after the completion of the assignment, the slowest girls can be helped by carefully outlining the originals in the minimum. Those trying maximum were given for each original merely a hint sufficient for an industrious girl of average ability. Those who tried additional maxima were told that sufficient help was given in the book.[15]

[15] Faculty of the South Philadelphia High School for Girls, *Educating for Responsibility* (The Macmillan Company, 1926), pp. 109-110. The quotation is from the chapter on the Dalton Plan in Mathematics by Miss Amy L. Clapp.

E. The problem-project method. There is little that is fundamentally different in the problem-project approach from the procedures already presented. However, there are several individual characteristics which should be analyzed. It has been noted already that this so-called method is largely a system of organizing teaching materials and not a method of instruction at all. Those phases which have to do with organizing materials have been treated elsewhere and only the aspects which are specifically related to method will be treated at this point.

All the general methods discussed in previous sections, as well as the problem-project, are attempts to develop a learning situation in which the child will experience a felt need or sense a difficulty which will stimulate his interest and will promote pupil leadership and followership in organizing, supervising, and completing a large unit of work, contract, problem, or project. The statement of the problem or project usually designates the goals to be attained and the standards which are involved in mastery.

1. *The problem method.* It is not difficult to prove that most adults are interested and actively engaged in solving or in attempting to solve problems of family life, finance, professional, business, or vocational occupations, etc. There are many courses of study and teachers to testify that students will develop an intense interest in problems which are related to their lives and are placed at the correct grade level to challenge them. Problem teaching can be characterized, therefore, as, first, promoting a problem which is both perplexing and challenging to the pupils; second, assisting in the formulation of the correct statement of the problem and procedures to be followed in its solution; third, the careful and intelligent supervision of the work of the class and individuals within the class, and, fourth, assisting the students to evaluate results and checking the attempts of the students to develop an adequate testing program.

It is apparent that the use of problems in classwork does not imply any particular formal method or plan of procedure. The pupil is presented with a problem which necessitates effort and some thinking on his part and which will result in the acquisition of knowledge, development of skills or the realization of attitudes, ideals, and habits. Different classroom procedures can be used in attaining these goals.

The organization of the classwork consists usually of a segmental set of problems. These are related so that the extensive tests of reference books and materials, which are essential, can be used throughout the semester or year. This makes it possible for the work to be developed through class discussions, research in reference material, experiments in the laboratory, etc. At the end of the problem-solving period, summarizations are made and generalizations developed. At this time the pupils usually make reports, while the teacher employs the lecture method, laboratory experiments, demonstrations, and other specific visual techniques.

The objectives attained through the use of the problem can be expressed as (1) the development of an objective attitude on the part of the pupils, (2) greater enthusiasm on the part of the pupils who are working with intriguing and stimulating materials, and (3) an easy approach on the part of the teacher to the objectives in terms of particulars and generalizations.

The problem may be of any length, from one recitation period to several weeks, but the procedures will not vary with the length. It is necessary for the pupils to have a clear understanding of the goals which are to be achieved; the statement of these goals, which is the statement of the problem, should institute a real challenge; and the data and equipment which will enable the pupil to undertake and evaluate his work must be available.

The procedure to be employed by the teacher can vary somewhat with the type of problem confronting the class. It may be that the class has the facts, data, generalizations, or definitions, and the problem is then the application of these to situations. This is known as a deductive procedure on the part of the pupils. If the class is faced with the problem of determining the law, definition, or rule, the procedure is inductive. While the inductive and deductive procedures are very different from the standpoint of the student, they do not necessarily require different teaching methods on the part of the teacher.

In both types of problems the following methods are essential:

a. Presentation of the problem to the class. This includes a clear statement of the problem which can be understood by every member of the group. An extended discussion at this point can be invaluable if a clear definition of the problem is the result.

b. Organization of the work of the class, as a whole, and the checking of the program for the individual members of the class. The teacher must note that the problem is either inductive or deductive and guide the endeavors of the pupils accordingly. This does not imply a different method of procedure, but rather an appreciation by the teacher of the type of thinking which will be developed through working with the problem and the guidance of the class through the stages of the inductive or deductive investigations and formulation of judgments.

Draper and Roberts make the following comment on materials which are available for the pupils using either type of procedure:

> Two questions are often asked: "Where do the problems come from?" and "How do the pupils work in their classes with this technique?" The problems grow out of the teaching and are developed in class discussion. A large variety of materials and reference books are placed within easy access of the pupils, who are trained to use them effectively. Class periods are spent in individual study of references, in individual or group laboratory work, in group or class discussion of various phases of the problem as it has been developed, in the organizing of the materials covered as a solution of the problem is sought. Pupils are trained to maintain an objective, questioning attitude until all data possible are in, and then the solution or solutions are summarized and presented in pupil reports, teacher demonstrations or talks, or group conferences and reports.[16]

The teacher has the responsibility, through individual and class discussion and presentation of new facts, of guiding the students to make careful evaluations of each new item of data.

---

[16] E. M. Draper and A. C. Roberts, *The Principles of American Secondary Education* (The Century Co., 1932), p. 460.

c. In summarization of the findings of the class, which may be either generalizations or the formulation of data concerning a new problem according to generalizations or rules which have already been established, the teacher should assist every pupil to formulate his own conclusions and verify them by every check available to the class. The pupils can be guided in making a careful analysis which will give them a mastery of either the details or the generalization.

2. *The project method.* In order that the pupils may make progress toward desirable goals, it is essential that problems be interrelated or that projects which include a number of problems be developed. The extensiveness of the project will be determined by the age-grade-ability level of the pupils but the teacher should have a progressive sequence in mind at all times.

Stevenson has indicated both the limitations and the possibilities of the project method for the teacher in the following general goals which he has proposed:

> *a.* Development of reasoning instead of memory for information
> *b.* Development of consciously deliberated conduct instead of information for its own sake
> *c.* A natural setting for the learning instead of an artificial setting
> *d.* A priority of the problem as against the priority of general principles [17]

From these general aims and the statements of others who have analyzed the project method, it could be assumed that the use of this method is limited to types of physical behavior and could not be developed as a procedure by teachers of subjects which do not lend themselves to the organization of physical activities. An excellent statement of a different point of view is found in the recent book by Powers and Uhl:

It has sometimes been assumed that the project must involve a preponderance of overt behavior. Without consisting of mere memory for information, information for its own sake, or abstract principles slavishly memorized, this need not be true. Psychologi-

[17] J. A. Stevenson, *The Project Method of Teaching* (The Macmillan Co., 1921), p. 4.

cally, it is entirely possible to have a mental project followed through in a natural setting with but little overt behavior. This is easily seen when one bears in mind the relation between language and thought as developed by such writers as Perrin.[18] Language is symbolical conduct. As such, it is used in the solution of problems. Psychologically the main requisite of the project which is solved through the use of symbolic conduct, language or thinking, is that such symbols are backed by and based upon actual experience. If this is the case, it is possible in the literal sense of the word to project oneself into a future situation, solve the problems therein presented, and base future action upon such solutions. It is not necessary in this discussion to decide whether such projection is always in terms of vocalized words, or whether it may likewise be conducted by imagery. This point has been discussed at length elsewhere.[19]

The possibilities which can be inferred from such a statement of principles are evidenced in the individualization of the work even though the work be organized as a class project. While standards of achievement can be maintained for the class and for the individual pupil, the emphasis can be placed upon improvement of habits, skills, and attitudes of each pupil.

The method involved in the particular project will be determined by the nature of the project. There are at least two, possibly three, distinct types of method in project teaching, and it will be necessary to analyze these types before developing the general principles which will govern procedure in project instruction.

a. The project which grows out of regular class work and serves to elucidate facts, clarify relationships, and motivate interest on the part of the pupils. This was the primary need and use of the project in its earliest development in the fields of agriculture and other practical types of training. To-day there is a tendency to supplement regular class work by projects carried out in school, under the daily observation of the teacher, as well as the home projects referred to above. The pupil, by handling materials, constructing apparatus, searching for data,

[18] Fleming Allen Clay Perrin, *Psychology, Its Methods and Principles* (Henry Holt and Co., revised edition, 1932), p. 267.
[19] F. F. Powers and W. L. Uhl, *Psychological Principles of Education* (The Century Co., 1933), pp. 276-277.

etc., relates the work more closely to his life situation than he would in regular classwork.

b. The project which grows out of distinguishable purposes of the pupils. This type was conceived by Kilpatrick [20] and worked out by Collings [21] while he was a county superintendent of schools in southern Missouri. An illustration from his book is summarized briefly for the reader.

The absence of two children of the same family from school due to attacks of typhoid fever led to a class discussion concerning the periodic epidemics of this disease in the family and provoked thought concerning the various causes of the disease. The class sought out the causes of typhoid fever and considered them in connection with the afflicted family. A visit was planned to the home in order to study the situation first-hand and determine which of the various causes probably operated in this situation. A study of conditions in the home and its environs led the children to tabulate the unsatisfactory conditions and compare them with the causes which had been discovered. A report was then made out for the father giving him the necessary information for the development of a new sanitary program.

A survey was then conducted for the purpose of determining the prevalence of this and other diseases in the community. Related activities, such as making fly traps, garbage pails, and plans for combating flies, were also introduced.

c. Possibly the third type of project can be designated, as it has been by its proponents, as a *real life activity.* According to this proposal, a real life activity can be distinguished from the purposes of children and from necessary supplementary work which can be carried on inside or outside the classroom. In order to be classified as a real life project, the work must be developed as an out-of-school experience or an in-school experience, which resembles closely the life situations outside the school and also stimulate intense enthusiasm in the pupils because of its being developed out of their immediate and vital life interests.

[20] W. H. Kilpatrick, *Foundations of Method* (The Macmillan Co., 1926), Ch. XVII.
[21] E. Collings, *An Experiment with a Project Curriculum* (The Macmillan Co., 1923), pp. 55 ff.

It should be apparent that the procedure of the teacher will vary from one type of project to another and will deviate to some extent from any standards which can be established for any one type. It is proposed to note some general approaches which can be applied to teaching any of the types and to allow the teacher or committee to determine the exact amount of emphasis upon particular procedures.

a. It is essential for the teacher to secure the individual coöperation of the pupils in planning and carrying out the work. In this respect there is a considerable variation from the contract procedure, in which the organization of the work is a unique responsibility of the teacher. This is a real task since all of the pupils must be occupied with the development of a major project or with supplementary aspects of the main problem. To accomplish this without wasting time and effort, it is necessary that an intense motivated interest be developed in this important first step.

b. A careful check should be kept on the work of the class and of each student. Since some projects are worked out in school, others develop entirely outside of the school, a few are organized as group endeavors, and many are individual in character, this step calls for insight, enthusiasm, and an innate desire to evaluate carefully each contribution. Otherwise, undesirable habits and damaging attitudes can be the chief educational results. Needless searching for material, procrastination, and the extension of projects beyond a justifiable time for satisfactory results can easily result if the teacher is not a real co-worker, guide, and friend of the pupils at this stage.

c. The completion of the project should represent a definite accomplishment in the education of the children. It should be apparent to them that with these new facts, skills, and understandings they are now ready to attack new projects and make further progress in their educational program. The evaluation of the results attained by the class should rest with the children as much as with expert opinion.

Draper and Roberts make the following statement concerning the use of this method by the inexperienced teacher:

The inexperienced teacher will meet certain dangers, limitations, and objections to over-use of the project as a teaching device. The logical sequences in the development of subject-matter are largely broken up; there is inevitably much non-educative activity in the procedure, especially when materials are being accumulated or booklets being developed; there is not a sufficient number of challenging projects to be developed which pupils will have an equal interest and desire to solve; there are greater demands upon the time and skill of the teacher in keeping a full program of projects alive and progressing; and some of the needs types of teaching must be either neglected or brought in deliberately to supplement the project. The strength of project teaching, on the contrary, lies in the greater interest, the adjustment of the work to individual differences of pupils, the possibilities of round-table discussion, the adaptation of the laboratory technique to many academic subjects, the rôle of the teacher as a co-worker in the solution of perplexing problems, the motivation that grows out of increased interest, and the possibility of the transfer of the technical skills to the solution of other and still more important problems as more difficult projects are attacked.[22]

F. The socialized procedure. Much that has been written in the preceding pages has had the socialization of the child as a goal. However, in view of the current use of the term in education it appears desirable to note the outstanding aspects of the socialized recitation.

The old textbook-recitation procedure tended to emphasize the average student to the detriment of the bright pupils as well as those of limited ability who began to crowd into the school. The work must be placed at some level, and often the teacher and the average student make good recitations during the class period. There was little responsibility placed on any one but the teacher; the excellent pupils were not challenged while those below standard could not accept the challenge when it was presented to them.

This situation not only effected a reorganized method but also new administrative devices, such as ability grouping, the development of new fields of subject-matter as well as the

[22] E. M. Draper and A. C. Roberts, *Principles of American Secondary Education* (The Century Co., 1932), pp. 463-464.

reorganization of many old subjects and the curricularization of the more highly organized extracurricular activities.

The socialized procedure permits the realization of the following desirable situations in the classroom:

1. The pupils can assume responsibility for certain phases of the work since they are encouraged to initiate various activities and prepare summaries of their endeavors. The pupils also have opportunities to visualize the goals to be attained by the group and can assist and coöperate in group activities. Much value can result from this coöperation with others, and the adjustment of individualities, tendencies, and opinions to the needs of the group and the results of work as prepared by all of the members of the class. There is also the possibility that the pupils will realize individual interests and ambitions and will learn to work in coöperation with the instructor on special problems.

2. The teacher assumes an entirely different position in the class since he is the friend and advisor of interested pupils rather than the director or the searcher for information or lack of information in the classroom. In using this approach, the teacher is able to promote greater interest and more effective mastery on the part of the pupils.

Powers and Uhl have an excellent summary of the psychological elements in the socialized recitation:

a. Fairly uniform pupil reaction. As in the case of the class where the teacher is in absolute control, so also in the socialized period, will certain students tend to dominate the situation. Socialization is not a passive but an active process. No student gains social competence from sitting and watching other students dominate the situation. Devices by which equality of reaction can be secured are numerous. A rotation method of assuming some responsibility in the class conduct may be used. The teacher may indirectly but effectively take care that each student is given an opportunity to react. It must be borne in mind that the main value of the socializing technique lies in the fact, that, properly used, it reaches the whole group. The aggressive, "extrovert" minority will become socialized in any case.

b. Full use of the socialized recitation should be made not only to secure unanimity of participation in recitation but also to inculcate many social amenities as well. Robbins has commented on the fact that noise and confusion may become the outstanding characteristics of this method.[23] Although possibly this may be the case in the early stages of the socialized period, it should in no sense be true of the final result. Otherwise, an opportunity has been passed to secure courtesy values fully as great as pupil autonomy in recitation periods.

c. The purpose of the socializing technique should be rationalized by the pupil or, at least, to the pupil. Socialization cannot be secured by merely turning a class loose to drift as it pleases. Even among adults the distinction between liberty and license is not completely clear. It is even less clear with adolescents. The lesson to be gained, namely that individual freedom of conduct carries an implication of social responsibility, can be gained by a long process of auto-inductive experience, but the acquisition may be quite as efficient and somewhat less painful and time-consuming when the result of direct socializing training.[24]

The socialized method involves at least two approaches. First, the formal organization of the work in which individual pupils, groups, or the entire class under the direction and guidance of the teacher attack the problem presented for solution or the materials organized for mastery. This can be accomplished through surveys conducted in the library, searching for materials outside the environs of the schools, and preparing reports or statements which present the conclusions arrived at by the individual or group studying the materials or data. Second, the informal phase of the work develops the class into a discussion group with the teacher or a designated student as chairman or leader. Here the results are reported and analyzed by the group, and the combined statements are formulated into a complete solution of the problem. There is another informal aspect of this procedure in schools which do not have ability grouping in that intricate points in the assignment must be cleared up and the work adjusted to the ability of particular groups of pupils before the investigations are initiated. Draper

[23] Charles L. Robbins, *The Socialized Recitation* (Allyn and Bacon, 1920), pp. 1-12.
[24] Powers and Uhl, *Psychological Principles of Education* (The Century Co., 1933), pp. 280-281.

and Roberts have evaluated this method in the following paragraph:

The problem-solving attitude, the project procedure, and the supervision of study make possible the organization of the classwork as a coöperative enterprise in which all share and carry some part of the responsibility for a complete and successful solution of the problems that have been set up. The advantages of this socialized procedure are obvious: interest, motivation, pupil contribution of worthwhile effort, the extending to the full of the powers of all pupils, the utilization of much more curricular and out-of-school material, a better relationship throughout the school, and, perhaps as important as any of the foregoing, the freeing of the teacher for more important tasks in directing the learning of the pupils.[25]

G. Supervised study. A recognition of the fact that many failing students, from the elementary school to the graduate level in the university, are in difficulty because of poor study habits has led to the development and the consistent spread of supervised study programs at all educational levels. Another important influence which forced administrators to reorganize their school programs to provide for supervised study was the impossibility of pupils' adjusting satisfactory study habits to conditions in the homes in which they were reared or were staying. In the college and university, living in large groups in fraternity, sorority and boarding houses presented many difficulties which were overcome by the exceptional rather than the average student. Lacking regular study hours and a knowledge of efficient study habits has produced an excessive mortality in every student body. The author, who has been affiliated with the educational program of a national fraternity, has found many students at the college level who could not make a concerted attack on a new problem or organize materials efficiently for classwork or examination.

Supervised study has been considered as an integral part of a number of the procedures analyzed previously. However, it can be highly developed and successfully used as a part of the

25 Draper and Roberts, *op. cit.*, pp. 465-466.

textbook-recitation method and for that reason it is accorded a separate treatment.

In supervised study, the teacher and the pupils study together as well as recite together. Many crimes have been committed in the name of supervised study; it can be a waste of time unless the period is one of directed studying and learning. Here again the objectives of the lesson must be clearly stated so that the pupils see the various phases of this lesson in their relationship to one another and to previous assignments. The teacher is available at all times to assist in the work and to promote good study habits and excellent organizations of material.

The mistakes which are commonly made in the supervised study period are: first, the attitude is easily developed that supervised study is an administrative device and that the period is of a certain definite length, *i.e.,* thirty minutes for recitation and thirty minutes for supervised study; second, the over-zealous teacher continues to lecture or discuss or make a presentation during the time when concentrated study is the need of the pupils; third, the indolent teacher merely assigns a lesson, advocates study, and retires behind the desk to carry on activities which are not related to the work of the class.

The advantages of this procedure are many if it is regarded as directed learning and not as a new type of administration. These can be listed as follows:

1. Every type of specific method can be more highly developed in the supervised study period than elsewhere. This may include drill, development of skills, appreciations, problem-solving, etc.
2. Individual differences can be adequately cared for in the development of the regular and supplementary materials.
3. The coöperative work of the teacher and the pupils enriches the experience of every one.
4. A new attitude toward study, organization of work, and the acceptance of responsibility can be attained.

IV. PLACE OF THE METHOD IN COURSE OF STUDY

The committee which is preparing the course of study will need to give serious thought to this problem. That a discussion of general method has a place in the course of study will be admitted by every one who advocated the preparation of teaching materials in advance. Merely bringing the child into contact with material will not guarantee educational progress; the presentation and the general procedure are absolutely essential and are so interwoven with content that they cannot be left out of the course of study.

It is safe to say that no subject will give general training to the mind if content alone is considered. Training is as much a matter of activity on the part of the pupils. Method is the procedure by which this activity of the pupils in the content of the subject can be guaranteed. Therefore, if the course of study is to contain content or activities through which objectives are to be realized, it is imperative that the committee and teachers devote considerable time and effort to the determination of the best possible approaches in assisting pupils to assimilate content in any particular field.

Since method is so closely related to objectives and content, it should be placed next to content in the course of study. This will enable the teacher to visualize at once the goals to be attained, the activities in which the child participates, and the teacher activities that will integrate most satisfactorily the objectives and child activities.

This raises an old question as to the extent to which teachers shall be required to follow a particular method of presenting content. This query can be answered partially by the statement that if the efficiency of the method in a particular field has been scientifically determined, the teachers should be permitted to substitute another method only when they have sufficient data to convince the administration that the new method is at least as effective as the one proposed in the course of study. In fact, teachers should be encouraged to challenge present methods and to compare results of teaching attained by the use of different procedures. If the experimentation is scientific, the results will be valuable for the school system, and the work will be doubly valuable in that it will add to the professional development of the faculty. Care must be taken by the administration, however, to see that propaganda in favor of certain methods is not the most important factor in the agitation for changes in teaching procedure.

V. EVALUATION OF GENERAL TEACHING PROCEDURES

The reader has had an opportunity to study several general methods which have been standardized and can be adopted more or less uniformly throughout the school system. This could be done in the case of the Morrison unit, the Miller challenge, the contract, and many others. By way of summarizing this study, it will be helpful to tabulate the essential principles which are inherent in the modern methods presented in this chapter.

A. Child activity is basic; no method can be tolerated which promotes passive, sponge-like reactions on the part of the pupil. The teacher can participate with the children, but the teacher must never dominate the classroom as in old textbook and recitation periods. The teacher should inspire and guide the activities of the pupils, but education is concerned with what the pupils think, do, feel, etc.

B. The pupils must be motivated, inspired, and challenged. If the pupils are to engage wholeheartedly in the "doing" of the work, they will need stimulation through relating their school activities to the life activities in which they are interested. The valid goals of the classwork must be understood and fully appreciated by the pupils and be constantly before them throughout the entire organization of the class program.

C. The principles of learning dictate the steps in the procedure. The method should be made to conform with accepted laws of learning.[26] Every teacher must recognize the following principles of learning which are briefly summarized at this point:

---

[26] F. F. Powers and W. L. Uhl, *op. cit.*, pp. 381-409. These authors present these principles in so far as they have been established by recent experimentation and research in this field. The above pages should be carefully studied by the reader.

1. The pupil must be ready to participate in the activities and experiences. Whether an individual acts or not is determined by his desire to act. It is satisfying to act and annoying not to act at this time.
2. The pupil must participate actively in these activities and experiences since exercise is basic in learning. The function of exercise is to establish associations and the frequency of stimulating the association is reflected in the fixity of the association.
3. The pupil must be motivated to participate since interest is a primal factor in learning. Interest and willingness to participate are determined by the effects upon the learner.
4. The pupil must appreciate the value of his participation in the activities and experiences. When the effects are satisfying and valuable, interest is easily motivated and active participation easily secured.

D. The learning process should proceed from psychological to logical and from concrete to abstract. Every step in the learning process should be based on the experiential life of the pupil, and each new experience should result in more adequate preparation and control for learning experiences which are to follow. The organization of content according to this criterion is a matter for the curriculum builder, but the teacher in the classroom must check the organization and assist in determining suitable procedures.

However, the opening statement of this paragraph should not be accepted as a shibboleth in education unless all of the ramifications and implications are understood. In certain instances the learning of an abstraction may be easier for the pupil than working with the concrete object. Powers and Uhl emphasize this fact:

... Whatever may be desired of the adult, the child's education must begin with the objects that are significant to him, however unimportant these objects may seem to the adult. Take the child to an intelligible environment of fields, hills, valleys, lakes, and woods, or bring chickens, dogs, cats, and guinea pigs, and samples of children's own collections to the school. Upon such object experiencing, lead the child to find his own problems and data.

Object teaching may be either direct or indirect. That is, either the object or a representation of the object, a rock or a word or idea referring to a rock, may be presented. In both cases an external object is involved. Objects have sometimes been called simple or complex according to whether or not the object itself or something in its place is presented. The fallacy of this judgment is due to overlooking the experience of the person to whom the presentation is made. One of the most difficult assignments for an adolescent pupil might be simply a rock. Assuming that the pupil had already learned to read and had seen many rocks, a chapter on petrology might be easier for him than the rock itself. The simplicity or complexity depends upon both the readiness of the pupil's organism and the desired outcome of the experience. Ordinarily, of course, the easiest situation for the learner is that in which both the object and indirect representations of or about the object are present.[27]

E. The pupil should be given an opportunity to evaluate the results of the educational program. Successful teaching demands that the learner be familiar with the goals to be attained and also with the degree of mastery attained by himself. Merely thinking about the objectives will be relatively valueless if the results are not carefully checked by the pupil. Much of the necessary incentive to learn will never be evidenced by the pupil unless he coöperates in evaluating his achievements. These evaluations are opportunities really to think through the complete problem which involves (1) goals to be attained, (2) procedures and materials to be manipulated, and (3) evaluations of results. If grading and evaluating are responsibilities of the teacher, memorization of facts can easily be substituted for thinking by the pupil.

F. The pupil should be given an opportunity to relate the learning in one field with all other subject-matter. The old textbook-recitation method emphasized the materials in one field which did or did not stimulate the pupil to further investigation and study in that field. A method to be acceptable at present should guide the student in relating his study and research to life and all subject-matter fields to give the pupil every possible opportunity for development of broad interests.

[27] F. F. Powers and W. L. Uhl, *op. cit.,* pp. 322-323.

VI. SUMMARY

The teacher and the administrator must recognize that learning within the school is developed through organized subject-matter. In working with this material, it is essential that the student *perform* and the teacher *guide* and *direct* and *motivate* the performance. The course of study is, therefore, a series of pupil experiences in the sense that education is based upon student activity.

The principles of learning should control and define the limitations of the teaching process. In a general way these can be summarized as (1) developing the correct attitude toward the work, (2) providing sufficient exercise, repetition, and use of the facts, skills, habits, etc., to insure mastery, and (3) attaining a pleasing, satisfactory reaction from the pupil. Effective teaching (procedures and methods) must include:

1. A presentation which is adequate and motivates interest of pupil
2. Assimilation and mastery of new materials
3. Application of new activities to practical life situations
4. Evaluation of results by pupils and teacher

BIBLIOGRAPHY

ALBERTY, H. B., and THAYER, V. T., *Supervising in the Secondary School* (D. C. Heath and Co., 1931).

ALMACK, J. C., and LANG, A. R., *The Beginning Teacher* (Houghton Mifflin Company, 1928).

BRUECKNER, L. J., and MELBY, E. O., *Diagnostic and Remedial Teaching*, (Houghton Mifflin Company, 1931).

BURTON, W. H., *Supervision and the Improvement of Teaching* (D. Appleton and Company, 1922).

COLLINGS, E., *Progressive Teaching in Secondary Schools* (The Bobbs-Merrill Company, 1931).

DOUGHTON, Isaac, *Modern Public Education* (D. Appleton-Century Company, 1935).

DOUGLASS, H. R., *Modern Methods in High-School Teaching* (Houghton Mifflin Company, 1926).

FONTAINE, E. C., *Ways to Better Teaching in the Secondary School* (Ginn and Company, 1928).

KILZER, L. R., *Supervised Study* (Professional and Technical Press, 1931).

MILLER, H. L., *Creative Learning and Teaching* (Charles Scribner's Sons, 1927).

MONROE, W. S., *Directing Learning in High School* (Doubleday, Page and Co., 1927).

MORRISON, H. C., *The Practice of Teaching in Secondary Schools,* Revised edition (The University of Chicago Press, 1931).

MUELLER, A. D., *Teaching in Secondary Schools* (The Century Co., 1928).

OSBURN, W. J., and ROHAN, B. J., *Enriching the Curriculum for Gifted Children* (The Macmillan Company, 1931).

STUART, Mary, and OAKDEN, Ellen, *Matter and Method in Education* (E. P. Dutton and Company, 1929).

WAPLES, Douglas, *Procedures in High School Teaching* (The Macmillan Company, 1924).

———, *Problems in Classroom Method* (The Macmillan Company, 1927).

WOODRING, M. N., and FLEMING, C. W., *Directing Study of High-School Pupils* (Bureau of Publications, Teachers College, Columbia University, 1929).

WRINKLE, W. L., and ARMENTROUT, W. D., *Directed Observation and Teaching in Secondary Schools* (The Macmillan Company, 1932).

YOAKUM, Gerald, *The Improvement of the Assignment* (The Macmillan Company, 1932).

CHAPTER XIII

INSTRUCTIONAL AIDS IN ACADEMIC UNITS

I. INTRODUCTION

The committee that is organizing the course of study and the teacher who will work with the completed course in the classroom are mutually interested in the general method suggested and in the specific methods and materials of instruction which will be included to guide the teacher in the presentation of the work. There can be close similarity in the general methods adopted for two different classes and striking variation in instructional aids and specific methods of approach. This variation may be due either to the divergent characteristics of two subject-matter fields or to the needs of different ability levels within the same field.

In the field of specific method, it should be noted that it is necessary for the teacher to have many lesson types at his command if the work is to make suitable progress at all points and the interest of the students is to be maintained at a high level. One general method can be used in an entire curriculum, but variations of specific method are often found desirable in every field and course of study.

The purposes of this chapter are, first, to discuss the common types of instructional aids and specific methods, and second, to indicate the use of these various materials of instruction and specific procedures in the different academic subject-matter fields.

II. TYPES OF INSTRUCTIONAL AIDS

There are various types of instructional aids, and these can be classified as follows:

First, those essential in the acquisition of knowledge, information, and understanding, such as laboratories, museum collections, plant and animal life, geological formations, stars, and social institutions of the community. Many of the materials of this type are experienced indirectly or vicariously by the pupils. Hollingworth lists several types of indirect experiencing which are of great educational value.

1. Seeing the actual events take place or handling concrete objects and materials
2. Seeing the events "acted out," as in drama or pantomime, by people who "represent" the actual characters of situations
3. Motion-picture portrayal of the events, or of actions intended to represent them
4. Photographs, still pictures of significant characters and objects
5. Maps, diagrams, blueprints, and similar graphic representations of objects, facts, and relations
6. Verbal account and description, heard or read, in the mother tongue, using the vocabulary of daily life
7. Description through the use of technical symbols and terminology, indices, coefficients, foreign speech, or similar sets of special and recondite signs [1]

Second, those essential in developing appreciation and expression of ability in the fields of painting, sculpture, music, photography, landscape gardening, home decoration, architecture, metalwork and woodwork, textiles and other crafts, drama, prose and poetry, dancing and sports. These will draw upon the rich heritage of the past as well as current innovations and inventions. The probable developments of instructional aids in these fields in the next decade are indicated by the announcement from the administration of the New York City schools that all classrooms will be wired for the use of the radio and motion pictures.

Third, those essential in developing a command of the fundamental processes. Here are included practice materials in all the basic subjects, work-books, the work-study type of text, and games which motivate interest and achievement.

This analysis of instructional aids suggests the variety and unlimited possibilities in the classroom. Only about 50 per cent

[1] H. L. Hollingworth, *Educational Psychology* (D. Appleton-Century Company, 1933), pp. 209-210.

of recent curriculum committees have developed courses of study that have presented adequate instructional aids. Miss Elma Neal, Assistant Superintendent of the San Antonio, Texas, schools calls attention to the criteria that have been formulated in that system for the purpose of determining the selection of materials of instruction:

1. The material should be suited to the physical development of the children, and should provide for normal physical growth. The material should be easy to handle and should be not so heavy or unwieldy as to strain muscles

2. The material should be suited to the intellectual and social development of the children, and should foster this growth. Such tendencies as the desire to imitate, to construct, to collect, to create, should be provided for

3. The material should be, as nearly as possible, of a type easily kept clean and sanitary

4. The material, as toys, should be simple and should stimulate activities rather than mere observation

5. The material should satisfy and develop children's esthetic nature [2]

The instructional aids selected according to these criteria included extensive provision of raw materials and a few simple tools for construction of various types, as woodwork, painting, and table representation, sewing, clay modeling, and weaving; room libraries; maps and globes; various musical instruments, phonograph, and radio; toys and games for dramatic play, for physical and intellectual recreation, and in some cases for arithmetic as a by-product; printing sets; visual aids, specifically including moving-picture projector, stereopticon, stereoscopes, films, slides, printed pictures, stereographs, and magnifying glass; materials for nature study, as collecting jars and nets, aquarium, pets and appropriate cages or pens; and playground centers, with equipment for play and for gardening.

A very interesting organization of instructional aids for formal, less formal, and informal classroom procedure is presented in Circular No. 2 of the "Informal Teaching Series" of the New York State Education Department, Materials and Sup-

[2] *Social Studies for the First Five Grades* (San Antonio Public Schools, 1929).

plies in Unit Teaching, 1933. Since it presents instructional aids from the standpoint of desirable characteristics, selection, storage, teacher responsibility, student responsibility, etc., a complete résumé is given:

VARIETY OF PROCEDURES IN HANDLING MATERIALS AND SUPPLIES

1. Who selects materials and supplies?

Formal	Less Formal	Informal
Central authority makes selection and determines distribution	Uniform supply list made by principals, special teachers, and classroom teachers working together.	Selected by those using them, teachers and children, in the light of the varied activities to be carried on
		Provision made by administrative officers for examination, experimentation, and evaluation of new materials

2. What are the desirable characteristics of materials and supplies?

Standardized	Planned to supplement the teaching of skills but used as individuals need them	Variety in type
Uniform for all children in each group	Limited to a few types	Adapted to variety of uses
Small enough to be used at desks	Printed directions for their use a common accompaniment	Lend themselves to uses made of them outside the school
Planned to supplement the teaching of skills		Suggestive of other needed materials
Limited to a few types		Suggestive of many and varied uses to suit individual's and group's growing demands
Use to be dictated by teacher		Use is determined by the individual's or group's purposes
		The use of such conducive to child health
		Tending to large rather than small activities
		Suitably esthetic

514   PRINCIPLES OF CURRICULUM MAKING

3. What is adequate storage space?

Formal	Less Formal	Informal
Small cupboards, narrow shelves	A few wide shelves	Well-lighted space conveniently arranged
Uniform spaces	Many book-shelves	Easily accessible to the work at hand
Placed for teacher's use	One or more cupboards available to children	Adjustable to changing demands
		Much storage space to care for large and small materials
		Conveniently placed for children's use

4. What is the teacher's responsibility in respect to materials and supplies?

Central office sends from supply list items needed to complete course of study	Coöperates in making up yearly supply list	Contributes to the general list of sources and supplies
Teacher selects, distributes and carries responsibility for care and economical use of these supplies	Appoints certain children to make available to the rest of the group the daily supply	Searches new sources for needed materials
		Contributes material of her own
		Constructs needed materials
		Experiments with possibilities of materials
		Makes available to children sources for and means of securing needed materials
		Makes children responsible for care and use of materials

5. What are the children's responsibilities with respect to materials and supplies?

Use materials given them as directed	Most capable children have opportunities for the selection, distribution, and care of material	Contribute materials from their own supplies at home
Distribute and collect materials when appointed to do so	All children made responsible for care and use of certain	Construct needed materials at home
		Seek available sources of material
		Seek needed material

Formal	Less Formal	Informal
	materials assigned to them	from available sources in a proper fashion
		Children develop a growing responsibility for the care and economical use of their own materials used by all the group

Effective instructional aids should be selected according to the criteria that have been developed in a particular school system. The following criteria have been selected from various recent courses of study and will be suggestive:

1. Instructional aids will be accepted which are definitely related to the current problems and experiences of the pupils.

2. Instructional aids will be accepted which are definitely related to the probable future problems and experiences of the pupils.

3. Instructional aids must supplement the active learning program of the pupil and therefore must be developed in accordance with his ability and powers of understanding and comprehension.

4. Instructional aids should provide for the growth of the individual pupil and the growth of the class as a whole.

5. The development of instructional aids and materials of instruction should be constantly evaluated by pupils and faculty.

III.   TYPES OF SPECIFIC METHODS

The distinction between general and specific method is one of gradation only. However, every field has its own particular problems of motivation and organization, and the definite helps included in the following pages should be of great value to the committee and to the individual teacher. These specific helps may, in general, be classified as follows:

A. The development lesson. The steps in this method are similar to those discussed in some of the general procedures. They consist of recalling previous work in the course, or in courses which have been completed, and introducing the new material either inductively or deductively, depending on the goals to be achieved. It is suggested here because it can be used for a phase of the course as well as for the entire year's work.

B. The lecture method. This method is used extensively in higher education and often in the secondary school. Undoubtedly, it is used too often at both levels, but there are several instances in which it is justified.

1. When material which is not available in the text or suggested readings needs to be presented.
2. When it is essential to make a personal presentation in order to establish relationships between a number of phases of the course.
3. To save time when materials are not available in sufficient quantity for class use. Recent publications and obscure and rare books and articles are examples of this need.
4. To give pupils practice in the organization of oral discussions. This requires concentration of attention in order that an accurate summary can be secured by the pupils.

"The lecture method as a means of communicating facts should have been dispensed with when the art of printing was invented," wrote President Nicholas Murray Butler, in his annual report for 1933. Many investigations have been undertaken to compare the lecture method with the reading method in teaching. A significant study was recently organized at the University of Nebraska Teachers College by S. M. Corey. In a class in freshmen orientation at that institution, emphasis is placed upon note taking. Corey selected two groups of students and gave them exactly the same materials, but, in the first instance, the lecture method was used, whereas, in the second case, the materials were given to the students in mimeographed form. The results are challenging and are summarized here for the student of special methods:

1. Immediate recall is better for materials students have used than for the same materials heard in lecture.
2. The two types of presentation have no very significant effect upon delayed (fourteen days) recall.
3. The scores on tests measuring retention of materials read are more closely related to standardized tests results for reading, vocabulary, and intelligence than are scores on tests measuring the retention of materials listened to in lecture.
4. There is a tendency for students scoring in the highest psy-

chological quartile to do relatively better on reading than on lecture tests.

5. When students in the highest psychological test quartile of the reading group are compared with those in the highest of the lecture group with respect to delayed recall, no significant difference appears. The same is true of other psychological test quartiles.[3]

C. The recitation method. This method is based on textbook teaching, which is, even to-day, the most popular method of giving instruction. A lesson is assigned in the text; individual pupils "recite" upon the material orally the next day or at the next class meeting; all the pupils "recite" the masses of facts that have been retained by them at the summarizing examination.

This method is an educational handicap if the teacher does not realize that (1) textbooks cannot be up-to-date and must be supplemented by recent and local material, (2) textbooks are not adjusted to the work of the individual pupil or groups of pupils, (3) textbooks are not final authority and should be questioned by both the teacher and the pupils, and (4) textbooks force the pupil to learn by the drill method and permit him to acquire command of small fragments of subject-matter.

However, there is no objection to the use of the textbook. Every class will profit from the use of such a scholarly accumulation of data. It is only when the textbook represents the scope of the educational program and learning stagnates under the use of recitation method, that criticism can be leveled against this system. If the recitation is only a phase of the classroom work and represents an opportunity for student discussion, challenges, and thinking, and if the text is used as only *one* reliable source of information, this method can be both stimulating and educative.

D. The discussion method. Since this method was introduced to eliminate the evils of textbook teaching, it could have been presented in the preceding section. It is a difficult proce-

[3] S. M. Corey, "Learning from Lectures vs. Learning from Readings," *Journal of Educational Research,* Vol. XXV (Sept., 1934), pp. 459-470.

dure to use for an extended period in the classroom, unless the teacher is a scholar and an artist in developing an issue or principle. Too often, it is merely a harangue by the teacher and silly conversation on the part of the pupils. Such an organization hinders thinking of either an inductive or a deductive type.

If the discussion method is to be effective in the classroom, the following steps should be observed:

1. The teacher guides the discussion, limits its scope, and participates sufficiently to help pupils progress in the direction of the objectives rather than merely talking around the subject.

2. The teacher stimulates all to participate in the discussion and does not permit it to center in a few individuals. If the students are assigned to different types of research to secure data, the problem is solved to a large extent.

3. The pupils must appreciate the worth of another's opinion and learn to engage in courteous, vigorous discussions.

E. The laboratory method. This method centers the activity upon the child rather than upon the teacher. The emphasis upon child activity has caused the extension of this procedure until many fields, particularly the social sciences and education, are using adaptations of the laboratory technique.

In having the pupil perform all these activities, care must be taken to evaluate them and to eliminate those which are not educationally sound. Pupils may prefer many activities in science laboratories and classrooms which are unprofitable and worthless. Experimentation indicates that the learning of the pupils could be advanced as rapidly and satisfactorily by a demonstration lesson and the expense of education reduced materially.

1. *Excursions,* which can be taken to the shop, industrial plant, greenhouse, fire-station, post-office, museum, farm, etc. Every community has its own contributions to the field of excursions which will be valuable types of visualizing important phases of life and activity.

2. *Pictures.* Motion pictures with or without sound, stereopticon views, lantern slides, flat pictures, and picture books. This wide range can make a contribution in every field from

the kindergarten through the university. The expanse of subject-matter which can be presented demands an extensive grasp of the material by the teacher. Improved teaching is usually the result.

3. *Demonstrations.* This technique is now being used in science and other fields in preference to the laboratory procedure. The teacher demonstrates and explains the new law, operation, or skill rather than asking every member of the class to perform the experiment or handle the machine. Later, the students will develop individual skills or attain personal results, but the preliminary learning is more rapid because of the demonstration by the teacher. Effective teaching is based upon demonstrations to a certain extent since visual appeal is fundamental in organizing learning activities.

The use of the observation technique does not require a rich and varied group of experiences for the children, but is dependent on the skill of the teacher in preparing for the demonstration and the resourcefulness of the instructor in following up the observations of the pupils. Unless these observations are related to previous experiences and other phases of the educational program, they are apt to remain isolated and of doubtful value. The true teacher will be sure that the children have opportunities to relate observations to known data and to develop new or broader ideas from their experiences.

In order to facilitate this growth on the part of the pupils, the teacher must know what objectives can be realized from this work and prepare the pupils by acquainting them with these goals, stated in terms of what they are to observe. Then, the work must be so organized that the important phases of the program will be apparent to the pupils. Otherwise the attention of the pupils will be diffused too widely, and essentials will be missed. Excursions can represent wasted time and effort unless they are carefully prepared for by the teacher's organizing the trip in a preliminary way so that each learner is aware of the objectives to be attained.

F. Drill as a specific method. It is necessary in many fields to secure rapid and repeated impressions in order to attain mastery of those facts, laws, etc., which must be learned verbatim. Every teacher must keep in mind the law of forgetting and recognize the importance of this technique in combating this enemy of mastery.

Drill cannot be overemphasized as the basis of classroom work. There are very few administrators who do not grant a place to this technique in supervising teachers' and pupils' work. However, drill is difficult to motivate, since it consists of the repetition of the same material. It is used for purposes which can be expressed only in terms of results and for this reason neither the pupils nor the teachers are enthusiastic about it. Recently, teachers in foreign languages, mathematics, and other drill subjects have introduced games, puzzles, and other motivating influences in order to increase the interest of the pupils in monotonous work. An example of this type of motivation in spelling is given at the end of this chapter in the work from the State of Oregon.

Powers and Uhl make the following summary statement of their discussion of drill:

Drill should be an attentive process if it is to be effective. The routine mumbling of verb forms or the mechanical parroting of formulæ is not productive of good learning. Only when attention is at a reasonably high pitch can material which is being gone over and over be expected to register. The teacher should ask students from time to time to explain material which is being memorized or drilled upon in other ways in order to insure that what is being covered is being understood and that active attention is being maintained. For this reason the practice of having students write exercises hundreds of times is probably not sound. Interest flags and desire to learn along with it. Indeed, the whole emphasis should not be upon any given set number of drills but pupil-needs to acquire mastery of the material. Obvious as this may seem, it is unfortunately not always the case, and many teachers still follow the practice of assigning the same class drills for all pupils. Only when drill becomes an active, attentive, rationalized practice pitched in terms of individual needs will a correct place be accorded it in the learning process.[4]

[4] F. F. Powers and W. L. Uhl, *Psychological Principles of Education* (The Century Company, 1933), p. 292.

G. The method of developing appreciation. Appreciation is based upon knowledge and understanding, but the approach cannot be through facts, drill, or analytical procedures. It is based on the emotional response of the child and is basic for the development of new feelings and attitudes. The material presented must be upon the level of the child, vitally interesting to him, and presented in a socialized atmosphere. Appreciation develops through discussing, comparing points of view, and developing standards by which future selection will be made. Appreciations are not developed unless new attitudes are induced. It is easier to teach literature as a drill lesson than as an appreciation lesson, and for this reason, teachers attempt to realize appreciation objectives through the drill technique.

H. The review-test technique. This technique provides for reflective thinking and the organization of facts and data which have been secured. It may take the form of oral quizzes and discussions, informal tests, and highly organized examinations. It is highly desirable in all fields to have old facts and associations revived. However, it is possible in the review lesson to do more than this since the repetition and reiteration can be productive of new ideas and new associations. Old and new facts, old and new associations are reflected in the thinking of the pupil. Drill subjects require frequent use of this type of review lesson.

IV. USE OF SPECIFIC HELPS IN VARIOUS SUBJECT-MATTER
FIELDS

The use that can be made of these specific procedures varies from one subject-matter field to another. A study of the procedures advocated in some of the best courses of study in the United States will be illuminating and suggestive to curriculum committees and teachers. It would be valuable to present data from a larger number of courses, but space demands that the author select the course or courses which, in his judgment, make the greatest contribution in this respect.

These direct quotations and summarizations from different courses of study are not presented as perfect specimens of the organization of specific helps for teachers. Neither are they presented as all-inclusive for a particular subject-matter field. They are excellent, however, in many respects and should be valuable in indicating and suggesting both the types of specific method which are to be adapted to a particular subject-matter field and the extent to which these types are being used in outstanding centers of curricular development and revision.

It would be well for the reader to note the specific types of teaching procedures which are being used in his subject-matter field and then ask himself the following questions concerning these accepted methods. Such a thorough examination of these procedures will serve two purposes: first, clarify the thinking of the reader concerning the place of specific method in the classroom, and, second, enable him to evaluate types of method.

1. Is the method adjusted to a course of study for this grade and age-level of pupils?
2. Does this method stimulate readiness on the part of the pupils to engage in this activity?
3. Did the course of study provide for individual difference through differentiated materials and methods?
4. Is this method the most effective procedure in realizing the objectives?
5. Is concomitant learning likely to be realized through the use of this method?
6. Is this method practical in your school with present equipment and scheduled time for the realization of these objectives?
7. Does this method provide for sufficient pupil activity to insure mastery of abilities, skills, etc.?
8. Does this method square with the principles of learning?

English

1. The junior high-school course of study in English published by the Denver public schools in 1931 indicates five specific ways in which the teacher can assist the students:

A. *Written Expression*
   1. Drill
      "There should be frequent drill upon matters of usage. The pupils should learn by repeated use and not by grammatical reasons." Drills should be built upon needs discovered as

important by the pupil in his own attempts to speak and write as well as upon the needs revealed to the teacher in oral and written compositions.

2. The laboratory method
Useful in written expression. Should not be strictly adhered to at all times. Many members of the group, having once learned the desirable procedure, will work more effectively as well as more happily if allowed to proceed independently. For the laboratory method, the following order of procedure is indicated.

1. Choice of subject
2. Planning what will be said
3. Writing rapidly, considering ideas rather than form
4. Appraisal by pupil, based upon the self-help questions or standards set up
5. Rough first draft accepted by the teacher unless the pupil desires to copy the paper to hand to teacher or to submit to the editor of the school paper.

3. Socialized conversation and discussion
4. Self-help questions
Questions are developed by teacher and pupils working together for pupils to use in rating their own work.
5. Supplementary reading assigned

2. The course of study in elementary-school English published by the Kansas City public schools in 1932 gives many valuable suggestions to teachers of this subject.

FUNDAMENTAL PRINCIPLES OF METHOD

A. *Language*
Some fundamental principles involved in a method of effective language training:
"Keep alive the child's natural desire to express himself through utilizing his interests and experiences and through providing a happy, free atmosphere. Develop language abilities and power in a school environment that is as lifelike as possible, that presents many interesting, worthwhile activities, and that calls for real interchange of ideas. Remember that, in developing a skill, a child should meet and feel a need for it, should practice it till mastered and should continue its occasional use—all in situations vital and worthwhile to him. Keep ever in mind that 'learning is never single but always multiple.' "
While the acquisition of a needed skill is taking place, various

learnings are accompanying it: habits and attitudes concerned with school, associates, work, thinking.

"Apply in all subjects and activities the standards of language expression developed and used in the regular language period.

"Provide abundant opportunity for pupils to hear good English. Never let them hear any but the choicest and best from the teacher.

"Use many models chosen from the writings of the best authors of to-day as well as from the literary masterpieces of the past.

"Emphasize the audience factor. Remember that language is the means by which we give our experience to others and get theirs in return.

"Require, in both oral and written expression, relatively short units of high standard.

"Use appropriate objective tests as means of survey, diagnosis, and motivation.

"Use the textbook as a source of needed information, standards, models of correct form, rules, and supplementary practice material rather than as a set order of procedure."

B. *Oral Expression*

Motive for oral expression:

1. Utilize child's interests
2. Base expression on child's experience
3. Provide an audience situation
4. Strengthen the desire to imitate

C. *Written expression—motives*

"Set up and carry on in the classroom activities and units of work so varied in character as to widen experience and stimulate desire to communicate ideas through written as well as through oral expression. Possession of ideas must always precede expression. Ideas come from a background of rich experience. The school must not only know and utilize the out-of-school experiences of pupils but must supplement them with others varying in kind and content. With the acquisition of ideas comes the desire for expression.

"Utilize, create, or recreate in the classrooms social situations that call for types of written expression similar to those used in life outside of school. For example, committee conferences result in written reports to class; club meetings necessitate the keeping of minutes of procedure; room programs call for written invitations, acceptances, regrets; favors from principal or parents must be acknowledged by notes of appreciation; class or school newspapers call for articles, descriptions, advertisements, stories, poems, jokes.

"Utilize expressional opportunities that occur in other subjects as

well as in the field of English. For example, frequent needs for reports, reviews, summaries, outlines, and taking of notes arise in
history, geography, and nature study; arrangement, spacing and
form are always necessary adjuncts of arithmetic and spelling."

D. *Creative expression* (*Language*)
  1. Helpful guides in developing creative expression:
     a. Utilize children's interests and experiences
     b. Seek to enrich and enlarge these interests and experiences
     c. Provide a changing environment and an atmosphere of
        freedom
     d. Establish a feeling of confidence and friendliness
     e. Give abundant opportunity for expression of ideas
     f. Recognize the creative moods of children and use them at
        the time they are manifest
     g. Respect sincere efforts, however crude
     h. Refrain from imposing unnecessary limitations, such as
        rhyme and meter
     i. Help the child build growing criteria.
  2. Types of activities
     a. Making titles, labels, signs
     b. Making plans and memoranda
     c. Making outlines
     d. Making summaries and reviews
     e. Making records
     f. Making speeches and reports
     g. Enjoying stories through listening and reproducing
     h. Enjoying dramatic expression involving life experiences

3. The following suggestions for the teaching of literature
are made in the elementary course of study in English published
by New York City in 1927:

  a. A work of literature is a work of art, and the presentation of
     it should not be minutely analytical.
  b. The goal of the teaching of literature is appreciation, not mere
     information, and the best approach to the subject is by way of
     a "recreational mood of curiosity, and not in the way of study
     and work."
  c. The material should be used at a time when it harmonizes with
     the immediate interest of the child.
  d. The treatment of the work should be primarily social; there
     should be adequate opportunity for free discussion of the ma-
     terial read.

    e. Every opportunity should be given for wide reading. The teacher should encourage the pupils to read related poems, stories, plays, and books.

    f. Appreciation of literature should be extended beyond the literature period through the enrichment of other subjects by literary references.

Reading

    1. *Detroit, Michigan.* (1931). The following statements concerning methodology in reading were selected from a course of study in this subject prepared for the elementary school. It is inclusive and is a very valuable summarization of some of the best work that has been done in the studying and teaching of reading.

    A. There are two phases to the teaching of reading which must be noted—the teaching of reading as a science and the teaching of reading as an art. One implies efficiency and skill, the other, the appreciation of literature. The former phase is emphasized in the reading period in the homeroom; the latter, in the literature room.

    B. The good reader makes fewer eye pauses and regressive movements, and has a greater perception span.

    C. As a result of scientific knowledge gained through laboratory investigations, reading methods of to-day have been greatly modified. The old A-B-C method of teaching beginning reading has been replaced by word and sentence methods. Whole sentences are learned and recognized before being broken up into elements. The first-grade child has made considerable progress in reading before he becomes conscious that words are composed of individual letters. In fact the entire reading program has seen a decided change.

    The method of long ago in which the child was given a book and told to read has given way to highly developed techniques in which means are consciously employed to produce rhythmical eye movements and to widen the perception span. The manner in which reading is done, as well as the fact that reading is done, has become significant.

    A discussion of certain typical current practices for the development of good eye movement follows:

    1. Pleasure reading of simple material in which few new words are encountered is probably one of the most effective

means of fixing and strengthening habits of good eye movement.

2. Another means of setting up such habits is requiring pupils to find answers to questions in rapid succession, under teacher supervision.

3. Before the reading of a selection words and phrases difficult to the majority of pupils are presented and developed for recognition and meaning.

4. Phrase drill is given to pupils who are inclined to be word-by-word readers, in order to aid the eye in taking in as much as possible at a glance.

5. In early stages of the learning process, opportunity is generally provided for silent reading before oral reading is attempted.

6. Re-reading selections promotes smooth, rhythmical reading. Since familiarity with material makes for better eye movements, it is an excellent practice to ask pupils to re-read, provided a new purpose is given for each reading.

7. Devices which stimulate speed in reading are bound to increase the perception span since the highest degree of attention is demanded. Flash card exercises and timing devices are illustrations.

8. Pupils who read under time pressure are likely to form permanent habits of reading more rapidly than they otherwise would read.

D. Vocational studies and scientific investigations in the field of measurement have greatly influenced teaching procedures.

"Since, by means of tests, it is possible to determine the reading age or grade of individual pupils, the practice of adapting materials and methods to their actual needs has developed, rather than the former custom of using like materials and instructions with large groups assumed to be at the same reading level."

The widespread use of the Thorndike and Gates vocabulary lists in the construction of reading books has eliminated the necessity of a basal text. Pupils may read a variety of readers and so get wider experience without having to encounter word difficulties at every turn. It has also been made possible to construct a reading test involving vocabulary suitable to the grade for which the test is intended.

E. Provide for individual differences through diagnostic testing, remedial drill, and careful selection of reading material.

Divide the class into three groups according to ability. If two or more classes are in a single room, disregard grade labels.

F. In order to develop conscious reading skills, certain organized procedures have come into practice, namely:
1. Measurement of reading growth by means of standardized tests
2. Provision for individual differences
3. Use of materials differing in degree of difficulty, to meet best reading needs in any one grade
4. Provision for a variety of phases of reading at each growth stage, with special emphasis upon those most needed at any particular stage.
   a. Acquisition of an adequate reading vocabulary. The following must be provided:
   (1) Power in effective work attack
   (2) The habit of associating recognition with meaning
   (3) Definite technique in vocabulary development
   (4) Steps in a vocabulary lesson
   (*a*) Selection of words
   (*b*) Presentation
   (*c*) Drill
   (*d*) Check on learning
   b. Ability to read narrative material in such a way as to comprehend the main points and as rapidly as is consistent with such comprehension.
   Typical procedure
   (1) Use of motive question
   (2) Giving several titles from which pupils select the one most appropriate to the story
   (3) Use of comprehension checks which take account of important incidents only. (A motive question is one which leads the pupil to read on until he finds the answer.)
   c. Acquisition of a rapid rate of reading. Use of contests, etc.
   d. Ability to read factual material in such a way as to get desired information and to acquire effective habits of study through the use of such material. The following must be provided:
   (1) A point of contact which insures the child's whole-hearted interest and attention as he reads
   (2) Practice in getting information
   (3) Practice in organizing material
   (4) Practice in retention of information—through

written checks at close of the lesson, discussion, written tests after several days, etc.

    e. Ability to read directions in such a way as to carry out the purpose indicated:
        (1) Constructing
        (2) Drawing
        (3) Acting
    f. Ability to read orally well enough to convey the thought to others.

2. A clear and carefully developed statement of procedures in reading is presented in the course of study for grades four to eight inclusive in the Philadelphia, Pennsylvania, public schools. This extended summary is presented because of its value to teachers and committees working in this field. The course was published in 1930.

PROCEDURES IN READING

A. *Choice of lesson type*—Three fundamental types of reading lesson
    1. Lessons primarily to secure and organize information (study type)
    2. Lessons primarily to improve techniques of oral reading (audience reading)
    3. Lessons primarily for appreciation and enjoyment (recreational reading)

B. *Preparation*
    1. Teacher aim: Central aim for the individual lesson. Every reading lesson should have a definite objective.
    2. The teacher's preparation for the reading lesson
        a. What specific objective is to be accomplished in this particular unit of reading?
        b. What is the relation of this specific aim to the broader aims of reading?
        c. Has the class a reading background adequate for the development of the particular reading unit?
        d. What difficulties should be anticipated and removed?
        e. What is there in the experience of the average pupil which will afford an adequate approach to the lesson?
        f. What definite and specific purposes should the child have in this lesson?
        g. What follow-up work is necessary?

     h. Is a check-up of outcomes necessary? What is the best way to make this check?
3. Enlistment of child purpose

    The fact that a pupil has had certain prerequisite experience is not enough; he must have it recalled to mind through his own pleasurable activity.

    The child's interest must be directed into desirable channels through introductory questions and suggestions; his purposes must be definite and specific.

4. Development of fundamental concepts that will not be grasped through context

    In preparing children for a lesson, it frequently becomes necessary to give them a knowledge of the meanings of key words or difficult expressions.

C. *Choice of material*
1. Should come from a variety of sources and from widely varied fields
2. Must be suited to reading abilities of the children. Comparatively easy material in greater amounts is more interesting and effective than the reading of more complex units.
3. Material must be appropriate to the objectives.

D. *Appropriateness of method*
1. Method must vary with the type of lesson.
2. Method must be appropriate to specific objectives.
3. Method must be appropriate to grade location of pupils.

E. *The teacher's questions*
1. The question is the chief means of guiding the mental attitude of pupils. It supplies motive for effort and a basis for the selection and organization of data.
2. In the lesson approach, the question serves to
    a. Recall past experience
    b. Stimulate interest
    c. Set the conditions of a problem
3. In the lesson development, the question should aim to:
    a. Give direction to pupil procedure
    b. Aid the pupil in determining the main idea
    c. Assist in the interpretation, organization, and summarization of data
    d. Help pupils to determine relative importance of different facts
    e. Prove or disprove statements

  f. Test comprehension by requiring pupils to indicate that they have understood what has been read
4. In testing pupil outcomes and attitudes, the question serves to
  a. Stimulate wider reading in search of further information
  b. Develop an appreciation of shades of meaning, niceties of difference and accuracy of expression
  c. Create definiteness of opinion
  d. Encourage desirable attitudes toward reading

F. *Pupil activity*

Emphasis should be on actual reading. In every lesson there should be some form of expressional activity.

G. *The audience situation*

Valuable reading experiences now become matters of common concern through the process of sharing. The audience situation should be characterized by mutual interest, adequate standards of expression, courteous attention, mental participation, self-criticism, helpful criticism by others when invited, and sportsmanlike acceptance of such criticism.

H. *Outcomes*

After each lesson or series of lessons the teacher should check to see what outcomes have been furthered.

I. *Individual differences*

Constantly observe the way in which pupils read silently. Study them from the point of view of ability to learn as well as of reading achievement. Slow learners need deeper and keener motivation, more cultivation of the fundamental habits, simpler material, more specific individual assignment, and closer supervision.

The multiple assignment is one of the best means of meeting individual differences. Two general types:

1. Different groups may be assigned work of varying difficulty.
2. The assignment may contain essential points to be accomplished by all, and additional work to be covered by those who are able to do it.

Diagnosis of individual weaknesses followed by remedial practice is necessary.

J. *Testing of outcomes*

Establishes goals for teacher and pupil and determines progress toward goals. Extent of child's reading can be measured only in terms of amount read. Attitudes can be measured only by indirect study of his reactions. Habits and skills can be measured by the use of oral, written, or action responses. Written responses are best on the whole.

K. *In the intermediate grades the fundamental habits of silent reading should be improved through:*

1. Continued development of independence in word recognition —to be secured through:
    a. Remedial treatment for those deficient in independent work analysis
    b. Care that all pupils know common sight words
    c. Checking habits of attack upon new words to discover pupils needing to improve ineffective habits

2. Growth in vocabulary—to be secured through:
    a. Extension of actual experiences and wide, varied reading
    b. Special attention to important words and idioms in geography, history, arithmetic, and other school subjects
    c. Study of difficult or unfamiliar words in context
    d. Preliminary presentation of the difficult words occurring in the selection to be read
    e. Training in the intelligent and rapid use of the dictionary
    f. Attention to words in context whose value will be increased because of study of certain prefixes, suffixes and stems provided for in the Course of Study in English
    g. Exercises in classifying words as to thought relationships

3. Increased comprehension of sentences, paragraphs, and larger units.

4. Improving rate of silent reading
    a. Procedure
        (1) Arouse a strong purpose to read rapidly in appropriate situations
        (2) Use material suited in difficulty to the child's level of development
        (3) Provide the sort of practice needed
        (4) Give the child objective evidence of his improvement
    b. Hindrances
        (1) Lack of will to read rapidly
        (2) Poor comprehension
        (3) Lip movements
        (4) Irregular and unrhythmic eye movements
        (5) Recognizing only single letters or words instead of larger units
        (6) Insufficient practice in rapid silent reading

5. Special remedial work
    a. Preliminary diagnosis

    b. Continuous diagnosis through the use of informal reading tests
    c. Individual diagnosis of special cases
        (1) Test of oral reading
        (2) Determination of visual, auditory, and speech defects
        (3) Determination of reading difficulties in content subjects such as history and geography
        (4) Determination of language handicap in the home
        (5) Determination of experience background
    d. Remedial instruction
        (1) Secure pupil's interest
        (2) Begin with exercises that are simple enough for the pupil to be fairly successful with them; this is very important
        (3) Be sure that the pupil gets plenty of successful practice in reading which is interesting to him
        (4) Use those teaching methods which any skilful teacher would use for pupils having difficulties
        (5) Keep a record of the pupil's progress

L. *Development of skills in reading for study*

Incidental reading activities are important. Specific training is necessary. Every lesson will involve:

1. Location of material
2. Comprehension of material
3. Retention and recall of material

Science

1. *Oakland, California.* A most complete, interesting, and suggestive discussion of methods appropriate to elementary science is presented in the course of study in science for the elementary schools of Oakland (published 1932). Because of its value, a rather comprehensive outline is included:

I. GENERAL SUGGESTIONS AS TO METHOD

Rightly viewed, the sciences that are taught in the elementary schools and in secondary schools are distinct and independent of each other in approach, method, and purpose. Elementary science should be approached as we approach the appreciation subjects—through the emotions. The appeal to the student should be through the senses and through enjoyment. In high-school grades the method is technically scientific; in the lower grades, informal and spontaneous. It is, however, noteworthy that elementary-school children can gain a scientific attitude and method. They are capable of drawing conclusions from observation and, with guidance, are capable of making correct generalizations. This ability safeguards them from current misconceptions and superstitions.

There can be little teaching of a direct nature on such themes as conservation or spiritual communion with nature, yet if these are held as goals in the teacher's mind throughout her handling of materials and problems, their accomplishment is much more probable. Both must grow from within the child out of a deep love of nature.

One of the important phases of science study is the teaching of conservation. Every child should have instruction in conservation in each grade.

The correlation of subject-matter in science with the Oakland course of study in social studies has been worked out rather fully. This section is intended to be used as a check-list from which the teacher selects material or subject-matter available to her for incorporation into work planned. This correlation will enrich both courses. It is not intended that science work stop at this point. It is in no degree subordinate to the social studies.

Adaptation of the content and methods of the course to special classes has been left entirely to the teachers of such classes. Children in the special classes seem to possess special aptitude and interest in nature study. Adjustment in some phases of the work, as in reading assigned, will be necessary. The concreteness of the content makes elementary science ideal as a center of interest in these special classes.

II. SUGGESTIONS TO TEACHERS

A. Types of activities

Large emphasis falls upon activity, since the course is constructed in terms of the child's first-hand experience and his real environment. He will, therefore, be engaged in carrying out purposes which to him seem worth while. Through his purposeful activity he will relate meanings. Out of these worth-while experiences other valuable experiences will come.

Reading is the central activity for most of the content subjects. There is a different emphasis upon activities in elementary science, since emphasis is upon first-hand, not upon vicarious experience. Reading, however, is an important activity in elementary science.

Observation occupies a prominent place among activities. Other activities of pupils are experimentation, construction and modeling, excursions, painting, drawing, writing, study, and discussion.

B. How to select activities

The teacher, according to the plan of the course of study, constructs her own course in subject-matter and activities. She thus has the thrill and inspiration of creating something for herself and her class from materials at hand.

The aim held in mind in the selection of content should be to assure the children at least the elements of a general view of material world and physical forces. Children must have the opportunity to come in contact with a great number of things and a great variety of situations. There should be numberless carefully planned sensory contacts for the enrichment of their experience.

The central aim, then, of the teacher's plan of selection, is to make the children know their natural environment.

C. How to prepare activities

1. *The approach to the activity.* First of all, the teacher must discover a vital approach, in order to launch the experience in an atmosphere of enthusiasm. Possible approaches are by discussion of the problem proposed and decision as to what the class desires to do, by reading a story or poem, by preparation of an exhibit of interesting objects showing correlated reading materials, by giving an informal talk or telling a personal experience, by showing a few well-chosen pictures, by demonstrating an experiment, by going on an excursion, by giving a browsing period in the library, by discussing the accomplishment of another group, by garnering experiences, or even by giving a test. The function of the approach period is to focus purposes and interests.

2. *Classroom procedures.* When the study is under way, the class will spend time in planning procedures; in informal exchange of ideas, experience, and materials; in problem solving; in using visual materials; in study of books; in observation of first-hand material; in experimentation; in making excursions; and in creative expression in language and art.

3. *First-hand materials and experience with nature.* Dr. M. A. Bigelow of Columbia University, in an article on "Evaluation of Nature Study," in *Nature and Science Educational Review,* April, 1930, maintains that "the most successful nature study is simple observational study of common things in nature as they interest us in everyday life." To be able to see, read, and understand the contents of the book of nature the child must spend time observing, manipulating, investigating, experimenting with, discussing, and drawing up generalizations about first-hand nature materials. With the teacher's guidance he can thus come to an elementary but truthful explanation of natural phenomena.

First-hand classroom activities in science and excursions afield should train the child to acquire facts and discover principles. The teacher should never rob the child of the thrill of discovery by telling him principles or facts which he may find for himself. It is the teacher's part to present materials calculated to arouse the child's interest and stimulate observation and investigation. She will aid him in planning activities and carrying them to fulfilment. She will keep curiosity alive and growing, never allowing it to become satiated. She will educate him in means by which he may satisfy his curiosity. Interest and curiosity, then, are the test of effective teaching.

Every normal child has attributes of the scientist—curiosity, wonder, an urge for investigation, and a desire for proof. Elementary science should encourage and cultivate these tendencies.

The setting for first-hand study may be either the classroom or points outside the school which may be reached by excursions. It is agreed that the most successful study of science comes with the subject-material before the child. Nature lessons should always be given with the concrete reality in view. This is possible through taking the class on field trips and excursions or by using material that is easily secured for the classroom. With objective material at hand in the classroom, children may watch growth and other changes of specimens.

Excursions are specially valuable because the child sees the object to be studied in its natural setting. By going out of doors with the class the teacher may increase the child's interest in outdoor observation and his love and understanding of nature.

The planning and organization of an excursion determines its educational value and scope. For a comprehensive summary of aims and procedures in excursions see *Visual Instruction in the Public Schools* by Anna V. Corris.

4. *Using casual science materials.* As the children grow interested in nature they will show this interest by bringing specimens which they think will be interesting to teacher and classmates. Such objects have an unfortunate proclivity for arriving just at the wrong time. They may, therefore, be put away for a more opportune time. The material cannot be permanently shelved without crushing the spontaneous interest of the bearer. No matter how brief the treatment of such materials must of necessity be, they should be examined and discussed in a way that really contributes to the child's background and leads given that may be followed, at home at or at school—in experimentation, observation, and reading activities.

It is a wise plan for teachers to set aside one period a week for class discussion and reports on casual materials which have been presented to the class and have aroused sufficient interest to have the children carry on independent study and observation.

5. *Experimentation.* Experiments in elementary science are necessarily very simple. This course recommends that all involving use of apparatus be left to the junior and senior high schools.

Since the controlled experiment is such an important tool of the scientist, experiments may aid in giving the child a concept of scientific method. The teacher may give demonstrations designed to suggest problems, to answer questions raised in advance, or to contribute to their solution. Perhaps the most valuable experiments are those which are suggested by the members of the class as study progresses.

6. *Questions.* Questions asked by teachers and by pupils are indicative of the type and extent of the teaching and learning going on in the classroom. By questions which motivate accurate observation, the teacher may lead the pupils to make definite observations. The teacher should check on their results.

Good science teaching will arouse in the child's mind significant questions, to which he may seek an answer by turning directly to nature or to available authority. The habit of turning to nature for an answer to problems should be cultivated early. The child must have knowledge of nature in order to be able to question her intelligently.

7. *Vocabulary.* With progress in knowledge, the child's science vocabulary will grow. Weekly lists of new words encountered may be kept. Spelling lessons, the labeling of projects, specimens and pictures, and the making of charts are incidental ways of keeping science terms before the child's eyes. If these terms are introduced through objective experiences, readings, and discussions, their repeated use should recall the connotation to the child's mind.

8. *Suggestions for caring for objective science material in the classroom.* All living specimens brought to class for study should be safely returned to their native environment. Children may be taught to respect the rights of lesser creatures and to enjoy and observe without disturbing or destroying. It is better to discard nature materials while they are still attractive and to supply fresh specimens than to allow the material to become old and uninviting in appearance.

Collecting rather than hoarding of material should be practised. A collection on display for too long a time loses its educational interest which may, however, be renewed by putting the material away for a time.

Displays of pictures and other material should be arranged with definite reference to the unit of work in hand. Tables and shelves may be placed near the wall display to contain related plants, minerals, ores, rocks, etc.

Questions listed opposite the display awaken keen competitive interest. Pictures or collections which pupils are to identify may be numbered.

D. How to evaluate progress

It is difficult to measure progress in the content subjects; so much of growth is shown in subtle and intangible ways. Teachers and pupils may to a limited degree appraise their progress in science content through reflective thinking. In the field of interests, attitudes, and appreciation—all intangible values—the results of the science course can only be inferred from changed conduct at home and at school. Does the pupil bring contributions to class in the form of books, pictures, objects? Does he give information gained out of school on subjects being studied? Are his questions intelligent and challenging? Does he tell at home what is studied at school? Does he use his play time for any activities stimulated in the science period? Does he show interest, understanding, and enjoyment of the activities of the science program? Affirmative answers to some of these questions may let the teacher know that the science work is having the desired effect of ingraining attitudes and exciting, worth-while interests. The appreciation phase of learning cannot be measured, although an increased enjoyment of nature may be observed.

None the less, specific learning should come, tangible results should as far as possible be sought, and objective measures should be made to evaluate outcomes. Some check, as problem exercises, work-sheets, or objective tests, should be used after every unit experience. This is primarily to let the children measure their progress rather than to allow the teacher to rate them. Tests should cover general ideas and relationships as well as facts.

E. Training versus science teaching

In the field of elementary science there is really much that is heartening on the horizon of the teacher who feels herself untrained. First, teachers with a fine background of science in college often have little knowledge of a first-hand nature that can function directly in the classroom situation. They also have to be enterprising. Children know their nature environment in a first-hand way. Even in a fifth-grade class they may be able to provide the best equipped teachers with information. Why, then, should any teacher feel ashamed to be taught by children? It should be the function of the science teacher to draw out the knowledge and experience of the child. The pupil-teacher relationship in science is unique in that here the child can teach his instructor much. A truly social situation is created wherein teacher and pupils share and give and take in knowledge and experience. Teachers are too often afraid to ask and be asked questions to which they do not know the answers. They can always lead in investigation and in finding out those things about which they themselves know little. John Fiske says, "A wise man of these days is not he who knows most but he who knows where to find most."

This is in no way meant to belittle specialized training in science. It is unequivocally true that elementary children can make the most technically trained ponder over questions and problems that occur to them. Some of these carry us into the realm of philosophy. An active attitude of interest and enthusiasm can make a teacher, no matter what her training is, a leader and inspirer of children, ready to adventure into their nature environment with them. Many teachers feel unduly embarrassed at having to say, "I don't know." They need feel embarrassed only if in the end they do not identify the item of knowledge that the class has come to know.

Entirely too much stress has been laid upon identification in science. It is part of our work to make children appreciate the fact that one can know a living creature well before knowing its name. The naming of animals, apart from other knowledge, is a futile activity. One may know the habits, movements, and songs of birds before he can apply the names. We should teach children that names are not of the first importance. Many true naturalists are unlearned in names.

2. Some valuable hints and references concerning methods and classroom procedures are given in the course of study in General Science and Earth Science for the junior high school which was published by the school system of Denver, Colorado, in 1931.

METHODS OF INSTRUCTION

Space is too limited here for a discussion of methods in science instruction. Many writers on the subject give helpful suggestions. The following magazines and books on method are especially valuable to science teachers:

Bureau of Education Bulletin No. 26, *Reorganization of Science in Secondary Schools* (1920), pp. 1-29.

Cunningham, H. A., *Types of Thought Questions in General Science Textbooks and Laboratory Manuals.*

FRANK, J. O., *How to Teach General Science.*
MORRISON, H. C., *The Practice of Teaching in the Secondary Schools,* Ch. XI.
TWISS, G. R., *Principles of Science Teaching.*
WATKINS, R. K., *Technique and Value of Project Teaching in General Science.*
WOODHULL, J. F., *Teaching of Science.*
Junior-Senior High School Clearing House.
Nature and Science Education Review.
School Science and Mathematics.
School Science Quarterly.
Science Education (formerly *General Science Quarterly*)

The following references will be found helpful in dealing with the slow-learning pupils:

BAKER, H. J., *Characteristic Differences in Bright and Dull Pupils.*
Denver Public Schools, Reprint from Course of Study Monograph No. 29, *General Principles for Differentiation of Courses for the Slow-Learning.*
KLAPPER, Paul, *Contemporary Education.*

Motivation. A few suggestions have been made throughout the course which may be of help to the teacher in capturing or stimulating the interest of the pupils. Motivation which borders on the entertainment variety with no effort on the part of pupils is considered worthless, even detrimental.

Learning devices. Balanced aquaria and potted plants add atmosphere to the science room which is helpful in motivating certain phases of work. A bulletin board for displaying pictures relative to current science interests or to the subject-matter under discussion is well worth the time it takes when handled by a committee of pupils, the committee being changed frequently enough to give each pupil in the class an opportunity to serve. Pictures may be collected from various sources. The *National Geographic Magazine* and *Nature Magazine* have attractive colored plates suitable for mounting on cardboard for use on the bulletin board. The greatest of care must be taken to see that such pictures are acquired through legitimate means. Only old or duplicate copies of such magazines should be used for this purpose. The rotogravure sections of the newspapers have many usable pictures especially for the unit dealing with the earth's surface.

Films, film-slides, and slides on many subjects may be rented from the Bureau of Visual Instruction of the University of Colorado, also the University of Kansas and others. They will gladly send catalogue upon request. Commercial firms also will rent or lend their educational films to the schools. The use of a moving-picture machine (for 16mm films) and any of the following films may be obtained on requisition through the principal:

Atmospheric Pressure
Compressed Air
Hot-Air Heating
Limestone and Marble
Planting and Care of Trees
Purifying Water
Reforestation
Sand and Clay
The Water Cycle
New York Water Supply

A set of fifty slides showing views suitable for use in connection with Unit VI, Geology of Denver and Vicinity, is furnished to each junior high school.

The Colorado Museum of Natural History has made for the use of the Denver schools loan exhibits of rocks and minerals, mammals and birds. These exhibits may be obtained on requisition. Pupils are urged to go to the Museum for instruction on the exhibits. The habitat groups are especially fine. The following pamphlets covering the loan exhibits have been prepared by the Museum and the Denver Public Schools and copies are in the school libraries.

Descriptions of Rocks and Minerals
Descriptions of Mammals
Descriptions of Birds

The National Health Service, New York City, publishes pamphlets for free distribution. These are usable for special reports.

Adapting the course to fit the locality. The course of study may be adapted to fit the local environment which is unique in many ways. Challenging problems may be worked out by the teacher. The following are suggested as possibilities of instructional material suited to the unit on air and water:

Compare the time required to hard-boil an egg in Denver with the time required high up in the mountains. Give reasons for the difference.

Make the report to the class on your experience with cooking in the mountains.

Would a pressure cooker be more useful at sea level or on top of Pikes Peak? Give reasons for your answer.

Why does one feel the heat less in Denver than in humid regions such as St. Louis?

Why do many people have nosebleed when going up into the mountains?

Make a report to the class on a trip to Cheesman Lake, Marston Lake, Watertown, or any place which is connected with Denver's water supply. How was the water protected from pollution, how was it being purified, how brought to Denver?

Coördination with other courses. No general science is given in Grade 8B. To develop better continuity in science education and to make a more common background among boys and girls in preparation for science in Grade 8A, certain adjustments have been made in the home-economics and industrial-arts program in coöperation with the science department.[5]

3. *A Tentative Course of Study in Chemistry for the Senior High School,* published by the Lakewood, Ohio, schools in 1932 indicates the emphasis which can justifiably be given to general and specific method in the development of the course.

GENERAL SUGGESTIONS ON METHOD

1. A modern concept of teaching implies that effective teaching procedures are to be found in the activities of the pupils. The teacher's method is important only in so far as it is effective in guiding pupil activities that will attain the desired ends of instruction. Projects of an individual nature extending throughout the semester enable each pupil to select some interesting principle which he wishes to apply through the use of chemicals and apparatus.
2. Investigations show positive results in favor of visual aids in science instruction.
3. Encouragement of extensive reading in the field is desirable. Lists of recent science books or magazine articles should be displayed on the bulletin board in every science classroom.
4. Science clubs should be encouraged.[6]

Each unit of the course contains Generalizations; Objectives; Teaching Units; Procedures—overview, suggested approaches, suggested activities in the classroom, class experiments; References; Desired Outcomes; and Tests to Measure Certain Outcomes. The section on procedures, which outlines concisely the overview, approach, class activities, and experiments is quoted in full in order

---

[5] *General Science and Earth Science,* Grades Seven, Eight, and Nine, Denver Public Schools *Course of Study Monograph* No. 2 (1931), pp. 16-19.

[6] *A Tentative Course of Study in Chemistry for the Senior High School* (Lakewood Public Schools, 1932), p. v.

that the reader can evaluate and compare these comprehensive suggestions.

I. Overview

The fundamental idea underlying chemistry is that of change, particularly those changes which are involved in the changing composition of materials. Nature furnished the raw or crude materials; man through chemistry adapts them to his own needs. The preparation of baking or washing soda from coal, limestone, and salt is only one of the many outstanding accomplishments in the ever-widening processes of man's adaptation of Nature's gifts.

These methods of adaptation are guided by a confidence in experimental observations and procedures gained through a critical study of fundamental physical and chemical laws; by controlling Nature but never by worshiping her or being satisfied with her crude or imperfect gifts.

For example, helium, which was discovered in the sun, has enabled man to circumnavigate the earth in palatial comfort and safety in our modern lighter than air craft.

At this point, read to class selected paragraphs from Slosson, *Creative Chemistry,* pp. 6-10, published by the Garden City Publishing Company.

II. Suggested approaches

1. Approach through interest in famous chemists, by reading interesting facts concerning the lives and works of certain great chemists such as: Charles Martin Hall and his problem of cheap aluminum; Perkins who found rainbows in coal; Joseph Priestley and his discovery of oxygen; the discovery of the element radium by Madame and Pierre Curie.

2. Approach through the interest in the uses of chemistry to society by noting the chemical work in which the people of the United States have excelled.

3. Talk over the problem of simple application of chemistry to the things close about the pupils. Mention paper, incandescent lamps, soap, ink, radio, paint, glass, foods, clothing, medicines, and so on.

4. Proceed through a general discussion and explanation of the part played by chemistry in the World War. Emphasize the horribleness of the part played by chemistry.

5. Proceed through a general discussion of the part played by chemistry in the development of any specific industry.

6. Through assignment to class find some typical industry

using chemistry, and show how chemistry is used to advantage.

III. Suggested activities within the classroom or laboratory

The teacher should instruct the pupils in the proper methods and then allow them to try the problems.

1. Examination of metals and non-metals by pupils
2. Illustrate solid element, liquid element, gaseous element
3. Illustrate solid compound, liquid compound, gaseous compound
4. Burn Mg, C, S, Fe, P, H (By teacher)
5. Dissolve salt or sugar in water
6. Try to dissolve sand in water
7. Separate mixture of sulphur and iron
8. Filter salt solution from sand
9. Make a compound from sulphur and iron
10. Introduce symbols and use simple formula of FeS
11. Point out the causes of chemical change as contact, solution, heat, light, electricity (Illustrate each)
12. Teacher demonstrate reaction between salt and silver nitrate solutions and explain
13. Have pupils try reaction between zinc and sulphuric acid dil. and test gas with splint
14. Measure and weigh materials and objects in the laboratory in terms of the metric system. Use meter stick to measure length of room and height of table. Compare measurements. Change metric measurements to English and vice versa, until pupils are proficient in performing individually assigned problems
15. Fill a burette with liquid. Instruct pupils about the meniscus, and have each pupil read the volume and record the measurements. Teacher change level each time by opening stopcock a little between readings. Teacher check each reading
16. Measure and compute volume of test tube, beaker, and bottle. Give results in cc. and in liters
17. Have pupils measure out 100 cc. of water and find weight in grams (platform balance)
18. Teacher show the different forms of chemical balances and weigh some five-cent pieces on a delicate chemical balance. Weigh a grain of sand
19. Through assignments to individual pupils to report on the work, handicaps, and successes of early chemists such as Priestley and Lavoisier

20. Have pupils list the names of the elements known at different times (years, 1800, 1930, etc.)

21. Ask for a list of all the elements having names which do not suggest correct symbols and then look up Latin origin and account for the symbols in use

22. To show the effect of water in chemical reactions, ask pupils to place water on baking powder and note all evidence of reaction

23. Ask pupils to place baking soda in a glass tumbler (a tablespoonful is enough) and cover with vinegar. Hold a lighted match down into the tumbler but not into the liquid. Report results and explain

24. Explain that the purest form of carbon may be obtained from sugar, and ask pupils to bring samples of pure carbon prepared at home. Ask them to tell what they did and to account for all changes

25. Show (demonstrate) experiment with silver nitrate and hydrochloric acid and one with silver nitrate and sulphuric acid, emphasizing the ease with which a chemical change is observed

IV. **Class experiments, to be performed individually by members of the class**

1. Laboratory manipulation
   Before the pupils begin work, each piece of laboratory apparatus in the equipment should be identified by the teacher. The pupils should be instructed that a future test will consist of identification of each piece of apparatus at sight. Proper spelling of the scientific names should be emphasized. The activities of laboratory manipulation for this unit are:

   a. Regulation of Bunsen burner
   b. Cutting glass tubing and glass rod
   c. Bending tubing
   d. Pouring from a bottle
   e. Preparing a filter
   f. Measuring liquids
   g. Fire polishing glass tubing and glass rod
   h. Fitting glass tubing in rubber stopper
   i. Boring a cork

2. To study chemical and physical changes
   a. Burn magnesium ribbon
   b. Burn copper foil
   c. Reaction of dilute sulphuric acid and zinc metal

     d. Reaction of silver nitrate solution and dilute hydro-
chloric acid

     e. Definition of chemical change from observed facts

     f. Definition of physical change from observed facts

     g. Listing chemical changes going on in daily life

   3. To study classes of chemical changes

     a. Synthesis (Suggest placing mixture of iron and sulphur
on center of asbestos gauze in forming FeS. This procedure saves test tubes)

     b. Publishing a chemistry newspaper

     c. Setting up science bulletin boards

     d. Preparing a school file of science materials

     e. Following up the chemical ads in a magazine

     f. Making charts on map cloth illustrating laboratory set-
ups occurring in this unit.[7]

4. An excellent organization of specific methods and helps
for teachers can be found in the *Tentative Course of Study in
General Science for Junior High Schools* prepared by the
teachers of the Lakewood, Ohio, schools and published in 1932.
The suggested procedures from the first unit, entitled *The
Value of Animals to Man,* is given in full:

A. *Suggested approaches*

   1. Arrange in advance for a talk by Miss Treat or some one at
the Museum of Natural History. A visit to the museum or a
combination of visit and talk by Miss Treat might be arranged.

   2. The teacher may give an overview of this whole unit by
means of a talk, pictures, charts, graphs, which would bring
out the economic value of different animals to man and raise
significant problems to be solved.

   3. Pupils who have traveled may give reports on the different
types of animals they have seen in their travels.

   4. Display on bulletin board clippings and pictures of recreational interest in connection with the various teaching units.

   5. Read to the class selections from any of the following:

     a. "Battle of the Ants" by Thoreau

     d. Roosevelt's experience with a python as told in his book,
African Game Trails

     c. Recreational reading on reptiles. See references.

     d. Stories of bird life. See references.

     e. Selections from *Captains Courageous* by Kipling

[7] *Ibid.,* pp. 1-4.

     f. Scenes from novels, etc., as found in *Romance of Labor* by F. D. Twomby, pp. 61-83

     g. "The Frog" by Hilaire Belloc in Burton Stevenson's *Home Book of Verse*

     h. "Whales at Play" as described in Paul Siple's book *A Boy Scout with Byrd*

     i. Accounts of the recent explorations in the Gobi Desert as told by Chapman

     j. Kipling's *Just So Stories* and *Jungle Books.* Read the story of Mowgli

     k. *Mighty Animals,* by Mix

     l. Selections from interesting books such as *Smoky, Star,* and *Tornado Boy*

6. Slides and films

     a. Slides from the Museum of Natural History may be secured for two days at any one time.

     b. Slides obtained from Ditmar's "Living Natural History Series" through Bell and Howell Company, 1801 Larchmont Avenue, Chicago, Illinois. These may be purchased in New York for sixty cents and $1.25.

     c. Films of R. L. Ditmar's "Living Natural History Series" 16mm. film. See references.

     d. Films of "Beavers at Work" and other animal films can be secured from the different motion-picture exchanges.

B. *Suggested activities*

In order to work out this unit in the short time available, the class may be divided into seven groups or as many groups as there are teaching units. During the overview pupils may decide which teaching unit or phase of animal life they are most interested in. During the assimilation period there will be wide reading by all pupils, working as members of specific committees, in the library, under the guidance of the teacher and librarian. Teachers must be ever watchful of the plans and progress of each committee and see to it that each child is supplied with reading materials and activities appropriate to his level of attainment.

The teacher is responsible for the use made of the library in these laboratory periods. The librarian is there to coöperate.

From time to time during the development of the unit, different committees will report upon activities being carried out. The work of all committees will be drawn together at the culmination of the unit. See "summarizing activities." [8]

[8] *A Tentative Course of Study in General Science for Junior High Schools* (Lakewood, Ohio, Public Schools, 1932), pp. 14-15.

Social Studies

1. The junior-high course of study in the social studies for the Cleveland schools indicates a number of approaches which are significant for the teacher. The contribution of this course, which was published in 1928, can be summarized briefly as follows:

I. **Units approached through:**
  A. *Finding a pupil interest (problem)*
    1. Use of visual aids, e.g., slides
    2. The development of socialized discussions leading to statement of the problem
    3. Industrial tours, trips, etc.

  B. *Solution of the problem*
    1. Committee and library work in which the class is divided into committees to study the different phases of the problem it has chosen
    2. Students bring in special reports
    3. Visual instruction is emphasized by:
      a. Stereographs
      b. Slides
    4. Socialized recitation is recommended
    5. Supplementary reading and organization of pupil work book
    6. No basic text is used.

2. *Denver, Colorado.* The course of study for the senior high schools, published in 1931, suggests specific procedures for the teacher by stating the exact activities of the boys and girls. These are so definitely and carefully stated that the methods of the teacher are largely predetermined. The ten items listed under visual activities for the pupils suggest rather accurately the procedure of the teacher in assisting in the work and stimulating and motivating the advancement of the pupils.

I. **Units approached through:**
  A. Use of a basic text.
  B. Use of the "interest question," first, to create interest in the pupil as a motive for attack, second, to explore the pupil's knowledge (socialized recitation).

C. Suggested activities:

Visual

1. Read written materials analytically
2. Read written materials for pleasure and general impression
3. Read written materials to locate information
4. Read aloud. Oral and silent reading are two different activities
5. Interpret charts, diagrams, graphs
6. Interpret maps
7. Observe pictures analytically
8. Observe pictures for pleasure and general impression
9. Observe models and relics
10. View actual or reconstructed scenes

Listening

11. Listen during formal presentation of materials
12. Listen during conversational discussions
13. Listen during personal interview
14. Listen to poetry
15. Listen to music

Oral

16. Answer a question
17. Ask a question
18. Take part in an individual interview or conference
19. Engage in group discussion
20. Conduct a meeting
21. Give a special report or "floor talk"
22. Engage in a debate
23. Take part in dramatization
24. Engage in singing
25. Engage in "reciting" or the interpretation of the printed page

Writing

26. Copy material
27. Complete a statement.
28. Make a list
29. Classify items
30. Write a single sentence
31. Make a summary or précis
32. Make an outline
33. Write an advertisement or slogan
34. Write a theme
35. Work a problem

II. *Visual aids*

Geography demands definite and accurate visual concepts on the part of the pupil if he is to receive its true educational value. Use:

1. Objects and models
2. Pictures
3. Lantern slides
4. Stereographs
5. Motion pictures
6. Maps, charts, graphs

III. *The class excursion*

1. Have a definite aim in mind
2. Plan the excursion carefully so as to avoid waste
3. Acquaint yourself with the places to be visited
4. Prepare the minds of the pupils for the particular geographical features to be seen
5. Arouse curiosity as a means of motivation
6. Notify the class in advance that the trip is to take place, and obtain permission of parents in writing
7. Obtain in advance the necessary permits for the places to be visited and make arrangements for guides, who are frequently needed
8. Excursions outside of school time should not be made compulsory; if made during school time, arrange for the care and occupation of those pupils who do not accompany the class
9. During the excursion continually keep the aim in mind; do not try to cover too much ground; avoid conducting an unwieldy crowd; keep the children under control by some simple, easily given signal such as a whistle or call
10. After the excursion, review in class the high points of the trip; if necessary, enrich the experiences through the use of textbooks and supplementary readers; encourage expression of the ideas formed during the excursion through compositions, conversations, and drawings

Spelling

1. *Long Beach, California* (1932). This course is very complete and outlines carefully and adequately the approach of the teacher. An extended statement is offered from this course because of the excellent suggestions which it gives to teachers in this subject-matter field.

I. **Some guiding principles**

   A. The basal list should include words selected on the basis of frequency of usage of both children's and adult's reading vocabularies.

   B. The grade placement of the words in this list should be determined on the basis of frequency of usage for children and on the basis of difficulty of spelling for children, with greater weight to the former.

   C. The emphasis should be upon the development of such habits of study and attitudes toward spelling as objective investigations have proved desirable rather than confined solely to the mastery of word lists.

   D. While it is recommended that in the elementary grades, beginning with the tenth week of the 2B semester, a separate period in the daily program be devoted to spelling instruction, this does not imply that the objectives which have been set up can be attained through the activities of this period alone. As conceived to-day, spelling is an integral part of the language arts and as such contributes to the effectiveness of written expression. Hence, attention has been directed throughout the course to the necessity of stressing spelling in every activity involving writing, in order that the pupil recognize that spelling serves a utilitarian purpose in the written expression of thought and feeling.

II. **Suggestions to teachers**

   A. *Developing a desire to spell correctly*

   If the acquisition of spelling skills is not an end in itself, but rather a means toward securing clearer and more nearly accurate written expression, it seems reasonable to assume that the desire to spell correctly is best developed in connection with varied pupil activities that involve writing. This does not mean that the fostering of such a desire must be deferred until a certain degree of mastery over the mechanics of writing has been acquired; even in the early primary grades, pupils engage in innumerable activities which give rise to a real need for spelling ability, as for example:

   1. Making signs for things constructed
   2. Making signs for the library corner
   3. Making labels for articles displayed
   4. Signing up for out-door play material
   5. Making captions for moving picture films.

In situations such as the foregoing the pupil's eagerness to proceed with the task in hand makes him conscious of his inability to write the words without help and not infrequently leads to an expressed desire to be able to spell. The interest thus aroused should be given every possible encouragement, for the amount of effort which the pupil expends in the mastery of any skill is commensurate with his evalution of its worth.

B. *Developing a technique for the study of spelling*

In Grades II and III one of the major responsibilities of the teacher is to help the pupil develop an effective method of studying spelling. Since the results of scientific investigations seem to indicate that only slight differences exist among individuals in so far as the methods by which they can learn to spell most economically are concerned, it is entirely justifiable to guide the work of all pupils according to the same study plan. To be psychologically sound, such a study procedure should involve visual imagery of the word; pronunciation of the word by syllables; writing the word; and sufficient repetition to automatize these associations.

The method of study presented here in detail is in harmony with these fundamental principles and is suggested for use in Grades II and III:

1. The teacher writes the word on the board and pronounces it distinctly so that the pupils hear the syllables.
2. The pupils pronounce the word, enunciating each syllable clearly, while the teacher underscores the syllables.
3. The meaning of the word is then considered in order that the pupils may identify clearly the word they are learning to spell.
4. The teacher directs attention to the difficult part of the word, if such exists.
5. The word is covered.
6. The pupils write the word on the blackboard or on paper, saying the syllables (or word) to themselves as they do so.
7. The pupils compare their work with the copy on the board.
8. The pupils cover their first copy and write again, then

check for accuracy. This may be done as many as three times.

9. All of the words are again written on the blackboard and each pupil studies those which he finds especially difficult.

While directed group study is most effective in Grades II and III, it need not be continued beyond this point, for by the time the pupil reaches Grade IV he is sufficiently mature for independent work. Individual study, therefore, should be begun in Grade IV and continued through Grades V and VI. Utilization of the general study procedure presented in the preceding grades should be definitely encouraged in order that these desirable habits of study may become more firmly entrenched.

C. *Word lists*

Two types of word lists are recommended; namely, (1) the basal lists as given in this course of study for Grades 2B to 6A inclusive, (2) supplementary lists to meet the individual needs of pupils in Grades 4B to 6A inclusive. The latter list should be recorded in the spelling note books under Special Assignment and should include: (1) words selected from the unit of work which will occur in activities involving writing with sufficient frequency to warrant mastery by the group, (2) words which the individual pupil has misspelled in his written work.

Once a week a test should be given on the words included in the supplementary lists. In conducting this test it will be found helpful to have the pupils work in pairs, each pronouncing for his partner the words he is to write. It is further suggested that in pairing pupils a strong pupil be selected to work with a weaker pupil, so as to equalize the time required to complete the work.

D. *Phases of a typical week's work*

The following plans for organizing the week's work are suggested for use in the grades indicated:

Grades II and III

Monday—Direct group study of the following words according to the procedure recommended on page 10: (1) words in the preceding week's list on which the Friday test revealed the need for further study, (2) a few new words selected from the current week's list.

Tuesday, Wednesday, and Thursday—(1) Give a written

test on the words presented the preceding day. (2) Direct group study of new words according to the procedure recommended.

Friday—Use the period for a written test on the week's work for the purpose of determining to what extent there is need for further study. The pupils' papers should be checked by the teacher and the words misspelled by a number of pupils included in the list for directed group study during the following week.

Grades IV, V, and VI

Monday—(1) Call attention to a chart or graph showing weekly class progress with a view to encouraging the pupils to get better results during the present week. (2) Call attention to the week's word list which has been previously written on the blackboard and concealed behind a map or roller shade. Pronounce each word distinctly, then have the pupils pronounce it. If the pupils appear to be in doubt about the meaning of the word, use it in a sentence. (3) Cover the words and give a written test on the entire list, in order to determine what words each member of the class needs to study. Let the pupils check their own work as the teacher spells the words orally. Papers reported as perfect should be collected and rechecked by the teacher.

Tuesday, Wednesday, and Thursday—(1) Excuse pupils who missed no words on Monday. (2) Call attention to the list of words for the week. Pronounce each and underscore the syllables in order to emphasize the importance of thinking of the syllables in connection with spelling. (3) Review the recommended method of study; namely, (a) Look at word and pronounce slowly in syllables. (b) Note any part likely to present difficulty. (c) Cover the word. (d) Write the word. (e) Check the spelling. (f) Repeat a, b, c, d, e. (g) Repeat a, b, c, d, e. (4) Let the pupils work independently, each member of the group studying only words misspelled on Monday. When these have been disposed of, the pupil should spend the remainder of the time in the study of the words included in his supplementary list. Supervise study habits of individual pupils, giving help where needed.

Friday—Give a written test on the week's list to all pupils. Collect and check these test papers so as to make possible the accurate charting or graphing of the results.

Words misspelled by a number of pupils should be included in the word list for the following week.

E. *Developing a "spelling conscience" and "spelling consciousness"*

The pupil's desire to write without errors in spelling, sometimes termed his "spelling conscience," is largely an outgrowth of the teacher's own attitude toward correctness of spelling. Consequently, insistence upon accurate spelling in all the written work of the school is of the utmost importance because of the part it plays in developing within the pupil an attitude whereby he will be satisfied only with correct spelling.

With this goal in mind every effort should be made to have the pupil establish the habit of checking his written work. His ability to do this is largely dependent upon his "spelling consciousness," or ability to recognize correct and incorrect spelling. The practice of guessing at the spelling of words when checking work should be definitely discouraged, pupils in the primary grades being urged to ask the teacher's help in case of a doubtful word and those in the intermediate grades being encouraged to use the dictionary for the purposes of verification.

F. *Use of the spelling note-books*

Spelling note-books may be requisitioned for the use of pupils in Grades 4B to 6A inclusive. These are intended to be used for the following purposes: (1) recording the correct spelling of words misspelled on the preliminary test, (2) the final test on the week's word list, (3) the supplementary word lists.

2. *State of Oregon* (1933). This course of study is also quoted extensively, since it is both recent and excellent in character. The first section summarized here deals exclusively with suggestions to teachers, while the following section presents an analysis of games, contests, and devices which will be valuable in the teaching of spelling.

Teaching Suggestions

1. First Grade
   a. During the first half year there should be no formal spelling. The time should be given to reading and recognition of word forms.

  b. The last half-year's work should include the learning of the sounds of the letters and writing the symbols representing them. The names of the letters should also be taught.

2. Grades two to eight inclusive, the text as listed for each grade.

3. Special emphasis on dictionary study. Intelligent use of the dictionary is not possible until there is an understanding of the following factors:

  a. Arrangement of material in alphabetical order

  b. Use of symbols to indicate pronunciation

  c. Use of symbols to indicate derivation

  d. Principles governing the explanation of meaning.

4. The relation of spelling to written work in other branches of study

  a. A paper receiving a perfect score should have all words correctly spelled, and be neatly written.

  b. After creative work is completed in language or other subjects, insist on correct spelling.

   (1) Pupils should have a note-book in which to list, in alphabetical order, words they frequently misspell in creative writing. Use this and the text as a source for spelling when they are writing and require help in spelling. Grades IV to VIII should form the habit of using the dictionary.

   (2) Place all new words called for upon the blackboard and have pupils copy them in the note-books later.

   (3) Check the papers and have the pupils correct them.

   (4) Train pupils to find and correct their own mistakes.

  c. Pupils should be encouraged to make lists of individual errors in composition.

  d. An alphabetical list of "words we need to know" may be placed on the blackboard or on a paper chart where the pupils may have ready access to it.

5. Methods of study

  a. A pupil cannot study until he has learned how to study. It is the duty of the teacher to teach him how to study. Heretofore, altogether too much time has been spent in testing spelling rather than in really teaching spelling. When a pupil has acquired a procedure for studying the words in his spelling assignment and has mastered a number of them, he is ready for testing. Until this end has been accomplished it is detrimental to encourage the habit of "guessing." The incorrect spelling may become fixed instead of the correct spelling. Therefore, it is advisable to use the Study-Test method in Grades I to IV. Above this classifi-

cation the Test-Study method may be found successful as
the right habits of study have been formed.

6. Adjustment of individual differences

   a. In teaching spelling it is important to determine the cause
      of misspelling, taking into consideration both the group
      and the individual. Pupils should be taught to recognize the
      causes of their misspellings and how to proceed to correct
      them.

   b. All children do not require the same amount of time in
      studying spelling. Pupils who are advanced may do sup-
      plementary work or be allowed to put the time on other
      branches. They may be permitted to read or to use refer-
      ence works in research on matters pertaining to directed
      activities. The teacher may then give her attention to those
      who need it most.

   c. Impressions of words should be acquired through as many
      sensory channels as possible—seeing, hearing, speaking,
      feeling, writing.

   d. The introduction, pages XXI-XXIV, should be carefully
      studied by the teacher to determine what causes misspelling
      and the remedy for it.

   e. The pupil should keep for his own convenience a list of
      troublesome words. Those he frequently misses should be
      made a part of his individual assignment for review in
      order to assist him in retaining the correct spelling. He
      may be interested in dividing them into groups, such as:
      1. Words I know
      2. Words I do not know
      3. Words about which I am not sure.

   f. The following suggestions for the teaching of spelling were
      compiled from *Spelling,* by Dr. Grace M. Fernald, asso-
      ciate professor of psychology in the University of Cali-
      fornia at Los Angeles:
      (1) The word should be written on the blackboard or on
          paper by the teacher. Underline each syllable.
      (2) The teacher pronounces the word very clearly and dis-
          tinctly. The pupil pronounces the word.
      (3) Time is allowed for each child to study the word. The
          object of his study is to develop an image of the word
          so that he will be able to think the word in all its
          details after the copy has been taken away.
          (a) The visual child tries to picture the word.
          (b) The auditory child says something to himself
              which he can write.

(c) The kinæsthetic child traces the word and so learns to think in terms of hand movement.

(4) When every child is sure of the word, it is erased or covered, and the child writes it from memory. (In learning the word through feeling, the tracing should be done with the finger rather than with pencil.)

(5) The paper should be turned over and the word written a second time. In no case should the child copy from the word he has written below.

(6) Some arrangement should be made so that it is natural for the child to make frequent use in his written expression of the words he has learned.

(7) It is necessary that the child be allowed to get the correct form of the word at any time when he is doubtful of its spelling.

(8) If spelling matches are desired, they should be written instead of oral.

III. Provision for measurement

1. The text provides reviews throughout the course in each grade, and special reviews at the beginning of each semester.

2. Pupils should be required to write original sentences using words learned in spelling exercises, thus providing additional drill in retaining the correct form when once learned.

3. Tests devised to be used in connection with the text are furnished separately.

4. Other tests:

   a. *Buckingham Extension of the Ayres Spelling Scale* (Public School Publishing Company), price 14 cents.

   b. *Morrison-McCall Spelling Scale* (World Book Company), price 25 cents.

   c. Ashbaugh-Ernest James, *The Iowa Spelling Scale,* Journal of Education Research Monographs, No. 3, 1922. (Public School Publishing Company), price $1.25.

Games, Contests, and Devices for Teaching Spelling

In all contests care should be given not to discourage the pupil who has difficulty in learning to spell. All too often a child is a "poor speller" because no one has faith in him. He hears his inability discussed at home and at school until he loses self-confidence and comes to believe that he never can learn to spell and that there is no use to make an effort to improve. In such cases the teacher should arrange exercises in which he can establish a record for himself. Then he may try to break that record on another day. Contests are often interesting to the best spellers only. Those who require the least time and drill are given the most. Poor spellers are eliminated early in the games and so gain little from the contest with others. If, on the other hand, the child who finds spelling difficult can be given a part that does not bring discomfiture and discouragement with it, he is made to feel that perhaps he can win a little approval and so makes a greater effort to improve.

1. Place a big word on the blackboard. Let the pupils write as many little words as they can, using the letters in the given word.

2. Place a miscellaneous list of words on the blackboard. Pupils arrange the words alphabetically.

3. Dictionary drills: Pupils have dictionaries at hand. The teacher announces a word. Pupils locate the word in the dictionary. First location scores a point.

4. Dramatize words in pantomime. Other pupils guess the word and spell it.

5. Sky writing: Writing words in the air. Play airplane. Start the motor (low buzz), then fly (trace word in air).

6. Give the class a list of sentences leaving blanks to be filled with words from the spelling lesson.

7. Time saving: The teacher in a crowded one-room school may go over the study procedure with pupils at least once a week, taking a different grade each day.

8. Spelling demons: Each child has a small note-book in which he writes the words that are particularly difficult for him. When he masters one of them and is able to recall the spelling at any time, he has slain his dragon and may indicate it in the note-book by some special mark after the word.

9. Cooky jar: In a jar or box place squares or rounds of heavy paper or cardboard on which are written words which the pupil has misspelled. The pupil's name is written on the back of the card. When the child can spell the word on his card he may take the *cooky* out of the jar.

10. Booklets: Make booklets with cover designs appropriate to the month—an apple for September, a pumpkin or jack-o'-lantern for October, Santa Claus for December, etc. Each child has a similar design colored and cut from heavy paper or cardboard to which is attached a string, clip, or clothespin. If the child has a perfect spelling lesson for the day he is given the privilege of fastening his apple, pumpkin, or other chosen design to a curtain or other object in the room for display. It is considered an honor to display the design. This device is best used in a one-room school.

11. Sentinel: Teacher or a pupil stands as sentinel at the door.

A poor speller may be chosen for this part. He may have a written list of words to be spelled for reference. The children all line up. The sentinel pronounces a word to the pupil in the line nearest him. If the word is spelled correctly it is considered as the *pass word* and the pupil spelling it is allowed to enter. Those who fail to give the pass word remain outside until all have had a chance, when they are given another word. They usually listen for the correct spelling of some word in the list and are able to spell it when given a second chance to try for entrance.

12. The last word: The pupils choose sides. The teacher gives the first word to the child at the head of one of the lines. He spells the word and his opponent on the other side must pronounce and spell a word which begins with the last letter of the word previously spelled. The next child on the opposite side spells a word beginning with the last letter of the word just spelled and so on, until some one fails to choose a word and spell it. This game is more interesting and of greater value if the words are written on the blackboard instead of being spelled orally. Poor spellers can play this game, as each one chooses his word, excepting that the beginning letter is specified.

13. Relay: The pupils choose sides. The captains go to the board first. The teacher or a pupil pronounces a word. Each writes the word. The one writing it correctly and neatly first scores one point for his side. The pair advances to the board, and another word is pronounced, etc. Before beginning to spell, the pupils agree upon the number of rounds which are to constitute the game. Four or five times around the line is usually enough.

14. Relay: This game is somewhat different from the foregoing, but even more exciting. If there are twenty children in the room, write five of the hardest words in the lesson on the board. The children pronounce and study each one carefully. When all are ready, the children are arranged in four equal rows. The first word is assigned to the first child in each row, the second word to the second child, and so on to the end of the rows. The words are then erased and at a given signal all those who are first in the rows run to the board and write the word assigned to them. As soon as the first child in a row has written his word and regained his place the second child goes forward and writes his word with the chalk given him by the first child. This continues until every child in any one row has written his word, when a signal is given to stop. The row finishing first with the lowest number of mistakes, wins, provided that each pupil has written his word carefully, even to the crossing of t's and the dotting of i's.

15. Baseball spelling: Divide the pupils in the room into two

sections. Have pupils choose a pitcher and a catcher for each section or team. The teacher may act as the umpire. When pupils become accustomed to the procedure, the honor of being umpire may be delegated to some efficient pupil. Team Number One goes to the bat first. The pitcher for Team Number Two pronounces a word to the pupil at the bat. If the batter writes the word correctly the pitcher pronounces another word. If this word is also written correctly, a third word is pronounced by the pitcher. The three words spelled correctly count as a score for Team Number One. Any word missed by the batter is written correctly by the catcher on the opposing team and is counted as an out for Team Number One. Team Number One continues to spell until three outs are registered, when it changes places with Team Number Two as is done in a baseball game. One member of each team must keep the score. If a child at the bat hesitates or erases in writing a word the catcher for the other team may put him out by pronouncing and writing the word. All words must be pronounced by the pupil before being written. A time limit should be set before beginning the game and the game called on the minute.

16. Cross question spelling: This game is good for review. The pupils choose sides. Each pupil on one side has a list of the words to be reviewed. The first pupil on this side defines a word in the list and gives the first letter. The first pupil on the opposite side spells the word or writes it on the board. If he misses it the word is dropped for the time being and taken up later in the review. The second child on the second side spells the word, etc. When all the pupils on one side have had an opportunity to spell they change with the other side.

17. Forward march: Have the class stand at the back of the room. Pronounce a word to each in turn. If he spells it correctly he advances one step toward the front of the room. The pupil reaching the front of the room first is permitted to take his seat. This may be varied by requiring the words to be used in sentences or defined. The pupils needing the most practice have an opportunity here, while the better spellers are soon eliminated.

18. Fish pond: Let each pupil draw a circle on a piece of paper for his fish pond. The teacher pronounces a word to each child. He spells it orally. If correct he writes it in his fish pond. At the close of the period each child counts the words in his fish pond. The one having the largest number is the winner. The poor speller may try to catch more fish for his pond than he had on the previous day. This game is best adapted to lower grades.

F. Foreign language

1. *Latin.* The course of study in Latin published by the State of Minnesota in 1932 considers teaching procedures, hints, and devices in great detail. An extended discussion is given to the methods of developing pronunciation, vocabulary, word study, inflection, syntax, writing of Latin, comprehension, and translation. Following this treatment, which merits the consideration of committees and individual teachers, devices, and specific plans are presented to assist in motivating the teaching of first and second-year Latin.

A. Construction

If the pupils are puzzled about what to give when a teacher asks for construction, let each pupil be supplied with a typewritten model, such as is given below, to use during the test. The answers will be more easily graded because of the uniformity of the points covered.

1. Noun (Word)
    a. Part of speech, declension
    b. Gender, number, case
    c. Depends on ....
    d. Rule for its use, or name of construction

2. Infinitive (Word)
    a. Tense, voice of ....
                                        (give principal parts)
    b. Subject (if it has one)
    c. Depends on ....
    d. Rule for use, or name of construction

3. Subordinate Verb (Word)
    a. Tense, voice, mood of ....
                                        (give principal parts)
    b. Introductory word
    c. Depends on ....
    d. Rule for mood, or name of the construction

4. Participle (Word)
    a. Tense, voice of ....
                                        (give principal parts)
    b. Gender, number, case
    c. Modifies ....
    d. Name of construction of the word it modifies

NOTE: The construction of an adjective follows the participle model except for the first points. It has no principal parts. Give declension.

Illustration: *Cum cīvitās ob eam rem incitāta armīs ius suum exsequī conārētur multitūdinemque hominum ex agrīs magistrātūs cogerent. Orgetorīx mortuus est.*

Incitāta
1. Perf. pass. part. of *incitō, incitāre, incitāvī, incitātus*
2. F. s. nom.
3. Modifies *cīvitās*
4. *Cīvitās* is the subject of *conārētus*

Exsequī
1. Pres. pass. (deponent) inf. of *exsequor, exsequī, exsecutūs sum*
2. No subject
3. Depends on *conārētus*
4. Use, complementary

Cogerent
1. Imperf. act. subp. of *cogō, cogere, coēgi, coactus*
2. Introductory word *cum*
3. Depends on *Orgetorix mortuus est*
4. *Cum* temporal, descriptive clause

Armis
1. Noun of 2d decl., *arma armōrum*
2. Neut. pl. genitive
3. Depends *exsequī iūs*
4. Ablative of means

B. Written composition

Young pupils find it hard to write in Latin because so many different mental decisions must be made before the correct form can be formulated. It is very helpful to have the child analyze each step and register his mental processes and conclusions. Let him copy down the English sentence, group carefully the words into phrases, and leave plenty of room between the phrases for analysis, as shown below.

The brave soldiers	of Galba	the leader
III mas. nom. pl. = *ēs*	I mas. gen. = *ae*	III = *is*

will |not|	be terrified	by great dangers.
II 3 pl.	fut. pass. = *bu — ntur*	II n. pl. abl. = *īs*.

Then in good Latin order, let him write: *Fortēs milites Galbae ducis magnīs perīculīs non terrēbuntur.*

Skilful grouping and picturing of agreements clarifies his ideas of the structure of the English sentences.

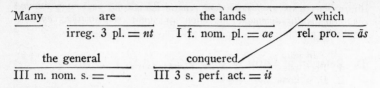

C. Drill work

Many devices can be adopted to make the Latin class interesting and even thrilling to the first- and second-year pupil. It is fun to answer roll call with *adsum* and sometimes with a Latin motto. Drill work should be rapid fire and competition between teams encouraged. Below are some games to be played with vocabulary, inflections, and briefly stated rules.

1. *The spell-down*

   The old-fashioned method is used except that meanings and facts are given rather than spelling. In small classes it is advisable to allow the pupil who misses his word to move to the end of the line twice before taking his seat at the third error. The side with the greater number standing when a certain unit of work has been finished wins.

2. *Pig or grunt*

   One pupil stands blindfolded in the middle of a circle of fellow pupils. The blindfolded one holds a stick and with this taps one of the moving circle. The pupil who is tapped has ready a question, such as "give the principal parts of *rego*," and, if the one within the circle can answer correctly, the questioner becomes "pig" and repeats the performance. The "pig" has the right, however, to challenge and, if the questioner cannot answer his own question, he becomes "pig."

3. *Baseball*

   The class is divided into teams with the two best pupils as catchers. The teacher is always the pitcher and she "throws" the words of a vocabulary to the first man at bat. If he gives the word correctly, he moves to first base. If he misses and the catcher of the other side can give the word, it is a strike. If the catcher misses too, it is not a strike but a ball. On four balls the batter walks to his base; on three strikes he is out. As the second batter takes his first base, the man there moves to second and so on until a home run is made. Innings should be limited by time.

   These games will probably suggest others modeled after popular sports. Many interesting ideas are to be found in

"Latin Notes" published during the school year at Columbia University, New York City, and conducted by Miss Frances Sabin's "Service Bureau for Classical Teachers."

D. Relation of Latin to English

1. *Derivative note-books*

Note-books are most interesting when profusely illustrated —originally or with magazine cut-outs.

2. *Posters for derivatives*

Gaily colored posters to which words may be added as the new derivatives are learned are valuable.

E. Study of Latin life

1. *The Roman people and their houses*

Pupils like to dress dolls in Roman costume and to build doll houses on the Roman plan. Trying to write letters is more fun if it is done with the sort of tools the Romans used.

2. *Military life*

In second-year Latin, if Cæsar is studied, plasticene maps with advancing and retreating lines of pins for soldiers are good. Details of military costume are appreciated if an occasional dramatization in costume is given.

F. The Latin Club

In a two-year Latin course, the advisability of organizing a Latin club should be considered. Pupils in the first two years of their high-school career have more time and energy for club work than in the last two years when they have become affiliated with so many other extracurricular activities and therefore they may thus form early some good habits of leadership and service. Unless there are so many other clubs already established that the administration objects of an additional one, the Latin club for first- and second-year pupils may become a real asset to any Latin department. If the teacher hesitates to undertake a formally organized club with regular meetings and all the responsibilities of continued programs, one meeting a semester may be substituted, with no obligations for future ones.

The object of the club is to give zest to the study of Latin, to vitalize the historical and cultural objectives for which the class period is not sufficient, and to teach pupils to conduct meetings in a simple, formal manner and to be of service to other departments of the school.

There is abundant material for club programs published and sold by the Service Bureau.

2. *French, Spanish, and German.* The following general procedures in modern foreign language teaching were selected from the course of study published by the State of Minnesota in 1932.

A. The fundamental methods of presenting material

There are two fundamental methods of teaching a modern language: first, that of analyzing it as to its grammatical structure until it can be reproduced, so to speak, synthetically, and second, the direct method whereby the imitative processes used by the pupil in acquiring his native tongue are stimulated in the classroom. These methods represent extremes. The tendency to-day is to combine the best features of both. The modern method may be styled eclectic. There is, however, a need for formulating a rather definite balance between the two methods if we are not to find ourselves in a chaos of complete individualism. Before attempting to make such a balance, we may first examine the two older methods in an effort to determine the limitations of both.

The analytical or grammatical method is the older, having been developed by analogy with that in common use for the teaching of Greek and Latin. The analogy is in many ways false. Besides the fact that the modern language is a living speech and should be taught as such, there remains the more important fact that modern languages, with the possible exception of German, are so lacking in complicated syntax as to render useless any extended analysis. Moreover, syntactical analysis looks toward reproducing of the written language, whereas such reproduction cannot be the aim of the high school course. The acquisition of style worthy of the name in a foreign tongue is the highest and most difficult accomplishment conceivable—an objective far beyond the economy of a high school course.

The chief fallacy of the direct method is that the imitative process by which we learn a native tongue begins in infancy and continues substantially throughout life. It cannot be supposed that in a classroom we can give a large group, already beyond the level of imitation, an amount of time or a diversity of language situations at all comparable to those afforded the home. Furthermore, the complicated coördinations required for the development of the powers to think and speak readily in a foreign tongue seem not to be natural to any great proportion of pupils. Again, the direct method shows a distinct waste of effort in failing to use the native tongue for needed explanations. There are a number of matters involved in learning a language which appeal more directly to logic than to memory and might better be presented for the sake of clearness through the native tongue. The reaction against the direct method, as applied in the strictest sense of the term, was due to a general feeling that there was lost effort. The success of a class hour so conducted was often only apparent; in reality the pupils were not understanding what was being presented. Skills based largely on imitation are slowly and inefficiently acquired and quickly lost with disuse.

B. The natural reading method

Considering the aims that have been sketched, much time would be wasted in pursuing either of the above methods as such. Reading for content is without question the most direct route to the building of the attitudes discussed above. The most rapid preparation for such reading is probably the natural reading method, whereby the pupil tries from the first to derive the meaning of a graded text. Grammar should be reduced to a minimum and should be specifically limited to frequency of forms in reading. Reading must be selected with care as to difficulty, content, and interest. Such oral practice and phonetic instruction as is given should be well defined and purposeful. Random oral practice is clearly wasteful.

Reading is most valuable when it unites form with content and interest. We must look for those poems, novels, histories, and art histories which give a broad and true cross-section of the fundamental ideals of the country and a clear picture of the foreign setting. Little time ought to be spent in setting forth the current colloquial speech involved in foreign travel. When the need arises for such diction, it can be acquired readily by one trained in the fundamentals of the language. The same is true of so-called "scientific" readings. Structurally, the language of science or business is precisely the same as that of the writer on general subjects. The vocabulary peculiar to the field can be acquired when need arises. An abundance of general reading, rich in content and cumulative in difficulty, is therefore recommended.

3. An excellent discussion of procedures and devices is presented in the course of study in modern languages developed by the public-school system of South Bend, Indiana, in 1930. It is so valuable that it merits the careful consideration of teachers in that field.

After considering objectives in the field of modern foreign languages, the course proceeds to discuss teaching devices as follows:

Some of the above mentioned objectives are, of course, of secondary importance. What we consider our primary objective has been very concisely stated by Professor Purin:

> The chief aim of a high-school course in a modern foreign language should be the acquisition of a ready and accurate reading knowledge. By a reading knowledge I understand (a) the ability to pronounce correctly, fluently and with proper intonation, and (b) the ability to understand, without recourse to translation into the vernacular or to the dictionary . . . the content of the piece read, in its parts or as a whole.
>
> This definition of a reading knowledge is to apply to the work of any one of the three or four years within the scope of the ground covered each year.[9]

We agree with Professor Morrison [10] that the proper method to be employed can be summarized as teaching pupils to read thought content by abundant experience in reading thought content from the beginning. Therefore the teacher must use great precaution to prevent the pupils from building up an initial habit of looking for word meanings rather than sentence meanings.

It should be our aim to bring the pupil as quickly as possible to the point at which he "sees through the printed page to the message beyond, much as a person gazes through a window without consciousness of the glass." In Professor Morrison's opinion the matter of critical importance is that there should be no transverbalizing, which would accustom the pupils to the notion that language learning is a matter of learning words and forms in isolation and afterward putting them together in discourse which has a meaning. The pupil builds up a vocabulary in which words have been learned from reading thoughts; in his language study the thought, not the word, is the unit.

By means of the thought content method of approach the pupil learns to read not only with greater speed but with greater interest and appreciation.

Oral Practice

Since our aim is to teach pupils to read, it would seem logical to require as much reading as possible. Yet we agree with Professor Bovée that oral practice is the vitalizing factor that renders reading more effective for [11] "if we push them ahead too far, and neglect oral practice, we do not do our work solidly. The oral practice so drills the material that it establishes the reading adaptation on a

[9] *Modern Language Journal,* Vol. VI, pp. 297-299.
[10] *The Practice of Teaching in the Secondary School,* p. 453.
[11] *Modern Language Journal,* December, 1928.

firmer basis, and insures greater permanency to the ability attained."
There must, therefore, be much oral practice although we regard
an oral command of the language as a subordinate objective.

In order to insure the permanency of the reading product, well-
arranged written exercises are equally necessary, but they must be
supplemented by the proper type of oral work in order to provide
for the number of supervised repetitions required.

Types of Oral Practice

Oral practice comprises such classroom activities as the following:

a. Well-prepared questions and answers based on the piece of
material assigned for reading. To train pupils to attend to the
spoken rather than to the written word the pupils' books should
be closed while the teacher is asking the questions printed in
the text or questions he himself formulates. To provide for
written as well as oral drill, after one pupil has answered a
question orally, another may be sent to the blackboard to write
the question and the answer while the class gives its attention
to the following question.

b. As one means of increasing their active vocabularies and
affording practice in grammatical forms and constructions,
pupils may be asked to memorize and to repeat, while standing
before the class, parts of the reading assignment or simple
selections from outside reading. As the study of the language
progresses, the giving of résumés will gradually replace the
repetition of memorized material.

c. Exercises in self-expression will include written as well as
oral work. Pupils may be asked to paraphrase parts of the
reading lesson or they may prepare original dramatizations
based upon material read. "Repeating anything by rote is
not self-expression," [12] says Professor Mercier. "Building in
power through the repetition and variation of language material is a step toward self-expression. But making some original combination of material learned, at the stimulus of one's
own idea, no matter how elementary, is real self-expression."
Opportunities for self-expression vitalize classroom practice
through the development of interest; therefore in addition to
drill repetition we should try to make ample provision for
genuine self-expression, within the limits of the material
studied. (In addition to suggestions found in our own basal
texts helpful material may be found in *Je Lis et Je Parle* by
Clement and Macirone, and *Junior French* by L. F. Mercier.

[12] *Junior French*, p. xiii.

  d. Vocabulary drill on words and terms of frequent occurrence. Sentences with blanks to be filled in provide not only written but oral and aural drill. While the pupils listen with closed books, the teacher reads a sentence, requiring the pupils not only to supply the missing words but repeat the entire sentence. In the exercises in antonyms, synonyms, etc., the teacher may pronounce the word or expression, requiring the pupil to repeat it and to use it in a sentence based on the selection being studied.

  e. Grammatical drill on the forms and constructions occurring in the piece read.

We are using texts which contain excellent exercises. The proper time for the pupils to practice these exercises is after they have been done under the supervision of the teacher, or after they have been approved by the teacher. Prof. O. T. Robert gives excellent advice concerning the treatment of such exercises.... "The exercises," he says, "should not be treated as mere tests, i.e., worked through once with more or less success and then discarded, for they aim not at testing the pupils' knowledge of vocabulary or grammar, but at adding to it. Rather should they be treated as musical scales or finger exercises. After the pupils have been shown how to do them, they should go over them until they are able to do them at a brisk pace and correctly, without reference to the text or notes of any kind. Furthermore, after adequate preparation and practice all types of exercises not requiring that the text be open before the students' eyes should be done with closed books, the instructor reading out the exercises one word or sentence at a time, and the pupil responding from memory. It is recommended that even the written translation exercises from English into the foreign language be gone over finally in that manner. It is scarcely necessary to add that these translation exercises, which are first to be written and later given orally, must be prepared under the careful supervision of the teacher; for they, too, are given not as tests but for the purpose of providing practice in the use of certain expressions found in the text or in the exercises." [13]

The Use of English

Conscientious effort on the part of both teacher and pupil will greatly reduce the loss of time caused by resorting too frequently to the mother tongue.

[13] Introduction to Méreimée's *Colombia,* D. C. Heath & Co.

Grammar

While insisting that our pupils should be thoroughly grounded in the principles of grammar, we agree with Professor Bovée that grammar should be presented as a function rather than as an abstraction. First, there should be presented many concrete examples of correct language usage; and second, correct language habits should be established through practice. At the proper time to clinch the matter, there should follow a clear statement of the grammatical principle involved. To quote Professor Bovée: "It is not a question of grammar or no grammar. It is a question of the most efficient way of studying grammar in order to promote the acquisition of a good reading knowledge and thus attain more speedily and effectively the ultimate objective of the study."

The grammatical principles selected for intensive drill should be those of frequent application and the ones needed as a preparation for future work.

After forms and constructions, whether of verbs or pronouns, have become familiar through usage, if the teacher organizes the material and then asks well-formulated questions, the pupils will be able to draw their own conclusions concerning grammatical phenomena. The exclusive use of the deductive method of teaching grammar deprives the pupils of the joy of discovering things for themselves. Challenging the intelligence of the pupils through inductive teaching leads to greater intensity of interest for it stimulates active thinking.

Pronunciation

Since sound is the basis of all language, inward pronunciation cannot be suppressed without harm even if the aim is primarily to teach reading. Correct pronunciation must, therefore, be stressed. Experiments have proved that it is practically impossible to secure correct pronunciation with a group of students merely by imitation. Teaching students by means of simple physiological explanations to account for tongue and mouth positions gives them a physical means of checking their own pronunciation.

Modern-language students must be taught that a language is made up primarily of sounds, not letters, and that the sounds of no two languages are exactly alike. They should learn, too, that the nature of a sound depends upon the position of the vocal organs, which are the lips, the teeth, the tongue, and the palate. The students may be reminded that an infant makes all kinds of sounds, including the French nasals and the German umlauted vowels. The process it goes through is to eliminate the sounds it does not hear, and to imitate those it does hear. By the age of twelve a child has formed the habit of using lips, teeth, tongue, and palate in a definite way, and this makes it extremely difficult for him to pronounce a foreign sound. Why? Simply because the foreign sound is produced by a relative position of the vocal organs which is entirely different from the various positions he is in the habit of taking in pronouncing the sounds of his native language. The pupils should understand that after the age of twelve the "organic basis" can be changed only by a conscious muscular effort. By "organic basis" is meant the general placing of tongue and voice. The German organic basis is situated farthest back in the mouth, the English relatively farther front than the German, and French language is spoken in the front of the mouth.

Even if the pupil's ear is keen enough to perceive the foreign sound to perfection, he may find difficulty in imitating it because his vocal organs often refuse to abandon old habits, and to form that relative position which is absolutely necessary for producing the correct foreign sound. How shall we overcome this difficulty? We have an extremely effective help in the science of speech sounds, in phonetics. It is helpful to tell our pupils that phonetics is to a large extent merely gymnastics, simply physical, and that we are going to attack the chief difficulties one at a time, and then combine them, in order that they may learn how to use their organs of speech in new ways.

Some of the mistakes Americans make are as follows: First, they pronounce too laxly, because their lips are not active enough. In French and Spanish, and to a large extent in German pronunciation, the position is taken very precisely, the organs of speech are not changed while the vowels are being produced. If the organs of speech are changed during the production of a vowel sound, a shading or gliding off into another vowel sound is the result. The pupil must be told repeatedly to open his mouth, to contract or protrude his lips, and to hold his tongue in the tense position required for each sound.

By Americans all consonants are under-voiced and voice begins too late.

It requires, also, constant vigilance on the part of the teacher to prevent the pupils from transferring to the foreign language the English rhythm and intonation, so different from the rhythmic-musical sentence melody of French and Spanish.

At all times the teacher should insist upon correct pronunciation. After the first few weeks of intensive study, throughout the remainder of their course, the pupils must have extensive practice in reading aloud and in all types of oral work if they are to acquire a pronunciation that would not offend the ears of a cultivated foreigner whose language they are studying.

At first it is probably best to correct each mistake as it is made. Later, corrections may be made after the completion of the sentence or entire paragraph.

From the very beginning the pupil should be encouraged to do much reading aloud in half-voice.

Dictation

Dictation exercises are valuable throughout the entire course. They sharpen the pupils' ears for the perception of foreign sounds, teach orthography, serve as a convenient means of checking the students' aural comprehension of first, known material and, later, unknown material. Dictation gives practice in four different activities: (1) The student hears the foreign language; (2) he writes it; (3) he pronounces it, for subconscious utterance of inner speech is always involved; and (4) he sees the foreign language. On account of this fourfold appeal dictation should not be neglected.

In elementary classes if the dictation exercise is not taken directly from a text previously studied, it should consist merely of an adaptation of material previously studied.

In the beginning oral dictation should precede written dictation, the teacher giving a sentence which is repeated by a single pupil or the entire class.

In the first written dictation exercises, it is helpful to redictate the same passage as soon as it has been corrected. When it is not feasible or desirable to send an entire class to the blackboard, one pupil may be asked to write at the blackboard in the rear of the room while the other members of the class write on paper. This makes it possible to have the mistakes corrected immediately after the dictation has been completed.

Translation from English into the Foreign Language

Translation into the foreign language should be required only as a final step after a long series of excellent direct-method exercises by means of which all the forms to be applied in translation have been so thoroughly reviewed that the translation may be a simple recasting of a thought into the foreign language by forms that have been thoroughly learned.

The temporary omission of translation by no means necessitates a reduction in the desirable amount of written work in the foreign language. In addition to various substitution and completion exercises there should be much writing of useful idiomatic expressions, and the changing of model sentences and sentences in series into all the most necessary forms employed in ordinary speech.

After direct-method exercises have resulted in the oral mastery of a certain portion of the work, its written reproduction should be required.

In an assigned question and answer exercise upon a prepared text, after a question has been answered orally by one pupil, a second pupil may be sent to the board to write both question and answer.

Translation into English

Translation into English should be reduced to a minimum. Nevertheless it is not desirable to discard it altogether. Occasionally pupils are able to give a creditable résumé of a passage or answer correctly questions on it in the foreign language although they fail to understand its exact meaning. And the weaker students are often considerably helped if the teacher calls for the translation of difficult passages.

If translation is used for isolated passages and is not permitted to consume a great deal of time, it will probably not destroy the foreign-language atmosphere of the daily recitation. Translation should be avoided, however, as much as possible in elementary work since its use prevents the growth of "Sprachgefühl."

In his chapter on "Reading" Professor Handschin [14] presents helpful suggestions for handling a reading lesson without much translation, summarizing his suggestions under the caption "Handy List of Teaching Devices." Helpful suggestions may also be found in the new "Tentative Course of Study in Foreign Language for Secondary Schools in Indiana."

Extensive Reading

In spite of our conviction that there should be much oral practice, we are equally convinced that the pupils should devote a large proportion of their time to what is known as "extensive reading." In the early stages of the work, the chief difficulty is in finding material sufficiently interesting and not too difficult. One of the teacher's chief tasks is to stimulate the pupil's desire to read, and to convince him that the only way to learn to read effectively is to read widely, regularly, and with understanding. Provided that extensive and intensive reading properly complement each other, extensive reading not only helps even the less gifted student in realizing his primary language objective; i.e., the ability to read, but it has a beneficial effect upon the other language objectives. As the psychologists re-

[14] *Methods of Teaching Modern Languages*, p. 169.

mind us, nothing can be retained permanently without frequent recall. Much extensive reading makes provision for this necessary frequent recall. "Reading," says Professor Hagboldt, "allows for the necessary respite between several recalls; it reviews vocabulary according to the subject-matter of the book; it repeats the same sentence structure according to the author's style; in fact, with every sentence it repeats some important elementary rule of the foreign language, correctly and vividly applied."

Many helpful suggestions for the handling of "extensive reading" are contained in Professor Hagboldt's pamphlet: "How to Study a Foreign Language in the High School." [15]

4. An interesting and valuable organization of teaching procedures in French is found in the Exploratory Course in French which was mimeographed for grades seven and eight by the Oakland Schools in June, 1927.

Suggestions as to General Methods and Teaching Procedure

As this course need not provide for correlation with a continued study of French, the method of procedure should differ materially from that of the ordinary French course. The important thing is to interest the pupils in the French people and their language. A means must be furnished, then, to stimulate their imagination, so that they may live with the foreigner in his own land.

The teacher should have at her command books on geography and on travel; collections of historical events simply told; English translations of some of the representative interesting stories which abound in French literature; and short biographies of great men of France. She must encourage the boys and girls to report to the class information culled from these books, supplementing their findings from her broader knowledge gained through study and experience. She must prompt them to do creative work in assembling outside material, making drawings, dressing dolls in French costumes, producing dialogues and playlets, etc. Scrap books of newspaper and magazine clippings, post-cards, cut-outs, and French advertisements will afford them much profitable enjoyment. The French flag should be conspicuously placed in the classroom, and on the walls should be physical and political maps, together with a map of the world which shows France in relation to other countries.

The recitation should be enlivened by learning French rhymes and

[15] *Courses of Study in the Modern Languages* (Board of Education, South Bend, Indiana, 1930), pp. 1-8.

jingles, playing short games, and singing easy, rhythmic French songs. The "Marseillaise" should be repeated often.

The teacher must constantly bear in mind that the purpose of presenting this colorful material to the children is to give them an interest in and an appreciation of a people who, through their high intelligence and prowess, have had a vital influence on civilization. Therefore, their outstanding contributions to world progress in science and the arts, and also, an insight into the finer side of the French nature, should be so stressed that it would make a lasting impression on the adolescent, and broaden his vision.

But he must not be led to believe that the study of French does not require serious mental effort. By employing a direct method, one is able to avoid much of the dullness of grammar rules and drill, but the little explorer should be shown that reasoning, application, and perseverance are necessary to acquire the correct use of the language. It is well, at first, to have copied in note-books the language material which has been taught objectively and then placed on the board to show accurate spelling. This material should include vocabulary, sentences, salutations, classroom expressions, songs, and a list of French words that have passed into the English language. Later a variety of exercises illustrating the simplest fundamentals of grammar may be added and also the conjugation of the present tense of such verbs as *avoir, etre, donner, marcher,* and others of common use. These conjugations should be in sentence form and should suggest content for detached sentences in conversation. A few of the common French idioms should be added in order that the pupil may have some idea of the peculiarities of the language.

As it is exceedingly difficult to find a reader suitable for a study of such short duration, it is advisable to introduce a very simple grammar book at the end of the third week. This is advised for several reasons. First, there comes a time in the first stage of language study when the young learner craves the joy of holding the book in his hands, or perusing its pages, and of studying out the English equivalents of the foreign words. If the vocabulary and other material already given by the teacher were based, at least in part, upon the first lessons of the book, the pupil will find a pleasant and encouraging familiarity in the printed pages he now sees for the first time, and he is soon well launched in systematic study. Next, he should know something of the nature of the textbook he will use, should he decide to study French. Again, the grammar furnishes a foreign text that he can read with facility. (The book chosen for this course is: *First French Book,* Greenburg, Merrill Book Co.)

In the brief period covered by this course there should be no attempt at a technical study of pronunciation. Care should be taken, however, that the sounds made by the teacher are imitated with reasonable accuracy, lest bad habits take form in the minds of those pupils who will continue the study. It will be well, also, to explain the pure vowel and nasal sounds and to call attention to the beauty and rhythm of the spoken word. As the facility or difficulty found in pronunciation often governs the child's decision about learning a foreign language, the teacher should avoid discouragement by giving sympathetic aid where it is needed.

Variety in each day's work must be the watch-word. From the first the children should hear spoken French. This may begin with classroom directions which are easily understood through the actions of the teacher and are soon in their possession. Salutations should be practised in dialogue form. Much concert work should be had until the pupils have gained sufficient confidence to hear their voices alone in the foreign tongue. Conversation should progress with the increase of vocabulary. The children should be encouraged to bring to class for translation any French words they may find in English texts. They should also contribute any interesting information about France and things French they may have gained from parents or friends. Throughout the course there should be that free give and take in the classroom which produces a lively interest and enjoyment.

It is suggested that a Saturday spent in the Palace of the Legion of Honor, in the Museum of Golden Gate Park, or at the French Theatre in San Francisco, will be pleasant and profitable. Even though the children will not be able to understand the French language, they will feel the fascination of the novelty and the sound. Such a production as "The Chimes of Normandy" easily holds the interest.

Finally, the content of this ten weeks' course should furnish material for correlation with the English classes through the stories read; with the social studies through the economic study of France; with the subject of music through French songs; and with drawing through the discussion of French art. If this is accomplished, the French people and their language will lose their strangeness, and the boys and girls will have new interests to enrich their experiences.

G. Mathematics

Two examples of teaching methods and procedures in mathematics are selected from the elementary school. The first was organized for grades one to six inclusive by the teachers of Greensboro, North Carolina, and the second was developed for grades seven and eight by the school system of Lakewood, Ohio.

1. *Greensboro, North Carolina* (1932–1933).

"Arithmetic in the grades should be taught as a tool subject in interpreting and solving the quantitative problems of everyday life."

"Street applications in meaningful activities and practical situations."

    a. Use of "Additive Method" in all grades. "By using the 'Additive Method' in subtraction, the teacher is allowed to present subtraction facts not as separate facts but as correlative facts of addition. The reverse form of each fact in each process is taught at the time the fact is introduced. Division and multiplication facts are taught as correlative facts. This method is observed in the basal textbook used." Pupils who have learned another method are not to be required to change. The three ways of using subtraction should be stressed in all grades.

        (1) How many more? Greater than

        (2) Difference or comparison

        (3) How many less? Less than

    b. Division. Division is to be introduced and taught, after the presentation of the primary facts, by the long division method. The psychological reasons for teaching the long division form are:

        (1) The long form shows all the work of division

        (2) The long form is less complicated for the pupil

        (3) There are few occasions when the short division form is necessary

    c. The arithmetic period should be a learning laboratory and follow closely Newcomb's "Purposes of the Arithmetic Period:"

        (1) To afford an opportunity for the pupil to review what has been studied

        (2) To allow the teacher to discover and clear up difficulties which pupils may have encountered

        (3) To give the pupil inspiration and guidance and a realization of the relative value of the several topics

        (4) To provide systematic drill under careful supervision, and an application of the general principles covered in the lesson

        (5) To give the pupil a chance to express his own views and measure his own accomplishments

        (6) To establish tentative and permanent aims

    d. Phases of the learning period:

        (1) The development lesson. All learning should start from the known and be developed through concrete illustrations and applications

        (2) Drill. In the *Third Yearbook,* Department of Superin-

tendence, Dr. F. B. Knight lists the following specifications for the preparation and organization of maintenance drills:

(a) Drill should cover the entire process
(b) Drill should come frequently and in small amounts
(c) Each unit should be a mixed drill
(d) Drill should have a time limit
(e) Drill should have accuracy standards
(f) Examples in a unit of drill should be in order of difficulty
(g) Drill units should include verbal problems
(h) Drill should facilitate diagnosis

e. Application. Arithmetic work should be closely correlated with the natural life activities and quantitative situations common to the pupil in his school, home, and community environment.

f. Problem solving
(1) Teach a simple technique from the very beginning
(2) Stress the analytic rather than the computational phase
(3) The child should be taught to interpret and understand a problem as a verbal presentation of a practical experience involving the application of arithmetical knowledge and skills
(4) Proficiency in problem solving is dependent not on any single ability, but on many specific abilities
(5) Stress thoughtful reading of the problem and selection of facts. Investigation shows a high correlation between reading ability and proficiency in problem solving
(6) The computational step is relatively easy since it involves the application of the facts and skills in the process learned
(7) Stress verification of the findings
(8) The keynote in the solution of problems is found in the accurate interpretation of particular phrases or of single words
(9) Problems should arise from the felt needs of the pupil
(10) Criteria of a good problem:
(a) The problem must be real; that is, it must relate to a situation that is common to everyday life
(b) The problem should be interesting and challenging
(c) The language used should be within the understanding and comprehension of the pupil
(d) The number of steps involved should be limited to ability and acquired arithmetical knowledge of the pupil

        (*e*) Computation should be limited to facts, principles, and processes taught within the grade, or in previous grades

  g. Testing; diagnosis; remedial measures

      (1) The purpose of the diagnostic test is to ascertain the specific needs and their *causes.*

      (2) Since each process in arithmetic involves many specific skills it is essential that the diagnostic test be limited to a particular phase of the work. Each test should be well planned and arranged in order of difficulty, steps, or levels.

      (3) Use pre-instructional tests.

      (4) Use intra-diagnostic tests to ascertain deficiencies in learning. It is important that incorrect practices be discovered early, in order to prevent the establishment of faulty habits or skills.

      (5) Use post-instructional tests to reveal needs for re-teaching and specific remedial measures.

      (6) For general purposes the group test is sufficient. In the individual diagnostic test, the pupil is required to execute his work orally when computing.

      (7) Teachers should analyze written work to discover abilities, errors, and causes of errors, rather than to grade or mark.

      (8) Diagnostic charts are used for particular processes or topics, with the specific skills listed opposite the name of each pupil. Weaknesses and progress are recorded in code.

2. *Lakewood, Ohio* (1932).

GENERAL TEACHING PROCEDURE

This course of study proposes the following plan for teaching procedure:

Step 1. *A class and individual inventory.* We must begin where the children are. During the first two weeks of any semester, the teacher will review the work of the preceding year to get a general picture of the status of her class. Besides the regular daily class work during this time, standardized tests in arithmetic will be administered to all Lakewood pupils in grades 3B to 6A inclusive. On the basis of the results secured, each teacher should prepare an inventory sheet for her class similar in form to the following:

ARITHMETIC CLASS INVENTORY

Gate													Grade
Names of Pupils	I. Q.	"G" Score	Number of Example Missed										
			1	2	3	4	5	6	7	8	9	10	etc.
Mary Jones	115	5.3				x		x					
George Jackson	95	4.6	x				x						
Etc.													

This inventory will indicate in a general way the remedial work necessary upon processes already taught. In addition to an analysis of the results of the standardized test, teachers will need to observe the lowest individual pupils at work. Have pupils talk as they work and tell exactly what they are thinking. Such analyses will often reveal counting, use of crutches, wrong procedure, etc.

In order to set up remedial measures to meet the needs revealed by the inventory test and by individual analyses, two plans for classroom organization of group work are set forth in the Appendix for remedial lessons, in grades four, five, and six. Pupils may be grouped according to their needs, or practice may be completely individualized by having each pupil work to overcome his specific weaknesses. Such re-teaching as may be required should also be done.

Step 2. *Introduction of a new process: A development lesson.* Each new process should be presented by the teacher to the entire class. Pupils should see how the process functions in life problems. One step of difficulty should be introduced at a time and understood before another step is presented. Good teaching arrangement of processes can be found in this course of study and in the adopted textbook. After the explanation pupils may work exercises from the blackboard or text while the teacher closely observes the work.

Step 3. *Providing practice for new process taught.* In order to fix more firmly the new skills just acquired, the teacher should provide adequate practice with effective drill materials. Many of these instructional materials will be found in the adopted text, which should be supplemented with practice materials from other modern texts and work-books for each grade in this course of study.

Step 4. *Diagnostic testing and remedial measures.* "Diagnostic tests should be given during and after the teaching of a process." ——*Second Yearbook,* National Council of Education. A policy of testing after teaching has been adopted in this course of study. The following procedure is advocated: teach—practice—test—re-teach—practice—until mastered.

Step 5. *Problem study in which the new process is applied and the power to solve problems is developed.* Pupils should see the application of arithmetic after the process is understood and practised. However well skill may have been developed in the steps given above, skill in itself is of but little value unless the pupil can use it in solving problems that arise in life. Each new process should begin with a problem (Step 2) and end with problems. The adopted textbook provides ample problem material for each process. Since children vary so greatly in intelligence, teachers cannot expect throughout a class the same degree of uniformity in problem solving as in computation. Suitable problems should be incorporated as extra work to challenge the brighter pupils, while other pupils are receiving the needed remedial instruction and practice.

Step 6. *Maintenance of skills previously acquired.* A systematic program to maintain the skills already acquired is provided for in this course of study in the following ways:
  1. Weekly mixed drills or progress tests—see adopted text.
  2. Group work—see Appendix.

Types of Work in Arithmetic

The majority of arithmetic periods may contain two or three of the following types of work:
  1. Development lesson (see Step 2 above). This type of work is given whenever a new process is introduced.
  2. Drill lessons (see Step 3 above)
  3. Remedial lessons (see Step 4 above)
  4. Problem solving lessons (see Step 5 above)
  5. Lessons of mixed type [16]

BIBLIOGRAPHY

Bibliography will be found at the end of the following chapter.

[16] *Arithmetic: A Tentative Course of Study for Elementary Grades* (Lakewood, Ohio Public Schools, 1932), pp. 5-6.

CHAPTER XIV

INSTRUCTIONAL AIDS IN NON-ACADEMIC UNITS

Instructional aids in the non-academic fields have the primary function of stimulating or arousing experiences for the pupils. This is true of academic fields to a certain extent, but it is fundamental in the development of the technical subjects that the pupils receive first-hand experiences in environmental situations such as the laboratory, shop, studio, gardens, and farms, as well as in the classroom. In order that environment may be understood as well as experienced, it is important that pupils organize as well as produce desirable experiences. Moving pictures, radio, phonographs, books, note-books, blackboards, work-books, etc., are effective means of organizing experiential activities.

This type of teaching and these methods of organizing experience were not introduced into the schools until comparatively recently. For centuries, it was assumed that experience was a part of learning in any situation, and it is only in the last two or three centuries that observation, experience, and practice with concrete materials have come into the school itself. Pestalozzi introduced object-teaching, home geography, and construction into his school, and Froebel organized much of this type of work for his kindergarten. Fellenberg introduced the theory into the United States through the manual-labor movement which emphasized agriculture. While the movement had only temporary success, school gardens and nature study followed in the curriculum. Gradually, progressive teachers in all units of American education have attempted to organize and direct the study of the natural world, and so the school museum, school exhibits, and school excursions as well as school laboratories are expressions of the same movement in 1935. This chapter will summarize the best practice in developing instructional aids in the non-academic fields in progressive educational centers.

A. Art

Two courses of study have been selected to indicate the important teaching devices in this field. Long Beach and Oakland have developed their courses so that every assistance possible is rendered the classroom teacher.

1. *Long Beach, California*. This course is for grades ten to twelve inclusive and was published in 1932.

A. Content and method are listed under three "periods," the acquaintanceship period, the enrichment period, and the creative period. In the acquaintanceship period the unit is introduced, interest is aroused, the unit is explored, discussion takes place. The teacher plays a larger part in this period than in the other two.

B. The enrichment period and the creative period are periods of pupil activity; the teacher takes part through encouragement, criticism, and suggestion. In the enrichment period drill takes place, research is carried on by committees and individuals, illustrative materials are studied, experimentation carried on, and appreciations deepened.

Knowledge and skills acquired in the enrichment period find application in the creative period. Here the imagination of the student is given free play. The students work from their own experience, independently or in groups. Exhibits of finished products are arranged to be criticized by pupils and teacher.

C. Some essentials to successful art teaching:
1. Preparation of the teacher
    a. Enriched background from which to draw for interesting presentation
    b. Definite recognition of aim of unit and purpose of immediate activity
    c. Recognition of the teaching advantage of linking present experience to past experiences
2. Attitude toward various phases of classroom activity
    a. As interesting presentation as possible
    b. Alertness to student interests
    c. Enthusiasm toward students' contributions and attempts

3. Technique of criticism
   a. Evaluation for the sake of future growth
   b. Recognition of endeavor and good points achieved
   c. Constructive attitude
   d. Approach which leads to student voicing his own criticisms. Recognition of such is evidence of growth in sensitiveness and power.
4. Responsibilities common to all class activities
   a. Leadership which effaces self and promotes student assumption of responsibilities
   b. Recognition of opportunities for the unexpected arising out of enlarged interests of students
   c. Responsibility for constantly increasing the student's art vocabulary and his ability to express himself in its terms
   d. Withdrawal of self during a creative experience on the part of a student
5. Consistent building of vocabulary
   a. Teachers are urged to use consistently an art vocabulary and to make opportunity for its use on the part of the students.
   b. To express a thought easily in terms suited to the subject clarifies a growing idea and increases appreciation and creative thinking.
   c. Repetition builds the words into the students' "everyday" vocabulary. They are among his essential knowledges as tools for practical use.

2. *Oakland, California.* This course in art for the junior and senior high schools was published in 1931. It is particularly valuable in illustrating the complete development of the learning and teaching of children in art.

SYSTEMATICALLY PLANNING THE ART LESSON

With art problems the lesson plan can be divided into three more or less distinct steps which combine teaching helps from the different systems previously outlined: (1) preparation, (2) experimentation, and (3) execution. These divisions may be interpreted to include the following general points in the process of art instruction:

1. Preparation, exploration, presentation (development of ideas and thought material)
   a. Understanding of needs of mankind
   b. Acquaintance with material and process

    c. Analysis, study, and comparison of art quality relating to the problem

    d. Principles involved

    e. Attitudes, interests, ideals, and appreciations

2. Experimentation, organization, development (development of fruitful knowledge, functional information, and mental technique)

    a. Supplementary practice and exercises to develop distinctive, original material

    b. Modification, refinement, and improvement of details

    c. Criticism and comparison

    d. Perfection of sketch or design

    e. Working plan or draft (working drawing)

    f. Generalization (functional information, using art knowledge in everyday life)

    g. Mental techniques—development of taste, discriminating judgment, creative ability, initiative, imagination, observation, etc.

3. Execution, completion, application (development of right habits and useful skills)

    a. Completion of object—drawing, painting, modeling, designing, or construction (pottery, woodwork, weaving, basketry, etc.)

    b. Application (using the object as a consumer)

B. Commercial Education

The following courses of study indicate valuable guide lines for teachers in preparing for the presentation of the lesson and the encouragement of active learning on the part of the pupils.

1. *Economic Geography.* This course was prepared and published by the State office of education in Minnesota in 1932. It was organized for the senior high school.

A. General suggestions to teachers

The teacher should make careful preparation before beginning the presentation of any given unit of this course. She should familiarize herself thoroughly with this syllabus. She should see that available wall and desk maps, charts, pictures, and other exhibit material are assembled and ready for use. Failure to do this is likely to result in haphazard and uninteresting presentation of the course.

In introducing a topic the first discussion should call for the knowledges and experiences of the pupils in relation to that topic. The problems to be solved should then be introduced. The use of maps, pictures, and exhibits at this time is invaluable.

The problem method adapts itself most readily to the teaching of economic geography, but the content of the course may easily be used with any other plan of presentation.

Field trips are very desirable projects in economic geography. If they are to be undertaken, the values to be obtained should be weighed against the time, effort, and expense involved. Such trips should be preceded by a preliminary study and followed by comprehensive reports.

The teacher should always keep in mind the physical basis of economic geography; failure to do so will result in waste of time and effort in teaching industrial processes, skills, or techniques not influenced or conditioned by one or more factors of the physical environment.

The equipment for the course in economic geography should include the following as a minimum:

A modern text for each pupil. It is highly desirable to supplement this with at least two additional up-to-date texts, one copy for every six pupils.

One school atlas

Latest agricultural and commerce year-books with bulletins and statistics for the United States

Statistical Abstract of the United States

Statesman's Year-book or World Almanac

Publications of various Minnesota State departments, such as *Minnesota Annual Crop and Livestock Statistics*

Desk-maps (physical-political) of the United States, Minnesota, and the world

One good geography magazine

Supplementary reading material

Pictures and exhibit material. (It is desirable to have a good opaque projector, if one is obtainable.)

The first class period or two should be devoted to orientation work. The pupils should be given an overview of the course. Its aims should be made clear to them and the content to be covered during the year should be outlined briefly. The pupils should be given needed directions for the effective use of the instructional equipment for the course. If this preliminary presentation by the teacher is to be made worth while, it is absolutely necessary that the teacher familiarize herself beforehand with the entire content of this syllabus.

B. Sample problems from division on resources of United States in relation to the rest of the world

Topic: Farming and grazing

Problem: To what extent can the American farmer produce the agricultural products needed by the nation?

1. Wheat

Problem: Is the contribution of wheat to man's needs worth the effort and land given to it?

The pupil may be requested to bring to class specimens of wheat and wheat products and pictures of the facilities used to produce, transport, and mill wheat.

    a. The uses and importance of wheat
    b. Wheat production
    c. Marketing wheat
    d. Pressing wheat
    e. Suggested questions, problems, and exercises for pupils
        (1) List the different forms in which wheat is used as a food.
        (2) Suggest substitutes for such foods.
        (3) Argue that wheat as a food cannot be driven out of use by other food.
        (4) Make a graph showing *per capita* consumption of wheat for the United States, England, France, Germany, Russia, Italy, Japan, and Europe as a whole. Do all people like wheat as a food and use it to the same extent as Americans?

2. Bookkeeping. The senior high-school course of study in commercial work published by the State of Minnesota in 1932 presents some excellent hints and devices for teachers of bookkeeping.

A. Orientation. The first regular class session or two may well be devoted to orientation work. Such topics as the following may be discussed: the purpose of bookkeeping, the value of bookkeeping to a business man, the place of accounting in business, the educational and vocational value of accounting, business forms, business operations, and practices.

B. Presentation of subject-matter. In general, bookkeeping is best presented by topics or by the introduction of principles separately. This should be done with all the aids available, *e.g.,* manuals, references, and tried and true methods. This should be followed by exercises or by the use of a practice set, with frequent testing and review work. This course is not outlined to show exactly what shall be taught in any particular period, nor should there be blind following of instructions. The teacher will predetermine her goal with well-planned lesson outlines and ultimately complete the course as outlined.

In the presentation of different devices, continuity should be emphasized. The journals, ledgers, statements, and other necessary devices are closely related. This relationship should be made clear to the pupil so that he will not, with each new division of the subject-matter, seem to be embarking on an unknown adventure.

C. **Practice sets.** The present tendency in bookkeeping instruction is to eliminate the use of long, tedious, and uninteresting practice sets. Little is learned by the continued filling-in of the same business forms or by a stereotyped routine in the disposition of various forms. The pupils, however, should be familiar with all the forms outlined in the syllabus. They should be able to identify them, to fill them in, to construct them, and to dispose of them correctly.

A limited use of practice sets for these purposes is recommended. A set carried on for one or two months during the first semester and a second set of the same length during the second semester should be adequate. Under no circumstances should time given to practice sets be a "rest period" for the teacher.

D. **Testing.** A carefully planned testing program is essential to the efficient teaching of bookkeeping. The tests should serve as a check-up on the pupil's knowledge and on the teaching; through their diagnostic function they should show where remedial work is needed; and they should help to motivate the work of the pupils. A few minutes may be taken from each period for a short test on the day's work. More comprehensive tests should be given on the completion of a given unit of the course.

Objective tests are recommended as the most satisfactory medium for sampling the knowledge of pupils. They are scored more easily, quickly, and accurately than the essay type. Tests prepared by the teacher may be supplemented by standardized commercial tests.

E. **Laboratory work.** In all laboratory work neatness and accuracy should be emphasized. The reason for the "no erasure" rule should be explained. It is suggested that the teacher draw up a "guide to better bookkeeping." (See below.) Actual problems illustrating principles should be introduced throughout the course. The entire subject in its various phases should be unified and the relationship to actual conditions of business established. In lesson development the subject should be related to individual experiences of pupils and should help them to solve their own bookkeeping problems.

F. Suggested guide to better bookkeeping:

1. Use pen and ink, not pencil, for all bookkeeping work.
2. Use blue or black ink for ordinary entries.
3. Always employ your best penmanship.
4. Always use a ruler for drawing lines.
5. Erasures are not to be tolerated, as they not only spoil the neatness of the page but often make entries look suspicious.
6. Make corrections in such a manner that the neatness of the books and their legal value are not affected.
   a. If a wrong name is written, draw a line through it and write the correct name either above or at the right.
   b. If a debit and a credit have been reversed, correct by writing Cr. after the debit item and Dr. after the credit item. Then post correctly.
   c. If an incorrect amount is written, cancel it by drawing a line through the figures and write above it the correct amount.
7. When writing an even number of dollars, place two ciphers in the cents column. This shows that there is no omission, and prevents the use of unauthorized figures.
8. Always fill in the explanation column. It is the experience of attorneys that very few books of record that are brought into court have any value as evidence, because of the incompleteness of the explanatory matter. If explanations are not clearly made, an entry is of little value as evidence.
9. If an entry is not to be posted to the ledger, place a check mark in the folio column. At the time of posting, indicate in the folio column the ledger page to which the item is transferred.
10. Indicate in the folio column in the ledger the page and kind of book of original entry from which the debit or credit is posted. To indicate the kind of book or original entry, use GJ for general journal, CRJ for cash receipts journal, CPJ for cash payments journal, PJ for purchases journal, SJ for sales journal.
11. When checking your work, use the check mark ($\sqrt{}$) to indicate correct entries and the cross to indicate incorrect entries. These marks should be written on the double vertical line to the right of the money column. Use small check marks.

12. Enter the year on both debit and credit sides of every account in the ledger.

3. *Penmanship.* The course of study for grades one to six inclusive which is published by the St. Louis public schools in 1930 is indicative of the contribution which a good course of study can make to teaching in any field.

I. The course of study in penmanship is planned to give the child the means to express his ideas through writing and to satisfy his desire for written expression in situations of real interest to him. The course is outlined under specific objectives and activities.

Manuscript writing, or printing, is taught in the first grade. The following advantages are claimed:

A. It makes use of letter forms similar to those the child sees in reading.

B. These printed forms are readily learned by the beginner because the strokes are few in number and greatly simplified in structure, consisting mainly of the straight line and the circle.

C. The child's use of printed words aids in learning to read.

II. Directions for teaching manuscript writing at the blackboard:

A. Position at the blackboard

1. The pupil should face the blackboard and stand about a foot away from it, as in the illustration on page 70.

2. The chalk should be held loosely with fingers on top and with thumb underneath, as in illustration 5, page 71.

B. *Movement.* The whole-arm movement such as is used in cursive writing should be used in manuscript writing at the blackboard. Resting the hand on the blackboard and making the letters with finger movement is incorrect.

C. *Quality of line.* The line should be distinct but not so heavy as to require undue pressure of the chalk on the blackboard.

D. *Size of letters and figures.* The capitals and extended small letters (*l, b, h, k,* and *f*) should be written about a space high, and the semi-extended small letters (*t* and *d*) a little shorter. The low letters (*a, c, e, i, m, n, o, r, s, u, v, w, x,* and *z*) should be written about half a space high. The letters *g, j, p, q,* and *y* should extend about half a space below the base line. The figures should be a little higher than the low letters; *7* and *9* should extend slightly below the base line. The alphabets and sets of figures on page 64 show the relative height of low letters, semi-extended letters, extended letters, and figures.

E. *Spacing.* Legibility in manuscript writing is, to a considerable extent, dependent upon good spacing. There should be more space between words than between letters so that the words will stand out as units.

F. *Forms of the letters and figures.* Letters and figures should be simply formed of straight lines, ovals, and parts of ovals. The alphabet and set of figures on this page will give the teacher an idea of how the forms should be made. The letters and figures should be written vertically.

G. *Writing on the line.* Making the letters rest on the base line as shown below is an important feature to be stressed in manuscript writing.

III. Directions for teaching manuscript writing at the desk

A. *Position at the desk or table.* The pupil should sit in the middle of the seat, with feet in front of body and with arms resting on the desk. Leaning over the desk with eyes close to the paper is undesirable from the standpoints both of health and results.

B. *Kind and size of paper.* The pupil should use wide-ruled manila paper, 9 × 12 inches in size, both for practice and for functional writing.

C. *Position of paper.* Straight position of paper (lines on paper parallel to lower edge of desk) is recommended.

D. *Pencil or crayola.* Either the drawing pencil or black crayola may be used. If pencil is used it should be held loosely with first finger back about an inch from the point. If crayola is used it should be held as the chalk is held (see illustration 5, page 71) and the writing done with whole-arm movement similar to that used at the blackboard.

E. *Size of writing.* The size and proportions of letters are fully described on page 63.

F. *Quality of line.* The line should be gray, but distinct. Heavy pressure of pencil or crayola on the paper should be discouraged.

G. *Direction of the movement.* The movement that forms the main strokes of the letters and figures should be to and from the middle of the body. With straight position of the paper this movement will produce vertical letters characteristic of manuscript writing.

H. *Ease of movement.* Speed should not be stressed; however, the movement should be sufficiently free to result in a smooth line.

The change to cursive writing may be begun at the beginning of the third quarter of Grade I. Manuscript writing should not be continued beyond the end of Grade I.

IV. Suggested steps in the transition from manuscript to cursive writing

It is recommended that, during the transition from manuscript to cursive writing which takes place during the last half of the first grade or at the beginning of the second grade, the practice be, for the most part, at the blackboard, until the basic principles of cursive writing have been learned. (See "Materials," page 66.)

To effect a ready transition from manuscript to cursive writing it is suggested that the following steps, in the order given, be taken:

1. *Legibility.* Assist the pupil to learn the cursive form so that his writing will be legible.
2. *Size.* Teach the pupil to write the low letters half a space high, the extended letters and capitals a whole space high, and the semi-extended letters and figures a little more than half a space high.
3. *Letter joining.* Teach the pupil to join the letters of the words.
4. *Ending strokes.* Teach the pupil to write words with ending strokes similar to those shown in the penmanship manual.
5. *Spacing.* Teach the pupil to write the letters of words and the words of sentences with spacing similar to that in the penmanship manual.
6. *Slant.* Teach the pupil to slant his writing slightly forward, as in the copies of the penmanship manual.
7. *Quality of line.* Teach the pupil to write at the blackboard with a line distinct enough to be seen from the opposite side of the room or, on paper, with a gray but distinct lead pencil line. Extreme effects—very heavy or very light —should be corrected.
8. *Letter form.* Assist the pupil to improve, by separate practice, the form of letters that he writes poorly or that impair the legibility of his writing. See illustration 2.
9. *Freedom of movement.* Assist the pupil to write with sufficient freedom of movement to produce a smooth line.

10. *Habituation.* Assist the child to habituate his cursive penmanship so that as soon as possible he may apply automatically the basic principles of penmanship.

It is suggested that the first lessons in cursive writing consist of easy subject-matter such as is shown on the initial two or three pages of the penmanship manual. Separate words rather than sentences should be practised, until the pupil can write them fluently and with good effect in form, including ending strokes.

In the development of good penmanship habits the writing of one word over and over with definite aim for improvement is decidedly preferable to the writing once of each of a number of different words. After first practice, a practised or key word may be used alternately with a new word for the purpose of aiding the pupil to write the new word well. Finally, the new word may be written independently.

When seat writing is introduced the most important considerations at first are these:

a. Sitting in an upright position with feet in front of body

b. Placing both arms (except elbows) upon the desk

c. Placing and holding the paper in correct relation to the body, as shown on back cover of penmanship manual

d. Holding the pencil loosely with first finger back about an inch from the point

V. Cursive writing at blackboard and on paper

A. *Aim.* The aim of penmanship in the second and third grades is to provide the child with an adequate tool for written expression. The blackboard is used at first to facilitate the development of good writing habits and the learning of good form for letters and figures. Gradually, as he becomes proficient in blackboard writing, the principles the child has learned are applied to writing on paper.

B. *Materials:*

1. For the teacher: course of study, primary pupils' manual, wall chart (arm and hand), wall chart (desk)

2. For the pupil: primary pupils' manual, school pencil, ruled manila practice paper

C. *Suggested outline.* On pages 68 and 69 is given a suggested outline of subject-matter and features to develop in second and third grades. This summary, arranged in progressive steps, includes both blackboard and pencil practice, and functional as well as formal subject-matter.

D. *Apportionment of lesson time.* The suggested division of weekly lessons between blackboard and lead pencil practice in grades two and three is indicated by the fractions below:

Grade	Blackboard Practice	Lead Pencil Practice
Second (first half)	¾	¼
Second (last half)	½	½
Third (first half)	½	½
Third (last half)	¼	¾

E. *Apportionment of practice time.* It is suggested that practice time in grades two and three be divided between formal and functional practice in the following proportions:

Grade	Formal Practice	Functional Practice
Second (first half)	¾	¼
Second (last half)	½	½
Third (first half)	½	½
Third (last half)	¼	¾

F. *Comments:* The penmanship lesson should be progressive in character, beginning with formal and closing with functional practice. The purpose of formal practice is to give training in the various principles of penmanship. Functional practice is intended to provide an opportunity for these principles to function in a practical way.

On page 69, under "Correction of Errors," it is suggested that a portion of the penmanship lesson be reserved at times for the correction of glaring errors found in the pupils' daily written work. These errors pertain to manner of writing as well as to effect in size, line, slant, form, spacing, and alignment.

Improvement in penmanship is brought about in three ways: (1) by giving penmanship lessons regularly, (2) by well-directed instruction, and (3) by systematic, sympathetic supervision of pupils' daily written work. All are necessary.

Classification of pupils during the writing period is necessary for satisfactory results. This classification may be into two general groups (of good and poor writers), or it may be according to a feature (position, movement, size, quality of line, slant, form, etc.) in which certain of the pupils need special attention.

4. *Stenography.* A short summary of teacher helps, which are found in the senior high-school commercial course for the State of Minnesota, is included for the guidance of course of study committees in that field.

A. *Alphabet.* Learning of alphabet in connection with penmanship drills, proportion of strokes, freedom of style, continuous motion being emphasized. Learning to associate a certain sound with the writing of a stenographic symbol.

The following order of presentation should be used:
1. A small group of consonants and vowels
2. Words in which the given consonants and vowels occur
3. Sentences in which these words occur

B. *Mastery of formation principles*—those rules governing the joining of strokes in word formation.

C. *Writing from dictation to train the ear.* Copying well-written shorthand is helpful, but since the aim of the course is to prepare the pupil to write from dictation, the earlier the dictation is started the easier it will be for him to attain the desired end.

D. *Reading written shorthand to insure legible notes.* The pupils should not be required to read back all they write. Their ability to read should merely be sampled from time to time.

E. *Reading shorthand plates.*

F. *Constant repetition and drill.*

G. *Shorthand sentences.* Dictation of sentences should be given as soon as vocabulary will permit, and transcription as soon as the student has acquired typewriting skill sufficient to enable him to concentrate on the shorthand outlines.

H. *Testing.*
1. Purpose of tests
   a. To inform pupils of their achievements
   b. To provide incentives to study
   c. To determine promotion
   d. To diagnose weak spots in the pupil's achievement
   e. To determine the quality of instruction
2. Abilities to be tested
   a. Ability to write vocabularies

        (1) Words to be written according to principles that have been presented

        (2) Brief forms, memory words for recall

        (3) Phrases consisting of brief forms

    b. Ability to combine good penmanship and speed

    c. Ability to take dictation

    d. Ability to read accurately written shorthand

In order that pupils may at all times know what progress is being made, tests should be given frequently.

5. *Typewriting.* The following valuable hints are found in the commercial course of study published by the State of Minnesota in 1932. The check list for students is very suggestive.

General suggestions to teachers. Much practice is needed to acquire speed and accuracy in the operation of the typewriter. Many pupils have difficulties which are troublesome. To assist the pupils in overcoming such difficulties the following *Technique Check Sheet* may be used. A copy of this sheet should be made for every pupil taking typewriting and should be used in accordance with the instructions on the sheet.

Name ⸺⸺ ⸺ ⸺

To the pupil: Keep this Check Sheet on your desk when operating the typewriter. Your errors in technique will be checked; when you have corrected the inaccurate technique, an o.k. will be given.

I. Position at the Typewriter

    A. *Body*

        1. Sit nearer typewriter

        2. Sit away from typewriter

        3. Lean from hips toward typewriter

        4. Keep shoulders erect

        5. Keep feet on floor

        6. Keep body well balanced

        7. Keep body relaxed, but not sagging

    B. *Eyes*

        Keep on copy

    C. *Wrists*

        1. Lower wrists

        2. Raise wrists

    D. *Fingers*

        1. Curve fingers more

        2. Curve fingers less

        3. Trim finger-nails

E. *Thumbs*
    1. Curve right thumb over space bar
    2. Curve left thumb under palm

II. Operating Technique
  A. *Machine adjustments*

  B. *Paper insertion*

  C. *Key stroke*
    1. Use snatch stroke (do not punch keys)
    2. Use more even touch
    3. Use lighter stroke (quick get-away)
    4. Use more forceful stroke (well-controlled)
    5. Correct fingering
    6. Do not raise the fingers so high
    7. Relax muscles of shoulder, forearm, and wrists

  D. *Rate*
    1. Too fast
    2. Too slow
    3. Jerky

  E. *Carriage Throw*
    1. Too much arm motion
    2. Sluggish movement

6. *Exploratory course in business.* This type of course is becoming important in every field. A rather extended outline of the course for the State of Minnesota, 1932, and the methods used in teaching the course are presented, because both will be helpful to teachers in this and other fields.

I. A unified course is recommended as a constant for the ninth year. This, like other courses of the junior high-school period, should carry no credit toward high-school graduation.

The course is in no sense vocational. It is not designed to give knowledge or skill having complete or immediate wage-earning value. This is in accord with the view that vocational training should be deferred until the senior high-school years, or later, and that the junior high-school period is properly one for general education which will broaden the outlook of pupils at the time when the urge to find their places in the social organization begins to assert itself. Those who hold to a different educational philosophy will find little or nothing in this syllabus to support their point of view.

II. Suggestions as to time distribution for the units

   1. Two weeks is suggested for penmanship. This time should be distributed throughout the year in short but frequent drill periods.

   2. Five weeks is suggested for typewriting. Sufficient time should be taken during the first part of the school year to familiarize pupils with the touch system so that they will strike the correct keys automatically without looking at the keyboard. The balance of the time should be distributed as practice periods throughout the year. In schools where facilities for typewriting are lacking, the time suggested for this unit should be distributed among the remaining units as needed, the major part of the time being given to the second unit, dealing with thrift, and to the last three units, which deal with occupational efficiency.

   3. Three weeks are recommended for business arithmetic. In addition to such arithmetic tests as may be given, there should be frequent short drills on arithmetic fundamentals and considerable work on problem solving. The three weeks suggested should be distributed throughout the year.

   4. The three weeks suggested for review and examination at the close of the year should be ample if the course as outlined in this syllabus has been covered satisfactorily during the year.

III. General suggestions as to method

   The course is recommended as a constant for all ninth-year pupils because of its general educational value.

   In teaching, provision should be made for the varying ability of pupils by means of elasticity in assignment. Material requiring varying degrees of independent thinking should be used. To make this possible, the teacher should have several well-chosen texts at her disposal. A carefully selected library for supplementary reading is also essential. Much value will be found in topical assignments requiring individual pupil investigation. The business activities of the community may well be assigned to pupils for individual or group study. Capable business men may be invited to address the class on topics of special interest. This procedure will result in valuable detailed information concerning business practices, ideals, and management, all of intense interest to pupils and to be secured by no other means. It should be so handled as to present a challenge to the maturity and ability of individuals in the class, and to the class as a whole.

The materials of the course can and should be richly supplemented by forms, booklets, rate-books, classification lists, and descriptive literature of all kinds. The securing of these materials may well be a class responsibility, the letters written being used as projects in typewriting and penmanship. Requests for material should be made far enough in advance of their use so that they may be available for class study. They should be preserved for future reference.

Pupils' work-books also contain many business forms, exercises, projects, and tests of decided value which might not otherwise come into the hands of the teacher. Most of the work-book material, however, is of highly formal nature.

Placed in the hands of the pupil for daily use, the work-book tends to overshadow the recitation. The objective too frequently in the mind of the pupil is the filling in of certain blanks, and the picture that remains is the tabulation in the work-book rather than a view of the business relations field. Therefore, great care should be exercised that the course is not taught mainly from work-books. The intelligent use of the work-book necessitates a proper balance at all times between work-book materials and direct instructional materials. The work-book should be a source of special exercises to supplement or complete the work already studied. Except under special conditions, it should be placed in the hands of pupils after and not before the completion of an exercise or group of exercises.

Tests should be given frequently throughout the year. There are some objective tests on the market that can be used in testing the information the pupil has on the general material of the course. Other similar tests should be constructed with great care so that each measures something that is definite and specific in character.

It is recommended that the first day or two at the opening of the school year be devoted to orientation work.

C. Physical education

1. *Denver, Colorado.* The following specific teaching suggestions are taken from the junior high-school course, published in 1927.

Specific Teaching Suggestions

The interest and coöperation of the children must be gained before one can make any satisfactory progress in posture work. The teacher must have an understanding of what correct posture includes, an appreciation of its value, and ability to sell the idea to pupils.

That there may be happiness and joy in the attitude of the child while striving for correct posture, many incentives can be used, such as posture campaigns, parades, posters, plays, and honor rolls. It would be helpful if good posture were made a necessary asset for holding prominent school office. Appeal to girls may be made through the relation of posture to complexion and beauty. Its value in obtaining good positions will probably have force with older boys and girls.

The posture tests are a means of grading posture and are also incentives to effort on the part of the individual. The tests must be given with much earnestness and care. A child failing in any particular test should know why he failed and be told how he can correct his fault.

It is usually best for the teacher to have some means of judging the straight line of the body; often the lines of the brick wall, a suspended rope with a weight on it, or a straight pole will be of much help.

It is sometimes found that an individual is able to hold correct posture during the test, while his habitual posture is not good. For checking such a tendency to carelessness, beside the grade of A, B, C, or D earned on the test, the children may be graded 1, 2, 3, or 4 according to habitual posture. Thus A, 1 would be the ideal grade.[1]

The teacher must insist upon correct posture while the posture training exercises are being done. The exercises are of little benefit and are often harmful, when done incorrectly. The need of manual correction is often present and the following suggestions may be of help:

1. For faulty head position it may be necessary to place the fingers on the bones behind the ears (mastoid process) and lift upward.

2. For flat chest, one hand may be placed just below the pupil's waist-line and the other on the back between the shoulder-blades. The hand at the waist controls and the hand at the back pushes the body forward into correct position.

3. For round shoulders and wing shoulder-blades, the fingers are placed on the front and top of the shoulders and the thumbs are placed on the shoulder-blades. A pressure is made inward with the thumbs while the fingers are used to pull the shoulders into place.

[1] George T. Stafford, *Corrective and Remedial Gymnastics*, Second Edition (University of Illinois, Urbana, 1924), p. 71.

The teacher should understand that during the junior high-school age (twelve to fifteen years) the rapid growth of the vital organs tends to pull the head and upper spine forward unless the necessary training is given to the extensor muscles of the neck and back.

The principles of hygiene should be emphasized when urging correct posture: for unless a child has plenty of rest and sleep, sunshine and fresh air, proper food and exercise and play, correction of posture is only temporary. There must be the necessary vitality, energy, strength, and muscle tone to support the body in correct position after that position is learned.

It is futile to expect the malnourished child to assume and maintain good posture. The corrective work in such cases is to build up the health of the child.

The posture exercises at the beginning of the class period are given so that the pupils will recognize the muscular feeling of good posture. Postural coaching is essential and should be repeated often because of its great value.

Helpful Cues	*Incorrect Cues*
Stand tall	Throw shoulders back
Grow an inch	Head back
Stretch the whole body upward	Chest out
Pull in at the waist	Stomach in
Chest broad	Hips back
Swing weight forward as if to raise heels	Heels together [2]
Feet parallel—a few inches apart	

2. Many valuable methods and procedures for elementary-school teachers are suggested in the *Health and Physical Education Course for Grades Four to Six,* published by the San Francisco schools in 1931.

A. *Teaching suggestions.* The specific period devoted to health instruction emphasizes the importance of the subject; it gives time for acquiring specific skills, for participating in activities, and for strengthening desirable attitudes toward the subject.

Incidental teaching plays an equally important part. It motivates the work by relating it directly to personal experience. Specific school and community problems, emergencies of various sorts, and correlation with other subjects of the curriculum enable the teacher to make immediate application of subject-content

[2] *Physical Education,* Course of Study Monograph Number Twenty-Three (Denver, Colorado Public Schools, 1927), pp. 41-43.

to the needs and interests of the group. The pupil sees health functioning as part of his daily existence.

Daily inspection and check-up are devices which enable the teacher to keep the subject before the child and to establish the desirable health habits.

B. *The teacher's responsibility.* In a program of health education which stresses positive health, the teacher is perhaps the most important influence outside the child's own home. The child of this age-group is extremely impressionable. The voice, carriage, dress, neatness and habits of the teacher are powerful factors in molding the lives of pupils. The teacher should permit no deviation from health habits practised at school and should motivate and check those which can be practised only at home. She should realize the importance of the classroom environment and should control it accordingly; she should be constantly watchful of her pupils and should bring the school, the home, and the community into close coöperation.

C. *Emphasis.* Emphasis should be placed upon the formation of proper health habits and attitudes rather than upon knowledge. The child must be made to want health; the boy must feel that health will enable him to make the team, to win the game; the girl, that it will make her more attractive. The activities must be connected with the child's innate desires.

D. *Methods of teaching.* There is no standardized way of teaching health. The project method, demonstration, the socialized recitation, visual education, field trips, or any other plans used in other departments of instruction, may be applied to health. The teacher is free to select the method best suited to the subject under consideration and to the ability and interest of her class.

E. *Devices used in forming health habits:*
  1. The morning inspection and check-up.
  2. Individual and class graphs and charts, showing results.
  3. Pupil organizations, useful in the formation of health habits and in checking health practices.
  4. Weighing and measuring.
  5. Spontaneous dramatization and the making of books, posters, rhymes, stories, or songs.
  6. Special campaigns, such as clean-up, anti-cold, and anti-fly campaigns.
  7. Competition between groups or between different classes of the school. Competition is most effective in arousing interest

when the child strives to better his own previous accomplishment.

F. *Caring for individual differences.* As occasion demands, the regular program of work should be modified to meet the individual needs brought about by illness, or physical defects, or fatigue. Periods of rest and mid-morning lunches should be provided for convalescent and under-nourished children. Those with defective hearing or vision should be seated so as to avoid unnecessary strain.

G. *The use of books.* No textbook is recommended for this course, but rather a number of books for the school library and reading table. These may be used during the class period to develop an appreciation of personal and community health problems, to secure knowledge for the solution of the particular problem under consideration, or to reinforce the formation of healthful habits of living. The alert teacher will find the selected materials rich in suggested activities and thought-provoking problems that may easily be adapted to the urgent needs and interests of her class.

D. Music

1. *Oakland, California,* published a course of study in music in 1931 for the junior and senior high schools. Excellent teaching procedures and devices, which are included, are summarized here as an aid to music teachers and committees.

A. *The recitation plan may be varied to substitute theory work for the new song, or an appreciation lesson.* More often, however, the theory and appreciation lesson will be given directly in connection with the song-singing. The time allotment in the above plan is purely suggestive and subject to change as the teacher sees fit.

B. *Voice-testing and classification.* Each student's voice should be tested at the beginning of each semester. It is generally advisable to let the class sing together for a few days before beginning the voice-testing. Watch voices carefully and test any doubtful or changing voices again, from time to time, throughout the semester. Classify voices by quality as well as by range.

C. *Seating.* Seating depends upon acoustics of the room and the balance of the parts in each group. Place students possessing truer sense of pitch and rhythm in the rear.

D. *Drill:*
1. Learn to work fast.
2. Acquire speed in knowing where to focus the energy of the drill; persist in the drill until the result is satisfactory.
3. Always establish the key and secure a full, true chord from all the parts before beginning.
4. Frequent practice in holding sustained chords will not only cure flatting but will improve the memory and appreciation for pitch.
5. The teacher should use her own voice in singing only to illustrate a point. When the class sings she should listen. Compel the class to become self-reliant. Teach them to go on even if they make mistakes.
6. Do not sing any part all the way through by itself. Work on those measures that need correction in any part, then start all parts together and sing the passage through.
7. Observe all marks of expression, holds, and changes of tempo.
8. Always require a correct and artistic rendition of a finished song every time it is sung. Always recognize and compliment good rendition, as it helps to fix in the minds of pupils the standard of work required.
9. The teacher must preserve a high standard as his ideal, and compel his classes to reach that ideal.
10. Interpretation should be added to any composition as soon as correct intonation and part-singing are secured.
11. Challenge every error in finished work and correct it immediately. Remember, however, that this suggestion does not apply to sight-singing and unfinished songs.
12. The use of the piano in choral classes requires the exercise of good judgment by the teacher. In many songs, the piano accompaniment is necessary to complete the beauty of the composition and should be used from the first. A good accompanist is essential to the best class work. Students should not be allowed to become dependent on the piano, however.

E. *Use of voice; tone quality.* The primary considerations in choral work are to secure good tone quality and correct use of the voice. The teacher should constantly strive to develop and maintain correct posture and breathing, relaxed throat, flexible articulation, clear enunciation, resonant tone, and legato singing.

F. *Organization of classes*
1. Choral classes
2. Glee clubs

3. Special voice classes
4. A cappella choir

Regular choral classes should be organized as mixed choruses (soprano, alto, tenor, and bass) because of the value of hearing the variety of voice quality in boys' and girls' voices and because of the fine literature of choral music written for mixed chorus. Glee clubs are best organized for boys and girls separately, with the possibility of arranging to combine them in programs and production of operas.

G. *Appreciation lessons.* A technical knowledge of music contributes much to appreciation. The appreciation lessons in connection with choral classes should tie up in a very definite and immediate way with regular class work, with other subjects studied by the pupils, and with their possible experiences in music outside the school, such as radio and concert programs. Whenever practicable, compositions to be given on radio or concert programs may be used as subjects for the appreciation lesson in advance of the programs.

The time given to appreciation work will vary from one to three periods a week, as the teacher desires and as the topics to be studied fit in with the rest of the week's work. Each appreciation period should include some class singing whenever there are songs available which are illustrative of, or connected with, the topic of the lesson.

H. *The music of each country, which makes up the units, is approached through:*
1. Its folk songs
2. Folk dances
3. The national instruments
4. Patriotic songs
5. Composed music.

I. *Glee clubs.* Glee clubs offer opportunity for more finished work than can be done in regular choral classes. Hold standards of performance and of selections given as high as possible. Frequent appearance at school assemblies is a vital part of the glee club program. The occasional production of an opera is valuable, or the organization of special trios and quartets. Membership should be determined by try-outs. Limit the size of the club and always keep a balance of parts. Stress the club feature—meetings, a uniform, emblems, etc.—to maintain interest.

J. *Voice culture.* Voice-culture classes should be planned as class singing lessons, with the specific aim of developing individual voices for solo singing. Limit the class to twenty-five. Have two or three meetings weekly, one for introducing new work, the other for routine drill. Require daily practice of from twenty to forty-five minutes. Start with songs of. small range in the medium voice, beginning a small amount of solo work in the sixth or seventh week. Increase the amount of solo work as much as possible.

K. *A cappella choir.* Like the glee club, the a cappella choir offers an opportunity for the more advanced performances. The choir should be organized on the same basis as the glee club. One of its greatest advantages is in the fine type of music written for this type of chorus.

Use great care in selection of voices, eliminating those with a tendency to tremolo or flat. The piano should not be used at rehearsals except in emergency. Secure the key-tone from pitchpipes used by two students seated advantageously in the group. Have more than fifty voices if possible, with more boys than girls. A good balance of parts for a group of sixty is as follows: soprano, twelve; mezzo-soprano, eleven; alto, ten; tenor, eight; baritone, nine; bass, ten. Begin each singing period with five to ten minutes of vocal exercises. Use humming frequently as it is valuable for the sense of pitch, for blending of parts, and for good tone quality.

L. *Harmony.* Each student should have a printed copy of the keyboard. Classes will be composed of all types of musicians, so that, outside of the fundamentals, a great deal of flexibility should be allowed. The class should be organized as a group for the initial lessons but later individual work brings better results. There are four chief types of activity: (*a*) the solution of harmonic problems, (*b*) rhythmic, melodic, and harmonic dictation, carried on during the entire course, (*c*) analysis, (*d*) melodic invention and free composition. Beginning with Harmony I, the creative faculty of students should be exercised by the evolution of melodies from given harmonies. This should be continued throughout the course. Practical application should be made by transposing the music for the band and orchestra, calling attention to the intervals in choral work, etc. The text is McCoy: *Cumulative Harmony.*

M. *Music history.* The teacher may choose between two approaches to this subject: (1) the evolution of music from primitive times down to the present, and (2) the interpretation of modern music. With either method of approach, visual aids, the phonograph, note-books kept by members of the class, and class discussion of concerts that pupils have attended are helpful.

N. *Orchestra and band.* Have two organizations—the *second* band or orchestra to afford training and practice in routine, and a *first* group of advanced musicians, chosen by examination from among those who have served at least one term in the second group. Some knowledge of music theory should be required of band or orchestra members, who must take a lesson a week, in school or out, and practise forty minutes a day. School lessons may be given individually or by groups.

O. *Helping the non-singer.* In every primary grade we find a considerable number of children who are non-singers or inaccurate singers. These must be given a chance to find their singing voices. The real monotone is extremely rare; there are very few children who cannot be taught to sing in tune. Problem cases must be given special, individual attention. They must sing softly and lightly. They must not be allowed to sing too low or too high. The range of the treble staff is the best limit for their songs. This necessitates frequent use of the pitch-pipe in order to maintain correct pitch. The following musical experiences are suggested for the improvement of inaccurate singing: singing of the teacher or child leader close to the child's ear; matching of the teacher's tone by the child; discriminating between various pitches; holding hands up high and standing on tiptoe to get the concept of the high tone; singing on high G or F with "nee-nee-nee" or "bow-wow-wow-wow" to develop the concept of head tone; singing "me-ow" as high as possible and listening for the highest tones; imitating the wind, the siren, "whee-whee," "oo-oo" on the same high tone; playing an imaginary violin accompaniment and singing "me" very softly on a high tone; singing "ding-dong" and listening for the clearest, highest, sweetest bells; playing peddler—calling wares; imitating bird and animal calls; throwing tones up like a ball bounced to the ceiling; blowing bubbles while singing "oo"; calling names on the octave or tonic chord tones.

E. Home Economics

Some of the necessary procedures and methods in home economics for the junior high school are presented in the course of study developed by the city of Oakland for these grades in 1929.

The all-important thing is to have interesting problems to solve. The solutions may involve any or all of the ordinary teaching methods.

The teacher who plans the work for the class, dictates directions, and hands out ready-made conclusions, cannot expect the pupils to plan or manage for themselves.

Specific problems to meet the immediate needs of pupils must be worked out by the teacher from day to day. They should be chosen with the idea of starting with situations that give in concrete form the application of the principles; then of leading up to a statement of the principles themselves. For example, in the unit on personal hygiene, to begin with a problem concerned with the principle that rest, exercise, sleep, and proper diet are necessary to health would probably kill all interest. On the other hand, the problem—*What may we do to improve our personal appearance?* or *Are you as attractive as you would like to be?* is already interesting to every girl and through informal discussion may lead pupils to formulate the abstract principle.

Pupil work-sheets, covering the various units in food work, have been provided for the seventh and eighth grades. They are an adaptation of the job-sheet and provide the girls with information and directions as to equipment, ingredients, operations, and precautions. Summaries or short objective tests are often included. The work-sheets are put in the girls' note-books and are used in connection with home projects.

The home-economics department provides a laboratory for the application of principles of health, science, color, and design to foods, clothing, and home furnishings. There are many opportunities for such application to social and community relationships.

It is possible, however, to carry the correlation between subjects so far as to weary pupils and waste their time by futile repetition in one course of what is being well taught in another. When a thorough course in a contributing subject is offered, the home-economics teacher need not take up in detail topics that are taught in the other class.

The Tentative Course of Study in Home Economics for Junior and Senior High School that was published by the State Board of Education of Idaho in 1932 is included in this chapter so that another excellent plan of relating specific instructional aids and pupils' activities can be compared with those developed at Oakland and Long Beach in the same subject-matter field.

FAMILY AND COMMUNITY RELATIONSHIPS

OBJECTIVES:

To develop an appreciation for home life and what it takes to make a desirable home.
To develop an appreciation of the necessity for leisure time for every member of the family.
To acquire some knowledge of ways of providing recreation and amusement for myself and my family.
To create a desire for my family's coöperation in community activities.
To learn to plan entertainment in my home, appropriate to the family income.

Reference and Illustrative Material	Content and Teaching Procedure	Pupil Problems and Activities	Outcomes
Teacher References Idaho News Letter (Feb., 1931) *Outline for Content and Teaching Procedure in Teaching Social and Family Relationships*, Jane S. Hinkley *Pupil References* The Family and Its Relations, Groves, Skinner, and Swenson	I. **The rights of others** A. What are the possible solutions for this problem? 1. Refuse to lend anything and keep everything locked up 2. Bawl Mary out 3. Do nothing—allow Mary to continue as in the past 4. Ask Mary to replace the hose with new ones 5. Talk it over with her, trying to make her understand that she is not being fair B. Which solution is best? 1. Judge according to the following standards: *a.* That solution which will be best for all concerned	*Problem:* Ruth finds that her sister, Mary, older than she, has been borrowing her clothes, handkerchiefs, and jewelry without permission. Once she borrowed a pair of cherished birthday hose and wore them until they needed mending before Ruth had ever had them on. What should Ruth do?	

Social Aspects of Homemaking, Bomar	b. That which will give the best present satisfaction c. That which will give the best future satisfaction	*Activity:* What would you do in this situation?	Learns to make her decisions in terms of the standards adopted.
Homemaking, a Profession for Men and Women, McDonald and McDonald	2. If No. 1 is the adopted solution then Ruth's clothes will be safe but it will be a nuisance to lock them, and Mary will probably be resentful. This will therefore not give satisfaction.		
	3. If No. 2 is adopted then Ruth may be temporarily compensated but the feeling between the sisters will not be pleasant and the probability is that Mary will not change her habits.		
	4. If No. 3 is selected the present acknowledged dissatisfaction will continue.		
	5. If No. 4 is the chosen solution, Ruth will be compensated but Mary may resent the action and the probability is that she will not change her borrowing habits.		
	6. No. 5 will be the best solution, according to the above standards, because *it is the best for both girls* (best for all concerned), probably will put Mary in an atti-		

Reference and Illustrative Material	Content and Teaching Procedure	Pupil Problems and Activities	Outcomes
	tude that will not be resentful (present happiness), and will lead to her being considerate of her sister and her sister's property (future happiness).		
Fourteenth Annual Reference Report, Pacific Region, Home Economics Education, 1931, *Principles in Subject-Matter in Social and Family Relations*	*Principle:* Respect for the rights and properties of others helps to make home life happy. C. What other applications can you give of the same trait? 1. Following their discussion the class should be led to suggest many similar positive or negative cases of respecting the rights of others, always making their decisions according to the standards set. 2. These problems will undoubtedly lead to other principles and personality traits that should be taken up in the same manner. The procedure is then, from the pupil's point of view, in five steps: 1. Face the problem	*Supplementary problems:* Last week the Home Economics Club was planning a party for their mothers and the State supervisor. Some one ate about one-fourth of the cookies made for the party and this discovery was made too late to make more. What embarrassments were caused by this? Why did it happen? How could it be avoided in the future?	Realizes that thoughtfulness of others is necessary in congenial family life.

2. Suggest the solution
3. Test suggestions in the light of the standards
4. Reach conclusions
5. Find other applications

D. Selection of problems to introduce the unit. Select from:
1. Own observation of girls in class or school
2. One brought to you by one of the girls.
3. One brought by a mother or principal.
4. Those secured by a question-box.

E. Selection may be made on the basis of the following points:
1. The problem should be on a true-to-life situation.
2. It should be interesting in itself or connected with something that is interesting.
3. It must be clear and definite in statement.
4. It should be of the proper scope and difficulty.
5. It should call for thinking of superior quality.

Supplementary problems:
The locker system had been used in the high school for some time but stealing continued. The superintendent, believing that students could be trusted further if trust were put in them, called in all the locks. A week later Norma saw Billie take a book from Pat's locker. The next day Pat missed her book and asked Norma about the book. Should Norma tell Pat about seeing Billie take the book?

Reference and Illustrative Material	Content and Teaching Procedure	Pupil Problems and Activities	Outcomes

Teacher References
 	
Understanding the Adolescent Girl, Elliott
Teaching of Ideals, Charters
 	
Pupil Reference
 	
Living with Our Children, Gilbreth
	II. Coöperation
	A. Carry through this or a similar problem as above in the case of regard for the rights of others so that a conclusion will be drawn following the judging standards set up—the desired result being that the girls get in the habit of making judgments in this way.
	B. Coöperation may be practised
	  1. In class
	  2. In school organizations
	  3. With school officials
	  4. In play
	  5. At home
	    a. work
	    b. amusements
	C. This is one of the most desirable and easiest traits to develop as a class project.
	
	Principle: Coöperation develops ability to get along with others, improves personality and creates happiness whether practised at home or at school.
		Problem: Leah and Jess are often given the use of the family car for their pleasures. Jess is older and feels that he should have preference over Leah. They frequently quarrel about it. What satisfactory arrangement can you suggest?
		
		Supplementary problems: Helen wants to try the things she has learned about cooking at home. Her mother dislikes to have her "messing" in the kitchen. How can Helen get her mother's coöperation?
		
		Supplementary problems: The student-body council put up a sign,	

	Keep Off the Grass, in a newly-grassed corner of the high-school campus. Students who are continually late pay no attention because by walking over this they shorten the distance to the door. How can these students be influenced to coöperate?	Learns how to coöperate—is not bossy or a slacker in doing her share.
Pupil Reference *Sorrell and Son*, Deeping	*Activities:* 1. List the ways that coöperation can be expressed at home. 2. How much of this do you practice? 3. Make a definite plan of coöperation to assist in some home problem. 4. List the ways that coöperation can be practiced in a class. 5. In Home Economics Club.	Learns that there is satisfaction in practicing coöperation.

III. **Loyalty**
A. To the family
  1. Most families have a skeleton
  2. To parents
  3. To brothers and sisters
  4. To the family intimacies
B. To your school
C. To your class
D. To friends
E. To your church
F. To your community, State, country
G. To your ideals
H. To yourself		

FAMILY AND COMMUNITY RELATIONSHIPS—*Continued*

Reference and Illustrative Material	Content and Teaching Procedure	Pupil Problems and Activities	Outcomes
		Problem: Carol is often telling something about their family life. Mother never told me not to do this but it does not seem fair to me. Is it?	Appreciates the value of loyalty as a stimulus to family happiness.
		Supplementary problem: Dorothy and Jean are very good friends. The other day Ruth came to Jean to tell her some gossip that she had heard about Dorothy. Ruth did not know whether it was true or not but did not believe it was. What should she say?	Is loyal to school, community, State and country.
			Is not afraid to express loyalty to her convictions.
	Principle: Loyalty builds confidence and character, the basis for any friendship in the home or out of it.	*Activity: Give examples* of loyalty to those things which are deserving of loyalty.	

Teacher and Pupil References	IV. Sharing responsibility	
	A. At home	Problem: Carl and Mary are active and popular at school and usually don't get home until 5:00 or 6:00. Their mother needs them to help her about the house or with the younger children. They often are at rehearsal, basketball games, or parties at night so that mother has to deny herself going many places to stay with the children. Is this fair?	Willing to assume her share of the household work.
Child Care and Training, Faegre and Anderson	1. Work	
	2. Pleasures	
Girls and Their Problems, Coss	3. Finances	
	4. Emergencies	
So Big, Ferber	5. Mishaps	
	6. Obedience	
Wild Geese, Ostenso	7. Keeping the family ideals	
Seventeen, Tarkington	*Principle:* A willingness of each person to take his or her share of the responsibility of the home promotes desirable relationships.	
Teacher and Pupil References	*Principle:* Family life is happier if each member considers the best interests of all concerned when deciding what to do in certain social situations.	
The Family and Its Relationships, Groves, Skinner, and Swenson	B. At school	Supplementary problem: Virginia assumes responsibility every place but at home. Her mother realizes it. What is wrong?	Shares in the making of a family plan for spending.
Girls and Their Problems, Coss	1. In class work, especially the laboratory	
Problems in Home Living, Just and Rust	2. In organizations	
	3. Student government	
On Being a Girl, Gibson	a. As an officer or on a committee	Supplementary problem: The Jones children have more than my brother and I. Father
	b. As a member	
	C. In the community	
	1. Church work	

Reference and Illustrative Material	Content and Teaching Procedure	Pupil Problems and Activities	Outcomes
	2. Charity 3. Clubs 4. Rotary or commercial club altruistic work 5. Community spirit 6. School 7. Keeping up the community standards 8. The community is composed of individuals *Principle:* The community improves as the members of the family concern themselves about and participate in desirable community activities.	says that they do not live within their income. I am sure that the Jones children do not know this for they do not hesitate to ask for what they want. Is this right? Does that give them more happiness than we have? How much experience should children have with the family finances? Who is responsible for the Jones condition? Should a father have all the responsibility for making and spending the income? *Problem:* Erma and Jane are partners in home economics laboratory. Several times	Does not shirk her duties.

Erma has left the cleaning up after the lesson to Jane because Jane did not go home for her lunch and Erma did. Is it all right for her to do this?

Problem: One of our reference books states that it is up to the women to see that the community has good water supply, milk supply, and general sanitary conditions. Is this true? Why? If so, what is your responsibility as a woman of your community?

Supplementary problems: There are several good churches in our community. What do these churches contribute to the community? In view of these facts, what support do we owe the churches?

Assumes responsibility in the community that she can do and should do.

FAMILY AND COMMUNITY RELATIONSHIPS—*Continued*

Reference and Illustrative Material	Content and Teaching Procedure	Pupil Problems and Activities	Outcomes

Pupil References
 	
The Bent Twig, D. C. Fisher
 	
The Homemaker, D. C. Fisher
 	
Pupil and Teacher References
 	
Problems in Home Living, Justin and Rust
 	
Girls and Their Problems, Coss
 	
Social Aspects of Home Making, Bomar
 	
Home Making a Profession for Men and Women, McDonald and McDonald
	V. **Family comparisons**
	A. The desirable family
	  1. Live within their income
	  2. Share work, play, joy and sorrow
	  3. Are considerable and thoughtful of one another
	  4. Are sympathetic and understanding
	  5. Are healthy
	  6. Coöperate
	  7. Plan for a division of responsibilities and money
	  8. Understand child development
	  9. Are hospitable
	  10. Use leisure time wisely
	  11. Enjoy one another
		Activities: 1. List the ways that you can share responsibilities at home. 2. At school 3. In community affairs
		
		Problem: The girls like to go to Ada's home more than to that of any other of the girls. What might be some of the things about her home that make us like to go there?
		
		Activities: 1. Think of a family that you admire very much. List all the things about their family life that are desirable. 2. Which of the qualities does your family have? 3. What other desir-
			Appreciates some of the important factors that make for desirable family life.
			
			Appreciates the loveliness in her family.
			
			Tries to make desirable changes in her family.
			
			Is more interested in her family.

The Family and Its Relationships, Groves, Skinner, and Swenson
 	
Earning and Spending the Family Income, Friend
 	
Maria Chapdelaine, Louise Hemon
 	
Making Homes, Shultz
	B. Families of other days
	  1. Primitive families
	  2. American family beginnings
	  3. American homes before electricity
	  4. The family in a machine age
	C. If possible some pioneer woman might be able to tell the girls many interesting stories.
		able qualities are in your family?
		4. What are some of the characteristics of the individual members of your family that make your home life happier?
		5. What qualities would you like to develop in your family? Would this be possible?
		6. Make a plan for that development.
		7. What is your responsibility for making your family life happier?
		8. Ask your grandmother or some elderly lady to tell you about life in her younger days.
		Problem: Pearl does not head a conversation well, not because she is timid but because

FAMILY AND COMMUNITY RELATIONSHIPS—*Continued*

Reference and Illustrative Material	Content and Teaching Procedure	Pupil Problems and Activities	Outcomes
	Principle: Determining reasonable standards of living for various aspects of family life help in developing satisfactory family relations.	she does not know what to talk about. What are some good topics of conversation? *Activity*: List and study some topics of conversation.	Gracefully leads versatile conversation.
	Principle: Understanding individual differences and the possibilities of individual expression and development helps in family relationships.	*Problem*: Mother says that I may select two new magazines for our family. I have three and a half dollars to spend. What would be a good selection?	Is up to date in current topics.
	Principle: Sharing in the formation of goals for the family adds interest and desire for maintaining them.		Develops social poise.
Pupil and Teacher References	VI. **Leisure** A. Conversation 1. Avoid gossip	*Activities*: 1. What magazines do my family read? Is the selection desirable? Is	Knows good magazines.
Readers' Digest	2. Avoid vulgarity in speech	it the best that could	
Literary Digest	3. Conversational topics are taken from your interests and those of the people to whom you are talking.	be made for the money?	Can plan and carry out pleasures for her family.
Newspapers	4. Know current topics. 5. Be a good listener.	2. Take an inventory of the magazines	

The Family and Its Relationships, Groves, Skinner, and Swenson	*Principle:* To take an active part in conversation one must have many interests, talk easily, and be a good listener.	Reads good books.
Problems in Home Living, Justin and Rust	**B. Amusements in the home**	

On Being a Girl, Gibson	1. Radio
	  a. Educational value
	  b. Up to date information
	  c. Variety
		Uses leisure time wisely.

	2. Magazines
	  a. Selection made according to
	    (1) Family interests
	    (2) Income
	    (3) Their influence especially on the younger members
	  b. Discuss values of certain magazines	

	3. Books
	  a. Use of public or school library
	  b. A good book
	  c. A poor book
	  d. Variety
		Recognizes the value of time and uses it to the best advantage.

in the school and city library. What use could be made of these by the family?

3. Make a list of the magazines sold in your town. List those that are good and those that should be tabooed, telling why.

4. Make a list of the books that you would select as a nucleus for a home library telling why you select each. What would this cost? How many of these books are in the public library?

5. Plan an evening at home with your family at little or no additional cost.

6. What amusements can your family afford?

FAMILY AND COMMUNITY RELATIONSHIPS—*Continued*

Reference and Illustrative Material	Content and Teaching Procedure	Pupil Problems and Activities	Outcomes
Pupil and Teacher References	e. Value of reading f. Some good authors	7. What games do your family enjoy? What others might add to the list?	Recognizes the value of desirable use of leisure time for herself and her family.
New York Times	4. Birthdays	8. Plan and carry out some amusement for the entire family, remembering the family budget.	
Book Reviews	5. Surprises		
School Reading lists	6. Gifts	9. Make a survey of the types of recreation available in your community. What is your responsibility in keeping these at a high standard?	
Child Care and Training, Faegre and Anderson, p. 225	7. Special occasions and holidays		
	8. Family guests		
Girls and Their Problems, Coss, pp. 110-113	9. Parties		
	10. Games	10. Does your mother have enough leisure time? If not, how could you help her plan her work so that she will have more time?	
	Principle: For happy family life provision for satisfactory group and individual recreation should be made.		
Pupil and Teacher References	C. Amusements away from home		
Choice of Motion Pictures	1. Church		
Liberty Magazine	2. Picnics or outings		

Parents Magazine Association of Motion Picture Producers, Inc., Hollywood, California	3. Movies
	   a. What is a good movie?
	4. Community activities
	5. Dances
	6. Musicals
	7. Plays
	   a. What is a good play?
	8. Car riding
	9. Vacations
		Goes to good movies.

Pupil References		11. Plan a time schedule for yourself or some other member of the family who needs it.
Social Aspects of Homemaking, Bomar		12. What is a hobby? Are hobbies foolish?

Encyclopedia Britannica	D. The fine arts
	  1. Music
	    a. What is good music?
	    b. Some of the noted musicians
	    c. Recognition of well-known musical compositions
	    d. With the coöperation of the music teacher, plan a music appreciation assembly
	  2. Art
	    a. Some famous pictures
		13. Plan a vacation that all your family would enjoy and could afford.
		14. Make a list of the objectionable features and good points of a recent movie. What good movies are booked at the local theater for the next month? If your family could go to only one as a group, which one would you choose?
		15. Study the pictures in the school building. Which are good? Why?

Reference and Illustrative Materials	Content and Teaching Procedure	Pupil Problems and Activities	Outcomes
	b. Some famous artists	Which are poor? Why?	Is familiar with noted works of art.
	c. If possible secure some prints of good pictures	16. The following magazines were the ones found to be most often in the homes in Idaho: *Good Housekeeping, McCall's, Colliers, Cosmopolitan, Delineator, Country Gentleman, National Geographic, Literary Digest, Pictorial Review, Woman's Home Companion, Better Homes and Gardens, Golden Book,* and *Saturday Evening Post.* Why do you think these were chosen? What are the values of each?	
	3. Drama		
	a. Good plays to see		
	b. Good plays to read		
	c. Notable actors		
The Boy and His Gang	E. Avocation		
	1. Plan to have one Home Economics Club meeting on hobbies		
	Principle: Good use of leisure time broadens one's poise, education, and interests.		
	Principle: Amusements participated in by the entire family allow the family to become better acquainted.		

The following unit of work from the Course of Study in Home Economics (Oakland Public Schools, 1932) for Grades Ten, Eleven, and Twelve presents an excellent illustration of the relationship of specific instructional aids to content or subject-matter.

UNIT I. STUDY OF TEXTILE FABRICS

SPECIFIC OBJECTIVE:
To give each girl a practical knowledge of textiles and to aid her in judging durability and quality of fabrics.

Subject-Matter	Pupil Problems and Suggested Procedure	References
A. *Seasonal fabrics* 1. Kinds 2. Uses 3. Quality 4. Cost	What are this season's silk and wool fabrics? Read style articles referring to suitable fabrics of the season. Get samples of kinds, prices, width, and colors of seasonal materials.	Current fashion magazines Denny, *Fabrics and How to Know Them,* pp. 17-116

B. *Basic differences in fabrics*
1. Color
2. Source
  a. Animal fibers
    (1) Wool
      (*a*) Virgin
      (*b*) Reclaimed
    (2) Silk
	What should a girl know about silk and wool materials?
	
	Mount samples and try to show basic differences. Use as distinctive samples as you can secure.
	
	Review fibers already studied and enlarge
		Small, *How to Know Textiles,* Ch. I
		
		Lectures and charts of Vogue Educational Service (free material)

UNIT I. STUDY OF TEXTILE FABRICS—Continued

Subject-Matter	Pupil Problems and Suggested Procedure	References
(a) Cultivated (b) Wild	on information. Review tests to distinguish fibers.	

(3) Hair
   (a) Goat's hair
   (b) Camel's hair
   (c) Rabbit's hair
	Secure samples large enough to be handled by students for texture, finish, and identity.	Dyer, *Textile Fabrics*, Ch. II

b. Vegetable fibers
  (1) Cotton
  (2) Flax
  (3) Jute, ramie, etc.
	Do you know a fabric's name by looking at it?	Baldt and Harkness, *Clothing Simplicity—Economy for the High School Girl*, pp. 66-74

c. Synthetic or manufactured fibers	Do we have sufficient raw material to meet trade demands?	Fales, *Dressmaking*, pp. 84-110
(1) Rayon (2) Paper cloth	Demonstrate how rayon is made.	Rathbone and Tarpley, *Fabrics and the Dress*, Ch. VII

d. Mineral fibers
  (1) Asbestos
  (2) Metallic
		Fales, *op. cit.*, pp. 76-84, 110-119

3. Construction	Use microscope.	Sage, *Textiles and Clothing*, pp. 45-50, 165-180

a. Woven fabrics
  (1) Plain
  (2) Satin
  (3) Twill
  (4) Pile
  (5) Gauze
	Demonstrate on loom, if one is available, and have students make various weaves on cardboard looms or with kindergarten construction paper.	*Premier Rayon Review*

b. Knitted fabrics c. Felted fabrics	Discuss and demonstrate "feel" of various finishes.	Baldt and Harkness, *op. cit.*, pp. 62-66, 74-85

4. Finish
  a. Mercerized
  b. Lisle
  c. Calendered
  d. Weighted
	What is the effect of finish on the likes and dislikes of the customer; on the value of the fabric?	McGowan and Waite, *Textiles and Clothing*, Ch. III
		Small, *op. cit.*, Ch. III and X
		
		Dyer, *op. cit.*, Ch. IV

C. *Physical characteristics of the five main fibers* 1. Length 2. Strength 3. Elasticity 4. Hygienic qualities 5. Fineness of fiber 6. Power of absorption 7. Affinity for dyes 8. Conductivity 9. Feel 10. Beauty	Class discussion. Examination of samples, illustrations, and materials. Show that certain characteristics result in different values and effects in fabrics, and that length and strength, elasticity and fineness contribute to strength and durability of fabrics. How does strength, hygienic quality, absorption of water, feel, etc., contribute to serviceability?	Small, *op. cit.*, Ch. XI Woolman and McGowan, *Textiles,* pp. 278-292 Dyer, Ch. III Sage, pp. 108-120 Matthews, *Elementary Home Economics,* pp. 499-538
D. *Special characteristics of wool* 1. Elasticity 2. Affinity for dyes 3. Felting properties 4. Effect of change of temperature 5. Cleanliness 6. Non-conductivity	Consult glossaries and trade magazines to increase vocabulary and ability to recognize fabrics. From discussions and demonstrations carried on above, the class should come to conclusions regarding the strength and durability of both wool and silk. Distinguish between woolens and worsteds.	Small, Ch. IV, V and pp. 260-264 Dyer, pp. 26-29 McGowan and Waite, pp. 133-139 Woolman and McGowan, pp. 105 and 106

UNIT I. STUDY OF TEXTILE FABRICS—*Continued*

Subject-Matter	Pupil Problems and Suggested Procedure	References
E. *Special characteristics of silk* 1. Beauty (luster) 2. Smoothness 3. Strength 4. Non-conductivity 5. Cleanliness 6. Power of absorption 7. Weighting	Silk dresses were formerly a luxury. Why is this not true now? Have students give reports on the culture of the silk worm and the manufacture of silks. What is meant by "pure dye" silk?	Sage, pp. 86-107 Dyer, pp. 27 and 28 Woolman and McGowan, pp. 204-206
F. *Simple physical tests* 1. Feeling 2. Breaking 3. Tearing 4. Moisture	Review, emphasizing testing of wool, silk, and rayon. How can you distinguish rayon from silk? Wool from cotton?	Dyer, pp. 37-39 McGowan and Waite, pp. 232-239

G. *Chemical tests for fibers*
1. Burning
  a. Orod
  b. Speed
  c. Residue
2. Action of alkali
3. Action of acids
4. Tests for rayons
  a. Breaking
  b. Burning
  c. Water
	Bring out that if fiber is dissolved in strong alkali, then strong washing powder is not good to use in laundering silk and wool.
	
	Bring out that wild silk dissolves less quickly than cultivated silk.
	
	Coöperate with science department. Choose simple tests that may be used by the consumer. Check results with physical properties.
		Sage, pp. 108-127
		
		Woolman and McGowan, Ch. XII
		
		Dyer, pp. 39 and 40
		
		McGowan and Waite, pp. 239-259
		Rathbone and Tarpley, pp. 96-100

An additional illustration is found in a unit from the Home-Making Course of Study for Junior High Schools of the Long Beach schools (1932), with its accompanying suggestions to teachers, from which the following excerpts are taken:

SUGGESTIONS TO TEACHERS

1. *General procedure*

In the outline of procedure the suggestions should be very definitely related to the needs and abilities of pupils. Teachers will discover much variation not only in the make-up of their classes, but within each class. Home experiences and conditions will differ considerably even within one school, and the first thing the teacher should endeavor to do is to discover the needs and abilities as a point of departure for her procedure.

In general, except as otherwise suggested in the approach to the different units, the material is arranged in the sequence which seems best adapted to the natural development of the phases of home-making covered in the special course of study; but the experience and judgment of the teacher must determine when the sequence should be changed. Equipment, number of pupils, number of sections, and other school conditions will also influence the sequence.

2. *Use of reference material*

The references for teachers given in the several courses of study have been selected according to (*a*) the books generally accepted as authoritative in their special fields, (*b*) those that the individual teacher either owns or should own, and (*c*) those that are obtainable in the school library, the Teachers' Library, or the Public Library.

The complete list will be found in the Appendix. To keep abreast of current publications is the responsibility of the teacher; this is particularly true in the field of periodical literature. Many references are included so that some, if not all, will be readily obtainable and their liberal use will visualize the teaching of a familiar subject and reveal new aspects of thought to help in interpretation to pupils.

Pupil references should be used with discretion, and to reveal the wealth of material within the covers of a book and the manner in which it may be related to the discussion. Assignments should be made in a way to provoke interest, to find the answer to a worth-while question, or to develop a higher level of appreciation. Written outlines or briefs often deaden or kill all pupil interest, especially when the directions are, "Make an outline of the subject from pages 20 to 30." A better plan is to place on the blackboard several questions that are of real interest in form as well as substance, suggest-

UNIT I. FOOD IN RELATION TO HEALTH

Time: Three Weeks

APPROACH TO UNIT I:

The teacher should find out how many pupils were in the sixth grade in Long Beach in order to review the 6 B course in foods, which emphasizes right food habits in relation to health, such as drinking milk, eating vegetables and fruit, and selecting suitable combinations of food in the school cafeteria. Use the information obtained as a point of departure for class discussion of the following topics:

Basic References—Illustrative Material	Content	Procedure	Specific Attainments
Teacher References Kinyon-Hopkins, *Junior Food and Clothing*, Part I. Why is Food Necessary to Health? pp. 3-70 Wellman, Mabel T., *Food Planning and Preparation*, Ch. III, How We Help Ourselves Grow, pp. 47-60 Rose, Mary Swartz, *Feeding the Family*, Ch. I, The Significance of Food, pp. 1-33; Ch. X, Food in Adolescence and Youth, pp. 185-206; Ch. XII, Food for the Family Group, pp. 218-243	A. Good health necessary for growing boys and girls in order 1. To be happy and comfortable 2. To work well 3. To play well B. Food as a factor in good health 1. To supply strength and energy 2. To build and repair tissue 3. To regulate body processes	Have pupils relate from observation or experience incidents that illustrate effect of health on class standing, keeping a job, making a team, being a useful member of the family. Have pupils suggest a few of the rules for good health which have been studied and observed in health and physical education classes. Ask pupils to list examples of foods which supply the various foodstuffs and classify in accordance with uses listed in "B."	An appreciation of the influence of health upon activities. Appreciation of food as a factor in good health.

Pupil References Kinyon-Hopkins, *op. cit.*, Part I, Why is Good Health Necessary to Growing Boys and Girls, pp. 3-6; Why do We Need Food and What is Its Use in the Body, pp. 6-9 Winchell, Florence E., *Food Facts for Every Day*, Ch. IV, Food as Fuel, pp. 32-56. Ch. V, Body Needs Food for Building, pp. 57-72; Ch. VI, Body Needs Vitamins, pp. 73-81 Kinyon-Hopkins, *op. cit.*, Part I, What Foods Shall be Chosen to Meet the Needs of the Body, pp. 9-30 What happens if a growing boy or girl continues to eat foods that do not meet the needs of the body? pp. 30-36. Why is it necessary to form right food habits early in life? pp. 36-43 Winchell, F. E., *op. cit.*, Ch. VII, Can you Choose Foods Wisely? pp. 82-87 *Teacher References* Brown-Haley, *The Teaching of*	C. Kinds of foods necessary for body requirements 1. Protein-rich foods 2. Carbohydrate-rich foods 3. Fat-rich foods 4. Mineral-rich foods 5. Water 6. Vitamin-rich foods 7. Roughage D. Some results to health if food is not well selected in kind and amount 1. Condition of under- or over-weight 2. Lack of energy 3. Poor posture 4. Low resistance to disease (colds, and so forth) E. Formation of desirable food habits in relation to health. Some of the desirable food habits for growing boys and girls to have are: 1. To eat three meals, including a well-balanced breakfast, at regular times every day.	Develop the importance of food to growth and good health by showing pictures of people and of animals who exhibit the effects of wrong diets; right diets. Ask pupils to compare the differences between the food habits of people and those of animals as a basis for discussion of habit formation, its characteristics and laws. Discuss the following: One of the best ways of keeping well is to learn to choose and eat the proper foods every day. How can boys and girls begin to form right food habits? What are habits? How is habit formed? Examples. Develop the three steps necessary in forming any habit: 1. A desire to do the thing 2. Frequent repetition of the act 3. Enough feeling of pleasure and satisfaction out of doing it to really want to do it over and over	An appreciation of the good habits already acquired and an interest in the formation of additional ones which will contribute to the girl's health and happiness.

UNIT I. FOOD IN RELATION TO HEALTH—Continued

Basic References— Illustrative Material	Content	Procedure	Specific Attainments
Home Economics, Ch. III, Habit Formation, pp. 22-37 Kilpatrick, W. H., *Foundations of Method, Value of Habit*, pp. 71-343; How Habit is Built, p. 320 Roberts, Lydia, J., *Nutrition Work with Children*, Ch. V. Causes of Malnutrition—direct causes, faulty diet, pp. 104-114; other factors, pp. 114-138; heredity, pp. 99-104 *Pupil References* Kinyon-Hopkins, *op. cit.*, Part I, Right weight for height, pp. 43-53 Height-weight-age charts, pp. 61-64 Wellman, Mabel T., *Food Planning and Preparation*, Health rules, pp. 57-60	2. To eat a variety of wholesome foods, some vegetables besides potatoes, and some fruits every day. 3. To eat slowly, chewing food well. 4. To eat candy and other sweets in moderation. 5. To drink milk every day, a quart if possible. 6. To drink four to six glasses of water daily. 7. To wash hands before eating. 8. To use an individual drinking cup and to avoid exchanging food. 9. To hold correct posture while eating. 10. To keep a record of weight as a check on diet.	How to form a new and desirable habit. How to break an undesirable habit. How to replace a poor habit with a good habit. Have pupils give examples of food habits. From response of the class, select and list desirable food habits which junior-high-school pupils should have. Compare this list with that in *Junior Food and Clothing*, pp. 41-42. If possible supply each pupil with a mimeographed copy of this list. *Assignment:* Each pupil should take home the list of desirable food habits and talk with parents about which ones are already formed and which seem to be most immediate in importance. Have pupils tell how these hab-	Stimulation of interest and coöperation of the home in the formation of good food habits.

References	Content	Teaching Procedure	Outcomes

Winchell, Florence E., *op. cit.*, Ch. I, Animals should be fed with care, pp. 1-10; Ch. II, How Parents Learn to Care for Babies, pp. 11-18; Ch. III, Should Animals Have Better Care than Boys and Girls? pp. 19-31
 	
Teacher References
McCollum and Simmonds, *Food Nutrition and Health*, Ch. XVIII, How to Reduce the Weight, pp. 93-101
Rose, Mary Swarz, *Foundations of Nutrition*, Height-age table for girls of school age, p. 480; weight increase in girls, pp. 417-418; Ch. V, Energy requirements of children, pp. 83-99
	F. Weight in relation to health
	1. Normal weight depends upon several factors.
	  a. Right kinds and amounts of food
	  b. The proper amount of exercise
	  c. Sleeping the required number of hours
	  d. Correcting body defects, e.g., bad teeth, eye strain
	  e. Plenty of fresh air
	  f. A cheerful disposition
	  g. Right food habits
	  h. Avoiding too many diversions in the evening
	2. Weight standards
	  a. Normal weight based on height and age; not more than 10 per cent below weight given for height; not more than 10 per cent above weight given for height.
		its can be formed. Emphasize the fact that only one or two should be attempted at a time. When one habit is established, another can be started.
		Show how a good habit often replaces a poor one; for example, drinking milk beverages at breakfast reduces the desire for coffee or tea; the eating of sufficient food regularly at meal times lessens or eliminates craving for food between meals.
		Begin the discussion of weight in relation to health with a brief review of health rules and habits.
		Emphasize the fact that health habits are factors affecting weight; that normal weight is one indication that a person has enough food to meet the needs of the body.
		Have the pupils secure records of height and weight from physical education examination, if possible.
			Knowledge of health rules and desire to practice them.
			
			An appreciation of normal weight as a factor in resistance to disease, appearance of health, and abundant energy.

Basic References—Illustrative Material	Content	Procedure	Specific Attainments
Illustrative Material Exhibit of 100-calorie portions of some of the common foods, such as cereals, bread, fresh and dried fruits, jelly or marmalade, sugar, milk, cream, butter, eggs, bacon *Pupil References* Bailey, Pearl L., *Foods, Preparation and Serving*, Food requirements for different conditions, pp. 367-369 Kinyon-Hopkins, Part I, *Junior Food and Clothing*, How may a growing boy or girl know how much to eat? pp. 53-56 Wellman, Mabel T., *op. cit.*, reckoning in calories, pp. 136-139 Winchell, Florence E., *op. cit.*, Ch. IV, Food as Fuel, pp. 32-56; Ch. VII, Can You Choose Food Wisely? pp. 83-87	3. Dangers of weight reduction to the growing girl. Underweight is apt to result in 　a. Lowered resistance to disease, as colds 　b. Pale color 　c. Poor posture 　d. Lessened energy 　e. Stunted growth 4. Value of height and weight chart 　a. Shows normal weight 　b. Records gains or losses 　c. Constitutes a check on physical condition G. Food requirements for health in terms of calories 　1. Explanation of the term calorie: *The calorie is a measure of energy.* 　2. Suggested division of calories of one day: 　　a. Breakfast, one-fourth	Compare the records with tables in *Junior Foods and Clothing*, pp. 63-64, to learn if the weight is approximately correct. Discuss weight standards approved by the Health and Physical Education Departments. Have each pupil make a chart of her height and weight. Indicate normal weight. Arrange a definite time each week to mark charts. Keep record for nine weeks. Encourage underweight girls to keep record for longer time. As an introduction to the study of the calorie, ask each girl to bring a list of the foods she ate for breakfast on a school day and to bring a list of what some boy of her own age ate for his breakfast. Discuss such questions as: How	An appreciation of the value of a weight chart as a factor in indicating good health.

References	Activities	Understanding
Kinyon-Hopkins, *Junior Food and Clothing*, Part I, Food Allowance Table, p. 54; Appendix B, Calorie value of servings of some common foods, pp. 239-247 Kinyon-Hopkins, *op. cit.*, Part I. Health Characteristics, p. 52; Rules of the Game, pp. 52-53	of the total day's requirement b. Luncheon or supper, one-fourth of the total daily requirement c. Dinner, one-half of the total daily requirement. H. Characteristics of a person who possesses good health 1. Is not often ill; has good vitality. 2. Has proper weight for height. 3. Stands and sits correctly (good posture) 4. Has healthy teeth and gums. 5. Has good digestion. 6. Has sweet breath. 7. Has good color. 8. Does not tire easily. 9. Sleeps well. 10. Is alert and happy.	may a growing girl know how much food to eat if she is of normal weight? Underweight? Overweight? Using the table on page 54, Part I of *Junior Food and Clothing*, have each girl determine her own daily food requirement. Show 100-calorie portions of some of the common foods used for breakfast. Using the exhibit and Appendix B, Calculate the number of calories contained in a typical breakfast. Allow each girl to calculate the calories in her usual breakfast. From class discussion list the characteristics of good health. Encourage the girls to score themselves on health characteristics and to suggest ways of adding desirable characteristics.	Some understanding of the calorie as a measure of energy requirement. A knowledge of good distribution of calories over the three meals of the day. An appreciation of the characteristics of a healthy girl and a desire to develop those that she does not possess.

STANDARDS OF ATTAINMENT:

Every pupil who has completed the work of Unit I should show development in ability
1. To know the characteristics of a healthy person
2. To appreciate the value of good health to successful, happy living
3. To appreciate the relation of food to good health
4. To know the steps in forming or changing a habit
5. To form and practise several good food habits

ing the references in which the answers may be found. It takes adult training and much experience to dig out the gold from reference material and leave the dross behind. The references are all from books either on the classroom reference-shelf or in the school library. Their special use is indicated in the procedure of the various courses of study.

3. Illustrative material

A liberal use of visual aids in teaching is of great importance. The wide-awake teacher should possess the collecting habit even though the school may own certain types of illustrative material for use at the psychological moment. The selective use as well as the possession of illustrative material is necessary to make it of value to pupils. This includes preparation of material before class, order and care in its storage, use as a stimulus to further investigation, knowledge or appreciation, and the encouragement of pupils to bring to school material of their own selection for class use. With a slow moving group, exhibits are usually more valuable than reference material to serve as the point of departure for the class discussion.

For excellent discussions and suggestions, Brown and Haley's "The Teaching of Home Economics," especially Chapters I, IV, X, XI, XIII, XVII, and XVIII, is recommended both as a stimulus to thought and as a guide to self-evaluation.

F. Mechanical Arts

Suggestions in this subject-matter field are selected from the Los Angeles *Course of Study in Mechanical Drafting—An Exploratory Course for Grade Seven.* This course was issued in 1928.

1. Methods of presentation

   a. *Drawing from Objects.* The copying of a drawing does not result in the pupil's being able to visualize its subject correctly. Unless he sees the actual object, he is likely to be confused. Whenever practicable, drawing should be done from life.

   b. *Blue-print reading.* Blue-prints are, for the most part, working drawings intended to give directions for doing work. It is important that pupils, as intelligent future consumers and future producers, be able to read working drawings. With this in mind several blue-print reading tests have been included in the exploratory courses. Prints may be had at the office of the supervisor.

c. *Occupational information.* Occupational information in the form of short talks, demonstrations, motion pictures, and exhibits, should be given throughout the course.

d. *Technique.* Special attention should be given to the technique of drawing. It is important that the correct use of instruments, methods of procedure, neatness, care and accuracy, good workmanship, etc., be emphasized.

e. *Inking.* Only one or two of the exploratory drawings need be inked. Additional inking may be considered a reward of merit for those pupils who have satisfactorily completed previous work.

f. *Atmosphere.* Pictures of characteristic types of architecture, interesting machine drawings, specimens of pupils' work, machine parts, maps, etc., displayed about the drafting room create an atmosphere favorable to accomplishment.

g. *Coöperation with other industrial arts.* The practical side of drafting is demonstrated by coöperation with other shop activities. The drafting room should be the headquarters for working drawings of all kinds.

h. *Instructional devices.* Teachers should use all possible instructional aids and devices. Plans of several devices for teaching mechanical drafting may be had at the supervisor's office.

i. *Supplies.* Two qualities of paper are furnished, sketch paper $9'' \times 12''$, and ledger paper $12'' \times 19''$ which can be cut $9'' \times 12''$, border line dimensions $8'' \times 10\frac{1}{2}''$. Each pupil should have thumb tacks, a soft eraser, an H pencil for sketch paper, and a 3-H for hard-surfaced paper.

j. *Equipment.* Each pupil is furnished with a drawing board $20'' \times 26''$, a $12''$ architect's scale, a $24''$ T-square, a 45 degree triangle, and a 30-60 degree triangle. Several sets of instruments are kept on hand in the instructor's desk and are given to pupils when needed.

k. *Test.* No textbook is used in the exploratory course. French and Svenson: *Mechanical Drawing for High Schools,* is used as a reference.

l. *Individual record.* An accurate record of the progress of each pupil should be kept by the instructor.

m. *Lettering.* Good lettering is essential, and a special effort should be made to develop a reasonable degree of skill. The style of lettering used in the exploratory course should be upper case slant Gothic. Lettering should be wholly free hand, but horizontal guide-lines are to be used. It is advisable to confine lettering practice to titles and to ordinary notes on drawings, accompanied by blackboard illustrations.

2. Methods of exploration

Two methods are used in the exploration of various industrial pursuits. One method consists of actual participation by the pupil in typical experiences of the occupations, the other of study and investigation of the occupations. The second method calls for short talks, demonstrations, visits to industrial plants, motion pictures of factory production, and other available information on the occupation being explored. Some occupations are explored by both the participation and information methods, while with others the information method only is used.

The course in drafting of the Sacramento high schools (Course of Study Monograph No. 35, Sacramento Public Schools, 1931), contains the interesting units in beginning architectural drafting found on pages 642-647. The reader should note the relationships of objectives, subject-matter and teaching procedures in these units.

Suggestions as to their procedure in project teaching are given to teachers in the Berkeley schools in the Course of Study in Industrial Education for the upper elementary grades and the junior and senior high schools (Course of Study Monograph, June, 1923). (See pages 649-652.)

PROCEDURE

The project

The procedure in manual-training instruction should be governed in a large degree by the essential features of the "project method" of teaching. Dr. H. B. Wilson, in the revised edition of "Motivation of School Work," has summarized the essential and desirable characteristics of a project as follows: "A good project (1) should be broad in scope, (2) should provide for the application of useful knowledge, (3) should grow out of the interest and expressed desire of the child, (4) should be understood so fully and its value should be so appreciated that the child has adequate motive for the undertaking, (5) should be conceived and largely projected by the child himself, (6) should be carried out under conditions, circumstances, or surroundings similar to those found in actual life practice, and (7) its success may be judged largely by objective standards of achievement."

The project method lends itself naturally to manual training instruction. The necessary practice work should be presented as a preparatory step in connection with a project in which the pupil is interested. The complete project in manual training should include on the part of the pupil: (1) conception or choice of project, (2) design and drawing, (3) making bill of material, (4) construction of project, (5) figuring of cost and value. Originality in design and construction should be encouraged by the instructor.

The place of the project

The "project method" of instruction should be the controlling method used. This should not mean, however, the entire elimination of the good features that are present in carefully planned, brief, snappy demonstrations of fundamental operation that are new to the class. Practice exercise unrelated to the project under construction should never be given to the class. Operations that are performed by a pupil as a necessary preliminary step to the successful beginning of his project should not be confused with formal and unrelated exercise work. Preliminary steps related to the project have a very necessary place in constructive training. "Is project work to replace drill? The correct answer to this question is, 'No, drill properly motivated and based upon the right technique is the most effective method of handling certain subject matter.' "——
H. B. Wilson, *Motivation of School Work* (Revised Edition).

Dangers to be avoided

The danger of the so-called "Individual method of instruction in manual training should be carefully noted. This desirable method of instruction, when misapplied, sometimes degenerates into a purposeless confusion of activity on the part of the instructor which resolves itself into the habit of doing the hard parts of a pupil's work while the remainder of the class is neglected. An abuse of this method is fatal to the best interests of the class. It encourages dishonesty because the pupil displays work as his own which was largely the work of the instructor. It encourages disorder because the instructor cannot observe the work of the class as a whole while working on a specific pupil's project. It induces discouragement because the boy is inclined to attempt projects that are too difficult. It retards the growth of self-confidence in the pupil because he relies to an increasing extent on help from the instructor over the difficult places. If petty details are allowed to monopolize the instructor's time, conscious planning and direction of instruction are impossible. Such absorption of the instructor's interest by petty problems involved in

UNIT I. TYPES OF DOMESTIC ARCHITECTURE

OBJECTIVE OF THIS COURSE: To teach the elements of architectural design and construction by means of drawing a complete set of plans of a two-story Dutch Colonial House.

Specific Objectives	Elements of Subject-Matter	Suggested Teaching Procedure	References
I. *Skills and abilities:* 1. To develop the ability to recognize the different types of domestic architecture used in home construction in and around Sacramento. II. *Knowledge:* 1. To know the main characteristics of the following types of domestic architecture: New England, Colonial, Southern Colonial, English cottage, Bungalow, Spanish, and Spanish-Mission. 2. To know the advantages and disadvantages of these types of architecture. 3. To know the relation between the type of architecture and the physical conditions of the country.	As a preparation for the successful study of this unit, students look up references given by the instructor, and try to discover, as they can, the salient features of each of the domestic types of architecture. Students bring to class the results of their research to form the basis for discussion.	1. Discussion. 2. Short talks by students. 3. Lecture by instructor. 1. Students present their results to class. 2. Group discussion guided and supplemented by the instructor. 3. The necessary illustrative material should be used in connection with these discussions. 4. Write the characteristic features of the style of domestic architecture on the blackboard as they are brought out in the discussion. Students copy these in their note-books. 5. A local architect could be in-	1. C. V. Bush and E. D. Townsley, *Problems in Architectural Drawing,* pp. 12-17 2. A. B. and C. H. Greenberg, *Architectural Drawing,* pp. 69-74 3. Any other standard work on architectural styles.

4. To know the origin and development of the different architectural styles.
5. To know that the style of architecture of a home is the expression of the wealth, ideas, and aspirations of the owner.
6. To know that any style of architecture is a harmonious combination of beauty and utility.
7. To know the importance of the following factors in the construction of a building or a dwelling; balance, unity, stability, proportion, fenestration, decoration.

III. *Appreciation of:*
1. The fact that architecture is a dynamic art; it grows and changes because it is vitally connected with life.
2. The fact that architecture constitutes an important means of expression of needs, wealth, ideals and aspirations of any given people at any given period.

vited to talk to the group or groups on domestic architecture.
6. This discussion could be closed by an excursion to different buildings under construction, students to be asked to identify the styles of architecture and to explain their salient features.

NOTE: In his lecture the instructor should stress the dynamic nature of architecture, point out how it expresses the ideals of communities, states, and nations by beautiful public structures: capital buildings, cathedrals, libraries, museums, etc., and could close his talk by a brief history of architecture of Egypt, Greece, Spain, Rome, France, Germany, and England, and point out how much we are indebted to them.

Time—two to four hours

Specific Objectives	Elements of Subject-Matter	Suggested Teaching Procedure	References
I. *Skills and abilities:* 1. To develop the ability to recognize the multiplicity of problems involved in the construction of a home. 2. To be able to select a type of domestic architecture that would fit a given site. II. *Knowledge:* 1. To know in a general way the main features of a desirable home site. 2. To know the relation between the cost of the site and that of the building. 3. To know how to arrange the rooms in reference to proper illumination—natural and artificial—economy of space—and conservation of human energy. 4. To know that the size of rooms is determined by definite requirements: use and equipment.	Students look up the references given and read on the points under consideration.	NOTE: The consideration of this unit must be brief, yet without eliminating salient points. A more detailed study of the different topics should be taken up as the need arises in connection with actual drafting. Discussion. Explanation. The method of procedure is the same, with some elimination and substitution as in Unit I. Time—two hours	1. Bush and Townsley, *Problems in Architectural Drawing*, pp. 5-10 2. G. W. Seaman, *Architectural Drawing*, pp. 10-13

5. To know, in a general way, about wall construction, materials used, thickness, etc.
6. To know in general about interior details: door and window openings, closets, size of different stairs, proper size of chimney flues, etc.
7. To know in general about fixtures: bathtub, lavatory, sink, etc.
8. To know definitely the relation of foundations to the superstructure.
9. To know the advantages and disadvantages of the different heating systems.
10. To know something about roof coverings.

III. *Appreciation of:*
1. The problems that enter into the planning and construction of a building.
2. The necessity of careful and intelligent planning of a building.
3. The need for good building construction.

UNIT III. PLANS

Specific Objectives	Elements of Subject-Matter	Suggested Teaching Procedure	References
I. *Skills and abilities:* 1. To make vertical architectural letters. 2. To use correctly architectural scale. 3. To use architectural symbols correctly. 4. To draw dimension plans correctly. 5. To be able to use standard reference works, mill books, etc. 6. To develop further the power of visualization, and to accentuate further neatness, accuracy, and logical planning. II. *Knowledge:* 1. To know the names, sizes, and uses of the following structural members: sills, girders, floor joists, studs, bridging, headers, and trimmers, corner-posts, plates, rafters, purling,	1. Size of lot: 60' × 110'. Lot faces south. On this lot must be placed a two-story Dutch Colonial house and a two-car garage. Over all dimensions of house: 23' × 43'. Size of garage 20' × 23'. 2. The rooms must be so arranged that every room gets sunshine sometime during the day. ——— Floor plans must show the arrangement and location of walls, partitions, closets, fire-place, flues, windows, doors, etc. They must also show the location of plumbing fixtures, lighting outlets, power-service outlets, heating apparatus. ———	NOTE: In order to obviate copying, it is necessary that all problems be given an isometric picture, students to translate these into orthographic drawings. The problems should never be given in orthographic form and students asked to draw them at larger scale. Such procedure has little, if any, educational value. ——— Lettering. The method of architectural lettering is the same as that of mechanical lettering, only that the former permits individual expression to a very large extent.	1. F. Halstead, *Architectural Details*, pp. 225–281 2. G. W. Seaman, *Progressive Steps in Architectural Drawing* 3. W. A. Radford, *Architectural Details* 4. Bright and Faber, *Simple Architectural Letters*

ridges, collar-beam, rough floor, finish floor, valleys, hips, eaves. 2. To know the proper method of blocking out drawings and finishing them. 3. To know in detail the architectural symbols of windows, doors, electrical equipment, lighting and plumbing fixtures, material in elevation and section. 4. To know the proper method of dimensioning. 5. To know the proper sizes of flues and fireplaces. 6. To know the proper method of laying out stair-well and the relation of the tread to the riser. 7. To know the thickness of lath and plaster, the thickness of outside wall finish, siding, rustic stucco, etc. 8. To know the proper thickness of concrete basement walls. 9. To know how to indicate conventionally the different materials used.	Scale: $\frac{1}{4}'' = 1'$ ___ Students draw one plate of each: First Floor Plan, Basement, Second Floor Plan, Roof Plan. 1. Basement: Plan must show laundry, heater room, coal-bin, play room, if possible, location for furnace, stairs to first floor, lighting outlets, etc. 2. First Floor Plan must indicate living room, dining room, kitchen, sun porch, stairs to second floor and to basement, vestibule, service hall, front and rear porches, fireplace, windows, doors, outlets for lighting, etc., material indicated conventionally, direction of floor joists. 3. Second Floor Plan should indicate: three bed rooms, closets, bathroom, stairs to attic, roofs of sun porch, front, and rear porches, lighting outlets, etc.	Students should practice lettering every day from five to ten minutes, using first pencil, later, ink. The teacher should insist on this practice. Vertical architectural lettering should be used. Methods: Demonstration Explanation Development (inductive method) Explain the relation between architectural and mechanical drafting. Point out that the principles of both are the same. Develop by the inductive method the concept of "plans." Demonstrate the proper method of blocking out drawings. Show proper method of dimensioning. Stress ac-

UNIT III. PLANS (*Continued*)

Specific Objectives	Elements of Subject-Matter	Suggested Teaching Procedure	References
10. To know the economic arrangement of floor joists. 11. The proper method of fenestration. 12. The different types of roofs: pitch, rise, run, span, etc. III. *Appreciation of:* 1. The important rôle plans play in construction activities. 2. Need of care, accuracy, and neatness in plan drawing. 3. The marvelous ability of man's brain to conceive and plan any structure on paper before it is executed in stone and steel.	4. Roof Plan must show every valley, hip, and every leader and gutter. Notes just be given as to roof covering, etc. Every floor plan should be carefully dimensioned, as the principal dimensions of the structure occur on these plans. Dimensions should also be given for the interior of the building, the dimensions being taken from centers of partitions to the face of the studding of a frame wall. In locating wall openings—doors and windows—it is necessary to work from center lines.	curacy and check dimensions closely. Be sure that students know the names and sizes of the structural members. Use standard reference works, mill books, etc. Subscribe for class use to several magazines, such as *American Builder, American Home, American Small Home,* etc.	

A similar treatment is shown in the initial units on woodwork for the junior high school (Junior High School Industrial Arts, Course of Study Monograph No. 3, Sacramento, 1931).

UNIT I. SHOP ORIENTATION AND TOOL CLASSIFICATION

Specific Objectives	Subject-Matter	Suggestive Teaching Procedure	References for Teachers
Knowledge of: Shop rules and regulations Shop systems Safety precautions Tools and their classification	Enrolment data Shop systems Lockers Tool room Shop tickets Foremen	Secure enrolment data. Assign benches. Seek to inspire appreciation of opportunities now offered.	*Woodwork in the Junior High Schools,* Roberts, Chs. I, II, III.
Appreciation of: A systematically arranged shop Orderly tool keeping Good shop sense Opportunity here afforded Rights of others	Shop rules and regulations Entering and leaving Shop behavior Relation with teacher, foreman, tool keeper, and other pupils	Pass out copies of shop regulations and discuss briefly. Explain the shop systems. Conduct pupils on a tour around the shop pointing out the dangers and safety precautions.	*Instructional Units in Hand Woodwork,* Brown and Tustison. Foreword and introduction. *How to Work with Tools and Wood,* Stanley, Ch. I.
Habits: Laying foundation for development of good habits, viz.: coöperation, caution, orderliness, open-mindedness and industry.	Shop precautions Running in the shop Distracting attention Relation to machines Care with hand tools Safety-first hints, etc. Classification of the wood-working tools 1. Laying-out tools 2. Cutting tools 3. Holding tools 4. Boring tools 5. Driving tools 6. Abrasive tools	Discuss briefly work to be accomplished in the course. Seek to lay the foundation for certain appreciations and desirable habits. Present pupils a list of tools properly classified for study. As enrichment work for some pupils have them prepare a small scrapbook of pictures of tools properly grouped.	*Essentials of Woodworking,* Griffith, Chs. I-V. *Principles of Woodworking,* Hjorth, Ch. I.
Ability: To coöperate with teacher and pupils in carrying out shop regulations and working procedure. To know tools by their correct names and uses	Tests in spelling, pronunciation, and classification of tools A true-false test	Other pupils may read certain reference material. Have pupils participate in handling the tools and separating them into proper classifications. Test pupils by presenting a mixed list of tools for classification.	*Prevocational and Industrial Arts,* Wood and Smith, pp. 3-34. *Tool Processes in Woodwork,* Laughlin, Chs. I-III.

UNIT II. PLANING AND SQUARING

Specific Objectives	Subject-Matter	Suggestive Teaching Procedure	References for Teachers
Knowledge of: Plane adjustment Posture at bench Stroke, angle and pressure in handling plane the six step method of squaring up stock How to whet a plane iron	Planing The jack plane The vise Soft pine board Plane adjustment Posture at bench Stroke	Give each boy a scrap piece of soft wood. With planes dull or maladjusted, have pupils proceed to make shavings. Now stop the work and have planes examined and adjusted.	*Instructional Units in Hand Woodwork,* Brown and Tustison, Units 4, 5, 6, 7, 10, 13, 14, and 15.
Appreciation of: The difference between a dull or badly adjusted plane and one in good condition Value of thin ribbon-like shavings Importance of accuracy	Face planing Edge planing End planing The six step method for squaring stock The laying-out tools The rule Try square	Proceed again with instructions as to posture, stroke, angle, etc. Direct practice in end-planing, discussing method of avoiding damaged corners. Explain and demonstrate the six-step method for squaring. Give each pupil a piece of soft wood using 1 x 4 x 13 Rough.	*Essentials of Woodworking,* Griffith, pp. 39-48. *Tool Processes in Woodworking,* Laughlin, pp. 28-33.
Habits: Attentiveness Carefulness Self-reliance Regard for tools and benches	Knife Marking gauge Use of: Bench vise Bench hook Bench saw	Using the six-step method, have pupils finish the piece to $\frac{7}{8}$ x $3\frac{1}{2}$ x 12. With proper laying-out tools, have pupils lay out half of the piece in $\frac{1}{4}$" sections around the block for a sawing exercise. The pupil should	*Squaring Chart,* Lukowitz. Stanley, *op. cit.,* Charts 111, 114, 115, 116.
Ability to: Properly adjust a plane Use the jackplane correctly Use the laying-out tools, jack plane and bench saw Properly square-up stock	Projects Sand block Bread-board A true-false test on squaring	test his own skill by observing the sawed-off pieces and the condition of the board after each sawing. The remaining half can now be used to make a sand block of desired size. Test for Unit II.	*Principles of Woodworking,* Hjorth, pp. 70-72.

UNIT III. ARRIS TREATMENTS

Specific Objectives	Subject-Matter	Suggestive Teaching Procedure	References for Teachers
Knowledge of: The difference between the common edge cuts, chamfer, bevel, taper, and round Use of the hand tools in executing these cuts	Squaring (reviewed) Chamfering Pencil gauging Planing chamfer End planing Beveling Tapering Rounding Hollowing Beading	Give pupil any scrap piece of soft wood for practice. By drawings, demonstrations, and models seek to teach the fundamental steps in chamfering, beveling, tapering, and rounding. Demonstrate the setting and use of the new tools.	Brown and Tustison, *op. cit.,* Units 14, 15, 16 Griffith, *op. cit.,* pp. 48 and 50
Appreciation of: The utility and beauty resulting from these various arris treatments The importance of accuracy in executing these processes	New tools T bevel Bench stop Pencil gauge Straight-edge Compass	Conduct a period of drill upon the laying out and making of arris cuts. Have pupils make a list or tell where the arris treatments can be used for beauty or utility in woodwork.	*Tool Processes in Woodwork,* Laughlin, pp. 37-38
Habits of: Clear thinking Accuracy in performance Attending strictly to one's own work Close attention to instruction	Projects Confined to one main piece Coat and hatracks Bases for ringtoss Calendar pads, bill-file, etc.	After sufficient practice have pupils choose and draw one or more one-piece projects and supervise the work of squaring the wood and submitting the arrises to the desired treatments.	*Woodwork in the Junior High School,* Roberts, p. 111.
Ability to: Lay out properly and successfully execute the edge cuts — chamfer, bevel, taper, and round	Orthographic drawing of the one-piece projects to be made A true-false test on arris treatments	The one-piece projects may be carried over into Unit IV if the boring of any holes is needed. Test for Unit III.	Hjorth, *op. cit.,* p. 182.

UNIT IV. BORING, DRILLING, AND COUNTERSINKING

Specific Objectives	Subject-Matter	Suggestive Teaching Procedure	References for Teachers
Knowledge of: How to lay out for boring holes The nature and use of the various boring devices How a bit cuts	Laying out for boring holes Try square Marking gauge Rule and pencil Use of the brace Operation of chuck	Briefly discuss the boring unit making it clear that all of the hand-boring devices will be studied, but special drill for mastery will be confined in this unit to the brace and auger bit.	Brown and Tustison, *op. cit.*, Units 22 and 23
Appreciation of: Difference between skilful and careless boring A properly sharpened bit or drill	Use of the ratchet Meaning of sweep Sight while boring	Conduct a brief study and comparison of the boring devices listed in sub-ject-matter column.	Hjorth, *op. cit.*, pp. 18-21
Habits of: Carefulness with reference to: Breaking through the wood when boring Boring straight and square Damaging bits on iron vise and otherwise	Bits and drills Judging kinds and sizes Judging condition Drilling for screws Hole for body of screw Pilot hole Use of countersink Use of hand drill Expansive bit	Demonstrate how to lay out and bore holes using the brace and auger bit. Conduct a period of practice on scrap pieces. Have pupils finish certain pieces started in Unit III.	Griffith, *op. cit.*, pp. 53, 55 Stanley, *op. cit.*, Chart 117
Ability to: Lay out accurately for bor-ing desired holes Identify bits and drills as to kind and size Use the hand-boring de-vices correctly	Forstner bit Projects Further development of pieces from Unit III Game boards, spool racks, ring-toss, line-winder, etc.	Fast pupils can study assigned refer-ences applicable to the boring unit and practice using the boring tools. A true-false test can be used to test the knowledge acquired.	

the successful completion of the individual pieces of work would retard his professional growth.

The child comes to the manual-training class for the first time with great enthusiasm to do, and with spontaneous activity-interest always present. He has the thought of free expression always uppermost in mind. This seems to be an ideal situation to keep within the fourth-grade shop.

At this age the child is enwrapped in his play, each part of the play being, to him, life itself. He is especially interested in toys and mechanical construction. The natural tendency of investigation and experimentation are prime factors of his child life and, if properly guided, he need have no other incentive. Hence we advocate toy making as most applicable to the fourth-grade age.

Another source of motivated projects may be found in connection with the classroom projects that are being developed by the class teacher in history, geography, and similar subjects. The opportunity for educative activities that will contribute toward the best procedure in other classes should be welcomed by the manual-training teacher. Situations that should be important to the room teacher as possible motives for projects in other subjects often develop because of the pupil's interest in his manual-training project.

It is always desirable that each pupil have in mind as thoroughly as possible the shape and representation of the project before he begins to work on it. In recognition of this fact we should encourage the pupil to draw a rough free-hand sketch representing the toy or other article that he may wish to make. When he has made his best effort he can complete his templet from his drawing. When the original drawing is not made the pupil should make a copy of the model templet on drawing paper and cut it out with the scissors.

G. Agriculture. *The Minnesota State Course in Agriculture for Junior and Senior High-School Periods* (Bulletin C-6, Department of Education, St. Paul, June, 1932) gives the following suggestions for vitalizing teaching.

I. TEACHING SUGGESTIONS

A. **Dairying**
1. *Agriculture I*
   a. When taking the class to a farm to score and judge breeds, have pupils take notice of such factors as buildings, equipment, system of ventilation, arrangement, size of stalls, and gutter.

   b. When using a large mounted picture of an animal to assist pupils in learning how to score and judge dairy cattle, have members of the class name and locate points, such as barrel, rump, milk-veins, withers.

   c. Have pupils make charts for display purposes showing value of milk as a food.

   d. Use class debates to bring out the advantages and disadvantages of each breed.

   e. When studying uses and qualities of dairy products, have on display as many samples as possible, such as cheese, butter, casein, products, candy made from powdered buttermilk, and poultry feed.

   f. If possible, have an actual demonstration of the way to fit and show calves.

   g. Visit an implement dealer to learn parts of the cream separator if there is none in the school.

2. *Agriculture II and III*

   a. Have pupils determine fertilizing value of rations when they are figuring cost of rations.

   b. Have samples of various feeds on hand.

   c. Study analysis given on several different kinds of commercial feed sacks and check with Minnesota Feed Inspection law.

   d. To bring out importance of cow-testing work, have records showing instances where "boarder" cows were discovered through testing.

   e. Compare profit from a high-producing herd in community with herd of average cows (190 pounds butter-fat) in Minnesota.

   f. Demonstrate testing of cheese, butter, sour cream, skim milk.

   g. Visit creamery to see testing, weighing, churning.

   h. Have pupils figure loss on their farm income in one year from use of an inefficient cream separator.

   i. A good way to learn principles and art of making ice-cream is to have pupils furnish necessary material and actually make some in class.

   j. When studying standardization of milk, have pupils determine nature of "doctored" samples.

   k. When studying clean milk production

      (1) Compare sediment tests of milk from small-topped pails and ordinary pails, cotton disc strainer and ordinary one, clipped cows and unclipped cows.

(2) Use bacterial counts to bring out comparisons more clearly.

(3) Have pupils make methylene blue tests of milk from home farms.

(4) Visit some dairies where clean milk is produced.

(5) Have on display cotton-disc strainers, small-topped pails, cream stirrers, model cooling tanks.

(6) Have pupils taste cheese or milk exposed to gasoline fumes to show them how important it is not to expose dairy products to contaminating odors.

(7) Have implement dealer discuss and demonstrate care and operation of cream separator.

l. When studying Mendel's law, use U. S. D. A. roulette wheel.

m. Have several pedigrees for examination.

n. Demonstrate prevention of horns on calves.

o. Demonstrate throwing an animal.

p. Visit local coöperative creameries, certified dairies, feed milling companies.

q. The teacher may compile a set of questions that he has been called upon to answer and give it to pupils to find correct answers.

B. Alfalfa

1. Have on display plants with nodules and long root.

2. Have pupils make diagrams or charts comparing alfalfa with timothy and other feeds.

3. Cite as many instances as possible where alfalfa helped to kill noxious weeds.

4. Have on hand samples of lime, marl, paper-mill and sugar-beet residue used for correcting acidity in soil.

5. Have pupils make several acidity tests of soil on home farms.

6. If possible, visit a field that shows benefit of liming or fertilizing.

7. Visit implement dealer to observe and learn care and operation of lime spreaders.

8. Show class a copy of certified seed laws, tags, and seals.

9. Have pupils make purification and germination tests of seeds.

10. Have some pupil demonstrate inoculation of seed.

11. Have successful alfalfa grower talk to class.

12. Make use of experimental undertakings carried on in State and county.

13. Have on display different kinds of fertilizers.

14. Have pupils make phosphorus tests of soil on home farms.
15. Visit farm or implement dealer to learn how to adjust parts on mower and on other hay machinery.
16. If opportunity offers, have class visit artificial hay-curing outfit.
17. Have preserved specimens of alfalfa insects and diseases.
18. Compare results from actual attempts to rejuvenate an alfalfa field.
19. Make a survey of community to find out what crops may replace alfalfa if it winter kills.
20. Compare value of farms with and without alfalfa.

II. FARM PRACTICE

The home-farm practice of pupils is regarded as an integral part of the course in agriculture. Two types of farm practice are emphasized. One is the definite short-time program of projects which should be required of all pupils in each year or work. The other is the long-time farm practice program which should be developed with each pupil according to his ability, opportunity, and need. The long-time program of farm practice which is considered most important should develop in scope and complexity as the pupil progresses through the three years of study. Each form of farm practice work should be preceded by a careful selection of the type of activity to be undertaken. The pupil and the teacher should select plans for the organization of problems which include opportunities to put into operation the activities selected. When the pupil has determined the kind of farm practice work he will undertake he should be given time and encouragement to make a thorough analysis of the problems involved. The outcome of the analysis and study of the farm practice problems should be a complete plan including objectives, information needed, plan of procedures, records, and arrangements for starting the work. The nature and scope of the farm practice work is an important index of the success of any teacher of agriculture.

A. The short-time program of farm practice. Careful and thorough planning is an essential phase of the farm practice program of any pupil. Good farm practice results are not accidental. They are possible only when the pupil makes a complete study of the problems involved in carrying on the practice activities and is able to make his plan coincide with what he can naturally perform at home. The following plan will assist pupils in preparing for effective farm practice work. Each pupil should have a separate note-book for each farm practice activity. Much of the work will be done on the individual basis. School-time preparation as well as outside study is essential for such individual work.

1. Suggested preliminary work by the teacher
   a. Make a farm survey of the community giving special attention to the home farms of prospective pupils in the classes in agriculture; also get acquainted with the boys and girls and their parents.
   b. Find out the pupils' chief interest in agriculture.
   c. Analyze data and facts presented by the pupil as his reasons for desiring a given kind of project.
   d. Help the pupil to select the short-time or definite project by questions and suggestions designed to stimulate his thinking.

2. The desirable characteristics of a short-time farm project are as follows:
   a. It must be of an agricultural nature; for example, raising a farm animal, raising a particular crop, constructing a farm building, making some convenience, beautifying the home, testing a herd, doing some particular farm improvement work.
   b. It must be adapted to community conditions (do not try to grow cotton in northern Minnesota).
   c. It must represent a coöperative effort by the pupil, the parents, and the teacher.
      (1) The pupil must know when he is working on the project and when he is not; when he is beginning the project and when it is finished; what he is to do (goal) and what the details of the work are. The project should lend itself to progressive planning. "The project plan should be the organized expression of the pupil's purpose and the procedure proposed for carrying out the activities involved."
      (2) The parents must be satisfied. If they are antagonistic the pupil will soon find it impossible to go on and the entire plan will fail. The pupil needs the encouragement and sometimes the financial aid of his parents.
      (3) The teacher should give adequate supervision and direction.
   d. It must be educational. The project is required as an essential part of the school work in agriculture. It should be of such a character as to increase the scope of the pupil's farm experience, extend his skill in range and degree and be a means of growth. It should provide opportunity for development "morally" as well as "mentally." When it is completed, the pupil should look back upon it as a worth-while experience.

e. It must be of pupil caliber. It should challenge and be within the range of the ability and the interest of the pupil, not beyond what he is able to do nor less than he will be interested in doing. It should not require unreasonable time and effort, neither should it require so little work and thought that it will tend to be forgotten or neglected. It should be suited to the pupil's physique, mental ability, and financial condition. It should not involve excessive financial responsibility. It should be performed largely by the pupil.

f. It should require at least six months' time for completion.

g. It should be possible of completion during the year. If the project is reported January 1st of one year, it should be completed that year, or in time to permit the records and report of completion to be sent to the State Supervisor's office in the spring of the following year.

h. It must lend itself to the keeping of records. Accurate and complete records are considered an essential part of the project activity.

i. It should have the "ownership" characteristic. The project subject or its returns, or both, should be owned by the pupil. He is entitled to a material compensation or satisfaction for his work. He will not do his best work or have the keenest interest in raising a calf that belongs to his father or in an acre of potatoes that is to be sold and the returns taken by some one else.

j. It should contribute to and stimulate interest in the long-time farm-practice program and should fit into it. A new plan should be set up for next year applying some of the principles learned for the current project.

k. It should give direction to other farm practices at home. The principles, the scientific attitude, and the educational value from it should be contagious.

B. The long-time program of farm practice. The long-time program of farm practice differs from the short-time program of farm practice in that it is broader in scope and involves several enterprises. The activities include working with many enterprises that require a year or more for completion. The approach to the broader program of farm practice is through a study of the needs of the home farm. Usually the study develops into a farm management problem involving a reorganization of the home farm procedures. The long-time practice program influences the work each pupil does in school. It forms the major basis for the individual study of each pupil in agriculture. The scope of the long-time program of farm practice is determined by (1) the interest and ability of the pupil, (2) the needs of the home farm, and (3) the opportunity the pupil has for making the needed changes. The selection and the planning of the long-time farm practice program proceeds in a manner similar to that of the special project. Each enterprise is developed in its relationship to the type of farming practised on the home farm.

The plan should be made at the beginning of the course in Agriculture I. The plan will develop in scope and detail as the pupil progresses to and through Agriculture II and III. Each of the enterprises will be analyzed and studied in a manner similar to the procedure suggested previously for the short-time practice plan. The pupil should emerge at the end of his agriculture course with a complete, improved and up-to-date farm management set-up for the type of farming considered most appropriate for the home farm. Naturally all the details of the plan are not intended to be in operation when the pupil has completed his school study of agriculture. Through follow-up work the teacher will continue his contacts, encouraging and helping the pupil as the opportunity presents itself to the end that the details of the plan may find expression in actual practice.

1. The long-time farm practice has the following desirable characteristics:
    a. It deals with the home farm of the pupil in high-school agriculture and is a continuous program of farm and country-home improvement carried out gradually through a period of several years.
    b. It has a definite, clear-cut goal or ideal of achievement.
    c. It requires complete, detailed, written plans showing the entire program, what is to be done each year, how it is to be done, and why.
    d. It involves the keeping of achievement records.
    e. It concerns the parents as well as the pupil.
    f. It should aim to:
        (1) Maintain the productivity of the soil
        (2) Pay all farm expenses
        (3) Pay interest on capital
        (4) Pay for work done by members of the family
        (5) Leave the operator a good labor income for his year's work
    g. It should be planned from the farm management point of view.
    h. It should be aided by the short-time definite farm projects of the high-school pupil.

  i. It should make use of and promote modern scientific practices in agriculture.

  j. It should promote efficiency in labor and management.

  k. It should provide for a secure income well distributed throughout the year.

  l. It should emphasize the saving of human energy for higher things than daily routine and drudgery.

  m. Coöperation should be a key word in the plans. It should suggest home, community, State and national coöperation.

2. Following is an example of the preliminary long-time program of home-farm activities as worked out by a pupil in a Minnesota high school department of agriculture:

As a pupil in the agriculture department, I shall have a good opportunity to make some careful studies of our home-farm business to discover some practical ways in which our business may be improved. This long-time plan of activities is simply a statement of present conditions at home and some of the results I hope to obtain in some of the enterprises and also of the ways in which I expect to make the improvements.

I shall fill out each year the farm survey sheet for my farm and out of the jobs and practices listed on the farm practice reporting form I shall select those jobs or practices that will help me to obtain the results I am after in this long-time program.

  a. Dairy program. About 50 per cent of our total farm income comes from the dairy enterprise. It will be necessary to find out how good this enterprise is at home and study ways of improving it in order to get as much profit as possible.

  (1) Present condition:

    (*a*) Six cows over five years old; three over four years old, five over three years old, three heifer calves two months old, and one two-year-old bull

    (*b*) Ten of the cows will freshen in September, two during October and November, and two during December and January

    (*c*) Herd butter-fat average for last year (1930-31) was 284 pounds. The two highest cows produced 257 and 346 and the lowest 257 pounds

    (*d*) We usually have plenty of concentrate feed for the cows except that we buy two tons of bran and a half ton of oil-meal each year

    (*e*) We have only ten acres of alfalfa (should have about 15 acres)

    (*f*) Have a silo

    (*g*) Our last crop of calves (1930-31) was out of a fair type bull, pure-bred sire and dam, but I do not know his production records

(2) Long-time objective:
Since higher production is economical production, I expect to raise the herd average to 400 pounds or more

(3) Methods of achieving the objective:
(a) Put cows on production test each year and keep feed cost record
(b) Cull out all cows that do not produce at least:
340 pounds at maturity
310 pounds as four year olds
280 pounds as three year olds
250 pounds as two year olds
The only exceptions to the above will be for some good reason, as sickness, milking too long, etc.
(c) At least 90 per cent of cows to freshen between September 1st and December 1st
(d) Each new bull bought will be of better type than the one before him and the production of his dams must average 500 pounds or more. For a while he will likely be bought under six months old
(e) Usually four heifers will be saved each year out of dams over 300 pounds
(f) The size of the herd will be kept at about twelve to fourteen cows

b. *Swine program.* About 35 per cent of total farm income comes from hogs. I believe we can make more profit from this enterprise than we have before.

(1) Present condition:
(a) Last spring (1931) 5 sows farrowed 43 pigs, of these 30 were saved to six months of age
(b) These pigs averaged only 175 pounds at six months on account of the fact that the sow dried up too soon. The pigs had to be weaned too young and they were always runty, weighing only 125 pounds at six months
(c) Total pork per litter was only 1,050 pounds

(2) Methods of achieving the objective:
(a) Keep feed cost record of the whole swine enterprise
(b) Mark all litters, study the difference between performance of litters, keep gilts from those litters making best showing, rapid gains, and showing uniformity of type
(c) Keep getting a better and better boar each year out of large litters making good, cheap gains
(d) Always flush sows
(e) Keep young sows growing and thrifty during gestation period
(f) Put guard rails in all pens
(g) Find a better system of feeding
(h) Run pigs on clean legume or oats and rape pasture

      (*i*) Wash sows before farrowing

      (*j*) Scrub pens with hot lye water before farrowing

c. Poultry. About 15 per cent of total income is from this enterprise.

  (1) Present condition:

We haven't made a practice of selling off the old hens each year. At present we have some one and a half and two and a half year old hens. Our pullets have been coming into production fairly early.

  (2) Objectives:

      (*a*) To raise production of flock to 225 eggs per hen

      (*b*) To develop good vigor and health and sell eggs to hatchery

  (3) Methods of achieving objectives:

      (*a*) Keep year-round egg record as a check on the health and productive ability of the flock and to test the efficiency of our feeding and management practice

      (*b*) Sell all old hens except about 50 of the best layers

      (*c*) Improve feeding practice for chicks and laying flock

      (*d*) Always buy chicks from high-producing flock

      (*e*) Grade eggs for market

      (*f*) Go through laying flock once a month at least and take out all birds showing low production and poor health

      (*g*) Develop a system of sanitation and clean range for the chick flock

d. Corn program:

  (1) Present Condition

      (*a*) Corn is our major feed crop for all livestock enterprises

      (*b*) We usually have about 25 to 28 acres of this crop each year

      (*c*) Last year (1931) our average yield was about 40 bushels

      (*d*) Our variety is a mixed Minnesota 13

  (2) Long-time objective:

      (*a*) Raise the yield average to 50-55 bushes per acre and in this way cheap production costs of the livestock products we sell

  (3) How the objective is to be achieved:

      (*a*) Raise the yielding ability of our present corn if possible, or bring a different variety or strain on the place that is capable of high yields

      (*b*) Select seed before frost from healthy, green, full stand hills

      (*c*) Store seed properly

      (*d*) Grade the seed

      (*e*) Run germination test

      (*f*) Make a check on our percentage of perfect stand each year

      (*g*) Use recommended methods of preparing seed bed and of cultivation

      (*h*) Check the value of fertilizers on different fields

      (*i*) Keep a cost account record of five or more acres

e. Small grain program
   (1) Present condition:
      (*a*) Small grains (oats-barley mixed) are an important feed crop on the farm at present. Usually have about 30 acres.
      (*b*) Average yield in 1931 was 40 bushels and in 1930 52 bushels
      (*c*) Our varieties are not on the recommended list for this section
   (2) Long-time objective:
   Raise average yield to 55-60 bushels if possible and reduce the production cost of our livestock products
   (3) How the objective is to be achieved:
      (*a*) Bring higher yielding varieties onto the place
      (*b*) Always clean seed before planting
      (*c*) Test for germination
      (*d*) Select the combination of grains that will produce the most pounds of feed per acre
      (*e*) Control weeks to increase yield and lower labor and power costs

f. Alfalfa. Alfalfa is the cheapest source of nutrient for sows. Hogs also can make very good use of this crop as pasture or protein supplement.
   (1) Present condition:
      (*a*) We have 10 acres of the crop at present
      (*b*) Last year (1931) two acres dried out pretty badly and yielded only 1½ tons an acre; on the other 8 acres we got 2½ tons per acre
   (2) Long-time objectives:
      (*a*) Increase acreage to at least one acre per producing cow
      (*b*) Secure an average yield of at least 3½ tons
   (3) How objectives are to be achieved:
      (*a*) Plow up the two acres of poor stand and seed 5 acres more this next spring
      (*b*) Use only recommended varieties, good germination, and clean seed

g. Weeds
   (1) Present Condition
      (*a*) We have a number of small patches of Canada thistle
      (*b*) We have several different kinds of weeds about the grove
      (*c*) There is some quack grass in all the fields
   (2) Long-time objectives:
      (*a*) Attempt to eradicate all noxious weeds
      (*b*) Keep all other weeds down as much as possible
   (3) Methods of achieving objectives:
      (*a*) Will not let any noxious weeds go to seed

(*b*) Will try best cultivating methods to keep weeds down
(*c*) Clean all small grain before planting
(*d*) Buy only clean legume and grass seeds
(*e*) Try chemical methods of weed control

h. Crop rotations

(1) Present condition:
Our present cropping system is not quite the way I would like it. We haven't developed the best system of manure application. We haven't got our legumes working around right yet.

(2) Long-time objective:
(*a*) Increase amount of legumes for soil fertility
(*b*) Develop regular system of manure application so that we can make heavy application every two years
(*c*) Use sweet clover for summer and fall pasture and for green manure

H. Adult Education. Three courses of study from the adult education program of the Minneapolis Public Schools have been selected as excellent examples of teaching devices in this field. These courses were organized and developed during the years 1934 and 1935.

1. New Deal legislation

A. *Teacher's Overview.* This unit is a study and discussion of various prominent legislative measures of the Roosevelt administration, in order to evolve an accurate interpretation of their objectives. The unit is divided into groups of discussions in order to present the problems that most vitally concern us as individuals. The students should be encouraged to submit topics for discussion, which they believe affect them and which in turn would interest others. Each discussion should include (1) a pooling of the experiences of members of the group, (2) an analysis of issues that appear, (3) a consideration of practical steps for improvements.

B. *Unit of work*

C. *The following topics were outlined for purposes of class discussion:*

(1) How are the NRA codes working out in industry?
(2) What are the points of view about the help provided by public works?
(3) How may debtors get relief?

(4) Must we reflate or repudiate?

(5) Will there be effective farm relief?

(6) Should the seller of securities also beware?

(7) Is stricter regulation of banks necessary?

(8) Of what value are the conservation and regional planning projects of the administration?

(9) How should unemployment relief be handled?

(10) Is nationalism a way out?

(11) How is public opinion reacting to economic planning?

(12) What is the consumer's part?

D. *Reference material.* The writer is indebted to the appendix of Landis: *The Third American Revolution* and to *Social Reconstruction: A Study Guide for Group and Class Discussion,* by Rugg and Krueger, for suggestions for the above syllabus. The writer believes that the above questions and issues should open up problems in which there is public interest and on which people will be developing opinions. The following are periodicals which interpret significant data for this course and which should be read because of the changing nature of the subject-matter. These are listed as suggested in Landis: *The Third American Revolution.*

United States News—record of activities of the United States Government without editorial comment

Business Week—interpretation of developments in the business world

New Republic—journal of opinions about the administration's program

Nation—variety of comment and data on the New Deal

Information Service of the Federal Council of Churches, 105 East 22d Street, New York. Interpretation of industrial and agricultural questions

Literary Digest—summaries and interpretation of newspaper opinion

E. *The outcomes were:*

(1) A knowledge of the provisions in the legislative measures of the New Deal

(2) An understanding of the following points:

(a) That the Roosevelt administration has attempted to help every class of industry and trade

(b) That the measures of the administration represent a movement of collectivism

(c) That the program aims at better urban-rural balance

New Deal Legislation

Main objective for this unit: To bring about an accurate interpretation of the legislative measures of the Roosevelt administration, with an emphasis upon the help which has been offered to industry and trade.

Means of arousing interest: Discussion of the aspects of the New Deal legislation as it has affected the students. Reports from people in the community. Discussion of radio addresses and the daily news.

Outline of Subject-Matter (Suggested)	Experiences to Aid Learning (Suggested)	*References:* For the Student (S) For the Teacher (T)
I. *Features of the Democratic platform*	Analyze New Deal legislation in conjunction with the following objectives:	McDonald, W., *The Menace of Recovery*, 1934
A. Reduction of expenditure	1. Elimination of special privilege in control of economic and social structure by numerically few but powerful groups	Landis, B. Y., *The Third Revolution*, 1933
B. Sound currency		
C. Tariff revision		
D. World Court adherence		Sprague, O. M. W., *Recovery and Common Sense*, 1929
E. Better financing of farm mortgage and home-mortgages	2. War on crime and graft	
F. Development of coöperative marketing	3. Seeking of swing of pendulum from concentration of wealth in hands of a few to a wide distribution of the wealth and property of the nation	Roosevelt, Franklin D., *Looking Forward*, 1933
G. Regulation of banks and securities		Roosevelt, Franklin D., *On Our Way*, 1934
H. Repeal of Eighteenth Amendment		
I. Non-cancellation of foreign debts	Discuss the following methods of carrying out the program of the New Deal:	Laski, Harold J., *Democracy in Crisis*, 1933
II. *Character of Roosevelt cabinet and advisers*	1. Organization and discipline of Industry by government, with bounty	Renatus, K., *Twelfth Hour Capitalism*, 1932

...and taxation of other people who cannot be organized
2. Created work and government dole
3. Reorganization of American society on collective lines with federal government as central source of authority
4. Artificial stimulation of business, industry, and farming
5. Artificial mitigation of unemployed and suffering
6. Increase of public debt
7. Off-gold standard with attempt to devaluate gold content of dollar in order to raise prices
8. Eventual stabilization of the dollar in relation to commodity prices

III. *Inauguration*
   A. Analysis of inaugural address
   B. Conference of governors
   C. Closing banks as first executive act

IV. *Key legislation in first session of the Seventy-Third Congress*
   A. Emergency Bank Act
      1. Licensing of reopened banks
      2. Issuing of Federal Reserve notes
   B. National Economy Act
   C. "Beer bill"
   D. Agricultural Adjustment Act
      1. Purposes
         a. To balance production and consumption
         b. To subsidize producer of basic commodities
      2. Farm Mortgage Bill
      3. Inflation Bill (Thomas)
   E. Civilian Conservation Corps
   F. Federal Emergency Relief Act
   G. Tennessee Valley Authority
      1. To reforest Tennessee Valley
      2. To control floods

Will and Walling, *Our Next Step: National Economic Policy*, 1934

Coughlin, C., *Labor, Capital and Justice* (Series of eight radio lectures)

Primer, F., *"New Deal" Economics*

Lindley, *Roosevelt Revolution*

Ayres, L. P., *Economics of Recovery*

Beard, C. A., *America Faces the Future*

Tugwell, R. G., *Industrial Description and Government Arts*

Wallace, H., *America Must Choose*

Lewis, *The Primer of the New Deal*

Chase, Stuart, *The New Deal*

(T) Rugg, Harold, and Kreuger, Louise, *Social Reconstruction* (Study guide for group and class discussion)

NEW DEAL LEGISLATION—*Continued*

Outline of Subject-Matter (Suggested)	Experiences to Aid Learning (Suggested)	*References:* For the Student (S) For the Teacher (T)
3. To develop cheap water power 4. To reclaim farm land H. National Industrial Recovery Act and Public Works Act I. Securities Act J. Home Owners Loan Act K. Glass-Steagall Act L. Farm Credit Act M. Emergency Railroad Transportation Act V. *Regular session of Seventy-Third Congress* A. Roosevelt message and budget report B. Monetary Bill 1. Government control of gold and devaluation 2. Stabilization fund		

C. Regulation of stock and commodity exchange
D. Housing Act
E. Guarantee of principle and interest of Home Owners' Loan
F. Federal Communication Commission
G. Federal Alcohol Control Administration
H. President's power in reciprocal tariff agreement
I. Frazier-Lemke Bill

2. SIMPLE CLOTHING PROBLEMS

Objectives: To develop some ability in the use of a sewing machine
To teach simple construction processes
To stimulate an interest and desire for well fitted undergarments
To create a desire for good standards in workmanship
To develop an appreciation of values in the choice of undergarments and footwear

Suggested Subject-Matter	Experiences to Aid Learning	Teaching Materials
Sewing equipment Needles—sizes and kinds Tape measure Pins Scissors Shears Thimbles Thread Gauge Emery	Discussion and demonstration of the use and care of sewing equipment	Various kinds of needles, thread, scissors, etc., to show class *Clothing Construction*, Brown and others *Sewing and Textiles*, Mathews *Essentials of Sewing*, Cook
A buyer's knowledge of textile materials suitable for undergarments Suitability Cleansing quality Color Cost Characteristics of cotton, silk, and synthetic fibers Knitted materials	Students discuss with the teacher what they want to know about materials. Teacher supplements the discussion with necessary points which may not have been emphasized	Samples of a great variety of materials suitable for undergarments *The Sewing Book*, Hyde *Fabrics and Dress*, Rathbone and Tarple

Selection of pattern for undergarment student desires to make Slip, pajamas, nightgown, panties, etc.	Demonstrate how to determine amount of material needed	Undergarments, Iowa State College The Well Clothed Family, University of Minnesota
The Sewing Machine Difference in: Makes Power Threading Handling	Discussion of various kinds and parts of machines Students compare parts and operations of machines in their home with the ones in the class room	The Sewing Book, Hyde Sewing Machine Manuals, Wall Charts for threading a machine
Parts Bobbin Bobbin case Presser foot Feed Take up Needle bar Spool pin Bobbin filler Stitch regulator Tension Treadle Hand wheel Bolt	Demonstrate treadling, threading, and winding a bobbin Students practise on paper or material stitching on the edge, away from edge, turning corners, etc.	
Testing and altering a pattern	Discussion and demonstration of the use of a simple commercial pattern Students test and if necessary alter patterns	Patterns of various makes to show markings, etc. McCall Butterick Pictorial Vogue Simplicity

SIMPLE CLOTHING PROBLEMS—*Continued*

Suggested Subject-Matter	Experiences to Aid Learning	Teaching Materials
Construction of undergarments Seams—French, fell	Discussion and demonstration of seams suitable to garments under construction	Samples of seams *Clothing Construction*, Brown and others *Clothing for Women*, Baldt
Finishes Hems Facings Bindings By hand By machine	Discussion and demonstration of suitable edge finishes and construction processes Hems, suitable widths for tops, bottoms, casing, etc. Facings—cutting, applying to garment, finishing Bindings—cutting, piecing, attaching to garment Straps for slips Joining of elastic in bloomers or pajamas Sewing on laces or edgings Application of decorative stitches	Samples of all suggested construction processes suitable for undergarments *Fabrics and Dress*, Rathbone and Tarple *The Sewing Book*, Hyde *Essentials of Sewing*, Cook Current Fashion Books
Pressing and folding garments	Demonstrate pressing and folding undergarments	
Home-made garments versus ready-made	Students put on garments and have class appraise and evaluate same	A display of ready-made garments varying in price, material, etc.

Materials Fit Construction Trimming Wearing quality Cost	Discussion of ready-made garments Students discuss points to look for in sale garments	A display of garments made at home or in class
Care of underwear Laundering Drying Ironing Mending	Demonstration of washing, hanging, and pressing knitted and woven garments Demonstration of mending knitted and woven materials	Samples to illustrate types of mending suitable for undergarments
Selection of hosiery Types of hosiery Fibers used Width and length Weight Cost	Discussion of hosiery Teacher stresses points which affect the wear of hose Students and teacher study and interpret advertisements	Materials to illustrate types of hose and other points discussed *Hosiery*, Iowa State College *The Well-Clothed Family*, University of Minnesota *The Manufacture of Hosiery*, Allen A Hosiery Mill
Care of hosiery	Demonstration of putting on and taking off hose; washing, and hanging; darning holes and runs Students bring hosiery or underwear to mend and darn	

Simple Clothing Problems—*Continued*

Suggested Subject-Matter	Experiences to Aid Learning	Teaching Materials
Selection of shoes Construction Importance of properly fitted shoes Weight Height of heel Care of shoes Use of shoe trees and shoe racks Cleaning and polishing	Lecture and discussion of shoes stressing points outlined in Subject-Matter	Shoes to illustrate points If possible a talk by a chiropodist or shoe salesman

3. **A tentative course of study in everyman's English**

   A. *Teacher's overview.* English is considered here as a tool which every one needs to use and is, therefore, approached from the standpoint of giving practice in the ways in which it is used in everyday life. The subject-matter of the course has been determined largely by studies which have been made to find out the most frequent uses of English by adults, both in expression and in reading.

   When the course is thought of in the usual terms, it includes oral and written composition, work-type reading, recreational reading, vocabulary building, and correct usage in grammar, spelling, punctuation, and capitalization. Since fundamentally these different phases of English are closely related, it seems difficult to classify them into separate units of work. Some of the points of relationship and integration have been noted in the course. There may be others.

   Another point of view in making out the course has been that the work should proceed from the level at which one finds the students. This can be found out by the student's writing and speaking, by tests, by conversation with the student, and by an informal questionnaire given at an early meeting of the class. The following questionnaire has been found to be helpful:

   1. Occupation, if not employed
   2. Vocational aim, whether employed in that vocation now or not
   3. Education in terms of number of school grades completed
   4. Leisure-time interests
   5. Approximate amount of time spent each day in reading
   6. Topics in which you are interested
   7. Names of magazines, newspapers, and books read the past week
   8. Benefits you expect to receive from the course

   B. *Unit of work in written expression*

WRITTEN EXPRESSION

Main objective for this unit: to develop ability in the effective use of written expression necessary for every-day intercourse in the social and business world.

Means of arousing interest: Informal discussion with the students of the situations in which they feel a need for being able to write well. As letter writing is the most usual way in which people express themselves in writing, lead into a discussion of the importance of the impression which a letter conveys.

Outline of Subject-Matter (Suggested)	Experiences to Aid Learning (Suggested)	References: For the Student (S) For the Teacher (T)	Comments

I. Writing letters
  A. Form
    1. Heading
    2. Complimentary close
    3. Salutation
    4. Body
    5. Address on envelope
    6. Color of paper
    7. Manner of folding
 	
  B. Informal news letter
    1. Importance of consider-ing to whom it is written
    2. Comparison of the letter to conversation
      a. Interest in everyday contacts
	Be sure that the following facts are made clear: (1) There are differences in let-ter forms used. (2) A given form should be used con-sistently throughout. (3) Certain forms are preferred to others.
	
	Discuss the characteristics of a good news letter.
	Give practice in writing, and evaluate according to stand-ards developed by the stu-
		(T) Johnson, R. I., Searcy, L. A., Charters, W. W., *Practical Studies in Com-position* (Macmillan, 1929)
		(T) Clark, T. A., *When you Write a Letter* (Sanborn, 1921)
		(T) Chapman, Lucy, *Using English* (Harcourt-Brace, 1929)
		(T) Cook, Luella B, *Experi-ments in Writing* (Har-court-Brace, 1927)	

b. Liveliness and also sincerity of tone
c. Correctness and effectiveness of expression
 	
C. Special types of social letters
1. "Thank-you" letter
  a. For a gift
  b. For special favors
  c. For hospitality
2. Letters of informal invitation, acceptance and regret
3. Letters of congratulation, sympathy, acknowledgment, formal invitation, formal acceptance and regret (only as requested by the group or as it seems to meet their needs)
 	
D. Business letters
1. Letters of inquiry or request (letters asking for information or giving notice of change of address)
	dents through class discussion.
	
	Apply the standard developed in the writing of informal news letters and such special standards as apply to the different types.
	Make the letter-writing situation as real as possible and use any situation that arises in the class which calls for the writing of letters.
	
	Show samples of good and poor business letters and develop standards before writing. Evaluate in terms of the standards developed through class discussion.
		
		In addition to those already mentioned:
		(T) Gardner, E. X., Aurner, R. R., *Effective Business Letters*. Revised edition (Ronald, 1928)
		(T) Smart, W. K., ed. *How to Write Business Letters* (McGraw, 1923)
			The aim is not to give a course in business correspondence, but to give the practice which the layman feels he needs.

WRITTEN EXPRESSION—Continued

Outline of Subject-Matter (Suggested)	Experiences to Aid Learning (Suggested)	*References:* For the Student (S) For the Teacher (T)	Comments
2. Order letters (letters subscribing to a magazine or ordering items in which interests of students lie)	Have students explore in magazines and write their subscription letter after they have made their choice.		Ties up with work in reading, skimming, and evaluating magazines.
3. Application letters *a.* Background of education and experience *b.* Special qualifications for the position *c.* Procedures in regard to (1) Recommendations (2) Interviews 4. Letters of courteous complaint and adjustment (if desired by the group)			Integrates with work in making applications Integrates with work in making interviews. (See *Oral Expression.*)
II. Writing personal memoranda A. Note-taking 1. Running notes 2. Outlining 3. Summarizing statements 4. Topical and card notes	Give practice in the various ways of taking notes. Read Walter Pitkin's informal discussion of note-taking, since he emphasizes note-taking as	(S) McNelly, A. E., *How to Study* (Adult Education office) (T) Pitkin, Walter, *The Art of Rapid Reading* (McGraw, 1929)	Ties up with note-taking in preparing either oral or written reports.

•	an everyday activity of the business man.	(T) Bird, Charles, *Effective Study Habits* (Century, 1931) (T) Yoakam, G. A., *Reading and Study* (Macmillan, 1928)	Ties up with work in reading, as the ability to pick out the main ideas is essential to good note-taking.
	Have students take notes on magazine articles and write a paragraph summary from the notes. Have students take notes on talks by speakers coming to the group and write a paragraph summary from the notes.		
B. A Diary or a note-book of daily experiences and observations	Aim to develop both the appreciation of everyday contacts and the ability to write about them effectively. Discuss the advantages of having an outlet for the expression of one's thoughts and of keeping them as a record. Motivate work in vocabulary building through creating a desire for the most exact and concrete words.	(S) "The Bristling Blue Jay," in mimeographed reading material from Adult Education office (T) Cook, Luella B., *Experiments in Writing* (Harcourt-Brace, 1927) (T) Craig, A. E., *The Speech Arts* (Macmillan, 1927)	See unit in *Vocabulary Building*.

WRITTEN EXPRESSION—*Continued*

Outline of Subject-Matter (Suggested)	Experiences to Aid Learning (Suggested)	References: For the Student (S) For the Teacher (T)	Comments
	Have students find the best words to express sense impressions, as, for instance: *Sight* Oak tree, moon, rainbow, factories, sailboat, frost, furnace, smokestacks *Hearing* Key in the latch, band, loon on a lake, pine grove, chimes, traffic, fire siren, an office *Touch* Fur of a dog, outside of a peach, morning dip, sand sifting through fingers *Smell* Lilacs, the market, morning air, soap counter *Taste* Green apples, spring water, fresh honey Read poems aloud to the students and discuss the poet's realization of beauty and in-		
		Suggested poems to read: "The Coin," Sara Teasdale *A Ballad Catalogue of*	

	terest in everyday contacts, his use of concrete and exact words to express his thoughts, his use of comparisons. Have students look for the same in other poems.	*Lovely Things*, Richard LeGallienne "Chicago," Carl Sandburg "Fog," Carl Sandburg "To a Post Office Inkwell," Christopher Morley "The Ticket Agent," Edmund Leamy "Stopping by Woods on Snowy Evening," Robert Frost "Who Loves the Rain," Mrs. Frances Shaw "Clean Curtains," Carl Sandburg "Lilacs," Amy Lowell "The Railway Train," Emily Dickinson "Smells," Christopher Morley	See *Reading: Locating information.*
III. Giving directions and explanations	Emphasize clear, logical thinking and expression. Integrate with work on the use of reference books, the library, the *Reader's Guide*, etc., by having students write out explanations based on their observations		See *Reading: Developing Reading skills.*

WRITTEN EXPRESSION—*Continued*

Outline of Subject-Matter (Suggested)	Experiences to Aid Learning (Suggested)	*References:* For the Student (S) For the Teacher (T)	Comment
	Integrate also, with reading for accurate comprehension by having students write our paragraphs containing directions to be followed. Have students make out their own questions testing ability to read directions and exchange papers.		
IV. Making reports A. Material as discussed under *Oral Expression* B. Bibliography C. Footnotes	Proceed as discussed under *Making reports* in *Oral Expression*. In addition discuss the appearance of the manuscript, especially in a long report, and the making of a bibliography and acknowledging of information. Adapt the forms in the latter to the level of the class. (A simple form is usually sufficient.)	(T) Bird, Charles, *Effective Study Habits* (Century, 1931) (T) Yoakam, G. A., *Reading and Study* (Macmillan, 1928)	Integrates with *Oral Expression* and with *Reading: Locating information and Developing reading skills.*
	Emphasize careful revision of the manuscript after the first draft, which should be written	(T) Bird, Charles, *Effective Study Habits* (Century, 1931)	Requests of this nature come: "I have to prepare a 30-minute paper

	spontaneously. Note the importance of a short lapse of time, when possible, between the first draft and the revision.	on present-day conditions in Russia for my study club. How do I go about it?"
V. Evaluating written composition A. Preparation of the students before writing through: 　1. Stimulating a desire for expression 　2. Assisting students to find information needed 　3. Assisting students to organize and present their material 　4. Developing an attitude of self-criticism before presentation, both for content and for mechanical errors B. Evaluation in terms of standards developed by the group in discussion before writing	Assist students before writing rather than mere correction afterwards.	(T) Hitchcock, A. M., *Bread Loaf Talks on Teaching Composition* (Holt, 1927) "Variety in unity—the secret of all interesting talk and thought."

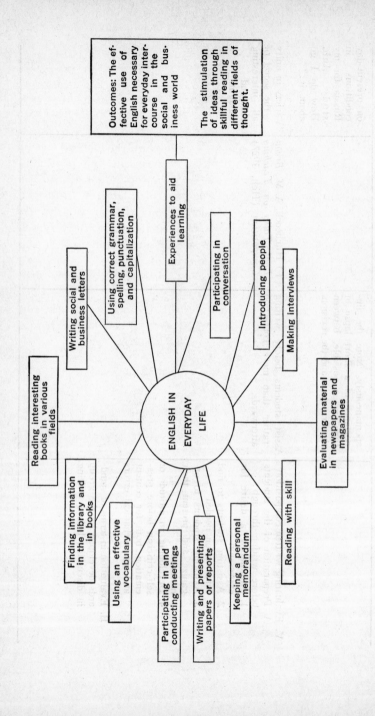

ENGLISH IN EVERYDAY LIFE

Reading interesting books in various fields

Writing social and business letters

Using correct grammar, spelling, punctuation, and capitalization

Experiences to aid learning

Participating in conversation

Introducing people

Making interviews

Evaluating material in newspapers and magazines

Reading with skill

Keeping a personal memorandum

Writing and presenting papers or reports

Participating in and conducting meetings

Using an effective vocabulary

Finding information in the library and in books

Outcomes: The effective use of English necessary for everyday intercourse in the social and business world

The stimulation of ideas through skillful reading in different fields of thought.

SUMMARY

This extended treatment of specific methods or definite procedure for teachers in various subject-matter fields has been presented for two reasons. In the first place, these suggestions taken from excellent courses of study will undoubtedly be of value to teachers who are facing problems in their own classroom or are assisting in the development of suggestions for teachers for courses of study in particular subjects. In the second place, it has been a concrete way of demonstrating the differences between methods and subject-matter. Every one who studies the best of modern courses of study will be surprised at the clarity of the thinking of teachers on that point.

The teacher should check at this time his professional reaction to the following generalizations:

1. Children are educated through self-activity. Their education is in terms of their *thinking* and *doing*. The teacher merely assists, motivates, and checks results.

2. The course of study furnishes or indicates the material to be *mastered* in attaining the objectives or goals.

BIBLIOGRAPHY FOR CHAPTERS XIII AND XIV

ANDERSON, H. A., and TRAXLER, A. E., "Group Corrective Spelling in the Junior High School: An Experiment," *School Review,* Vol. XLI (October, 1933), pp. 595-603. They reported satisfactory results in group work in the field of junior high school.

BARTGES, Paul F., "The Melody Method of Teaching Sight Reading of Vocal Music versus the Mechanical," Master's Thesis (Pennsylvania State College, 1932). He found the mechanical method superior to the melody method in teaching sight-reading.

BRUECKNER, L. J., and MELBY, E. O., *Diagnostic and Remedial Teaching* (Boston, Houghton Mifflin Co., 1931), Ch. X, "Diagnostic and Remedial Teaching in Spelling." They classified probable causes of frequent misspellings.

BURNS, S. T., "The Value of Prognostic Tests for Instrumental Pupils," *School Music,* Vol. XXXI (April, 1931), pp. 6-9.

BUTLER, Charles Henry, "Mastery of Certain Mathematical Concepts by Pupils at the Junior-High School Level," *Mathematics Teacher,* Vol. XXV (March, 1932), pp. 117-172. He made an investigation by means of the test method to measure the mastery of sixty-three concepts listed by Schorling in his study of objectives in teaching mathematics, and found that while the median seventh grader has mastered only one-third of the sixty-three, progress is uniform and by the end of the ninth grade, he has mastered two-thirds of them.

CARNEY, E., and LEUENBERGER, C., "Experiment in Remedial Reading in Senior High School," *High School Teacher*, Vol. VII (February, 1931), pp. 71-72.

CONGDON, R., "Training in High School Mathematics Essential for Success in Certain College Subjects with Special Reference to Physics," *Teachers College Record*, Vol. XXXI (March, 1930), p. 568.

CONNELLY, Elizabeth A., "An Experiment in Spelling," *English Journal (High School Edition)*, Vol. XXI (October, 1932), pp. 666-669. Using modern procedures, she found satisfactory results in group work in the high-school level.

COOK, M., "Stimulating Interest in Mathematics by Creating a Mathematical Atmosphere," *Mathematics Teacher*, Vol. XXIV (April, 1931), pp. 248-254.

COOK, Walter W., "The Measurement of General Spelling Ability Involving Controlled Comparisons Between Techniques," *University of Iowa Studies in Education*, Vol. VI, No. 6 (Iowa City, the University, 1932). On the strength of an unusually detailed and elaborate investigation, he reported methods for selection of test items, of test technics, and time of administration for given tests.

CREAGER, M., "Are You a Spoon Feeder?" *High School Teacher*, Vol. VI (January, 1930), pp. 11-13, 36, 38.

CROWLEY, Edna E. E., "An Experiment in Methods of Teaching Design," Master's Thesis (University of Chicago, 1931). She reported that, in the effectiveness rating of five methods of teaching design, the direct observation method was highest.

DAVIS, G., "Procedures Effective in Improving Pupils of Poor Reading Ability in Regular Reading Classes," *Elementary School Journal*, Vol. XXXI (January, 1931), pp. 337-348.

DEXHEIMER, Lora M., "Systematizing the Use of Pictures in Teaching Sixth-Grade Geography," The Teaching of Geography, National Society for the Study of Education, *Thirty-Second Yearbook* (Bloomington, Illinois, Public Schools Publishing Co., 1933), pp. 507-519. She made an experiment concerning the systematic use of pictures in sixth-grade geography classes.

DORRIS, A. V., *Visual Instruction in the Public Schools* (Ginn and Co., 1928). Part II takes up visual instruction applied to the teaching of the various subjects of the curriculum.

DUNCAN, M. B., "Civics Vitalized in Roanoke," *Journal of Education*, Vol. CXII (November 10, 1930), pp. 368-369.

EARHART, Will, and GATTO, Frank M., "An Experimental Study of Creative Work in Public School Music," *Pittsburgh Schools*, Vol. VIII (November-December, 1933), pp. 44-56. He accords the creative approach a much superior rating, on the basis of tests of sightreading, taste, musical knowledge, and musical performance.

ENLOW, E. R., "Visual Instruction," *High School Teacher*, Vol. VI (May, 1930), pp. 200-201.

Federal Board for Vocational Education, "Teaching of Art Related to the Home," Bulletin No. 156, "Home Economics Series No. 13 (Washington, D. C., Government Printing Office, 1931). After studying the relation of art in the home, they recommended certain teaching methods and listed reference and illustrative material.

Fowlkes, J. G., "The Wisconsin Experiment in Radio Education," *Wisconsin Journal of Education* (December, 1930), pp. 167-169.

Fulcher, G. S., "Use of Printed Practice Sheets and Standardized Test Sheets in Teaching School Subjects," *School and Society,* Vol. XXXII (August 23, 1930), pp. 264-265.

Garcia, Edward C., "Reading Method and Culture Study," *Modern Language Forum,* Vol. XVI (April, 1931), pp. 60-61. He asserted the maximum vocabulary progress which can be made each year.

Garrison, S. C., and Heard, M. T., "An Experimental Study of the Value of Phonetics," *Peabody Journal of Education,* Vol. IX (July, 1930), pp. 9-14. They reported that spelling is benefited by phonetical training.

Garver, F. M., "Principles of Method Revealed by an Analysis of a Spelling Pre-Test," *Educational Outlook,* Vol. V (March, 1931), pp. 147-153. After analyzing and pre-testing, they classified likely causes of errors in spelling.

Gates, A. I., "An Experimental Comparison of the Study-Test and the Test-Study Methods of Spelling," *Journal of Educational Psychology,* Vol. XXII (January, 1931), pp. 1-19. He reported the test-study method superior in grades high three to eight, the study-test method superior in two and low three.

Gates, A. I., and Bennett, C. C., "Two Tests versus Three Tests Weekly in Teaching Spelling," *Elementary School Journal,* Vol. XXXIV (September, 1933), pp. 44-49. They concluded that, save in the earlier grades, methods of instruction differed insignificantly, and that improved interest and ability as a result of skilful teaching were the most important factors.

Geck, E. E., "The Large Unit in History Teaching," *High School Teacher,* Vol. VI (January, 1930), pp. 31-32.

Gilbert, Luther C., "Experimental Investigation of a Flash-Card Method of Teaching Spelling," *Elementary School Journal,* Vol. XXXII (January, 1932), pp. 337-351. He found evidence that flash-card exercises speeded up perception, and resulted in improvement in spelling.

———, "Experimental Investigation of Eye Movements in Learning to Spell Words," *Psychological Monographs,* Vol. XLIII, No. 3, Whole No. 196. (Princeton, New Jersey, Psychological Review Co., 1932). In order to prevent poor study habits, he recommended a definite instruction method for early grades, after he found significant differences in the eye movements of good and poor spellers.

Gruen, F. B., *English Grammar in American High Schools since 1900* (The Catholic University of America Publications, 1934).

Guiler, W. S., "The Spelling of Graduates," *High School Teacher,* Vol. VI (February, 1930), pp. 53-55.

GUIN, R. L., "Cash and Carry On," *High School Teacher,* Vol. VI (March, 1930), pp. 99-100. The stimulation of the work in an English class by selling themes to the newspapers.

HANSEN, L. B., "Creating Interest in Mathematics through Special Topics," *Mathematics Teacher,* Vol. XXIII (January, 1930), pp. 3-6.

HARLAN, F. B., "Some Learning Implications of the New History," *High School Teacher,* Vol. VI (September, 1930), pp. 274-275.

HARTMANN, George W., "The Relative Influence of Visual and Auditory Factors in Spelling Ability," *Journal of Educational Psychology,* Vol. XXII (December, 1931), pp. 691-699. He concluded that ability to spell is dependent rather on a special form of visual reaction than on general superiority in any sense modality.

HENNESSEY, J. A., "Boston's Use of Motion Pictures," *Journal of Education,* Vol. CXII (November 10, 1930), pp. 365-366.

HILLARD, G. H., and BARNES, M., "The Effect of Specific Drill on Reading Ability," *Elementary School Journal,* Vol. XXXI (February, 1931), pp. 417-426.

HURD, A. W., *Coöperative Experimentation in Materials and Methods in Secondary-School Physics* (New York, Teachers College, Columbia University, 1933). He presented conclusions which he drew after making a series of extensive and significant investigations in the reorganization of content to suit the needs of pupils enrolled in secondary-school physics classes.

IRWIN, M. E., and ODIEN, E. C., "Building English Contracts for the Dalton Plan," *Elementary School Journal,* Vol. XXXI (October, 1930), pp. 136-141.

JACOBSEN, O. Irving, "Methods of Research in Reading Music," *Supervisors Service Bulletin* (November-December, 1931). By photographing eye movements during the reading of music, he concluded that difficulties in music-reading are due to unfamiliarity with the keyboard and notation of the instrument, or, in vocal music, to unfamiliarity with the Latin syllables, or to the pitch-relation of notes of the scale.

JARVIS, E. D., "Equipping the School for Radio Reception," *American School Board Journal,* Vol. LXXXII (February, 1931), pp. 61-62.

JENSEN, M. B., "The Influence of Class Size Upon Pupil Accomplishment in High School Algebra," *Journal of Educational Research,* Vol. XXII (May, 1930), pp. 337-356.

JONES, R. G., "Arithmetic by Radio in Cleveland," *Journal of Education,* Vol. CXII (November 17, 1930), pp. 391-392.

KATZ, Elias, "Educational Possibilities of Films in Art Courses," *Educational Screen,* Vol. XII (February, 1933), pp. 60-61. He concluded that films could be used to distinct advantage in the art curriculum.

KILZER, L. R., "Making Supervised Study More Effective," *Education,* Vol. LI (April, 1931), pp. 478-482.

———, "Introducing Supervised Study," *American School Board Journal,* Vol. LXXX (April, 1930), pp. 45-46.

KING, Luella M., "Learning and Applying Spelling Rules in Grades Three to Eight," *Contributions to Education*, No. 517 (Teachers College, Columbia University, 1932). She continued investigating possibilities and limitations of rationalization, and reported the effect of teaching seven rules selected on the basis of their relation to words in common usage. Her data show the need for further investigation in this field.

KNIGHT, W. H., "Improving English Expression of High School Pupils," *High School Teacher*, Vol. VI (March, 1930), pp. 106-108.

KOOSER, V. L., "Present Trends in the Use of Visual Instruction," *American School Board Journal*, Vol. LXXX (February, 1930), p. 56.

KURRIE, J. J., "Inexpensive Visual Aids," *High School Teacher*, Vol. VI (February, 1930), pp. 57-58.

LAMONT, F., "Arousing Interest in Chemistry," *High School Teacher* Vol. VI (February, 1930), pp. 56, 85.

McCALLISTER, J. M., "The Effectiveness of Remedial Instruction in Reading in the Junior High School," *School Review*, Vol. XXXIX (February, 1930), pp. 97-111.

McGUIRE, M., and HEDELSON, E., "Learning to Teach Larger Classes," *Educational Administration and Supervision*, Vol. XVI (January, 1930), pp. 34-38.

McDILL, R. M., "Laboratory Work in Geometry," *Mathematics Teacher*, Vol. XXIV (January, 1931), pp. 14-21.

MONROE, W. S., and CLARK, J. A., "The Teacher's Responsibility for Devising Learning Exercises in Arithmetic," Bureau of Research Bulletin, No. 31 (University of Illinois, 1926).

MONROE, W. S., and ENGLHART, M. D., "Stimulating Learning Activity," Bureau of Research Bulletin No. 51 (University of Illinois, 1930).

MURSELL, J. L., "The Economy of Learning," *School Music*, Vol. XXIX (November and December, 1929), pp. 3-8.

O'BRIEN, I., "A Comparison of the Use of Intensive Training and of Wide Reading in the Improvement of Reading," *Educational Method*, Vol. X (March, 1931), pp. 346-349.

PARKS, C. B., "Poetry as a Recreation: An Inducement," *English Journal*, Vol. XVIII (December, 1929), pp. 810-817.

PEARSON, F. B., "Projects in English," *High School Teacher*, Vol. VI (December, 1929).

PHILLIPS, D. P., "Comparison of the Two-Response and Dictated Recall Types of Spelling Tests," *Journal of Educational Research*, Vol. XXIII (January, 1931), pp. 17-24. He compared two-response and dictated recall types of tests.

PITTS, L., and DAVIS, R. A., "A Comparison of the Analytic and Synthetic Methods of Teaching Geometry," *School Science and Mathematics*, Vol. XXX (March, 1930), pp. 333-339.

RADEMACHER, E. E., "Making Posters for Chemistry," *Journal of Chemical Education*, Vol. VIII (April, 1931), pp. 688-698.

ROBINSON, R., "A Study of Pre-Tests in Geography," *Journal of Geography*, Vol. XIX (December, 1930), pp. 389-400.

SCRUGGS, S. D., "Remedial Teaching for Improvement in Handwriting," *Journal of Educational Research,* Vol. XXIII (April, 1931), pp. 288-295.

SEARS, Edith K., "The Vocabularies of Two Direct-Method French Grammars for Beginners," *Modern Language Journal,* Vol. XV (May, 1931), pp. 599-606. She studied two recent French grammars, and showed the large size of the vocabularies, and their disagreement and lack of repetition.

SELZER, Charles A., "Lateral Dominance and Visual Fusion; Their Application to Difficulties in Reading, Writing, Spelling, and Speech," Harvard Monograph in Education, No. 12 (Cambridge, Mass., Harvard University Press, 1933). He decided that spelling disabilities were an indication of lateral cerebral dominance.

SHAFFER, Laurance F., "Children's Interpretations of Cartoons," *Contributions to Education,* No. 429 (New York, Teachers College, Columbia University, 1930). He investigated the value of the use of cartoons in grades 4 through 12 and pupil ability to interpret them.

SHANKLE, G. H., "Aims and Methods of Teaching English Grammar in American Schools," *Education,* Vol. LI (September, 1930), pp. 41-43.

SHEFFLER, N., "How to Make Textiles Interesting," *High School Teacher,* Vol. VI (October, 1930), pp. 328-330.

SMITH, Nila B., *American Reading Instruction* (Silver, Burdett and Co., 1934).

THURSTONE, Thelma G., "The Difficulty of a Test and Its Diagnostic Value," *Journal of Educational Psychology,* Vol. XXIII (May, 1932), pp. 335-343. She investigated the difficulty of test items in relation to their reliability.

TOHILL, L., "Method in the Teaching of the Social Studies," *Historical Outlook,* Vol. XXII (January, 1931), pp. 21-24.

TORMERY, Thomas J., "The Effect of Drill Upon Specific and General Comprehension of Historical Content" (Abstract in *University of Iowa Studies,* Series on Aims and Progress of Research, No. 38. New Series No. 248, April 1, 1933). He conducted an experiment, the results of which indicated that history textbooks authors should be more critical of specific geographic terms.

TWOGOOD, A. P., and CRAMLET, R., "Film Slides in Teaching Mechanical Drawing to Beginners," *Industrial Education Magazine,* Vol. XXXI (January, 1930), pp. 254-255.

WASHBURNE, Carleton W., "Mental Age and the Arithmetic Curriculum: A Summary of the Committee of Seven Grade Placement Investigations to Date," *Journal of Educational Research,* Vol. XXIII (March, 1931), pp. 210-231.

———, "Individualizing English," *Modern Education* (December, 1929).

WEAVER, Robert B., "The Relative Value of Intensive and Extensive Reading in United States History," *School Review,* Vol. XXXIX (March, 1931), pp. 217-226. In this work he studied the relative

value of extensive and intensive reading, and concluded that there
was a great deal to be said in favor of extensive reading.

WETZEL, W. A., "Large-Group Instruction," *School Review,* Vol. XXXIX
(April, 1931), pp. 288-292.

WIVEL, C. B., "Education by Radio," *Education,* Vol. LII (April, 1931),
pp. 470-477.

WOODRING, M. N., and FLEMMING, C. W., "Directing Study of High
School Pupils" (Bureau of Publications, Teachers College, Columbia Unversity, 1929).

CHAPTER XV

TESTING ACHIEVEMENT IN UNITS OF WORK

I. INTRODUCTION

Briefly stated, the purpose of teaching is to take the individual from his present educational situation to that which has been determined as desirable for pupils of his interests, abilities, and attainments. Considerable time has been spent upon the problem of establishing valid goals of education. It is imperative, however, for teachers to realize that instruction is a process by which advancement is made. As such, it is necessary for the teacher to know more than the goals to be achieved. In the first place, the teacher must determine the educational and intellectual status of the pupil at the beginning of the process. Unless a point is established from which to measure, any measurement attempted will be little better than guessing. In the second place, the progress of the pupil in the work must be determined. The distance traversed by the pupil from the starting point toward the goals will determine the emphasis at a particular time, the remedial work, and the speed or tempo of the classroom. In the third place, the teacher should know, in addition to goals, the achievement of the pupil at the end of the course in terms of skills, habits, appreciations, ideals, etc.

Lacking a knowledge of the students' attainments up to the time of the beginning of the class, the progress of the pupil during the semester or year, and the final result of the work, the teacher is handicapped in making an original outline of his course, adjusting it to the needs of the individual students, or evaluating it in terms of pupil modifications. The problems involved in checking, adjusting, and evaluating the course of study and the achievements of the pupil represent the most scientific and professional opportunities of the teachers. A course of study would not be worth the time devoted to its preparation if it failed to provide for the guidance of teachers in determining both the educational status of students as they begin the work and the attainments realized by them throughout the course as outlined.

This chapter is included in order that the teacher and the committee can have accurate and practical information concerning tests and the construction of tests. There are many varieties of examinations, each with its advantages and disadvantages. Also, there is much perplexity regarding the construction of tests, and it is proposed to clarify that issue as much as possible. The following pages will attempt to include all the constructive suggestions which have appeared in recent studies concerning the construction of tests, so that the readers may have an adequate background in this field.

II. CLASSIFICATION OF TESTS

Tests can be classified according to use, form, and function. An analysis of these classifications will serve as an introduction to the field of testing.

A. The use of tests. The use of the written examination is not new; it is as old as formalized education itself. However, the so-called objective test is of comparatively recent date (about 1907-1915), while the essay type of examination represents the procedure down through the centuries.

By 1913 the use of standardized tests had been accepted, and by 1919 they had become popular among teachers and administrators. A few years later, the movement for the scientific improvement in course of study construction was under way. With the new emphasis on course of study construction, standardized tests became satisfactory, only in part, since these tests often measured progress toward objectives which were not included in the individual course of study and did not measure achievement in certain materials and activities which were included. The new-type test retains many of the advantages of the standardized test and, in addition, permits the teacher to deal with the particular subject-matter field in the local school which is adapted to the needs of the community.

1. *Supervision and administration.* Examinations, particularly the standardized type, are invaluable to supervisors and administrators. The ease with which comparisons can be made between grades, schools, ability levels, teachers, etc., makes them a valuable tool in organizing and supervising an educational program. Weak spots in the system can be segregated at once and corrections made. These may involve readjustments of students, reassignment or dismissal of teachers, or reallocation of equipment and personnel.

2. *Measurement of learning.* It is possible, through the use of tests, to determine the knowledges, skills, abilities, etc., which the pupils possess when they enter a course. Their achievement can be measured at various times during the semester and at the end of the course. The pupil, as well as the teacher, can evaluate his progress.

In order that accurate comparative results can be obtained, the mental ability of the pupils can be determined as they enter the school, the work adjusted to their ability, and the examination made to serve the purpose of determining the pupils' progress in terms of his ability and not in comparison with superior or inferior classmates. The opportunity to achieve at his level and to measure his improvement at that level often motivates the student to improve his standing through greater efforts.

3. *Measurement of teaching.* The attempt has been made to evaluate the effectiveness of teaching in terms of the improvement of pupils. For example, knowing the ability and the achievement of the class at the opening of school, the quality of teaching can be determined by the scores which the pupils make at the end of work. These results can be compared with both means and results in other classes in the school system. While the classes can be carefully organized as far as ability and achievement of the students are concerned, there are other variables which make it impossible to measure accurately the effectiveness of teaching by merely checking the scores made

by pupils on the examinations. Nevertheless, supervisors are of the opinion that tests have made supervision more scientific and represent a great advance over the old system of classroom visitation for the purpose of checking ventilation, discipline, poise of teacher, type of questions asked, etc.

4. *Diagnosis of pupil progress and attainments*. It is essential that an accurate measure of the specific progress of the pupils be developed. This means that the teacher should be concerned with the attainment of the child in a particular phase of the work and not with the general rating of the individual student or of the class. It is a problem for the teacher to determine the adequacy of performance (mastery) in the skills, habits, etc., presented in the unit. In those instances where individual attainment is low or inadequate, additional work can be prescribed and the desired efficiency realized. Many other problems enter at this point: (1) the determination of the grade-level of work and the mental level, age-level, grade-level of attainment of the pupils, (2) the reorganization of the course of study to meet particular situations, and (3) the development of satisfactory remedial measures to insure reasonable progress. But little progress can be made in diagnosis unless reliable and valid tests have been developed. Carefully constructed remedial work must be developed which will eliminate difficulties and prevent the recurrence of these faults in the future.

5. *The development and grade placement of learning activities*. The organization of valid tests demands that the materials in the curriculum be scrutinized carefully. If they are not satisfactory, new and valid activities must be introduced before the test can be constructed. This interaction among objectives, valid learning activities, and valid tests has been of great service to the committees in charge of course of study construction.

Standardized tests have been particularly valuable as a standard or criterion by which learning materials can be correctly placed in the various grades and adequate time allotted to their mastery. It is possible to determine the relative difficulty of various units before they are included in the course of study and thus be reasonably accurate in checking their grade placement. For example, pupil records on such matters as reading ability, arithmetical ability, etc., can be checked and compared with the material included in textbooks for particular grades or with the activities included in units of the course which are to be included in different grades of the school system.

B. The types of tests. Three common types or forms of subject-matter tests are used in schools. Also, there are forms of examinations not specifically related to the work of the classroom but useful in measuring intelligence, aptitudes, etc. The discussion at this point will be centered upon the subject-matter examination.

1. *The essay examination.* This type has been used for so many years that it is unnecessary to discuss its form either extensively or intensively. It consists of questions or problems (usually ten or less) to which the student reacts by (1) presenting the information he has secured in this field, (2) organizing his ideas on the subject, and (3) formulating conclusions on part or all phases of the problems. Since the answer or the statement is complete and is developed as an essay, the organization of the content and the style and neatness of the paper have often received greater consideration than the accuracy of the pupils' thinking or reasoning. The essay test has advantages that cannot be gainsaid. The fact that the child must organize his reactions carefully and accurately and express his ideas clearly is a valuable consideration. As a teaching device it is more valuable than as a checking instrument by which to measure the progress of the pupils. Some of the apparent defects in the essay examination as a testing device are:

(*a*) It covers, at best, only a few of the items presented in the course. The five, ten, or, at most, twenty questions are not extensive enough to permit the pupils to indicate a fair sampling of their knowledge or conclusions drawn from the course.

(*b*) It forces the teacher to distinguish between the pupils' knowledge of the course and their ability to organize material well, even if their grasp of the content is weak. Neatness and excellent handwriting are further variables which distort the grading of essay examinations.

(c) Furthermore, the teacher faces the difficulty of attempting to make a diagnosis of the pupils' real difficulties in the work from a paper which presents facts, conclusions, handwriting, neatness, and other considerations.

(d) It is a subjective examination, and, therefore, the scoring of the paper is inaccurate. It is difficult to distinguish between facts and suppositions, beliefs and definite conclusions, memorization of key words and phases and valid thinking. Teachers in the same subject often disagree concerning the grading of a particular paper. Three additional factors must be considered in this connection: (1) the essay type of examination must be thought out carefully or these criticisms become more evident; (2) the questions or problems are usually involved and require extended periods for giving the examination; and (3) comparisons are difficult or impossible, and norms cannot be established.

(e) It can be scored only by the teacher, and this requires hours of time after school. Correcting essay examinations takes energy and produces nervous strain as well as consuming an excessive amount of time. Student assistance is undesirable and cannot be used effectively in scoring this type of examination.

2. *The new-type tests.* The weakness of the essay examination led to the development of tests which would more nearly meet the criteria established for the effective examination. There are various forms of these new tests, none of which are perfect, but all present some advantages over the essay type. In general, it can be said that these new-type examinations are more comprehensive, since it is possible to include an extended list of questions or statements which completely cover the pupils' knowledge of all phases of the unit or semester's work. It is a matter of hundreds of items rather than five or ten important phases of the work. Such an examination requires much effort and time in preparation, an extended period of time in which to determine the reliability, and to effect standardization, if this is considered desirable in the system, but requires only a short time to give and score the tests. Another feature closely related to the scoring of the tests is that any one can check the results and secure the correct grade for every participant, since the standards remain the same for all examinations.

Furthermore, it should be pointed out that the construction

of the new-type test is related intimately to course of study construction. This is true, because the teacher, who is constantly constructing and reconstructing tests of two hundred to four hundred items and noting class results, has an opportunity to reorganize and revaluate the subject-matter of the course. Since the new-type-test results can be submitted to statistical treatment, norms can be established, and the standardization of a particular test for a school system is not difficult. This permits supervisors and administrators to check and compare the results of different schools, teachers, and classes of varying abilities with required and elective subject-matter. Since the results can be analyzed accurately, specific weaknesses can be determined and the causes of deficiencies noted at once. Remedial instruction can be organized for a class or individual members of the class, and teaching can be effectively supervised.

The readers should not accept the principle that the new-type test is an unmixed blessing and the solution of every teaching and subject-matter problem. While such a test can measure the pupil's knowledge and not his ability to write a composition neatly, yet, one must recognize that the pupil has neither to furnish any material for the test nor to organize any material while checking his answers. Everything is furnished in the test, and the pupil has merely to make a plus ($+$) or minus ($-$) sign, write *yes* or *no,* or write in a word or phrase. There is little effort made to determine the initiative of the pupil or to measure his ability to organize material, both of which are of great significance in education. For these reasons the teacher who relegates the essay examination completely from his class work will be committing an educational blunder. Its value cannot be overemphasized.

(*a*) The true-false test. This type of test is made up of questions which can be answered by *yes* or *no* or statements which can be checked as *True* or *False,* or $+$ or $-$, depending on the pupil's reaction to the statement. Since an examination of this type can be quickly filled in by the pupil and easily corrected by the teacher, a list of two or three hundred statements is not excessive. Wood [1] found that examinations made up of less than one hundred items or statements did not have satisfactory reliability.

Example of statement: (Check yes or no)
—— Seattle is the largest city on the Pacific Coast.

Example of question: (Check yes or no)
—— Does the Columbia River rise in the State of Washington?

Provision is usually made for the student to mark his answer or reaction at the left of the sentence or question.

In addition to the problem of scoring, the true-false test presents the challenge to the teacher of formulating statements which are definitely and completely right or wrong. Naturally, ambiguous statements, which can be misinterpreted or misunderstood, which are partly true and partly false, which relate to beliefs rather than facts, must be eliminated or the validity of the test is lowered. The teacher will have to check the reactions of various classes to the particular test in order to determine its weaknesses. Such a test is not constructed over night, but is the result of continuous experimentation.

(*b*) The multiple-choice type of test. In this examination, each statement is followed by several alternatives which complete the sentence. The problem for the pupil is the selection of the two or three words or phrases, out of the total number, which constitute the best or most correct completion of the sentence.

An example of this type of test is:

The best generals on the American side in the Revolutionary War
    were (   )

            (1) Gates
            (2) Greene
            (3) Cornwallis
            (4) Washington
            (5) Lee

[1] B. D. Wood, "Studies of Achievement Tests," *Journal of Educational Psychology,* Vol. XVII (January, 1926, February, 1926, April, 1926), pp. 1-22, 125-129, 263-269.

The numbers preceding the names of the outstanding generals will be included in the parenthesis. In the above instance, the numbers 2 and 4 are the best answers and would be graded as perfect. Since there are two correct answers to be inserted in the parenthesis, the problem counts for two points. The omission of either 2 or 4 or the insertion of any other number would cost a penalty of one point for each error.

(c) The matching test. These tests are easily constructed and scored, and they can be made objective and highly reliable. They consist of two columns of parallel facts, items, dates, or words. Each item in column one should be related definitely to an item in column two. However, more items can be included in the second column than in the first for obvious reasons. The order of the items in the two columns should not be suggestive to the pupils. One column should include parentheses in front of each item. The number or letter indicating a fact in the first column which matches an item in the second column can be placed in the parenthesis opposite that item.

An example of this type of test:

1. Kansas-Nebraska Bill	( )	1820
2. Missouri Compromise	( )	1857
3. Dred Scott Decision	( )	1854
4. Formation of the Republican Party	( )	1856
5. Harpers Ferry	( )	1856
6. Lincoln-Douglas Debates	( )	1848
	( )	1858
	( )	1859

(d) The completion test. This test consists of a number of statements in each of which an important word or important words are missing. The problem for the student is to fill in the blank spaces correctly. The following are examples:

1. The first battle of the Civil War was fought at ———— in ————.

2. The ———— Compromise established ————° ————′ as the line of latitude dividing the slave from the non-slave sections.

(e) Recognition test. The distinguishing feature of this test is that several options (usually four or five) are given, only one of which is correct. In many respects this test is similar to the multiple-answer type. It differs only in that one answer is correct rather than two or more of the completing words or clauses.

An example of this test is:

The boundaries of Europe were changed at the end of the World War
   (1) According to plebiscites
   (2) On the basis of racial prejudice
   (3) Through secret treaties
   (4) In accordance with the ideals of President Wilson
   (5) In the peace treaty at Versailles

There are additional types of tests which have been developed and advocated by research experts and writers in the field. Those which have been discussed here are most commonly used and are satisfactory for the use of teachers who are initiating that phase of the organization. Several excellent books on this subject will prove invaluable for teachers who are undertaking to organize tests. Reference is made to them at the end of the chapter.

C. The function of tests. It is implied here that tests have a particular function in education. Tests can be made to function in the development of the teaching program (teacher) and in the learning program (pupil). Neither of these points can be disregarded in an educational institution.

1. *The teacher and testing.*

(*a*) The pre-test. By far the most important test from the standpoint of the teacher is the pre-test. It serves to orient him to the particular class in terms of the general requirements of the course. The level of the classes, as well as the range of individual differences, varies from year to year, and no teacher can take the students of a previous class as establishing a standard for a new class with which he is relatively unacquainted.

(*b*) The diagnostic test. It is possible through tests to diagnose the individual or the class. A general achievement test, which has been standardized, can be given and the results will enable the teacher or the administration to evaluate the status of the class or individual pupil in terms of national or city norms. While these standardized tests enable the teacher to compare the status of his class with national norms, they do not assist him greatly in determining the reasons for the success or lack of success of his pupils. For example, a student may be doing poor work in all fields, particularly in social science. His difficulties are appearing because he reads at a sixth-grade rate and seventh-grade comprehension when he is in high school. No standardized test, which merely indicates that he is below the norm, will present the solution of this problem. However, if a number of standardized tests are given, the particular weakness of the student will be apparent since a comparison of the results of a number of tests measuring different skills and abilities will point out the outstanding weaknesses. Further diagnostic work can be carried on by the teacher as soon as the lead has been established.

(c) Tests of achievement. Most tests are organized so that pupil attainment in terms of the objectives of the course, which have been determined, can be measured. This test is different from the pre-test since it measures accomplishment of the class during the semester or year. The following diagram will illustrate the relationship of pre-testing, achievement-testing, and the objectives of education.

The pre-test indicates pupil level at beginning of course	The outcome established by the achievement test at the end of the term or during the course	The objectives to be achieved by the class

D. The examination as an educative or teaching device. A good examination must motivate the attainment of the objectives of the course. In doing this, it will point out and emphasize again these objectives, indicate the essential facts, skills, etc., to be mastered, show at once the short-comings of the individual pupil in the attainment of them, and tend to encourage the student to properly review the course and develop adequate habits of study. Of course, all these desirable results will be frustrated if the examination is used as a threat to insure cramming on the part of the pupil rather than as a stimulant to insure study and careful organization of the materials of the course. It should serve both as a check upon the content of the course and the methods used by the teacher in the presentation of his work.

1. *The pupil and testing.* As suggested in the preceding paragraph, the pupil may regard the examination as a menace and a threat or as a means of help and assistance in studying and diagnosing his difficulties, and in analyzing the requirements of the course. The pupil can evaluate his work in terms of the progress of his fellow students and adjust his tempo of work. Competition of this kind is a desirable form of motivation. However, if there are extended ranges of ability in the same class, this should not be overdone. Motivation cannot make up for natural endowment, and such procedure may stultify as well as promote growth.

III.   CRITERIA FOR THE CONSTRUCTION OF TESTS

There are primary and secondary criteria for the construction of tests. Primary criteria are essential in every examination, while secondary criteria must be used in the construction of certain types of tests.

A. Primary criteria. There are at least three criteria which represent standards to be attained in every examination. It must be admitted that it is difficult to attain these standards and they usually represent aspirations and hopes rather than actual attainments even by experienced and highly-trained teachers.

1. *Validity.* In simple language this means that the test should measure those specific objectives which it is supposed to measure. However, the problem of constructing a valid test is not as simple a matter as one might infer from this brief definition. Tests which are developed to measure specific skills, habits, and attainment of information can be reasonably valid if care is taken in their organization. But tests which purport to measure appreciation, attitude, proficiency in methods, or procedures

are apt to be less valid. Hence, the first reason for the development of invalid tests is that teachers have assumed they could
measure these latter qualities by asking questions which purport to test proficiency in certain skills or the accuracy and
extent of information.

The second reason for low validity is due to a number of
factors, other than the attainment of the pupil, which play an
important part in the grading of his papers. In the first place,
typed papers are compared with those written in long hand;
second, poorly organized papers must be evaluated in comparison with well-organized papers; third, poorly written papers
must be compared with clearly written papers; and fourth,
questions and problems are often improperly weighted by the
teacher. These items serve to indicate the critical problems
which are presented to the teacher in developing and grading
an examination. To what extent does the grade on the paper
indicate a measure of the pupils' achievement? If the examination fails to measure the competence of the pupil, validity is
below a desired standard.

2. *Reliability.* The reliability of an examination refers to the
accuracy or degree with which the test measures whatever it does
measure. Hence, if a test is developed in grammar, it should
measure the comprehension and achievement of the pupil in
grammar with a high degree of reliability so that the teacher
can say that the pupil is either competent or not competent in
that field as a result of the examination. The distinction between validity and reliability is evident at this point since validity would be concerned with whether or not the examination
measured ability in grammar or handwriting or composition,
while reliability is concerned with the accuracy of measurement
in one of these fields.

Several methods can be used to determine the reliability of
an examination. First, the content and construction of the examination can be checked by dividing the test into two approximately equal parts and comparing the scores made by the pupils
in the two sections of the test. Naturally, it is possible to develop two separate examinations covering the same material

and equal in every respect, which can be given on successive days and the results compared. Since these two examinations have high validity, in theory, they will present a high correlation if they are reliable. The same examination can be given to two sections of the same class, and comparisons made of the scores by determining the coefficient of correlation. Second, the grading of the examination introduces many errors which contribute to unreliability. A check upon the grading of the papers can be established by grading an examination at the time the papers are handed in and then putting the test away for a definite time and regrading it without referring to the previous grades. A comparison of the two sets of grades will demonstrate the reliability of the grading.

3. *A good test contributes to the realization of the objectives of the course of study.* If there is no relationship between the examination and the important items of the course, the student may waste his time concentrating on non-essentials or spend an unprofitable amount of time memorizing unimportant materials and cramming for the test. However, if the examination emphasizes the important materials and activities mentioned in the course of study, it can be of inestimable value in promoting good habits of study, proper review techniques, and organizing ability. An examination should be diagnostic to the extent that it indicates clearly to both the teacher and student the degree of mastery of all units. Such an examination is an excellent teaching device.

B. Secondary criteria. Other factors need to be considered if the test is purchased and given in the system so that the achievement of the pupils can be compared with national norms. First, the test should be one that can be given and checked by the classroom teacher. Therefore, it must be easy to give the test, correct the papers, and evaluate results. Second, the norms and standards should be adequately established through a wide sampling of pupils in all sections of the country. Third, tests, which have a number of equivalent forms, should be selected. This provision will make it possible to test pupils several times during the year or over a period of several years. The results of tests of this type can be used in the guidance of pupils and in the supervision of teachers. In "The Work of the Bureau of Measurement, Statistics and Research" issued by the Baltimore schools in 1933 appears the following statement:

The entire school system has been gradually instructed in the techniques of testing and organizations have been built up in the school staff to carry out this work. The old method of judging the efficiency of instruction and the progress of pupils by the opinion of teacher and administrative officers alone has been found to be inadequate. These older methods have been supplemented and supplanted by the use of standardized tests and related procedures. By common consent one of the most significant single discoveries in the field of education that has been made in the past two decades is the standardized test. No single device has been developed which has as far-reaching significance in the promotion of efficient instruction and administration. Despite much blather about intelligence tests, standardized tests involve no mystery or magic. They have no relation to the superstitions of fortune-telling, hypnotism, or phrenology. On the contrary, they are but common-sense applications of questions dealing with the courses of study. They are technical measuring tools of the teaching art, and their value is no longer debated by school people. Through the use of tests it has become possible for the first time in the history of education to obtain impartial measurements of the status and progress of each pupil in the basic subjects of the curriculum which the schools are organized to provide.

To-day through the use of standardized tests we measure with accuracy a child's status in, for example, reading ability, the basic art governing almost all other forms of learning, and which in a printing age constitutes the major source of all other knowledge. We measure whether he has made, in a five-month term, five months of progress, two months of progress, or ten months of progress. Similarly, we measure each child's status and progress in arithmetic, in spelling, in history, in geography,—in fact, in all of the subjects of the curriculum. In the last analysis, the mastery of the basic subjects of the curriculum constitutes the whole business of the schools, for it is through this process that the total educational development takes place. It is for this purpose that schools are maintained. Maximum educational progress in the subjects which constitute the program of the school is by definition the justification for every dollar that is expended in teachers, for buildings, and for all other activities which comprise the total school expenditures. *It is evident, therefore, that an instrument as important as the standard test which so greatly facilitates instruction is a necessity of first importance.*[2]

If the test is for the purpose of grading or determining the level of mastery of a particular student in comparison with the class as a whole, it is well to use a scaled examination. That is, the test should sample the field vertically in the direction of increasing difficulty. Such a test can be arranged so that no one in the class can secure a perfect grade, and the score made by each individual will give his position in the class.

If the test is arranged for the purpose of determining pupils' mastery of the whole field of work, then a wide horizontal sampling is desirable. It is not only a question of measuring the amount of knowledge acquired, but also of determining if the ability to use that knowledge is satisfactorily developed. If some objectives of the field have been sufficiently mastered, such a test will indicate this fact. Of course, this test can be scaled, but it is possible that sufficient individual comparisons have been made in the progress tests which have been given from time to time.

IV. SELECTION OF MATERIALS FOR TESTS

Most authorities on testing agree that the materials for a good test should be determined by an analysis of objectives rather than of content, and that the situations determined by such analysis should be put in terms of student behavior, rather than simple factual recall. The material of the tests used will almost inevitably, consciously or unconsciously, affect the character of the teaching. Therefore, the elements of the test used should be aligned with the valid social objectives of education, but in actual practice, only a few tests rest upon a systematic survey of social needs. In other words, the material of the test is too often determined by a "logical" analysis of the subject rather than an analysis of the objectives sought.

In applying these data to the specific problem of the selection,

[2] *The Work of the Bureau of Measurement, Statistics and Research* (Department of Education, Baltimore, Maryland, May, 1933), pp. 5-6.

construction, and placement of tests in courses of study, the following working principles have been developed:

1. Tests shall be used whenever information as to mental and educational status of the learner is desirable. Information concerning the pupils' mental level and educational progress is essential, first, before instruction begins, as a basis for adapting the level of instruction by segregation, grade placement, etc. Second, it is desirable to know throughout the teaching-learning process just what progress is being made. If progress is generally unsatisfactory, probably the method or materials, or both, are at fault. By changing the methods and the materials and retesting after a definite period, data will be furnished on these points. If progress is generally satisfactory, but unsatisfactory in some specific cases, diagnostic testing is called for. Third, at the end of the unit, it is necessary to know if the unit has been mastered and if reteaching is necessary or if the next unit may be attacked. Finally, for grading purposes, the comparative level of achievement of the different pupils of the class should be known.

2. The nature of the test is to be determined by its specific use. In selecting the type of test to be used, two general principles may be put down: (*a*) the test or examination shall be adapted to its specific use, and (*b*) the test must attain its objectives without producing harmful effects on the educative process. Under the first of these will come considerations of validity and reliability, and under the latter a consideration of the third criterion.

The teacher must know the educational status of the child at the beginning of the course and the preliminary or pre-test measures this level of development. It should therefore be a scaled test and should sample the field vertically in the direction of increasing difficulty. Norms should be available. Since only the level of attainment is wanted, the simplest and quickest form of reliable test is suggested. This will be an objective test and probably a true-false test.

For the progress test, if a skill is involved, both rate and accuracy must be measured. The type of test will of course depend upon the subject-matter, but will usually consist of measured performance of the skill being learned. In other types of learning, the level of development, which calls for a scaled test, and the method of work, which again calls for a performance test, are the factors to be measured. Diagnostic tests which have been previously mentioned should be used here.

In the case of the final test, the teacher is not concerned with the class level which the learner has attained, since that level has already been determined by the progress tests. Rather it is important to determine if the learner has mastered the whole field, or if he has omitted some parts. To answer this question, the range of development must be measured. A wide horizontal sampling is desirable which will measure not only the knowledge acquired, but also the ability to use these facts. It is possible to use extensive recall and recognition tests similar to those developed by Odell [3] and called rearranging tests, verification tests, and analogies. Here is also the place for the essay-type test. In connection with the final test, a scaled test for the purposes of comparative grading, if it is used, is necessary. This should be varied to include true-false, multiple-choice, and other forms of tests, and be as objective as possible. The three criteria—validity, reliability, and contribution to the educative process—must be constantly in the mind of the teacher.

Specifically, the course of study should include:

(1) Pre-tests
(2) Progress tests
(3) Provision for diagnostic tests
(4) Final or mastery tests.

The form of these shall in general be determined by the points just discussed, and the material shall be determined by the objectives of the course of study.

V. THE CONSTRUCTION OF THE TEST

The reader who has read carefully the preceding pages is ready to undertake the development of a test. The following discussion will simplify this work and assist one in gaining proficiency.

A. Review the course of study, noting objectives, activities of pupils, materials assigned, etc. Those materials which are really significant in the course should be considered for inclusion in the test. An early inventory of the classwork will guarantee the comprehensiveness of the examination.

B. Different subject-matter fields lend themselves to particular types of tests. A study should be made of the types which can be used to advantage. It is possible, of course, to use several types of tests in the same examination. As a very short

---

[3] C. W. Odell, *Traditional Examinations and the New Type Tests* (The Century Company, 1928).

objective examination has little validity, an approximation should be made of the items necessary to develop a valid examination of the unit or course. It is worth while to write out more statements than one can use and then discard those which are not clearly stated or are of little significance.

C. Every examination should contain stimulating thought questions or statements. Of course, certain items in the examination will demand only memory, but they should be in the minority.

D. If the purpose of the test is to arrive at a grade for each student, it should commence with easy questions or statements and build up to very difficult ones. Every student should be able to answer some of the questions, and very few should be able to answer all of them. An examination which can be answered correctly by every student has no value as a basis for grades. If the easy questions are at the beginning of the test, it tends to build up confidence in the students who are taking the examination.

E. It is well to remember that a fair test will not confuse students by introducing complicated statements, double negatives, or new terms, which do not assist the examiner in determining the knowledge of the pupils. The teacher should be familiar with the following facts secured by Brinkmeier and Ruch[4] from a study of a large number of tests prepared by teachers:

1. Four out of five statements containing *all* are false.
2. Three out of four statements containing *always* or *never* are false.
3. Four out of five statements containing *no, none,* or *nothing* are false.
4. Nine out of ten statements containing *only* or *alone* are false.
5. Two out of three statements containing *clauses* of *cause* or *reason* are false.
6. Four out of five statements containing *evaluations* are true.
7. Two out of three statements containing *may* expressing possibility are true.

[4] I. H. Brinkmeier, and G. M. Ruch, *Journal of Educational Research,* Vol. XXII (September, 1930), pp. 110-118.

8. Three out of four statements containing such words as *most, some, often, generally, etc.,* are true.

It is extremely important that no ambiguity be permitted to appear in the test so that the student who has a partial mastery of the course can indicate the exact degree of that mastery. It is also essential that the phraseology shall not reveal to the clever student the correct answer to the questions and enable him to secure a higher grade than he deserves.

F. If the test is made up of a number of different types, it is desirable to keep each type segregated as a unit of the examination. These units can be preceded by directions and examples, if desired. It is particularly essential that the true and false test be organized so that no definite scheme is apparent. Only a random development of true and false questions can prevent the smart pupil from guessing and making a good score.

G. When the test has been completed, the teacher should analyze it carefully by asking himself the following questions concerning it:

1. *Is the meaning of every question clear?* This can be further checked by having other teachers assist in work. If the examination is given to older or more advanced students, their reactions will assist in clarifying the meanings of words, phrases, or statements. No involved or awkward English should be tolerated; the question or statement must have only one correct answer.

2. *Is the test composed of too much factual or memory material?* A careful study of each statement will reveal the percentage of the test which is devoted to thought-provoking material.

3. *Can a well-read person, with a limited knowledge of the course, answer these questions?* Statements may be too general as well as too specific. All statements which have little significance or which are extremely easy should be eliminated.

4. *Are the statements arranged in order of difficulty?* The scaling of the examination will add greatly to the service it can render as a measuring device.

VI. THE TEST IN THE COURSE OF STUDY

The place of the test in the course of study can best be illustrated by referring to one of the excellent courses of study and noting the practice in a leading curriculum center.

Lakewood, Ohio. Social Sciences for the Third Grade, 1931.[5]
The Unit on *Books, Newspapers, and Printing Make the
World a More Delightful Place in Which to Live* is selected
to illustrate the use and place of tests.

The objectives of the unit are:
A. To learn about books and printing
B. To make paper

The desired outcomes are:
A. Knowledge and understanding
  1. Thousands of years B.C. man kept a permanent record of
     his happenings. *Example*—the Bible
  2. Civilization advanced with the invention of:
     a. Paper
     b. Means of writing
     c. Printing presses
  3. A knowledge of the many ways in which records were
     kept—tablets of clay, wax, stone, bamboo, leaves of gold,
     etc.

B. Habits and skills
   Growth in habits:
  1. Of reading for information and for pleasure a variety of
     materials such as history, biography, poetry, stories
  2. Of ability to comprehend facts
  3. Of correct language forms
  4. Of self-expression, ability to form judgments
   Increased skill in:
  1. Organizing materials for oral and written reports
  2. Asking questions
  3. Arousing interest
  4. Study habits

C. Attitudes and appreciations
  1. An appreciation of effect of inventing on our lives
  2. Consciousness of dependence of people upon different
     countries for their contributions to civilization
  3. Greater appreciation of use and necessity of modern in-
     ventions
  4. Appreciation of the value of good books and of libraries
  5. Keener interest in reading for information and pleasure

[5] *Tentative Course in the Social Sciences for the Third Grade* (Lakewood Public Schools, Lakewood, Ohio, 1931).

The following tests are included:

FACT TEST

Objective: Ability to comprehend facts.
Directions: Number the lines of your paper from 1-23.
Write the correct word to fit each blank opposite the correct number of your paper.

1. The Chinese first learned to make paper from watching the —————.
2. The Chinese learned to make paper from ————— before any other people.
3. People of Egypt made paper of the ————— —————.
4. Paper was first made by —————.
5. In the United States ————— is used more than anything else for paper.
6. Old ————— are often used to make paper.
7. The ————— people discovered how paper could be made from cotton.
8. ————— and ————— are used a great deal in paper making.
9. The Congressional Library is in ————— —————.
10. "Memory aids" in form of knots was used by ————— natives.
11. Cuneiform characters are ————— writing.
12. Hieroglyphics were written on ————— tablets.
13. Straight line writing was done by the —————.
14. Papyrus is made from the pith of a —————.
15. Parchment is made of —————.
16. ————— is made of calf-skin.
17. ————— introduced paper making into Europe.
18. A printer's folio is a printer's —————.
19. A ————— sets type up in separate letters.
20. A ————— sets type up a line at a time.
21. The matrix is a ————— —————.
22. The most ancient volume on record was made in —————.
23. The ————— Stone was found in the Louvre in 1868.

Answers:

1. wasp		8. hemp, straw
2. wood		9. Washington, D. C.
3. papyrus plant		10. Peruvian
4. hand		11. picture
5. wood		12. clay
6. rags		13. Irish
7. Chinese		14. reed

15. sheepskin
16. vellum
17. Arabs
18. page
19. monotype

20. linotype
21. metal mold
22. Egypt
23. Moabite

FACT TEST

Objective: Ability to comprehend facts.

Directions: Number the lines of a piece of paper from 1-25. Opposite each number on your paper write "Yes" for each true statement and "No" for each false statement. Do not copy statements.

1. The Chinese made picture signs on bamboo tablets.
2. The Hindus invented alphabetical characters.
3. Clay tablets were used by the people of Nineveh.
4. The Rosetta Stone was important to civilization.
5. The Arabs of the tenth century used linen rags to make paper.
6. The wasp helped us to make paper.
7. Charles Watts perfected the art of printing.
8. Chinese and Japanese use parts of the mulberry tree in paper making.
9. Papyrus was first made in Italy.
10. Experimenting with woodcuts later led men to the art of engraving.
11. Movable type printing press was much experimented with in the country of France.
12. A linotype works on the same order as a player piano.
13. William Penn set up the first printing press in Philadelphia.
14. Many cheap books have type set by hand.
15. A linotype is used in a printing office.
16. Libraries provide pleasure and information to thousands of people.
17. For years stories and songs of men were handed down orally.
18. Some of man's early writings have been saved.
19. Man first made symbols on the bark of trees and on rocks.
20. The cave men drew pictures on the walls of their cave homes.
21. Early Indians of North America wrote on vellum..
22. The first books were made by machinery.
23. Books have always been made of paper.
24. In Egypt books were in the form of rolls.
25. Books and newspapers make it possible for man to know the happenings of the world.

Answers:

1. Yes	6. Yes	11. No	16. Yes	21. No
2. No	7. No	12. No	17. Yes	22. No
3. Yes	8. Yes	13. Yes	18. Yes	23. No
4. Yes	9. No	14. No	19. Yes	24. Yes
5. Yes	10. Yes	15. No	20. Yes	25. Yes

INCOMPLETE OUTLINE TEST

Objective: Ability to organize facts.

Directions: Fill in each blank with the correct word from the list of words below the test.

1. What peoples have preserved records in their earliest forms of writing?

   I——   G——   J——
   H——   E——   S——
   R——   C——   A——

2. Paper was and is made of many different materials.

Ancient Times	*Modern Times*
V————	L————
P————	P————
P————	S————
	P————
	R————

List of words to be used above:

vellum, parchment, rags, papyrus, linen, pine, spruce, poplar, clay, wax, Romans, Assyrians, Japanese, Irish, Hebrews, Greeks, Chinese, Egyptians, Scandinavians

ORGANIZATION TEST

Objective: Ability to organize ideas.

Directions: On your paper write the main topics below. Match the detail sentences with the main topics to which they belong. Write the number of each detail sentence after the appropriate main topic.

Main Topics:

A. Kinds of Paper: 1, 5, 9
B. How Records Were Kept: 3, 4, 8, 10
C. Types of Printing: 2, 7, 12
D. Work of Gutenberg: 6, 11
   1. The ancient Egyptians wrote on papyrus.
   2. A linotype works faster than a monotype.

3. Gutenberg was said to have made the first movable type printing press.
4. The Chinese kept records on bamboo tablets.
5. Linen paper is expensive.
6. Gutenberg experimented with woodcuts.
7. Types of printing vary greatly in size.
8. Ideographs are picture signs.
9. The wasp taught us how to make paper.
10. Stone and metal imprints of the Hebrews have been discovered.
11. Gutenberg's Bible is in the Congressional Library.
12. Setting type is more complicated to-day than ever before.

Judgment Test

Objective: Ability to use judgment in independent thinking.

Directions: Number the lines of a piece of paper from 1-10. Opposite each number on your paper write the letter preceding the best reason given.

1. Much of our paper is made of wood pulp because:
   a. It is inexpensive
   b. It is the easiest way
   c. The people prefer this kind
2. Parchment was used in ancient times because:
   a. It was easy to write on
   b. It would wear well
   c. People didn't know of any other way of keeping records
3. Records were kept in many ways because:
   a. People did not want their records mixed
   b. People could not agree on one certain form of writing
   c. Each country had different ways of interpreting its own language
4. Hieroglyphics mean much to us because:
   a. Their interpretation connects us with the ancient world
   b. They are old
   c. They are of Egyptian origin

5. Printers have certain units of measurement because:
   a. They can use linear measure
   b. It is a systematic way of setting type
   c. That is the custom
6. A proofreader must be accurate because:
   a. This is a slow process
   b. An error is expensive in both material and time
   c. The public demands that reading material be accurate

7. Gutenberg worked to establish printing because:
    a. It would be of great benefit to the world
    b. He wished to become famous
    c. The people did not like woodcuts
8. Printing progressed slowly because:
    a. There was not enough money to experiment
    b. People were not interested
    c. It was so different from anything they knew of at the time
9. Much money is expended in public libraries because:
    a. It benefits the public
    b. Children like to visit them
    c. Schools demand them
10. People go to the libraries because:
    a. It is quiet there
    b. They want to read for information or pleasure
    c. They are conveniently located

VII. THE TEST IN THE ACTIVITY SCHOOL

Many leaders in the progressive education movement have maintained that tests should not be introduced into the activity program, since, first, such an analysis would limit the value of the movement, and, second, the results of the work in the activity school are too indefinite and intangible to respond to careful evaluation. Adams secured some interesting data when the problem of testing the results of the activity school was presented to 949 specialists, supervisors, teachers, student-teachers, administrators, and university professors. The following table (reproduced from the study by Fay Adams) [6] summarizes the results of this investigation.

A. *Excellent solutions*
    g. Evaluate the outcome by observation of pupil activity together with the results of standardized and teacher-prepared tests ....

B. *Good solutions*
    d. Use a combination of teacher-prepared and standardized tests ....

[6] Fay Adams, "The Initiation of an Activity Program into the Public Schools," Contributions to Education, No. 598 (Bureau of Publications, Teachers College, Columbia University, 1934), p. 34.

    e. Evaluate the outcomes by observation of the activities of the group ....

    f. Evaluate the outcomes by observing the activity of each child ....

C. *Solutions having some merit*

    b. Test the results by means of teacher-prepared tests........

D. *Solutions having little merit*

    c. Test the results by means of standardized tests............

E. *Undesirable solutions*

    a. Make no attempt to test the results of an activity..........

Adams says:

The best solution for this problem is solution *g*. Note that it provides for the evaluation of an activity program upon three bases:

    1. Observation of pupil activity, both group and individual
    2. The results of standardized tests
    3. The results of teacher-prepared tests

The rating assigned this solution by supervisors was one of the highest given to any solution. Its composite score was 2.93; twenty-six out of twenty-seven specialists rated it excellent. The significance of a score of 2.93 will be seen when it is recalled that the highest possible composite score is 3. While other groups gave solution *g* a very high rank, their ratings were not so consistently high as were those of the specialists. The critical ratio of this difference is 7.42.

The writer is not aware of any definite techniques which have been developed to aid teachers in the observation of pupil activity. However, as has been revealed in the rating of adjustments each individual child is making to other children and to his work, they should note any significant responses which help them to understand better the way in which the child is growing and developing. The following questions may suggest the type of conditions and reactions for which teachers should watch. Is the child happy? Is he well? Does he show a growing interest in his work? Does he demonstrate an increasing willingness to assume responsibility? Has he made definite contribution to the group enterprise? Does he coöperate wholeheartedly with other children?

Most teachers will find it advisable to keep records which will show the development of the children. It has been suggested that this can be done by keeping a special card for each child and record-'ng upon it brief notes whenever the child reacts in a significant manner. By experimenting, teachers will be able to determine the techniques and types of records which will be most helpful to them in observing and evaluating pupil activity. In any case, the keeping of record cards should not be time-consuming or burdensome.[7]

VIII. THE DEVELOPMENT OF TESTS IN THE DENVER PUBLIC SCHOOLS

The following quotation from *The Denver Program of Curricular Revision* [8] will serve as an excellent summarization of procedures in developing tests for the teacher or committee. While it is limited to three academic fields, the suggestions are general enough to be valuable to any course of study committee.

"Analysis of typical procedures in testing." As a summary of the procedures used in preparing and using curriculum tests, the detailed and definite steps in the procedure followed in three typical cases will be given.

Procedure of testing in junior high-school English, grammar, and punctuation. The detailed steps in the procedure were:
1. Content prepared by chairman of curriculum committee
2. Types of tests to be used selected by chairman of committee in conference with director of measurements
3. Test written by chairman and criticized by committee members
4. Judged by director of curriculum for content
5. Judged by director of measurements for form and English
6. Score key prepared by chairman
7. Test checked with key by members of committee
8. Test given by English teachers under carefully controlled conditions
9. Test scored by teachers and returned to director of measurements
10. Tabulations made by director of measurements
    a. Medians for city and for schools
    b. School mark equivalents for scores for city and for schools
    c. Per cent missing each question by schools and for city
11. Giving the test a second time to secure more reliable figures regarding errors of various types

[7] *Ibid.,* pp. 34-35.
[8] *The Denver Program of Curriculum Revision* (Denver Public Schools, Denver, Colorado), pp. 58-60.

12. Summary of tabulations. Collecting under each head the test items referring to it and giving an example of each. Prepared by chairman of committee

13. Averaging of per cents missing under the summary of tabulations by director of measurements

14. Preparation of report showing for the city and for each school by grades the difficulty of each type of error, with suggestions as to their significance and remedial measures

15. Presentation of report to principals and curriculum committee

Procedure of testing in senior high-school science. The detailed steps in the procedure were:

1. Material selected by chairman of committee with the aid of one member

2. Type of test to be used selected by chairman of committee and director of measurements

3. Test written by chairman of committee and sometimes read and criticized by committee members

4. Judged by director of curriculum for content

5. Judged by director of measurements for form and English

6. Score key prepared by chairman

7. Test checked carefully with score key by a member of committee

8. Test given in schools by social-science teachers under carefully controlled conditions

9. Test scored by teachers and returned to director of measurements

10. Tabulations made by director of measurements
    a. Median for city and for schools
    b. School mark equivalents for scores for city and for schools
    c. Per cent missing each question by schools and for the city

11. Criticisms of test by teachers of social science sent to chairman of committee

12. Course of study modified according to results as shown by studies made by director of measurements and criticisms of test results made by teachers

13. Form of test modified according to criticisms before being reprinted

Procedures of testing in elementary-school arithmetic. The detailed steps in the procedure were:

1. Content at first selected by chairman of committee, super-

visors, and director of measurements; later by supervisors and director of measurements

2. Tests at first prepared by chairman of committee, supervisors, and director of measurements; later by supervisors and director of measurements

3. Tests checked by director of measurements, a principal, and a teacher

4. Decision by schools whether or not they wished to give the tests

5. Tests given by teachers

6. Tests scored by teachers

7. Scores tabulated by teachers as follows:
    a. Tabulation Number 1—Scores distributed into five groups
    b. Tabulation Number 2—(Optional). Showing individual problems missed by each child
    c. Tabulation Number 3—Per cent missing each problem by grades

8. City tabulations made by director of measurements as follows:
    a. Medians, twenty-five percentiles, seventy-five percentiles for city
    b. Percentile ranks for all tests
    c. Per cent missing each problem for the city by grades

9. Report prepared showing tabulations of scores and norms, with analysis of difficulties and suggestions for remedial treatment

10. Research Monograph Number Two prepared by listing the types of examples that are significant in the mechanical processes together with the mental processes involved in working them and citations to the pages in the course of study showing the methods of reteaching or remedial work

11. Presentation of report and research monograph to principals of elementary schools

12. Supervision of instruction, making use of facts discovered as the basis for work needed

IX. SUMMARY

A course of study should include tests to be used as well as presenting suggestions and illustrations which will serve to assist teachers in the construction of them. This discussion will vary from one subject-matter field to another and cannot be standardized for all courses of study. It should be indicated, however, that there are results of teaching and learning which cannot be accurately measured, and the teacher will have to make an evaluation. Appreciation of literature is an example of this. However, if the teacher assumes that no one wishes an evaluation of this phase of the work, emphasis will be placed upon those aspects of the course which will indicate results in the examination. If the teacher of literature ignores or minimizes appreciation, the results will be disastrous to the student.

An important objective of testing is to secure a diagnosis of the weaknesses and difficulties of children. This type of test can be given before, during, or after instruction. It is the basis of the remedial teaching which is developed in the school.

Much time and money have been wasted by school systems which have engaged in testing programs because it was the "fad" rather than realizing it was part of a complete educational program involving the analysis of subject-matter, determining what to teach, and what achievements to test.

The teacher should realize that standardized tests are valuable for purposes of checking achievements in a particular system against norms, established either nationally or locally. They are usually of little value as teaching instruments, because they do not correlate with the course of study with respect to emphasis in the subject-matter, time allotment, or grade placement. The important test is the one which has been constructed from the particular course of study.

The testing program which is outlined in the course of study in mathematics for the junior high schools of Kansas City, Missouri, indicates both the scope of the testing work and the relationship of each type of test to the course of study.

In recent years educational and intelligence tests have so fully demonstrated their worth that they are now regarded as essential in all the more progressive school systems. They are no longer used only by school surveyors, research workers and supervisors, but they have become everyday tools of teachers and principals. Every progressive teacher now realizes that these tests give types of information more accurate and more reliable than the usual subjective school judgments and that attempts at guidance, counseling, and classification of pupils without the accurate objective results secured by means of tests are unwise.

A carefully organized testing program enables the teacher to find the weaknesses of her class, to make provision for those weaknesses, and to test the effectiveness of her teaching. Such a program is also valuable for pupils, especially if individual records of achievement and progress are kept. These records enable the pupil to compare his attainment with class and national standards. They also show his growth and progress and serve as an incentive to maximum achievement.[9]

A well-planned testing program will probably include the following items:

1. *Inventory test*
   This type of test is valuable if given at the beginning of the year to acquaint the teacher with the previous attainments of her pupils. By revealing group and individual weaknesses, the results of this test enable the teacher to provide the necessary remedial measures and to avoid waste of time through reteaching what has already been acquired.

2. *Diagnostic test*
   This test is perhaps the most valuable of all in the testing program of the teacher, for upon its results she may base her entire remedial and corrective program. The diagnostic test may be used for inventory purposes or may be given at the completion of a topic to determine group and individual mastery and difficulties.

3. *Practice test*
   This test serves two purposes—it is diagnostic in that it reveals deficiencies and remedial in that it provides practice material for the correction of deficiencies. Suitable material of this nature should be on hand to meet the needs of the group.

4. *Achievement test*
   This type of test measures class progress and effectiveness of teaching. It should be given either at the beginning and end of a term or at the end of the term.

   Objective classroom tests of the teacher's own making may profitably be given at frequent intervals.

5. *Records of test results*
   Results of tests should be recorded for the purpose of analysis and comparison. These results, if recorded in some form—chart, graph, or table—which can be posted, will serve as an incentive

[9] *Bulletin of the Bureau of Research and Efficiency* (1927), excerpt included in *Curriculum Bulletin* No. 4 (Kansas City, Missouri, 1929).

to the pupils for greater achievement. Individual score-sheets, charts, or graphs kept by the pupils themselves also serve as a spur to maximum attainment. Suggestive pupil graphs may be found in the Course of Study in Arithmetic for Grades I-IV, pp. 153, 264.[10]

The results of the test are important for the student, because they indicate his proficiency in realizing the objectives of the course. He will be interested in tests for the measurement of attainment in specific skills and habits and in the tests which determine his mastery of the general objectives of the unit. The latter can be determined, in many instances, by having the pupil develop a test for himself, engaging him in conversation or making use of the essay examination.

An adequate appraisal of the attainments or degree of mastery achieved by the students necessitates the use of a well-planned system of testing. This system will necessarily include: questioning and discussing in the class or in conference; the written examination, both essay and new-type or objective; written reports and subjective evaluation of pupil behavior.

The teacher or committee should realize that all examinations and other methods of evaluating the immediate results of teaching are concerned with specific objectives. Any type of general objective, which cannot be attained during the class or the semester cannot be measured specifically except to the extent and the degree to which they have been mastered. The final examination in many subject-matter fields cannot be given or evaluated until reaction to life situations are noted.

It should be realized at this point, however, that the problem of testing is intimately related to the validity of the specific objectives. To the extent that the specific objectives are valid and the mastery of them will result in the ultimate attainment of the general objectives and principles of education, an accurate measure of the former will result in careful evaluation of the mastery of the latter in so far as the specifics represent a section of the complete field of general objectives. In regard to

[10] "Course of Study in Mathematics for Junior High School Grades," Kansas City Public Schools, Kansas City, Missouri. *Curriculum* Bulletin, No. 4, 1929.

the general objectives and principles of education, it must be admitted that the validity of the examination will depend on the validity of the specific objectives.

BIBLIOGRAPHY

ADLER, Mortimer, J., "Music Appreciation; an Experimental Approach to its Measurement," *Archives of Psychology,* No. CX (New York, Columbia University, 1929). His study disclosed the fact that most listeners prefer the obvious to the more subtle in music.

ANDERSON, Howard R., and LINDQUIST, Everett F., "The Improvement of Objective Testing in History," Classroom and Administrative Problems in the Teaching of the Social Sciences. National Council for the Social Studies, *Second Yearbook* (Philadelphia, McKinley Publishing Company, 1932). By presenting results of an extensive test in world history, they revealed a cross-section of the knowledge of a large group of high-school students.

BERNSTEIN, L., "A New Type Examination in History," New York Bulletin of High Points (March, 1923), pp. 15-20.

BOWMAN, Horace B., "The Standardization of the Kwalwasser-Dykema Tests," Master's Thesis (Syracuse University, 1931). He presents in this statistical study on the Kwalwasser-Dykema Tests, which was based on approximately 2,000 cases, norms, reliability coefficients, and intercorrelations.

BRIGGS, T. H., "An Examination in First-Term Latin," *Classical Weekly,* Vol. XVI, No. 19 (March 19, 1923).

BRINKLEY, S. G., *Preparation and Use of New Type Examination.* (Bureau of Publications, Teachers College, Columbia University, 1924).

BRUECKNER, Leo J., *Diagnostic and Remedial Teaching in Arithmetic* (John C. Winston Co., 1930).

BRUECKNER, Leo J., and MELBY, E. C., *Diagnostic and Remedial Teaching* (Houghton Mifflin Co., 1931).

CHURCH, Esther, "The Use of Tests and Measurements in Grouping Music Students of the Junior High School," *Music Supervisors Journal,* Vol. XVI (December, 1929), p. 79. She pointed out the uses of tests and measurements in grouping junior high-school pupils in music.

COOLEY, A. M., "Some Investigations Concerning the Use of Certain Home Economics Information Tests," *Teachers College Record,* Vol. XXIV (September, 1923), pp. 374-392.

CUBBERLEY, Ellwood P., Introduction to Brueckner and Melby, *Diagnostic and Remedial Teaching* (Houghton Mifflin Co., 1931).

DOUGLASS, H. R., *Modern Methods in High School Teaching* (Houghton Mifflin Co., 1926), Ch. XII, Quizzes, Examinations, and Markings. Ch. XIV, New Ideas in Written Examinations.

DUNLAP, Knight, "Mental Tests," *Progressive Education,* Vol. VII (March, 1930), pp. 57-67. A clear discussion of mental tests as differing from measurements, their value of the distributions, and the dangers of using mental tests as a diagnosis by one untrained in their underlying psychology.

EURICH, A. C., "Four Types of Examinations Compared and Evaluated," *Journal of Educational Psychology,* Vol. XXII (April, 1931), pp. 268-278. A determination of the relative value as measuring instruments of four types of tests, essay, completion, multiple-choice, and true-false, covering the same subject-matter.

FARNSWORTH, P. R., "Psychology and Music," *School Music,* Vol. XXXII (November, 1932), pp. 3-4. He discussed the value of tests and measurements in determining the extent of musical talent.

FRASIER, G. W., and ARMENTROUT, W. D., *An Introduction to the Literature of Education* (Scott, Foresman and Company, Chicago, 1931), Ch. IX, Measuring in Education.

GILLILAND, A. R., and JORDAN, R. H., *Education Measurements and the Classroom Teacher* (The Century Co., 1924), Ch. IV, Requisites for Giving Objective Tests.

GRANICH, Louis, "A Technique for Experimentation on Guessing in Objective Tests," *Journal of Educational Psychology,* Vol. XXII (February, 1931), pp. 145-156.

GREENE, Harry A., and JORGENSEN, Albert N., *Diagnostic and Remedial Techniques: Arithmetic* (Longmans, Green and Company, 1929). Summarizes and evaluates various research studies dealing with diagnostic and remedial techniques in arithmetic.

——, *The Use and Interpretation of Educational Tests* (Longmans, Green and Co., 1929).

HARAP, Henry, and BAYNE, J., "A Critical Survey of Public-School Courses of Study," *Western Reserve University Leaflet* No. 28 (October 1, 1932).

HARRISON, Margaret, "Testing the Appreciation Hour in Rural Schools," *Music Supervisors Journal,* Vol. XVIII (December, 1931), pp. 37, 43. She found a definite increase in musical information in rural schools where Damrosch concerts were heard.

JACOBSON, P. B., and VAN DUSEN, E. C., "Remedial Teaching in Reading in the Ninth Grade," *The School Review,* Vol. XXXVIII (February, 1930), pp. 142-146.

KAULFERS, Walter, "Why Prognose in the Foreign Language?" *Modern Language Journal,* Vol. XIV (January, 1930), pp. 296-301.

KELLY, T. L., *Interpretation of Educational Measurements* (World Book Co., 1927).

KIMMEL, W. C., "Practice Tests in the Social Studies," *Historical Outlook,* Vol. XIV (December, 1923), pp. 354-358.

KINDER, J. S., "Educational Tests for Use in Institutions of Higher Learning," Educational Research Circular No. 55, *University of Illinois Bulletin* (Urbana, Ill., 1930).

KLINE, Linus W., and CARY, Gertrude L., *Measuring Scale for Free-Hand Drawing,* Part 2, "Design and Composition" (Baltimore, Johns Hopkins Press, 1933). This test deals with design and composition.

KREY, A. C., and WESLEY, Edgar B., "Does the New Type Test Measure

Results of Instruction in the Social Studies?" *Historical Outlook,* Vol. XXIII (January, 1932), pp. 7-21. They attempted to differentiate between factual knowledge and understanding of ideas as results of history courses.

LANG, A. R., *Modern Methods in Written Examinations* (Houghton Mifflin Co., 1930), Ch. V, New Type Examinations; Ch. VI, True-False Tests; Ch. VII, Multiple-Choice and Matching Test; Ch. VIII, Recall Tests; Ch. IX, Combination Tests.

McCALL, W. A., *How to Measure in Education* (The Macmillan Co., 1922), pp. 119-133.

METCALF, A. N., "Diagnostic Testing and Remedial Teaching," *School Executives Magazine,* Vol. XLIX (April, 1930), pp. 358-360.

MICHELL, Elene, *Teaching Values in New-Type History Tests* (World Book Co., 1930). Ch. IV, Using Tests to Improve Instruction.

Music Teachers' National Association, "Report of the Committee on Tests and Measurements," *Proceedings, 1930* (The Association, Oberlin, Ohio, 1930). In their report on tests and measurements in music education, they showed that new tests are contributing much of value to musical pedagogy, vocational guidance, and psychology.

ODELL, Charles W., *Statistical Method in Education* (D. Appleton-Century Company, revised edition, 1935).

PEASE, G. R., "Should Teachers Give Warning of Tests and Examinations?" *Journal of Educational Psychology,* Vol. XXI (April, 1930), pp. 273-277.

PETERS, Charles C., and ALTMAN, John E., "A Critical Study of the Content of Standardized Tests in American History," *Journal of Educational Research,* Vol. XXIII (February, 1931), pp. 153-161. They critically analyzed twenty-three standard tests in American history, and reported percentages of test items.

PRESSEY, S. L., and PRESSEY, L. C., *Introduction to the Use of Standard Tests* (World Book Co., 1931). Ch. I, How to Use Tests; Ch. II, Tests in School Subjects; Ch. III, Tests of Mental Ability.

RUCH, G. M., *Improvement of the Written Examination* (Scott, Foresman and Co., 1924).

———, *The Objective or New-Type Examination* (Scott, Foresman and Co., 1929). Ch. VII, The Building of an Objective Test.

RUCH, G. M., and RICE, G. A., *Specimen Objective Examinations* (Scott, Foresman and Co., 1930). Ch. II, Trends in Objective Examination Practice as Revealed by Analyses of the Examinations Submitted in the National Contest.

RUCH, G. M., and STODDARD, G. D., *Tests and Measurement in High School Instruction* (World Book Co., 1927).

RUSSELL, Charles, *Standard Tests* (Ginn and Co., 1930).

SHYROCK, H. W., "New Tests for Old," Historical Outlook, Vol. XIV, No. 8 (November, 1923).

SICELOFF, Margaret McAdory, and WOODYARD, Ella, *Validity and Standardization of the McAdory Art Test* (New York, Teachers College, Columbia University, 1933). This is one of the best known of the standardized tests to determine ability in art skills and appreciation, and has age, grade, and adult norms for each sex.

SMITH, H. J., "Objective Measurement in Industrial Education," *Industrial Education Magazine,* Vol. XXXI (March, 1930), pp. 331-336.

STANTON, Hazel M., and KOERTH, Wilhelmina, "Musical Capacity Measures of Adults Repeated After Music Education," *University of Iowa Studies,* Series on Aims and Progress of Research, First Series No. 189, No. 31 (Iowa City, University of Iowa, October, 1930). They reported on the measures of musical capacity of adults after music education.

STENQUIST, J. L., "Baltimore Constantly Checks Results," *Journal of Education,* Vol. CXII (September 22, 1930), pp. 183-185.

SYMONDS, Percival M., *Measurement in Secondary Education* (The Macmillan Co., 1929),

TEN EYCK, H. E., "The Testing Movement," *The Balance Sheet* (January, 1931), pp. 149-152.

TEST, Flora C., "A Study of the Predictive Value of Tests in a Music School," Master's Thesis (Syracuse University, 1931). She discussed the predictive value of tests in music.

THORNDIKE, E. L., and GATES, A. I., *Elementary Principles of Education* (The Macmillan Company, 1929). Ch. XIII, Appraising the Results of Education.

THURSTONE, Thelma G., "The Difficulty of a Test and Its Diagnostic Value," *Journal of Educational Psychology,* Vol. XXIII (May, 1932), pp. 335-343. She investigated the difficulty of test items in relation to their reliability.

TODD, Jessie M., "Test in Art for Grade Children," *School Arts Magazine,* Vol. XXX (February, 1931), pp. 365-368. This test measures improvement under supervised practice.

TURNEY, Austin, "The Effect of Frequent, Short Objective Test," *School and Society,* Vol. XXXIII (June 6, 1931), pp. 760-762.

TYLER, Ralph W., "A Generalized Technique for Conducting Achievement Tests," *Educational Research Bulletin,* Ohio State University, Vol. X, No. 8 (November, 1931), pp. 199-208.

——, "The Master-List as a Device," *Educational Research Bulletin,* Ohio State University, Vol. X, No. 1 (January 7, 1931), pp. 1-11.

WHITE, C. W., "The Effects of Exemptions from Semester Examinations on the Distribution of School Marks," *The School Review,* Vol. XXXIV (April, 1931), pp. 293-299.

WHITLEY, Mary T., "A Comparison of the Seashore and the Kwalwasser-Dykema Music Tests," Teachers College Record, Vol. XXXIII (May, 1932), pp. 731-751. She outlined the relative merits of the Seashore and the Kwalwasser-Dykema music tests.

WILLIAMS, C. O., "A Critique of Measures of Musical Talent," *Music Supervisors Journal,* Vol. XVI (October, 1929), pp. 67-81, 95. He offered a critique of measures of musical talent.

WILSON, G. M., *How to Measure* (The Macmillan Company, 1930).

WILSON, W. R., *Improvement of the College Examination* (University of Washington Press, Seattle, Washington, 1932).

PART IV

ADMINISTRATION AND ORGANIZATION
OF CURRICULUM DEVELOPMENT

CHAPTER XVI

ORGANIZING AND WRITING THE COURSE OF STUDY

I. INTRODUCTION

It has been emphasized in previous chapters that the functional aspect of the course of study is all-important. The committee must ascertain if it is teachable and if it will be used in a professional way by the teachers in the system. Furthermore, the committee must determine if the course of study will make supervision a reality in the system in that both teachers and supervisors will have a definite, specific outline of objectives, activities, methods, and tests through which classroom progress can be ascertained and evaluated.

It is generally known that many teaching hours are wasted and thousands of dollars of tax money squandered in the development of courses of study which are not used in the classroom and which have little, if any, influence upon the educational program of the community. The questioning attitude which has developed toward education and educators is justified. The production of teachable courses of study which can and will be used as a basis of good teaching and supervision will do a great deal to alleviate this tension between society and educators. Confidence in the educational program can easily be secured through the establishment of a fine professional attitude on the part of teachers, supervisors, and administrators toward the problem of scientifically determining *what to teach, when to teach, how to teach,* and *how effective the teaching has been* in building character through the development of desirable attitudes, ideals, and appreciations, as well as information.

There is a high correlation between the character of the writing and general plan of organizing the course of study and the

731

functioning of the course of study in the school system. This is the only justification for the extended treatment of the phases of the work which were presented in the preceding chapters, and for the present chapter, which considers the structural aspects of the course. It is not enough to develop valid objectives and effective learning experiences and methods; it is essential that the course be so organized that it becomes at once a usable source of information and a guide to the professional teacher.

II. WRITING THE COURSE OF STUDY

The most scholarly minds in the school system should be assigned to the writing and the checking of the course of study. So much is dependent on this phase of the construction of the course that several professional people, representing different groups in the system, should have an opportunity of reading and evaluating the composition of the course. The following criteria will be suggestive to those teachers who are assigned to the task of evaluating the course.

A. *Is the course easy to read?* The ease of reading will determine, to a large extent, the frequency of reading. Since a course to be of value must be translated into better teaching, it is essential that it be read and studied by the teachers for whom it is prepared. Any course which is ponderous rather than scholarly, and which sacrifices clarity for profundity, will not represent full value on the investment.

B. *Is the course of study simple in organization?* An involved course, which requires the teacher to read extensively rather than study intensively, is not often used. The various aspects of the course should be so related that it can be used effectively without laborious effort on the part of the teacher. For example, when the specific objectives of the course are not definitely related to the activities of the child, teachers who have not participated in the organization of the course are apt to be confused. Only expert and laborious supervision can prevent "muddling along" under these conditions.

In some cases, members of the course of study committee

appear to have only a hazy idea of the relationships of different phases of the course. Unless the course of study is well and thoroughly organized, it cannot function adequately in the teaching of children.

C. *Is the course of study a scholarly production?* Unless the course of study is clearly written and its composition presents evidence of marked scholarship, it will receive little attention from the faculty. Poorly written and poorly organized courses represent merely wasted time and money. The emphasis should not be upon "fine writing," but upon clear, accurate, and concise use of the professional language of the teacher.

D. *Can the course of study be translated into improved teaching?* This, after all, is the final test of the course. The course which represents high scholarship and careful organization, and which affords a clear picture of the relationships of the many details which must be considered, rests its case on everyday use by the teaching staff. The effectiveness of the course cannot be evaluated until it has been introduced into the classroom, but the importance of a scholarly committee and editor cannot be overemphasized.

III. THE ORGANIZATION OF THE COURSE OF STUDY

There is wide variation in the general organization of courses of study at the present time. It will be impossible and unnecesary to indicate all of these divergences of procedure on the part of individual cities and committees. However, it is imperative that the general characteristics of those which have little value and cannot be recommended be presented and illustrations of excellently organized courses of study be outlined for the guidance of teachers and committees.

A. Some characteristics of poorly organized courses of study. The following are not all-inclusive, but are representative of common mistakes in organization:

1. Overemphasis in the grouping of objectives, methods, content, etc. In some courses, objectives for the entire year or semester are grouped on pages one and two. Content and methods are grouped

in separate sections, and no attempt is made to indicate any relationship. Such a course probably influences teaching very little, if at all.

2. Objectives ignored in the development of the course. Often the content is outlined in great detail, but no attempt is made to relate this material to teaching goals.

3. Overemphasis on the objectives. In a few instances, extended lists of objectives have been developed, while practically no suggestions are offered for their realization.

4. Omission of specific objectives. There is a tendency to develop general objectives and content and ignore completely the necessity of relating specifically the objectives and the child's learning experiences.

5. Lack of provision for individual differences. A number of courses appear to assume that a general course will inspire the teacher to make such adjustments as are necessary for the purpose of meeting individual differences.

6. Lack of a testing program. While such a program should not be rigidly prescribed, often no suggestions or samples of tests are included. The determination of mastery is too important to be left to chance.

7. Lack of bibliographies for teachers and pupils. Most courses include suggested reading lists for teachers and pupils, but many of these are inadequate and out-of-date.

B. Some characteristics of a well-organized course of study. Only four items will be included here, since this topic will be extensively treated in the remaining sections of this chapter.

1. The course of study must be comprehensive. It should include general objectives, specific objectives, content, suggested types of method, equipment and instructional aids, a testing program, complete reference lists for both teachers and pupils, etc.

2. The work of the year or semester should be divided into units, topics, contracts, problems, projects, or challenges.

3. Each subdivision should be correctly placed according to grade and be within the capacity of the pupils.

4. Each of the subdivisions should be organized in terms of the objectives of the course and the preceding units of work.

IV. SPECIFIC PLANS OF COURSE OF STUDY ORGANIZATION

Teachers or committees engaged in this work are faced with the problem of organizing the course so that it will be of greatest service to teachers, pupils, supervisors, and administrators. The problem is not so much what items should be included in the course as it is in what form the relationships of the various items can be shown to greatest advantage. The course of study must stimulate the teacher to continuous research; it must be practical in the sense that it can be translated into improved teaching; it should facilitate supervision and administration as well as teaching.

This problem has not been satisfactorily solved up to the present time, but great improvement is being evidenced in course of study construction as research experts, and teachers are giving more and more time to investigation in this field. The results which have been realized to date can be classified under five types of organization. There is wide variation within each of these classifications. It will be necessary to include several illustrations in order to indicate the possibilities of each group.

A. The several elements of each unit are organized in columns so that the teacher can see at a glance the relationship between objectives, pupil activities, teaching procedures, and results to be attained. The reader will profit from (1) a study of the number of columns, (2) a comparison of the titles of these, (3) the arrangement of the columns in the unit, and (4) methods of organizing the content within each column.

1. The course of study in art for the senior high school published in 1932 by the Long Beach, California, schools provided for the organization of the units under Content and Method and Attainments after the objectives have been stated. The following unit will serve as an excellent illustration of developing pupil activity in columns under Content and Method.

ATTAINMENTS

Knowledges:
1. Expulsion of air from clay is necessary to assure success in firing
2. Wedging and building up with a forcible movement are methods used to accomplish air expulsion—(*Contd. on page* 739)

CONTENT AND METHOD

UNIT: Clay construction processes of the slab and coil methods and the reproduction of objects by means of molds

OBJECTIVE: To grow in appreciation of fine structural design in clay; to gain knowledge of the essential techniques of the clay craft; to grow in appreciation of the beauty created by great potters

Acquaintanceship Period	Enrichment Period	Creative Period

I. Demonstrate slab method, for tile or box
 	
A. Wedging—purpose explained
B. Building up slab—purpose explained
C. Rolling
D. Cutting to size and shape
E. Reproduction of pattern
F. Mitering corners
G. Fitting slabs together, as parts of a box
H. Essential points in making cover
 	
II. Demonstrate
 	
A. Use of incising tool
  1. Depth and shape of cut
  2. Rounded edge
B. Hollow relief
	I. Demonstrate ability to wedge and roll clay for tile or box (individual choice or class choice of problem according to experience of group in previous classes).
	
	A. In case of box, demonstrate ability to miter corner and join slabs
	
	II. (Following the demonstration of the coil method in Acquaintanceship Period)
	Experimental work in forming a vase
	
	A. This work to perfect technique may be in the nature of a one- or two-coil tray. Under-glaze painting may carry out a design, if desired. The purpose
		I. Create tile and/or box, personally deciding:
		
		A. Size
		B. Shape
		C. Method of reproducing chosen design (chosen at close of Unit III-A)
		
		Note: A second problem in design may very naturally develop at this point—the designing of one's own mark. Such an interest may be made the basis for group discussion and research of the Acquaintanceship and Enrichment Period type of teaching, or for individual design and evaluation as part of the work of this Creative Period.

C. Surface planes—geometric areas forming pattern

Note: Previous experience of students on a lower level may make the above demonstrations and those of the coil method following unnecessary. In this case, a review to bring to mind the essential elements of the performances and to reveal needs for clarification will take the place of the demonstrations. Carry this experience through the study of the Enrichment Period and the production of the Creative Period before demonstrating the Coil Method (III following).

III. Demonstrate coil method (following creative experience with tile and/or box)
A. Building up base of bowl
B. Rolling coil
C. Attaching coil to base and to coil
D. Starting new coil

Note: Complete experience with coil method through enrichment

of this exercise, however, is to give opportunity for individual help in rolling of coil, joining, etc.

III. Class evaluation for technique, proportion, shape

IV. (If unit is extended to include Acquaintanceship Period, IV) Group or individual study of molds and casts in the room

A. Indicate grasp of directions given during demonstration.
B. Written or verbal review of facts concerning use of plaster of Paris

Materials and Media

Clay	Cardboard (or other stiff paper)
Knife	
Scissors	
Plaster of Paris	Scraps of Linoleum

II. Create bowl by coil method using shape chosen after experiments of Enrichment Period or create directly in clay a new form of fine proportion

A. Decorate by some method suited to shape and use if interest warrants.
1. Edge—incised
2. Surface—under-glaze painting
3. Variation in surface elevation

III. Form for casting

A. Block form — mold poured while clay is damp
1. One piece mold
B. Block form of character requiring more complex mold

CONTENT AND METHOD—Continued

Acquaintanceship Period	Enrichment Period	Creative Period
process (II and III) and creative production (III). In case of a more extended experience the technique of the plaster mold—one piece and a more complex form—should become a part of the experience with clay.		*Materials and Media*

IV. Demonstration
A. Mixing of plaster of Paris for a mold
  1. Variation in quality of plaster of Paris on the market
B. One-piece mold
C. Two or more piece mold
  1. Undercuts
		Clay Plaster of Paris
		Simple tools Linoleum scraps

Illustrative Material		
Clay—moist Incising and other simple tools Some illustrative material from preceding unit Some designs created by students (Unit III-A) Molds and casts Plaster of Paris Scraps of linoleum		

3. Slab and coil methods are used in forming clay articles
4. In building clay articles, care must be taken in all processes to expel air and leave no joinings incompletely sealed
5. The process of clay modeling is building up rather than cutting away, as in sculpture
6. A mold is made by pouring plaster of Paris over a form
7. Care must be taken in creasing the form so that no undercuts appear in the mold
8. In case the form is too complex for a one-piece mold, as many particles of clay are attached to the form as are necessary to separate the plaster when poured
9. These separate plaster walls are bound together when the clay slip is poured
10. Clay slip is clay mixed with water to a consistency thin enough to pour

Appreciations:
1. Some appreciation of the skill evidenced in clay objects of fine craftsmanship
2. Greater sensitiveness to beauty of form
3. Greater appreciation of the "hand-made" quality of objects built in this way and retaining evidence of the process
4. Joy in producing by hand objects of beauty and usefulness
5. Sensitiveness to clay as a medium for self-expression

Habits and skills:
1. Skill in building both by the slab and the coil method
2. Ability to complete a simple form with evidence of good craftsmanship in the result
3. The habit of careful consideration of each step of a technical procedure
4. Skill in producing satisfactory molds of one or more pieces [1]

2. Oakland, California, published in 1929 a course of study in Home Economics for Grades Seven, Eight, and Nine, which follows the same general plan of organization, but includes some interesting and valuable variations. The unit on the Preservation of Food under the larger unit of Home Planning and Preparation of Dinners is presented. New titles for the columns make necessary a new organization within the columns.

[1] *Art Course of Study for Senior High Schools* (Long Beach City Schools, 1932), pp. 104-105.

HOME PLANNING AND PREPARATION OF DINNERS [2]

Unit I. Preservation of Food

Specific Objective: To gain knowledge of the industry of food preservation and to acquire some skill in the preservation of food in the home.

Problems	Subject-Matter	Suggested Procedure	References

A. *Why should we preserve food?*	*Reasons for preserving food*
	
	1. Economic
	
	   a. To have foods out of season
	
	   b. To conserve when there is a large supply
	
	   c. To cut cost
	
	   d. To permit transportation
	
	2. Scientific
	
	   a. To meet nutritional needs all the year round
	
	   b. To kill micro-organisms
		List foods which, if preserved when cheap, will save cost when supply decreases and price grows higher.
		
		List foods which may be preserved in season and out of season.
			Cornell University Reading Courses, Lesson 136, p. 95, "Food Preservation"
			
			Bitting, A. W. and K. G., *Canning and How to Use Canned Foods,* p. 9
			
			"Canning by Safe Methods," *Good Housekeeping* (July, 1925)
			
			Harris and Lacey, *Everyday Foods* (adopted text), p. 336

[2] *Home Economics for Grades Seven, Eight and Nine* (Oakland Public Schools, 1929), pp. 150-157.

B. *What are the agencies which bring about deterioration in food?*	*Agencies which bring about deterioration in food:* Micro-organisms:	Review use of microscope.	Buchanan, R. E., *Agricultural and Industrial Bacteriology*, p. 173

What conditions develop in foods caused by micro-organisms in the food itself?	1. Intrinsic, i.e., those which are present in the food itself Bring conditions of over-ripeness
	   a. Hydrolizing
	      Bring rancidity in fatty food
	   b. Oxidizing
	      Bring discolorations
		Study methods of cultivating bacteria so that they may be seen under the microscope.	Broadhurst, Jean, *Home Community Hygiene*, pp. 1-11

What are the types of micro-organisms which attack from the outside?	2. Extrinsic, i.e., those which attack from without, (*a*) bacteria, (*b*) yeasts, (*c*) molds	Make chart giving meaning and application of terms. Continue chart through the unit. If possible cultivate bacteria, yeasts, or molds, and study them under the microscope	Powell, Ola, *Successful Canning and Preserving*, pp. 15-27 Harris and Lacey, p. 336
C. *What foods are affected by extrinsic micro-organisms?*	*Food affected and conditions of growth* 1. Protein (*a*) bacteria, (*b*) much water, slightly acid. 2. Carbohydrates (*a*) yeasts, (*b*) much water, usually acid.	Classify foods under protein and carbohydrate which are easily affected by micro-organisms	Cohn, H. W., *Yeasts and Molds*
	3. Any food (*a*) molds, (*b*) less moisture; acid; alkaline; or neutral.	List foods which are easily affected by molds.	Buchanan, pp. 174-182

HOME PLANNING AND PREPARATION OF DINNERS—*Continued*

Problems	Subject-Matter	Suggested Procedure	References
D. *What are the methods of preventing deterioration of Food?* How could this statement be proved? Canned foods hold to-day a large place in the food supply.	*Methods of preventing deterioration of food* 1. Heating to a temperature and for a time sufficient to kill micro-organisms and enzymes (*a*) canning (*b*) preserving, (*c*) pasteurizing 2. Holding foods at temperatures so low that changes cannot take place (*a*) cold storage, (*b*) freezing 3. Elimination of water (*a*) drying, (*b*) evaporation 4. Use of chemicals (*a*) salting, (*b*) pickling, (*c*) fermentation	List foods which are produced and canned in California. Visit pasteurization plants and canneries. Show by outline the difference between sterilization and pasteurization. List foods which are kept in cold storage. Study location of canneries and determine what governs location.	Matthews, *Elementary Home Economics*, p. 257 Cruess, W. V., *Home and Farm Canning*, p. 3. College of Agriculture, University of California Farmers' Bulletin No. 984, *Drying of Fruits and Vegetables* Harris and Lacey, p. 335 Round and Lang, *Preservation of Vegetables by Fermentation and Salting*, Farmers' Bulletin No. 881

	Dangers resulting from canning		
E. *What are the different kinds of spoilage affecting canned foods?*	1. Fermentation 2. Flat sour 3. Botulism 4. Putrefaction	Discuss the difference between flat sour and botulism. Study method of disposing of a doubtful canned product.	Harris and Lacey, p. 337 Bitting, pp. 11-14
F. *What are the different problems in the canning process?* What are the various methods which may be used for home canning? What is the difference in packing fruit and vegetables?	*Canning* 1. Types of containers and rubbers (a) advantages, (b) disadvantages, (c) testing 2. Methods of sterilization (a) water bath, (b) open kettle, (c) oven, (d) pressure cooker, (e) commercial steamer 3. Selection of food 4. Preparation 5. Packing (a) syrup for fruit, (b) salt solution for vegetables, (c) addition of acid for some vegetables 6. Sealing jars (a) methods, (b) tests for keeping 7. Storing (a) methods, (b) labeling	Study methods of testing cans and rubbers Discuss standards for canned fruits and vegetables. List factors to consider in selecting fruits and vegetables for canning. List advantages and disadvantages of open-kettle and cold-pack methods of canning in the home. Can foods which are in season by both open-kettle and cold-pack methods. Make an outline to follow in the selection, preparation, and canning of most vegetables.	*Cornell University Reading Courses,* Lesson 136, pp. 98, 99 Powell, pp. 36-92 Parloa, Maria, *Canned Fruit, Preserves and Jellies.* Farmers' Bul. No. 203 Wellman, W. T., *Food —Planning and Preparation,* pp. 353-364 Benson, O. H., *Home Canning by the One-Period Cold-pack Method.* Farmers' Bul. No. 839 Matthews, pp. 260-267 Harris and Lacey, pp. 338-343 Powell, p. 76

HOME PLANNING AND PREPARATION OF DINNERS—*Continued*

Problems	Subject-Matter	Suggested Procedure	References
G. *What factors should be taken into consideration in preparing fruit juice?*	*Fruit Juice* 1. Preliminary work 2. Extraction of juice 3. Clearing of juice 4. Canning or bottling (a) filling bottles or jars, (b) sealing, (c) sterilization, (d) paraffining	Make and bottle the juice of some fruit. Study how bottled fruit juice may be used in the home.	Cruess, W. B., *Fruit Juices and Jellies*, College of Agriculture, Univ. of California Powell, Chap. VIII
H. *What factors should be taken into consideration in making jelly?* Successful jelly is standard jelly. What is the standard?	*Jellies* 1. Boiling the fruit 2. Clearing the juice 3. Testing for pectin 4. Testing acidity 5. Addition of sugar 6. Tests for completion of cooking 7. Sealing, labeling, storing 8. Standards for judging jelly (a) appearance, (b) consistency, (c) flavor, (d) container 9. Use of pectin extracts	Tests for pectin. Tests for acidity. Make jelly for school use or for a hospital. List the steps in jelly making.	Powell, Chap. XIII Harris and Lacey, pp. 346-352 Greer, C. M., *School and Home Cooking*, pp. 496-500 Wellman, pp. 364-367 Powell, p. 342

I. *What factors should be taken into consideration in making pickles?* What are the various kinds of preservatives?	*Pickling* 1. Utensils 2. Preservatives (a) vinegar, (b) salt, (c) spices or sugar or both 3. Methods (a) brining, (b) open-kettle, (c) cold-pack 4. Kinds (a) sweet pickles, i.e., peaches, watermelons, (b) mixed pickles, i.e., combinations of vegetables, (c) relishes, i.e., Chile sauce, Chow Chow, (d) cucumber pickles (e) ketchup and sauces (f) dill pickles (fermentation)	List different kinds of pickles you have purchased or seen advertised, noting preservatives used. Investigate this statement: Excessive use of spiced foods is not good. Make a sweet pickle, a sour pickle, a relish. Study the pure food laws as applied to preservation of foods. Determine what "dill" is and how we get it.	Wellman, p. 369 Harris and Lacey, pp. 473–475 Greer, pp. 500–502 Powell, Ch. XIV Sherman, W. S., *Food Products*, pp. 448–458
J. *Why are fruits and vegetables absolutely necessary for health and well-being?*	*Relation of Canned Goods to a Well-Balanced Diet* Provide a well-balanced diet for all the year round, to supplement the fresh supply.	Review place of fruits and vegetables in well-balanced diet.	Powell, Ch. XVII

3. The kindergarten course of study published by the Berkeley schools in 1931 presents another form of column organization. The objectives are stated in terms of pupil participation in meaningful situations, and the classroom program is organized in columns. It is interesting to note that teaching procedure and content, are combined, while materials occupy a separate column. The sample on pages 748-751 will illustrate the characteristics of this type.

4. The State of Idaho published a course of study in Home Economics, in 1932, which illustrates another variation of the column plan. In view of the fact that it is organized differently from any of those previously included in this section, a short selection is presented. Note the order of the columns and the introduction of a column of Outcomes (pages 752-754).

B. A course of study which represents a transition between the column type and the type next to be discussed was published by the Kansas City Schools in 1928. The course considers arithmetic for Grades One to Six inclusive. The unusual feature of this course is that specific objectives and suggested activities are arranged in columns. A complete treatment of these two aspects of the course is followed by consecutive and sequential discussion of teaching procedure, minimum attainments for the grade, and references. Preceding the column of specific objectives and suggested activities are sequential outlines of general objectives, general suggestions, preview of the year's work, and the inventory of previous arithmetical attainments.

A short section from each phase of the organization of the work for the second grade will be presented as illustrations:

COURSE OF STUDY IN ARITHMETIC [3]

I. **General Objectives**

To extend the child's quantitative thinking about the common experiences in his daily life.

To develop skill and accuracy in using the number facts of the fundamental processes such as a second-grade child encounters in life situations.

[3] *Course of Study in Arithmetic for Grades I-VI* (Kansas City Public Schools, 1928), pp. 77-110.

To realize the necessity for measurement and to make use of measurements and comparisons as occasion arises.

To develop interest and joy in the use of acquired facts and skills in practical situations.

To continue the development of habits of neatness, order, and accuracy.

II. General Suggestions

The basis for arithmetic instruction in the second grade should be child experiences in home, school, and community. The teacher should utilize these vital interests, incorporating them into the quantitative thinking children should do in this grade. Through them will come the realization of the importance of number in daily activities and the need of accuracy and skill in their use to solve the problems that arise. The working out of large activities will provide real situations that necessitate an accurate knowledge of fundamental facts and measures and practice to acquire skill in their use. (Law of readiness, exercise, and effect.) Children can not trade intelligently at a real or toy store unless they know the combinations. They do not enjoy games unless they can use number facts with facility..............

III. Preview of the Year's Work

1. *Integers*—To develop

   A. Ability to count
      (1) by 1's to 100
      (2) by 2's to 100
      (3) by 5's to 100
      (4) by 10's to 100
      (5) by 4's to 40
   B. Ability to read numbers to 200
   C. Ability to write numbers to 200
   D. Addition
      (1) Automatic control of combinations to 10
      (2) Decade addition involving combinations taught (sums not to exceed 39)
      (3) Single columns, 3 addends, involving combinations taught
      (4) Double columns, 2 or 3 addends, involving no carrying
   E. Subtraction
      (1) Automatic control of combinations involving no number greater than 9
      (2) Two-digit minuend, two-digit subtrahend, involving combinations taught—(*Contd. on page* 755).

PLAN FOR KINDERGARTEN [4]

Pupil Participation in Meaningful Situations	Teaching Procedure and Content	Materials	Desired Outcomes
The child relaxes.	The teacher should provide proper resting places for her pupils according to room conditions and see that regular habits of relaxation are formed. These may take the form of a regular rest period, children lying on the floor, on tables or chairs pushed together, or occasional exercises which produce relaxation. If rest period is used, the child should be encouraged to lie in a comfortable position with eyes closed. The teacher offers suggestion to gain a relaxed state: Lie flat on back, arms at side, slowly inhale, raise arms at same time, above head. Exhale as arms come down. Repeat with arms raised sideways.	Rugs, mats, paper, etc. If individual rugs are used, they should be of material that can be laundered; preferably woven rag rugs. They should be marked with individual name of owner and always folded with the clean side inside and kept in clean place, free from damp and dust. Pupils should be taught to care for own rugs.	Lessening of nervous tension Renewal of energy Habit of relaxation

[4] Kindergarten, Course of Study Monographs Number Sixteen (Berkeley Public Schools, 1931), pp. 224, 227.

Personal cleanliness Use of rest room The child uses the lavatory and toilet.	The teacher explains the correct use of toilet facilities: 1. Flush toilet. 2. Wash hands after using toilet. 3. Economy in use of soap and towels. 4. Necessity of drying hands thoroughly to avoid chapping. 5. Clean wash basin after using. 6. Dispose of towels in basket provided. 7. See that one person at a time uses equipment.	Toilet Lavatory Paper towels Soap	The child acquires: 1. Regular toilet habits 2. Ability to wash and dry hands properly 3. Self-respect through the feeling of cleanliness
The child brings and uses his handkerchief.	The teacher: 1. Sees that handkerchiefs are used at proper time, and that they are kept out of sight, preferably in pocket. 2. Encourages covering coughs and sneezes. 3. Gives single nostril breathing drill daily. (See Supervisor's Outline) 4. Encourages child in keeping hands away from mouth and nose.	Handkerchiefs Paper towels Cheese cloth or old clean cloths brought from home	Habits of personal cleanliness. The child unconsciously acquires: 1. Refinement 2. Thoughtfulness and consideration for others. 3. A rudimentary knowledge of the prevention of communicable disease.

PLAN FOR KINDERGARTEN—*Continued*

Pupil Participation in Meaningful Situations	Teaching Procedure and Content	Materials	Desired Outcomes
The child uses the drinking fountain.	The teacher explains the proper use of drinking fountain: 1. Do not put mouth to bulb. 2. Keep fingers off bulb.	Drinking fountain with water flowing at an angle.	He acquires knowledge of the need of plenty of drinking water.
The child has health examinations by nurse and physician.	The teacher sends notices to parents of the examination. Parent returns note with consent or refusal. Doctor examines. Nurse keeps records, makes calls, gives advice. The teacher: 1. Keeps health records. 2. Measures and weighs each child once a month. 3. Notifies parents of underweight. 4. Provides milk for undernourished children if necessary.	Scales Charts Consent cards Usual supplies used by nurse in school	Freedom from fear of nurse or doctor. Helpful advice to parents as to adjustment and diet. Child acquires a better viewpoint of health in general. Child learns obedience to health laws. Child and parent learn necessary precautions to avoid communicable diseases. Maintenance and steady gain in health and vitality

The child has inspection by dental hygienist.	Inspections are made and cards given regarding dental attention. Dental hygienist: 1. Gives a thorough examination once a term. 2. Follows examination with data to parents. 3. Keeps "follow up" records of parents' responses to cards. 4. Visits the class at intervals telling stories and giving demonstration relative to oral hygiene. The teacher follows up these lessons daily with tooth inspection and further encouragement for daily practice in brushing teeth, emphasizing the need of a new tooth brush. The teacher should encourage parents to take children to dentist each semester, since the hygienist is not allowed by law to examine teeth above the gum line.	Pictures Stories Large tooth brush Large set of papier-mâché teeth	Knowledge of the necessity of brushing teeth Favorable attitude toward brushing teeth Correct use of tooth brush The habit of brushing teeth three times daily established.

FOOD PRESERVATION [5]

Objectives:

To know how to decide when home preservation of foods is advisable.

To develop ability in the processes of food preservation.

To be able to recognize differences in standards of various commercially canned products.

Reference and Illustrative Material	Content and Teaching Procedure	Pupil Problems and Activities	Outcomes
	A. Why foods are preserved: 1. To keep the excess fresh food available for later use 2. To furnish a variety of fruits and vegetables in meals the year round 3. To have a supply of foods to make the meals more attractive 4. To save time and money in meal preparation. Have students find out the types of foods which are stored in their homes.	*Problem:* Since it is essential that fruits and vegetables be included in everyday meals, it is necessary to make a variety of these foods available during the whole year. What foods are in season now? What provision should be made for having these foods later on in the year? What fresh fruits and vegetables do you have at home now? What fruits and vegetables do your mothers can, dry, pickle, or preserve?	Has knowledge of why foods are preserved. Has knowledge of kinds of fruits and vegetables available for canning.

[5] *Tentative Courses of Study in Home Economics for Junior and Senior High Schools* (Idaho State Board of Education, 1932), pp. 54-55.

Teacher References		
R. Cook, "Economy of Canned Goods," *Home Economics News* (September, 1930) Blinks and Moore, *Food Purchasing for the Home*	B. Factors which determine when it is advisable to can foods at home: 1. Supply of fresh food available—at home or in the market 2. Cost—fresh food, canned food 3. Nature of the product 4. Time available 5. Needs of the family 6. Food preferences	*Problem:* Ellen's mother says it does not pay her to can food. She is sure that she can buy it cheaper already canned than can it. Would this be true under all conditions and of all foods? What would make it vary? How can you estimate whether home-canned products are less or more expensive for your family than those canned commercially?	Knows how to decide when it pays to can at home.
Powell, Ola, *Successful Canning and Preserving* *The Delineator Cook Book*, "Canning, Preserving and Jelly Making," pp. 658-686. "Pickles and Relishes," pp. 687-700	C. Commercial methods of food preservation: 1. Canning — vegetables, fruits, meats, fish 2. Drying—fruits, vegetables, fish, meat 3. Pasteurization, evaporation, condensation—milk 4. Pickling and spicing—fruits, vegetables, spices 5. Preserving with sugar—fruits 6. Brining, salting—olives, fish 7. Smoking—meats, fish	*Activities:* Make a list showing the approximate amount and kinds of canned foods that are used in your home for two weeks. Compare the cost of these if purchased commercially canned and if all of them are canned at home. (This problem will be completed at the end of the unit.)	Appreciates the type of commercially preserved foods available.

FOOD PRESERVATION—Continued

Reference and Illustrative Material	Content and Teaching Procedure	Pupil Problems and Activities	Outcomes
	8. Cold storage — fruits, eggs, meat, fish	*Problem:* What methods of food preservation does your mother use? Have you helped in canning foods at home?	
Farmer, *Boston Cooking School Book* (1929 Edition) "Canned Fruits and Vegetables," pp. 719-727. "Jellies, Jams, and Marmalades," pp. 712-718. "Pickling," pp. 728-737. "Drying," pp. 738-740	D. Home methods of food preservation: 1. Canning: *a.* Open kettle method—tomatoes, fruits *b.* Hot pack method—vegetables and fruits —use of hot water bath, oven, and pressure cooker, in processing	*Activities:* Find out the advantages of the different methods in preserving fruits, tomatoes, chicken, peas, corn, string beans.	Knows methods used in home preservation of different kinds of foods. Uses judgment in deciding which method to use for certain foods.
Pupil References Lanman, McKay, Zuill, *The Family's Food,* "Home Care of Foods," p. 220; "Canned Foods," p. 326; "Frozen Foods," p. 330	2. Drying—cherries, berries, prunes, beans 3. Pickling and spicing—vegetables and fruits 4. Preserving with sugar—jams, marmalades, jellies		

F. Multiplication
  (1) Ability to multiply by 2, products to 20
  (2) Ability to multiply by 5, products to 50
G. Division
  (1) Ability to divide even numbers to 20 by 2
  (2) Ability to divide multiples of 5 to 50 by 5
H. Ability to interpret and use $+$, $-$, $\times$, $\div$, $=$
I. Ability to apply acquired arithmetical knowledge and
   skills to practical problems of real interest

....

IV. Inventory of Previous Arithmetical Attainments

Teachers and texts often waste time reteaching knowledge
and skills which children already possess. A teacher must
first know the strength and weaknesses of the class. What
they have retained of previous teaching may be learned by
giving an inventory test. The amount and nature of the
review of first-grade work should be determined from the
results. They will show individual weaknesses which may
require special attention and individual help to bring the
child to the standard of the class. It is only by careful diagnosis in the beginning that effective teaching can be done.

....
....

V. Specific Objectives and Suggested Activities for Realizing Them

Specific Objectives	*Suggested Activities*
1. Ability to count	Counting
a. By 1's to 100 (review)	Members in family
	Children in class
b. By 2's to 100	Materials for class (pencils, scissors, crayolas)
c. By 5's to 100	
d. By 10's to 100	Scores for games
e. By 4's to 40	Amount of bank money
	Seats in row
	Things needed for a party
	Articles needed to set table
	Characters needed in dramatization
	Pairs of eyes, arms, etc.
	Cost of two-cent stamps in post office
	Children in groups for games

2. Ability to read num-
bers to 200

Reading
Scores in games
Prices on menu in cafeteria
(real or play)
Page numbers in a book
Calendar numbers
House numbers
Price list in store
Street numbers
Health record—height, weight
Numbers on blackboard

3. Ability to write num-
bers to 200

Writing
Numbers for calendar
Numbers for flash cards,
dominoes, etc.
House numbers
Price lists
Price tags
Numbers from dictation

. . . .

VI. Suggestions as to Teaching Procedure

Counting. The teacher should begin with review of counting
as listed in first grade. Next, children, hands, eyes, shoes,
desks, books, may be counted in pairs, the children touch-
ing them as they count. Fingers, toys, cents, marbles, etc.,
may be counted by fives and tens. After some objective
counting the children will enjoy counting rhythmically.
They may count by rote from 100 to 200 by ones, twos,
fives, tens in order to sense the serial order of larger
numbers.

Reading and writing numbers. To read and write larger
numbers the children must first be able to sense the serial
order beyond 100. They already know the serial order of
the units and tens. The teacher may develop the serial order of hundreds by counting 100, 200, 300, etc. Filling the
gaps should then be developed, as writing the numbers
from 120 to 140. Later in the year, as the need for larger
numbers occurs, writing serially, as 565 to 580, may be
used. At all times the pupils should be able to read numbers
as large as needed, to write from dictation, and to copy
accurately. The teacher should help the children "see" the
numbers correctly in copying and reading; e.g., when the
number is 91, a pupil may call it 19. She should also watch
closely to be sure that no incorrect habits are formed.

The reading and writing of Roman numerals to XII should be taught in connection with the clock face.

. . . .

VII. **Minimum Attainments for the Grade**

All abilities listed for the first grade
Ability to count by 1's, 2's, 5's, and 10's to 100
Ability to read and write numbers to 500
Ability to read and write Roman numerals to XII
Automatic control of the 100 addition combinations
Automatic control of the 100 subtraction combinations
Automatic control decade addition (sums to 39) involving no bridging
Tables of 2's, 5's, 10's, 4's
Single column addition, three addends
Column addition, two orders, two or three addends
Subtraction, two orders, involving no carrying
Ability to use in concrete situations measures listed
Ability to tell time by the hour and half-hour
Ability to use intelligently the cent, nickel, dime, quarter, in money experiences
Ability to use $+$, $-$, $=$, $\times$, $\div$, $\$$, $\cent$
Ability to think through to completion a simple one-step reasoning problem applying accurately acquired arithmetical knowledge and skills
Ability to use intelligently the vocabulary listed
Ability to do board or seat work with neatness, accuracy, and order
Joy in acquired knowledge and skills
A growing appreciation of the value and importance of number of the child's life activities

VIII. **References**

BUCKINGHAM-OSBORN, *Searchlight Arithmetics, Introductory Book* (Ginn & Co., 1927). Especially helpful in methods of teaching the basic combinations, including also suggestive devices, games, tests, and problems.

GUILER, W. S., *Objectives and Activities in Arithmetic* (Rand, McNally & Co., 1926). See especially "Activities for Grade II," pp. 47-64. Games are listed under the abilities they are supposed to help develop.

HILLEGAS, M. B., *Teaching Number Fundamentals* (J. B. Lippincott Co., 1925). See especially pp. 15-58, "First Steps in Teaching Number."

MORTON, R. L., *Teaching Arithmetic in the Primary Grades* (Silver, Burdett and Co., 1927). See especially Chapter IV.

"Teaching the Addition and Subtraction Facts," and Chapter XI, "The Course of Study."

SLOMAN, L. G., *Some Primary Methods* (The Macmillan Co., 1927). Chapter II, "Projects, or Class Activities," and Chapter VI, "Arithmetic," contain many helpful suggestions as to class activities and methods of teaching.

Books suggesting exercises, activities, and games:

HARRIS and WALDO, *First Journeys in Numberland* (Scott, Foresman & Co., 1911).

———, *Number Games for Primary Grades* (Beckley-Cardy Co., 1917).

HOWARD, HAWTHORNE, and HOWARD, *Number Friends* (The Macmillan Co., 1927).

Iroquois Arithmetic, Grade Three (Iroquois Publishing Co., 1926).

KENT, R. A., *Bobbs Merrill Arithmetic Friends,* Book One (Bobbs, Merrill Co., 1927).

LOCKHART, ELDRIDGE, and BROWN, *Number Helps* (Rand, McNally and Co., 1924).

STEVENSON, Maria A., *Primary Number Book,* Grade Two (Regan Printing Co., 1925).

STONE, J. C., *A Child's Book of Number* (Benj. H. Sanborn and Co., 1924).

THIELE, SAUBLE, and OGLESBY, *My First Number Book* (Rand, McNally and Co., 1927).

THORNDIKE, E. L., *The Thorndike Arithmetics,* Book One (Rand, McNally and Co., 1924).

C. The elements of each unit of work are presented in consecutive or sequential order. While these courses are not so easy to read as those of column type, and are more difficult to interpret to the classroom teacher, they afford means for the adequate presentation of every phase of the work. Many excellent and scholarly examples of this type of organization are being developed in the public schools. Excerpts from a few of the outstanding courses are presented, in order that the reader may compare headings, content, and order of presentation in these courses with similar features of courses of study of the column type.

1. Lakewood, Ohio. *Social Sciences,* A Tentative Course for Third Grade, published 1931.

THE VIKINGS [6]

Time: 4 to 6 weeks

General Theme: The tendency of man to move from place to place in quest of adventure and a higher standard of living

Aspect of the theme: How early man ventured out upon the sea for adventure and trade

I. **Objectives**
   A. To learn about the Vikings
   B. To make Viking tools, weapons, and designs, ships
   C. To enjoy tales of adventure

II. **Major Problem:** Where did the Vikings live and travel?
   A. What was the natural environment of the Vikings?
      1. Rocky shores, fiords, islands, difficult passages
      2. Mountains, valleys, fields
      3. North Atlantic drift tempers climate
      4. Forests, unfertile soil
   B. What would you expect to be the characteristics of people living in such a land?
      1. Love of truth
      2. Hardy endurance, love of sea, love of adventure
      3. Faithfulness to plighted word
      4. Strong, fearless, heroic, crude courage
   C. How did the Vikings live?
      1. Homes: materials used, how built?
         a. Storehouses
         b. Stables
         c. Feast hall: size, shape, furnishings, decorations, use
         d. "Tun"
      2. Dishes; food—how served
      3. Dress
         a. Women
            (1) Materials: Velvets, silks, linen, wool
            (2) Where obtained
            (3) Jewelry
            (4) Colors: red, purple, blue, etc.
         b. Thrall
            (1) Iron collar for identification
            (2) Long loose coat of white wool
         c. Men
            (1) Tights
            (2) Cape of velvet

[6] *Social Sciences, A Tentative Course of Study for Third Grade* (Lakewood, Ohio Public Schools, 1931), pp. 54-62.

       (3) Jewelry
       (4) Weapons and armor
          (*a*) Shields
          (*b*) Spears
          (*c*) Sword and scabbard
          (*d*) Helmets

4. Occupations
   a. Trading with other countries: countries visited, articles of trade, means of exchange
   b. Traveling upon the sea in search of adventure
       (1) Trips to Iceland
       (2) Greenland
       (3) France
       (4) British Isles
       (5) America
   c. Metal working: weapons, armor
   d. Wood carving: chairs, tables, doors, etc.
   e. Fishing: method, vessels, how fish were preserved
   f. Farming
   g. Making boats and ships
       (1) Trading vessels: size, shape, materials used
       (2) War vessels
          (*a*) Size and shape
          (*b*) Materials used
          (*c*) Benches and desks
          (*d*) Decorations
          (*e*) Sails
          (*f*) Equipment
          (*g*) Naming of vessels
          (*h*) Ceremonies attending journeys, method of carrying on a sea fight
   h. Carrying on war
       (1) Weapons used
          (*a*) Kinds: offensive and defensive
          (*b*) How made
          (*c*) Decorations
          (*d*) Names
       (2) How a sea fight was conducted
       (3) How a land battle was conducted

5. Customs and ceremonies
   a. Naming a child
   b. Taking a vow
   c. Burial after battle, etc.

6. Games

D. How did these Vikings explain everyday happenings such as terrible storms, northern lights, etc.?
  1. Valhalla
  2. Stories of Odin, Thor, Baldur, Loki, Frigga, Freya
  3. Sagas
  4. Skalds

III. **Procedure—Activities**
  A. Suggested approaches
    1. Show pictures which illustrate physical features of the country, boats, feast hall, runes, dress of the people, tun, etc.
    2. Visit a wharf in Cleveland.
    3. Teacher tell about the physical and climatic conditions of the country, about its natural resources and how the people use them.
    4. Pupils read stories about Norway and its people.
    5. Interest may be aroused to know more about the Vikings by reading some of the Norse myths to the class.
    6. Some one may want to know the meaning of the Viking car.
    7. Interest in Vikings may develop from the unit on boats.
    8. Discuss who first discovered America.
  B. Suggested activities
    1. Orienting activities to get new experiences
      a. Look at Viking pictures depicting dress, ships, etc.
      b. Read "Viking Tales" by Jennie Hall.
      c. Excursions
        A trip to a boat
        A trip to the lake where children may try to row a boat
        A trip to a historical museum
    2. Research activities to get new experiences
      a. Children use the *World Book* and other reference books to get information.
      b. Bring to the classroom illustrative materials such as pictures.
      c. Pupils may read and tell Norse myths.
    3. Group discussion activities to use experiences
      a. Discuss the interior of a feast hall
      b. The size and shape of a Viking boat
      c. The arrangement of a "tun"
      d. How a long winter night was spent
      e. Harold's dress
      f. Weapons of war

      g. Conditions found in Iceland, Greenland, and Vineland

      h. Racial characteristics

      i. Customs of warfare

      j. Make plans for constructing a feast hall, Viking ships, etc.

      k. Discuss designs for jewelry, pottery, etc.

      l. Discuss the poetical names given by the Vikings to their ships and weapons.

1. Practice activities to assimilate experiences

      a. Booklet containing stories and pictures about:
        (1) Wild and tame animals used by the Vikings
        (2) Weapons and warships

      b. Dramatize
        (1) Scenes in a Viking feast hall
        (2) The return from a trading voyage
        (3) A field day for Viking boys
        (4) Work of the women
        (5) Skald with his harp reciting a saga
        (6) Christening a baby

      c. Develop vocabulary through group discussion, conversation, and stories:

Viking	dragon myth	Worship	hearth
skald	high seas	runes	foster father
thrall	Valhalla	forge	burial ships
tun	Thor	nobility	mound
Sibula	Odin	head dress	helmet
mead hall	adventure	stern	conquest
feast hall	pine knots	rudder	plundering
bower	ale	symbol	expedition
bodice	superstition	tapestry	islands

      d. Silent reading exercises from the blackboard and from flash cards, such as:
        Name one of Harold's weapons.
        Draw the "tun."
        Tell about a sea fight.
        How did Harold dress?

      e. Printed reading slips which find their authorship in the teacher, about such topics as the following:
        Fiords
        A sea fight
        A dragon ship
        Valhalla
        Jewelry

      f. Informal tests from time to time as the unit develops

     g. Learn the Viking Code.

     h. Write scenes to be dramatized.

5. Construction and original creative activities to express ideas

     a. Write coöperative stories and rimes about any topics similar to these: Nights in Norway, The Feast, The Voyage, Harold's Weapons, The Sea Battle.

     Examples written by third-grade pupils:

The Wave Runner

I am a "Wave Runner." My sides have been scratched by spears and stones. I sail on rough seas and have many fights with enemies. I see men killed.

A Viking

> I am a Viking bold
> My ship sails far and wide
> My friends are faithful
> My enemies are fearful
> I brave both wind and wave
> I am a Viking bold

The Weapons of the Norsemen

The weapons of the Norsemen were inlaid with gold. They named their weapons. Sometimes the Norsemen poisoned the ends of their weapons, so that they killed the enemy if the wound was small. Some of the weapons were battle axes, swords, spears, bows and arrows, slings and knives.

Harold's Clothing

Harold's clothing is different from ours. He wears a gold band around his long yellow hair. He wears a tight scarlet jacket and gray woolen tights. His long velvet cape lined with scarlet hangs from his shoulders. It fastens with a gold buckle in front. His shoes are fastened with gold lacings that wind around his legs to the knees. He looks very gay and handsome.

Song of the Vikings

What does my dragon smell?
A hungry battle
A brave fight
A stormy sea
My sword tastes the blood of my enemies
The ships side by side
The spears flying through the air
King Halfden shall go to Valhalla by my sword

The Bloody Battle

I am "Bloody Foes Fear." Harold and I are going to battle. There are many men lying dead. Their flesh is all red with blood running everywhere. I protect Harold from the other swords. Harold has to wipe the blood off me.

    b. Children create own games similar to those played by Viking children.

        Examples:

        (1) contest with rope or skin to determine who is strongest

        (2) throw balls or stones to see who can throw farthest

        (3) jump over imaginary chasms

    c. Construct a "tun" on the floor

    d. Build a feast hall

    e. Construct dragon ships, with carved head, or trading vessels.

    f. Model in clay or soap: weapons, pottery.

    g. Draw designs of jewelry, shields, weapons.

    h. Use designs on wall hangings for feast hall.

    i. Make and dress Viking dolls.

    j. Make and paint Viking shields, helmets, spears, battle horns, swords, etc.

    k. Draw or paint a panorama of Viking life.

    l. Compose Viking songs depicting various phases of that rugged life.

IV. References—Materials

Books

Authentic excerpts taken from Du Chaillu's "Viking Age" have been mimeographed and sent to each building for reference.

SNEDDEN, *Leif and Thorkel* (rich in content, and easy)

HALL, *Viking Tales*

HOLBROOK, *Northland Heroes* (contains Viking code)

CLARK-GORDY, *The Early Story of Mankind* (contains simple forms of myths)

LANSING, *Great Moments in Exploration*

TERRY, *The Beginnings*

JOHNSTON, *Our Little Viking Cousin of Long Ago*

BROWN, *In the Days of Giants* (Norse myths in what is probably their best form for children)

COLUM, *Children of Odin*

ADAMS, *The Swords of the Vikings*

MACGREGOR, *Story of the Vikings*

FRENCH, *Story of Rolf and the Viking's Bow*

MABIE, *Norse Stories* (to be read or told by teacher)

BULFINCH, *The Golden Age of Myth and Legend* (adapted by teacher)

BALDWIN, *Story of Siegfried*

ANDERSON, *Viking Tales of the North* (for teachers)

National Geographic Magazines: August, 1922; June, 1924; April, 1928; October, 1928; October, 1899, 1901, 1902; January, October and December, 1903; April and July, 1907; June, 1908; February, 1910; January, 1913; January, 1908; February, 1912; January, 1913; August, 1927 (Amundsen); November, 1926; September, 1926; September, 1927; January, 1928.

Compton's *Pictured Encyclopedia*

Pictures

Mimeographed reference pictures sketched from Du Chaillu's *Viking Age* have been supplied to every school. These materials will remain permanently in each school.

V. Desired Outcomes

A. Knowledge and understanding of:
1. Courage and daring of the Vikings
2. Conditions under which they lived
3. Natural environment in Norway
4. Topography of the coastline of Iceland and Greenland
5. Icebergs
6. Contrast between Vineland and Iceland

B. Habits and skills

Members of the group show growth in:
1. Good workmanship
2. Responsibility for materials and results
3. Ability to reproduce facts
4. Ability to get information from reference books
5. Ability to express their thoughts more adequately in oral and written work

C. Appreciations and attitudes

Members of the group show growth in:
1. Enjoyment of tales of adventure
2. Interest in the habits and customs of early man
3. Courtesy and helpfulness in working together

VI. Informal Tests to Measure Certain Outcomes

Fact Test No. 1

Directions: Number the lines of your paper 1 to 30. Opposite each number on your paper write "Yes" for each true statement and "No" for each false statement. Do not copy the statements.

1. The Vikings got their name from *viks* or bays which were all along their coasts.

2. The Vikings spent summers in their boats.
3. When winter came, the Vikings went home to rest.
4. The Norsemen thought it was a disgrace to work.
5. The Kings went to the fields to oversee the work done there.
6. Barley was the grain most cultivated by the Norsemen.
7. Oats, rye, and wheat were unknown to the Norsemen.
8. The Vikings threshed their grain with a flail.
9. Children turned the handles of the mills which ground the grain.
10. The Northmen were their own carpenters.
11. The Northman's house usually had one room.
12. The sides of the walls were high and filled with many windows.
13. The windows were filled with tiny panes of glass.
14. The entrance of the house was at the gable end.
15. The outside door opened into a feasthall.
16. A hole was cut in the center of the roof to let out smoke.
17. The roof of the house was covered with turf.
18. The bare walls were decorated with bright-colored pictures.
19. The silk cloth which was used to hang on the walls for feasts was bought at the stores.
20. The floor was made of hard-beaten clay.
21. The fire was at one end of the room.
22. The hearth was made of flat stones.
23. The houses were filled with all kinds of beautiful furniture.
24. Large chests were used to keep their treasures in.
25. The Norsemen buried their treasure chests.
26. A Norseman always told his family where the treasure chest was buried.
27. The rooms were lighted by wax candles.
28. The Northmen used dishes made of china.
29. The Northmen ate wild game and bread and drank milk and mead.
30. Honey was used for sugar.

Fact Test No. 2

1. The Northmen who were rich and those who were poor ate the same kinds of food.
2. The Northmen made their clothes of cotton material.
3. The Northmen liked bright colors.
4. Their favorite color was scarlet.
5. A Northman's coat was called a kirtle.
6. The color of this kirtle was often scarlet.
7. A belt was always worn.

8. A scarlet cloak was flung over the kirtle.
9. Northmen wore leggings of wool, or tan boots.
10. The cloak was stitched to the coat at the shoulder.
11. A Northman always wore a helmet.
12. A woman's dress was often called a kirtle.
13. The women wore very short dresses.
14. The sleeves were long and flowing.
15. A belt of gold or silver was fastened about the waist.
16. A careful housewife wore an apron.
17. From her belt hung a bag in which a handkerchief was carried.
18. The women always went about with their heads bare.
19. The Northmen hunted only for pleasure.
20. Their favorite sport was hawking.
21. While the men were hunting, the women went visiting.
22. When a baby was born, it was bathed, dressed, and taken to its father.
23. The father laid the baby on the cold ground.
24. The father felt the baby's limbs and listened to its cry.
25. If the father was satisfied with the baby, he carried it to its mother.
26. Weak babies were left outside to die.
27. Babies left outside to perish were often taken by kind neighbors.
28. These men and women were called foster-parents.
29. A Northman's child was taught early to be brave and endure hardship.
30. The Norsemen discovered America.

Fact Test No. 3

1. What were the history books of the Northmen called?
2. Before the sagas were written, how did the people hear stories of heroes, and what they did on the battlefields?
3. What were these poets called?
4. How did the skalds know so many stories?
5. Were these stories always true?
6. In what did the Vikings believe?
7. What did they think they often saw on the battle-fields?
8. How did the Valkyries go about?
9. In the early days how many Valkyries were there?
10. Where did the Valkyries live?
11. Who else lived in Valhalla?
12. How did warriors often feel after battle?
13. What one thing did a Viking not fear?

14. What was it that he did fear?
15. What did every Viking long to do?
16. What power did he believe some people were given?
17. How could a man make himself very fierce?
18. When a Northman died, where did he wish his body to rest?
19. Describe a Viking's grave.
20. Where did a Viking wish to be buried?
21. What things were buried with the dead?
22. What strange duty did the nearest kinsman have to perform?
23. What sometimes happened to the graves?

Fact Test No. 4

1. Where were most of the Vikings' battles fought?
2. What were their war-ships called?
3. In what ways did a war-ship differ from a merchant vessel?
4. Name two ways a ship could be sailed.
5. Where did the rowers sit?
6. Why was the center of the boat so low?
7. Describe the sails.
8. What shape were the sails?
9. Where was the gunwale?
10. What was hung along the gunwale?
11. What color were the shields painted?
12. What was at the prow of the boat?
13. Where is the stern of the boat?
14. What was in the stern of the boat?
15. What was in the prow of the boat?
16. Who went along besides the rowers?
17. How many men would a fighting vessel hold?
18. How many rowers' seats were there?
19. How could a merchant ship be told from a fighting ship?
20. What kind of weapons did the Vikings use?
21. What would a Viking fleet do when it met an enemy?
22. What did they call their flag?
23. What means did they have of drawing an enemy's boat to theirs?
24. Give their battle formation.
25. What weapons did they use for close fights?
26. What weapons did they use for long-distance fights?
27. If a Viking chief knew he was going to have a battle, what did he do?
28. How did he choose his men?
29. In what part of the boat was the struggle fiercest?
30. Where did the chief stand?

Fact Test No. 5

1. Name five things that a Northman did to occupy his time.
2. Where did the people live?
3. When the father died, to whom did his property go?
4. What did the other sons do?
5. Name two things which a Northman did well.
6. Name three things which a Northman valued for himself.
7. Where did the Northmen believe the gods dwelt?
8. How was Asgard connected with the earth?
9. Who was the All-father?
10. What name was given to the feast hall in Asgard?
11. Who poured mead for the warriors?
12. What did the heroes in Asgard do all day?
13. Who was the god of war?
14. Who was the god of thunder?
15. Who was the god of goodness, wisdom, purity, and innocence?
16. Who was Odin's wife?
17. Who was the goddess of love?
18. Who was Idun?
19. What was the name of the giant's home?
20. How did the Northmen worship their gods?
21. Where did they offer sacrifices?

2. A similar unit is selected from the Tentative Course of Study in Social Studies for the Elementary Grades, published by Greater Greensboro School District, Greensboro, North Carolina, 1932–1933. The reader should note the differences in the outlines from Greensboro and Lakewood.

Social Studies—Grade IV [7]

Foreword: The work in social studies for Grade Four consists of a tour around the world, a series of trips to type countries—cold countries, hot, dry countries, etc.—in company with great men of history, beginning with the stumbling upon our continent by the Vikings down to the settlement of America.

During this trip, pupils acquire a knowledge of those geographical principles which control or affect man and his mode of living, with emphasis upon *why* the members of the big human family are different rather than *how*.

[7] *A Tentative Course of Study in Social Studies for Elementary Grades* (Greensboro, N. C., School District, 1932).

They also gain an elementary idea of the big movements in American history up to this point, and its leaders in early discoveries, explorations, and settlements.

The theme that dominantly characterizes the geography phase of work is: Man's life and activities are controlled or affected by his environment.

1. Geographic controls
   a. Distance from the equator, latitude, vertical ray
   b. Tilt of the earth on axis as it travels around the sun
   c. Height from sea level—altitude
   d. Distance from water
   e. Winds, their direction
   f. Surface—mountains, plains, sea-coast, soil
2. Man changes his environment, when he can, to meet his needs
   a. Spans the seas
   b. Tunnels mountains
   c. Irrigates land
   d. Digs canals
   e. Builds dikes, etc.

Objectives
   a. To awaken an appreciation of how the Vikings stumbled upon America about five hundred years before Columbus discovered it
   b. To develop an understanding of how the slant of the sun's rays (latitude) and the tilt of the earth as it travels around the sun determine man's mode of living, materials for his home, his food, his clothing, and his activities

Unit: Cold Country Life
   a. Vikings or Norsemen, Norway, Leif Ericsson
   b. Lapps, Northern Europe
   c. Eskimos—Greenland, Northern Canada, Alaska, North Cold Cap; Peary
   d. Antarctica—South Cold Cap, no human life, Amundsen, Byrd

The above unit, with its sub-units, is an introduction to the study of the vertical ray as a life control, heat belts, and latitude.

Desirable attainments and outcomes
Each child should show growth in the following:
   a. Appreciations and attitudes
   b. Habits and skills
   c. Knowledges

d. Social gains

e. Study outcomes

(Listed under the unit "Cold Country Life")

Cold Country Life Unit

I. **Initial Stimulation**

At the beginning of school a child brought a toy sail boat that he had made. This led to an informal discussion of water transportation and its development. One child said the boat looked like the one Columbus came in. This brought forth the question, "Who was Columbus?" The immediate reply was, "He's the man who discovered America." I disagreed with the children and told them I knew of some one who discovered America long before Columbus. Many questions arose.

II. **Problem Questions**

A. Who did discover America first?

B. When?

C. How did Leif travel?

D. What kind of country did he come from?

E. How did he happen to come across the ocean in this tiny sail boat?

F. Why did people forget about Leif's discovery?

III. **Development of Problem Questions**

Viking story told in form of an imaginary trip, children taking part in judging what happened next.

Our steamer traveled northeast across the Atlantic for nearly two weeks.

A. Viking country—Norway. Locate on map, in northern part of Europe. Locate New York and Norway on the world map.

1. Very cold most of the year

2. Mountainous, rugged

3. Beautiful glaciers, fiords, water falls, fir trees

B. The people, called Vikings, Northmen or Norsemen.

1. Tall, fair, light hair, blue eyes

2. Brave, strong, adventurous

C. How they lived.

1. Shelter

a. Rude cabins

b. Crude furniture but gold and silver dishes and bowls

c. Boats—carving of dragon's head

2. Food

a. Fish, seals, whales

    b. Goats in south and reindeer of north furnished milk, butter, cheese, and meat

    c. "Flat-bread" of barley and rye

   3. Clothing

    a. Furs and skins

    b. Woolen clothes

  D. Government—how united and result.

   1. Many tiny kingdoms.

   2. "Might made right." Robbed one another.

   3. King Harold's motto: "One country; one king."

   4. Many objected and left, going to Denmark, Germany, France and England.

  E. Home in Iceland.

   1. Vikings on continent "harried" King Harold until he whipped them.

   2. They left for Iceland where Eric again committed murder and was driven out.

  F. Eric's boat, drifted by the winds, landed him in Greenland.

   1. Life in a country too cold to grow trees.

   2. His return visit to Iceland and his "Greenland" story.

   3. Leif's attempted return to Norway, drifted by winds to North America.

  G. "Wineland" discovered. Finally forgotten because of lack of books. Stories handed down in the form of ballads and songs.

IV. New Stimulation

"Land of the Midnight Sun"

  A. Problem questions

   1. Why does the sun never set in mid-summer?

    a. Study motions of earth (simple form)

    b. Axis, poles, cold caps

   2. Why is it so cold in the far north?

    a. Draw diagram on board showing relation of rays of the sun to earth.

   3. Do any other people live in countries similar to Norway?

  B. Study of Lapps and Eskimos

   1. Countries—Northern Norway, Finland, Russia, Greenland, Alaska.

    a. Long winters, short summers, only two seasons

    b. No night in summer

    c. No trees, tiny bushes and moss

    d. Northern lights

2. Personal appearance of Lapps and Eskimos
   a. Small, yellow
   b. Small nostrils
3. Clothing
   a. Furs and woolen clothes
4. Homes
   a. Winter—igloo, entrance a tunnel
   b. Summer—tent or hut, no windows
5. Furniture
   a. Move too often to have much furniture
   b. Bed of skins
6. Food
   a. Sea food
   b. Goat and reindeer milk and butter
7. Occupations
   a. Hunting and fishing
   b. Making weapons to hunt animals
8. Transportation
   a. Sledge
   b. Dogs—huskies
   c. Kayaks
9. Animal life
   a. Polar bear, dog, reindeer, musk ox, whale, seal, walrus, birds, fish
10. Plant life
    a. Trees, shrubs, vines, mosses, lichens, and flowers

C. Other questions leading on:
   1. Is it cold at the South Pole?
      a. Discussion of Byrd's trip to Antarctic. Many pictures may be secured from the public library on Byrd's trip.
   2. Is the South Pole just like the North Pole?
      a. Show more land about South Pole and mountains making it harder to reach and colder. Slanting rays and elevation combined make it colder. No human life there, just penguins, seals, and whales.
   3. Discuss value of radio and airplanes in these explorations.
   4. Compare with other trips to the poles.

V. **Subject Correlation Which Helped to Solve Problems**
   A. Reading and literature
      1. Material found in text and reference books
      2. Myths

B. Arithmetic
   1. Measuring distances on map
   2. Cost of trip to Norway, Alaska
   3. Reading figures in exports, imports, and population
   4. Original problems dealing with expense of Byrd's ex-
      pedition
   5. Cost of Alaska

C. Language
   Written:
   1. Imaginary journeys with Leif
   2. Letters asking for information on countries
   3. Riddles
   4. Original poems and stories

   Oral:
   1. Telling in clear, concise, interesting way new informa-
      tion learned
   2. Dialogue between Leif and King Harold

D. Social studies
   1. Place geography. New York, Norway, Russia, Greens-
      boro, Canada, Alaska, Antarctica
   2. Motions of earth
   3. Axis and effect of its inclination upon the earth
   4. Poles and ice caps
   5. Heat belts. Ten months of winter in the cold belt, two
      of summer
   6. How cold country people live and why
      a. Eskimo winter homes, rounded huts of stone and
         sod, or igloo (igloos usually while traveling);
         summer homes, tents of skin called tupiks
   7. Discovery of North Pole—Peary. Discovery of South
      Pole—Amundsen. Byrd, the only man to fly over both
      poles; his life in Antarctica.

E. Science
   1. Whales, seals, bears, fox, wolf, etc.
   2. Earth's relation to the sun
   3. Northern lights, electricity

F. Writing
   1. Improvement of letter formation by practice through
      writing letters, stories, etc., with supervision and
      guidance

G. Drawing
   1. Sketch maps
   2. Posters

   3. Viking boats, etc.
   4. Reindeer and dog teams
   5. Eskimo scenes
   6. Drawing heat belts
H. Health
   1. Open life of Vikings made them sturdy. Factors that make us strong.
I. Spelling Words We Needed to Know
J. Activities
   1. As listed under correlation of subjects
   2. Lantern slides, illustrative talks
   3. Posters
   4. Sand tables
   5. Frieze
   6. Dressing dolls as Eskimos, etc.
   7. Make movie machine and reel for movie show
   8. Puppet shows
   9. Sand table scenes—Eskimos, Byrd's "Little America"
   10. Make Viking boats, shields, etc.
   11. Collect pictures for bulletin board or class use
   12. Library activities and discussions

VI. Outcomes
A. Attitudes and Appreciations
   1. Developing desirable attitudes in group work
   2. Appreciation of inventions
   3. Appreciation of climatic control of human life and man's adjustment
   4. Appreciation of the ideas of early peoples
   5. Increased interest in
      a. Other countries
      b. Science
      c. Books
   6. Attitude of quiet in the library
B. Skills and Habits
   1. In doing neat work
   2. In using reference material
   3. In using clear and correct English
   4. In giving floor talks effectively
   5. In listening and concentrating
   6. In ability to follow directions
   7. Increased reading ability
   8. Careful use of books and materials

9. An increase in vocabulary and ability to spell, as needed, such words as:

axis	ocean	Polar bear
Arctic	glacier	whales
Antarctic	waterfall	kayak
circle	horizon	zero
equator	Peary	soapstone
mountains	seals	blubber
fiords	fir trees	explorers
continent	reindeer	

10. Place geography—ability, with map of any size before one, to point out promptly:

Norway (country)	Antarctic Circle	Europe (continent)
Atlantic	Antarctic Ocean	Canada
Arctic Circle	North Carolina (state)	Alaska
Arctic Ocean	Greenland	North America
Antarctica	Iceland	New York (city)

C. Knowledges—as shown in correlation of studies
D. Study gains
    1. How to use reference materials, how to study
    2. How to draw conclusions
    3. How to talk to the point
    4. How to read for something definite
E. Social gains
    1. Ideals of courtesy in all things
    2. Growth in judgment
    3. Development of initiative
    4. Coöperation through group work

VII. **Bibliography**

SMALLIDGE and PAXSON, *Finding America* (Houghton Mifflin Co., 1929).

GAMBRILL, *How the Old World Found the New* (Ginn & Co., 1929).

CROWE, *Studies in American History* (Lyons and Carnahan, 1924).

GREEN, *Pathfinders by Land and Sea* (World Book Co., 1932).

ANDREWS, *Each and All.*

———, *Seven Little Sisters,* pp. 4-22.

CHAMBERLAIN, *How We Travel.*

PERDUE, *Child Life in Other Lands,* pp. 25-35.

PERKINS, *The Eskimo Twins.*

CARROLL, *Around the World,* Book 3, pp. 9-46, 78-128.

STEFANSSON and SCHWARTZ, *Northward Ho!*

LUTHER, *Trading and Exploring,* pp. 81-147.

CHANCE, *Little Folks of Many Lands.*

AITCHISON and UTTLEY, *Across Seven Seas,* pp. 183-237.

MULLER, *Little People of the Snow* (A geography story).
———, *In Storyland*, Book I, pp. 66-78.
———, *Thought Study Readers*, Book 5, p. 71.
MYRICK, *Home Life Around the World*, pp. 1-24.
PEARY, *Snow Baby* (story).
———, *Lands and People*, Vol. 2, pp. 1-23.
———, *Little Journeys, Norway and Sweden*.
———, *Little Journeys, Alaska and Canada*.
———, *Peeps at Many Lands*, pp. 24-37; 110-131.
FAIRGRIEVE, *Homes Far Away*, Book 2.
HILLYER, *Child's History of the World*.
———, *Child Geography of the World*.
Lantern slides.
Eskimo Unit, Industrial Arts Coöperative Service, 121st St., New York.
Byrd Unit.

3. The Detroit public schools published a *Course of Study in the Social Sciences*, Grades 1 to 6, in 1932. The sequential order and content of the phases of the various units are illustrated in the following selection, which takes up the Southern States.

UNIT III. SOUTHERN UNITED STATES [8]

Time: ten days

A. **Introduction**
There is a certain part of our country that is known as the Southern States, or, in short, the South. The South differs from the northeastern section and from our own state in many ways. For one thing, the climate is warmer and, because of that, the things the people do differ from the things we do. Just as many people go to the New England states in the summer because the climate there is cool, so many people go to the South in the winter because the climate there is warm. It would seem strange for us to spend Christmas in a place where we could pick flowers and go in swimming. That is what people in the far south can do. Do you know why it is warm in the south while we are having snow and ice?

There are places in this section that are interesting for other reasons. There is the city of Washington where Congress meets and where the President lives. Just a short distance from Washington is Mount Vernon which was the home of George Washington. The home is furnished just as it was when he lived there. When he died,

[8] *Course of Study in Social Science*, Grades 1 to 6, 1932 (Detroit Public Schools).

he was buried on the grounds of his home. On February 22d, the Boy Scouts march out from Washington and decorate his grave.

While farming is the chief industry of the south, there are other things that the people do to earn a living. Manufacturing is done in some of the cities. There is also some mining and lumbering. In the western part of this section where it is too dry for farming, great herds of cattle are pastured. Perhaps some of you have been to Palm Beach, Mount Vernon, or some other place in the South. If you have, you can tell the class about what you have seen. This is truly a wonderful part of our country.

B. **Unit Objectives**
1. To understand why agriculture has always been the chief industry of the South.
2. To understand what the farmers of the South raise and why they raise these products.
3. To understand why other industries have developed in this part of our country.
4. To understand to some extent the principle of a republican form of government, and to associate the name of the President of the United States in office with the name and location of the seat of government.
5. To show the interdependence between the South and the rest of the United States as well as the rest of the world.
6. To acquire an interest in the early-history stories of the South.

C. **Content in Terms of Subject-Matter**
Southern United States
1. Natural conditions that influence the industries
   a. Farming—rich level land, long growing season
   b. Manufacturing—water power and coal in the mountains
   c. Lumbering—southern or Georgia pine
   d. Mining—coal and iron
2. Products—cotton, sugar cane, rice, lumber, oil, coal, and iron
3. The capital of the United States and other important cities
4. History stories—De Soto, Ponce de Leon, Raleigh, John Smith, George Washington

D. **Procedure**
Problems for classroom activities
Problem One: We have learned that the people of New England found it very hard to make a living by farming. On the other hand, there are many large farms in the South and agriculture is one of the chief industries. Why is this?
Problem Two: The farmers of New England and the Middle Atlantic States raise hay, wheat, and oats, and hardy fruits

and vegetables. The farmers of the South raise entirely different crops. What do the farmers of the South raise, and why are their crops different from the crops in the northeastern part of the United States?

Problem Three: There are many cotton mills in the New England States. At one time all the cotton raised in the South was shipped to New England or to foreign countries to be made into cloth. Our third problem is to find out why the raw cotton was shipped to the North to be manufactured. Are there any cotton mills in the South now?

Problem Four: Some countries are ruled by a king, some by an emperor, while other countries have a president. What is the difference? What kind of a government do we have in the United States, and why do we have that kind of a government?

Problem Five: Transportation has made it possible for us to enjoy many things which our grandparents and great-grandparents had to do without. If we in Michigan were cut off from all other states, what are some of the things that we would miss that the South gives us?

Problem Six: Have you ever heard of Captain John Smith and Pocahontas, Ponce de Leon and the Fountain of Youth, Sir Walter Raleigh and Virginia Dare? What have they to do with this unit of work?

Suggested Pupil Activities

1. Indicate the Southern States by printing or writing in the names of the States on an outline map of the United States. Then color the States.
2. Make a relief map of the Southern States.
3. Look at and discuss the following classroom films: cotton growing, cotton goods, rice, and sugar.
4. Make a miniature cotton plantation.
5. Make a cotton poster.
6. Make a chart showing the products of the Southern States.
7. Make a model of the capitol at Washington, D. C.
8. Dramatize the story of John Smith and Pocahontas.

E. **Suggestions for a summary discussion**
   1. Why is farming an important industry of the South?
   2. Would you like to work on a southern plantation? Why?
   3. Who is it that does most of the labor in the cotton fields?
   4. Do you think the South could get along without the negro laborers? Why?
   5. If you owned a plantation in the South, what would you raise? Why?

6. If you had your choice, in what southern state would you like to live? Why?

7. If you had your choice of just one city in the South that you could visit, what city would you choose? Why?

8. In what month would you like to visit the South? Why?

9. How does the South help us to enjoy our meals in the winter time?

10. For what should we thank the farmers of the South?

11. For a great many years all the cotton raised in the South was sent north to be manufactured into cloth. Now there are many cotton mills in the South. Why?

12. Why is it that levees or dikes have to be built along the banks of the Mississippi River?

13. Why is Birmingham sometimes called the Pittsburgh of the South?

14. Would you rather live in the North or the South? Why?

F. References for the Unit

Text

Brigham and McFarlane, *Essentials of Geography,* Book I, pp. 109-122

Supplementary Books

a. Branom and Ganey, *Western Hemisphere,* pp. 69-93
b. Winslow, *The United States,* pp. 91-120
c. Carpenter, *North America,* pp. 124-210

School Readers

a. *Lincoln Readers,* III
    (1) How to Tell Linen from Cotton, p. 135
    (2) How to Know Cotton from Wool, p. 154
    (3) A Queer Garden Bed, p. 149
b. *Bolenius,* IV
    (1) A Literary Journey Through the South, p. 233
    (2) A Letter from the Jamestown Colony, p. 97
c. *Winston Third Reader*
    (1) The Fountain of Youth, p. 154
d. *Horace Mann,* IV
    (1) George Washington, p. 59
e. *Study Readers,* IV
    (1) The Story of Captain John Smith, p. 295
    (2) A Plan of the City of Washington, p. 214
f. *Thought Test Readers,* II
    (1) George Washington, p. 58
g. *Silent Readers,* II
    (1) Washington's Love for Animals, p. 174
h. Natural Method, III
    (1) The Boy Surveyor, pp. 21-26
    (2) Washington's Birthday, p. 204

i. The Pathway to Reading, IV
  (1) George Washington and the Colt, p. 200
j. Easy Road to Reading, IV
  (1) George Washington, p. 286
k. Baldwin and Bender, IV
  (1) Washington and the Sorrel Colt, p. 140

G. Visual Aids

1. Maps
   a. Wall map of the United States
   b. Blackboard outline map of the United States
   c. Individual outline map of the United States
2. Globe
   One twelve-inch globe
3. Classroom Films (Visual Education Department)

		Call No.
a.	Chesapeake Bay	55
b.	Cotton Goods	" " 56
c.	Cotton Growing	" " 7
d.	Electric Power in Southern Appalachians	" " 23
e.	Producing Crude Oil	" " 40
f.	Rio Grande	" " 35

4. Auditorium Films (Visual Education Department)

		Call No.
a.	Cotton Production	347, 317
b.	Land of Cotton	D18
c.	New Orleans	192
d.	Seminole Indians	160
e.	Sugar Cane	187
f.	Washington, D. C.	30
g.	Rice Industry in the United States	316
h.	Cotton Goods	395

5. Slides (Visual Education Department)

a.	Washington, D. C.	46, 47, 48, 49, 50, 51, 52
b.	Virginia	53
c.	New Orleans	59
d.	Florida, St. Augustine	54
e.	Negro life in the South	60
f.	Jamestown Colony	108
g.	Cotton (Stillfilm)	1051

6. Materials from Children's Museum, 96 Putnam Avenue
   a. Trays or separate specimens:
      Coal, cotton, plants, cotton and its products, rice, sugar
   b. Specimen collections:
      Products of the South Atlantic States; products of the South Central States
   c. Specimen charts:
      Cotton manufacture

 d. Picture collections:
   South Atlantic States; South Central States; Washington,
     D. C.; Colonial Period including Colonial Virginia and
     Georgia; lumbering in the South; turpentine industry
 e. Large pictures:
   The Capitol; Library of Congress; White House; Oklahawa
     River, Florida; the lake, Magnolia-on-the Ashley, South
     Carolina
 f. Locked case collections of specimens:
   Seashore life, cotton, Colonial America

D. The Cleveland Course of Study in the Social Sciences
for Junior High Schools, published 1927-1928, follows the sequential plan of organization, but includes such a unique feature
of course of study construction that a separate treatment is accorded to it.

The course of study is made up of four separate bulletins
which were published at different times by the Bureau of Educational Research of the Education Department. In the first
place, there is a teacher's manual and teaching units for the
junior high-school years. This contains suggestions as to methods, articulation with other fields of study, testing programs,
and outlines of teaching units. In the second place, there is a
publication for the pupils in each grade of the junior high
school which outlines the work for the year. The material in the
teacher's course of study is in perfect harmony with that presented in pupil's course of study or textbook.

In order that this treatment can be clearly understood, the
unit "Our Latin American Neighbors" is presented from both
the pupil's and teacher's manuals.

Teaching Unit No. 8-A-9 [9]

For the Teacher

Our Latin American Neighbors

This teaching unit aims to bring before the American boy and
girl the growing importance of the countries beyond our southern
border, in relation to our affairs. Products obtainable from the Orient
only can now be had at near-by ports. Our dependence upon Latin

[9] *Course of Study in the Social Studies for Junior High Schools,*
Part I (for the teacher) (Cleveland Public Schools, 1928), pp. 181-183.

America has become sufficiently well developed to make friendly trade relations very important. To help our young citizens to have a more tolerant and gracious attitude toward these neighbors for the sake of a much needed reciprocation on their part is one of the chief reasons for including this unit.

I. **Objectives**
   A. *Major:* To acquire knowledge of the interdependence of peoples, States and nations through a study of our International Relations; specifically here, our relations with Latin America.
   B. *Minor:*
      1. To help pupils develop an attitude of tolerance toward races and policies of our neighbors.
      2. To show pupils the need of coöperation with other nations.
      3. To teach pupils the duty of recognizing and accepting responsibilities to other nations.
      4. To help pupils to acquire knowledge of neighboring nations.
      5. To help pupils to realize the advantages of peace between nations.

II. **Approach**
   A. A study of this unit may be made more interesting through a discussion of some current happening in relation to Latin American countries.
   B. An account of our interference in Nicaraguan affairs, with a report on our treaty with that country granting us a canal right of way, will lead to an interesting and provocative discussion.
   C. An account of Colonel Lindbergh's good-will flight to the Latin American countries will provide an excellent stimulus for the introduction of this unit.
   D. General Pershing's official representation of the United States in 1925, at the Pan-American Convention in the City of Mexico, is a significant example of our relations with these lands.
   E. A class may study the world map for places touched by Columbus in his four voyages to America, discussing the significance of Spanish control of the island-locked Caribbean Sea and of later Spanish exploration of lands skirting the Caribbean.
   F. Pictures of Latin American countries showing life and industries of the people, together with social conditions,

will help pupils to understand the primitive states of some of these countries.

G. Some short reports might help pupils to realize the needs of these lands and the reasons for unstable governments, as well as the customs and traditions of the people.

H. A class discussion of races, languages, and cultures of European countries contributing to the population of Latin America will lead to further interest in this teaching unit.

III. **Solution**

A. Pupils may appoint committees to canvass school and neighborhood libraries for available references and present to class lists of books and pictures.

B. The class may choose a day when an interesting review or an especially inviting chapter of some book may be given or read by classmates or teacher.

C. Maps and graphs may be made by pupils to show our dependence on these lands for material and food supplies.

D. An interesting "store window" may be developed to show how our luxuries and our industries would suffer if Latin American trade were withdrawn.

E. An imaginary trip may be taken into the jungle in line with lessons given to the pupils at the Museum of Natural History.

F. Pupils may list parts and material in automobile construction and operation, and check all material found to be of Latin American production. (Include oils, enamels, etc.)

G. A frieze may be constructed by the class in which is shown the effects of the westward movement and the industrial revolution on Latin America.

H. Maps and models of the Panama Canal and trade routes to Latin American countries may be made.

I. Lists and statistics may be prepared to show our interchange of products with countries to the south. These items may be shown graphically.

IV. **Outline**

A. Geographic locations and conditions in Latin America
   1. Surface features
   2. Climatic conditions
   3. Soils
   4. Vegetation

B. Historic and economic relations with Latin America
   1. Spanish and Portuguese colonies established south of British settlements

2. Commercial relations between English and Spanish colonies
3. Growth of Spanish West Indies
4. Independence won by American colonies
5. Exploitation of colonies by Spain
   a. Independence won by Latin American republics
   b. European interference
6. The Monroe Doctrine
   a. Its policy
   b. Relations established
   c. Its application
7. United States expansion into Latin America
   a. The Panama Canal Zone
   b. The Virgin Islands
   c. Supervision and protection in
      (1) Cuba
      (2) Panama
      (3) Santo Domingo
      (4) Haiti
      (5) Nicaragua
8. Effect of expansions
   a. Investment of American capital
   b. Improved living conditions
   c. Advanced ideas and means of production
   d. Increased means of transportation
9. Important diplomatic relations with South
   a. The Venezuelan boundary controversy
   b. Brazil-Argentine boundary dispute
   c. Tacna-Arica dispute
   d. Colombia-Panama claims
C. Attitude of Latin America toward our country
   1. Opposition due to:
      a. Past neglect of southern neighbors
         (1) Lack of international interest
         (2) Commerce chiefly with Europe and Asia
         (3) Difference in races
         (4) Lack of common language
         (5) Difference in customs, manner, sports
         (6) Unstable governments
      b. Fear of strong countries on the part of weak countries
   2. Future relations to secure friendship of Latin America based on
      a. Sympathetic understanding of traditions and ideals

        b. American study of Latin American languages

        c. Closer coöperation

           (1) In economic development

           (2) Investment of capital

           (3) Placing of progressive men and women in positions of trust

           (4) Encouragement of economic, political, and social systems in keeping with best ideals of Latin Americans.

        d. More stable governments.

V. Readings

    A. West and West, *Our Country*

    B. Gordy, *History of the United States*

    C. Atwood, *New Geography,* Plate A, Appendix, pp. 111, 157, 545, 549, 605

    D. Smith, *Human Geography,* pp. 181, 183-217. Supplementary sets in school libraries

    E. Woodburn and Moran, *Elementary American History and Government,* pp. 417, 418, 424, 425, 514

    F. Brigham and McFarlane, *Essentials of Geography,* Second Book, pp. 211-240

    G. Tarr and McMurry, *New Geography,* Book Two, pp. 171-186

    H. Nida, *Panama and Its Bridge of Water*

    I. Carpenter, *South America*

    J. Bowman, *The New World,* pp. 523-580

    K. *National Geographic Magazine,* May, 1928.

TEACHING UNIT 8-A-9 [10]

For the Pupil

Our Latin American Neighbors

When your fathers studied about the Latin American countries they learned of a vast area of unsettled wilderness, much of which was pathless jungle and impassable mountain. Other areas of tall grass and treeless plains were overrun with fierce animal and reptile life. These regions, half a century ago, were settled with primitive natives, cowboys, and backward peons or peasants.

This wilderness of the older geography books does not represent Latin America to-day. Much of this country is still unchanged. However, the past forty years have produced a more rapid advancement in these lands than the preceding four centuries. In this lesson you have an opportunity to learn how improvements have worked their way into the most remote places.

[10] *Course of Study in Social Studies for Junior High Schools,* Part II (for the pupil) (Cleveland Public Schools, 1928), pp. 70-72.

The story of Latin America's resources came to be known to the world when the Great War shut off trade from the East and from Africa. Her national riches rival those of the United States. You will be interested to learn how her people are achieving so much in such a short period of time, just as we achieved a century ago. You will understand why nations are seeking the good will of Latin America, and why it is important that we should show them the respect and friendship they so richly deserve.

I. **Some Ways to Work**
   A. Make lists of products shipped to us from Latin American countries, together with lists of products which we ship to them in turn. This will show you the interdependence between the peoples of the two continents.
   B. You might make a world map, showing the four voyages of Columbus. Mark possessions in the Caribbean Sea claimed for Spain as a result of these voyages.
   C. Prepare a floor talk on any other of the explorers who visited South American or Mexican lands.
   D. Look for information concerning the early history of these countries to help you understand the reasons for their being called Latin American.
   E. Find statements in your geographies and histories that will help you to compare the classes of people to be found in the Latin American countries.
   F. Committees might be chosen to discuss the geographic conditions that help or hinder development in Latin America. Maps might be prepared by these committees to show important conditions, products, industries, etc.
   G. A collection of pictures made by the class would show the progress of these people in architecture, road building, recreation, occupations, etc.
   H. An interesting display of Latin American goods might be made from materials easily obtained. This might be assembled according to lists you have prepared.
   I. Appoint committees to canvass school and neighborhood libraries for available references, and present to class lists of books and pictures available.
   J. Choose an interesting review or an especially inviting chapter of some book to read to classmates concerning Latin America.

II. **Outline of Subject**
   A. Geographical conditions of Latin American countries
      1. Surface
      2. Climate

  3. Soils
  4. Vegetation
  B. History and progress of Latin America
   1. Spanish and Portuguese colonies
   2. Trade relations with Europe and the United States
   3. Spanish oppression of colonies
   4. Independence won by these colonies and republics established
   5. European interference with new republics
  C. The Monroe Doctrine
   1. Meaning of new Latin American countries
   2. Significance at the present time
  D. United States expansion into Latin American regions.
   1. Panama Canal Zone
   2. Protection of Cuba, Panama, etc.
   3. The Virgin Islands
  E. Effects of United States expansion on Latin American regions
  F. Our present-day attitude toward Latin America
   1. Commercial
   2. Diplomatic

III. **References**
  A. West and West, *Our Country*
  B. Gordy, *History of the United States*
  C. Halleck, *History of Our Country*
  D. Beard and Bagley, *History of the American People*
  E. Long, *America*
  F. Burnham, *The Making of Our Country*
  G. Atwood, *New Geography*, Book II
  H. Smith, *Human Geography*
  I. Brigham and McFarlane, *Essentials of Geography*
  J. Jackard and Sinnott, *Nations as Neighbors*
  K. Allen, *South America*
  L. Carpenter, *South America*
  M. Warshaw, *The New Latin America*
  N. Current publications as *The National Geographic Magazine, Pan-American Bulletin,* etc.

IV. **Quotations**
  Note: The best source of quotations for this lesson will be found in current events, magazines, newspapers, and periodicals of the times. As you find suitable quotations you might place them in your notebook. Special attention should be given to the *National Geographic Magazine* for May, 1928. It contains the story of Colonel Lindbergh's visit to some Latin American countries.

V. **Tests**
  A. Locate important countries of Latin America with capitals and ports.
  B. Name Latin American products useful to our manufacturers and merchants.
  C. Tell of the languages, customs, and sports of Latin American people.

VI. **Leisure Time**
  A. Many thrilling stories of adventure in the jungles of South America may be had at the library.
  B. Stories of hunting and exploration expeditions into Brazil and the Andes regions have been written by Roosevelt and others.
  C. You might visit a factory where some raw product of Latin America is being prepared for us. Some of these products are rubber, cocoa, chocolate, fine woods, etc.
  D. It might be interesting to start an exhibit of Latin American products.
  E. Many men and women are finding opportunities in Latin America for which extra preparation in languages is necessary. It would be profitable to look up opportunities for employment there to-day.

E. The fifth and last type of organization is that of the narrative or essay, which presents a descriptive account of the unit. There is no attempt in this general discussion to designate or emphasize objectives, methods, and other elements under separate headings. It will be apparent, at once, that this type of organization requires more than average ability in composition on the part of the committee and a high professional spirit among the faculty. Otherwise it is apt to be ignored.

This form of course of study construction is found in the kindergarten and elementary school, but is rarely used at the secondary level or in higher education. This is probably because courses at the high-school and college grades must be more intensely and extensively developed.

Two excellent courses of study have been selected as illustrations of this type.

1. The following Farm Unit was selected from the *Suggestive Course of Study for the First Grade* which was published

by the Dayton Schools in 1931. It should be pointed out that the first half of the course deals with goals for the subject-matter fields of the first grade, teaching procedures, standards of achievement, etc. The second half presents the teaching units, one of which is given here.

FARM UNIT [11]—FIRST GRADE

This unit was carried on in one first grade.

With the idea of telling and dramatizing the story of "The Little Red Hen," some wheat was cut in the summer and saved for the first day of school. After the story was told and dramatized several times, it was set up in the sand table.

Equipment: A china cat, hen and little chicks, a celluloid pig, and some wheat, but—no goose. How could we make a goose?

A plasticene goose appeared in the afternoon, made by one of the children. The child turned the head of the goose so that it seemed to be talking to the little red hen.

A pig pen was made. The pig was placed in it.

In the afternoon a child brought in a little brown pig.

The following stories were written on charts to keep for a class book:

> A little pig! A little pig!
> Clarence brought a little pig.
> The pig is brown.
> The pig is in the pig pen.

> A goose! A goose!
> Allan brought a goose.
> The goose is green and yellow.
> The goose is in the farmyard.

The farmyard needed a barn, the barn a farmer, the farmer a house. Work began on the barn. It was made of blocks. A cow, a horse, and a little red wagon were contributed. Stories followed:

> A barn is in the farmyard.
> Allan made the barn.
> The barn is big.
> A horse is in the barn.
> A little wagon! A little wagon!
> Victor brought a little red wagon.

The following books have been examined by the children and appropriate stories read to them by the teacher:

[11] *A Suggestive Course of Study for the First Grade* (Dayton Public Schools, 1931), pp. 142-148.

Nida, "Grandfather's Farm," in *Social Science Readers* (D. C. Heath and Co.)
Bolenius Primer (Houghton Mifflin Co.)
Tippett, *The Singing Farmer* (World Book Co.)
Marjorie Hardy, *Wag and Puff* (Wheeler Co.)

New words in the children's vocabulary so far are: *silo, silage, tractor*. A tractor has been contributed and also a silo made of cardboard.

Then came a horse and a cow (celluloid) followed by a discussion of the old and new ways of plowing, milking, making butter, etc. A dairy was made of blocks, and a real little butter churn and little pail were contributed by the teacher.

Next came a shed for the farmer's tools. Then another barn for his implements (this was made at home by an interested parent) was followed in quick succession by a dog house, a china dog, three glass puppies, a chicken coop, three chicks and a hen, corn for the hen, a rabbit family, a house for the rabbits, a cat family (a mother and three kittens were put in the hayloft), and so it went. A fence was cut from paper. A pig trough was made of paper. Pumpkins were cut and colored. Real corn shocks were put in the field. The silo was filled, and that brings us to Halloween.

Reading: Made booklets: The first booklets had "My Book" on the outside and contained pictures of the cat, hen, goose, pig, chicks, and wheat, drawn and cut by the children, under which were printed "This is the cat," "This is the Goose," etc. The second booklets contained pictures of the different animals on the farm, and a sentence or two more was added describing the color of the animals.

Chart Stories:

Rolland's Dog

Rolland brought a dog.
The dog is little.

Ben's Dog

Ben brought a dog.
The dog is big and brown.

The Cow

A cow! A cow!
A cow is in the barnyard.
The cow is red and white.
The cow is friendly.

The Donkey

See the donkey!
The donkey is black and white.
Ben bought a donkey, too.
His donkey is brown.
His donkey is big.

The Dog House

A little house!
A little house!
The house is a dog house.

> The puppy is in the dog house.
> Draw a dog house.
> Color the house green.

The words *mother, father, sister, brother* have been developed by matching words with pictures and singing "The Family Song."

Now, *mother* and *baby* will be introduced into the farm stories.

The Cat

A mother cat is in the barn.
She has three baby kittens.
One kitten is black and white.
One kitten is yellow and white.
One kitten is yellow and white and
  brown.
Draw the mother cat.
Cut out the cat.
Color the cat black.

The Rabbit

A mother rabbit is on the farm.
The rabbit is brown.
She has three baby rabbits.
They are in a little house.
Margaret made the rabbit house.

Draw the mother rabbit.
Color the rabbit brown.
Cut out the rabbit.

The farmer's pumpkins, cut out of paper and placed in the field near the corn shocks, were picked at Halloween and converted into Jack O'Lanterns.

> Cut out one big nose.
> Cut out one big mouth.
> Cut out two big eyes.
> Cut out the pumpkin boy.
> Color the pumpkin boy orange and green.

The farm was about to die a natural death when a little girl brought in a doll dressed as a farmer. This was followed by a bag of hay for the hayloft.

A farmer! A farmer!
Verna Jane brought a farmer.
Verna Jane's mother dresses
  the farmer.
His overalls are blue.
His shirt is blue and white.

Some hay; same hay!
Robert brought some hay.
The cow will eat the hay.
The horse will eat the hay.
The sheep will eat the hay.
The cat will not eat the hay.

A rubber mouse was put in the hayloft. Similarity between *mouse* and *house* was shown and how phonics aid in telling which is which.

With the idea of vivifying the story of "The Boy and the Goat," part of the sand table was changed into a woods. A ten-cent store was visited, and a goat, a boy, and a fox were added to the farm. The woods, the boy's home, the squirrel, and the bumblebee were made from paper.

When the goat was introduced to the farm, the story from the board read: "This is the goat that would not go home," "This is the boy that ran after the goat," etc.

Then, as Thanksgiving approached, a turkey came to live on the farm. The song, "There's a Big Fat Turkey," was taught and the following story for the board was made:

The Turkey

Farmer Brown had a turkey. (Draw a turkey.)
The turkey ran into the woods. (Color the turkey red, yellow, black, and green.)
He flew up into a tree.
He would not go home. (Cut out the turkey.)
Farmer Brown did not have turkey for his Thanksgiving dinner. (Take the turkey home.)

The next story from the basic text was "The Wee Wee Woman." The words table, chair, door, window, and candle were put about the room, naming the different objects. Much action reading was done. "Run to the chair," "Walk to the table," "Skip to the door," etc.

Many tables, chairs, and beds were constructed of paper. Candles were drawn on the tables from blackboard direction. The Wee Wee Woman's house was set up in the sand table, but the "Home Unit" did not follow. As fast as things were put in the house, they disappeared, the interest in construction being only to take the article home.

So "Making Things to Take Home" became the Christmas project:

Christmas is near. See the presents!
We will make a present for mother.
We will make a present for father.
We made a present for mother.
It was a vase.
We put many colors on the vase.
The colors ran into each other.
They looked pretty.
Look at the colors.
Some are red and black.
Some are yellow and blue.
Some are green.
We will make an ash tray for father.
We will make the outside black.
We will paint another color inside.
Look at the colors!
Look at the presents!

There is a vase for mother.
There is an ash tray for father.
Who made the presents?
Did the boys and girls do this?

2. The Raleigh Elementary Education Council, of the Raleigh Public Schools, Raleigh, N. C., published a *Study of Language Expression in the Elementary School* in 1932. The following quotation from the Foreword indicates the scope of the course of study:

The teachers have had in mind throughout this study certain generalizations agreed upon as basic in the development of the work in language. No fixed rules are given for the teaching of language, but each group has agreed upon certain desirable outcomes for the guidance of the work in the grade. Means for securing the outcomes which have proved effective in Raleigh classrooms are given. Ways and means of checking on the progress made are suggested.

Recognition is made of the fact that through participation in rich and varied experiences many occasions arise for purposeful speaking and writing. The child experience program in Raleigh classrooms affords many opportunities for practise along definite lines which make for effective use of language as a means of both oral and written expression.

When a group of teachers recognize a definite need for study of some particular phase of their program, survey the situation and determine ways of solving problems and improving the work, real growth results on the part of each individual who has entered purposefully into the study. As a result of this year's study teachers will be better able to provide real opportunities for growth in language abilities for the individual pupil and for the group.[12]

The unit on *Christmas in Other Lands* will illustrate the form of organizing teaching materials and learning activities.

Christmas in Other Lands

Blanche Holt, Second Grade
Hayes-Barton School

It was the first day after the Thanksgiving holidays when Betty chanced to find a beautiful new book in the library entitled "Tales Told in Holland," and edited by Olive Beaupre Miller.

Naturally she was interested because her group had been studying

[12] *A Study of Language Expression in the Elementary School* (Raleigh Public Schools, 1932), pp. v-vi.

about Holland. She found a story about how the children in that country celebrate Christmas. The story was illustrated to show Dutch Christmas customs.

After reading a few minutes she exclained, "Say, girls, did you know that children in Holland don't hang up their stockings at Christmas?" "No," they replied. "I'm glad I don't live in Holland." "I bet they don't have a very good time at Christmas." "Don't they have any Santa Claus?" came from the group.

Betty, feeling very proud of her recently gained knowledge, replied: "Yes, they have a Santa Claus and are just as happy at Christmas as we are. They put out their wooden shoes for Good St. Nick to fill."

"What else do they do at Christmas time?" asked Jack. Geraldine said, "I will look in *My Book House*. I believe I can find something there." "I will bring my *Compton*—it has most everything in it," said another eager youngster. "I will go down to the library and get some books. That's where my sister finds what she wants to know," offered Helena.

Many books were brought in, some from home, some from the school library, and some from the city library.

While reading one of the books entitled "Christmas in Other Lands," they found that Holland was not the only country that did not celebrate Christmas as Americans do. The group studied these countries in the short time between Thanksgiving and Christmas:

Italy
Spain
Sweden
England
Germany.

Just a week before the holidays, when the real Christmas spirit was permeating every young American, some one decided that a play should be given and all the mothers should be invited. Nobody knew where to get a play. In the midst of suggestions and discussions Emily, a very resourceful child, said, "I think it would be nice if we could write a play and tell about how children in other countries celebrate Christmas. We could just tell about what we have learned."

The suggestion was met with enthusiastic approval, but the next difficulty was how to start. It so happened that in the group was the daughter of a returned missionary, who had lived in China four years. She told the group about her trip across on the boat, adding, "Daddy thinks we'll go next time on an airplane. Uncle Tom is coming home that way." (Uncle Tom was really in China at the time, but in order to introduce children from the different countries it was pretended that he had been around the world and was bringing some little children to America to spend Christmas.)

"Let's have a bedroom scene," said Jean. "Then we can use the furniture that we have made." "And we can play that we have to clean up the house before the guests arrive," chimed in Mary.

So it was decided that Ben and Betty should be brother and sister, and Ben should run in and wake Betty very early the day Uncle Tom was expected to come.

"What are we going to say?" one child asked.

"I know," said Mildred, "Betty, Betty, wake up, quick! Uncle Tom is coming home to-day to spend Christmas with us. He is going to bring some little children from all the countries he has visited on his trip around the world."

"And what will Betty say?"

"I will jump out of bed in a hurry and say, 'Oh, let's get the house all nice and clean before the guests get here.' "

Once started, the questions and answers came fast enough, and the lines were easily made. Each country was studied for the purpose of finding out how other children celebrate Christmas.

The following is an example of how the work was carried on:

It was decided that Germany would be taken first, probably because it was better known to them. Each child found all he could. Reading material above their level was brought in by the children and read to them by the teacher. After getting all the information possible, they came together for discussion.

The following is the pooled knowledge of the group:

In Germany Christmas lasts three days, the 24th, 25th, and 26th of December. Each member of the family makes a gift for every other member. Everybody, rich or poor, has a Christmas tree, but they do not put presents on the tree.

They call their Santa Claus, Kris Kringle. He carries toys to every good boy and girl, and switches to the naughty ones.

After the candles are lighted, the family gathers around the tree and sings Christmas carols.

Other countries were studied in a similar manner. The play contained only a summary of the information they had gained in their study.[13]

V. CRITERIA FOR USE IN COURSE OF STUDY CONSTRUCTION

The discussion of the various plans for the organization of courses of study makes it imperative that the essential criteria which should determine the scope and character of course of

[13] *Ibid.,* pp. 87-91.

study construction be considered and studied. The previous pages of this chapter have shown that many common features can be observed in courses of study even though radically different plans of organization have been followed. If those common elements which appear in courses of study in every subject-matter field and in every school system are studied and analyzed by qualified people, a list of criteria which will have real significance in establishing definite bounds and limitations in course of study construction can be formulated and presented to the teaching corps.

Naturally, it is wasteful in terms of time, money, energy, and professional spirit for an administration to institute course of study construction without establishing definite criteria for the guidance of the teachers and others engaged in the work. What are the essential items to include in the course of study? What aspects of the course of study are so important that failure to include them will affect the service which the course of study can render to the corps? The problem is one of determining standards or criteria by which excellent courses of study can be distinguished from the mediocre and the worthless. Such criteria if placed in the hands of the course of study committee will do much to simplify procedures and guarantee satisfactory results.

A. Securing the criteria. In attacking the problem of formulating criteria for course of study construction, the author began with the seminar classes in curriculum under his direction. During the period of three years, these students worked with problems centering on the comparison of various courses of study and analysis of the lists of criteria that had been organized as a result of investigations organized in various curriculum centers, by graduate students in other universities, by the Bureau of Research of the National Education Association, and by the Society for Curriculum Study.

These preliminary lists of criteria were submitted to professional teachers who were working with curriculum problems or were members of committees considering course of study construction. In this way, additional criteria, restatements of criteria, and the elimination of questionable criteria were realized and a master sheet of criteria attained. These were, theoretically, of value for course of study construction in every field of instruction. However, it was felt that this list should be validated by referring it to the experts who were directing and supervising course of study committees in organizing experiments, carrying on investigations and producing courses of study.

The master list was forwarded to the most prominent directors of research and curriculum specialists in the country with the request that they evaluate each item which had been included. The following points were suggested to them as a basis for the comparison of the criteria:

1. Is this item absolutely essential in the construction of the course of study?
2. Is this item of sufficient importance that its elimination would affect the value of the course of study organized in any academic field?
3. Is this item important in particular subject-matter fields but not in others? Could the matter of using this criterion be left to the judgment of the committee?
4. Can this item be disregarded in organizing a course of study?
5. Should this item be disregarded in organizing courses of study in every field?

B. **Evaluating the criteria.** The criteria which had been developed into a master sheet and which were sent to the experts for final evaluation were as follows:

1. The course of study should contain an introduction stating:
   a. Philosophy of the school system and relation of general objectives to that philosophy
   b. Procedure followed in constructing the course of study
   c. Means of validating objectives
   d. Sources of objectives
   e. Methods of selecting content
   f. Basis for the selection of general and specific teaching procedures
   g. Development of the testing material, types of tests, standardization, scaling, validity, reliability, etc.
2. The general objectives should be stated in order that new and approved trends can be noted.
3. The validated specific objectives should be stated for each unit.

4. A prospectus of the work of the lower and higher grades should be included.

5. An overview of the purpose and content of the unit should be included.

6. The course of study should be organized into well-articulated teaching units, having definite progression toward the stated objectives.

7. Each unit of the course of study should be concise and self-explanatory to both teacher and pupil.

8. Each unit should contain an adequate bibliography of reference material.

9. The course of study should contain various types of specific pupil activities and teaching procedures definitely for the guidance of the teacher.

10. The suggested materials, activities, and methods should be practical for use in the particular school system.

11. The course of study should provide for individual pupil differences.

12. The course of study should provide both situations and content materials which will help the child make normal social adjustments.

13. The course of study should be an outgrowth, in part at least, of the pupil's past and present experiences, characteristics, and needs.

14. The course of study should be an outgrowth of the community interests and activities.

15. The course of study in any field should develop the interests of the child in one or all of the following life problems:
    a. Vocational pursuit
    b. Avocational interest
    c. Citizenship

16. The material retained in a course of study should be organized in accordance with the principles of interest, use, and difficulty. These will determine grade placement.

17. The course of study should suggest the necessity of evaluating the achievement in the subject by the best methods available.

18. Evaluation based on objectives should be a definite part of each unit.

19. The course of study should provide stimulation through the inclusion of supplementary materials and specific methods.

20. The course of study should serve as a motivating influence for independent and creative thinking.

21. Every course of study should be so flexible that an effective correlation can be made with other subjects in the curriculum.

22. The organization of the course of study should be consistent throughout and indicate the results of real planning.
23. The preliminary organization of the course of study should be tried out for at least two years before publication.
24. The course should be carefully edited by competent people.
25. The mechanical aspects of the course should guarantee adequate use by pupils and teachers, and long service.
26. The course of study should be carefully indexed.
27. The typography and type of paper used in the revision of the tentative course should be of the best.
28. A pocket should be included in the course of study, preferably on the back cover, so that revisions can keep the printed course up-to-date for a number of years.

As a result of the consideration of these aspects, certain criteria can be designated as absolutely essential, others as valuable, and a few as meriting practically no place in the thinking of the curriculum committee.

The following criteria were regarded as absolutely essential in the construction of the course of study: 2, 3, 5, 7, 8, 9, 10, 11, 12, 13, 16, 20, 22, and 24.

Those which were highly important but not absolutely essential were designated as follows: 1a, b, c, d, e, f, g; 14; 15a, b, c; 18, 21, 23, 25.

The following were judged to be relatively unimportant: 17, 26, 27, and 28.

C. Developing the score-card. The course of study committee may find the score-card on page 801 of value in checking their course of study from time to time and at the completion of their work:

In making use of the score-card, it will be helpful for the teacher or the committee to have a very careful analysis of various phases of the course of study in order that the checking may be more than a mere guess. Most of the criteria concern the following divisions of the course: (1) objectives, (2) materials, (3) content, (4) methods, (5) measurement, and (6) references. A common understanding and agreement regarding the essentials of each of these will enable the committee or indi-

viduals who evaluate the course to have a definite basis for
agreement or disagreement.

SCORE-CARD FOR COURSE OF STUDY

*Name of Course*_____ *Date Issued*_____

*Name of Committee Chairman*_____

*Total Score*_____ (Each item evaluated 0-10)

Indicate criteria, regarded as absolutely essential or highly
important, which have not been realized by the committee

_____

*Remarks:*_____

_____

_____

· ·

INTRODUCTION [14] Is the philosophy of the school system stated and the relationship of the general objectives of the course to that philosophy indicated?	*Yes*	*No*	*Score*

---

1. *Objectives.* These should be definite and attainable and
should consider, first, knowledge as an end in itself and as the
foundation of ideas; second, habits and skills, together with the
knowledge which is essential for their realization; and third,
attitudes, appreciations, and ideals basic in American life. It is
not sufficient that these be adequately stated, but evidence should
be apparent that subject-matter has been selected which will attain them. It is not sufficient that they be high-sounding phrases,
but they must be specific, and the methods of determining their
validity should be indicated.

2. *Materials.* The course must indicate the basic material to
be used. This may be a text, although it is probable that in many
courses the references will reflect many textbooks and other
sources of information. An adequate bibliography of supple-

[14] The score-card can be completed by selecting from the list of criteria
and from other sources those items which are considered essential by the
committee or the director of research.

mentary materials should be included. If this is annotated, much confusion will be eliminated in determining what to use and the sources of the materials selected. It is particularly important that those materials which will make adjustments for individual ability and group levels be indicated.

3. *Content.* It is important that emphasis be centered on the selection of the content in terms of the objectives. Unless this has been done, little consideration can be given the work of the committee on that phase of the work. It is here that the fundamentals of the learning program should be indicated, and the selection and organization of the subject-matter should be made after a consideration of the research studies in the field. Unless definite adaptations have been made to local environment in this phase of the course, the course should be returned to the committee for further consideration.

Osburn has formulated the "Earmarks of Desirable Curriculum Content" which will be suggestive to the teachers who are trying to revise a course of study or to organize new teaching materials for the classroom. The following statement by Osburn will indicate clearly how an exact and accurate analysis of a course of study can be made with the application of these "earmarks."

These earmarks are to be used as a check-list first with reference to the present course of study, if one is being used, then as applied to content found elsewhere. The use of any check-list in connection with a course of study requires some training and practice. The meaning of each earmark must be gotten clearly in mind, and care must be taken not to overlook any earmark when examining a course of study. Each earmark is to be tallied as it is found. This matter is so important that detailed illustrations of the process are desirable.

Having secured a copy of the course of study to be appraised, the next thing to do is to get a copy of the earmarks upon which the tallies may be recorded. Begin with the first sentence in the course of study. Read it carefully. For each idea that it contains make a check opposite the corresponding earmark. Check the same idea twice or more, in proportion to the number of times that it functions as an earmark. Continue in this manner until the course of study or desired portion of it is tallied. Count the tallies opposite each earmark. The numbers thus obtained will show how much emphasis each earmark receives and thus give an appraisal of the course of study as a whole or as checked.[15]

The earmarks which are suggested by Osburn for use in evaluating courses of study are included to show the implications of this technique and the comprehensiveness of the treatment. The author says that up to the present time this list of "earmarks" has provided a place to tally every element that he has found in courses of study. The following items are included in the "Earmarks":

I. **Individualistic Values**
   A. *Provisions for routine*—Include all references to habit-formation abilities and drill. Do not include exercises designed as study guides. See IV, I.
   B. *Provisions for thinking*—Include references to any of the twelve types of thinking, namely: cause-effect, comparison, manner, exposition, generalization, classification, functional-relation illustration, advantage, disadvantage and limitation, hypothesis, quantitative relation, and condition. Include also problem solving, decisions, discussions, studies, and research activities. Do not include questions and problems set as study-guides. See IV, I.
   C. *Provisions for differentiation*—Include all actual differentiated content.
   D. *Cultural content*—Include all items which are of widespread application or which require the activity of evaluation. Include also interpretations. See II, E.
   E. *Remedial content*—Include all material given with the *explicit* purpose of aiding in diagnosis and in the correction of disabilities.
   H. *Freedom*—Include non-functional factual content, social graces, and activities leading toward the achievement of economic freedom. Include also material which refutes superstitions and current fallacies. Include privileges, ideas of growth, benefits, activities initiated by pupils, and the provision of opportunities for pupils.
   I. *Thrift*—Follow the ordinary interpretation of thrift and include in addition all content that has to do with the elimination of waste.

[15] Osburn, W. J., "Earmarks of Desirable Curriculum Content," *Educational Research Bulletin* No. 1, Department of Education, Ohio State University, p. 11.

    J. *Ideals and attitudes*—Include content which promotes feelings and sensitivities of all kinds.

    K. *Responsibility*—Include also content which involves duties.

II. Social Values

    A. *Social utility*—Include all material which is introduced with explicit reference to social usage.

    B. *Promotion of like-mindedness*—Include all material which promotes social sympathy, toleration, and social solidarity. Include also open-mindedness and loyalty.

    C. *Promotion of social participation*—Include all elements that require the learner to take part in group activities. Include coöperation here. See II, F.

    D. *Training in leadership*—Include all content relating *explicitly* to pupil initiative and resourcefulness.

    E. *Social heritage*—Include all knowledge listed *explicitly* as worth-while content handed down from the past. See I, D.

    F. *Provision for self-realization*—Include only material which mentions self-realization *explicitly*. See II, C.

    G. *Social interdependence*—Include content which relates to conditions of dependence between individuals or groups.

    H. *Social progress*—Include material relating to the advancement of nations and the growth of civilization.

III. Psychological Values

    A. *Guidance*—Include information concerning social, industrial, and occupational needs. Include also all items relating to the perpetuation and stabilization of pupil interests.

    B. *Adjustment to learner's level, gradation*—Include mental, chronological, grade, social, emotional, and physical levels.

    C. *Adjustment to learner's experience*—Include also the provision of experience for the learner.

    F. *Transfer values*—Include all material listed *explicitly* as prerequisites, and all listed as *explicit* applications.

IV. Pedagogical Values

    A. *Goals*—Check all statements of aims and standards. Check pupil aims as immediate, if no remote time element is implied. Check teacher's aims and pupils' aims with implied remoteness under remote aims.

    B. *Motivation*—Ends which grow out of activity pursued for its own sake are intrinsic. All activities which are means to other ends are extrinsic.

    C. *Functional facts*—Include all facts, information, and ideas which by implication lead to conclusions, ideals, attitudes and activities. Include understanding, ideas, recognitions, acquaintances, learnings, visualizations, and knowledges.

D. *Activities*—Include all activities not listed under II, C. Do not include thinking. See I, B. Include expressions.

E. *Material aids*—Include all material aids except books. See IV, G.

F. *Provisions for measurement*—Include all suggestions for test construction.

I. *Supervised study*—Include all exercises designed as guides in study whether of thought or routine type. See I, A and B.

J. *Provision for teacher freedom*—Include all provisions for choice on the part of the teacher.

K. *Devices, methods, and procedures*—Include here all suggestions of TEACHER activity.

V. Organization

A. Integration
B. Deductive basis
C. Difficulty basis
D. Interest basis
E. Experiential basis
F. Utility basis
G. Inductive basis
H. Recognition of relative values

VI. Mechanical Make-up [16]

4. *Methods and Procedures.* It is of prime importance that the course of study provide for pupil activity. The committee must recognize the fact that children learn through their own activity and the teacher's place in the classroom is to stimulate this activity. The following points should be considered by the committee:

a. Method is related closely to content, but can be treated separately in the course of study.

b. In any case, suggestions regarding methods which have been tried and proved valuable should be included in every unit of the course.

c. Pupil difficulties that are due to the material or methods of procedure should be pointed out and the results of research indicated.

d. The ability and initiative of the individual teacher should be

[16] *Ibid.,* pp. 7-10.

recognized by allowing freedom in the selection of both materials and methods of procedure. Otherwise, all creative power would be lost in the teaching corps.

e. Reference to all experimental work in the field should be made available to the faculty.

f. Emphasis should be placed upon the problem of handling individual differences, academic guidance, and adjustment.

5. *Measurement of Results.* There must be some tests by which the outcomes can be measured in terms of the objectives established for the course. These will have to be rather definitely indicated as habits, skills, attitudes, appreciations, etc. Either the examinations for the various units and for the course will be included in the course or the types of questions which should be included in a comprehensive examination will be indicated as well as the standard of performance which should be expected.

6. *References.* There is no occasion to give an extended list of references. Only those of real value should be included in the course, and these should be adequately annotated so that their value and use to the teacher is indicated at once. A bibliography which is not annotated will merit a very low score.

The Department of Instruction of the Oakland Public Schools has developed a score-card for the evaluation of the course of study. A copy of this card is included so that the teacher or committee may have as many suggestions as possible in formulating a score-card for their own use.

OAKLAND PUBLIC SCHOOLS
DEPARTMENT OF INSTRUCTION

General Rating

	Ex.	V.G.	G.	F.	P.
EVALUATION OF COURSE OF STUDY					

Subject .... Grades Covered .... Date of Course..........

Name of Course ....Date of Evaluation...............

I. OBJECTIVES

	Ex.	V.G.	G.	F.	P.	None

A. *Validity*

	Ex.	V.G.	G.	F.	P.

Much	Little	None	
			1. Recognition of child needs, interests and abilities
			2. Recognition of adult needs and interests
			3. Recognition of needs of society
			4. Emphasis on present reality
			5. Use made of studies and research
			6. Consistent with general educational objectives

B. *Arrangement*

	Ex.	V.G.	G.	F.	P.

—— 1. A few broad general objectives
—— 2. Specific objectives in sufficient detail as to indicate:
    —— Habits and skills
    —— Necessary facts
    —— Broad understandings
    —— Attitudes and appreciations
—— 3. Clearly stated

II. CONTENT

	Ex.	V.G.	G.	F.	P.	None

A. *Nature of material*

Ex.	V.G.	G.	F.	P.

—— 1. Closely related to objectives
—— 2. Selected on basis of children's needs and interests
—— 3. Selected on basis of studies and research
—— 4. Provides for correlation and integration with other fields
—— 5. Provides for individual differences
—— 6. Includes visual aids
—— 7. Includes supplementary sources
—— 8. Can be easily adapted to different teaching situations

B. *Arrangement*

Ex.	V.G.	G.	F.	P.

—— 1. Arranged in large "natural" units
—— 2. Can be easily located
—— 3. Summary or overview given
—— 4. Pupil references given
—— 5. Additional teacher references given

III. ACTIVITIES

Ex.	V.G.	G.	F.	P.	None

A. *Nature of Activities*

Ex.	V.G.	G.	F.	P.

—— 1. Closely related to objectives
—— 2. Selected on basis of children's needs and interests
—— 3. Selected on basis of studies and research
—— 4. Provide for correlation and integration with other fields
—— 5. Provide for individual differences
—— 6. Involve intellectual effort
—— 7. Involve creative effort
—— 8. Involve planning and evaluating
—— 9. Considerable variety in type
——10. Involve vital contact with out-of-school life.

B. *Arrangement*

Ex.	V.G.	G.	F.	P.

—— 1. Suggested in connection with large "natural" units
—— 2. Can be easily located
—— 3. Large number of suggested activities, none prescribed

IV. EVALUATION AND MEAS-
    UREMENT

Ex.	V.G.	G.	F.	P.	None

—— 1. Evaluation a definite part of each unit
—— 2. Evaluation based on objectives
—— 3. Objective tests given or referred to
—— 4. Other evaluating devices suggested and described
—— 5. Evaluation not confined to facts and skills; work habits, attitudes, and appreciations given due weight

V. GENERAL

Ex.	V.G.	G.	F.	P.

—— 1. Not bulky or cumbersome
—— 2. Important phases emphasized in mechanical make-up
—— 3. Usable table of contents
—— 4. Usable index
—— 5. Artistic in typography and make-up

VI. SUMMARY

The framework of course of study construction consists of studies concerning content, method, grade placement, etc., and the organization of all of these into a usable volume which will be basic in the promotion of good teaching. The "lag" between educational theory (based on research) and educational practice is due to the fact that the practitioners in course of study construction and in teaching are not familiar with recent research and those who are directing the construction of courses of study are not aware of the most desirable content, methods, tests, and standards for the determination of grade placement in the field. It is apparent on every hand that those who are in charge of this work do not have the training to conduct scientific investigations or even to use the results of research which are available. It should be pointed out that using research in the field of the curriculum is difficult and often misleading to any one but the expert in education.

Some of the difficulties which face the teacher, supervisor, or administrator who is directing the reorganization of curricula or the development of courses of study are:

1. Scientific studies are often fragmentary, and the results cannot be applied directly to the work of the staff. In few cases do results of studies present a complete and satisfactory solution to any problem.
2. In many cases the results of these investigations are contradictory or appear to be contradictory unless the educator has been trained to interpret statistical data.
3. A critical evaluation of every previous study plus a knowledge of all current investigations are essential in determining criteria for course of study construction and standards by which content, methods, etc., can be selected.

Critical thinking by every member of the committee and administrative and supervisory staffs is essential to the development of the correct pattern for the course of study. The criteria and the current patterns of courses of study which have been presented in this chapter are only suggestive. The teacher should approach the problem of classroom teaching with the attitude of improving present practice through research in his field and a critical evaluation of all studies relating to the organization, presentation and evaluation of his work. The professional teacher will not look for ready-made solutions to his problems, but will constantly and untiringly seek to develop new investigations which will produce valid results and refine and redefine the results of previous and current studies in the educational field.

BIBLIOGRAPHY

BARR, A. S., and BURTON, W. H., *The Supervision of Instruction* (D. Appleton and Company), Chs. VI, VII, VIII and IX.

COCKING, W. D., *Administrative Procedures in Curriculum Making for Public Schools* (Bureau of Publications, Teachers College, Columbia University, 1928).

Curriculum Bulletin Number One, Dayton Public Schools (Board of Education, Dayton, Ohio, 1931). Under "Criteria of Procedure" on page 8, ten suggestive criteria for the evaluation of the first-grade curriculum are included.

Denver Program of Curriculum Revision (Denver Public Schools, 1927). A clear and concise statement of the organization of teaching materials in the Denver schools.

GREENE, C. E., and GUMLICK, H. R., "Some Techniques in Installing a New Course of Study," *Teachers' Journal and Abstract,* Vol. III, No. 4 (April, 1928), pp. 257-262.

HARAP, Henry, *Technique of Curriculum Making* (The Macmillan Company, 1928). Beginning with the Thirty-Eighth Meeting on page 181, an excellent and detailed discussion of the significant qualities of the good teaching unit and procedures for evaluating the unit of work is presented.

HILL, P. S., *A Conduct Curriculum* (Charles Scribner's Sons, 1923). This book will be particularly helpful to those who are engaged in developing activity materials.

HOPKINS, L. T., *Curriculum Principles and Practices* (B. H. Sanborn & Co., 1929). Committees and individuals working with this problem will find Chapter XI of great value.

JUDD, C. H., "The Place of Research in a Program of Curriculum Development," *Journal of Educational Research,* Vol. XVII (May, 1928), pp. 313-323.

KYTE, G. C., "The Coöperative Development of a Course of Study," *Educational Administration and Supervision* (December, 1923), pp. 517-536.

————, "Installing a New Course of Study," *The Nation's Schools,* Vol. XIV, No. 6 (December, 1934), pp. 34-37.

————, "When Supervisor and Teacher Talk It Over," *The Nation's Schools,* Vol. XV, No. 6 (June, 1935), pp. 29-32.

Lincoln School Staff. *Curriculum Making in an Elementary School* (Ginn & Co., 1927). The material in Chapter III on "Criteria for the Selection of Units of Work" merits consideration.

MINOR, Ruby, "Making a Course of Study," *Elementary School Journal* (October, 1920), pp. 381-387.

National Society for the Study of Education, *Twenty-sixth Yearbook,* Part I (Public School Publishing Company, 1927), pp. 194-203, 151-162.

Research Bulletin of the National Education Association, Vol. III, No. 4 and No. 5 (National Education Association, 1925). Criteria for special subject-matter fields as well as general course of study construction will be found in this publication.

RUGG, Harold, and SHUMAKER, Ann, *The Child-Centered School* (World Book Co., 1928). This volume will be especially valuable for those interested in activity curricula.

SMITH, Fred C., *Curriculum Problems in Industrial Education* (Harvard University Press, 1930). This study is particularly valuable for those working in vocational and industrial fields, but can be used profitably as a general reference.

STRATEMEYER, Florence, *The Effective Use of Curriculum Materials* (Bureau of Publications, Teachers College, Columbia, 1931).

STRATEMEYER, Florence, and BRUNER, H. R., *Rating Elementary School Courses of Study* (Bureau of Publications, Teachers College, Columbia University, 1926). An important source of criteria for general course of study construction and for the organization of materials in the various subject-matter fields of the elementary school.

THORNDIKE, E. L., "Curriculum Research," *School and Society,* Vol. XXVIII (November 10, 1928), pp. 569-576.

WADDELL, C. W., SEEDS, Corinne, and WHITE, Natalie, *Major Units in the Social Studies* (The John Day Company, 1932). An excellent source of criteria for those interested in formulating materials for the activity school.

WELLS, M. E., *A Project Curriculum* (J. B. Lippincott Co., 1921). Can be read with profit by those interested in the activity school.

CHAPTER XVII

ADMINISTRATION OF COURSE OF STUDY CONSTRUCTION

I. INTRODUCTION

In many school systems, both large and small, the problems pertaining to course of study construction are administrative, in part at least. Unless there is stimulation, direction, and evaluation on the part of the administrative and supervisory officers, the work accomplished is likely to be both haphazard and ill-advised. This concluding chapter should serve to indicate the essential relationship between the administrative and supervising officers and the classroom teacher in the successful accomplishment of the task. Building a course of study is a community program; it is not the responsibility of any particular group.

It is true that these relationships have been mentioned in previous chapters, but the emphasis, so far, has been upon the teacher rather than upon administrative or supervisory phases of the program. While many teachers may be compelled to introduce and develop their own techniques in a particular system, it is important that these relationships be understood so that teachers can adjust themselves in systems which have highly-developed administrative programs.

II. ORGANIZING THE SCHOOL FOR COURSE OF STUDY CONSTRUCTION

The establishment of a curriculum revision program necessitates the inclusion of representatives from every division of the educational staff. This will be apparent as soon as the reader considers that responsibility must be assumed for the initiation of the work, planning its scope, guiding and directing its development, evaluating the results, and instituting as well as modifying the new organization of activities, procedures, and materials in the system.

A. Superintendent of schools. The initiation of the program is the responsibility of the superintendent. It is he who must provide for the necessary financial support through the board of education and who must present this phase of activity to the community so that continued support will be forthcoming. In developing a policy to govern this revision, he must train his immediate staff and ultimately the entire teaching corps so that they can intelligently participate. Much of this work can be specifically allocated to associate or assistant superintendents or to the director of curriculum and research, but no subordinate can be permitted to assume all of the responsibility entailed in the multifarious duties of course of study construction.

B. The expert in curriculum construction. This official may have the title of Associate Superintendent or Director of Curriculum Research. In any case, he is closely associated with the superintendent in formulating a policy and is individually responsible in the system for the maintenance of a program which will harmonize with the principles agreed upon as fundamental. He is constantly in contact with the personnel in all units of the system; directs all agencies and committees in their work; formulates the educational program needed to make every project a success; advises with every committee appointed and provides it with all available research bearing on the problem; passes on all research that will be organized in connection with the work; and devises procedures for evaluating results attained through the experimental period of trying out the new course of study. This work brings him constantly into contact with the superintendent's office, assistant superintendents who have charge of various units of the school system, pupils, supervisors, heads of departments, and classroom teachers. No revision can be carried on at one level that will not affect all preceding and succeeding units—any revision of a particular course at one level will affect all other courses in the same subject-matter field and often in related fields. Problems of articulation and integration will have to be handled through the office of the curriculum expert.

C. Principals. Since principals have both administrative and supervisory duties in their buildings, they are intimately related to a number of phases of course of study revision. In the first place, every principal should, as a member of committees or individually, study the latest research and investigations in one subject-matter field during each school year. In this way he becomes an authority to whom criticisms and complaints can be forwarded. He is familiar with the course of study in use in the system and in his building and is in a position to evaluate demands from the corps for revision. When a program of revision has been instituted, principals should be ready to serve on the committee or to be attached to a committee temporarily in an advisory capacity.

There are numerous opportunities for principals to render valuable service through coöperation with, rather than participation in, the program. In the first place, it is often necessary for them to make adjustments so that their best teachers can be released for committee duty. Second, after the tentative course of study has been developed, it is necessary for the principals to reorganize the work in their schools so that the material can be adequately tested. In the third place, many research projects will be instituted throughout the system, and it is important that the administrative heads of the schools be informed and ready to coöperate with this essential unit.

D. Supervisors, E. C. A. directors, heads of departments. These officers, whose duties are partially administrative and supervisory, must be represented on the committee and participate both in the development of objectives and the determination of learning activities, methods and tests. They assist in directing the try-out of the tentative course and in the evaluation of the results. Such changes as are necessary in the tentative program are made under their direction and the installation of the final course is consummated with their advice and guidance. Naturally, they coöperate with the director of curriculum research and the principals in the installation of the courses.

The research instituted in a system is usually directed by one of these groups. The allocation of this work to schools and classes depends upon their active interest and coöperation. Those who are not participating in the work of the committee can be called in at any time for advice and assistance.

E. The classroom teachers. Since the organization and revision of courses of study is for the purpose of improving teaching in the system and stimulating professional activity of all the teachers, it is essential that as many as possible of the corps be included in the program. The following opportunities for service are present in every system engaged in this work:

1. Service on committees charged with the responsibility of studying and revising courses of study. Only a few can be selected for active membership, but the ramifications of the program can be made to include practically every teacher and to affect the work in every classroom.

2. Develop and carry on research studies which are needed by the committee. Many of these will be extensive enough to include a large number of teachers.

3. As units are developed or the tentative course is organized, there is need for every one to use the new course, criticize it, and prepare reports for the consideration of the committee.

The following excerpts from tentative courses in the Lakewood schools and the Kansas City, Missouri, schools illustrate the type of definite provisions which are being made to secure teacher reaction to provisionary objectives and learning experiences.

CRITICISM NOTES BY THE TEACHER

In order that curriculum building may be coöperative, every teacher taking part, this preliminary or tentative course is issued. Criticisms, additions, and eliminations are invited. As this course is tried out during the school year 1932-1933, teachers are urged to coöperate in the following ways and thus contribute to the building of the course:

1. On the blank side of each page in this course teacher reactions should be made to every division of each unit. Thus, criticisms will be written just opposite the part of the course to which they refer.
2. Many of these tentative units are "thin" or weak in many parts. Therefore, some most valuable contributions can be made in the following ways:
   a. Check time allotment
   b. Improve objectives
   c. Indicate better organization of the elements of the unit
   d. Check approaches used. Add others

e. Check activities used and found to be profitable. Indicate those not so valuable; add others

f. Revise outcomes. Show those actually achieved

g. All errors in tests should be recorded. Work out tests to measure other outcomes.[1]

INTRODUCTION

These units in general science have been outlined with two ends in view: (1) to be of service to classroom teachers, and (2) to provide a frame-work for the building of a modern course of study. It is felt by the committee that application in the classroom and the creative work of the classroom teacher will contribute suggestions which will result in a piece of work worthy to be put in printed form.

With these thoughts in mind, the committee asks that teachers give this outline a thorough trial and assist in its improvement.

Blank pages throughout the bulletin may be used for comments, suggestions, recommendations, etc. Some of the lines along which contributions can be made are as follows:

1. Scope and content
   Do the units cover the field?
   Does each particular unit cover its particular field?
   What changes, eliminations, or additions are desirable?
2. Organization
   Comment on the organization as a whole; on that of each particular unit.
   What phases are most helpful?
   What parts can be eliminated?
   What additions are suggested?
3. Reference material and enrichment reading
   Note those that are especially helpful.
   Add others that are valuable.
4. Time allotments
   Note changes deemed advisable as a result of actual trial in the classroom.[2]

4. Teachers formulate different methods and procedures in the same subject-matter field. Those who rendered good service through introducing innovations in preparing materials, methods of instruction, or testing can be called into a conference of the committee in an advisory capacity in order that their advice can be secured or their results studied and checked.

5. All teachers will have to coöperate in the installation of both the tentative and final course of study. This involves careful study

[1] *General Science, A Tentative Course of Study for Junior High Schools* (Lakewood, Ohio, Public Schools, 1932), pp. 4-5.

[2] *General Science for High School* (Kansas City Public Schools, Kansas City, Missouri, 1930), p. 1.

and evaluation, prompt reports, and regular attendance at departmental and group meetings.

III. PROMOTING COURSE OF STUDY CONSTRUCTION

In order that an intelligent decision can be made concerning
the desirability and advisability of course of study revision, it
is important that some organization in the school system devote
its entire time to the study of curricular problems in particular
subject-matter fields. This can be accomplished by councils of
teachers in that field or groups of principals and administrative
officers who take up the intensive study of a particular subject-
matter field for the year. The latter plan can be developed only
in systems where a large number of administrators makes it
possible to organize a sufficient number of such committees.

Such committees as those mentioned serve as a balance to a
program which usually arises out of the discontent and criticism
of the teaching corps. A complaint representing a part of the
teaching corps can be forwarded to such a professional committee for investigation and recommendations. If the group
which has been studying the research in this field believes that
a revision of the old course or the construction of a new course
is justifiable, then the director of research and curriculum who
is not a subject-matter specialist can proceed to appoint a committee to undertake the actual work. The curriculum specialist
can thus develop a smooth-working organization, which is always striving for the realization, in a conservative fashion, of
progressive principles of living. Harmony is the essence of this
program and is secured because every one has a voice, while
no small group is permitted to steer a department off on a
tangent.

It is only necessary to read again the discussion of the programs presented in Chapter V to appreciate both the prominent
place given to classroom teachers in course of study construction and the reasons for that prominence. The work is necessarily both stimulating and professional in character if the
administration of the system is carefully integrated into the
movement.

IV. ORGANIZING THE PROGRAM OF STUDIES

The number and character of curricula offered will be determined by the community, college-entrance requirements, vocational and social needs of the pupils, and the State. All these factors are important in shaping the program of studies. Another way of stating this fact is to say that life goals—health, worthy home membership, worthy use of leisure time, etc.— determine the general outline of the program and the extent to which opportunities shall be offered for the realization of these aims in a particular school system will depend upon the above-mentioned factors.

Surveys have indicated that in the United States high schools exist which present only a college-entrance curriculum, when less than 5 per cent of their graduates ever enter institutions of higher education. The program of studies in such cases is determined largely by State accreditation requirements, and the needs of the community and the students are overlooked so that the school can be placed on the accredited list.

No school system can assume that all its graduates will remain in the community. However, if a survey indicates that a considerable percentage of graduates and students who leave school before graduation are entering activities such as farming, office-work, ship-building, or repair plants, it is evident that curricula are needed which will offer training toward those vocational fields. Such curricula will demand the development of course materials not offered in the college-preparatory curriculum or necessitate the revision of content in particular courses in order that they can contribute to the objectives of these new curricula.

A curriculum is established in a school to realize life goals, and they are usually stated in terms of vocational activities. The student is planning, with the assistance of the guidance department of the school, to be a lawyer, doctor, farmer, engineer, machinist, beauty-parlor expert, or homemaker. The curricular organization of the school enables pupils with similar tastes and interests to achieve the same goals.

The extracurricular program is organized to cut across curricula and permit students with varying vocational interests to attain leisure, vocational, and health goals that are not included in the regular curricular offering.

V. LACK OF UNIFORMITY IN CURRICULA

One might expect to find divergencies in the development of curricula in different cities and States, since consideration must be given to different communities, different clientele, different legislative requirements in various States, different forms of higher education, etc. A careful study of the present situation is, nevertheless, astounding as regards both the number of curricula and the titles given to these different groupings of subject-matter.

Good and Good [3] made a survey in 1927 to determine the lack of uniformity in the selection of titles of the various curricula offered in the schools. They found a total of one hundred and thirty curricula in the schools studied. However, as they admit, many of these curricula are similar in everything but name. For example, an examination of home-economics curricula indicates the following among the titles used: college-entrance home economics, dietetics, domestic arts, general home economics, girls' vocational home economics, home training, household arts, industrial home economics (girls'), and vocational home economics. One common title could have been used in all cases. Consequently, a number of educators have raised the question of the desirability of greater uniformity and standardization in curricula as a means of simplifying language and facilitating the transfer of students from one section of the country to another.

Another study [4] in which one of these investigators partici-

---

[3] C. V. Good and R. E. Good, "Titles of Curriculums Offered or Suggested in Secondary Schools," *School Review,* Vol. XXXV (1927), pp. 503-509.

[4] Carter V. Good and Edward D. Roberts, "Curriculum Titles and Curriculum Constants in Senior High Schools," *School Review,* Vol. XXXVI (November, 1928), pp. 679-684.

pated reports an even more astounding divergence of terminology in curricular organization. Sixty-five senior high schools, located in cities of more than 30,000 population and representative of all sections of the United States, offer a total of 466 curricula which have been grouped by the authors under 184 different titles. In order that the lack of uniformity in the same curriculum fields can be noted, the following table is reproduced:

FREQUENCY OF CURRICULUM GROUPS AND NUMBER OF DIFFERENT
CURRICULUM TITLES IN EACH GROUP [5]

Curriculum Group	Total Number of Curriculums	Total Number of Titles
Academic and college preparatory......	91	45
Art and fine arts....................	16	6
Commercial	110	45
English	6	3
Foreign language	11	6
General and miscellaneous	41	4
Home economics, household arts, and girls' vocational	45	13
Manual, industrial, and agricultural arts and boys' vocational and technical...	83	38
Mathematics	2	1
Music	7	2
Physical education	1	1
Science	26	8
Social studies	4	3
Teacher training	14	9
Total	466	184

This study presents significant data concerning the content of the various curricula offered in the various fields. Using the same headings for curriculum groups as in Table I, the authors proceeded to tabulate the required courses in each curriculum for each year of the senior high school. This material is so valuable that a compilation of these data is reproduced:

[5] *Ibid.*, p. 681.

SUBJECTS REQUIRED OR RECOMMENDED IN 466 SENIOR HIGH-SCHOOL CURRICULA IN SIXTY-FIVE SCHOOL SYSTEMS [6]

Division of Subject-Matter	Academic and College Preparatory	Art and Fine Arts	Commercial	English	Foreign Language	General and Miscellaneous	Home Economics, Household Arts, and Girls' Vocational	Manual, Industrial, and Agricultural Arts and Boys' Vocational and Technical	Mathematics	Music	Physical Education *	Science	Social Studies	Teacher training	Number of times subject appears in all curriculums
Grade IX															
Art	8	3	0	0	0	6	5	8	0	0	:	2	0	1	33
Commercial subjects	9	0	56	0	0	0	1	0	0	0	:	0	0	0	66
Education	0	0	0	0	0	0	0	0	0	0	:	0	0	0	0
English	64	8	69	3	9	32	30	48	1	3	:	16	2	7	292
Foreign language	53	2	9	0	8	4	1	7	0	1	:	8	1	5	99
Guidance	5	2	4	0	1	1	1	1	1	0	:	2	0	0	18
Health	42	7	49	3	5	20	20	29	1	2	:	11	0	4	193
Home economics	4	2	9	1	1	4	27	0	1	0	:	2	0	1	52

* Curriculum is not offered before Grade X.

Industrial arts	4	1	7	1	1	2	0	37	1	0	...	2	0	1	57
Mathematics	58	2	18	3	9	24	18	39	1	2	...	15	2	6	197
Music	9	2	5	1	1	6	1	3	0	2	...	0	0	1	31
Science	30	3	41	2	1	17	20	24	0	0	...	10	0	5	153
Social studies	38	6	40	2	3	13	13	21	1	1	...	7	2	5	152

Grade X

Art	6	10	5	0	0	3	9	10	0	0	0	2	0	1	46
Commercial subjects	1	0	117	1	0	0	0	1	0	0	0	0	0	0	120
Education	0	0	0	0	0	0	0	0	0	0	0	0	0	0	0
English	91	16	119	6	11	41	45	83	2	7	1	26	4	14	466
Foreign language	98	5	7	3	12	7	3	10	1	4	1	14	2	7	174
Guidance	7	3	3	2	3	0	1	1	1	0	0	1	0	1	23
Health	53	10	71	3	6	25	26	40	1	1	1	18	1	7	263
Home economics	2	0	7	0	0	2	42	0	0	0	0	2	0	0	55
Industrial arts	4	0	3	1	0	2	0	68	0	0	0	2	0	2	82
Mathematics	86	6	19	1	8	26	16	67	2	2	1	24	4	14	276
Music	11	4	10	1	1	4	5	6	0	7	0	2	0	2	53
Science	19	6	13	3	2	10	18	21	2	1	1	16	1	6	119
Social studies	29	6	79	3	2	20	14	35	1	3	0	4	4	9	209

Grade XI

Art	2	10	3	0	0	4	7	6	0	0	0	1	0	6	39
Commercial subjects	1	1	102	0	0	1	0	1	0	0	0	0	0	0	106
Education	0	0	0	0	0	0	0	0	0	0	0	0	0	4	4
English	91	14	119	6	11	41	41	74	2	5	1	26	4	12	447
Foreign language	91	4	5	0	11	6	2	8	0	2	1	12	1	5	148
Guidance	7	3	3	1	2	0	1	1	1	0	0	1	0	1	21
Health	43	8	60	2	5	22	19	27	1	1	1	14	1	6	210

SUBJECTS REQUIRED OR RECOMMENDED IN 466 SENIOR HIGH-SCHOOL CURRICULA IN SIXTY-FIVE SCHOOL SYSTEMS—*Continued*

Division of Subject-Matter	Academic and College Preparatory	Art and Fine Arts	Commercial	English	Foreign Language	General and Miscellaneous	Home Economics, Household Arts, and Girls' Vocational	Manual, Industrial, and Agricultural Arts and Boys' Vocational and Technical	Mathematics	Music	Physical Education *	Science	Social Studies	Teacher training	Number of times subject appears in all curriculums
Home economics	3	1	6	0	0	1	38	0	0	2	0	2	0	1	54
Industrial arts	2	1	1	1	0	3	0	61	0	0	0	0	0	0	69
Mathematics	49	0	8	3	7	3	5	36	2	0	0	16	1	3	133
Music	9	3	4	1	1	4	2	1	0	6	0	2	0	2	35
Science	35	2	21	0	1	14	18	43	1	3	1	21	0	9	169
Social studies	50	9	94	4	2	27	24	39	1	4	1	8	4	14	281
Grade XII															
Art	0	9	0	0	1	7	4	0	0	0	0	0	0	1	22
Commercial	1	0	95	0	0	4	1	0	0	0	0	0	0	0	101

														Total
Education	0	0	0	0	0	0	0	0	0	0	0	0	0	6	6
English	83	12	88	6	8	36	34	57	1	6	1	22	3	14	371
Foreign language	66	2	2	0	6	3	2	5	0	1	0	2	0	3	92
Guidance	7	3	5	0	1	0	1	1	1	0	0	1	0	4	24
Health	43	7	39	2	3	17	18	21	1	1	1	11	0	5	169
Home economics	0	0	1	0	0	0	30	0	1	0	1	0	0	0	32
Industrial arts	1	2	0	0	0	2	0	50	0	0	0	0	0	1	56
Mathematics	43	0	9	0	0	2	1	20	0	0	0	0	0	6	91
Music	10	4	4	1	1	4	3	1	1	6	0	3	0	5	42
Science	35	2	4	3	0	8	13	38	1	1	1	20	2	8	136
Social studies	74	14	94	5	9	28	39	65	2	7	1	15	4	14	371
Number of curriculums	92	16	119	6	11	41	45	83	2	7	1	26	4	14	466†

† Of the 466 curriculums, 292 are first offered in Grade IX, while the remaining curriculums, with few exceptions, are first offered in Grade X.

The tendencies indicated in this study are:

1. Most frequently required subjects in all curricula: English, foreign language, health, mathematics, science, and social studies.

2. As pupils make progress through all curricula they encounter less emphasis on English, foreign language, health, and mathematics; continued emphasis on science; and increasing emphasis on social studies.

3. Extensive variations between curricula in different fields can be noted by referring to the table.

The constants or core curriculum materials which appear in this study are being questioned more and more by American educators. Since there is little scientific evidence bearing on this problem, administrators are inclined to permit traditions to dominate and continue to build curricula to meet diverse vocational goals with the same basic core materials.

Siebold[7] has attacked this acceptance of tradition and has attempted to show that the Seven Cardinal Principles cannot be realized through the inclusion of present core materials. His method is based on opinion and is entirely subjective. Nevertheless, his challenge deserves the consideration of persons whose responsibility is building constants for the realization of curricular objectives. He lists as the basic subject-matter fields, English, music, physical education, homemaking, art, history, science, mathematics, and languages. A direct comparison of his core materials with those found in the larger high schools by Good and Roberts shows little correlation:

Siebold's List	*Good and Roberts' List*
1. English	1. English
2. Music	2. Foreign language
3. Physical education	3. Health
4. Homemaking	4. Mathematics
5. Art	5. Science
6. History	6. Social studies
7. Science	
8. Mathematics	
9. Languages	

[7] Richard Siebold, "A New Deal for the Curriculum," *Junior-Senior High School Clearing House*, Vol. IX (Oct., 1934), pp. 68-71.

Admitting the subjective development of Siebold's list, how many educators and parents have revolted against cutting the school program during the depression according to the Good and Roberts' findings rather than the list submitted by Siebold? Further expressions of discontent will produce research in the public schools to test the two types of core materials. However, little can be accomplished until a more enlightened set of college entrance requirements has been proposed and generally accepted.

The following quotation from Siebold expresses an ever-increasing sentiment concerning this problem:

> ... the work of the committee which set up the Seven Cardinal Principles of secondary education was incidental to an effort by the National Education Association to articulate the high school and the college. This committee urged the modification of college entrance requirements in order that the secondary school might adapt its work to the varying needs of its pupils in meeting the requirements of democracy, without closing to them the possibility of continued education in higher institutions. To this end, the committee took the position that the satisfactory completion of any well-planned high-school curriculum should be accepted as preparation for college. It is a sad commentary upon our educational leadership that we have made so little progress in the direction so wisely recommended twenty-three years ago.
>
> The world's troubles of recent years indicate the need for education in worthy social behavior. It seems obvious that education in the past has not accomplished that end. Let us revise the curriculum in the direction of preparing our people not preëminently for the so-called "practical" ability of making a living, but for what we now recognize as the more important and more practical ability of living with one another and at the same time achieving a fuller measure of social justice. The above examination contains some implications for such revision which lend weight to an important truth uttered by Joy Elmer Morgan recently when he said that the most important subjects in the high-school curriculum are those which have been added last, because they have been added to meet to-day's needs and demands.[8]

These facts are challenges to administrators and teachers. Unless they adopt a social philosophy, unless they can see in

[8] *Ibid.*, p. 71.

the program of studies something more than the traditional core of materials, unless far-reaching changes are effected in the near future, the American people are likely to become the impoverished victims of destiny rather than riding with their hands on the throttles of the various aspects of social and industrial development. Newlon makes the following pertinent comment:

The next few years will probably determine whether the men who now hold positions of leadership and authority in school administration can rise to the social responsibilities imposed on them by the present critical period. The alternatives are educational stagnation or indescribable confusion, or the usurpation of the direction of education by fascists who will know exactly what they want and who will violate every cherished democratic tradition.[9]

VI. FORMULATING CURRICULA

The most important problem after a particular curriculum has been accepted and prescribed for a school is that of determining its basic content and the elective fields. Even though administrative curricula are not outlined for the guidance of the teachers and students, this problem is not minimized in the least, since some one must advise with every pupil concerning his curriculum. If *administrative* curricula are not available, the problem of organizing *individual* curricula becomes more difficult and, if anything, more important.

The administrator must accept the responsibility for directing this phase of the program although teachers should coöperate and not merely follow directions. In the organization of the course of study, scientific techniques can be introduced, but in the development of the program of studies and the included curricula, a thorough knowledge and understanding of philosophy, educational principles, evolution of American culture, development of present industrial, economic, and social problems are essential. Since these are all related to politics and basic problems of citizenship, careful attention must be centered on a

[9] J. H. Newlon, "The Bearing of Administrative Theory and Practice on Social Education," *Junior-Senior High School Clearing House,* Vol. IX (Sept., 1934), p. 9.

school which is proposing to function for all students with varying capacities and life goals.

The present tendency is to have definitely organized curricula for the guidance of teachers and pupils or to have no

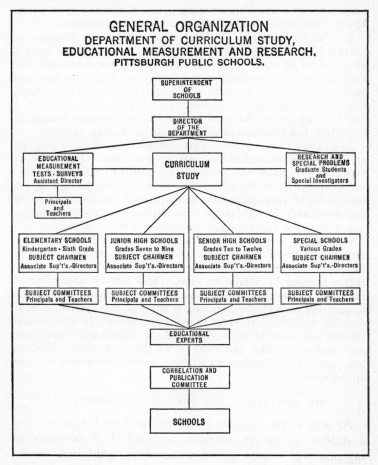

curricula—merely prescribing constants for graduation—and placing upon the teachers, guidance officers, extracurricular directors, and others the responsibility of developing adequate individual curricula. In case definite administrative curricula are developed in the school, they conform to one of the following types:

1. *Single curriculum.* This is used in the very small high school where facilities permit only the development of one grouping of subject-matter fields. This grouping is determined to a great extent by the State department or college-entrance requirements.

2. *Multiple curricula.* The first illustration in the introductory chapter is of this type. Several curricula are offered, and each is standardized as far as constants and electives are concerned. The student selects a curriculum at the beginning of his first year and follows the outlined program throughout his stay in the school, unless he changes his curriculum. It should be noted that such a change often retards the pupil by one semester or more because of the established constants in each year of the various curricula.

3. *Constants and variables.* This system of organizing a program of studies is illustrated in the introductory chapter also. A list of constants is included which must be completed by all students who are graduated from the school. Provision is made through an extensive list of variables for the completion of curricula interesting and worthwhile to each pupil. Free electives are also included so that avocational and extraclass interests can be developed.

4. *Multiple curricula with constants, variables, and electives.* This type of organization does away with the complete segregation of the pupils into curricula too early in their school careers and permits a transfer of interest to another field without undue loss of time and inconvenient readjustments. The various avenues are mapped out through the curricula established, but specialization is reserved until the last years of each curriculum. In case certain subjects are required in the first years of a particular curriculum, the possible variables and electives of the later years afford an opportunity to the student transferring to this curriculum to make up the work.

VII. ORGANIZING THE PARTICULAR CURRICULUM

As soon as the program of studies has been determined and a skeleton of various curricula proposed, it is necessary to organize the various subject-matter fields which will be included. Several factors will need to be taken into account by the administration of the school.

1. *Constants required by State law.* If the legislature has passed laws concerning either the subject or topics within the subject-

matter fields, these can be set in at once. No discretionary power is allocated to the administration in these instances. If, on the contrary, the State has decreed that a subject or part of a subject-matter field should not be taught, the work of the administration committee is simplified to that extent.

2. *Constants essential for high-school graduation.* These are often determined by State boards of education or accreditation committees from institutions of higher education and can be set into the curricular program at once.

3. *Constants required for graduation from a particular curriculum.* These are often influenced by State board and accreditation committees also, but the school system has some voice in the determination of these items. The nature of the curriculum will demand certain constants.

4. *Designation of electives which will be open to the student.* The administration will find it necessary to consider such items as, (1) time, (2) teacher supply, (3) physical equipment of the school, and (4) community needs and interests.

5. *The amount of time to be assigned to each subject-matter field has to be determined.* The particular field will have to be measured in terms of the objectives of the curriculum.

6. *Arrangement of courses in the curriculum.* This involves the problems of determining the correct sequence or grade placement in a field of work as well as the correct placement of material in one field in relationship to materials included from other fields.

There is a real scarcity of objective methods of solving many of these problems. The administrative committee will have to weigh values in terms of curricular goals and resort to surveys of community needs and opportunities, current practice and consensus. It is the obligation of the committee to meet the needs of the pupils who will probably enroll in the curriculum. Those subjects which have high value will be included at once, and those which are being included in the program of studies for purposes of enrichment and meeting avocational interests must be given immediate consideration.

The committee should determine upon criteria which will be of value in allocating materials to curricula. The following list was secured by presenting the problem to experts and is suggested to those interested in this work. No doubt others will be presented as the labors of the committee are centered in this field.

1. Each curriculum should be developed in terms of one or more principles which have governed the organization of the program of studies. Its relationship to the principles of education and life goals should be apparent at once.

2. Each curriculum should provide for social and vocational growth. These aims are not antagonistic, but are supplementary to each other.

3. The early years of every curriculum should include opportunities to explore in vocational, social, and educational fields. Recognition must be given to the general social, cultural, recreational, and political needs of the entire school population as well as the highly specialized needs of those with great endowment and ability. This means that elements from all recognized fields of learning can be included, but the usual practice of requiring certain subject-matter fields in their entirety as constants will have to be ignored in the future.

4. Individual differences must be provided for in all curricula through differentiation of work in all courses of study. This is particularly true of the constants which are required in all curricula and for this reason become program-of-study constants.

5. Curriculum prescriptions should provide for high standards of attainment. Those not adapted to the work should be transferred to other curricula or registered in special courses in the curriculum which do not have specialized work. An illustration of the differentiation of curriculum prescriptions was given in an earlier chapter in the discussion of work in commercial education at the South Philadelphia High School for Girls.

6. Provision must be made in every curriculum for meeting individual interests and needs through variables, electives, and extracurricular activities.

VIII. ADMINISTRATION OF CURRICULA

The administration of the curricula in any school system involves four important principles which merit analysis and discussion. These are broad enough to be stated in terms of the program of studies, but they are related to adjustments within one or several curricula of the school.

1. *Graduation.* Two questions are immediately raised as to the present basis of graduating students. What does graduation mean now? What should it mean in any school at any level of the educational program? In answer to the first, it can be pointed out that graduation signifies completion of a certain number of

courses—required and elective—in a particular curriculum. It is granted when the principal or the registrar certifies that fifteen or one hundred and eighty credits have been earned in required and elective courses. Thus, graduation has become a mathematical problem to a large extent rather than indicating the development of an ability or power as a result of organizing a synthesis from the pupil's classroom exposures to facts and philosophies. The only check—other than the more or less inaccurate one of grades acquired—is the number of exposures of a particular variety, independent of achievement. Every one realizes that there are freshmen in every institution who are more adequately educated than some of the students who receive degrees or diplomas as seniors.

In answer to the second question, it is imperative to organize curricula to provide training so that the individual pupil can be educated and realize the goal of the curriculum and at the same time provide training for those who cannot be educated in terms of those goals. These latter can be given a leaving certificate to indicate that they have served the required amount of time and have enjoyed the social and intellectual contacts provided in that phase of the school work.

2. *Extracurricular activities.* The extensive offering in this field in every high school has developed without scientific study or attempts at evaluation and often with little, or untrained supervision. This problem can be ignored no longer. Extracurricular offerings must be studied and evaluated according to the same standards as the materials presented in the classroom. Adequate supervision must guarantee that proposed objectives are realized or the activities must be eliminated or revamped. A conservative estimate is that 50 per cent of these activities would be eliminated if they were forced to attain educational objectives. Probably many of those remaining would be rapidly curricularized. This would mean the development of objectives and student experiences in each field and the allocation of the course of study in the extracurricular field to a required or elective basis in a particular curriculum.

3. *Integration of curricula.* This problem of determining

constants for the school system is particularly important, since students' interests change and necessitate their transfer from curriculum to curriculum. Few experiments have been performed in this field, but it is worthy of serious attention and experimentation in every school system.

4. *Guidance.* The organization of more than one curriculum or the development of constants and variables demands both educational and vocational guidance. Provisions for group guidance and individual counseling in the system is essential if adjustments are to be made. Chance or haphazard guessing or advising does not have a place in a system which is striving for the realization of educational goals.

IX. ADMINISTRATION OF COURSE OF STUDY PRODUCTION

The attention of the administration staff should be centered upon course of study construction throughout all phases of work. Every step in developing the course of study is of paramount importance since failure to complete one phase accurately and adequately not only produces a weak link in the chain of sequential activities but devitalizes every other aspect of the construction and evaluation of the course. In addition to the production committee, many individuals, committees, and teachers must participate in the work before it is accepted for introduction into the classroom. The various steps in the organization of a course of study will be considered from an administrative point of view.

A. Production committees. The scientific character of the work which can be prepared by production committees is illustrated through a study of the actual work of revising courses of study in several cities which have Bureaus of Research and Curriculum Directors.

1. *Baltimore, Maryland*

In 1921 work was started on our present course of study, and the same plan that was started in 1921 has been used in reorganizing the various curricula since that time. In most cases a general meeting of all teachers of a certain subject is called. Generally, one person, either a supervisor or some one connected with the Bureau of Research, is in charge. Each school selects one representative to work with the person who is in charge. In the senior high school this representative is generally a department head, and in the junior high school, where we have no department heads, one teacher is either appointed by the principal or elected by the other teachers of that subject. The committee for revision of a senior high-school subject would have one representative from each senior high school, and probably one or two from the junior high schools. The committee working on the junior high-schools curriculum would have one representative from each junior high school and one or more from the senior high schools. This enables each group to work hand in hand with the other, and in the past it has been found that the overlapping of these two committees has been a great help. Just as the one in charge of the whole revision works with each committee, so each member of the committee works with his group within his own school. Frequently, experts on the subject are brought in to stir up enthusiasm on the part of the teachers and committee members, and as often as possible the superintendent and assistant superintendents meet with the various committees. Both the expert's opinion, that is gotten from leaders in the field, and the contribution of the individual faculty members in the various schools, are most beneficial. The general tendency, however, is to build up the course of study through the teachers rather than the experts, although the opinions of both are used. In all cases, those in charge try to make use of all scientific investigations that have been made in the field, and no amount of effort or time is spared to make results complete.

In the past this work has generally been carried on under the leadership of one of the supervisors or department heads, but at present we are revising our English Course of Study, and Dr. Angela Broening, recently appointed as Research Assistant, has been given full charge of this work.[10]

2. Oakland, California

In our administrative organization, the final authority on course of study problems is the Superintendent's Council. By this council course of study committees are appointed and the finished courses approved. In the field of secondary education, the junior and senior high-school principals have a conference which recommends to the Superintendent's Council. Committees of secondary-school principals are organized in each subject field. To each of these committees, also, is added the subject supervisor, two outstanding class-room

[10] Report made to the author by Mr. G. C. Taylor, assistant superintendent of the Baltimore schools.

teachers, and the director of research and the assistant superintendent in charge of secondary schools as ex-officio members. The formulation of duties of these committees and the assignment of problems to them from time to time is made by the director of research, who is also the director of curriculum development.

It is these committees which determine when it is necessary for course of study committees to be appointed in any given field. At the suggestion of the director of research and the supervisor, the personnel of committees is proposed, sometimes through the principals' committee, but more often directly from the office of the director of research to the Superintendent's Council.

After the course of study committees have been appointed, they work under the immediate supervision of the subject supervisor if such supervisor is willing and able to undertake such supervision; otherwise they work directly under the supervision of the director of research, who makes editorial suggestions, approves outlines, provides clerical assistance, conducts investigations, and assembles printed material for the guidance of the committee.

After the course is prepared, it is submitted to the Committee on Improvement of Instruction in that field for suggestions and final approval, going through the usual channels of recommendation to the Principals' Conference and the Superintendent's Council. Having been approved by the Superintendent's Council, it is referred back to the office of the director of research for final editing, publishing, and distribution.

The new course is then presented to the teachers of the subject at a required meeting, and is also presented to the Principals' Conference by the supervisor or the chairman of the committee which wrote it, usually the latter.

If the work of the committee has been completed, the course of study committee is discharged until the Committee on Improvement of Instruction feels that another revision should be made. However, in actual practice, the course of study committees usually find that in addition to preparing the course, teachers are desirous to have them prepare unit tests to accompany the course and to assemble lists of teaching aids, such as slides, reference books, etc., as such material becomes available. The course of study committee, therefore, frequently continues for years.

The usual life of a course of study is four years, although the printed course usually represents the result of our experimentation and thinking in the field at the date of publication and becomes the point of departure for further experimentation rather than a definite procedure to be followed.

In the *Handbook for Course of Study Committees,* we define the course of study as a "handbook for the teacher." Page 21 in the Handbook shows our check sheet for progress of courses of study through the committees.

I might state that the one defect of this plan is the lack of articulation between the elementary- and the secondary-school course of study committees, although this is not serious since in several instances the secondary-school supervisor also works in the elementary schools and knows the program there. We also have on our Superintendent's Council both the assistant superintendent in charge of elementary schools and the assistant superintendent in charge of secondary schools. We make arrangements for joint meetings of the principals' committees from both elementary and secondary schools in any given subject field whenever questions or problems of articulation arise.[11]

3. Cleveland, Ohio

Cleveland sets up three types of curriculum committees to deal with course of study problems in junior and senior high schools. In the first type, the assistant superintendent for junior high schools appoints a committee made up of principals, the director of research, and himself. The general curriculum outline is determined in this committee, and special committees controlled from it. Special committees (committees of the second type) are set up under the direction of the Bureau of Research to deal with specific subjects, such as social studies, science, mathematics, and English.

The third type of committee is the special coördinating committee. Such committees are appointed from time to time to arrange continuous sequences throughout the six years. The last such committee was in the field of science. The assistant superintendents for both the junior and senior high schools had committees on science going at the same time. One member of each subject-matter committee, general science, biology, chemistry, and physics, made up the committee which arranged the continuous sequence. Not all courses of study are made in this way. Some of the directors made their own and administered them. However, the tendency is in the other direction and growing stronger.

The evidence from tests and measurements tends to confirm the opinion that the general practitioner as represented by the assistant superintendent, the director of research and his assistant, the principal, the head of the department, and the teacher, working together, are generally more effective than the directing supervisor-teacher combination in securing high-grade results. However, in two or

[11] Dr. Richard E. Rutledge, formerly Director of Research and Auxiliary Agencies, prepared this excellent statement.

three cases where the directing supervisors work well in the circle of general practitioners results are apparently very good.

Apparently, all the factors which may conceivably belong in any job of curriculum revision have to be there in order to produce a highly satisfactory result. For example, the Bureau of Research, with a committee of teachers, may produce a course of study, get it into operation, and prove by tests and measurements that it is a fine course of study, but nobody believes it unless everybody has been in on it. The director of a special subject may, in coöperation with a few of his most gifted teachers, produce a course which they like and believe in, but it seldom measures up when the Bureau of Research tests the results. Courses gotten up by principals and teachers are usually conservative and results ordinary when checked by tests. Only those courses in which every one has a hand seem to prosper.[12]

4. *Chicago, Illinois*

The policy of a Bureau of Curriculum of the Chicago Public Schools in the matter of organizing committees for curriculum revision and methods of procedure is that of providing for a fair representation of district superintendents, principals, and teachers on our subject committees. Inasmuch as the financial situation in the Chicago public schools will not admit of the practice of releasing teachers wholesale for serving on the various committees, we are rather largely restricted when it comes to the matter of asking teachers to serve in this capacity. However, the practice is rather generally followed by the principals of referring many matters pertaining to the revision of our courses of study to the teachers in their schools. In this way we feel that the teachers are having a great deal to say regarding the construction and organization of our courses of study.

Although it may seem that working through committees is a very slow process, which it is, the situation is such in Chicago that, in our opinion, we will make much more satisfactory progress by working through the district superintendents, principals, and teachers, as I have just outlined above.

In the final analysis, the success of courses of study is determined almost entirely by the extent to which they are used in the classroom. We feel that unless there is a rather wide participation in curriculum work by teachers and principals they will not be very keen about using the materials that supervisors and directors work

[12] Dr. William L. Connor, Chief of the Bureau of Educational Research of the Cleveland schools, prepared this fine summarization of the work, which is organized under the direction of his bureau.

out. We have been following this plan for the last two years, and we believe that our underlying philosophy is sound.

The size of our committees ranges from a few (five or six) to as many as twelve or fifteen. It is our experience that a good deal of time is wasted in pointless discussions, but for reasons stated above, we are quite certain that we must expect this and be more or less tolerant of it in order that we may accomplish the bigger things that we have in mind. The willingness of many teachers to give a great deal of their time outside of regular school hours to this kind of work is one of the most encouraging features of our curriculum work in Chicago. Of course we make it a point to give due recognition to every one who participates in these curriculum activities. This all means that there is a very large number of teachers who are intensely interested in teaching and believe the work to be significant.[13]

5. *Detroit, Michigan*

Our high-school curricula are under constant revision. We do not plan any drastic changes in the near future.

Revision or the construction of a new course is usually accomplished through the guidance of a general steering committee, consisting of the assistant superintendent, one or more secondary-school principals, the supervisor of the subject concerned and a member of the department of curriculum research. General policies are outlined by this group.

Our purpose in having classroom teachers work on the course is (1) to get the benefit of the experiences and points of view of those in direct contact with the students in order to get a more usable course, (2) to develop teacher initiative as well as an understanding of the purposes and problems involved in building a course, and (3) to insure the existence of a group possessing the philosophy guiding the work, as well as skill in its interpretation.

Our purpose in having teachers, principals, and supervisory officers coöperate in the making of a course of study is to make for balance in the course, since (1) supervisors are experts in the knowledge of the content of their field and of the best teaching methods known, (2) principals are experts in the problems involved in administering the course, and (3) teachers are experts in the translation and adaptation of purpose, theories, and methods into practical forms suitable to their particular classroom situations.

Our general procedure in organizing the work of the various

[13] Dr. Eston V. Tubbs, Director of Curriculum in the schools of Chicago, Illinois, submitted this summary of the work in course of study construction in Chicago.

committees is (1) to submit an outline to the sub-committees, (2) the sub-committees work on the various units of the course, (3) the steering committee then reviews the various units and offers suggestions for their improvement and articulation, and (4) after the final revision the special subject supervisor edits the entire material and prepares it for publication. They are first tried out by a few teachers in mimeographed form, next they are revised and tried out by a larger number of teachers in multigraphed form, then finally they are printed and prepared for city-wide distribution.[14]

6. *Lakewood, Ohio*

The curriculum of the Lakewood Schools is an outgrowth of the traditional American philosophy of education. At periodic intervals it has undergone change and modification largely through the addition or subtraction of some subject. These changes have occurred pretty generally as a result of one of the following influences:

1. The initiative and vision of supervisory officers or individuals within a given department in the local school system.
2. A national movement toward the improvement of teaching within a given field, such an incentive as that offered by the National Council of English teachers.
3. Advance in the knowledge of the science of education gained by teachers through professional study and reading.
4. Activity of community minority or majority groups centered about special interests which have resulted in state or local legislation requiring the inclusion within the school curriculum of such movements as safety, temperance, fire prevention, the national constitution, bird study, etc.
5. The publication of certain important books or reports of educational organizations devoted to isolated subject-matter fields.
6. The discovery of new facts in science and the application of these facts to life activities.

As in other American public school systems, these changes have made themselves felt in the curriculum slowly.

It is obvious that this method of curriculum modification has resulted in a somewhat unbalanced program of education. It has been concerned with a small segment of the entire program and has been developed intermittently by a small group of persons within the system. Consequently the material developed has not always been used to the best advantage in the actual teaching of children. Be-

[14] Mr. Manley E. Irwin, Assistant Director of Curriculum Research in the Detroit schools, presented the plan of reorganizing and revising courses of study at Detroit.

cause the program of revision has been carried on in isolated segments of the whole field of study, repetition and duplication of work within different divisions of the school and from one department to another has sometimes resulted.

In February, 1930, a permanent and continuing organization for the study of the curriculum was instituted. The entire educational staff has participated in the work. They have helped to formulate the guiding principles of education upon which all units and subjects are based. They have actually tried out in the classroom these units, have written them, helped to install them, have made suggestions for their revision after they have been tried out. They have planned in terms of the entire period of public education instead of planning for one grade or one subject, with the object that no part of the entire program should be isolated from or unrelated to any part and division of the total school educational experience of children.

Each year since 1930 is seeing the publication of some new curriculum materials in many fields. They are developing slowly but surely according to a definite plan, and are modifying definitely our school procedure. It is our belief that the actual school experience of our Lakewood children through the effort and planning of our teachers in this way, is each year more valuable, more closely related to child needs as well as to the changing demands of a changing society.

The entire teaching staff is indebted to those whose names appear as authors of these courses of study. The director of curriculum study, the chairman and members of this committee have given willingly and unselfishly of their time in the carrying on of the investigations and studies which have made this course possible.[15]

7. The steps which are outlined for the guidance of curriculum committees at Baltimore will be helpful in further analyzing the scientific attack being made by school systems in determining necessary data:

a. Procedure for revising the English course of study for the Baltimore secondary schools.

The starred (*) activities were already under way with all teachers of English working with Angela Broening, from 1927 to 1930. Preliminary investigations on the other items listed have been made up by Angela Broening and are being discussed with teachers as the work progresses.

[15] This statement by Julius E. Warren, formerly Superintendent of Schools at Lakewood, Ohio, is taken from the "Foreword" of the tentative courses of study published by the Lakewood schools.

I. Survey of pupil and adult needs in oral and written expression and oral and silent reading.

    A. Research studies, e.g., Johnson's *English Expression*, Public School Publishing Company, 1926.

    B. Courses of study prepared since 1924 (Pendleton's study brought up-to-date).

    C. Investigations conducted by agencies outside public schools, e.g., Koos' nation-wide research in literature (Personnel Department, Washington, D. C.). Job analyses undertaken by specific trades and professions, also by National Council of Education (Dr. Mann).

    D. Textbooks and other instructional equipment based on experimental study of pupil's needs, interests and capacities.

   *E. Baltimore English Teachers' analysis of pupils' needs in English discovered in the entire curricular and extra-curricular activities.

II. Examination of all available instructional materials.

III. Study of experimental research in the teaching of reading, spelling, appreciation, oral and written expression—Stephens, Broening, Coryell, Gates, Horn and Asbaugh, Lyman, etc.

IV. Experimental teaching by Baltimore teachers:
Of units already in the Baltimore course of study.
Of new units prepared by individuals and committees of Baltimore teachers.

Note: These activities were conducted through:

    1. General conferences with all teachers.

    2. Faculty meetings in schools to discuss coördination of English and other departments.

    3. Committee meetings of groups working on specific units.

    4. Demonstration lessons (city-wide and within school buildings) conducted by Dr. Broening and teachers in the department.

    5. Record keeping of units of work noting learning difficulty, pupil reactions to instructional materials and management problems.

Since September 16, 1930

Step I. With the launching on a city-wide scale of the English curriculum research at Dr. Weglein's meeting on October 15, 1930, the above activities will be extended to all teachers of English in junior and senior high schools.

Step II.   Following this meeting, teachers have selected the phase of English of greatest interest to them.

Step III.   Within the selected phase of English, each teacher has chosen the problem which he or she can most conveniently investigate.

Step IV.   Individual and group conferences will be held with the curriculum groups.

Step V.   At one or more of Dr. Taylor's conferences with the Secondary Principals, time may be allowed for discussing the work in progress.

Step VI.   At one meeting of Dr. Weglein's administrative council the work will be presented to the principals.

Step VII.   1930-31 should see the publication of a monograph on "Differentiation in English at Various Grade Levels Experimentally Determined."

Step VIII.   Publication, 1931-1932 of the *English Course of Study for Secondary Schools*. (This will give two terms for testing out in sequence the experimentally determined units.)

8.   The following coöperative project in building a course of study in English in the Denver school system [16] illustrates the contributions of the pupils, teachers, principals, supervisors, administrators, and outside authorities in a scientific attack on this problem. There is no attempt, however, to evaluate either the procedure used by the committees or the objectives, content, methods, or tests of the course. The author has merely summarized the plan presented by the teachers in Denver who were chairmen of the junior and senior high-school committees in order that the reader may appreciate the place of every member of the staff in the undertaking.

I.   *Purpose:* to provide for all grades a unified course in usage, composition and literature allowing pupil interests and immediate needs to dictate the content.

II.   Committee represented the elementary, junior high, and senior high schools in order to prevent overlapping and provide for advancement from grade to grade.

[16] Kate W. Ashley and Mary A. Dodds, *Coöperation in Building English Courses of Study in Denver.* Junior-Senior High School Clearing House, Vol. VI (April, 1932), pp. 488-492.

III. *Procedure:*

A. A small group of teachers were called together to judge the major objectives of the old course of study.

B. An appraisal was made of the content of the old courses by all principals and teachers who were willing to participate. The following questionnaire was used in the appraisal:

In your judgment does the course provide pupils of limited ability with work which:

1. Challenges their best efforts?
2. Is within their ability?
3. Allows sufficient time for mastery of essentials?
4. Is rich in concrete, illustrative material?
5. Is easily adaptable to individual differences?
6. Is of such importance for these pupils that it should be included?

Summaries of the results of the questionnaire were sent to all participating teachers. These were used as the basis for informal discussions later on.

C. A careful study was made of many courses of study, English textbooks and published committee reports by the committee chairman who prepared a list of six general objectives and twelve hundred specific objectives. The specific objectives were so definite that each could be used as the center of a teaching unit.

D. These objectives were then submitted to eight groups of Denver teachers, each group composed of three members representing the elementary, junior high, and senior high schools.

1. Each group criticized the general objectives.
2. Each member of each group rated the specific objectives according to:
   a. Grade placement
   b. Importance
   c. Required of all pupils or should provision be made for individual differences.
3. Six authorities in the field of English in various parts of the country were asked to rate these specifics according to the same plan.
4. Teachers who participated in this phase of the work stated they had had an invaluable experience professionally.

E. The results of the voting of the teachers and outside authorities were tabulated on charts by the chairman of each committee and the foundations of the work in English for each grade in each unit were apparent.

F. All English teachers met in small groups with the director of curriculum for free discussion of the old course of study and the new appraisal sheets. A record of these discussions was kept for reference. The committees considered every question and suggestion which were raised in these meetings.

G. A study of the ratings given to the various objectives indicated the functional centers for oral and written work. Usage requirements were discussed and research in the field studied in order that most important learning activities could be assigned to various levels of work.

H. As sections of the course were organized they were studied by the committees. Further study and research often led to revision of the proposed sections.

I. As soon as a general agreement had been reached on objectives, purposes and plans, Dr. R. L. Lyman of the University of Chicago was called in to work with the committees for a week. At a later date, he was called in for a conference of one day.

J. There were two meetings of the combined committees in which outlines for the elementary, junior high, and senior high were presented and discussed. Principals, teachers, and college professors of English were present at these meetings. The plans were reformulated as a result of these conferences and were then sent to all teachers and principals for their consideration. More than ninety per cent responded and, therefore, the plans were further extended and revised.

K. Mimeographed courses of study were tried out in the fall of 1930. Teachers were asked to note:
   1. Pupil reactions
   2. Effectiveness and adaptability of the course
   3. Faults which might be corrected.

L. In 1931, Dr. S. A. Leonard spent a day in conference with the chairmen. A short joint committee meeting was held also. As a result of these conferences and the reactions of teachers to the points suggested in K, further modifications were made in the courses.

M. 1. Work-books and hand-books were developed to realize objectives of the course of study.
   2. Diagnostic tests were developed by the department of research.

B.   Trying out the course of study. The final test in validating objectives, as well as determining time allotment, sequence of units, modification of content and grade placement is the tryout of the material in the grade and unit of the school system for which it was prepared. Otherwise overlapping and duplication will not be indicated until the students insist that the essence of the new material has been presented in the previous unit or grade of the school system.

This tryout program should conform as nearly as possible with the standards of experimental research. If possible, controlled groups, which have been selected and equated as far as intelligence and knowledge is concerned, should be used. In the smaller systems, this may not be possible, and the teacher will have to note difficulties, duplication of material, etc., and make suggestions for change. Tests can be used effectively in both the controlled and uncontrolled situations. However, care must be exercised in the use of standardized tests since they will not always parallel the objectives of the course.

All teachers of the subject in the system should participate in the tryout of the tentative course. Some provision should be made for the teachers to indicate their criticisms to the administration. Blank pages have been included and found to be effective in attaining results. Teachers should be invited particularly to note critical phases of the course and present reactions. As indicated above, these critical aspects will center in validation of objectives, modifications of content, grade placement, sequence of units, time allotment, etc.

C.   Editing the course of study. This work will be performed by the director of curriculum or under his direction. The same principles hold for this work as for any other type of publication. Sentence structure, punctuation, capitalization, paragraphing, trite words and phrases, and coherence are a few items that must be particularly checked.

The mechanical make-up of the course is of vital importance. The use of the course by the faculty will depend upon its usability and attractiveness. The general organization of the course, which was considered in the last chapter, is of vital significance to the teachers who will use it. In this connection, a check upon the indexing, table of contents, paging, methods of presenting graphs, charts, and photographs will be advisable.

D. Installing the course of study. It is important that the teachers, principals, and supervisors be prepared for the installation of the course. In particular cases, they will be fully prepared for new work, but in other schools extensive preparation must be made. This may mean changes in both personnel and equipment. An indication of the type and amount of equipment needed has been presented by the course-of-study committee, but as soon as the course of study has been accepted it is the obligation of the administrative staff to see that all facilities are available for the successful début of the new course.

E. Supervising the new course of study. Unless the course of study results in improved teaching, the time and money allocated to its construction have been wasted. Since the objectives to be attained are listed in the course of study, it is only fair to the teacher, the student, and the taxpayer, that the actual outcomes of every classroom be compared to these goals. That means that every teacher, head of department, supervisor, curriculum director, and pupil will be a vital factor in the final success of the project. Dr. I. Keith Tyler of the Oakland schools outlines the new program in Oakland as follows:

> As a means of making possible the centering of attention upon instruction and curriculum in the senior high schools in Oakland there were appointed this year vice-principals in charge of instruction in five of the eight schools. In the three remaining schools present members of the staff will undertake the same responsibilities. These vice-principals have no administrative authority, but are given the responsibility for improving instruction and encouraging experimentation.[17]

Inviting the teacher to study the course as a basis for continuous revision usually insures coöperation on the part of the teaching staff. When supervision and teaching can be directed toward constructive goals, valuable results are possible. How-

[17] I. Keith Tyler, *News from the Pacific Coast,* News Bulletin of the Society for the Study of Curriculum, Vol. V., No. 7 (Nov. 28, 1934).

ever, the course of study which has definite objectives and reasonably valid and reliable tests by which achievement in a particular classroom can be measured is a powerful stimulant to the teacher to improve both his technique and results.

F. Selection of textbooks. The selection of textbooks is closely related to the organization of the course of study. A new course of study necessitates the appointment of a committee to analyze textbooks and make recommendations or report the data secured from the study to the director of curriculum or other administrative officer. In some instances, a permanent textbook committee receives the report of the special committee appointed to study the problem in a particular subject-matter field.

Since the selection of a textbook involves an analysis of many books over an extended period of time and the actual tryout of books in the classroom in which the course of study is being used, it is advisable for the administration to have a definite schedule planned for all committees assigned to this work. The following steps are essential in order to insure definite and orderly progress on the part of the committee:

1. Several samples of textbooks for the particular class must be secured from each publishing house and made available to the committee.

2. A set of criteria should be available to the committee or the committee should develop one for the selection of textbooks for the class or grade. The weight given a criterion may change from grade to grade.

In case the committee is faced with the problem of determining criteria, the following items are suggested for inclusion in a score-sheet:

a. Publication
   (1) General
   (2) Training of author
   (3) Educational experience of author
   (4) Author's background
b. Content
   (1) Purpose
   (2) Proportional distribution of subject matter
   (3-6) Illustrations

    (7) Proportional distribution of illustrative material
    (8) Space
    (9) Validity and reliability
    (10) Style or nature
    (11) Organization
    (12) Aids in using the book
c. Mechanical makeup
    (1) Binding and size
    (2) Paper
    (3) Typography
    (4) Quality of illustrations
d. Adaptability [18]

In another book, the same authors present the following suggestive outline:

a. By whom has the book been written? The teacher will have to determine how important this question is, and then evaluate his training and educational experience in elementary, secondary, and collegiate work. This enables the teacher to interpret the material which is presented in the text. Two points will receive particular attention here. The first is the philosophy of the author and the school of educational thought to which he belongs; and the second is the experimental work which he has done in preparation for writing such a book.

b. By whom has the book been published? Many of our book companies have become specialists in certain fields or at least have made outstanding contributions in publishing textbooks in these fields. Men of national reputation have been secured as editors in these fields; and for these reasons the publishing house should receive consideration.

c. How nearly does the content of this particular book make possible the realization of the objectives of the course of study which has been worked out in the school? The objectives of the author may be tabulated, and the content he has included may be summarized by pages. The number of pages devoted to each topic or unit should be listed as the basis for comparison. The number, distribution, and desirability of illustrations may be checked. In a similar manner, the matter of organization, validity, and reliability of the testing material included, and related problems should be given careful thought and objectively checked.

d. Is the general organization of this book such that it will meet the needs of the children of the particular age and grade for

[18] A. C. Roberts and E. M. Draper, *The High School Principal as Administrator* (D. C. Heath and Co., 1927), p. 120.

which it is being considered? In this connection, the size of type used, the quality and number of illustrations presented, the grade of paper selected, the durability of the binding, and the size of the book should be carefully considered.

c. If this book should be selected, would it be adaptable to all of the children of a particular age and grade or suited only to the needs of certain ability levels? This problem is one of great importance to the superintendent and the school directors. Many districts are constantly faced with the financial problem of securing large numbers of supplementary texts in order to meet the needs of the students for whom the text has been adopted.[19]

Score-cards for the evaluation of textbooks have been developed in most of the curriculum centers mentioned in this book, and can be secured upon request.

3. All the textbooks submitted to the committee should be evaluated according to these criteria. Representatives of the various companies will have to be heard at this time concerning the particular merits of their respective books.

4. The books should then be rated and ranked according to the results attained through the use of the criteria. There will usually be two or three books of outstanding merit, and the recommendation of the committee can be made to the curriculum director for the adoption of a text or the trial of the excellent texts over a period of time for the purpose of securing a more accurate evaluation of them in terms of actual class use.

G. Promoting continuous revision. Although the terms "tentative course" and "final course" have been used, the reader must bear in mind that no course of study is ever accepted as final or complete. It is necessary in the professional development of the staff to have an "open season" at all times on every course of study. It is probable that little will be accomplished in such a continuous program unless the administration promotes research and investigation.

Partly with a view to keeping the faculty alert, many investigations can be organized, in evaluating objectives, developing experimental studies in method, and reading and reporting on current professional literature and reports of committees in

[19] E. M. Draper and A. C. Roberts, *Principles of American Secondary Education* (The Century Co., 1932), pp. 387-388.

subject-matter fields—the Coleman report on the modern foreign languages, the Krey report on the social studies, the Classical investigation, and others. Reports of national councils in the various subject-matter fields and numerous year-books will add challenges to the teacher in the classroom and to the supervisors and administrator.

H. Providing for individual differences. This phase of course of study construction is a direct responsibility of the administrative force. Too often courses of study are developed which meet the needs of only one group—the average—and the teacher is responsible for the *diluted* or the *concentrated* doses to be given to those of low and high ability. While many school systems are working with ability grouping or differentiated assignments, few are attempting to:

1. Develop definite courses of study which provide differentiated materials and methods to realize pupil objectives at different levels. In most instances, rate of progress is the only differentiating factor.
2. Develop pupil classifications on other bases than intelligence.
3. Provide for different levels of work in different subject-matter fields for individual pupils.
4. Provide for readjustment from one level to another in the school. The application of the individual student, as well as his intelligence quotient, must be taken into account in adjusting him in the academic offerings of the school.
5. Develop different students for promotion from each level of each class or grade.
6. Select and train teachers for special work with particular levels within the school.

The administration of the Eureka Schools, Eureka, California, developed the following principles to govern this problem in their school system:

1. That every individual, regardless of age, race, color, or creed, has an inalienable right to receive at public expense that training which will best fit him for the job of life; but that no individual, either because of unwillingness to work or mental inability to maintain a reasonable standard, has a right to interfere with the growth of another.
2. That there are at least four branches to every well-organized school system: the home; the employing establishment; the school

proper; and all other organizations of the community; and that, if the training is to be proper, each of these branches of the school system must assume its full responsibility, for responsibilities cannot be delegated; they can only be assumed or neglected.

3. That there are at least three distinct types of students in any modern high school, with radically different objectives; and that the school has an obligation to serve each of these types efficiently.

4. That it is wrong and vicious to set a standard for an individual lower than that which can be reached by the individual; and that it is equally vicious to set a standard too high for the individual. Inasmuch as individuals differ and differ widely, there must be a wide range in standards.

5. That "academic" and "industrial" education do not represent two different kinds of education, but that these merely represent two different means for arriving at the same ends—that of preparing for life. That knowledge, skill, and ideals are constant underlying objectives utterly regardless of the subject.

6. That a lateral extension of the curriculum cannot take care of a vertical difference in mental ability or in willingness to work.

7. That the leadership for bringing about the general recognition of the above principles rests largely with school officials, because they have control of large, well-organized agencies (the schools) and are in touch with practically every home of the communities. This gives school officials a near-monopoly which, if capitalized, can in a short time bring these or any other principles into being. The subtle force of propaganda can be properly used.[20]

These basic principles were carried into practice in the following manner:

1. All boys and girls are given a full opportunity. Different levels of work and an elastic program which allow each individual to find his level. Each is permitted to move at his own rate. Students who will not or cannot work are not permitted to clog the machine. This system is not yet complete, but a very decided step has been taken.

2. The home, the employing concerns, and other elements in the community have been recognized as a part of the educational system and are rapidly coming to coöperate with the school in the proper training of youth.

3. The school is now organized to take care of all classes of students: those who are seeking positions as well as those who expect to go to college. It recognizes the validity of other objectives than that of college training.

[20] A. C. Roberts and E. M. Draper, *The High School Principal as Administrator* (D. C. Heath and Co., 1927), pp. 288-289.

4. Different mental and ability standards are recognized and the students considered accordingly.

5. Industrial education has been put on the same level as academic work. We refuse to recognize any fundamental difference in the two —merely a difference of means. We recognize that every job well done is honorable and that a successful mechanic or laborer needs to use his brain as well as the lawyer or the teacher.

6. We add no subjects merely for the purpose of taking care of students who are disinterested. Courses are added only when there is need for a specific type of training.[21]

No school system can proceed effectively in course of study construction until these basic administrative problems have been studied and machinery developed to meet the situations they present. Although the ultimate decisions rest with the administrator, teachers are involved in securing data and coöperating in the formulation of effective principles and the making of intelligent decisions. The organization of classes for the slow-learning child proceeds as follows in the schools of Grand Rapids:

The work with slow-learning types may be divided into four groups: (1) a centralized group of pupils of the lowest mental ages in a unit by themselves, (2) special classes known as auxiliary in grade buildings, for pupils with I.Q.'s of from 50 to 75, (3) ungraded opportunity classes for pupils two or more years behind the grade in which they should be according to their chronological ages and for pupils who for various reasons might be unevenly graded, (4) a junior vocational school for boys and girls who are unable to adjust themselves successfully to the life of the traditional school.

Pupils not making normal progress are reported by the principals to the special class department. Arrangements are made for mental tests. School and family history is obtained. After due investigation and consideration, treatment or placement is advised. If there is a special class available in the building or in an adjacent school, parents are interviewed and asked to coöperate in a plan of education adapted to the needs of the child.

Each case requires individual adjustment. In general, pupils with I.Q.'s from 50 to 70 are regarded as belonging in auxiliary classes. It has been found, however, that no distinct demarcation can be made between the mentally defective and the merely backward pupil; therefore, many high-grade subnormal pupils have found places in

[21] *Ibid.*, pp. 290-291.

ungraded classes, and on the other hand, many backward children are found in auxiliary classes. This overlapping has been due in some instances to the convenience of location of classes of certain types or to the desirability of chronological age grouping.

Though surveys in some buildings have proven the permanence of coaching results, we know that every school has a residue of all-around retardates who cannot be classified other than as slow-moving normal individuals. These pupils are difficult to fit into the later elementary grades, due to the more definite program of work that must be accomplished there, the current idea that grade standards and not individual standards should be considered, and the lack of provision of suitable industrial activities in these higher grades. Added to this group of all-around retardates is a second group composed of emotionally unstable or socially maladjusted children. These two make up the ungraded group.

The segregated auxiliary, or ungraded, room is an attempted solution of the problem. It provides a session room where individual help may be given and concrete work and activities suitable to each individual presented. The training of children of low mentality is, in general, vocational and homemaking in its nature. Boys are taught how to use tools and are given the experience of manipulating various materials such as clay, cloth, paper, cardboard, beaverboard, and wood. Older boys and girls learn to wash, iron, set a table, clean a room, wash cars, and cook in a simple manner. When possible, pupils have flower and vegetable gardens. Methods as well as subject-matter are adapted to the limited capacity of pupils of the group. For instance, successive steps each day finally lead to the serving of a complete luncheon. Connection is made between the utilitarian and the academic. Teachers of these classes work with the practical-arts teachers in their grade buildings.

In the work of the junior vocational school, the objectives are the formation and development of such habits, attitudes, and interests as lead to wholesome living and good citizenship. These objectives are taught to a great extent through show and manual activities. Provision is made for the academic branches and promotion is open to pupils whose achievement along these lines is successful. It is hoped that the wide range of activities provided by the school will at least give an opportunity for the joy of success and will send the pupil out into the community with greater courage and self-confidence.

X. SUMMARY

1. Allocation of administrative duties in course of study construction. The preceding pages have indicated that course of study construction involves members of every professional group in the system. Some phase of the work will be overlooked or will lack completeness if any group is ignored.

Course of study revision is carried on primarily for the benefit of the faculty and the pupils. In the definite organization of teaching materials and learning experiences, according to the data secured from the most recent research, are possibilities of improved teaching, more definite and worthwhile supervision, valid pupil objectives and learning experiences and an accurate evaluation of the achievements of pupils. Every aspect of the educational system should be involved in this comprehensive program and make a contribution to its ultimate realization. The following groups, which are primarily interested in course of study construction and revision, have been emphasized in this chapter :

a. Administrative officers. The superintendent and his assistants and associates plan the program and provide for its satisfactory development. The director of research and the subject-matter specialist, as well as other groups and individuals who have special training and experience, are called in as advisers concerning the scope of the work, expense involved, allocation of teachers, buildings, etc. The education of the faculty and the community is planned in this office. The editing, publishing, and installing of courses of study are additional responsibilities of the superintendent's office.

b. Building principals. These administrative officers assist in determining aims and objectives, grade placement and time allotment. They are particularly influential in formulating programs of study and curricula since these are related to the educational program presented in their building. They coöperate in organizing the experimental work which is essential in determining objectives and teaching materials. Trying-out new courses of study and installing those which have been tentatively accepted places a great responsibility on the building principals who direct and supervise this work in coöperation with the central office, the director of research and the supervisors in the subject-matter field.

c. Supervisors and teachers. Their coöperation is essential in the solution of practically all of the problems facing the building principal, but they are more intimately associated with the determination of subject-matter and methods of instruction and with the development of tests.

2. Principles governing the administration of course of study construction.

a. Course of study committees should produce tentative courses of study. Constant revision is imperative for teacher growth. Through revising and reorganizing courses of study teachers have the opportunity to familiarize themselves with recent research and to evaluate the results in terms of the conditions existing in their own school systems.

b. Education of the faculty must precede the allocation of curricular tasks to a committee or individual teachers in the system. Understanding and intelligent participation are more fundamental than willingness or enthusiasm in this work.

c. The most important criteria for the selection of members of curriculum committees are: (1) special training, (2) experience, and (3) physical and mental fitness. Age and length of service should be disregarded.

d. The teacher or the committee should have access to recent books, courses of study, results of experimentation in the field in which the course is being formulated. Unless adequate facilities and materials can be provided, it is inevitable that results will be limited.

e. Course of study construction should be based, in part at least, upon experimentation in the school system. The administrative staff should provide the facilities for research work and coöperate with the teachers and supervisors in directing the research and evaluating the results.

f. Provision should be made for the training of the faculty in the use of the new course of study. Improvement in teaching is evidenced only when the course is made an effective instrument in the classroom.

BIBLIOGRAPHY

ADAMS, Fay, and WALKER, Brown, *Teaching the Bright Pupil* (Henry Holt & Co., 1930).

ADAMS, Mary A., "City-Wide Experimentation in the Intermediate Curriculum Program in Geography and History," *Baltimore Bulletin of Education,* Vol. IX (April, 1931), pp. 172-177.

ARGO, A. C., "Administrative Aspects of Curriculum Construction," *Junior-Senior High School Clearing House,* Vol. IX, No. 6 (February, 1935), pp. 350-355.

BARR, A. S., *An Introduction to the Scientific Study of Classroom Supervision* (D. Appleton, 1931), Ch. II.

BENTBACK, Emil, "Standards for the Selection of Arithmetic Textbooks," *Educational Research Record,* University of Nebraska (February, 1929), pp. 85-90.

BUCKINGHAM, B. R., "The Scientific Development and Evaluation of Textbook Materials," National Education Association, Department of Superintendence, *Official Report* (1933).

BURR, S. E., "Instituting a Program of Curriculum Reconstruction," *Curriculum Yearbook* (Lynn Public Schools, 1928-1929).

CLARK, Helen T., *A Plan by Which to Organize a Group of English Teachers for the Purpose of Course Revision* (University of California, Berkeley, 1930).

COCKING, W. D., *Administrative Procedures in Curriculum Making for Public Schools* (Teachers College, Columbia University Contributions to Education, No. 329, 1928).

———, "Program of Curriculum Construction," *Seventy-Second Annual Report,* Board of Education of the City of St. Louis (1926), pp. 36-45.

COLEMAN, R. M., "An Experiment in Meeting Individual Differences in First Term Civics," *New Jersey Journal of Education* (February, 1930), pp. 4-5.

CONRAD, E. B., and HICKOK, K., "Placement of Literary Selections for Junior and Senior High Schools," English Journal, Vol. XIX (May, 1930), pp. 377-384.

COUNTS, G. S., "Who Shall Make the Curriculum?" *School Review,* Vol. XXXV (May, 1927), pp. 332-339.

COURTIS, S. A., "Curriculum-Construction at Detroit," *Twenty-Sixth Yearbook,* National Society for the Study of Education (Public School Publishing Co., 1926).

CROFTS, T. J., "A Scale for Arithmetic Texts," *Chicago Schools Journal* (June, 1929), pp. 363-366.

Curriculum Revision and Development in Houston, Texas (Houston Independent School District, 1924-1930.

DALE, George A., *Use of a Modified Course of Study in Arithmetic for Borderline Children* (Master's Thesis, University of Iowa).

DAVID, F. L., *The Selection and Organization of Personnel for Curriculum Revision* (Bulletin No. 30, Curriculum Laboratory, Western Reserve University, 1932).

DAVIS, C. O., *Our Evolving High School Curriculum* (World Book Company, 1927).

Denver Program of Curriculum Revision (Denver Public Schools Monograph No. 12, 1927).

Department of Superintendence, National Education Association, *Fourth Yearbook* (1926).

DESCOEUDRES, Alice, "Arithmetic," in *The Education of Mentally Defective Children* (D. C. Heath & Co., 1928).

DOUGLASS, H. R., "Steps in Curriculum Construction in Junior and Senior High Schools," Second Yearbook, Eastern Commercial Teachers' Association.

DOWNING, Elliot R., "Teaching Units in Biology—An Investigation," *North Central Association Quarterly*, Vol. V (March, 1931), pp. 453-470.

DYER, A. R., "The Placement of Poems in the Grades," in Bobbitt, *Curriculum Investigations* (Chicago, Ill., University of Chicago Press, 1926).

———, *The Placement of Home Economics Content in Junior and Senior High Schools* (Bureau of Publications, Teachers College, Columbia University, 1927).

Evaluation of Arithmetic Textbooks, California State Department of Education Bulletin, No. 19. (Sacramento, California, 1932.)

FOSTER, C. R., "Teacher Participation in Curriculum Building," *Chicago School Journal*, Vol. VIII (December, 1925), pp. 142-145.

FULLER, Florence D., "Evaluation of Geometry Textbooks," *Los Angeles Educational Research Bulletin*, Vol. X (October, 1930), pp. 5-10.

GREEN, C. E., and GUMLICK, H. R., "Some Techniques in Installing a New Course of Study," *Teachers Journal and Abstract*, Vol. III (April, 1928), pp. 257-262.

HAGAN, Forrest P., *An Objective Appraisal in Eight Grade Arithmetic Textbooks* Master's Thesis (Iowa City, Iowa, State University of Iowa, 1930).

Handbook for Course of Study Committees (Oakland Public Schools, June, 1928).

HARAP, H., "A Critique of Public-School Courses of Study," *Journal of Educational Research,* Vol. XXI (February, 1930), p. 116.

———, "Evaluation of Curricula and Texts," *Review of Educational Research* (January, 1931), pp. 43-45.

———, *The Technique of Curriculum Making* (The Macmillan Company, 1928).

HARRING, Sydney, "What Primer Shall I Use Next?" *Elementary School Journal*, Vol. XXXII (November, 1931), pp. 207-213.

HERRIOTT, M. E., "How to Make a Course of Study in Arithmetic," Bureau of Educational Research, Circular No. 37, *University of Illinois Bulletin,* Vol. XXIII, No. 6.

——, "How to Make a Course of Study in Reading," Bureau of Educational Research, Circular No. 42, *University of Illinois Bulletin,* Vol. XXIII, No. 18, p. 38.

——, "Textbook Adoption and Evaluation Procedures, Los Angeles Secondary Schools," *Los Angeles Educational Research Bulletin,* Vol. X (October, 1930), pp. 2-5.

——, "The Selection of a Physics Textbook," *Los Angeles Educational Research Bulletin,* Vol. X (October, 1930), pp. 15-21.

HOPKINS, L. T., *Curriculum Principles and Practices* (Benjamin H. Sanborn and Co., 1930).

——, "Who Makes the Curriculum?" *Teachers Journal and Abstract,* Vol. VI (September, 1931), pp. 381-384.

HORN, E., "Who Shall Make the Courses of Study and How?" *Addresses and Proceedings,* National Education Association, Vol. LXI (1923).

Introduction of the Suggested Courses of Study, St. Louis Public Schools, Curriculum Service Bulletin No. 1 (1926).

JACOBSON, J., "The Machinery and Organization for Devising, Revising, and Supervising the Curriculum—The Viewpoint of the Classroom Teacher," *Second Yearbook,* Department of Superintendence, National Education Association (1924).

JENSEN, Frank A., *Current Procedure in Selecting Textbooks* (J. B. Lippincott Co., 1931).

"Keeping Pace with the Advancing Curriculum," Research Bulletin of the National Education Association, Vol. III (September, November, 1925), pp. 119-124.

KNOWLTON, P. A., "Publishers and the Curriculum," *Elementary School Journal,* Vol. XXXIII (March, 1933), pp. 502-513.

KYTE, G. C., "The Coöperative Development of a Course of Study," *Educational Administration and Supervision,* Vol. IV (December, 1923), pp. 517-536.

——, "Installing a New Course of Study," *The Nation's Schools,* Vol. XIV, No. 6 (December, 1934), pp. 34-37.

——, "When Supervisor and Teacher Talk It Over," *The Nation's Schools,* Vol. XV, No. 6 (June, 1935), pp. 29-32.

LANGVICK, Mina M., *Current Practices in the Construction of State Courses of Study,* U. S. Bureau of Education, Bulletin No. 4 (1931).

LINDAHL, H. M., "Teacher Participation in Constructing a Course of Study," *Educational Method,* Vol. IX (February, 1930), pp. 288-289.

LOGAN, A. E., "The Cincinnati Program of Curriculum Revision," *Second Yearbook,* Department of Superintendence, National Education Association (1924).

Los Angeles City Schools, Course of Study Monographs, No. 30 (1924).

MCCLURE, W., "Adapting New Courses of Study to Classroom Use," *Teachers Journal and Abstract,* Vol. IV (February, 1929), pp. 120-216.

———, "The Principal and the Machinery for Devising, Revising, and Supervising the Curriculum," *Second Yearbook,* Department of Superintendence, National Education Association (1924).

MARYE, Mary E., "A Form for Rating Textbooks in English Composition Prepared for the Ninth and Tenth Grades," *School Review,* Vol. XXXVIII (February, 1930), pp. 124-137.

MAXWELL, C. R., "The Use of Score Cards in Evaluating Textbooks," *Thirtieth Yearbook,* Part II, National Society for the Study of Education (1931).

MINOR, R., "Making the Course of Study," *Elementary School Journal,* Vol. XXII (May, 1922), pp. 655-664.

Minnesota Curriculum for Secondary Schools, State Department of Education, Bulletin No. 1, August (1931).

MONROE, W. S., "Making a Course of Study," Bureau of Educational Research, Circular No. 35, *University of Illinois Bulletin* (1925), pp. 13-17.

NETTELS, Charles H., "The Selection of a Textbook for 8B Science," *Los Angeles Educational Research Bulletin,* Vol. X (October, 1930), pp. 10-15.

NEWLON, J. H., and THRELKELD, A. L., "The Denver Curriculum-Revision Program," *Twenty-Sixth Yearbook,* National Society for the Study of Education (Bloomingdale, Ill., Public School Publishing Company, 1926).

NORTON, M. A., "Leadership in Curriculum Building in 168 Large City School Systems," *School and Society,* Vol. XXXIII (January 3, 1931), pp. 17-20.

OTTO, H. G., *Elementary School Organization and Administration* (D. Appleton-Century Co., 1934).

Preliminary Reports on Approaches to and Theories Regarding Curriculum Construction, General Aims and Guiding Principles of Education, South Dakota State Superintendent of Public Instruction, Bulletin No. 1 (1930).

Report of the Board of Education, District of Columbia, 1927-1928 U. S. Government Printing Office, 1928.

Report of St. Louis Board of Education, 1925-1926.

RUGG, H. O., *Statistical Methods Applied to Education* (Houghton Mifflin Co., 1917).

Seventh Yearbook of the Department of Supervisors and Directors of Instruction of the National Education Association, *Scientific Method in Supervisory Programs,* Chapter VII discusses "How to Use the Scientific Method in Curriculum Studies."

SMITH, D. V., "Evaluation of Composition Textbooks—A Report of National Council Committee," *English Journal,* Vol. XXI (April, 1932), pp. 280-295.

STINGLEY, C. L., "Curriculum Practices in 95 Junior High Schools in Ohio," *High-School Teacher,* Vol. VI (March, 1930), pp. 114-116.

STRAYER, G. D., and Others, *Report of the Survey of the Schools of Chicago,* Vol. III (Bureau of Publications, Teachers College, Columbia University, 1932).

SVANE, Phyllis, *A Score Card to be Used in the Selection of a 'Language' Textbook for the Ninth Grade in a Junior High School* (University of California, Berkeley, 1930).

THRELKELD, A. L., "Curriculum Revision: How a Particular City May Attack the Problem," *Elementary School Journal,* Vol. XXV (April, 1925), pp. 573-582.

————, "The Denver Plan of Curriculum Revision," *Second Yearbook,* Department of Superintendence, National Education Association, (1924).

TRILLINGHAM, C. C., *The Organization and Administration of Curriculum Programs* (University of Southern California Press, 1934).

United States History Textbooks (American Association of University Women, 1930).

WEBB, L. W., *High School Curriculum Reorganization* (The North Central Association, Ann Arbor, Michigan, 1933).

WILLIAMS, L. A., *A Rating Scale by Which Teachers Are to Select Textbooks* (Oakland School Department, 1929).

WILSON, H. B., "Machinery and Organization for Devising, Revising, and Supervising the Curriculum—The Administrator's Viewpoint," *Second Yearbook,* Department of Superintendence, National Education Association (1924).

————, "The Course of Study in the Work of the Modern School," *Course of Study Monograph* (Berkeley Public Schools, 1921), p. 12.

INDEX

Typewriting, instructional aids used in State of Minnesota, 597-598

Uhl, W. L., on types and characteristics of mental functions, 264; on inducting pupils into learning activities 268-269; on project method, 495-496; socialized procedure, 500-501; drill, 520
Units of instruction, definition, 32
Units of work, 249ff.; 293ff.; a large division of work, 299ff.; a sub-division of work for year or semester, 308ff.; a section or major topic, 313ff.; a sub-division of a major topic or section, 323ff.; criteria essential in developing course of study units of work, 325ff.; constructing units of work at Ann Arbor, Mich., 332-334; as centers of interest, 338ff.; can be complete educational experiences, 338ff.; the problem-project type, 350ff.; an illustration of a unit as a large center of interest, 374ff.; for individualized learning, 384ff.; the contract plan, 384ff.; samples of contracts, 386ff.; organization of contracts, 398-403; criteria for development of contracts, 403ff.; Winnetka Plan, 409ff.; samples of individual work at Winnetka, 410ff.; child-centered, 418ff.; organizing activity unit, 420-421; aims of activity school, 421-422; developing materials in activity school, 423-425; organizing daily programs in activity school, 425; initiating activity programs, 426-427; difficulties in organizing activity units, 427-428; activity unit on the "Early Hebrews," 428ff.; activity unit on "Building a Playhouse," 433ff.; activity unit in social science from Lakewood, Ohio, schools, 436-449; purposes of activity units

in Kansas City, Mo., 449; activity units from kindergarten, Kansas City, Mo., 449-452; activity unit in elementary science, Kansas City, Mo., 452-460; activity unit from fine and practical arts, Long Beach, Calif., 460-461; activity unit from elementary science, Oakland, Calif., 461-464; evaluation of activity program, 464ff.; criteria for organization of units, 469-471; teaching procedures, 474ff.; function of method, 476-477; general methods, 477ff.; Herbartian steps, 478-479; Morrison steps, 479-484; Miller steps, 484-487; contract method, 488-491; problem-project method, 492-499; socialized procedure, 499-502; supervised study, 502-503; place of method in course of study, 503-505; evaluation of general method, 505-507; instructional aids in academic units, 510ff.; types of instructional aids, 510ff.; instructional aids in San Antonio schools, 512; organization of instructional aids in New York State, 512-515; developmental lesson, 515-516; lecture method, 516-517; recitation method, 517; discussion method, 517-518; laboratory method, 518-519; drill, 519-520; developing appreciation, 521; review-test, 521-522; instructional aids in non-academic units, 583ff.; testing achievement in, 692ff.
University of California at Los Angeles, aims of activity school, 421-422; developing materials in activity school, 423-425; unit on "Life of Early Hebrews," 428ff.; unit on "Building a Playhouse," 433ff.

Validation of objectives, 188ff.; summary sheet for, 208-209

(2)